D1067379

CAPITAL IN TRANSPORTATION, COMMUNICATIONS, AND PUBLIC UTILITIES: ITS FORMATION AND FINANCING

NATIONAL BUREAU OF ECONOMIC RESEARCH

Studies in Capital Formation and Financing

1. Capital Formation in Residential Real Estate: Trends and Prospects
   Leo Grebler, David M. Blank, and Louis Winnick

2. Capital in Agriculture: Its Formation and Financing since 1870
   Alvin S. Tostlebe

3. Financial Intermediaries in the American Economy since 1900
   Raymond W. Goldsmith

4. Capital in Transportation, Communications, and Public Utilities: Its Formation and Financing
   Melville J. Ulmer

Capital in Transportation, Communications, and Public Utilities: Its Formation and Financing

BY MELVILLE J. ULMER
THE AMERICAN UNIVERSITY

A STUDY BY THE
NATIONAL BUREAU OF ECONOMIC RESEARCH

PUBLISHED BY
PRINCETON UNIVERSITY PRESS, PRINCETON
1960

Copyright © 1960, by Princeton University Press
All Rights Reserved

L.C. Card No. 59-11082

HD
2766
U4

Printed in the United States of America

This monograph is part of a larger investigation of trends and prospects in capital formation and financing made possible by a grant from the Life Insurance Association of America

Relation of the Directors to the Work and Publications of the National Bureau of Economic Research

1. The object of the National Bureau of Economic Research is to ascertain and to present to the public important economic facts and their interpretation in a scientific and impartial manner. The Board of Directors is charged with the responsibility of ensuring that the work of the National Bureau is carried on in strict conformity with this object.

2. To this end the Board of Directors shall appoint one or more Directors of Research.

3. The Director or Directors of Research shall submit to the members of the Board, or to its Executive Committee, for their formal adoption, all specific proposals concerning researches to be instituted.

4. No report shall be published until the Director or Directors of Research shall have submitted to the Board a summary drawing attention to the character of the data and their utilization in the report, the nature and treatment of the problems involved, the main conclusions, and such other information as in their opinion would serve to determine the suitability of the report for publication in accordance with the principles of the National Bureau.

5. A copy of any manuscript proposed for publication shall also be submitted to each member of the Board. For each manuscript to be so submitted a special committee shall be appointed by the President, or at his designation by the Executive Director, consisting of three Directors selected as nearly as may be one from each general division of the Board. The names of the special manuscript committee shall be stated to each Director when the summary and report described in paragraph (4) are sent to him. It shall be the duty of each member of the committee to read the manuscript. If each member of the special committee signifies his approval within thirty days, the manuscript may be published. If each member of the special committee has not signified his approval within thirty days of the transmittal of the report and manuscript, the Director of Research shall then notify each member of the Board, requesting approval or disapproval of publication, and thirty additional days shall be granted for this purpose. The manuscript shall then not be published unless at least a majority of the entire Board and a two-thirds majority of those members of the Board who shall have voted on the proposal within the time fixed for the receipt of votes on the publication proposed shall have approved.

6. No manuscript may be published, though approved by each member of the special committee, until forty-five days have elapsed from the transmittal of the summary and report. The interval is allowed for the receipt of any memorandum of dissent or reservation, together with a brief statement of his reasons, that any member may wish to express; and such memorandum of dissent or reservation shall be published with the manuscript if he so desires. Publication does not, however, imply that each member of the Board has read the manuscript, or that either members of the Board in general, or of the special committee, have passed upon its validity in every detail.

7. A copy of this resolution shall, unless otherwise determined by the Board, be printed in each copy of every National Bureau book.

(*Resolution adopted October 25, 1926*
and revised February 6, 1933 and February 24, 1941)

NATIONAL BUREAU OF ECONOMIC RESEARCH

1959

OFFICERS

George B. Roberts, *Chairman*
Arthur F. Burns, *President*
Theodore W. Schultz, *Vice-President*
Murray Shields, *Treasurer*
Solomon Fabricant, *Director of Research*
Geoffrey H. Moore, *Associate Director of Research*
William J. Carson, *Executive Director*

DIRECTORS AT LARGE

Wallace J. Campbell, *Director, Cooperative League of the USA*
Solomon Fabricant, *New York University*
Gabriel Hauge, *Chairman, Finance Committee, Manufacturers Trust Campany*
Albert J. Hettinger, Jr., *Lazard Frères and Company*
Oswald W. Knauth, *Beaufort, South Carolina*
H. W. Laidler, *Executive Director Emeritus, League for Industrial Democracy*
Shepard Morgan, *Norfolk, Connecticut*
George B. Roberts, *Larchmont, New York*
Beardsley Ruml, *New York City*
Harry Scherman, *Chairman, Book-of-the-Month Club*
Boris Shishkin, *American Federation of Labor and Congress of Industrial Organizations*
George Soule, *Professor Emeritus, Bennington College*
N. I. Stone, *Consulting Economist*
J. Raymond Walsh, *New York City*
Joseph H. Willits, *Director, The Educational Survey, University of Pennsylvania*
Leo Wolman, *Columbia University*
Donald B. Woodward, *Vick Chemical Company*
Theodore O. Yntema, *Vice-President–Finance, Ford Motor Company*

DIRECTORS BY UNIVERSITY APPOINTMENT

V. W. Bladen, *Toronto*
Arthur F. Burns, *Columbia*
Melvin G. de Chazeau, *Cornell*
Frank W. Fetter, *Northwestern*
H. M. Groves, *Wisconsin*
Gottfried Haberler, *Harvard*
Walter W. Heller, *Minnesota*
Maurice W. Lee, *North Carolina*
Lloyd G. Reynolds, *Yale*
T. W. Schultz, *Chicago*
Jacob Viner, *Princeton*
Willis J. Winn, *Pennsylvania*

DIRECTORS APPOINTED BY OTHER ORGANIZATIONS

Percival F. Brundage, *American Institute of Certified Public Accountants*
Harold G. Halcrow, *American Farm Economic Association*
Theodore V. Houser, *Committee for Economic Development*
Stanley H. Ruttenberg, *American Federation of Labor and Congress of Industrial Organizations*
Murray Shields, *American Management Association*
Willard L. Thorp, *American Economic Association*
W. Allen Wallis, *American Statistical Association*
Harold F. Williamson, *Economic History Association*

RESEARCH STAFF

Moses Abramovitz
Gary S. Becker
Gerhard Bry
Arthur F. Burns
Morris A. Copeland
Frank G. Dickinson
James S. Earley
Richard A. Easterlin
Solomon Fabricant
Milton Friedman
Raymond W. Goldsmith
Leo Grebler
Millard Hastay
W. Braddock Hickman
Daniel M. Holland
Thor Hultgren
C. Harry Kahn
John W. Kendrick
Simon Kuznets
Clarence D. Long
Ruth P. Mack
Ilse Mintz
Geoffrey H. Moore
Roger F. Murray
G. Warren Nutter
Lawrence H. Seltzer
Robert P. Shay
George J. Stigler
Leo Wolman
Herbert B. Woolley

FOREWORD

by Simon Kuznets

I

THIS is the fourth in a series of monographs resulting from an inquiry initiated by the National Bureau of Economic Research in 1950, with the financial assistance of the Life Insurance Association of America.[1] The inquiry examines long-term trends in capital formation and financing in the United States, and is organized primarily about the principal capital-using sectors of the economy—agriculture, mining, manufacturing, the public utilities, residential real estate, and governments. The analysis for each sector summarizes the major trends in real capital formation from 1870 (or the earliest year for which data are available), and in financing from 1900, or somewhat earlier. In each, an effort is also made to discover the factors determining these trends, and, so far as possible, to suggest the significance of these factors for the future. In addition to the sector studies, the inquiry comprises two others. One deals with trends in external financing channeled through intermediate financial institutions and attempts to link the major types of institutions with the various groups of capital users. The second integrates the results of all the other studies, within a framework provided by country-wide estimates of national product and relevant components, and of country-wide estimates of assets and debts.

Some of the findings have been presented in part or in preliminary form in a series of Occasional and Technical Papers.[2] This monograph, like those to follow, presents the full results of a specific study together with supporting data. The three others, near completion, deal with trends in capital formation and financing in mining and manufacturing, and in governments, respectively; and

[1] The first three monographs are: *Capital Formation in Residential Real Estate: Trends and Prospects*, by Leo Grebler, David M. Blank, and Louis Winnick (1956); *Capital in Agriculture: Its Formation and Financing since 1870*, by Alvin S. Tostlebe (1957), and *Financial Intermediaries in the American Economy since 1900*, by Raymond W. Goldsmith (1958), all published for the National Bureau of Economic Research by Princeton University Press.

[2] Leo Grebler, *The Role of Federal Credit Aids in Residential Construction*, Occasional Paper 39 (1953); Daniel Creamer, *Capital and Output Trends in Manufacturing Industries, 1880–1948*, Occasional Paper 41 (1954); Raymond W. Goldsmith, *The Share of Financial Intermediaries in National Wealth and National Assets, 1900–1949*, Occasional Paper 42 (1954); Melville J. Ulmer, *Trends and Cycles in Capital Formation by United States Railroads, 1870–1950*, Occasional Paper 43 (1954); Alvin S. Tostlebe, *The Growth of Physical Capital in Agriculture, 1870–1950*, Occasional Paper 44 (1954); Israel Borenstein, *Capital and Output Trends in Mining Industries, 1870–1948*, Occasional Paper 45 (1954); David M. Blank, *The Volume of Residential Construction, 1889–1950*, Technical Paper 9 (1954); all published by the National Bureau of Economic Research.

with a summary presentation and analysis of trends in capital formation and financing for the country as a whole.

II

The regulated industries, whose long-term record is analyzed in Dr. Ulmer's monograph, have a number of distinctive characteristics. At the risk of repeating the obvious, it may be useful to list them briefly.

First, most regulated industries are products of modern technology—of new ways of providing energy for industrial and household uses, of harnessing energy to the transportation of goods and persons and to the communication of messages, written and oral. Many of these industries could not have existed a hundred or a hundred and fifty years ago because neither the practical inventions, nor even the theoretical discoveries underlying their operation, were known.

Second, because of the large volume of concentrated power involved in the modern technology of regulated industries, they require—for *minimal* operation—huge investments of durable capital: in roadbeds or roadways, terminal stations and airfields, power equipment, transmission lines, control stations, etc. For optimum *economical* operation such durable capital investment must be even larger relative to current rates of output—to exploit the internal economies of large-scale production and to provide for the secular rise in demand.

Third, since so many of the regulated industries are concerned with transportation and communication, the efficiency of their output depends upon a rapid integration of local and regional units into a country-wide—and sometimes international—network. A single railroad is far less effective economically than one which is part of a country-wide system; and the same can be said of a single truck company, air transport company, or telephone firm, unless, of course, each is already so large as to be able to provide effective integrated service throughout the country. Hence, once such a transportation or communication industry emerges, it is under great pressure to extend its network—and thus its capital investment—to cover the country; and perhaps link up with similar industries in other countries.

Fourth, the large size of durable capital investment relative to current output makes for a high ratio of fixed to variable costs—and leads to the classical case where, in the long run, competition within the industry ends in monopoly by killing off all competitors but one. By their very structure as producers, many regulated industries are naturally monopolistic.

Fifth, since the industries in the group are in the business of supplying power and other necessities (like water), or of providing transportation and communication services, the products constitute a basic framework for much of economic and social life. All of us need the products; and their availability, once established, permits changes in the pattern of life designed to take advantage of them (e.g. of new transportation facilities). The consequence is that the withdrawal of the products of regulated industries, an interruption in their supply, would create severe and widely ramifying difficulties throughout the country's economy. In other words, regulated industries are suppliers of goods that can be viewed practically as basic necessities.

Sixth, it is, of course, this combination of monopolistic position and provision of necessities that results in the industries[1] being regulated—treated as public utilities[3]—in countries where nationalization can be avoided. Were the industries concerned with minor luxuries, such as artificial hair buns or fancy cigarette holders, few would care about the monopolistic power of the producers—where the latter happened to possess them. If the goods were necessities, but the industry naturally competitive (as with many agricultural and industrial products), reliance could be placed on the free competitive market and little special regulation would be required. A public utility must be regulated for the joint reason that, as the term implies, it is of wide and basic use, and yet its technology and economics bar the possibility of effective intra-industry competition.

Finally, even though the degree of monopoly is high *within* each regulated industry, in the long-term perspective one can observe a great deal of *inter-industry* competition. Surely the railroads have been affected in recent decades by the competition of motor trucks and of airplanes; electric power competes for certain types of household use with gas; there is even competition, limited though it may be, between the telephone and telegraph. Indeed, it may be suggested that the very origin of regulated industries in recent technical progress and the wide field which they cover raise the probability that, as time passes, competitive pressure on some already existing industries will be exercised by newly emerging methods of providing power, transportation, or communication services—methods so new as to provide a base for new industries. And one may add that as such new industries are born, and exercise

[3] Dr. Ulmer's definition of regulated industries embraces a group somewhat wider than public utilities, but sufficiently close to it to say that by far the predominant part of the group are privately owned public utilities. (Government-owned units are excluded by Dr. Ulmer from the analysis; but in many of the subsectors, government ownership in this country is insignificant.)

competitive pressure on those already existing, the new sectors—even though still undergoing internal competition—may promptly be subjected to special controls and thus be added to the regulated group.

III

The characteristics just listed go far to explain the long-term movements of output, capital formation, capital-output ratios, and sources of financing, which are so clearly portrayed and cogently analyzed in Dr. Ulmer's monograph. His main conclusions can be briefly stated.

(1) As each of the major industries with which Dr. Ulmer deals separately (steam railroads, electric light and power, telephones, street and electric railways, local bus lines) emerges, its output grows at high rates—far higher than those in country-wide output. As a result, its share in total national output also rises rapidly. The steam railroads, much of whose early growth preceded the period covered here, accounted for about 5 per cent of gross national product in 1886 (their share in the 1830's must have been nearly zero), and rose to almost 9 per cent by the early 1920's. Electric light and power, whose share was close to zero in the early 1890's, rose to over 4 per cent of gross national product in the 1950's; the share of telephones, from close to zero in the early 1890's to over 1.5 per cent in the 1950's; and that of street and electric railways, which emerged in the 1890's, to a peak of about 1.4 per cent in 1916.[4] But such rapid growth—greatly in excess even of the vigorous growth of national output—ceases, after some decades. The timing differs from one industry to another, depending upon its scope and its susceptibility to competitive pressure from new industries. From a peak level in the early 1920's of 9 per cent of gross national product, the share of steam railroads drops to 5 per cent by 1950; that of street and electric railways declines from 1.4 per cent in 1916 to 0.2 in 1950; and even for those industries that are still growing relatively vigorously, such as electric light and power and telephones, the rise in share of total output, rapid at first, slows down materially.

This pattern of a life cycle of growth of output in the regulated industries is clearly associated with their origin: their emergence as a product of a major technological change which, as Dr. Ulmer points out, fills the vacuum of a felt need, of a wide potential market. The improvements that follow soon upon the introduction of the new technology, and the pressure on transportation and communication to build quickly toward an integrated country-wide

[4] All of these figures are from Tables 22 and 23 in the monograph.

framework, provide the continuous stimulus to a high rate of growth in the early phases of the industry's history. Then, as the national network is completed, as the original need is gradually satisfied, and as competitive pressures arise because of new technological changes, the rate of growth diminishes; and in some cases absolute and relative declines may set in.

(2) The long-term trends in capital formation are similar to the trends in output in that high rates of growth prevail in the early phases and then retardation begins. Plant and equipment grew in the regulated industries at rates averaging over 30 per cent per decade for the period from 1870 to 1910; but at a rate averaging only about 10 per cent per decade for the period from 1910 to 1950 (see Table 5). Net additions to durable capital of public utilities accounted for well over a fifth of all additions to durable capital in 1880–90; probably appreciably less than that in the earlier decades; about a fifth for the period 1880–1912; but less than a tenth for the period 1912–48. In other words, capital formation in the regulated industries, like output, first grew more rapidly than that for the nation and then declined materially as a share of the national total. This finding—that the trend pattern of capital formation reproduces that of output but in a magnified fashion and within a shorter time span—was to be expected. For the capital plant had to be built in advance of prospective demand and output, and as the technology became stabilized and the turbulent growth of output itself slowed down, higher rates of utilization and capital-saving economies made it possible to reduce the rate of growth of capital investment even more than the rate of growth of output was reduced.

(3) This relation between growth of output and of capital formation is reflected most clearly in the trends of the capital-output ratios. Among regulated industries the ratios of capital to output, which in most cases were much higher than for the country as a whole, have declined precipitously—if not from the very beginning, then from not long after the industry's birth. In steam railroads the ratio declined from about 16 in 1880 to less than 3 in the 1950's; in electric light and power, from 16 and more in the early 1890's to less than 2 in the 1950's; in telephones, from 4 or 5 in the 1890's to less than 2 in the 1950's; and in street and electric railways, from about 7 at the end of the 1890's to less than 3 in the 1950's (all of these figures from Charts 17 through 20 in the monograph). It is clear that the very large volume of durable capital investment, relative to current output, which was required in the regulated industries—particularly during the early phases of extensive growth and construction of the networks—provided the opportunity and

the incentive for reducing the capital-output ratio, so that the resulting reductions were greater, both absolutely and relatively, than in most other industries in the country.

(4) The rate of growth of gross capital formation fell markedly from the high levels of the early decades—partly because of the slowing down in the rate of growth of output, and even more because of rising rates of utilization of capacity and of capital-saving innovations. But this meant that the ratio of capital depreciation to current capital formation would, all other conditions being equal, grow; and as Dr. Ulmer demonstrates, growth in the ratio of depreciation to gross investment was a major factor contributing to striking long-term changes in the sources of financing. Whereas in the early decades financing was almost wholly from external sources and came largely from new issues of stocks and bonds, in the later decades internal financing—retained profits and especially depreciation charges—loomed much larger; in some industries, such as steam railroads, dominating the picture completely. True, other factors were involved; and we must always consider the effect of price changes, in scanning movements of capital formation in constant dollars to infer trends in sources of financing. But even some of these other factors—for example, changes in the future prospects of the industry which clearly affect its chances of securing external funds in long-term capital markets—are, like the growing ratio of capital depreciation to gross capital investment, aspects of the life cycle pattern of growth traceable to the distinctive characteristics of the regulated industries.

(5) Finally, attention must be called to the long swings that so clearly characterized capital formation in the regulated industries—particularly in steam railroads, whose record is the longest. The association between them and long swings in other important aspects of the economy is discussed in detail in Chapter 7 of the monograph. In the present context, it is important to stress that many of the regulated industries provide consumer goods and should, in general, be quite sensitive to population movements; and additions to the durable capital in them, like additions to residential housing, should be responsive to additions to population and to internal migration. Given the long swings in additions to population and in internal migration, it is this association that may be at the root of long swings in capital formation in the regulated industries.

Two comments should be added to this too-brief summary of Dr. Ulmer's findings. First, the trend patterns in output, capital formation, capital-output ratios, and sources of financing—as well as the susceptibility to long swings—that are so clearly apparent in the regulated industries can be found also in many other sectors. New industries, emerging as a result of new technological changes, are likely to go through similar life cycles of output, capital formation, capital-output ratios, and sources of financing; and if they happen to be responsive to population changes, may also show long swings. But because of the distinctive characteristics of regulated industries, these trends and long-term movements stand out with special prominence, and possibly provide a clearer insight into the causal mechanisms that bring them about.

Second, regulated industries are a category that includes subsectors at different stages of growth, and hence at different phases of their life cycle pattern. Any attempt at projection of the future from the past must, as Dr. Ulmer clearly shows, take account of this diversity of behavior within the group; and particularly of the possibility that the scope of the group will be expanded in the future by the addition of new industries, now in their very early stages or still to be born. It is the difficulty of appraising the potentials of the future with respect not only to the industry already existing and with clearly observable trends, but as well to new industries in the making, that renders projection so hazardous. And the rapidity of change, the short period of two to three decades in which an industry could grow, in the past, to unprecedented importance, is a warning that should be given due weight in avoiding oversimplified projection from the record.

IV

The comments above can hardly do justice to the analytical framework and to the empirical foundation of Dr. Ulmer's monograph. The intention here is to provide a brief view of the findings, and to introduce the reader to an intriguing account of long-term movements in capital and output in an important and distinctive sector of our economy. Even a brief glance at the discussion will reveal the variety of analytical suggestions advanced to account for the findings; and skimming through the appendixes will indicate the time-consuming effort that has been made to organize the underlying statistical data. One can trust that the data, findings, and hypotheses will be quickly absorbed in the stream of current work and thinking on economic problems; and thereby contribute to more reasoned views of them and so, hopefully, to more intelligent solutions.

PREFACE

THIS study grew out of a general inquiry into the secular growth of capital undertaken by the National Bureau of Economic Research in 1950. It was made possible by a generous grant from the Life Insurance Association of America.

It is a pleasure to acknowledge, and express gratitude for, the many debts incurred in the course of this study. The manuscript was read by Moses Abramovitz, Solomon Fabricant, Michael Gort, Simon Kuznets, and Geoffrey H. Moore, all of whom offered valuable suggestions. Periodic meetings during the planning stages made possible a fruitful exchange of views, also, with Morris A. Copeland, Daniel Creamer, Raymond W. Goldsmith, Leo Grebler, and Alvin S. Tostlebe. I had the benefit of useful comments from several Directors of the National Bureau—M. G. de Chazeau, Oswald W. Knauth, and Harold F. Williamson. In the extensive preliminary task of constructing statistical estimates, I was fortunate to have the competent assistance of Celia Gody. Milton Abelson and John Coleman also contributed to the statistical work in its earlier stages. I am grateful, also, for the skillful draftsmanship and imagination of H. Irving Forman, who prepared the charts, and for the editorial assistance of Mary Phelps and Emilie M. Hatfield. As with any strenuous and sustained effort, the sympathetic support of one's family and friends is vital. I acknowledge that in this regard my wife and children performed with extraordinary forbearance.

All the authors of the monographs in this series had the benefit of the aid of the Advisory Committee on the Study of Capital Formation and Financing, which assisted in drafting plans for the over-all inquiry and reviewed the final manuscripts. The committee was composed of Leo Wolman, Chairman; Sherwin C. Badger, Donald R. Belcher, Claude L. Benner, Percival F. Brundage, Arthur F. Burns, W. Braddock Hickman, Edgar M. Hoover, DeLong H. Monohan, and Geoffrey H. Moore.

MELVILLE J. ULMER

Gilmanton, I.W.
New Hampshire

CONTENTS

TABLES

TABLES

APPENDIX TABLES

CHARTS

APPENDIX CHARTS

CAPITAL IN TRANSPORTATION, COMMUNICATIONS, AND PUBLIC UTILITIES: ITS FORMATION AND FINANCING

CHAPTER 1

The Background

THIS study is an essay in the new and swiftly burgeoning field of growth economics. It is a localized analysis, focusing upon one important aspect of the American economy—the long-range behavior of capital formation and financing in transportation, communications, and public utilities. Of course, it is hoped that some of our findings will have significance beyond this framework—that they will illuminate, to some extent, the phenomena of industrial growth in the American economy generally, and, to at least a sparing degree, in the world at large. Our objective is nonetheless specific. The segment of the economy with which we are concerned is of obvious importance in itself. Taken together, the industries involved have in recent years accounted for nearly one-third of the gross capital expenditures on plant and equipment by private non-agricultural industry in the nation as a whole. In the earlier years within our purview their relative importance was even greater. They represent, also, an industrial area in which the degree of public regulation is sufficiently higher than elsewhere, in general, to warrant special consideration. We shall begin by describing the plan of the study, some of the underlying concepts and definitions, the character of the industries reviewed, and the scope and nature of the statistical materials.

Framework and Objectives

The few particular theories which bear upon long-term developments are discussed in the body of the text, as (and if) their applications arise. They will not be reviewed here. But a few prefatory remarks seem in order at this point on the underlying conception of secular development which enters our analysis. And this, fundamentally, turns on what we are trying to find out.

In one respect, this study springs from an interest in the long-run future. What are the prospects for capital formation over the next several decades? To what extent, and in what form, will they be reflected in financial markets? No illusions are entertained concerning the degree of reliability of any answers which may be made to these questions. For one thing, complete answers can be framed only on the basis of considerations which far transcend the ordinary borders of economic inquiry—entering into such disciplines as political science, international relations, and sociological history. Even within economics, the uncertainties faced are overwhelming.

But this is not the same as saying that *nothing* may be said, on the basis of economic analysis, about the future. It is, we think, not too much to hope for conditional statements about future trends (rather than prophecies) of practical interest to economists and men of affairs in politics and business.

But totally aside from this, an interest in the future provides a particularly fecund approach to a study of the past. Especially in fields in which formalized theory is scanty, it aids in lending purpose to description and discrimination to the accumulation of facts. It obviously heightens the need for hypothesizing and probing historical relationships, and for distinguishing the more enduring patterns from the primarily fortuitous.

TYPES OF PATTERNS

Indeed, patterns of uniformity in past behavior must comprise the central foundation for an appraisal of the future, and their analysis necessarily occupies a considerable portion of this study. Such patterns are of two general kinds. The first of these may be termed the *sequential pattern*, which refers to uniformity in the nature of the temporal sequence of events in single series of the same general classification. One of the best examples of a sequential pattern is the logistic curve, found by Pearl to be characteristic of growth in the populations of certain organisms under given conditions,[1] and used extensively by Kuznets to describe the growth of production.[2] But a sequential pattern need not be of mathematical form. Indeed the application of mathematical equations to sequential patterns have been, for the most part, deliberately eschewed in the body of this work. Few, if any, of the trends we have defined are sufficiently distinct, or sufficiently simple, to justify their use. And yet much can be said in quantitative terms, without formal mathematics, concerning the directions in which series move, the pace at which they progress, and the comparative behavior of different series of the same general kind or of any given series at different stages of development. To attempt to caparison all in a neat mathematical "law" would grossly violate the complexity and volatility of the multitude of forces which, in fact, act upon capital formation.

But a sequential pattern is essentially a relationship between the

[1] Raymond Pearl, *The Biology of Population Growth* (Knopf, 1925). Pearl and L. J. Reed applied the curve to the human population in their study, "On the Rate of Growth of the Population of the United States since 1790 and its Mathematical Representation," *Proceedings of the National Academy of Sciences*, Vol. 6, 1920, pp. 275–288. For an application of the curve to the population of business firms see Melville J. Ulmer, "Industrial Patterns of the Business Population," *Survey of Current Business*, May 1948, pp. 10–15.

[2] Simon Kuznets, *Secular Movements in Production and Prices* (Houghton, Mifflin, 1930).

variable of interest and time. No matter how broadly or narrowly defined, it is limited to purely descriptive services unless underlying economic factors, operating over time, are at least to some extent exposed. Whether the pattern may be extrapolated can be judged only by a study of the forces by which it was molded, and by the likelihood of their persistence. Often the underlying forces are susceptible to qualitative study only. But in some cases they may be represented quantitatively. Under these circumstances the possibility arises of defining quantitative relationships between the variable of principal interest and affiliated ones. Such relationships may be termed *affinitive patterns*. For example, the volume of residential housing may be related to such variables as changes in population, income, and interest rates.

A study of long-term trends, when most fruitful, yields uniformities or patterns, both of the sequential and affinitive variety. And a search for patterns and underlying forces obviously requires guides in the form of hypotheses and theories. In this regard, as already suggested, the store of available tools is far from abundant. For example, static theory suggests a relationship between the volume of investment, the prospective rate of return over costs, and the cost of money capital. But in seeking long-run determinants of investment, or of the methods by which they are financed, explorations inevitably move beyond this framework. We must inquire generally into the factors which generate enduring changes in the prospective rate of return, and are led to investigate long-run changes in the stock of capital, technological innovations, trends in the capital-product ratio, the role of population, tastes, urbanization, shifts in competition, and the like. The direction in which these factors *may* operate is in most cases obvious. But beyond this—the extent to which such forces *have* influenced investment over time, the relative importance of each, the directions in which they are tending—little can be said before examination of the facts. And in the realm of finance, in seeking shifts in the sources of funds, we must similarly rest on a loose and flexible system of ideas which only a background of factual study can reinforce and amplify.

THE TIME FACTOR

How to define the long run! Is it not, after all, merely the sum of its parts? And just when does the successive summation of short runs add to a total which may be termed long?

We shall think of the long run as any movement which persists over the course of more than one business cycle. For example, if one business cycle develops at a higher level than the previous cycle, we shall consider this a long-run upward movement. This view is premised on the observation that certain underlying economic forces generate movements which, in fact, do persist over the course of more than one (and often many) business cycles. An obvious illustration is the phenomenon of "linked" innovations.[3] The invention of the steam engine led to new modes of production in a multitude of industries to which its employment was adapted, to additional innovations in rail and water transport, in metallurgy, shipbuilding, coal mining, the construction of harbors, and so on. The development of a transcontinental railroad system was itself the initial link in a chain of innovations leading to the opening of new regions, to the appearance of new products, and new alignments of industry and distribution. Trends attributable to such cumulative innovation patterns are, by any standard, long-run.

There are others which we shall consider within our purview, in accord with the definition cited, though their classification may not be quite so distinct or unequivocal. Such is the twenty-year building cycle. The possibility of similar movements in the capital formation of regulated industries is a matter which receives some attention in subsequent pages. Their potential importance in the development of the regulated industries is such as to compel their inclusion. Furthermore, no statement of possible practical interest about the future (say the probable level of capital formation in the decade of the 1960's or 1970's) can afford to neglect the possible significance of waves of this kind.

But the business cycle is considered beyond the scope of this study. Though on occasion we may note the implications of our observations for such "short-run" phenomena, and though in many places we shall have to take them into account, they shall not be considered an object of the present study.

Characteristics of the Industries

In most industrial classifications the segment of the economy included in this study would be covered by the phrase, transportation, communications, and electric and gas utilities. For brevity, we shall refer to our group throughout this volume as the "regulated" industries. This is a matter of convenience, although it also serves to call attention to one of their more important characteristics. In our group, social control of business activity is generally more traditional and more extensive than elsewhere in the economy. Among the branches of industry we *exclude*, the most closely

[3] See B. S. Keirstead, *The Theory of Economic Change* (Macmillan, 1948), p. 136.

approaching in this respect are probably finance, agriculture, and housing.

The regulated industries, as we have circumscribed them, do not quite coincide with the segment of the economy covered by the legal definition of public utilities. Our concept is slightly broader. A few of the smaller components we include, such as radio broadcasting, have been denied public utility status by the courts. However, the legal concept does cover the more important industries in our group, and the others are at the very border of public utility status —at least when judged by the very high degree of government regulation now accorded legal approval.

One prominent characteristic of the regulated industries is a relatively high degree of monopoly. This, to be sure, is not *universally* true. There are minor exceptions, such as taxicab service, which is included in our group along with other types of transportation. But, generally speaking, the regulated industries are monopolistic, and it is this factor, when coupled with others, which most often justifies the public control exercised over their activities. In many cases, the companies in the various segments of our group operate under franchises, which confer exclusive rights for providing particular types of service in restricted areas. This is true, for example, of electric light and power, railroads, and telephone companies. In no case, of course, is the degree of monopoly unlimited. Obviously, the several types of transportation, of power supply and communication, compete. But in many cases, as in the provision of power for illumination in a particular locality, or the long distance hauling of coal in bulk along certain routes, the practical degree of monopoly enjoyed is very high.

All the regulated industries operate either under franchises or under licenses. Along with the exclusive rights they provide, franchises entail a threefold duty of serving all who apply, at "reasonable" rates, without discrimination. The granting of franchises thus implies some degree of public control over both investment and disinvestment. But it is important to note that this is tenuous and indirect, at most. The acceptance of a franchise by a private company is itself a voluntary act. And once accepted, only a minimum amount of service becomes mandatory. Facilities may be built with a level far above the minimum in mind, and later may be substantially contracted—all without public intervention. Considerable latitude ordinarily exists in the quality of the service performed and in the manner of its production. Furthermore, franchises may be abandoned.

Licenses are of course not so binding as franchises. Typically, the rights are not exclusive, and no obligation for the provision of service is entailed. Both licenses and franchises are associated with public regulation. The principal industries in the regulated group—e.g., the railroads, electric and gas utilities, telephones, street railways, and bus companies—operate on franchises and are subject to government regulation of the prices charged for their services.

The regulated industries are in many respects characterized by great diversity. Though it is of interest to deal with their totality—as we do in subsequent pages—the distinctive attributes of individual components can at no time be overlooked. To subject each component to detailed statistical analysis, however, is a task which would require more time—and space—than could be devoted to this study. Accordingly, a compromise was achieved. All statistical data have been provided for the sum of all regulated industries as a group and for six components: the railroads, electric light and power, telephones, local bus lines, street and electric railways, and "all other" regulated industries. These industries were selected because of their quantitative importance—now or historically—and because of the widely different stages of development they represent.

It should be borne in mind that the regulated industries are privately owned and operated. Our analysis, therefore, does not include the growth of public power facilities, publicly owned municipal transportation systems, or other public projects, except insofar as it must be taken into account when appraising the behavior of private business in the same or related fields. Our basic statistical series, unless otherwise indicated, cover private operations alone. A study of publicly owned projects would obviously have introduced a wide variety of special elements to our analysis, springing from the different motivations and the different conditions shaping the development of such enterprises. Their activities are worthy of a separate study.

The Data

It is a commentary on the paucity of our knowledge of long-term growth, that *not one* of the series employed in this study was heretofore available in its entirety. Accordingly, much of the time devoted to this project was concerned with the construction of the statistical foundation. New annual series from 1870 through 1950 are presented herein for the totality of the regulated industries and for each of the six segregated components on gross capital formation, capital consumption, net capital formation, and the aggregate value of plant and equipment. They are presented both in current and in 1929 dollars. Of these, only fragmentary figures on gross capital expenditures in current dollars were previously available, covering some of the recent years for some of our components. In addition, data on the output of the regulated industries—in the aggregate and for components—are presented in 1929 dollars for the period from 1880 through 1950. For the latter series, however, considerable groundwork had been laid by the earlier measurements of Gould[4] and Barger,[5] who, between them, covered most of the regulated industries and most of the time period of interest.

A word is in order here concerning the nature of these data, although full descriptions of their characteristics and their derivation are provided in Appendixes A through I. In general, the degree of their accuracy is directly correlated with time. For the years prior to World War I, in particular, the annual figures are subject to a considerable margin of error. There is, however, no evidence of any consistent bias, and tests suggest that moving averages succeed in eliminating, i.e. smoothing, most of the error in the estimates for the earlier years, as indicated in Appendix A. Accordingly, our analysis has been confined to a study of the nine-year moving averages, which prove to be a sufficiently sensitive tool for the object in hand of illuminating long-term trends.

Except for Chapter 8, in which explicit attention is given to financial relationships, analysis is focused entirely upon "real" quantities. Gross and net capital formation refer to flows of expenditures measured always in terms of the prices prevailing in 1929—and in this sense may be interpreted as physical quantities. Capital consumption and the stock of capital are similarly measured in dollars of constant purchasing power. This, of course, is a necessary procedure where the intent is to explore the characteristics and causes of growth, for the essential features of the phenomena under review would remain hopelessly obscure unless the influence of price level changes were segregated. On the other hand, when problems of financing are raised, as in Chapter 8, the analysis is extended to the flows of money capital unadjusted for alterations in purchasing power.

For the same reasons, output is likewise measured in "physical" terms. Thus railroad output refers to quantities of freight ton-miles and passenger miles, appropriately weighted; electric light and power, to units of electrical energy sold, weighted in accord with type of consumer; telephone output, to the weighted number of

[4] J. M. Gould, *Output and Productivity in the Electric and Gas Utilities, 1899–1942* (National Bureau of Economic Research, 1946).

[5] Harold Barger, *The Transportation Industries, 1889–1946* (National Bureau of Economic Research, 1951).

local and toll calls, and so on. To provide comparability with our measures of capital formation, the output series were valued at 1929 prices, and hence are similarly expressed in terms of money of constant purchasing power. Of course, measures of the physical quantity of capital formation as well as of output are subject to a common bias, inherent in *all* estimates of this kind. They do not reflect alterations in the *quality* of goods and services over time. In this sense, since the trend of quality has been upward, our figures understate the growth of capital and of output. A departure from the purely quantitative concepts employed, however, is neither feasible nor necessarily desirable.[6]

Certain peculiarities of definition in our series may be noted. Capital formation (whether net or gross) refers to accumulations of plant and equipment; the stock of physical reproducible capital similarly refers to the value (in constant dollars) of plant and equipment. The point is that inventory accumulations are consistently omitted from our series—a procedure justified by the fact that inventory accumulation is a matter of distinctly minor consequence among the regulated industries. Over the long run in this segment of the economy not more than 2 per cent of all money capital, and probably considerably less, was used for this purpose. On the other hand, the statistical resources available for estimating inventory trends are scanty over the period of interest; it was felt that the time required for constructing such estimates would not be warranted in the light of their negligible quantitative importance. It should be noted also that our figures on capital formation exclude land. Although for brevity the word is often omitted, our reference throughout this volume is to *reproducible* capital. Only in Chapter 8, where we focus on money flows and financing, do we consider expenditures on land and on inventories.

Our series on output are gross measures, in that they represent the *total* volume of goods and services produced. No deduction is made for the materials *consumed* in their production, which were purchased from other branches of industry. An analysis of the relevant data shows that the trend of output would be about the same whether measured in gross or in net terms.[7] Where the

[6] A passenger mile today may be a much more comfortable one than fifty years ago. *How* much more, could be measured only in terms of some unit of consumer satisfaction or utility. But the satisfaction actually experienced by a consumer would depend also on (among other things) the alternatives available now and fifty years ago, and these were very different. Neither the meaning of, nor a general way of measuring, a qualitative change is entirely clear. Considerations of much the same kind apply to qualitative changes in capital goods.

[7] See discussion in Chapter 4 in the section on *The Data*.

distinction in concept is significant for other purposes, at later points, particular attention is called to the matter and, where necessary, appropriate adjustments made.

In the next two chapters we shall review the record of the regulated industries, employing all of these data. Our discussion in these chapters, and to a large extent in Chapter 4 as well, will remain primarily on the descriptive level, laying the necessary groundwork for the analysis undertaken later.

CHAPTER 2

The General Secular Pattern

In 1870, the initial year covered by this study, the regulated industries were the giants of the American economy. It was in these that the newly won technological wonders of the industrial revolution found—and for the next two decades continued to find—their most dramatic manifestations. To them, capital had been drawn from all sectors of the nation, and continued to flow in very large quantities. By 1870 the net value of the plant and equipment of the regulated industries had reached $8 billion, measured in terms of 1929 prices. This was somewhat more than the entire gross national product in that year. In the following decade, the average annual gross flow of capital to this segment of the economy, again figured at 1929 prices, exceeded $500 million. This was about 15 per cent of the entire nation's annual gross investment in this period—an aggregate which includes public as well as private construction, residential as well as industrial building, and producers' durables purchased by farms as well as by nonagricultural industries.

The principal components of the regulated group in 1870 were the steam railroads and privately owned water transportation and water supply. Of these, the railroads were the youngest and by far the most important. They accounted for 85 per cent of the total value of the plant and equipment of all regulated industries, and more than 80 per cent of their gross capital formation, net capital formation, and output.

Large as it was in 1870, the subsequent growth of the regulated group was very substantial. The size of the railroads, as measured by the constant dollar value of their road and equipment, increased more than threefold in the years subsequent to 1870. Street and electric railways by 1870 had made but a modest start with the horsecar toward the elaborate network which reached, with the application of electric power, almost every sector of the nation just forty years later. The commercial beginnings of telephones and electric light and power were not realized until the early 1880's. Local bus lines, and a number of the industries we embrace in the "all other" group, such as air transportation, motor trucking, radio communication, and pipe lines, were developed in the main in the period after World War I. This chapter focuses upon the growth of the group as a whole, mindful that its several parts bear common as well as many distinctive characteristics, as detailed in the following chapter.

An Over-All View, 1870–1950

Net capital formation, measured in constant dollars, represents net additions to the physical stock of capital—within the statistical limits described in the previous chapter. The uneven, gyrating pace of growth in the facilities of the regulated industries, so measured, is depicted by the broken line in the center panel of Chart 1. There is, of course, no purely straightforward way to pierce the swift procession of lofty peaks and cavernous troughs, so pronounced in this series, for a glimpse of the longer-term trend. Even the nine-year moving average, illustrated in the solid line of the center panel, leaves cycles of great magnitude and duration—the long cycles to be described in Chapter 7. Accordingly, several vantage points have been taken.

The first of these is the tabulation of the annual average net capital formation in regulated industries, for overlapping twenty-year periods, as given in Table 1. These figures suggest a gradual

TABLE 1

Annual Average Capital Formation of All Regulated Industries, by Twenty-Year Periods

(*millions of 1929 dollars*)

Period	*Net Capital Formation*	*Gross Capital Formation*
1870–1889	413	642
1880–1899	460	830
1890–1909	636	1,245
1900–1919	713	1,662
1910–1929	740	2,036
1920–1939	328	1,858
1930–1949	175	1,864

Source: Appendix Table B–1.

rise from an annual rate of somewhat more than 400 million 1929 dollars in the first twenty years to a peak of 740 million in the period 1910–29. Then there is a steady decline to a rate of less than 200 million in the final twenty years of the tabulation. The location of the peak before or after World War I, however, remains uncertain in this compilation. For net capital formation in the period 1900–19 is almost as great as in the period 1910–29. Furthermore, a comparison of the post World War II peak with those in previous periods is not possible within this framework.

Some further light is cast on these questions by the compilation of Table 2. This presents nine-year averages of net capital formation

TABLE 2

Annual Average Capital Formation of All Regulated Industries in Nine-Year Periods, Selected Dates

(*millions of 1929 dollars*)

Central Year of Nine-Year Average	*Net Capital Formation*	*Gross Capital Formation*
1876	273	464
1886	413	713
1896	452	949
1906	968	1,781
1916	368	1,566
1926	1,132	2,615
1936	−388	1,230
1946	717	2,542
1880	393	620
1890	562	925
1900	405	1,009
1910	1,137	2,113
1920	363	1,684
1930	433	2,003
1940	−73	1,573
1950	1,610	3,690

Source: Appendix Tables K–2 and K–4.

taken at selected dates at ten-year intervals. Here we discern a gradual rise in net capital formation from about 270 million 1929 dollars per annum in the 1870's to a peak in the neighborhood of the first fourteen years of the twentieth century, when investment proceeded at a rate of $1 billion a year or more. From this point onward the general drift of net capital formation was downward, at least until the years following World War II. To be sure, another peak is reached in the 1920's, about equal to that achieved around 1910, but it is apparent now that the high level of investment at the later date is not so sustained as at the earlier one. Thus, the peak nine-year average centered in 1926 of $1,130 million is preceded by figures of less than 400 million for the nine-year averages centered in 1920 and in 1916. It is followed, moreover, by an investment rate of little more than 400 million in the nine years centered in 1930. On the other hand, the 1910 peak of about 1,140 million 1929 dollars is preceded by a figure almost as large—nearly 1,000 million —for the nine years centered in 1906.

Similar consideration may be brought to bear upon the evaluation of the post-World War II peak, though here the picture—at least as it appears in Table 2—is not so clear. In order to provide full consideration for the buoyant years following World War II, a special estimate was compiled for net capital formation of the regulated industries in the years 1951 through 1954, essentially beyond the time span established for this study. It will be observed that in the nine years centered in 1950 an additional investment peak was achieved, materially greater than those of 1926 and 1910. Here again, however, we may note that the peak is preceded by years of unusually low investment, as the tabulation shows. Indeed —to an even greater extent than in the 1920's—the huge post-World War II capital flow represented in important degree a process of recuperation from an extraordinarily severe and prolonged investment contraction. Nevertheless, it is apparent that proper perspective, from a secular standpoint, can be obtained only by taking explicit account of the long cycles which so clearly dominate this series. The computations of Table 3 were designed for this purpose.

TABLE 3

Annual Average Capital Formation of All Regulated Industries during Long Cycles, Dated from Nine-Year Moving Averages

(*millions of 1929 dollars*)

Long Cycle[a]	*Net Capital Formation*	*Gross Capital Formation*
1876–1898	432	765
1898–1918	722	1,620
1918–1935	483	1,961
1935–1946[b]	63	1,743

[a] Measured from trough to trough.

[b] Terminal date of series rather than cyclical trough.

Source: Appendix Tables K–2 and K–4. Terminal years of cycles are weighted one-half.

For this tabulation, cycles were marked off from the nine-year moving averages, which succeed in smoothing the shorter fluctuations. For the periods intervening successive troughs, the dates of which are given in the first column, annual averages of the nine-year moving averages of net capital formation were computed. Viewed in this framework, the general growth pattern is more distinctly outlined. The investment peak falls quite definitely in the earlier of the three doubtful periods—that is, in the dating of Table 3, somewhere in the span 1898–1918. This conclusion stands even when use is made of the special estimates for the years after 1950. The average annual net capital formation from the nine years centered in 1935 to the nine years centered in 1950 was 367 million 1929 dollars, 25 per cent less than that of the 1918–35 period, and only half the rate prevailing in 1898–1918. Thus, this approach suggests that the secular peak in this series must be dated somewhere in the years preceding World War I.

Consideration of all three tables together, however, impels a more circumspect conclusion. It is true that placed against the broad historical background, the buoyancy of the years following World War II appears less dominating and impressive than it might otherwise seem. Nevertheless capital formation reached heights in these years well in excess of all previous levels. It is reasonably clear, at least, that the secular trend since 1910 has not headed *sharply downward*. On the other side, our analysis precludes the judgment that the long-term movement was still heading *sharply upward*. Beyond this it is difficult to go. Three possibilities must be admitted: (1) that the long-term trend since 1910 was horizontal; (2) that it was rising slightly; (3) that it was falling slightly. For brevity we shall speak of the secular trend in net capital formation of the regulated industries as being "virtually horizontal" since about 1910.

A somewhat different impression of the development of the regulated industries is obtained from examination of the bottom panel of Chart 1. Gross capital formation embraces the *entire* flow of machines, buildings, and other capital equipment to the regulated industries, including that required both for the maintenance of their stock of plant and equipment as well as for expansion. It is thus the total demand made upon the economy by the regulated industries for capital goods, and is equal to net capital formation plus capital consumption.

The gross flow of investment evidences no downward tendency after World War I, or even a suggestion of a horizontal movement, as was the case for net capital formation. The general drift of the charted data appears distinctly upward. The figures of both Tables 1 and 3 show that the gross investment peak of the 1920's was substantially larger than that of the immediate pre-World War I period. And the data of Table 2, including the preliminary estimate for the relevant years of the 1950's, show that the post-World War II peak was, by a substantial margin, the greatest of all. In the nine years centered in 1950, gross capital formation proceeded at the annual rate of 3,690 million 1929 dollars, fully eight times the rate which had prevailed in the 1870's.

Of course the difference between gross and net capital formation is capital consumption. And the divergent behavior of the first two implies the general trend of the last. Capital consumption rose from about 180 million 1929 dollars per annum in the 1870's to a rate of nearly 1,800 million a year in the 1940's as shown in Table 4. In the 1870's capital consumption was about half the size of net capital formation. By the 1940's capital consumption had reached a rate about three times as great as net capital formation.

This phenomenal increase is, of course, inevitable in a growing industry. As long as net capital formation remains positive on balance—that is, as long as the total stock of capital continues to grow—capital consumption must increase. A logical exception—though hardly of practical import—would occur if the economic life

TABLE 4

Annual Average Capital Consumption of All Regulated Industries, by Decades

(*millions of 1929 dollars*)

Decade	*Capital Consumption*
1870–1879	178
1880–1889	279
1890–1899	461
1900–1909	757
1910–1919	1,141
1920–1929	1,449
1930–1939	1,612
1940–1949	1,766

Source: Appendix Table B–1.

of new capital used for replacement and expansion were materially expanded. And even this would arrest the advance of capital consumption only for a limited time, unless the economic life of plant and equipment was subject to *indefinite* and *continuous* extension.

Furthermore, barring the improbable exception noted above, the expansion of capital consumption to a size greatly exceeding net capital formation is also inevitable. For net capital formation is bound—ultimately—to decline relative to the total stock of capital; to maintain even a constant ratio it would have to increase (absolutely) to infinitely high amounts. If the ratio of capital consumption to the total stock of capital remains constant, increases, or declines only modestly, capital consumption must sooner or later equal and then exceed net capital formation. In the regulated industries as a group, the period of equality was reached—roughly—in the 1890's. And we have seen how rapidly after this date capital consumption outstripped net capital formation. A special circumstance, however, accelerated this movement. This was the growth of new industries such as telephones, electric light and power, trucking, local bus lines, and air transportation, virtually all of which had higher rates of capital consumption than the older giant of utilities, the railroads. Thus, in the regulated industries as a group, the ratio of capital consumption to the stock of capital increased rapidly. And in absolute magnitude, capital consumption swiftly dwarfed net capital formation.

The net result of the growth of the regulated industries is reflected in the expanding volume of their total stock of plant and equipment, depicted in the top panel of Chart 1. Physical capital exclusive of land, and measured in 1929 dollars, aggregated about $8 billion in 1870; by 1889 it amounted to $16 billion, and by 1912—at $32 billion—it had doubled again. By the end of 1950 it was at a new peak of 48 billion 1929 dollars. Net capital formation, discussed above, is of course identical with *changes* in the volume of plant and equipment; it measures, strictly speaking, the absolute rate of growth. And it will be recalled that the trend of net capital formation was approximately horizontal after 1910; when expressed as a ratio to the stock of capital, therefore, it would be expected to decline. In other words, the trend of net capital formation as described above indicates that the *relative* rate of growth in the stock of capital must have been retarded, at least after World War I. That indeed it was, is shown directly by the data of Table 5.

Percentage changes in the stock of capital appear to reach a peak in the ten or fifteen years prior to World War I. After this date they decline swiftly. Even the post-World War II flurry of investment fails to approach, on a relative scale, the previous peak. Furthermore, prior to the pre-World War I high the rise is not nearly so steep, when measured relatively, as it was in the absolute terms of net capital formation. Indeed the percentage increases in the 1870's and 1880's were but little below the peak rate reached in the decade or so before World War I. Relatively, the growth of the entire stock of plant and equipment of the regulated industries sloped slightly upward from 1870 to about 1910, and declined sharply thereafter. In contrast, the *absolute* rate of growth (net capital formation) had advanced vigorously up to 1910, and leveled off in the neighborhood of the peak in subsequent years.

In Table 6 the trend in the relative growth of the value of plant and equipment, measured in constant dollars, is shown in a different framework. Long cycle peaks were marked off in the nine-year moving averages of the series, and average annual percentage changes were computed for the intervening periods. Because of the great

CHART 1

Value of Plant and Equipment and Capital Formation, All Regulated Industries, 1929 Dollars, 1870–1951

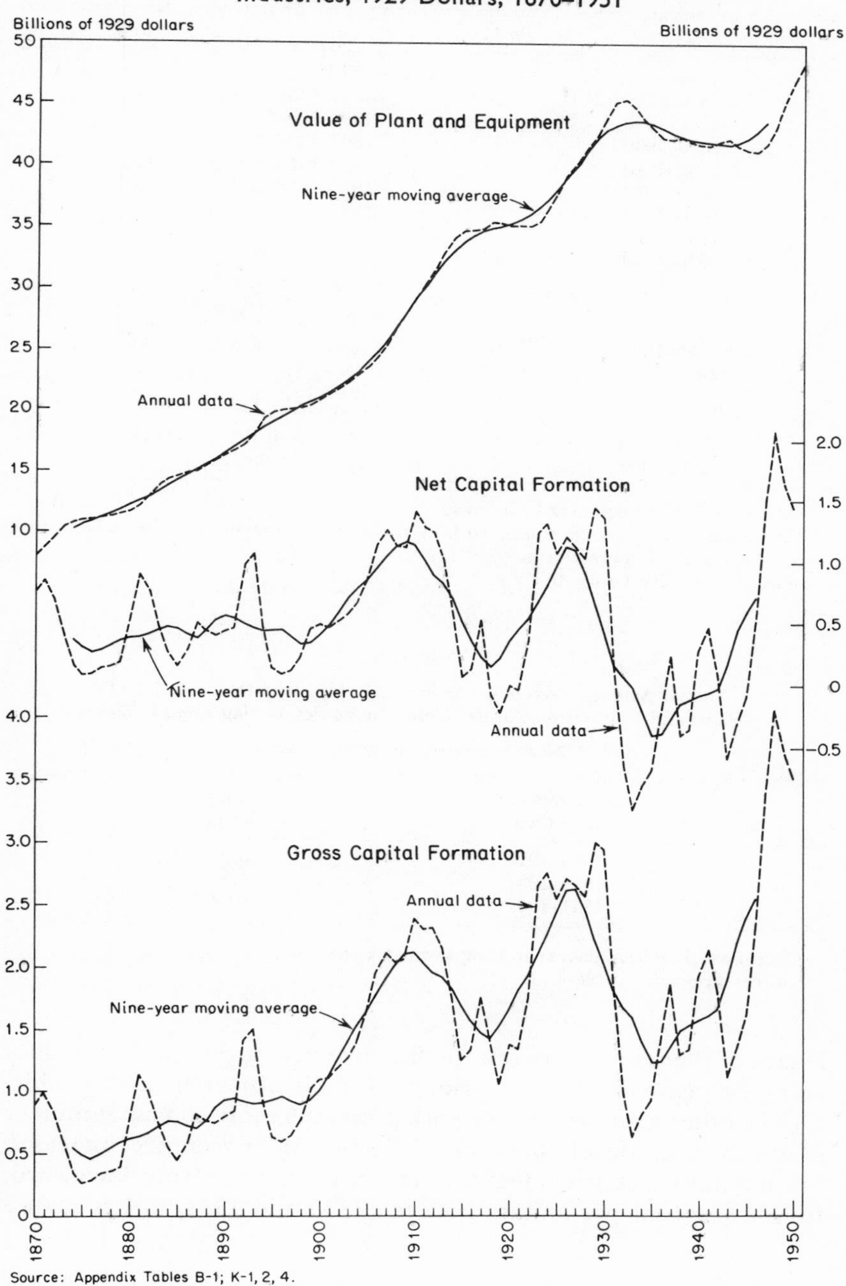

Source: Appendix Tables B-1; K-1, 2, 4.

TABLE 5

Percentage Changes in Constant Dollar Value of Plant and Equipment and of Output, All Regulated Industries

Years	*Per Cent*	*Years*	*Per Cent*
	PLANT AND EQUIPMENT[a]		
1870–1880	38	1876–1886	34
1880–1890	38	1886–1896	35
1890–1900	27	1896–1906	23
1900–1910	43	1906–1916	42
1910–1920	15	1916–1926	13
1920–1930	29	1926–1936	8
1930–1940	−8	1936–1946	−3
1940–1950	16		
	OUTPUT[b]		
		1886–1896	84
1890–1900	91	1896–1906	120
1900–1910	100	1906–1916	72
1910–1920	57	1916–1926	36
1920–1930	16	1926–1936	0
1930–1940	51	1936–1946	119
1940–1950	65		

[a] Values as of the beginning of the year.
[b] Percentage changes were computed from the nine-year moving averages, except that for 1950 the annual figure was used.
Source: Appendix Tables B–1 and K–9.

TABLE 6

Annual Average Percentage Increases in Constant Dollar Value of Plant and Equipment, All Regulated Industries, during Long Cycles

(*based on nine-year moving averages*)

Peak Dates of Long Cycle	*Percentage Increase*
1875–1914	3.0
1914–1931	1.6
1931–1947[a]	0.03

[a] Terminal date in nine-year moving average series.
Source: Appendix Table K–1.

length of the period between the first two peaks, the stage of slightly rising percentage increases prior to 1910 is obscured in this table. On the other hand, this framework presents a more concise summary of the magnitude of the over-all decline in percentage increases. For it is more clearly evident here that the trend is sharply downward, from 3 per cent per annum between 1875 and 1914, to less than 2

CHART 2

Output and Changes in Output, All Regulated Industries, 1929 Dollars, 1880–1950

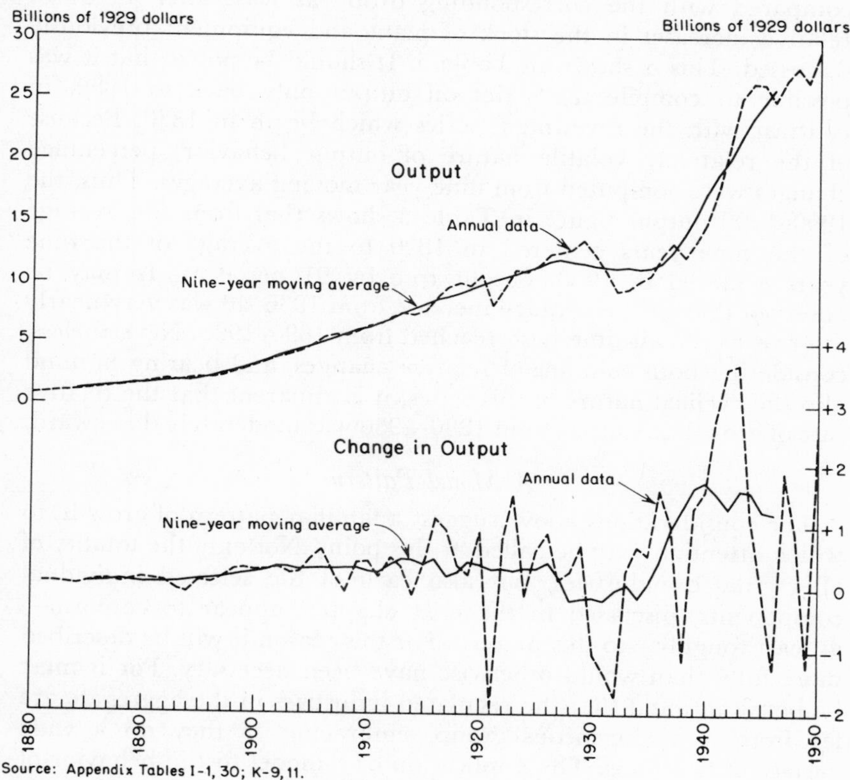

Source: Appendix Tables I-1, 30; K-9, 11.

per cent per annum between 1914 and 1931, and finally to a fraction of one-tenth of 1 per cent between 1931 and 1947.

The striking thing about the production of the regulated industries from 1870 to 1950 is the vigor of its rise. This is illustrated in the upper panel of Chart 2. Measured in terms of 1929 dollars, it rose from less than 1 billion in 1880 to more than 2 billion in 1897, to more than 4 billion in 1905, to more than 8 billion in 1918, and to nearly 17 billion in 1948. Nor did the absolute rate of increase tend to level off. This is illustrated indirectly by the general curvature of the series depicted in the upper panel of the chart, for it rather obviously heads upward at an ever-increasing pace. It is shown directly in the lower panel in which year-to-year changes in output are plotted. Despite the highly erratic behavior of this series it is apparent that the general trend is upward.

Moreover, though the general trend of relative increases in output is downward, the decline is fairly modest, especially when compared with the corresponding drop—at least after 1910—in relative increases in the stock of plant and equipment previously discussed. This is shown in Table 5. It should be noted that it was possible to compile the series on output only back to 1880, in contrast with the investment series which begin in 1870. Because of the relatively volatile nature of output behavior, percentage changes were computed from nine-year moving averages. Thus, the 1890–1900 output figure in Table 5 shows that from the average of the nine years centered in 1890 to the average of the nine years centered in 1900, output rose by 91 per cent. It may be observed that the percentage increase from 1936–46 was very nearly as great as the all-time high reached from 1896–1906. Nevertheless, considering both columns of relative changes, and bearing in mind also the cyclical nature of this series, it is apparent that the relative rate of growth in output from 1880–1950 was moderately downward.

A Model Pattern

The considerations above suggest a familiar pattern of growth, to which attention may be called at this point. Not only the totality of all regulated industries, but also each of the selected individual components, discussed in the next chapter, appear to conform—at least roughly—to this pattern. For this reason it will be described more fully than would otherwise have been necessary. For it must be borne in mind that the regulated industries in the aggregate are far from a homogeneous group, embracing as they do a wide variety of functions. The application of a model to the behavior of the totality, therefore, can at best be of descriptive utility only.

An ideal model of the pattern is illustrated in the solid lines of Chart 3. The form of the curve in the upper panel of the chart is of course similar to that employed frequently in the past to describe the time path in the output of many mining and manufacturing industries.[1] It is used here to depict the secular behavior of the physical stock of reproducible capital as well as of output. It is composed of the following "stages," of importance to our analysis: (1) it initially rises by increasing amounts per unit of time until it reaches an inflexion point at A; (2) it continues to rise, but by diminishing amounts, up to the peak at B; (3) it declines by increasing amounts

[1] Cf. Arthur F. Burns, *Production Trends in the United States since 1870* (National Bureau of Economic Research, 1934).

CHART 3

Model Pattern of Secular Growth in Industry

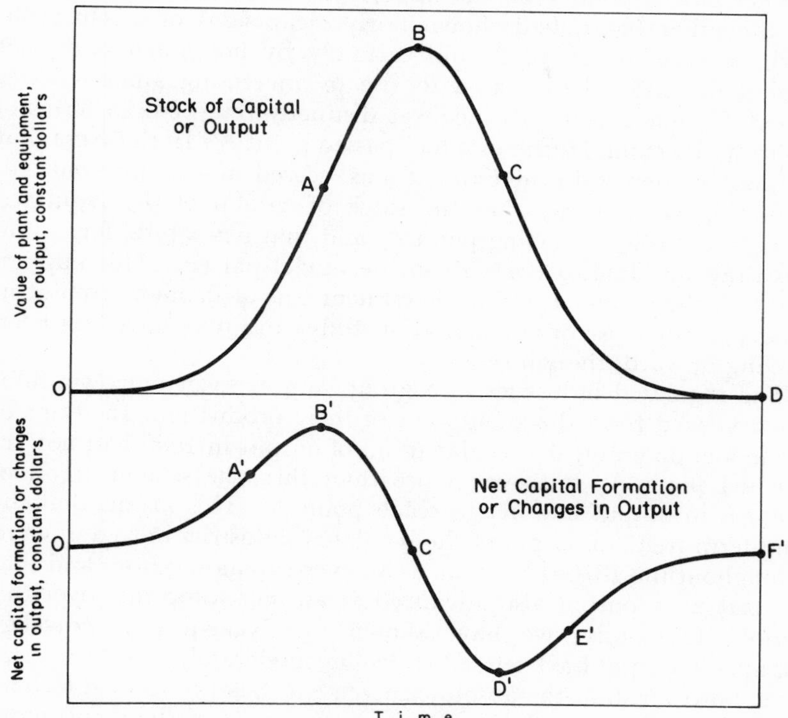

up to the inflexion point at C; (4) it continues to decline, but by diminishing amounts, until it reaches zero at D.

The curve in the lower panel of the chart is designed to depict the secular pattern of net capital formation or of *changes* in output, and is therefore the derivative of the one above. It, too, contains component stages of interest here. It rises at an increasing rate until A′, continues upward, but at a diminishing rate, until B′ (corresponding to point A in the upper curve); declines at an increasing rate until zero is reached at C′ (corresponding to B above), declines at a diminishing rate until D′ (corresponding to C above), rises at an increasing rate to E′ and at a diminishing rate until zero is reached again at F′ (corresponding to D above).

With this model as background, we may compare the behavior of capital formation and of output in the aggregate of the regulated industries. Throughout almost the entirety of the span of study the constant dollar value of plant and equipment rose at an increasing rate. In terms of Chart 3, this means that the stock of capital had not yet passed point A in the upper panel. Net capital formation, on the other hand, had shown fairly clear signs of leveling off. Perhaps even before 1870, and certainly by not much later, net capital formation had ceased to rise by increasing amounts over time.[2] The pace of its advance was distinctly retarded. In terms of Chart 3, net capital formation had passed point A′. In the sense that a *rising* tendency in investment has ceased to be pronounced, secularly, we may say that the stock of capital of the regulated industries was approaching point A, and that net capital formation was drawing close to point B′ in the model pattern. This implies, too, that the secular trend in investment was at its highest point in history at the close of our period of study, and may have still been moving upward, though slowly.

The regulated industries as a group appear even more youthful when viewed from the standpoint of their production. In terms of the model diagram, the secular trend of output in 1950 had not yet reached point A; but even more than this, the secular trend of changes in output had yet to reach point A′. This means that the long-term trend of output of the regulated industries moved upward throughout the 1870–1950 span at an ever-expanding rate; and that the *changes* in output also advanced at an increasing rate over this period. Previously, we have shown that year-to-year *percentage* changes in output have tended to decline moderately. We emphasize here, however, that the absolute increments have continued to tend upward—a fact which for some purposes is perhaps of more significance. A more vigorous pattern of growth is barely possible in an industry group which is among the oldest in the American economy.

Significance of the Model

Observations made in the section on the model pattern are of course consistent with the conclusions drawn in earlier pages from an analysis of tabular materials. The pattern served only as a descriptive device. In the following chapter it shall serve also as a framework for ready appraisal and comparison of the several individual regulated industries selected for separate study.

It may also be suggested, perhaps, that the growth model adds an entirely new dimension to the analysis thus far undertaken. For does it not imply something about both past and future? Should

[2] A mathematical curve approximating our model was fitted to the data, and suggested a date for inflexion point A′ at about 1875.

not mathematical curves—empirical approximations of our model—be fitted to the data and employed for predictive purposes of interest? With reference to the period *prior* to 1870, fragmentary evidence permits us to say that what such curves would imply, broadly, is very likely true. Extrapolating them over future years presents other problems. Past experience provides sufficient caution against mechanical projections of this order. For economic history is larded with mathematical patterns adhered to for a time and then abruptly broken.[3] The very nature of economic activity warns against excessive confidence in a mere mathematical model. The power of these warnings is increased manifold when, as in the present case, the model applies to an aggregate of many industries with a wide variety of heterogeneous characteristics. Until, or unless, a model of this type can be supplemented with considerations of another order—those referring to *causal* relationships and the reasons for the behavior summarized—it must remain of descriptive utility only. We should caution, in particular, that no assumption can be made about the chronological *duration* of the various stages of the model. Indeed, as the next chapter shows, these may vary almost without limit. Hence their value for some *mechanical* scheme for prediction is next to nothing.

In the broadest terms, however, some analytical justification may be suggested now for the use of a model of this general type when applied to more homogeneous groupings, as it is in the following chapter. This stems from the expectation, on theoretical grounds as well as on the basis of previous studies,[4] that the rate of growth of an industry is *ultimately* retarded. This idea—which is expanded in Chapter 5—suggests a tendency for each of the regulated industries to follow our model pattern of growth (or some similar version of it) at least part way. The model is therefore illustrative of certain observable uniformities of behavior. As such, it provides a useful framework for the broader analysis of trends which is undertaken later.

[3] Cf. Harold T. Davis, *The Theory of Econometrics* (Principia, 1941), Chapter 11. Numerous mathematical "laws" are defined for industrial growth; virtually all have since been flagrantly violated.

[4] Burns, *op. cit.*, and Simon Kuznets, *Secular Trends in Production and Prices* (Houghton Mifflin, 1930).

CHAPTER 3

Variations in Secular Patterns

In at least one respect the utilities group is far from cohesive. It includes industries in widely diverse stages of development—from the venerability of the steam railroads to the robust middle age of electric light and power and the swiftly growing adolescence of pipe lines and air transportation. Stage of development is of course not a mere matter of chronology, for there is great variety in life spans, and maturity arrives much more quickly for some than for others. This will be apparent when we apply to their growth trends, the model pattern of secular development introduced in Chapter 2, and note the progress made by each of the components.

As indicated earlier, the individual regulated industries we have selected for special study were chosen—at least in part—with an eye to the proper representation of this heterogeneity. The components so selected are listed in Table 7, where the relative importance of each with respect to the stock of reproducible capital and capital formation is also given.

The preponderant share of steam railroads in the total during the first decade of our time span is clearly evident in this table.[1] By the early 1900's, however, this situation had been substantially altered. The proportion of the total physical stock of capital held by the railroads declined from nearly 85 to less than 70 per cent; their share of gross capital formation declined from about 82 to less than 45 per cent, and their share in net capital formation from more than 80 to less than 40 per cent.

The industries which had made the most significant relative gains from the 1870's to the 1900's were street and electric railways and electric light and power. The growth of both, of course, reflected the quick spread of the commercial application of electricity. The former in the first decade of the twentieth century accounted for 12 per cent of the constant dollar value of plant and equipment, and for about 20 per cent of the total capital formation of all regulated industries. Electric light and power—a much younger industry—accounted for less than 5 per cent of the stock of reproducible capital, but for more than 15 per cent of the total capital flow. Telephones had also made substantial gains. The all other group—roughly—maintained its relative position.

[1] Note that the term steam railroads is used loosely here and throughout this volume; it covers roads which in the modern era have used diesel or electric power as well as steam. We use the term because of its historical importance, and also to assist in avoiding confusion with the electric street railways prominent in urban transportation.

TABLE 7

Percentage of Total for All Regulated Industries Accounted for by Each Component in Stock of Reproducible Capital and Capital Formation, Selected Decades

(*based on values in 1929 dollars*)

Industry	*1870–1879*	*1900–1909*	*1940–1949*
	VALUE OF PLANT AND EQUIPMENT		
Steam railroads	84.8	67.4	52.7
Electric light and power[a]	0	4.6	17.4
Telephones	0	3.1	7.0
Street and electric railways[a]	1.5	12.2	2.7
Local bus lines[a]	0	0	0.8
All other transportation, communications, and utilities	13.7	12.7	19.5
Total	100.0	100.0	100.0
	NET CAPITAL FORMATION		
Steam railroads	80.7	39.1	3.8
Electric light and power[a]	0	17.8	30.0
Telephones	0.3	8.1	41.6
Street and electric railways[a]	3.6	20.9	−9.3
Local bus lines[a]	0	0	2.4
All other transportation, communications, and utilities	15.4	14.0	31.6
Total	100.0	100.0	100.0
	GROSS CAPITAL FORMATION		
Steam railroads	81.7	44.1	23.8
Electric light and power[a]	0	15.1	22.0
Telephones	0.2	9.4	20.3
Street and electric railways[a]	3.6	18.1	1.1
Local bus lines[a]	0	0	2.5
All other transportation, communications, and utilities	14.6	13.3	30.3
Total	100.0	100.0	100.0

[a] Excludes publicly owned facilities.

Source: Appendix Tables B–1, C–1, D–1, E–1, F–1, G–1, and H–1. Detail may not add to 100 because of rounding.

By the 1940's further significant revisions had occurred in the relative importance of the principal regulated industries. Telephones exceeded all other components in net capital formation, accounting for about 40 per cent. Electric light and power and the all other group—reflecting the growth of pipe lines, gas utilities, trucking, air transportation, and other new industries—were not far behind with about 30 per cent each of the total net capital formation. The railroads' share in the net flow of capital had been reduced to less than 4 per cent. It is important to note, however, that the railroads still—in the 1940's—owned more than half the reproducible capital of all regulated industries and, because of the large replacement demand stemming from this ownership, accounted for a significant proportion of the total gross capital formation. Of course street and electric railways were actually contracting in this period. Local bus lines were growing, but accounted for only a modest share of the total investment flow.

The relative importance of each of the components in terms of output (as measured by the constant dollar value of their services) is shown in Table 8. The share of the railroads in this total declined

TABLE 8

Percentage of Total for All Regulated Industries Accounted for by Each Component in Output

(based on nine-year averages of values in 1929 dollars)

Central Year in Nine-Year Average	*All Regulated Industries*	*Railroads*	*Electric Light and Power*	*Telephones*	*Street and Electric Railways*	*Local Bus Lines*	*All Other*
1886	100	80	...	...	...	0	...
1890	100	80	...	...	...	0	...
1896	100	77	1	2	9	0	11
1900	100	74	2	3	9	0	12
1906	100	68	2	6	10	0	13
1910	100	66	3	7	10	0	14
1916	100	64	5	7	9	0	15
1920	100	60	7	7	9	0	16
1926	100	52	11	9	8	1	19
1930	100	45	15	9	6	1	23
1936	100	37	19	9	5	2	28
1940	100	41	19	8	3	2	27
1946	100	38	20	8	2	2	30

Detail may not add to 100 because of rounding.
Source: Appendix Table K–9.

sharply from 1896 to 1946, though at the latter date they still accounted for nearly 40 per cent of the production of all regulated industries. Street and electric railways, which had once accounted for 10 per cent, had dropped to 2 in the 1940's. Aside from the all other group, the second most important in the 1940's, in terms of production, was electric light and power with 20 per cent. Telephones had also achieved a relative standing of significance, with 8 per cent of total output. The all other group, with its many new and widely publicized segments, accounted for 30 per cent.

Capital Flows

The rate of growth of the various components is shown in the center panels of Charts 4 through 9. The diversity of behavior is

CHART 4
Value of Road and Equipment and Capital Formation, Steam Railroads, 1929 Dollars, 1870–1951

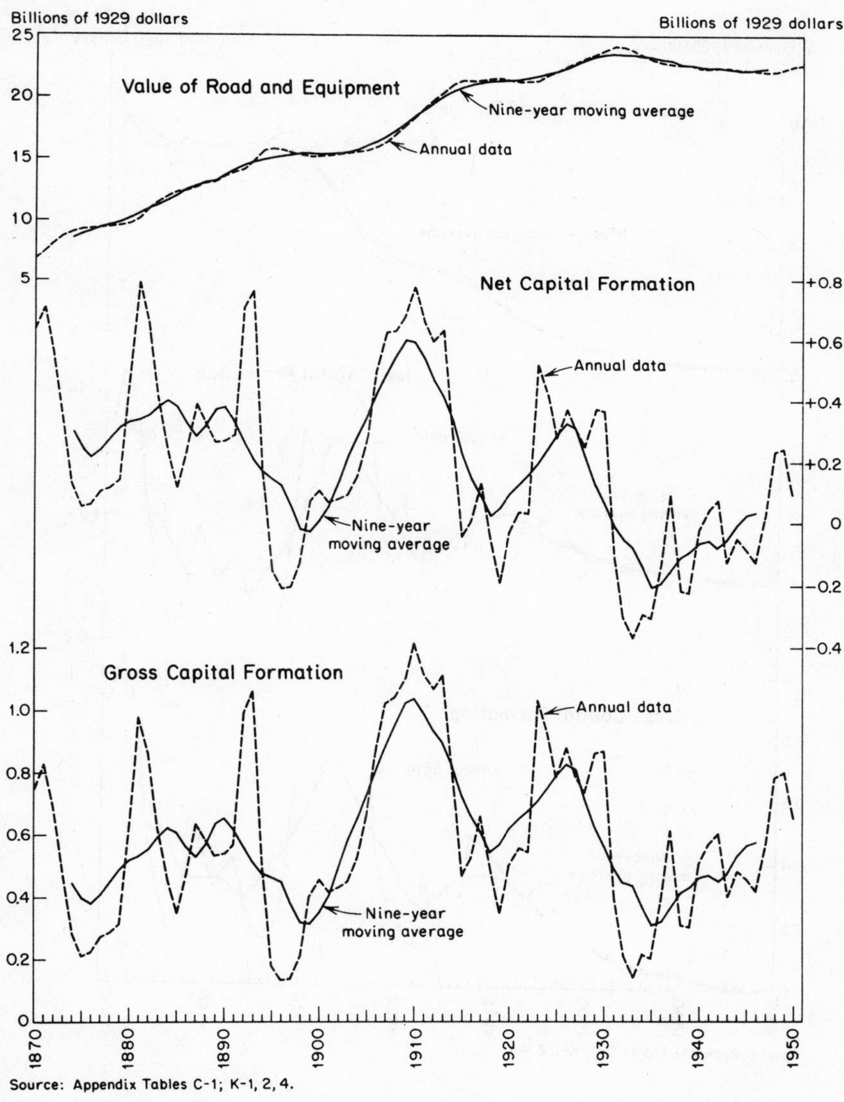

Source: Appendix Tables C-1; K-1, 2, 4.

CHART 5

Value of Plant and Equipment and Capital Formation, Electric Light and Power, 1929 Dollars, 1881–1951

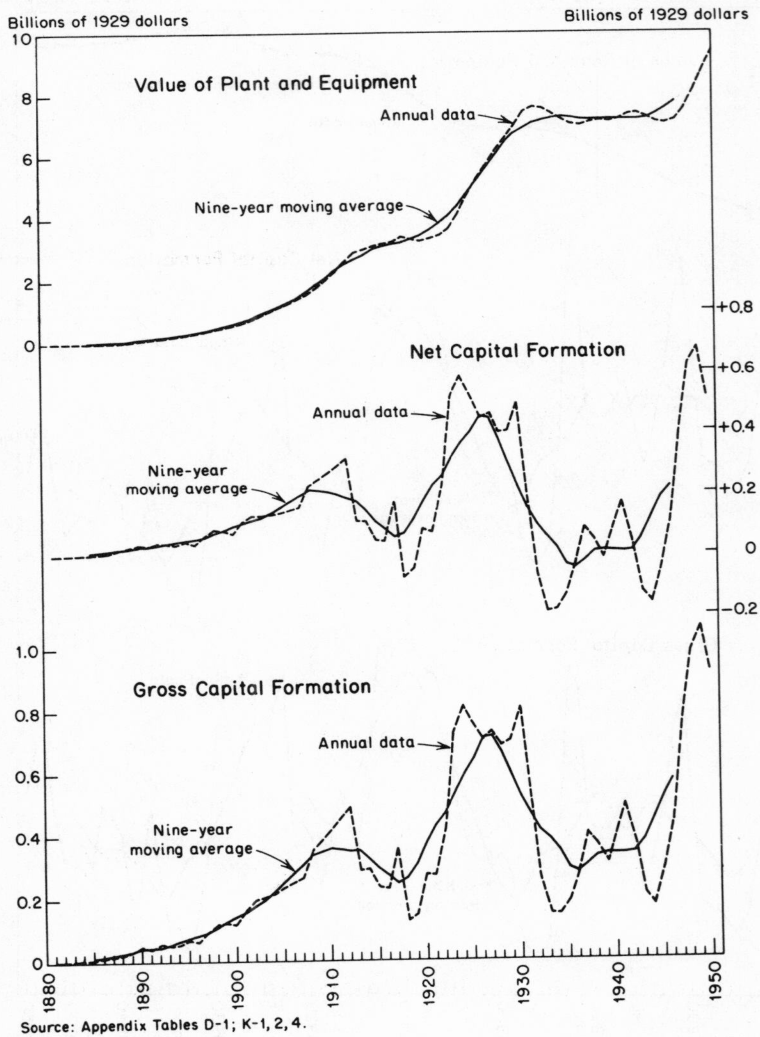

Source: Appendix Tables D-1; K-1, 2, 4.

CHART 6

Value of Plant and Equipment and Capital Formation, Telephones, 1929 Dollars, 1880–1951

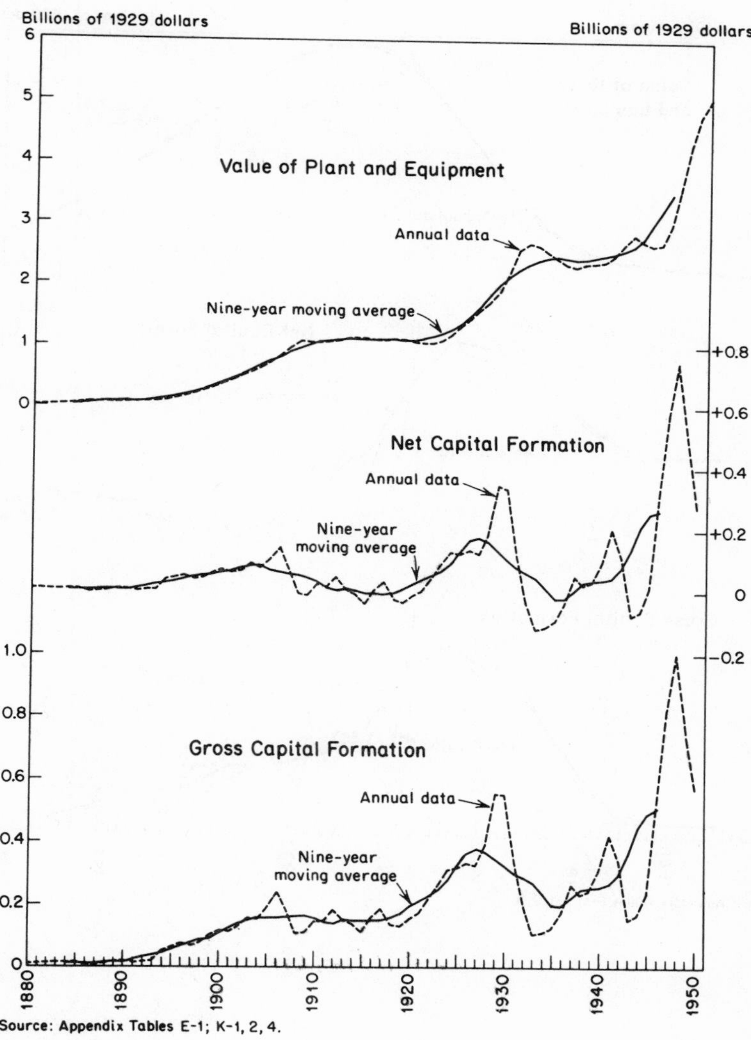

Source: Appendix Tables E-1; K-1, 2, 4.

CHART 7

Value of Road and Equipment and Capital Formation, Street and Electric Railways, 1929 Dollars, 1870–1951

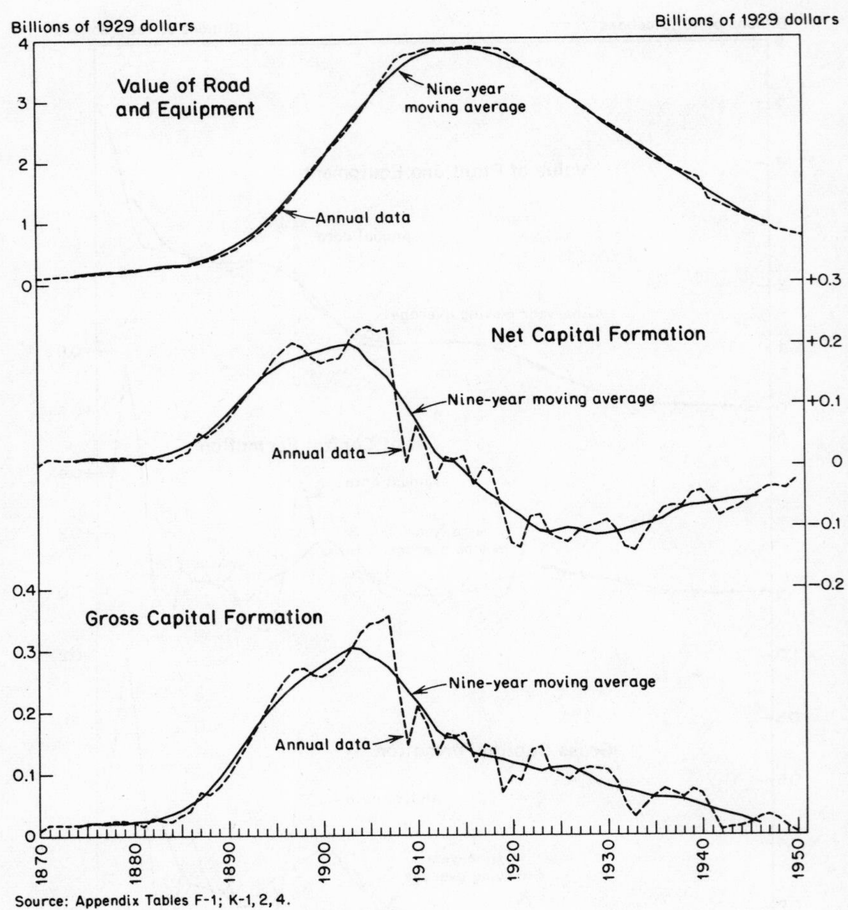

Source: Appendix Tables F-1; K-1, 2, 4.

CHART 8
Value of Plant and Equipment and Capital Formation, Local Bus Lines, 1929 Dollars, 1910–1951

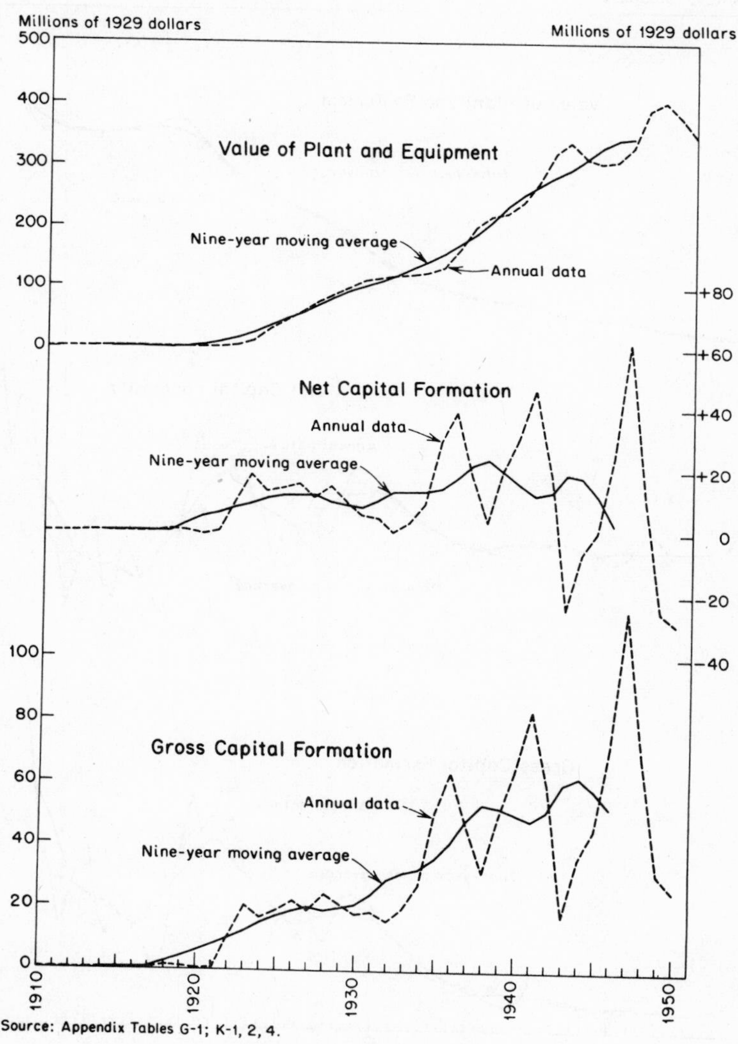

Source: Appendix Tables G-1; K-1, 2, 4.

CHART 9

Value of Plant and Equipment and Capital Formation, All Other Utilities and Transportation, 1929 Dollars, 1870–1951

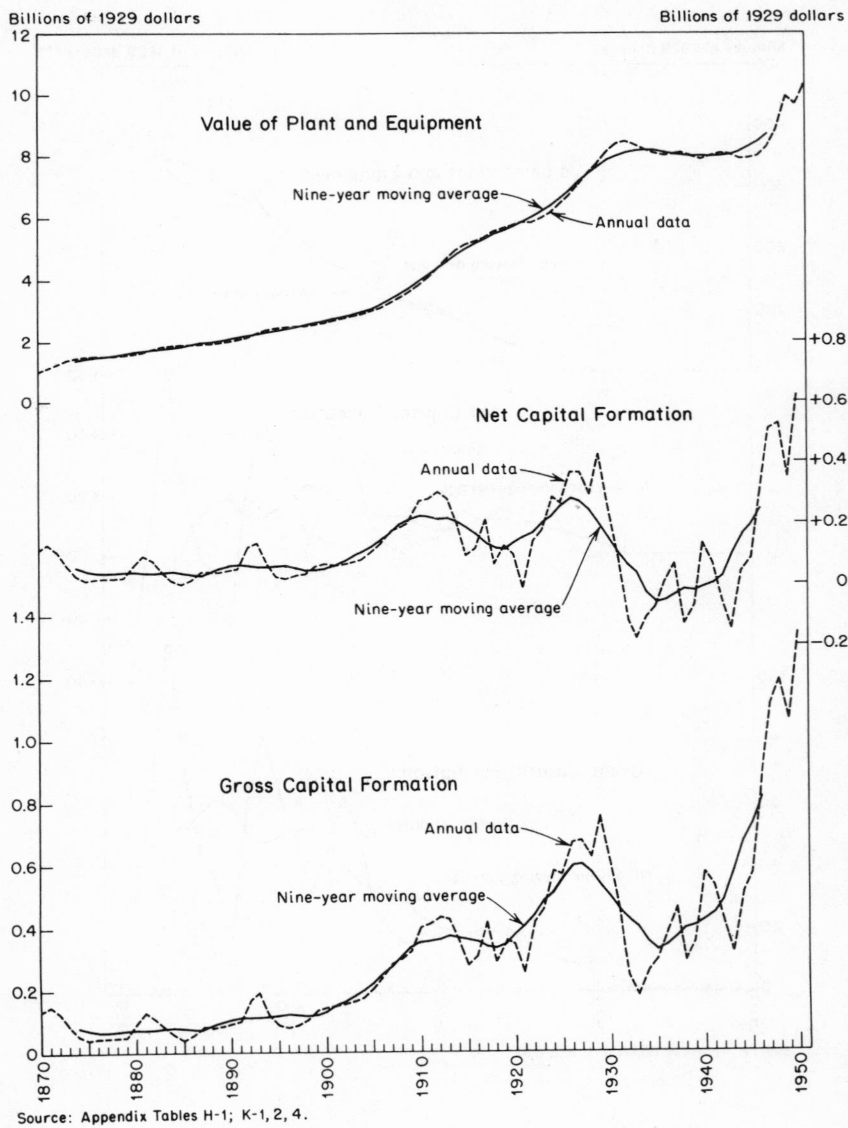

Source: Appendix Tables H-1; K-1, 2, 4.

striking. At one extreme is the sharp upward trend for telephones, at the other the inverted U-shaped curve for street and electric railways, with its sharp downward movement over the last several decades.

Despite the inherent volatility of net capital formation series, the general long-term trend in rate of growth is reasonably clear for most components. The charts and Tables 9 and 10 tell the gist of the

TABLE 9

Net Capital Formation, All Regulated Industries and Components, Annual Averages by Decades, 1870–1949

(millions of 1929 dollars)

Decade	*Total*	*Steam Railroads*	*Electric Light and Power*[a]	*Telephones*	*Street and Electric Railways*[a]	*Local Bus Lines*[a]	*All Other*
1870–1879	352	284	0	0	13	0	54
1880–1889	474	388	9	7	27	0	43
1890–1899	447	157	48	31	152	0	60
1900–1909	826	323	147	67	173	0	116
1910–1919	600	281	122	2	−1	0	196
1920–1929	880	256	367	116	−109	11	240
1930–1939	−226	−148	16	14	−92	13	−29
1940–1949	576	22	173	240	−54	14	182

Based on Appendix Tables B-1, C-1, D-1, E-1, F-1, G-1, and H-1. Detail may not add to totals because of rounding.

[a] Excludes publicly owned facilities.

story. The trend for telephones was sharply upward throughout the 1870–1950 span, with the annual net capital flow amounting to 240 million 1929 dollars in the final decade. The trend of net capital formation in electric light and power and in the all other group was also upward throughout the period of study, and was especially vigorous during the earlier years in the former. In both cases, however, the rate of advance was distinctly retarded after World War I, and even more so after the 1920's. The net flow of physical capital to the railroads expanded until the first decade of the twentieth century, moved down slightly in the next two decades, and then in the final twenty years, on balance, turned moderately negative. For street and electric railways the peak was also reached in the first decade of the twentieth century, but in this case the subsequent decline was precipitous. Capital moved out of this industry, on balance, in each of the subsequent decades. Thus, in the inverse order of relative maturity, as judged from the net capital flow, we would rank these components as follows: telephones,

TABLE 10

Net Capital Formation, Component Regulated Industries, Nine-Year Averages, 1876–1950

Central Year of Nine-Year Average	*Millions of 1929 Dollars*	*Central Year of Nine-Year Average*	*Millions of 1929 Dollars*
RAILROADS			
1876	218	1880	331
1886	322	1890	379
1896	125	1900	4
1906	425	1910	598
1916	149	1920	99
1926	324	1930	66
1936	−196	1940	−61
1946	32	1950	92[a]
ELECTRIC LIGHT AND POWER			
1886	14	1890	28
1896	54	1900	91
1906	174	1910	207
1916	82	1920	172
1926	445	1930	213
1936	−47	1940	7
1946	221	1950	513[a]
TELEPHONES			
1886	6	1890	8
1896	41	1900	63
1906	62	1910	32
1916	−4	1920	26
1926	168	1930	107
1936	−23	1940	38
1946	262	1950	271[a]
STREET AND ELECTRIC RAILWAYS			
1876	14	1880	13
1886	36	1890	84
1896	169	1900	191
1906	161	1910	72
1916	−26	1920	−74
1926	−102	1930	−113
1936	−86	1940	−64
1946	−51	1950	−24[a]
LOCAL BUS LINES			
1916	[b]	1920	5
1926	12	1930	8
1936	17	1940	16
1946	3	1950	−29[a]

(concluded on next page)

TABLE 10 (concluded)

Central Year of Nine-Year Average	*Millions of 1929 Dollars*	*Central Year of Nine-Year Average*	*Millions of 1929 Dollars*
	ALL OTHER		
1876	40	1880	41
1886	36	1890	63
1896	62	1900	55
1906	145	1910	227
1916	166	1920	135
1926	285	1930	152
1936	−54	1940	−10
1946	249	1950	621[a]

[a] For 1950 only.
[b] Less than 500,000.
Source: Appendix Table K–7.

electric light and power, the all other group, railroads, and street and electric railways.

Only local bus lines remain unranked. In this case, the period of operation is so short that definition of the secular trend becomes most difficult. The decade averages of Table 9 suggest a slight upward movement from 1920–50. But Chart 8 provides a different impression, and so does the more detailed tabulation of Table 10. It would appear from these that the peak rate of growth in local bus lines occurred in the 1930's, and that the subsequent decline from these very high levels has been substantial. This does not deny, of course, that the industry remains in a stage of expansion, for net capital formation in the 1940's as a whole remained positive.

Of course the impression gained from examination of the gross capital flow, shown in the bottom panels of Charts 4 through 9, is a more buoyant one. Secular declines, where they occur, are dampened or delayed, and upward trends become even steeper. Thus, the gross flow of capital to the railroads continued to rise through the 1910–19 decade, as Chart 4 and Table 11 show. Although decade averages in the latter table indicate a high for electric light and power in 1920–29, Chart 5 shows that the rate of gross investment in the years 1948–50 reached unprecedented heights. The upward trends for telephones and for the all other group are materially accelerated when attention is shifted from net to gross capital formation. Decline is virtually obliterated in the gross investment flow of local bus lines. For street and electric railways it is apparent that despite a precipitous decline, gross capital formation had not ceased entirely, for as a practical matter, as long as *any* lines remained in operation the need would persist for some replacement investment.

TABLE 11

Gross Capital Formation, 1929 Prices, All Regulated Industries and Components, Annual Averages for the Decades 1870–1950

(millions of 1929 dollars)

Decade	*Total*	*Steam Railroads*	*Electric Light and Power*[a]	*Telephones*	*Street and Electric Railways*[a]	*Local Bus Lines*[a]	*All Other*
1870–1879	530	433	0	0	19	0	77
1880–1889	753	612	10	12	40	0	79
1890–1899	908	468	70	50	204	0	115
1900–1909	1,583	698	239	149	286	0	211
1910–1919	1,742	777	304	147	147	0	366
1920–1929	2,330	760	608	304	107	15	535
1930–1939	1,387	361	342	234	66	34	350
1940–1949	2,342	557	516	475	25	59	710

Based on Appendix Tables B–1, C–1, D–1, E–1, F–1, G–1, and H–1. Detail may not add to totals because of rounding.

[a] Excludes publicly owned facilities.

TABLE 12

Capital Consumption, 1929 Prices, All Regulated Industries and Components, Annual Averages for the Decades 1870–1950

(millions of 1929 dollars)

Decade	*Total*	*Steam Railroads*	*Electric Light and Power*[a]	*Telephones*	*Street and Electric Railways*[a]	*Local Bus Lines*[a]	*All Other*
1870–1879	178	149	0	0	6	0	23
1880–1889	279	224	1	5	14	0	35
1890–1899	461	311	22	20	52	0	56
1900–1909	757	375	92	82	113	0	95
1910–1919	1,141	497	182	145	148	0	169
1920–1929	1,449	504	241	188	217	5	295
1930–1939	1,612	509	326	220	158	21	379
1940–1949	1,766	535	343	235	79	45	528

Based on Appendix Tables B–1, C–1, D–1, E–1, F–1, G–1, and H–1. Detail may not add to totals because of rounding.

[a] Excludes publicly owned facilities.

The growth of capital consumption, which is the difference between gross and net capital formation, is shown in Table 12. The trend has been sharply and steadily upward in all industries except street and electric railways. The general reasons for this were cited in the previous chapter. It is significant to note that an investment of nearly two billion 1929 dollars was required annually in the 1940's simply to keep the physical stock of capital of the regulated industries intact, and that more than one-fourth of this was accounted for by the railroads. By the 1920's capital consumption had grown to exceed net capital formation for every component except local bus lines and electric light and power, and during the next two decades capital consumption was considerably greater for these two components as well. For regulated industries in the aggregate in the 1940's, capital consumption amounted to more than three times the volume of net capital formation, and this was only in small part due to the restrictions on investment during the war years.

The Stock of Capital

In the top panels of Charts 4 through 9, the growth of the regulated industries is shown directly—at least in terms of their physical stock of capital. In this series the trend is upward for all components except two: railroads and street and electric railways. In the case of the former, the downward trend did not start until the 1930's, and it progressed only slightly after that date. For street and electric railways, the drop was sharp and started early in the twentieth century.

But even among those components for which the trend is regularly upward, there is great diversity in the pace of the movement. This was evident in our discussion of net capital formation. It is also evident, visually, in the top panels of the charts. In the earlier stages of all series, growth proceeds at an expanding rate, with the slope of the stock of capital curve gradually increasing. In the case of telephones, this condition seems to persist throughout the 1880–1950 span. For electric light and power, the all other group, and local bus lines, the rate of growth—after a time—loses some of its vigor, and in the latter, tends to flatten out. In the case of railroads and street and electric railways, this flattening out period is followed by actual cessation of growth and subsequent decline. It should be borne in mind that the latter two components were in fact fairly well developed even in 1870, and accordingly the earliest stage of growth at an increasing rate is barely evident, if at all, within the limits of the time span we cover.

Declining Relative Rates of Growth

In one respect, however, there is agreement among *all* components in the secular trends in the stock of reproducible capital. In all cases, the *relative* rate of growth progressed at a declining rate, and the stage of decline set in at very early periods in the history of each component. This is seen, in the broadest terms, in the data of

Table 13. Here annual percentage changes in the constant dollar value of plant and equipment are given between long cycle peaks. From an annual rate of growth in their facilities of 2 per cent in the 1875–1914 period, the railroads dropped to less than 1 per cent in 1914–31, and to a slightly negative annual change in the final period of 1931–47. Electric light and power dropped from a nearly 20 per cent annual increase during the first cycle to about 5 per cent in the second and to less than 1 per cent in the third. Over the

TABLE 13

Average Annual Percentage Changes in Constant Dollar Value of Plant and Equipment during Long Cycles, All Regulated Industries and Components

	PEAK DATES OF LONG CYCLES BASED ON NINE-YEAR MOVING AVERAGES[a]		
Industry	*1875–1914*	*1914–1931*	*1931–1947*[b]
All regulated industries	+3.0	+1.6	+0.04
Steam railroads	+2.2	+0.9	−0.3
Electric light and power[c]	+19.6[d]	+5.4	+0.7
Telephones	+11.8[e]	+4.2	+2.8
Street and electric railways[c]	+8.6	−2.3	−5.8
Local bus lines[c]	...	+39.1	+7.3
All other	+3.1	+3.1	+0.5

[a] Peak dates based on data for all regulated industries.
[b] Terminal date in nine-year averages.
[c] Excludes publicly owned facilities.
[d] 1885 (the earliest available date) to 1914.
[e] 1884 (the earliest available date) to 1914.
Source: Appendix Tables B–1, C–1, D–1, E–1, F–1, G–1, and H–1.

entire time span, telephones dropped from a rate of nearly 12 per cent to one of less than 3 per cent, and street and electric railways from a 9 per cent per annum rise to an average annual decline of nearly 6 per cent. Local bus lines, during their brief history, dropped from an annual average increase of nearly 40 per cent in the 1914–31 period to one of less than 8 per cent in 1931–47. Only in the all other group was the decline anything but constantly progressive. In this case the rate of growth remained unchanged at slightly more than 3 per cent through the first two periods, and then dropped to one-half of 1 per cent in the final cycle.

When the percentage changes are examined in detail, as in Table 14, it is of course observed that the declines in relative rate of growth are by no means perfectly progressive in every case. Given the sharp cyclical fluctuations in these series, this is not surprising. Even after allowance for these fluctuations, however, it is apparent that in every component the period of declining relative rate of

TABLE 14

Percentage Changes in Constant Dollar Value of Plant and Equipment, by Decades, 1870–1950, Component Regulated Industries

Decade	*Per Cent*[a]	*Decade*	*Per Cent*[b]
RAILROADS			
1870–1880	35	1876–1886	53
1880–1890	36	1886–1896	26
1890–1900	10	1896–1906	2
1900–1910	25	1906–1916	33
1910–1920	10	1916–1926	5
1920–1930	14	1926–1936	1
1930–1940	−8	1936–1946	−3
1940–1950	2		
ELECTRIC LIGHT AND POWER			
1890–1900	421	1886–1896	136
1900–1910	262	1896–1906	307
1910–1920	45	1906–1916	151
1920–1930	122	1916–1926	65
1930–1940	−3	1926–1936	34
1940–1950	30	1936–1946	c
TELEPHONES			
1880–1890	357	1886–1896	182
1890–1900	443	1896–1906	370
1900–1910	137	1906–1916	29
1910–1920	−1	1916–1926	32
1920–1930	142	1926–1936	60
1930–1940	−3	1936–1946	15
1940–1950	103		
STREET AND ELECTRIC RAILWAYS			
1870–1880	123	1876–1886	79
1880–1890	132	1886–1896	299
1890–1900	280	1896–1906	157
1900–1910	74	1906–1916	21
1910–1920	−5	1916–1926	−20
1920–1930	−29	1926–1936	−36
1930–1940	−47	1936–1946	−49
1940–1950	−45		
LOCAL BUS LINES			
1910–1920	2,400	1916–1926	9,717
1920–1930	4,504	1926–1936	178
1930–1940	138	1936–1946	91
1940–1950	28		

(concluded on next page)

TABLE 14 (concluded)

Decade	Per Cent[a]	Decade	Per Cent[b]
	ALL OTHER		
1870–1880	42	1876–1886	25
1880–1890	25	1886–1896	31
1890–1900	29	1896–1906	24
1900–1910	51	1906–1916	69
1910–1920	44	1916–1926	28
1920–1930	44	1926–1936	19
1930–1940	−6	1936–1946	0
1940–1950	29		

[a] Computed from end-of-year figures.
[b] Computed from middle-of-year figures.
[c] Rise of less than 1 per cent.
Source: Appendix Tables B–1, C–1, D–1, E–1, F–1, G–1, and H–1.

growth is preceded by at least a few years in which the relative rate of growth is rising. In electric light and power, telephones, and local bus lines, this rising period appears to have lasted little more than a decade, and possibly less. The somewhat longer period of rise in the case of street and electric railways reflects the virtual transformation of this industry in the late nineteenth century as electricity replaced cruder means of motive power. In the case of the railroads, there is no preliminary period of material rise within the time span covered by this study, but of course by 1870 this industry was nearly forty years old.

In any event, one important generalization concerning the regulated industries appears warranted from this segment of our analysis. The stock of reproducible capital grows by relative amounts which, from the secular standpoint, decline progressively from almost the very beginning of an industry's history. The lone exception among our components is the all other group; but this is a conglomerate aggregate and its sporadic relative rate of growth reflects essentially the development of new industries within the total.

This generalization is of some importance for later stages of our analysis—particularly in connection with the financing of these industries—and a further word concerning it may be in order here. The early declining relative rate of growth noted above appears to stem from characteristics typical of the regulated industries. We may consider, in contrast, the conditions attendant upon the development of a small, little-known industry, characterized by small business units. Such an industry would by its nature be expected to depart materially from the pattern described above. For its growth would depend upon the slow, gradual accumulation of capital by individual proprietors. The high risk involved would preclude for some time access to organized capital markets, and would narrowly limit the availability of credit generally. As the industry expanded, and as the business units within it grew, these barriers might be expected to weaken. Provided that we are dealing with an industry destined for ultimate success, it is likely that its relative rate of growth would remain stable or upward for several decades as, within an ever greater radius, the nation's capital was mobilized for its use. If technological developments in this industry were such as to engender a rise in the ratio of physical capital to output, this would be an *additional* factor for an increasing—rather than a decreasing—relative rate of growth in the stock of plant and equipment, at least for some considerable period. A number of manufacturing industries would conform in whole, or in substantial part, to this pattern.

The regulated industries, however, were differently situated in every respect. In the most prominent and important cases, the individual business units involved were, out of technological necessity, large at the very outset. They were highly publicized and typically endowed with a substantial degree of monopoly. From their very beginnings, they attracted investors by what appeared to be a relatively low element of risk and a relatively large promise of profit. The accessibility of capital permitted a swift burgeoning at the start, which in relative terms, as we have seen, very soon diminished. And the decline was accelerated by technological developments, which in this segment of the economy, resulted in a pronounced and fairly steady reduction in the ratio of fixed real capital to product, as shall be described in Chapter 5. Of course these comments are not meant to deny the historical fact that the railroads, and some of the other utilities, at times experienced difficulty in obtaining all the capital they wanted. But in such instances capital was scarce primarily *in relation to* their own huge requirements. The point is that these industries were able to draw funds from *national* and sometimes *international*, money markets. This is something that smaller, less well-known, and riskier business units could not have accomplished.

Output

The diversity of behavior among the individual regulated industries is less pronounced in output than it is in investment. The general trend in production over the 1890–1950 period is upward for every component except street and electric railways, as the top panels of Charts 10 through 15 show. The data of Table 15, consisting of nine-year averages centered at the selected dates indicated,

TABLE 15

Output per Annum, Component Regulated Industries, 1929 Dollars, Nine-Year Averages, 1886–1950

Central Year in Nine-Year Average	*Millions of 1929 Dollars*	*Central Year in Nine-Year Average*	*Millions of 1929 Dollars*
	RAILROADS		
1886	1,013	1890	1,329
1896	1,778	1900	2,334
1906	3,477	1910	4,179
1916	5,557	1920	6,013
1926	6,229	1930	5,251
1936	4,442	1940	7,231
1946	9,846	1950	8,451[a]
	ELECTRIC LIGHT AND POWER		
1896	22	1900	51
1906	128	1910	197
1916	431	1920	684
1926	1,345	1930	1,719
1936	2,257	1940	3,251
1946	5,100	1950	6,806[a]
	TELEPHONES		
1896	46	1900	111
1906	296	1910	423
1916	583	1920	725
1926	1,032	1930	1,094
1936	1,100	1940	1,350
1946	2,059	1950	2,591[a]
	STREET AND ELECTRIC RAILWAYS		
1896	211	1900	297
1906	507	1910	651
1916	814	1920	892
1926	894	1930	742
1936	536	1940	539
1946	548	1950	339[a]
	LOCAL BUS LINES		
1926	108	1930	145
1936	188	1940	301
1946	475	1950	411[a]
	ALL OTHER		
1896	255	1900	380
1906	671	1910	892
1916	1,321	1920	1,616
1926	2,286	1930	2,613
1936	3,312	1940	4,806
1946	7,904	1950	10,274[a]

[a] For 1950 only.
Source: Appendix Table K–9.

also make this clear. Perhaps the most spectacular rise is that of electric light and power, for which output advanced from about 22 million 1929 dollars per annum in the 1890's and not much more than 100 million in the first decade of the twentieth century to over 5 billion in the 1940's. But, with the exception noted, the advances for all other components are large too. Even railroad output rose from about 1 billion 1929 dollars per annum in the 1880's to about 6 billion in the 1920's and again to between 7 and 10 billion per annum in the 1940's. It is significant, however, that output of street and electric railways in 1950 was not much greater than it had been 60 years before, and that—at 340 million 1929 dollars—it was far below its peak of nearly 900 million annually in the 1920's.

When attention is directed to changes in output, greater differences appear among the several industries. These changes are shown in the lower panels of Charts 10 through 15. In Table 16 there are presented average changes in output computed between nine-year averages at selected dates for each of the components. Thus, the top figure in the second column under railroads shows that between the nine-year average centered on 1886 and the nine-year average centered on 1896, railroad output rose by an average of 77 million 1929 dollars per year.

Most striking are the progressive advances in the rate of output growth in electric light and power, telephones, and the all other group. In electric light and power, production rose at the rate of 284 million 1929 dollars per year between the 1930's and the 1940's, and in the decade of the 1940's by about 350 million per year. This compares with increases of from 10–15 million per year in the 1890's and early 1900's. Production of telephone service rose by about 124 million 1929 dollars per year in the 1940's, compared with 25 or 30 million in earlier years. The all other group reached the spectacular rate of increase of about 450 million per year between the 1930's and the 1940's, and nearly 550 million per year in the decade of the 1940's. For all three of these groups, output rose at an ever-increasing absolute rate over the 1870–1950 span.

The picture is less buoyant for the other segments. The great demands for local transportation, when use of private passenger cars was restricted during the war, boosted production of local bus lines greatly in these years. The output increment from the 1930's to the 1940's is therefore very substantial. But aside from this, it is apparent that the secular trend in output increments in this segment had turned downward in later years, and that the peak had been reached somewhere in the 1930's or 1940's. This does not mean, of course, that production was headed secularly downward. It *does* mean that

TABLE 16

Average Changes in Output, per Annum, All Regulated Industries and Components, 1886–1950

(*average annual change between nine-year averages centered on the indicated years*)

Central Years of Nine-Year Averages	*Millions of 1929 Dollars*	*Central Years of Nine-Year Averages*	*Millions of 1929 Dollars*
	ALL REGULATED INDUSTRIES		
1886–1896	105	1890–1900	151
1896–1906	277	1900–1910	317
1906–1916	364	1910–1920	361
1916–1926	318	1920–1930	161
1926–1936	−6	1930–1940	591
1936–1946	1,411	1940–1950[a]	1,139
	RAILROADS		
1886–1896	77	1890–1900	101
1896–1906	170	1900–1910	185
1906–1916	208	1910–1920	183
1916–1926	67	1920–1930	−76
1926–1936	−179	1930–1940	198
1936–1946	542	1940–1950[a]	122
	ELECTRIC LIGHT AND POWER		
1896–1906	11	1900–1910	15
1906–1916	30	1910–1920	49
1916–1926	91	1920–1930	103
1926–1936	91	1930–1940	153
1936–1946	284	1940–1950[a]	356
	TELEPHONES		
1896–1906	25	1900–1910	31
1906–1916	29	1910–1920	30
1916–1926	45	1920–1930	37
1926–1936	7	1930–1940	26
1936–1946	96	1940–1950[a]	124
	STREET AND ELECTRIC RAILWAYS		
1896–1906	30	1900–1910	35
1906–1916	31	1910–1920	24
1916–1926	8	1920–1930	−15
1926–1936	−36	1930–1940	−20
1936–1946	1	1940–1950[a]	−21
	LOCAL BUS LINES		
1926–1936	8	1930–1940	16
1936–1946	29	1940–1950[a]	11
	ALL OTHER		
1896–1906	42	1900–1910	51
1906–1916	65	1910–1920	72
1916–1926	97	1920–1930	100
1926–1936	103	1930–1940	219
1936–1946	459	1940–1950[a]	547

[a] The figures used for 1950 represent production for that year only.
Source: Appendix Table K–9.

CHART 10
Output and Changes in Output, 1929 Dollars, Steam Railroads, 1880–1950

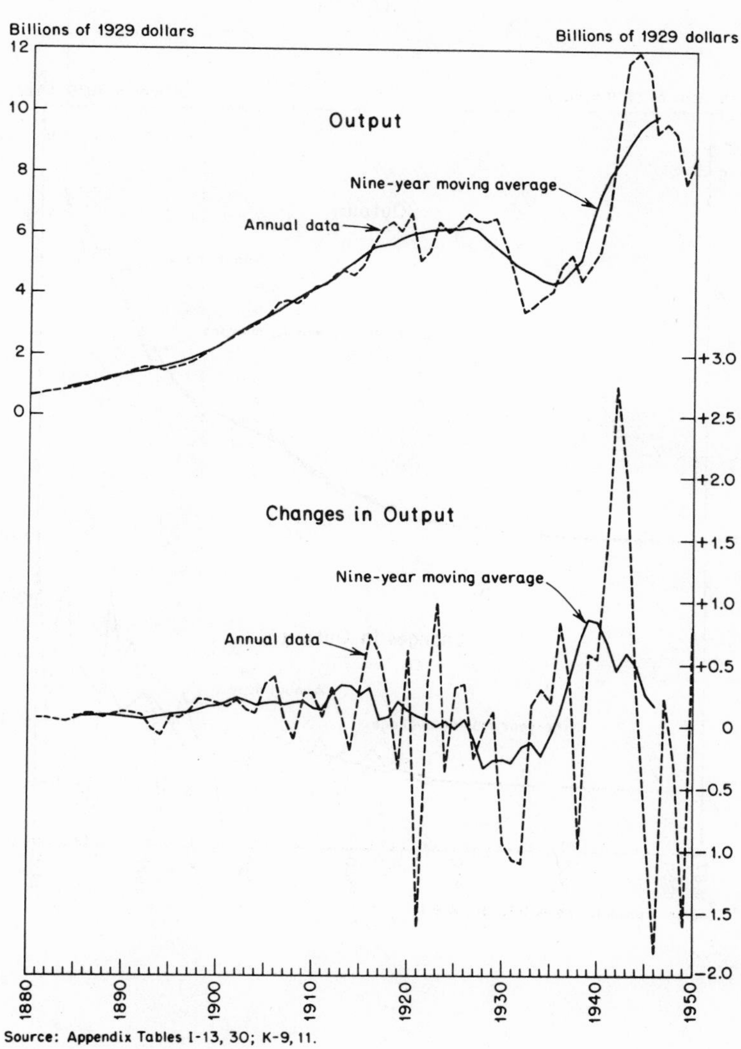

Source: Appendix Tables I-13, 30; K-9, 11.

CHART 11

Output and Changes in Output, 1929 Dollars, Electric Light and Power, 1887–1950

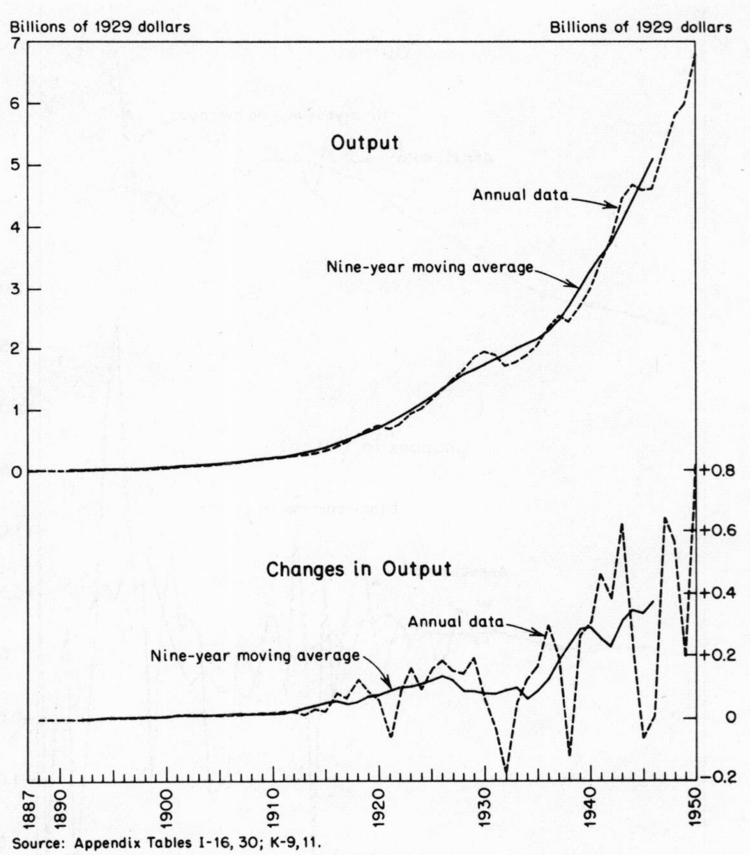

Source: Appendix Tables I-16, 30; K-9, 11.

CHART 12

Output and Changes in Output, 1929 Dollars, Telephones, 1890–1950

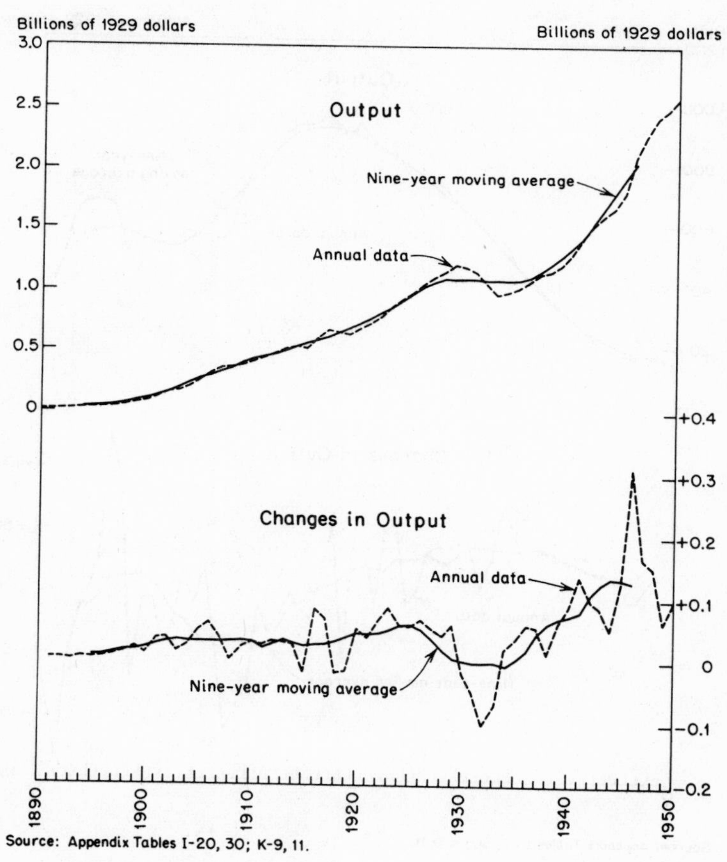

Source: Appendix Tables I-20, 30; K-9, 11.

CHART 13

Output and Changes in Output, 1929 Dollars, Street and Electric Railways, 1890–1950

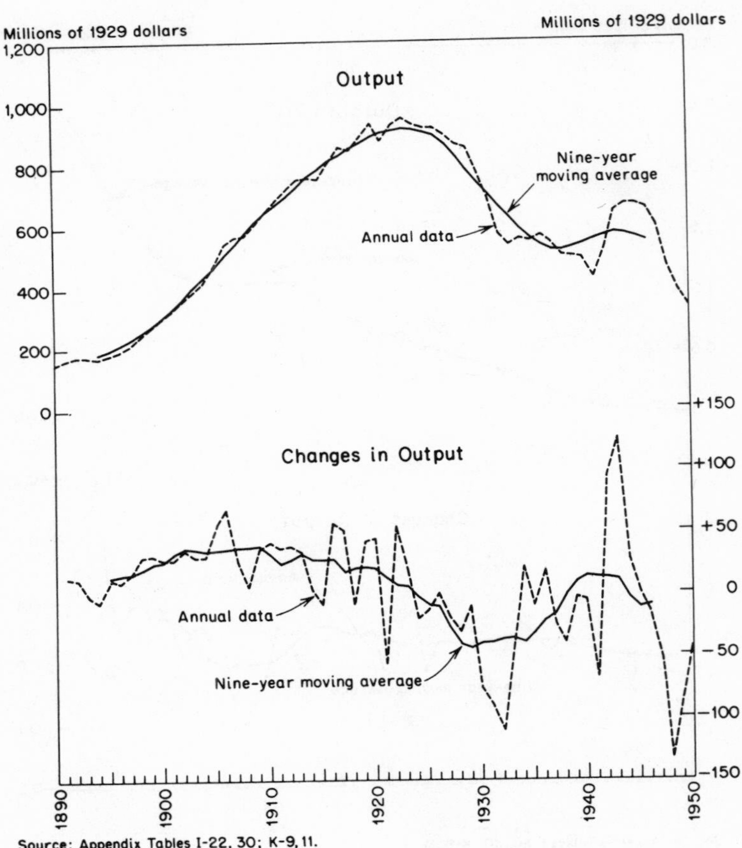

Source: Appendix Tables I-22, 30; K-9, 11.

CHART 14
Output and Changes in Output, 1929 Dollars, Local Bus Lines, 1922–1950

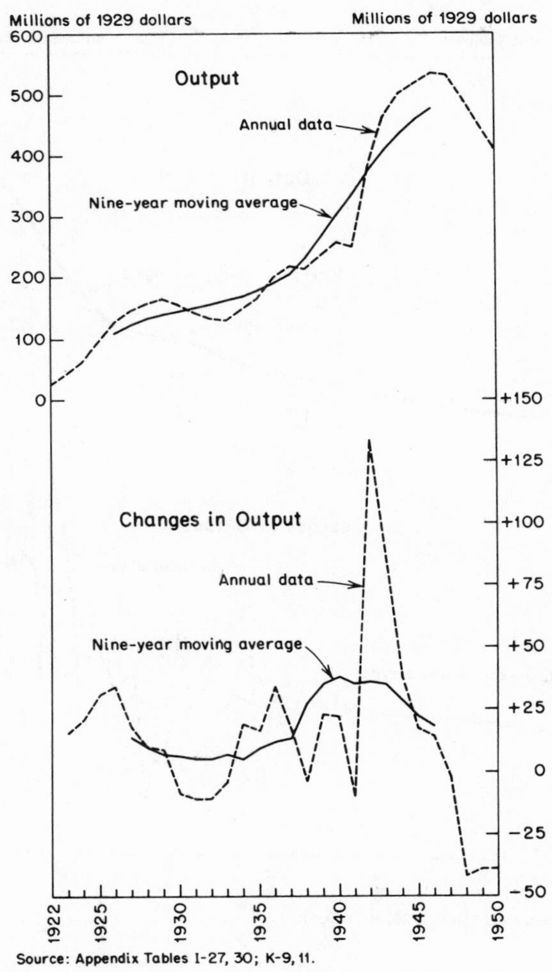

Source: Appendix Tables I-27, 30; K-9, 11.

CHART 15
Output and Changes in Output, 1929 Dollars, All Other Utilities, 1890–1950

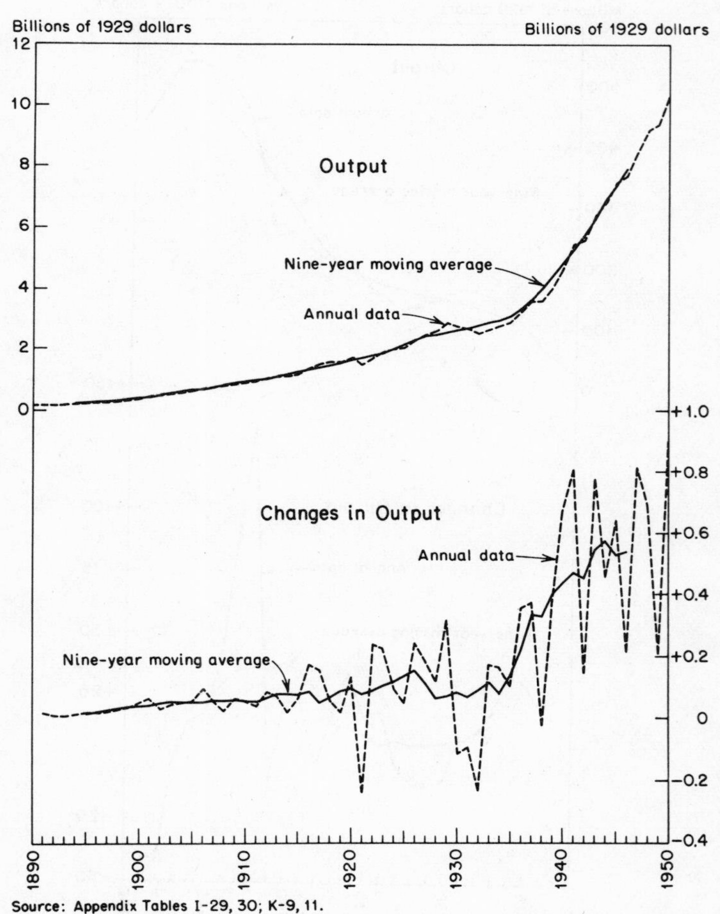

Source: Appendix Tables I-29, 30; K-9, 11.

the secular *rate of growth* in the output of local bus service had begun to decline.

It seems evident, likewise, that the rate of growth in railroad output was headed downward. Here, too, the febrile activity of the World War II period obscures the secular movement, but in this case analysis may be placed on a broader historical base. Though the downward trend is sufficiently clear, the approximate date of the turning point remains indistinct. The most likely times are the immediate pre-World War I period and the early 1940's, with perhaps some favor to the latter because of the pronounced all-time peaks persisting over a significant span in this period. Street railways, on the other hand, present a case with few complexities. Output increments turned downward in the first decade of the twentieth century, and by the 1920's had become negative. They remained negative thereafter, on balance, except for a brief flurry in the World War II period.

The *relative* rate of growth in output is measured in the data of Table 17. In every component, these relative output increments display a pronounced declining secular trend. The declines commence at very early dates—though just how early is obscured by the fact that the output series do not begin for some components until the 1890's. In two cases—the railroads and local bus lines—the largest percentage increases in output actually occurred in the 1936–46 period, reflecting the wartime bulge in activity previously noted. But even in these components the secular downward trend, stemming from the earliest date, seems apparent. Indeed in all cases the declines are spectacular—for example, the drop from the 543 per cent rise in 1896–1906 to the 92 per cent rise in 1940–50 in telephones, or the drop from a 76 per cent rise in 1886–96 to a rise of 17 per cent in 1940–50 in railroads.

It is by no means inevitable for the percentage rate of growth in output to decline from the earliest days of an industry's development, as appears to be the case in each of the components we have examined. Rather, this phenomenon seems to stem from characteristics indigenous to the regulated industries, and perhaps to certain other industries which closely resemble them. The considerations bearing on this were discussed in the section above, dealing with the diminishing rates of growth in capital.

Application of the Model Pattern

In the previous chapter, we described a model pattern of secular growth, which was accordingly applied to the capital formation and output series of all regulated industries in the aggregate. We now

TABLE 17

Percentage Changes in Output, by Decades, Component Regulated Industries, 1886–1950

(based on nine-year averages of values in 1929 dollars)

Central Years of Nine-Year Averages	*Per Cent*	*Central Years of Nine-Year Averages*	*Per Cent*
	RAILROADS		
1886–1896	76	1890–1900	76
1896–1906	95	1900–1910	79
1906–1916	60	1910–1920	44
1916–1926	12	1920–1930	−13
1926–1936	−29	1930–1940	37
1936–1946	122	1940–1950[a]	17
	ELECTRIC LIGHT AND POWER		
1896–1906	482	1900–1910	287
1906–1916	237	1910–1920	247
1916–1926	212	1920–1930	152
1926–1936	67	1930–1940	89
1936–1946	126	1940–1950[a]	109
	TELEPHONES		
1896–1906	543	1900–1910	281
1906–1916	97	1910–1920	71
1916–1926	77	1920–1930	51
1926–1936	7	1930–1940	23
1936–1946	87	1940–1950[a]	92
	STREET AND ELECTRIC RAILWAYS		
1896–1906	140	1900–1910	119
1906–1916	61	1910–1920	37
1916–1926	10	1920–1930	−17
1926–1936	−40	1930–1940	−27
1936–1946	2	1940–1950[a]	−37
	LOCAL BUS LINES		
1926–1936	74	1930–1940	108
1936–1946	152	1940–1950[a]	37
	ALL OTHER		
1896–1906	163	1900–1910	135
1906–1916	97	1910–1920	81
1916–1926	73	1920–1930	62
1926–1936	45	1930–1940	84
1936–1946	139	1940–1950[a]	114

[a] The figures used for 1950 represent production for that year only.
Source: Appendix Table K–9.

apply this model to the several individual industry groups within that aggregate, which we have selected for special study. The several stages of development inherent in this model should be recalled at this point. They are listed again, at least with reference to the behavior of the net capital formation series, in the first column of Table 18, and in the second and third columns they are related to the key points indicated by capital letters in Chart 3. The key dates in the secular development of each of the regulated industries, in accord with this pattern for capital formation, are given in this table.

These key dates were selected as follows. Tables 9 and 10 and the relevant charts were studied, as previously described, to determine whether the series on the stock of plant and equipment and on net capital formation had advanced throughout the period of study, secularly, or had reached some turning point in the intervening period. In the latter case, long cycles were marked off in the nine-year moving averages of the series concerned, and the cycle with the highest average level then selected. Within this cycle the highest nine-year average was determined, and the year about which this average was centered was designated as the peak. Of course the selection of a peak in the net capital formation series automatically determined the inflexion point (point A in the upper panel of Chart 3) in the stock of capital series, since these are necessarily simultaneous. An exception to the general practice described was made in the case of local bus lines, for which the investment series do not conform to the long cycle patterns of the other regulated industries. In this case the peak of net capital formation was dated in 1938, which was the all-time high in the nine-year moving averages, and both from its graph and a study of the data in Table 10 appeared to be followed by a definite secular downtrend.

The inflexion point in net capital formation (point A′ in the lower panel of Chart 3) was determined from mathematical curves fitted to the data.[2] However, in cases where the peak of net capital

[2] The form of the curve fitted to the constant dollar value of plant and equipment is:

$$\text{I.} \qquad \log y = a + bt + ct^2,$$

where y is the stock of capital and t is time measured in years.

The differential of this curve is the trend of net capital formation, drawn in the center panels of Charts 1 and 2. The form of this curve is:

$$\text{II.} \qquad \frac{dy}{dt} = y(b + 2ct),$$

where $\frac{dy}{dt}$ is net capital formation.

The inflexion points in net capital formation are found by taking the second differential of equation II (equivalent to the third differential of equation I), setting this equal to zero and solving for t. This solution yields three values of t, which provide the timing of inflexion points A′, C′ and E′ respectively in Chart 3. However, point C′ is equivalent to point B—the maximum level of the stock of capital; this point, as described above, is determined by another method. Therefore, except for street railways, where point E′ is required, our interest is in A′ only.

TABLE 18

Key Dates in Pattern of Secular Growth of Capital, All Regulated Industries and Components

STAGE IN PATTERN AS DEFINED BY BEHAVIOR OF NET CAPITAL FORMATION	TERMINAL POINTS IN STAGES AS DESIGNATED IN CHART 3:		APPROXIMATE DATES OF STAGES IN:						
	Net Capital Formation	*Stock of Physical Capital*	*Total Utilities and Transportation*	*Steam Railroads*	*Electric Light and Power*	*Telephones*	*Street and Electric Railways*	*Local Bus Lines*	*All Other*
Increases by increasing amounts	A′	–	Up to 1875	1840–1857	1881–1909	1878	1850–1889	1910–1930	Up to 1919
Increases by decreasing amounts	B′	A	1875–	1857–1881	1909–		1889–1905	1930–1938	1919–
Decreases by increasing amounts but remains positive	C′	B		1881–1931			1905–1916	1938–	
Becomes negative and decreases by decreasing amounts	D′	C		1931–			1916–1933		
Increases by increasing amounts but remains negative	E′	–					1933–1949		
Increases by decreasing amounts but remains negative	F′	D					1949–		

For derivation, see accompanying text.

formation had not yet been reached, the existence of inflexion point A′ was first checked by a study of the detailed data of Table 10, before resorting to curve fitting. Inflexion point E′, on the negative branch of the net capital formation curve, had to be dated only for street railways. This date was fixed from the mathematical curve.

It must, of course, be realized that all the key dates listed in Table 17, no matter how great the care taken in their determination, are by their nature rough approximations. Secular movements cannot be said to change pace or direction in a particular hour, day, month, or year. Although for convenience secular stages have been marked off for each component as well as for all regulated industries by specific years, each of these dates should be interpreted as the central point in a time range or period (perhaps of five to 10 years in length) within which the secular turning point falls. And of course no purely objective method is available for determination of these central points. Moving averages of a length different from nine years may have been studied and the form of the curves employed modified in one way or another. Such alterations in approach would surely have altered some of the results obtained. But if judged as approximations within a fairly broad range as indicated, the key dates provided in Table 17 possess considerable substance; alternative approaches resulting in minor revision of conclusions can, from this point of view, be adjudged irrelevant. And the pattern of growth, thus liberally interpreted, nevertheless fulfils its intended mission of providing a broad framework for the comparative analysis of the secular development of the regulated industries.

That the growth of capital in each of the regulated industries—at least roughly—followed the outline of the model pattern, was indicated in our examination, earlier in this chapter, of the detailed data dealing with the stock of capital and capital flows. For, though not overtly acknowledged, this model provided the framework for that analysis—the underlying structure around which the figures were organized. The extent to which the several components progressed along this model pattern, however, varied greatly. At one extreme was telephones. From the standpoint of its investment behavior, this industry was by far the least mature of all, for not only did its stock of capital rise by increasing amounts, but its net capital formation itself rose at an increasing absolute rate throughout the period from the industry's beginning in the late 1870's to 1950. With reference to the model in Chart 3, the development of the industry had not only failed to reach point A, but had not even reached the earlier point A′. The position of telephones was well within the very earliest stage.

At the other extreme was street and electric railways, a prime example of an industry whose life span in nearly its entirety was covered by the period studied. In this most mature component, the change-over from an increasing to a decreasing rate of advance in net capital formation came at the end of the 1880's. The peak in net capital formation—equivalent to a change-over from an increasing to a decreasing rate of growth in the stock of capital—came in the middle of the first decade of the twentieth century. Net capital formation then turned downward in this component, diminishing at an increasing rate until it reached zero around 1916. At this point the stock of capital was at its peak. Subsequently it was subject to continuous contraction. Net capital formation turned negative, continuing to decrease—though by diminishing amounts—until the early 1930's. At this juncture, while remaining negative throughout, net capital formation began to rise. This means that the net capital formation series was moving back toward zero—i.e., that the reductions in the stock of capital were becoming smaller over time. In the late 1940's it appeared that this approach to the zero line—at which point the entire stock of the industry's plant and equipment would be dissipated—became subject to some retardation.

Among the other components, steam railroads came closest to matching the maturity of the street railways—though it still remained a substantial distance away. For steam railroads the change-over from an increasing to a decreasing rate of growth in the stock of capital—the peak in net capital formation—came in the early 1880's; the peak in the stock of capital itself seemed to fall in the early 1930's. But in the years between 1931 and 1950, the railroads did not progress very far along the stage from C′ to D′ in the model pattern, i.e., the reductions in the stock of capital were modest. In contrast street railways had not only completed the stage from C′ to D′, but had finished the following one from D′ to E′, and had apparently—in addition—made a start on the final stage leading to F′. Thus steam railroads were a much less mature component. Though their stock of capital had indeed headed downward since the early 1930's, the negative balance of their net capital formation was only moderate, admitting substantial spurts of net investment over protracted periods.

Electric light and power and the heterogeneous all other group ranked somewhat behind telephones in the inverse order of maturity. After World War I, in both cases, the pace of expansion evidenced some loss of vigor. Somewhere between the years just preceding and immediately following that conflict, they appear to have passed the point at which net capital formation changes over from an increasing to a decreasing rate of advance. Local bus lines progressed one stage further in the model pattern. Just before or after World War II, this industry passed the point at which the *stock of capital* changed over from an increasing to a decreasing rate of advance. In 1950, in all three cases, the stock of capital was still heading secularly upward, but in local bus lines its rise was proceeding by diminishing amounts.

The fact that several industries are in the same stage of development, of course, casts faint light upon the relative duration of their remaining life spans. Indeed it should be emphasized that there was wide variation among components in the length of any given stage of development, and there was but little similarity in the duration of the various stages in any given component. Thus, for steam railroads, electric light and power, street and electric railways, and local bus lines, the first stage (during which net capital formation increases by increasing amounts) ranged in length from 17 to 39 years. The second stage for the same components varied in length from 15 to 24 years. The third stage ranged from 11 years for street and electric railways to 50 years for steam railroads. And it will be recalled in the case of telephones, that by 1950 the first stage of development had lasted some 70 years and still had not ended.

Such wide variations, however, befit the nature of the causal factors at work—especially the long-term growth characteristics of demand together with the ubiquitous, and capricious impact of technological change. The role of the latter, in particular, enters in quite different ways in the history of our industries. For example, it is this factor, especially, which accounts for the fact that the first stage of secular development had by 1950 lasted 70 years for telephones (and was still in progress), while during roughly the same period street and electric railways had passed through five of the six stages which carry an industry from its birth to its final demise. This is an extreme example of variation—and a dramatic illustration of the distinction between chronological age and degree of maturity.

For it is obvious that there is but slight connection between chronological age and the relative positions in the model pattern of growth occupied in 1950 by the five components studied. The first street railways were established around 1850, some ten years *after* construction of the first steam railroads. The former nonetheless was a considerably more mature industry, reflecting the greater, swifter, and more conclusive impact of competitive forms of transportation upon its business. Chronologically, telephones is a slightly older component than electric light and power and it is much older than local bus lines, but from the standpoint of the secular growth pattern it is more youthful than either. Electric light and power was less mature than local bus lines, though it predates that component by some 40 years.

In Table 19, key dates in the model pattern of growth are presented for each of the regulated industries, based upon the behavior of output. Of course, if the technical relationship between capital and production had always remained unchanged, there would have been no need for this additional tabulation. Analysis in terms of the stock of capital and net capital formation, as provided in Table 18, would have sufficed. But this technical relationship did indeed change, in a significant manner which we analyze in detail in the following chapter. And accordingly the patterns of growth described by the production series differ materially from those already defined in investment.

Determination of these dates presented a slightly different problem from that encountered in the capital formation series. For, though quite volatile, there is no distinct or pronounced evidence of long cycles in the production series. Consequently, the methods of determination employed for capital formation were revised somewhat. Thus, principal reliance for the location of peaks in output and in changes in output was placed upon a study of the nine-year averages given in Tables 15 and 16. In fact, in connection with the discussion of these tables, the general areas of the peaks were pointed out. In the general time spans cited, the maximum points were selected, and designated as peaks, from examination of the nine-year moving average series, shown in Charts 10 through 15. For those components for which the peak in changes in output had not yet been reached, Table 16 was also used to explore the existence of inflexion point A′. When it appeared that this inflexion point had in fact been reached, its date was determined from a mathematical curve of the same form as those employed in the study of capital formation.

Though the picture of growth patterns derived from the study of production differs from that provided in our analysis of capital formation, it does so in a systematic way. Generally speaking, the industries appear less mature within this framework. The telephone industry still appears in the earliest stage of most vigorous growth, as it did in the capital formation study, but it is now accompanied in this standing by electric light and power and the all other group. In all three cases, not only did output increase at an increasing rate, but changes in output also advanced at an expanding rate through

TABLE 19

Key Dates in Pattern of Secular Growth of Output, All Regulated Industries and Components

STAGES IN PATTERN AS DEFINED BY BEHAVIOR OF ANNUAL CHANGES IN OUTPUT	TERMINAL POINTS IN PATTERNS AS DESIGNATED IN CHART 3:		APPROXIMATE DATES OF STAGES IN:						
	Annual Changes in Output	*Output*	*Total Utilities and Transportation*	*Steam Railroads*	*Electric Light and Power*	*Telephones*	*Street and Electric Railways*	*Local Bus Lines*	*All Other*
Increases by increasing amounts	A′	–	[a]	1840–1891	1881–	1878–	1850–1893	1910–1928	[a]
Increases by decreasing amounts	B′	A	–	1891–1942			1893–1906	1928–1943	
Decreases by increasing amounts but remains positive	C′	B		1942–			1906–1923	1943–	
Becomes negative and decreases by decreasing amounts	D′	C					1923–1948		
Increases by increasing amounts but remains negative	E′	–					1948–		
Increases by decreasing amounts but remains negative	F′	D							

Chart 3 presents the secular pattern of capital formation. An analogous pattern is assumed for output. The pattern for output corresponds with that for the stock of capital (upper panel of Chart 3) and the pattern for changes in output corresponds with that for net capital formation (lower panel of Chart 3). For derivation, see text accompanying Chart 3.

[a] This stage had not been completed by 1950.

the entire period of analysis. The latter two components had been in a significantly later stage of development when appraised from the standpoint of capital formation. Indeed, they had each reached the point at which net capital formation (analogous to output increments) had not only ceased to rise by increasing amounts, but had actually begun to decrease.

Ranking on a par behind these three, in the inverse order of maturity, are steam railroads and local bus lines, when production is used as the standard of secular development. The latter—alone among the components, except for telephones—reached the same stage of growth in terms of output as it did in terms of capital formation. Output increments passed the point of change-over from an increasing to a decreasing rate of advance in the late 1920's, and appeared to reach their peak in the early 1940's. Hence, total production of local bus line service was still rising, secularly, in 1950, though by diminishing absolute amounts. Substituting the stock of capital for output, and net capital formation for output increments, we see the same pattern of growth noted previously for this component.

In the case of railroads, however, the change is substantial. It will be recalled that the stock of capital had begun to decline, with net capital formation turning negative for this component as early as the 1930's. Production provided by the railroads, on the other hand, was still pointed secularly upward in 1950. Output increments had ceased to rise by increasing amounts in the early 1890's, but they continued to advance until the early 1940's. Since then they appear to have been declining, though remaining substantially positive. Stated alternatively, production of railroad service since the early 1940's continued to advance, secularly, but by diminishing amounts.

To a lesser degree street and electric railways also have a slightly more youthful look, when judged by production, though still ranking as by far the most mature of the components studied. In terms of the model pattern of growth, this component in 1950 stood between the points D′ and E′ when judged by production, instead of between E′ and F′ as in the capital formation analysis. Nevertheless—and most important—production of street railway service like the stock of capital in this component, was headed secularly downward in 1950, and had been tending in this direction for at least twenty-five years.

Thus the relative standing of the several regulated industries, with respect to the model pattern of growth, is much the same when judged by the behavior of production as by that of capital formation.

But in the former framework, the various components appear to be in significantly earlier stages of development, reflecting systematic changes in their respective capital coefficients, as shall be discussed more fully later. An apparent exception is telephones, but in this case no earlier stage than that reached in the capital formation framework is possible. A real exception is local bus lines, for in this case—unlike the others—the secular relationship between capital and output remained relatively unchanged.

CHAPTER 4

Trends in Capital Coefficients

ONE of the findings drawn from our analysis of secular trends in the regulated industries thus far is the disparity in behavior of output and capital formation. We have seen, however, that the differences in growth rates between the two evidenced a certain regularity. Their relative behavior suggested a systematic, progressive divergence rather than capricious differences following no apparent pattern. We may be thus encouraged in our expectation of finding a regularity of behavior in the ratio of capital to product studied directly.

Before proceeding to an examination of the record, we may take cognizance of the needs of the following chapters, in which the factors underlying capital formation are explored. In particular, we may distinguish the forms—of possible interest here—in which the ratio may be defined.

Principal Concepts and Their Relationships

The first of these concepts of the capital-product ratio is highly abstract. It cannot be measured directly, and yet it represents a relationship of interest. Consider an industry operating in long-run equilibrium, in the sense that its output has been attuned to demand and its stock of reproducible capital has been adjusted to output, in the most profitable way possible, given the factor prices prevailing and other relevant conditions. Now suppose there is an enduring change in the volume of demand (a shift in the demand curve) to a new and higher level which is maintained without revision. To this change the industry will adjust by expanding its stock of capital and its output as well, until a new equilibrium (in the sense defined above) is attained. The ratio between the increment in the stock of reproducible capital (net capital formation) and the increment in output, between these two equilibria, we may term the capital coefficient.

Thus defined, the capital coefficient is in considerable part a technological concept. For prevailing technology will establish the limits of its dimensions, in many cases—and in the regulated industries especially—rather narrowly. But technology will not fix its magnitude uniquely, unless we assume that the relative prices of the factors of production are unchanged between the two equilibrium positions—and unchanged, strictly, in terms of efficiency units. For many analytical purposes the latter assumption is too restrictive, and may accordingly be omitted. This means that the capital coefficient, so defined, may vary over time because of: (1) technological changes; or (2) changes in relative factor costs; or (3) discontinuities (i.e. indivisibilities) in the units of the physical capital stock, which irresistibly limit the adjustment to equilibrium required between two particular levels of demand. The model should be further elaborated to permit short-run fluctuations about the enduring levels of demand at each equilibrium. Then, in equilibrium, allowance may be made for the maintenance of a certain "normal" reserve capacity. Insofar as such concepts may be applied at all to observable growth phenomena, this is the framework which appears most pertinent for the present study. It is the ratio of concomitant changes in capital and output between such equilibria, which we term the capital coefficient. It is, of course, not directly observable.

The observable concepts are the actual average and marginal capital-product ratios. The first of these may be defined as $\frac{C}{O}$, where C is the stock of reproducible capital and O is the volume of output, both measured in constant prices. The marginal capital-product ratio may be defined as the ratio between the change in the stock of reproducible capital and the change in output—i.e. as $\frac{\Delta C}{\Delta O}$. The familiar relationship between average and marginal quantities would suggest that when the average ratio is stable, then—during this period of stability—it is equal to the marginal ratio. Otherwise, they would differ in the following way: (1) So long as the average ratio is moving downward, it must remain higher than the marginal ratio. (2) So long as the average ratio is moving upward, it must remain lower than the marginal ratio. (3) The slower the movement in any direction, the smaller is the difference between the two. (4) Whenever the two ratios change direction, it is the marginal ratio which turns first. In the present case, however, such relationships would hold only approximately. For the *efficiency* of the capital stock may be improved merely through replacement. Hence, the *average* capital-product ratio could decline over time even in the absence of *net* changes in that capital stock—i.e. while the *marginal* capital-product ratio was zero.

The relationship between the observable ratios and the capital coefficient, defined above, cannot of course be framed with exactitude. But attention may be called to one possibility. The long-run average behavior of the marginal capital-product ratio may approximate that of the capital coefficient, at least broadly. In the long run there is an opportunity for the errors born of uncertainty, lack of knowledge, etc., to cancel out. And insofar as investment is made on the basis of estimates of the most profitable level of output in the future, we should expect that this estimated production would tend to converge with *actual* production in the long run. For though expectations may at times diverge sharply from current realizations, business—including utilities—will not *indefinitely* act upon hopes or fears which run counter to experience. Such reasoning implies that the marginal capital-product ratio, on the average in the long run, would resemble the capital coefficient, though we must be alert to allow for possible exceptions. Thus, such enduring catastrophes as the Great Depression of the 1930's and the war years of the 1940's represent obvious occasions for substantial differences between the two.

The Data

In Chart 16 the average capital-product ratio is depicted for all regulated industries in the aggregate from 1880–1950. Similar data are shown for the several components in Charts 17–22. The ratios were computed by dividing the value of plant and equipment in 1929 dollars existing at the beginning of each year by output in 1929 dollars in that same year. It should be borne in mind, however, that the measures of output employed in this study are gross, in the sense that no deduction is made for the quantity of goods and services consumed by these industries which were produced elsewhere in the economy. Thus, railroad output is measured in terms of freight ton-miles and passenger miles, appropriately weighted and valued at 1929 prices. No deduction from this figure is made for the coal, oil, and other materials used by the railroads but produced outside this industry.

Had we employed the concept of net rather than gross output, the capital-product ratios we show would have been in general about 50 per cent higher. There would have been, however, no substantial differences in their trends. This is shown in Table 20, which presents the ratio of net output (national income originating) to gross output (operating revenues) in selected years for the major divisions of the regulated industries of interest here. It will be observed that the ratios remain remarkably constant over the long run in every case, despite moderate short-term fluctuations reflecting—among other things—relative price changes as well as statistical errors. We may conclude, therefore, that the secular behavior of gross and net physical output is, in the case of our industries, much the same. This means, of course, that the trends in capital-product ratios would be about the same, whether the denominator was measured in net or in gross terms.

TABLE 20

Ratios of National Income Originating in Regulated Industries to Operating Revenues, Current Dollars, Selected Years, 1890–1946

Year	*Railroads, Pullman and Express*	*Street and Electric Railways and Affiliated Bus Lines*	*Telephones*	*Telegraph*	*Electric Light and Power*	*Manu-factured Gas*	*Weighted Totals, All Included Industries*
1890	0.52						
1902	0.66		0.75		0.46		0.66
1907	0.61		0.65		0.47		0.60
1912	0.62		0.68		0.48		0.61
1917	0.61		0.63		0.47		0.60
1922	0.63	0.61	0.71	0.72	0.54	0.33	0.62
1927	0.67	0.59	0.68	0.79	0.61	0.50	0.65
1929	0.69	0.60	0.69	0.74	0.75	0.41	0.68
1932	0.62	0.51	0.61	0.62	0.66	0.39	0.61
1937	0.65	0.50	0.63	0.68	0.54	0.51	0.60
1939	0.64	0.52	0.63		0.51		0.59
1946	0.68	0.54	0.68		0.54		0.63

Ratios are based on comparisons between net income originating and operating revenues in current dollars. The industries listed accounted, in 1929, for 91 per cent of income originating in transportation and public utilities as defined by Kuznets in *National Income and Its Composition, 1919–1938* (National Bureau of Economic Research, 1941); water transportation and pipelines are omitted here. The data for income originating for 1922–37 were taken from Kuznets (*ibid.*). The Kuznets figures, which are available for 1919–38, were extrapolated to 1890 by use of data shown by Robert F. Martin, *National Income in the United States, 1799–1938* (National Industrial Conference Board, 1939) and extrapolated to 1946 by use of Department of Commerce national income data. The figures for operating revenues (or sales) were obtained from the Bureau of the Census, the Interstate Commerce Commission, the Federal Power Commission, the Federal Communications Commission, and trade sources.

The Aggregative Trend

The general trend in the average capital-product ratio of all regulated industries, shown in Chart 16, is so pronounced that, despite the volatility of the series, it is quite evident in the annual data. But it is even more clearly represented in the nine-year moving averages, and more unequivocally still in the trend lines fitted to the data. The movement is progressively downward over the 1880–1950 span, and at an extraordinarily brisk rate.

Most striking, perhaps, is the very high level from which this decline begins. For in the 1880's the ratio of capital to product exceeded 12, meaning that on the average the regulated industries possessed 12 dollars in plant and equipment for every one dollar of

CHART 16

Capital-Product Ratios, All Regulated Industries, 1880–1950

(ratios of value of plant and equipment in 1929 dollars to output in 1929 dollars)

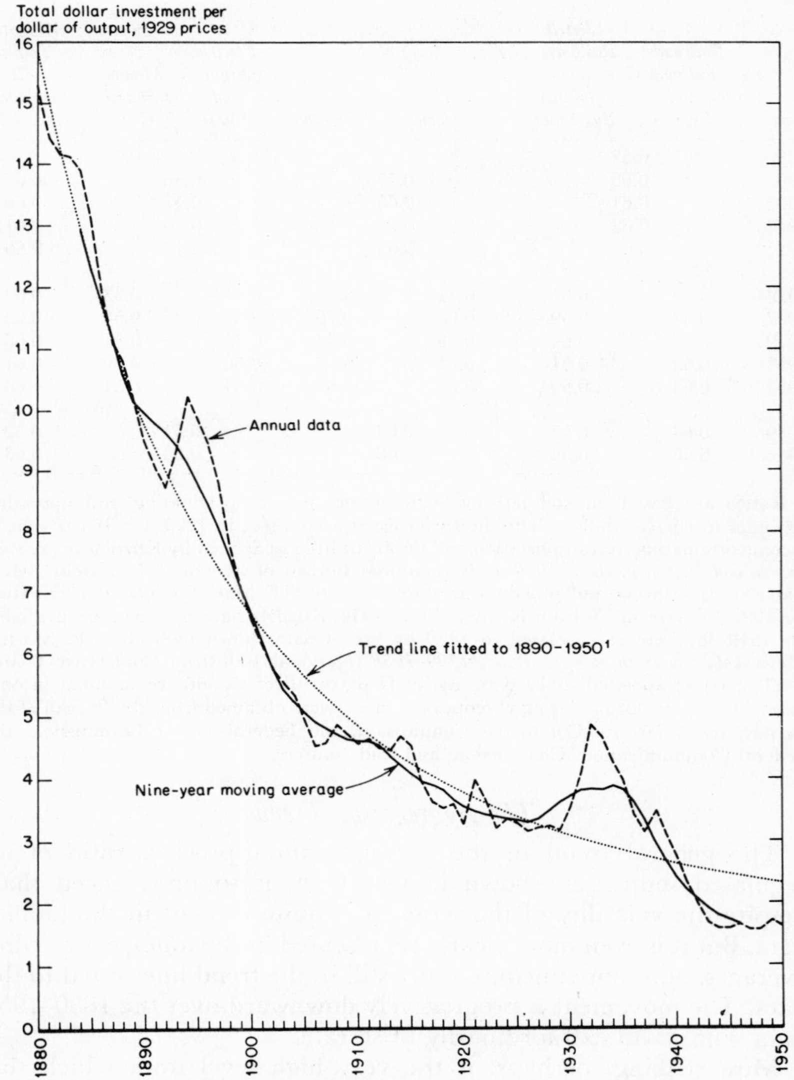

[1] Capital-product ratio (1929 dollars) = $(1.36)(7.2197)^{0.97836^t}$ where t is measured in years with 1890 as origin.

Source: Appendix Tables I-1, K-10.

CHART 17

Capital-Product Ratios, Steam Railroads, 1880–1950

(ratios of value of plant and equipment in 1929 dollars to output in 1929 dollars)

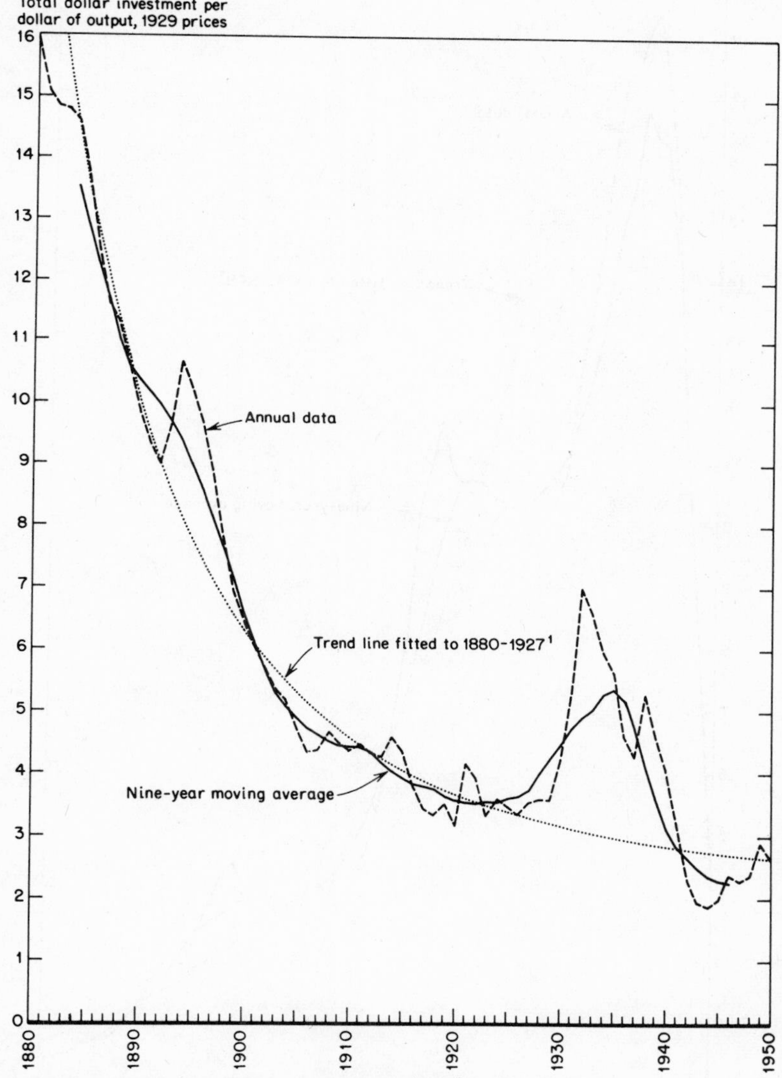

[1] Capital-product ratio (1929 dollars) = $(2.26)(8.7263)^{0.9633^t}$ where t is measured in years with 1880 as origin.

Source: Appendix Tables I-13, K-10.

CHART 18

Capital-Product Ratios, Electric Light and Power, 1887–1950

(ratios of value of plant and equipment in 1929 dollars to output in 1929 dollars)

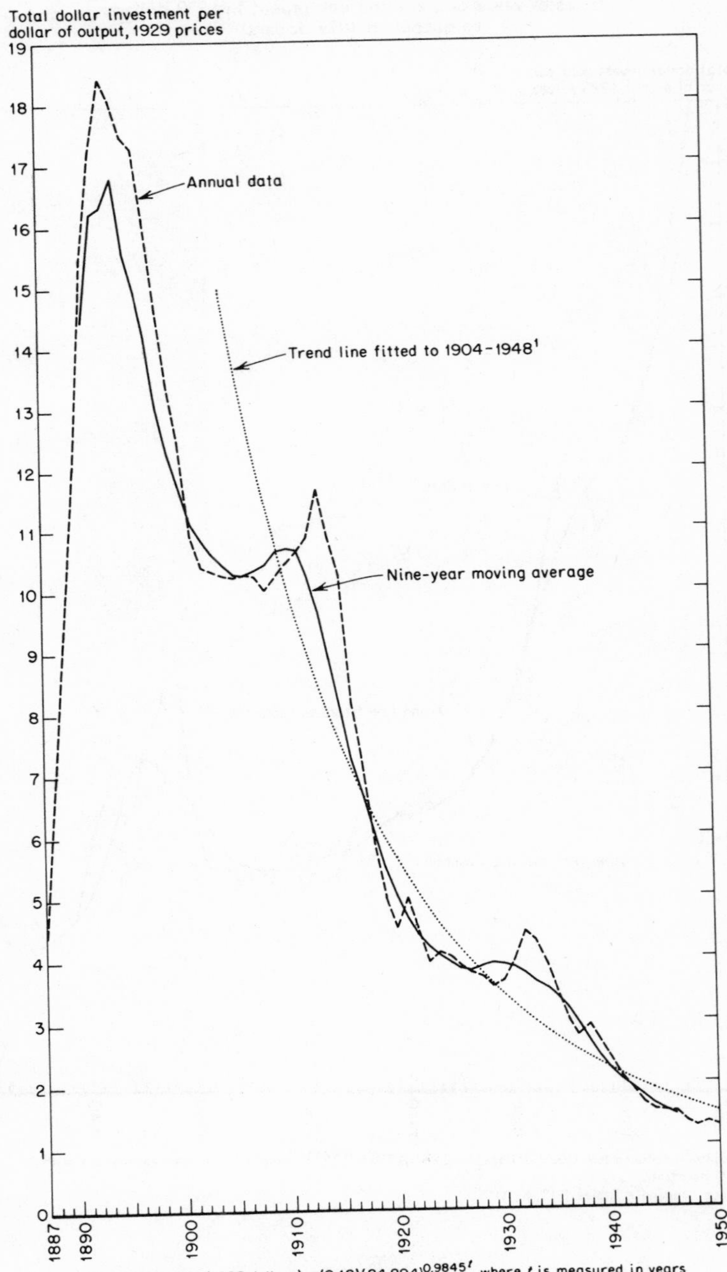

[1] Capital-product ratio (1929 dollars) = $(0.18)(84.894)^{0.9845^t}$ where t is measured in years with 1904 as origin.

Source: Appendix Tables I-16, K-10.

CHART 19

Capital-Product Ratios, Telephones, 1890–1950

(ratios of value of plant and equipment in 1929 dollars to output in 1929 dollars)

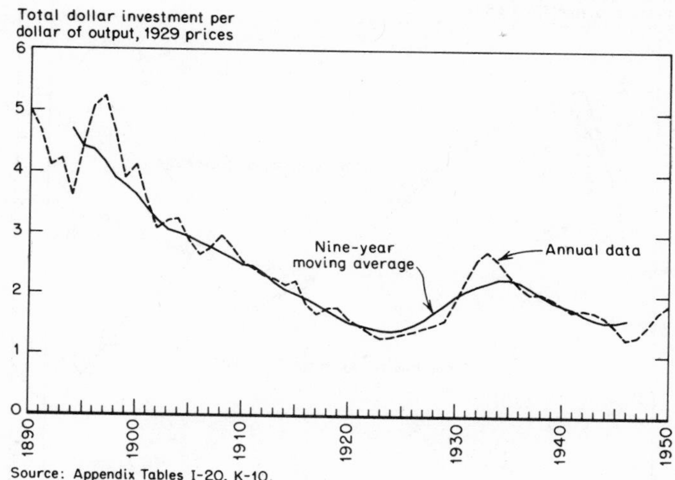

Source: Appendix Tables I-20, K-10.

annual output. This compares with average capital-product ratios of less than one for manufacturing, and of less than two for agriculture and mining in the same period.[1] Since the ratios for the other industries were computed in terms of net output, the comparison here actually understates the difference. It is also slightly understated by the fact that in the numerator of our ratio we include only *fixed* capital, while for the other segments *total* reproducible capital is included; but the variation arising from this factor is for most purposes—including this comparison—negligible.[2]

The subsequent decline in the average capital-product ratio for all regulated industries is sharp, though it gradually loses momentum. By the turn of the century it was down to about 6.5; by the 1920's, to about 3.5; and by 1950, to 1.7. Of course the latter figure may be abnormally low, still reflecting some of the remaining backlog of capital requirements accumulated during the years of privation in World War II. This is suggested, albeit very roughly, by the position

[1] Simon Kuznets, "Capital Product Ratio and Technological Change," *Conference on Quantitative Description of Technological Change*, Social Science Research Council, 1950, Table 4.

[2] In the regulated industries, inventories typically account for less than 2 per cent of total reproducible capital. See Chapter 8.

CHART 20

Capital-Product Ratios, Street and Electric Railways, 1890–1950

(ratios of value of plant and equipment in 1929 dollars to output in 1929 dollars)

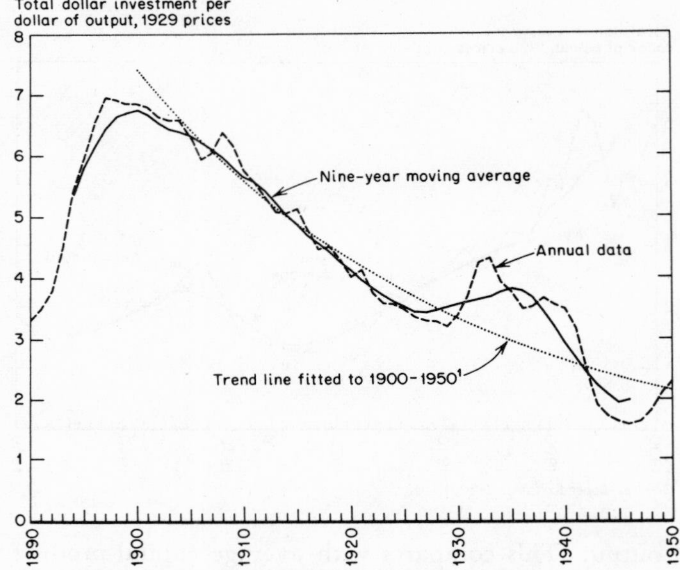

[1] Capital-product ratio (1929 dollars) = $(0.10)(70.902)^{0.9931^{t}}$ where t is measured in years with 1900 as origin.

Source: Appendix Tables I-22, K-10.

of the trend line, which ranges somewhat above the actual capital-product ratio throughout the 1940's. But even if—illustratively—we take the *trend line* capital-product ratio in 1950 as more representative of its "true" long-run value than the actual figure in that year, we note that it is still little more than 2, or about a sixth of its size of seventy years before.

The tendency of the absolute rate of decline in the ratio to diminish gradually is reflected in the form of the curve fitted to the data. Its equation is given in the footnote to the chart. It is the declining branch of a Gompertz curve, and falls gradually toward a fixed lower limit—the value of which in our fit is 1.4. Taken literally, this would imply that the long-run value of the average capital-product ratio will continue to decline very gradually in the future, approaching by ever smaller amounts the floor of 1.4. But there is no intention here to employ the curve for a mechanical

CHART 21

Capital-Product Ratios, Local Bus Lines, 1922–1950

(ratios of value of plant and equipment in 1929 dollars to output in 1929 dollars)

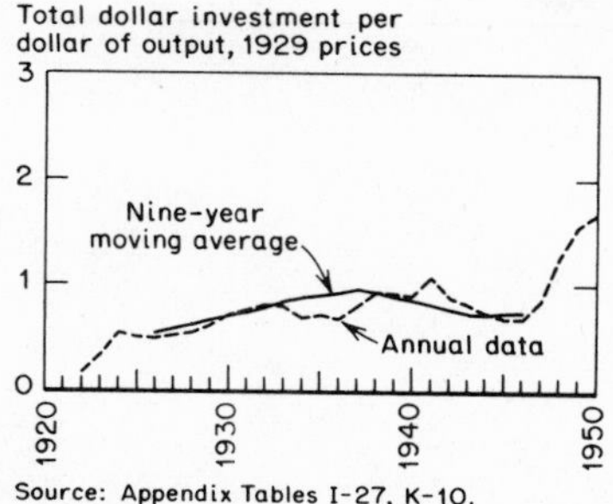

Source: Appendix Tables I-27, K-10.

extrapolation of this kind. It serves as a descriptive, smoothing device, and aids in the detection and—to some extent—the appraisal of periods such as the 1930's and the 1940's when the ratio departed from its general long-run drift.[3]

Despite the substantial decline in the capital-product ratio over the 1880–1950 span, and despite the repression of this ratio by the special conditions of the 1940's, it remained considerably above similar ratios computed for other segments of the economy. Thus, in manufacturing, the average capital-product ratio in 1948, computed on the same basis as ours, was 0.65,[4] compared with 1.7 in the regulated industries. In mining the ratio was 1.3.[5] Accordingly, the regulated industries remained a segment in which reproducible capital played an extraordinarily large role in the productive process, though the differences in this regard are very much smaller than they were seventy years before. It should be noted, however, that disparities in the capital-product ratios among industries provide only a rough guide to divergences in the amount of capital *consumed* for each dollar of output. In the regulated industries, capital is on the average considerably more durable than in the economy as a whole. In the 1930's the average depreciation rate in this segment was 1.9 per cent compared with from 5.4 to 9.2 per cent in manufacturing industries, 4.9 in mining, and to 3.5 per cent in the

[3] These remarks apply as well to the curves fitted in Charts 17, 18, and 20. Nothing in the mechanics of the curves themselves justifies extrapolation.

[4] Daniel Creamer, *Capital and Output Trends in Manufacturing Industries, 1880–1948* (National Bureau of Economic Research, Occasional Paper 41, 1954), Table 8, p. 43.

[5] Israel Borenstein, *Capital and Output Trends in Mining Industries, 1870–1948* (National Bureau of Economic Research, Occasional Paper No. 45, 1954), Table 13, p. 54.

CHART 22

Capital-Product Ratios, All Other Utilities and Transportation, 1890–1950
(ratios of value of plant and equipment in 1929 dollars to output in 1929 dollars)

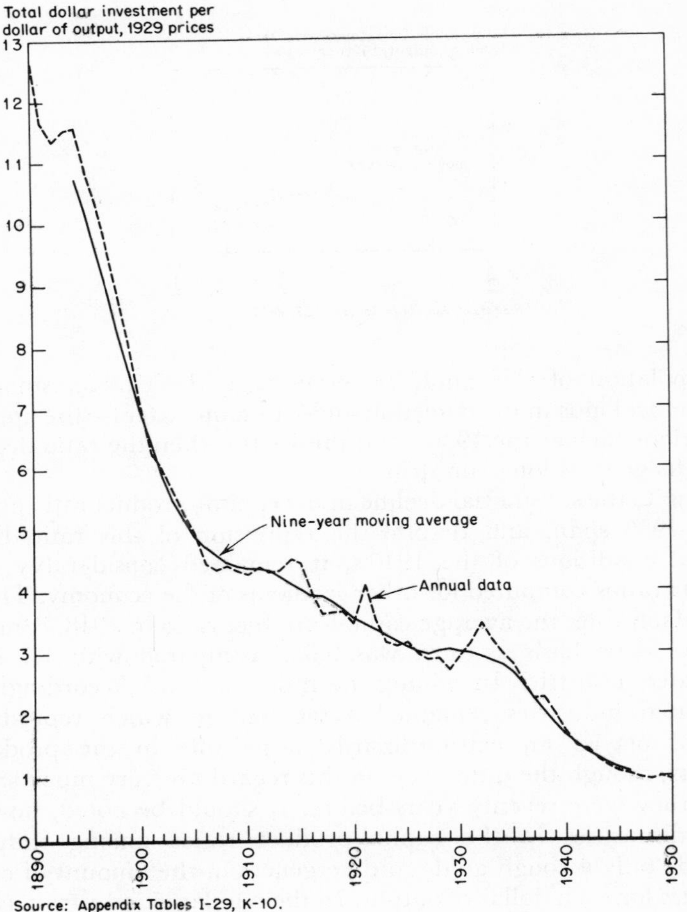

Source: Appendix Tables I-29, K-10.

economy in the aggregate.[6] Such discrepancies alone, other things being equal, would result in observed differences in capital-product ratios at least as large as those in the 1940's, though not nearly so large as those observed in the later decades of the nineteenth century.

Perhaps the most important aspect of the capital-product ratio is the light it casts upon the impact of an alteration in demand upon

[6] Solomon Fabricant, *Capital Consumption and Adjustment* (National Bureau of Economic Research, 1938), p. 34.

investment—i.e. upon the capital coefficient. Of course no simple, empirical ratio can measure this exactly, for the causal relationships will typically remain, to a large extent, obscure. In practice, investment is always undertaken with *future* needs in mind, and may have little relationship with current changes in output. But as noted earlier, in the long run, business expectations are brought closer in line with actualities, errors in one direction find compensatory counterparts in the other, and sufficient time elapses for adjusting the stock of capital to realized requirements as they appear. We may countenance, therefore, the possibility of at least approximating the general drift of the capital coefficient and—over sufficiently long periods—its general magnitude. For this purpose the *marginal* capital-product ratio is most pertinent.

Measuring the trend of the marginal capital-product ratio, however, presents some difficulties. Because of its highly erratic nature, values in particular years have little or no meaning for the purposes in view here. Values computed over a considerable span remain peculiarly sensitive to the choice of end years—a difficulty which is modified, but not often eliminated, by the use of broad averages. In Table 21 we have tried to refine the measurements

TABLE 21

Marginal Capital-Product Ratio,
All Regulated Industries and Components, Selected Periods

Period	*All Regulated Industries*	*Railroads*	*Electric Light and Power*	*Telephones*	*Street and Electric Railways*	*Local Bus Lines*	*All Other*
To 1891[a]	9.2	10.2	16.9	4.6	5.9	...	11.4
1891–1910	2.9	1.8	11.5	2.4	5.9	...	2.4
1910–1927	1.9	2.0	3.0	1.0	−4.5	0.8	2.2
1927–1950[b]	0.4	−0.2	0.6	2.2	4.0	0.9	0.4

These are the ratios of the change in the stock of reproducible capital between the ends of the indicated years to the change in the nine-year averages of output, centered in the indicated years. Both numerator and denominator are measured in 1929 dollars.

[a] From the starting date of the industry.

[b] Data used for 1950 are for the single year only.

further by selecting end periods which are centered about the peak years of long cycles. The numerators of the ratios therein presented are the changes between the ends of the indicated years in the stock of reproducible capital, measured in 1929 dollars—i.e. net capital formation. The denominators are the changes in the nine-year averages of output, centered on the years indicated. An exception was made for the terminal year, since here it was desired to extend the period as far as possible in order to reflect the activity of the post-war period; rather than stop with the nine-year average centered in 1946, we terminate the change with 1950, for which output in that year alone was employed.

The data show a sharp and progressive downward trend in the marginal capital-product ratio. In the period prior to the 1890's, an increase of one dollar in the output of the regulated industries was accompanied on the average by an increase of 9 dollars in capital formation. In the 1891–1910 span, an increase of one dollar in output was accompanied by one of only 3 dollars in capital formation, in 1910–27 by one of only 2 dollars, and in the 1927–50 span, by only a 40-cent advance in capital formation. Thus the impact of an expansion in demand upon investment grew steadily weaker over time. This conclusion is reinforced when we examine the record of individual components.

Individual Industries

The trend of the average capital-product ratios in the components is depicted in Charts 17–22. In every case but one—local bus lines—the general long-run drift is downward, in keeping with that of the aggregate. But there are some important distinctions to be noted in the pace and the regularity of this movement.

Most similar to the aggregative average capital-product ratio in the regularity and general form of its decline is that of steam railroads. Here, the ratio dropped from about 16 in 1880 to somewhat over 6 at the turn of the century, to less than 4 in the 1920's, and finally to about 3 in 1950. The pace of decline was progressive, proceeding by diminishing amounts, and broken mainly by cyclical fluctuations—especially the severe depressions of the mid-1890's and the early 1930's, when output was contracted sharply and the ratio correspondingly boosted. Like the aggregative ratio, its trend is well described throughout its range by a Gompertz curve. No one of the other components adheres to this pattern so closely.

In electric light and power the trend is also sharply downward, but is broken by a temporary "bottoming out" and modest rise in the first twelve years of the twentieth century. Nor can this interruption be explained by cyclical changes in the level of business activity. Only in the last forty years of the time span covered is the movement of the average capital-product ratio in electric light and power adequately described by the Gompertz curve. Nevertheless, the over-all drop in the ratio was substantial, extending from about 15 in the early 1890's to about 10 in the 1900's, to about 4 in the 1920's, and to less than 2 in 1950.

In street and electric railways there is also a divergence from the over-all pattern. From 1890 to 1910 the average capital-product ratio in this segment rose very sharply, from slightly more than 3 to nearly 7. Thereafter, the Gompertz curve pattern is evident, and the decline proceeds from somewhat less than 7 in 1900 to between 3 and 4 in the 1920's and to a bit more than 2 in 1950.

Although both declined over the long run, in neither telephones nor the all other group does the average capital-product ratio follow the Gompertz pattern. In the former, the ratio declines sharply from about 5 in 1890 to less than 2 in the 1920's. But in the mid-1920's the ratio began a significant rise. The advance was powerfully accelerated in the early 1930's by the effects of the Great Depression. However, when the influence of the depression had subsided, and—still later—when in 1950 the influence of the wartime squeeze on investment had been largely erased, the ratio stood at a level slightly above its previous low point of the 1920's. In short, over the last thirty years, taken as a whole, stability in the neighborhood of 1.5 to 2, rather than continued decline, was characteristic of the ratio in this component.

In the all other group the decline in the average capital-product ratio is progressive, but not at the same evenly diminishing rate which characterized behavior in the aggregate and in steam railroads. From 1890 to 1906 the ratio dipped sharply, from somewhat less than 13 to a little more than 4. During the next twenty years the decline proceeded, but very slowly, with the ratio ranging in the neighborhood of 3 in the late 1920's. In the following years there was a moderate acceleration in the pace of decline, and by 1950 the average capital-product ratio in the all other group was slightly less than 1.

As indicated earlier, the ratio for local bus lines departs materially from the general trend, though it must be borne in mind that the history of this industry is very brief. The general trend of its average capital-product ratio was upward, rising from about 0.5 in the mid-1920's to about 1.7 in 1950. A substantial part of the increase in the post-World War II period, however, was of short-run nature, reflecting both the cutback in traffic from the wartime high as private passenger cars came into wider use, and the extension of lines into new suburban areas where the intensity of traffic was at least initially light. Save for this brisk post-war advance in the average capital-product ratio for local bus lines, the over-all secular upward trend was of narrowly limited dimensions.

With the exception of this small component, however, the broad generalization reached in connection with our study of the aggregate, holds as well for its several parts. The over-all trend of the average capital-product ratio was distinctly downward over the 1880–1950 span. In the case of telephones, this decline was substantially arrested in the last thirty years, though it was by no means reversed. In all other components the reduction in the average capital-product ratio has proceeded progressively for at least the past forty years and, in two of them, for the entirety of the seventy-year period of record.

In the same way, the generalization concerning the *marginal* capital-product ratio holds for the components as well as for all regulated industries in the aggregate. This is shown in Table 21, where data are presented for each of the components computed by the same method as that employed for the aggregate. But for local bus lines, the marginal capital-product ratio moves downward in every case. The declines are most pronounced in railroads, electric light and power, and the all other group. In the first, the reduction proceeds briskly from somewhat more than 10 dollars of capital formation for every one dollar advance in output, to a long period of stability at a level of about 2 for 1 during 1891 through 1927. Then in the final twenty-three years the ratio actually turned negative, for in this period output was substantially increased even though the stock of reproducible capital was reduced. In both electric light and power and in the all other group, however, the decline in the marginal capital-product ratio was sharp and progressive throughout the period, proceeding from nearly 17 to 0.6 in the former and from more than 11 to 0.4 in the latter.

For telephones the reduction was much smaller. Indeed, after the initial drop from the pre-1891 period, there was on balance but a moderate downtrend. In street railways the reduction in the marginal ratio was also relatively modest, though it should be remembered that in this component the stock of reproducible capital had been contracting since early in the twentieth century. During the 1910–27 period, this contraction was accompanied by a rise in output. During 1927–50, output also declined. The data for local bus lines suggest virtual stability in the marginal capital-product ratio, but here the historical base for defining the secular trend is very small.

Thus, with a minor exception, advances in output were accompanied by progressively smaller amounts of capital formation over the 1880–1950 span—in each of the regulated industries as well as in the aggregate. Moreover, the dimension of this change in the long-run relationship between demand for final product and investment was very substantial. Both the reasons for the trend, as well as its implications, present an intriguing and challenging problem for analysis. Some tentative explorations in this area are included in the subject matter of Chapter 6.

CHAPTER 5

Factors Underlying Long-Term Trends: Output

OUR previous analysis has led us through an examination of the secular trends in capital formation, in output, and in the capital-product ratio. Distinctive patterns, it was observed, characterize each. It should be recalled, however, that investment in the regulated industries constitutes the principal interest of this study, and it is only insofar as this central core is thereby illumined, that the trends in the other variables have warranted attention. That all three variables—capital formation, output, and the capital-product ratio—are related in a complex system of mutual interaction, common to most objects of economic study, is obvious. Yet in an analysis confined to secular trends in particular industries, it is possible to simplify. The trend in capital formation may be viewed, *in the main*, as the net result of the factors underlying the trend in output on the one hand, and those underlying the trend in the capital-product ratio on the other. This is a hypothesis on which we shall amplify later. It may be summarized in the equation:

$$\frac{\Delta O}{\Delta t} \cdot \frac{\Delta C}{\Delta O} = \frac{\Delta C}{\Delta t} \qquad (1)$$

where O stands for output, C for the stock of reproducible capital, and t for time measured in some convenient unit.

The equation is of course a truism. It serves here, however, as a frame of reference convenient for assembling the host of events and conditions which together have influenced the pace of investment in the regulated industries. We shall be concerned in this chapter with one compartment of this framework—those factors which have affected the secular trend of output.

In our previous discussion of output, one outstanding characteristic observed was the secular tendency for its *percentage* rate of increase to diminish over time. The decline set in at a very early date—in every component and in the total for regulated industries as a whole. Another characteristic concerns the *absolute* rate of change in production. We noted the tendency of the regulated industries to follow a path marked by at least one or more of the following stages:

Stage	*Output*	*Change in Output*
I	Increases by increasing amounts	Increases by increasing amounts
II	Increases by increasing amounts	Increases by decreasing amounts
III	Increases by decreasing amounts	Decreases by increasing amounts but remains positive

OUTPUT

Stage	*Output*	*Change in Output*
IV	Decreases by increasing amounts	Becomes negative and decreases by decreasing amounts
V	Decreases by decreasing amounts	Increases by increasing amounts but remains negative
VI	Decreases by decreasing amounts until it reaches zero	Increases by decreasing amounts, remaining negative until it reaches zero

The aggregate of all regulated industries, it will be recalled, remained in stage I throughout the 1880–1950 span for which data are available. So did three of the components—electric light and power, telephones, and the all other group. The steam railroads and local bus lines, on the other hand, had by 1950 progressed to stage III. Thus, for these components the peak of output increments had been passed, and total production was advancing by diminishing amounts. Street and electric railways had progressed to stage V, with production moving secularly downward at a pace which had finally begun to level off.

This pattern of relative as well as absolute changes in production is not confined to the regulated industries. Previous studies have established that it is common to the growth of output in most industrial segments of the economy,[1] though progress beyond stage III is rare in the United States. We may inquire now concerning the factors which combined to determine this behavior in the regulated industries.

The Vacuum Effect

The uppermost limit to the growth of a new industry is set by the size of its principal market—in the case of most regulated industries, the size and the purchasing power of the national population. In none of our components would it have been technologically or financially possible for the first productive units to satisfy fully the ultimate demands of the then existing population. Typically, there was—and perforce *had* to be—an experimental period, in which the beginnings made were modest in the extreme. In this category were the first railroad line, operated with thirteen miles of track by the Baltimore and Ohio in 1830; the first electric company, with a distribution area of less than a mile, in New York City; and the first telephone exchange, with twenty-one subscribers, in New Haven.

In this experimental period the commercial feasibility of the productive process, as well as the receptivity of consumers, was tried.

[1] Cf. Simon Kuznets, *Secular Movements in Production and Prices* (Houghton Mifflin, 1930), and Arthur F. Burns, *Production Trends in the United States since 1870* (National Bureau of Economic Research, 1934).

As both tests were passed, innovators were free to expand and imitators were inspired to activity. Each year brought larger, more ambitious productive units, and elicited them in greater number over an ever-widening circle. Given this modest start and the subsequent tendency toward cumulative expansion, which in the earliest days even business depressions fail to retard, spectacular rates of increase in output were virtually inevitable. The data of Table 17 start at or close to the beginnings of electric light and power, telephones, and local bus lines. They show percentage rates of increase for these components ranging from 7 to 15 per cent *per year* during the first two decades of operation. Of course under these circumstances, too, growth at least for a time in the manner of stage I above acquired a high degree of probability.

But there were other factors which helped to generate this swift advance. The market potential itself grew progressively. The population of the United States prior to World War I expanded by increasing amounts, and even in subsequent years has grown substantially. Per capita incomes increased steadily. The point at which decreasing returns might have retarded the growth of output was continuously raised to higher levels, and was so raised throughout much of the eighty-year time span covered by this study. In the absence of a check, it was to be expected that output would rise with the spectacular vigor evidenced by the data for all components in the earlier decades covered by Table 17.

Nor does this exhaust the list of stimulating factors which operated in the earlier days of the regulated industries. The first essays in a new productive process are typically crude, and the possibilities for improving efficiency are correspondingly manifold. Such improvements, reducing costs and increasing sales, further stimulated output. Combined with this was the gradual extenuation of consumer resistance. For before general acceptance is accorded, each new product must surmount a threshold of habit and inertia. And along with these factors was the conflict with, and the final victories—total or limited—over, competing products. Thus the success of the early railroads overcame the opposition of wagon and stagecoach operators, water carriers, and canal enterprises.

Hence the equilibrium point—at which production might stabilize—was, at the beginning, far above the capacity of the first tentative units established. And before it was even approached, a host of factors operated to raise this point rapidly and progressively to higher levels, each new obstacle overcome disclosing a wider range of profit opportunities. Meanwhile, the report of these opportunities was communicated over more extensive geographical and financial ranges. Stated alternatively, in their beginnings the regulated industries were ones in which the marginal efficiency of capital was much higher than the rate of interest or the prospective rates of return in most other lines, and they were generally in a position to have their situation widely publicized. The response of the economy may be likened to the rush of air into a vacuum.

Brief mention may be made of the role of financing—a topic treated more fully in Chapter 7—in shaping this stage in the pattern of development. The vacuum effect is symbolic of the rush of resources into a pocket of the economy in which the prospective returns are unusually high. How swiftly it moves depends in part on how quickly capital is mobilized for its use. In this respect, the regulated industries enjoyed a distinct advantage. For the individual firm in this segment of the economy is by nature large, endowed with high prestige, and some degree of monopoly, along with an apparent promise of substantial profit and *relatively* small risk. Hence capital in larger amounts and over a greater area was made available with less reservation than would have been true of the average industry in the United States. It was a factor which lent additional power to the vacuum effect in the regulated industries. This is not to say that raising all the capital desired was at no point a difficulty for any of the regulated industries—e.g. the railroads. It obviously was an obstacle at a number of stages in their development. It must be recalled, however, that their requirements were huge. The only point made here is that the requirements were satisfied more easily *because* of the special characteristics of the regulated industries, than they would have been otherwise.

Output and National Aggregates: The Vigorous Industries

Quantitatively, the vacuum effect may be defined as an advance in production substantially in excess of the long-run growth of an industry's potential market. It is characterized by an initial rush which gradually subsides—slowly or swiftly petering out, depending upon the relative strength of retarding or stimulating factors in an industry's history. But that it must diminish in intensity rather quickly, at least in some degree, is clearly evident from the data of Table 22.

For example, in 1896 electric light and power output represented 0.07 per cent of the gross national product. By 1906 this percentage had grown to 0.28, despite the fact that the national aggregate had itself expanded substantially. Now if the advance of this component had continued at the same percentage rate in subsequent years as had prevailed in the decade prior to 1906, its output would have amounted to more than 80 per cent of the gross national product by 1950. Even if we allow for the fact, previously pointed out, that electric output is measured on a "gross" basis,[2] this extrapolation is obviously far beyond the realm of practical possibility. Nor does this conclusion apply only to electric power. Study of the rates of growth prevailing in the earlier years in *any* of our components would yield roughly similar results. Note that this includes railroads and street and electric railways, even though in these components the full strength of the vacuum effect had been appreciably attenuated by the earliest years for which data are available. In every case rates of growth had been established which could not possibly have been sustained.

Yet in some of our components the pace of expansion remained remarkably high throughout the period of study. These are the ones which, throughout this period, were in stage I of the model pattern. They are grouped in Table 22. Their output is compared in this tabulation with the progress of population, income, and urbanization. For these factors set limits of a kind to the development of nearly any industry, though—depending upon other factors—they may be far from definite. Of course, the phenomena described above—under the vacuum effect—explain the fact that in the earlier years the growth of production in the regulated industries far outstripped that of population and of income too. But for the components in Table 22 the continued rise in output, relative to the national aggregates, went far beyond this. That it persisted over so long a period—indeed through the entire span of study—can only be explained by the development of especially favorable circumstances. One factor or another served over the years to sustain demand for the output of these vigorously growing components, relative to the national income. Chief among these factors appear to have been:

1. The development of new uses for the product. This almost always involved technological advance, as embodied, for example, in the electric dishwasher, the vacuum cleaner, and other appliances.

It often involved, also, continued victories over competition, as illustrated by the displacement of gas stoves and iceboxes by electric models.

2. Virtual immunity to competition. This was the case for telephones, for which no reasonably close substitute has been developed. Accordingly, the industry was free to expand unimpeded, as its service was transformed from a luxury item to an everyday household necessity.

3. Technological innovations and economies of mass production, permitting a secular decline in price relative to the price level in

[2] See Chapter 4, section on *The Data.*

TABLE 22

Output of Vigorously Growing Industries in Relation to National Income and Population

(*based on nine-year averages, constant dollar values*)

Central Year of Nine-Year Average	ALL REGULATED INDUSTRIES: As percentage of: Gross National Product	As percentage of: Urban Population Income	Per Capita	ELECTRIC LIGHT AND POWER: As percentage of: Gross National Product	As percentage of: Urban Population Income	Per Capita	TELEPHONES: As percentage of: Gross National Product	As percentage of: Urban Population Income	Per Capita	ALL OTHER GROUP: As percentage of: Gross National Product	As percentage of: Urban Population Income	Per Capita
1886	5.9	20.2	$ 21.7	...	...	...	...	...	...	...	...	...
1890	6.9	21.6	26.4	...	...	...	...	...	...	...	...	...
1896	7.8	22.8	32.6	0.07	0.2	$ 0.31	0.15	0.4	$ 0.62	0.86	2.5	$ 3.60
1900	9.0	25.0	41.8	0.14	0.4	0.67	0.31	0.9	1.46	1.07	3.0	5.00
1906	11.1	28.5	59.5	0.28	0.7	1.50	0.65	1.7	3.47	1.46	3.8	7.86
1910	12.4	30.5	69.0	0.39	0.9	2.15	0.83	2.0	4.60	1.75	4.3	9.70
1916	14.5	33.4	86.4	0.72	1.7	4.23	0.97	2.2	5.72	2.20	5.1	12.95
1920	14.5	32.0	94.3	1.00	2.2	6.48	1.06	2.3	6.86	2.36	5.2	15.30
1926	13.9	29.0	101.4	1.58	3.3	11.5	1.21	2.5	8.81	2.69	5.6	19.50
1930	14.1	28.5	94.3	2.20	4.2	14.0	1.34	2.7	8.92	3.07	6.2	20.40
1936	14.1	28.4	92.4	2.69	5.4	17.6	1.31	2.6	8.60	3.95	6.5	25.80
1940	16.2	32.6	133.2	3.00	6.1	24.6	1.25	2.5	10.30	4.44	9.0	36.60
1946	18.3	36.1	185.5	3.60	7.1	36.4	1.45	2.9	14.65	5.58	10.9	56.50
1950[a]	17.5	33.0	191.5	4.12	7.75	45.2	1.57	3.0	17.20	6.24	11.7	68.30

[a] Based on data for 1950 only.

Source: Gross national product in 1929 dollars, from revised annual estimates of Simon Kuznets, National Bureau of Economic Research (Variant I); urban population income, from Table 23; total continental population, from Bureau of the Census.

general. This was an influential factor in both telephones and electric light and power. It obviously encouraged the expansion of consumption in relation to that of the national income.

4. A favorable shift in consumer tastes. We use the term "tastes" here in the objective sense of the propensity to purchase in a given environment of income and price structure. Tastes, in this sense, may be altered by other changes in the environment, including urbanization, advertising, mode of employment, and other influences in great number. The growing complexity of modern life has, through this channel, promoted the use of both telephones and electric power. Swift and frequent communication, via the telephone, and abundant illumination are attributes especially of city life. Hence progressive urbanization powerfully raised the level of demand in both cases. So did the revolutionary changes during the last seventy-five years in the commercial and industrial configuration of the country. The gradual movement of wives from housework to industry and professional careers is an additional example of a social change stimulating the use of electric power—in this case, through accelerated adoption of household electric appliances.

All of these factors in combination account for the continued gains, over the entire 1880–1950 period, of output of telephone service and electric light and power relative to population and income, as measured by the data of Table 22. In addition, the development of new industries help to explain the similar results shown for the all other group and for all regulated industries in the aggregate. Figured on a per capita basis, production actually rose by increasing amounts over the seventy-year span in each of the vigorously growing groups. Production of all regulated industries in the aggregate advanced from $26 per person in 1890 to $69 in 1910, to $94 in 1930, and to $191 in 1950. The general pace of the rise is of similar order for telephones, electric light and power, and the all other group. It should be borne in mind that the cyclical influence in the data of Table 22 have been partially smoothed by the use of nine-year averages.

The movement of the national income over time, of course, reflects the advance in population and the steady ascension of per capita incomes in combination. The gains in output of the vigorously growing industries, relative to this aggregate, are therefore somewhat less spectacular than when population was considered alone, though they are very substantial still, as Table 22 shows. Production of all regulated industries amounted to 7 per cent of the gross national product in 1890, to 12 per cent in 1910, to 14 per cent in 1930, and to 17 per cent in 1950. There is some suggestion here that the pace of the relative advance—though still quite large—was leveling off. Similar evidence is apparent in the behavior of the separate industry groups. In telephone service, where this tendency was most pronounced, output accounted for 0.8 per cent of the gross national product in 1910, 1.3 per cent in 1930, and 1.6 per cent in 1950. In no case, however, is there doubt concerning the persistence of the relative gains, secularly, throughout the entire period.

Though our interest is primarily in the trends evidenced by these figures, attention may be called once again to the nature of our output data. They are gross figures, in the sense described earlier,[3] and hence tend to overstate the importance of our components relative to national income. The degree of overstatement is generally about one-third: that is, if calculated on a "net" basis, fully comparable to the income data, output of the regulated industries would have amounted to about 12 per cent of the gross national product in 1950 rather than the 17.5 per cent shown. But this matter does not affect the relative trends of these series, in which our interest now centers.

Reference has already been made to the influence of urbanization on the demand for the products of the regulated industries. This consideration leads to the calculation of another tentative ascending "limiting" factor—the data shown in Table 23. This series represents the product of the urban population and the per capita income of the total population in each period. It is somewhat less than the true figure for urban income, since per capita incomes in cities (for which no figures are available over the period of interest) were higher and probably rose somewhat more than did per capita incomes in the nation as a whole. The difference in the aggregate, however, would not be great,[4] and our series in any event retains the advantage of representing in combination the shift to cities superimposed upon the growth of population and the rise in per capita incomes. Does the expansion of our vigorously growing components outstrip this even higher and more swiftly rising "ceiling"? For all regulated industries in the aggregate, the answer must be in the negative. In the proportion of their output to urban population income, there is but little evidence of a secular trend over the last thirty-five years, as the relevant data in Table 22 show. From the period of World War I, and perhaps from some years earlier, through 1950, this percentage has remained roughly stable. But the result reflects, in part, the downward pull of retarded and declining

[3] See Chapter 4, section on *The Data*.

[4] Particularly because the urban population was important in the total throughout the period and since 1910 has been in the majority.

TABLE 23

Nine-Year Averages of Urban Population Income

(billions of 1929 dollars)

Central Year of Nine-Year Average	*Urban Population Income*
1886	6.2
1890	7.7
1896	10.1
1900	12.7
1906	17.8
1910	20.8
1916	26.1
1920	31.1
1926	41.1
1930	40.5
1936	41.8
1940	53.6
1946	71.9
1950	87.8[a]

Figures are nine-year averages of net national product per capita of total population, multiplied by urban population. Net national product is from revised annual data of Simon Kuznets, National Bureau of Economic Research (Variant I); total and urban population, from Bureau of the Census, with intercensal years interpolated.

[a] Based on data for 1950 only.

industries included in the total. For when attention is centered upon the vigorously growing components, it will be seen from Table 22 that they pierce this higher ceiling too.

Output of electric light and power amounted to 0.9 per cent of urban population income in 1910, to somewhat more than 4 per cent in 1930, and to nearly 8 per cent in 1950. Output of telephone service grew from about 2 per cent of urban population income in 1910 to 2.7 per cent in 1930, and to 3.0 per cent in 1950. The all other group, with an influx of new industries, also advanced progressively. However, the pace of this *relative* increase in output of electric light and power, and in even greater degree, of telephones, clearly leveled off in later years. The comparatively modest gains in percentage over the last decade or two was by a wide margin smaller than those which had been scored before. It is clear that in the rising population, in the shift to cities, and in the advance in per capita incomes, we have in combination the principal factors underlying the continued powerful upward surge in output by these components in recent years.

But these are not the only factors. Nor do these influences in any event operate in isolation from those other specific considerations described earlier. The development of new uses, the favorable swing of consumer tastes, the price-reducing inventions, and continued success against actual or potential competition, would in some part have been necessary of production in these components even to keep pace with the sharp rise in urban population income. That the advance in output was still greater throughout the 1880–1950 period is a tribute to their power.

It would appear reasonably clear, too, that the somewhat poorer performance of telephones, when compared with electric light and power, may be explained in terms of the relative force of such attendant circumstances. Thus, new product uses have obviously proved more influential in the latter component than in the former. It is possible, also, that telecommunication has approached the point of market saturation; that is to say, its use has been spread, approximately, as widely as possible within the existing market, and further expansion is dependent more directly upon over-all national growth. The aggregate income elasticity of demand for telephone service, for this reason, may have begun to diminish more rapidly, though it may still remain above the critical level of unity. Surely this is a natural development, ultimately, for a commodity which has reached the stage of mass distribution, unless fully counteracted by the gestation of new uses and the evolution of favorable environmental circumstances affecting tastes. It is a development which would stem from the limits of the average family budgetary income itself as well as from the "law" of diminishing utility. And it is a hypothesis which is consistent with the behavior of the relevant data in Table 22. But this raises the question of retarding influences, which are by definition barely evident in the vigorously growing industries. We turn now to a discussion of their nature and their effect upon the other components.

Retarding Influences

One important factor making for a subsequent retardation of growth is the very force of the vacuum effect. As observed above, it established in the regulated industries a rate of expansion that could not possibly be maintained. Some diminution was inevitable. Thus, in the 1890's and 1900's, the secular rate of increase in the gross national product was about 5 or 6 per cent per annum.[5] The yearly

[5] Simon Kuznets, *Long-Term Changes in the National Income of the United States of America since 1870* (Preliminary manuscript of Part I, National Bureau of Economic Research), pp. 28–32.

increase in production during the same period in electric light and power was nearly 20 per cent. In telephone service, output rose by more than 20 per cent per year. Even in street railways, where the full power of the vacuum effect had appreciably subsided, the rate of growth achieved in this period was nearly 10 per cent per year, and in railroads about 7 per cent. In the post-World War I period, when the growth of the national product was materially slower than in previous years, output in local bus lines rose by about 7 or 8 per cent per year. All these rates of growth declined substantially later on. But in the especially favored industries, the rate remained well above that of the national income even in the most recent decades for which our record was prepared. By 1950, when the secular rate of increase in the gross national product was about 2 or 3 per cent, electric output was still headed upward at a rate approaching 8 per cent per year. Telephone service was expanding by about 7 per cent per year. In other components (except for the all other group), growth had declined close to, or below, the expansion rate of the gross national product. This difference in behavior reflects the more forceful impact in the latter components of the particular retarding influences to which we now turn briefly.

One of these is the tendency for income elasticities of demand to decline, once a product ceases to be a luxury and achieves mass distribution, and once older competition has been thoroughly routed or subdued. The power of this tendency is especially great in industries which by their nature lack resiliency—in lines in which the development of new uses is not feasible, and quality upgrading is narrowly limited. Another retarding factor is the rise of new and effective competition of related goods and services. Unless counteracted, it is nearly certain to enter the scene, sooner or later, wherever technological and institutional conditions permit. Its effect is obviously to cut, or to limit the growth of, the industry's market. It intensifies the decline in the income elasticity of demand, or stimulates its reduction if not already under way. And in extreme cases it relieves the industry of its market entirely.

Both of these retarding factors are evident even in our vigorously growing components, although in these cases their influence has been over-shadowed by others. Some reduction in the income elasticity of demand for telephone service seems apparent in the secular trend of this component's output relative to the national income, as observed above. But thus far it has been moderate. In electric light and power, the competition of government projects has assumed increasing significance. Publicly owned facilities accounted for less than 3 per cent of the nation's total generating capacity in 1920, and for fully

16 per cent thirty years later.[6] But in these industries, there were counterpoising factors stimulating growth, as pointed out in the previous section. A similar degree of resiliency (as in electric light and power) or virtual immunity to competition (as in telephones) did not prevail in the other components.

Thus the rise of motor vehicles and air transportation have materially limited the growth of railroad freight and passenger business. Bus service and automobiles dampened the growth of, and then reduced drastically the business of, street and electric railways. In local bus service, with the continued rise in levels of living and the expanding ownership of passenger automobiles, there is evidence that the income elasticity of demand has declined to less than one.[7] Railroads and local bus lines had by 1950 progressed to stage III of the model pattern; their production continued to increase, though at a rate which was diminishing. Street railways ran almost the gamut of the model pattern of development, and by 1950 was in stage V.

It is not without significance that once retardation appeared in these industries, it persisted, or was intensified. There are a number of reasons why a retardation in the secular rate of growth, once established, is seldom reversed. If a decline in the income elasticity of demand has set in, it is most unlikely that it can be turned back—though it may be slowed. A "rich man's good" does not become a "poor man's good" and then a rich man's good again; and, secularly, per capita incomes in the United States have moved progressively upward. If the industry's looming difficulties have stemmed from successful competition, this too will most likely prove to be a self-perpetuating, dilating obstacle to continued growth. For inter-industry competitive advantages ordinarily inhere in the nature of the industries and their products. They are not easily obliterated and reversed. The advantages of the automobile over the railroad (say the flexibility of its routes) and of the airplane over the auto (say its speed) are indelible, technical characteristics of the vehicles concerned. Their economic effects endure accordingly.

True, the pressure of competition may be steady rather than overwhelming, gentle rather than devastasting, and the decline in the income elasticity of demand over time may be slight. If so, there may be no apparent limit to the duration of stage III of the model pattern—the position of railroads and local bus lines in 1950. But on the other hand, the inroads of competition may be swift and comprehensive. Then progress from stages III to IV and onward will be relatively quick and certain, with production plunging. This was the fate of street railways.

[6] See Appendix D, Table 32.

[7] See pages 90 and 92.

Combined with these factors is the observation that the pace of favorable technical changes slackens as an industry matures. This may be due, as described in an illuminating essay by Kuznets,[8] to the fact that the flood of early technological and organizational advances gradually leaves less and less in the productive process subject to further improvement. Moreover, as Kuznets points out, the gains accruing from additional innovations tend in the long run to peter out, for as the price of a product is reduced, its price elasticity of demand may be expected, ultimately, to decline.

Output and National Aggregates: Retarded and Declining Industries

To summarize, railroads, street railways, and local bus lines clearly lack the relative immunity to competition with which telephones have been favored. They lack the numerous facets for new uses characteristic of electric light and power. To only a limited extent have they been able to produce services over a range of grades sufficient to counterbalance the tendency toward a declining income elasticity of demand. Though cost-reducing innovations have been steady—especially in railroads, but also in local bus lines and streetcars—they have not been sufficiently profound and persistent to permit substantial and continued price reductions relative to the general price level.

True, all of these components have been favored by the growth of the nation at large—a common supporting influence for all industry. They have also benefited, particularly, from the growth of cities. But in their earlier years—in every case—output advanced at a rate which far outstripped these general sustaining factors. Given the retarding influences which gradually dominated these components, it was a rate which was bound to diminish by large amounts in subsequent decades.

Railroad output amounted to less than 5 per cent of the gross national product in the 1880's and to about 16 per cent of urban population income,[9] as Table 24 shows. Thirty years later these proportions had been stepped up to 9 per cent and 21 per cent, respectively. It should be borne in mind that railroads had their beginnings in the 1830's. It is testimony to the size of their market, as well as to the magnitude of the construction job faced, that so large a differential rate of growth could have persisted after nearly

[8] Simon Kuznets, *Economic Change: Selected Essays in Business Cycles, National Income, and Economic Growth* (Norton, 1953), Chapter 9.

[9] Since the output figures were not computed on the same basis as the national income, the comparisons given in this section overstate the relative importance of the regulated industries by about one-third. See pages 64–65.

TABLE 24

Output of Retarded and Declining Industries in Relation to National Income and Population

(based on nine-year averages, constant dollar values)

Central Year of Nine-Year Average	RAILROADS: As percentage of: Gross National Product	RAILROADS: As percentage of: Urban Population Income	RAILROADS: Per Capita	STREET AND ELECTRIC RAILWAYS: As percentage of: Gross National Product	STREET AND ELECTRIC RAILWAYS: As percentage of: Urban Population Income	STREET AND ELECTRIC RAILWAYS: Per Capita	LOCAL BUS LINES: As percentage of: Gross National Product	LOCAL BUS LINES: As percentage of: Urban Population Income	LOCAL BUS LINES: Per Capita
1886	4.8	16.3	$17.5	...	...	...	...	...	...
1890	5.6	17.3	21.1	...	...	...	...	...	...
1896	6.0	17.6	25.1	0.71	2.09	$2.98	...	...	...
1900	6.6	18.4	30.7	0.84	2.34	3.91	...	...	...
1906	7.6	19.4	40.7	1.10	2.85	5.93	...	...	...
1910	8.2	20.1	45.5	1.28	3.13	7.08	...	...	...
1916	9.3	21.3	54.5	1.36	3.12	7.98	...	...	...
1920	8.8	19.3	56.9	1.30	2.87	8.45	...	...	...
1926	7.3	15.2	53.2	1.05	2.18	7.61	0.13	0.26	$0.92
1930	6.4	13.0	42.8	0.91	1.83	5.80	0.18	0.36	1.18
1936	5.3	10.6	34.7	0.64	1.28	4.18	0.22	0.45	1.47
1940	6.7	13.5	54.9	0.50	1.01	4.09	0.28	0.56	2.28
1946	7.0	13.7	70.4	0.38	0.76	3.92	0.34	0.66	3.41
1950[a]	5.1	9.7	56.3	0.21	0.39	2.25	0.25	0.47	2.73

[a] The comparisons are based on data for 1950 only.

Source: Gross national product in 1929 dollars, from revised annual estimates of Simon Kuznets, National Bureau of Economic Research (Variant I); urban population income, from Table 23; total continental population, from Bureau of the Census.

eighty years. This was a period, of course, in which expansion thrived, at least in part, at the expense of older industries, as previously described. But once these had been definitely downed, given the characteristics cited above, reduction in the proportion of this component's output to national income was clearly in the offing. The way was open for the more dramatic manifestations of retarding factors.

Streetcars, too, had established a rate of growth in their early days, that exceeded the pace of the general sustaining influences upon which it must in the long run be dependent. Indeed, the differential rate of growth in this case was even greater, though it should be borne in mind that with the establishment of the first successful electrified streetcar system in 1887 there arose a virtually new industry, while the railroads at this time were roughly fifty years old. In the 1890's the output of the street railway component represented 0.7 per cent of the gross national product, and in just twenty years this ratio had nearly doubled. Its proportion of the swiftly growing urban population income in the same period rose from 2 to 3 per cent. Underlying this advance was a speculative splurge which reached almost every city, large or small, in the country. It is virtually certain that some modification of this differential rate of increase would have occurred, given this industry's characteristics, even if competition had not entered the scene. There is some evidence of this in the gradual tendency toward stability in the ratio of street railway output to urban population income, even before bus lines and other motor vehicles had become an important element.

The vacuum effect displays its typical power also in the case of local bus lines. In a mere ten years the proportion of its output to the gross national product had advanced from 0.13 per cent in the 1920's to 0.22 per cent in the 1930's, and the proportion to urban income in the same period from 0.26 to 0.45 per cent.

Thus, in all three cases initial rates of advance had been established which seemed destined for later reduction. The effects of competition, and other retarding factors, insured and intensified a radical change in trend. For street railways, of course, this was a sharp and drastic decline—sharp in relation to urban income and to national income as well as to the population. By 1950 production by this component amounted to 0.2 per cent of the gross national product, less than one-sixth of the percentage prevailing at the peak. For railroads the rate of increase dropped from one which far exceeded that of the gross national product to one which appeared to match roughly the growth of population, if we ignore the abnormal bulge in the period of World War II and make due allowance for cyclical swings. In

1950 railroad output amounted to about 56 dollars per person, about the same as thirty years earlier.

The picture is somewhat distorted for local bus lines—particularly in the light of the brevity of historical experience in this case—by behavior in the war years. For in this period use of bus service was greatly augmented by the prevailing limitations on the use of passenger automobiles. The decline in the ratio of the production of this component to the national income from the 1940's to 1950, therefore, must be in some part discounted. Even so, it will be noted that this ratio in 1950 was only slightly more than that prevailing in the mid-1930's—a difference which contrasts signficantly with the very sharp advances prevailing in earlier years. There seems little doubt that the income elasticity of demand for local bus service had declined materially between these periods, as pointed out in the preceding section. And judging from behavior in post-World War II years, there is the suggestion that it may have fallen below unity. If so, unless some new element is introduced in this situation, future increases in national income will bring less than proportional advances in the output of the local bus component.[10] In this respect, then, it will more closely resemble the behavior of the other industries treated in this section.

[10] Whether something new is on the horizon is not easily determined. The parking and traffic problem in many large cities has thrown many car owners back on bus service, and as this problem worsens bus service will continue to profit. But at the same time there is a trend toward the two- or even three-car family, a factor which reduces the use of buses for many local purposes.

Furthermore, the growth in popularity of the small car, and the geographical dispersion of industry too, help to alleviate the parking problem.

CHAPTER 6

Factors Underlying Long-Term Trends: Capital-Product Ratios and Capital Formation

IN the previous chapter we proposed a general framework linking the secular behavior of net capital formation in the regulated industries to the long-run trends in two series: the marginal capital-product ratio and the *increments* in output. In addition, we explored the factors underlying the secular pattern of production in this segment of the economy. In the present chapter we turn to the determinants of the capital-product ratio, and then once again to our central problem—the long-run trend of investment.

Determinants of Trends in the Capital-Product Ratio

The average capital-product ratio is essentially an inverse measure of the efficiency with which capital is employed. It is one-dimensional, of course, since it takes no account of the length of life of capital, its cost, or the cost of the other principal factor of production —labor. Nevertheless, other things being equal, a decline in the capital-product ratio is a gain in efficiency. In a business economy, therefore, there are bound to be forces making for its reduction, though these might indeed be counterbalanced by others. Thus, in the static framework often employed in theoretical analysis, a rise in the capital-product ratio would occasion little speculation: it would represent rather obviously an adjustment to an increase in labor costs relative to that of capital. But in the actual long-run behavior of industry, pronounced alterations in other conditions greatly overshadow adjustments of this kind. For one thing, technological advance has been a continuing phenomenon, and may result in economies in the use of any or of *all* factors of production. Other conditions of dynamic change also enter into the determination of the capital-product ratio, as we shall see, so that the causal nexus binding the actual events of history is necessarily clouded with the complexities of a variety of interconnections. Through it all, however, remains the tendency for increasing the productivity of capital (i.e. reducing the capital-product ratio) as well as that of labor.

It is of some significance, therefore, that a *rising* capital-product ratio in the initial period of an industry's existence is evident in the records in every case in which our analysis covers the activity of an industry from its inception. Reference to the charts in Chapter 4 will call to mind that for electric light and power there was a very sharp rise in the capital-product ratio from about 4 in 1887 to more than 18 in 1893. For telephones the advance was very much more modest, though quite perceptible, and lasted from 1890 to 1897. The application of electricity to street railways—and the subsequent swift growth of a virtually new industry—is reflected in the substantial rise in the capital-product ratio for this component from 3 in 1890 to nearly 7 in 1897. A similar development could have been observed for railroads in the earliest days, not covered in our charts.

This phenomenon springs at least in part from an outstanding characteristic of the regulated industries—the indivisibility of their most important capital units. In order to provide any service at all between two points a railroad must undertake some minimum amount of investment in the grading of roads, the purchase of equipment, and the construction of track, terminals, and auxiliary structures. Electric light and power and telephone companies, street and electric railways, and most other utilities must similarly make substantial investments in central facilities as well as in lines of communication or transportation before any output at all may be expected. In the earliest days of an industry's history, while many large units are being put in place and very few are actually in operation, it may be expected that the capital-product ratio will increase. It is possible that such "extensive expansion" in new or radically reorganized industries accounted in part for the upward trend in the capital-product ratio in manufacturing and mining for at least a portion of the latter decades of the nineteenth century. But since indivisibility is not so pronounced a general characteristic, the advance in these segments was much smaller,[1] though it was prolonged by the development and spread of a series of radical technological innovations. These innovations required large aggregations of capital, and were profitable because of the correspondingly large savings achieved in the use of labor—particularly since wage rates rose through most of this period in relation to the cost of capital. Once the *regulated* industries were established, however, innovations of this type in this segment of the economy were in the minority.

The initial rise in the capital-product ratio in the regulated industries, then, was in part a manifestation of early extensive expansion in a technological environment characterized by a high degree of indivisibility. By its nature, an upward trend so generated cannot last for very long.[2] It denotes, after all, a gestation period

[1] Daniel Creamer, *Capital and Output Trends in Manufacturing Industries, 1880–1948* (Occasional Paper 41, National Bureau of Economic Research, 1954), Table 8, p. 43, and Israel Borenstein, *Capital and Output Trends in Mining Industries, 1870–1948* (Occasional Paper 45, National Bureau of Economic Research, 1954), Table 7, p. 34.

[2] Cf. the remarks of Simon Kuznets in his Introduction to Creamer, *op. cit.*, pp. 8–10.

only. In the regulated industries for which we have early records, the gestation period was relatively short, lasting for barely a decade, in which many facilities were gradually brought to the point of completion at which their use could begin. As soon as this point is reached output may be started and expanded rapidly. Moreover, once a given installation is complete, its initial operating capacity may typically be further extended by substantial amounts with relatively small additional investment. Thus, after the huge outlays required for the building of roads and terminals, a railroad may double or triple the capacity on a given line with relatively small expenditures for additional rolling stock, double track, or passing track. The latter phenomenon would appear to have been evidenced in the steady increase in the relative importance of equipment, especially rolling stock, in the total volume of fixed operating capital of the railroads, from 9 per cent in 1880 to 26 per cent in 1917 and to 35 per cent in 1951.

These factors would alone explain a distinct tendency for the capital-product ratio to *decline*, after the first brief period of increase. But there were in fact other influences operating in the same direction and intensifying this decline, which in the regulated industries were both pronounced and prolonged. One was the distant horizon typically envisaged by the utility builders, perhaps most notable in the case of the railroads. In numerous instances the completion of lines was followed by strenuous efforts to encourage the establishment of towns and industries along an otherwise barren way. The capacity of roads as initially established—both because of techniques and ambitions—was geared to a volume of business which could be realized only with the passing of decades. The same influences, though not so spectacular, were in operation in other components, and reinforced the effect of capital indivisibility upon the capital-product ratio. Thus, central telephone facilities and electric generating plants were necessarily constructed with relatively distant needs in mind, for economical planning precluded frequent and small additions later as actual needs arose. Some weight must be given, too, to the role of speculation and promotion in the construction of the regulated industries—especially steam railroads and street railways. The financial rewards of promotion were typically great and tended to vary, moreover, with the size of the project; often in the calculations of the organizers the subsequent profitability was apparently a matter of consideration secondary to the gains obtained from initial construction and financing. Here was an additional factor making for initial capacity greatly in excess of immediate needs. But most important for our analysis is the fact that the very existence of such capacity virtually compelled a *decline* in the capital-product ratio as output expanded in subsequent years. Reference once again to the data of Chapter 4 will remind us that this reduction proceeded at an extremely swift pace in the early years, shortly after an initial increase where our records cover the industry's beginnings. In the aggregate of all regulated industries, of course, the initial rise in industries which made their start in the 1870's or 1880's was overshadowed by the continuing decline of the capital-product ratio in the older and larger segments.

Were these the *only* influences depressing the capital-product ratio, one would expect that the decline might persist for as long as an industry expanded, but not after growth had ceased. For once growth is at an end, the factors discussed above lose their force. Yet, as we have seen, a gradual reduction in the capital-product ratio persisted, though at a progressively slower pace, even in the case of declining industries such as steam railroads and street and electric railways—and long after expansion of facilities had ended. Obviously, certain influences, other than those already mentioned, were at work.

Chief among these were changes in the *nature* of the capital stock and changes in the way this stock was used. In the first connection, a nearly constant stream of technological improvements occurred in the industries under review. A few of the improvements were capital-*using* inventions, in that they led directly to larger proportionate increases in capital formation than in output. Such was the introduction of the dial system which induced the sharp rise in the capital-product ratio of telephone communication which began in the mid-1920's. In the same class were the revolutionary changes in generating facilities of electric utilities in the first decade of the twentieth century. And in manufacturing and mining until 1910 technological advances of this type were the rule, making for a gradual rise in the capital-product ratio during the period of these industries' most rapid expansion. But the great bulk of all innovations which occurred in already established regulated industries were capital-*saving*, in the sense that they increased output per unit of capital.

Introduction of alternating current and the transformer and the resulting interconection of plants, and later the successful introduction of high-voltage lines and system interconnection, gradually made possible steadier electric light and power service, smaller reserve capacity requirements, and the ability of central installations to service far more extensive areas than had previously been possible. In the railroads, the work-capacity of freight cars, passenger cars, tracks, ties, locomotives, etc., has been steadily enhanced. Similar capital-saving improvements mark the history of most of the other regulated industries. By their nature, such innovations lower the capital-product ratio.

Aside from changes in the physical characteristics of capital, there have been changes in its use which have operated in this direction. This factor was most pronounced in the railroads and was of particular importance in the years succeeding World War I. Thus, there was a substantial rise in the average length of haul in freight cars and in the average distance traveled by passengers. The former rose by more than 30 per cent and the latter by nearly 70 per cent between 1919 and 1950. These advances mirror in part the development of the western states and the concomitant rise in transcontinental traffic, and in part the greater diversion to the automobile and truck of short-distance business.[3] Their effect was to augment the capacity output (as measured in passenger miles and freight ton-miles) of existing road and equipment.

There is a third, and related, factor which served to depress the capital-product ratio. Since the work capacity of capital is almost constantly improved, replacement investments are nearly always something more than the name implies. A capital unit purchased today, even if it sells at the same price, is likely to have a substantially greater productive capacity than one obtained twenty years ago. Since price indexes do not reflect alterations in the volume of productive service that goods can perform, it is apparent that even if the growth of an industry ceased entirely, the decline of its capital-product ratio would be likely to proceed. Furthermore, as an industry matures its relative rate of growth is retarded, and the proportion of replacement to the total stock of capital expands.[4] Here, then, we have another factor operating to reduce the capital-product ratio long after the industry's gestation period and its aftermath have passed. Its role was undoubtedly significant through most of the history of the regulated industries.

A concluding factor, also related to the character of our measurements, may be noted. The numerator of the capital-product ratio is of course the *net* depreciated stock of capital. But as industries mature the volume of *accrued* depreciation rises. The physical reality behind such accruals are units of capital which have partly aged but remain in use. In some cases, partly depreciated units remain *fully and*

[3] For a description of these trends see Harold Barger, *The Transportation Industries, 1889–1946: A Study of Output, Employment, and Productivity* (National Bureau of Economic Research, 1951).

[4] Cf. the Introduction by Simon Kuznets to Creamer, *op. cit.*, p. 7.

efficiently in use. Nonetheless, accrued depreciation is deducted in full from the net stock of capital. Thus, a machine which costs a thousand dollars, and with an expected life span of ten years, may at the end of five years perform with its original efficiency completely intact. But—assuming straight line depreciation—one-half of its value (the five hundred dollars of accrued depreciation) would already have been deducted from the net stock of capital. Clearly, this too is a factor which served to depress the capital-product ratio as we have measured it.[5]

From these observations there emerges a general pattern of events shaping the capital-product ratio in the regulated industries. Initially, there is a period of gestation in which preparatory investment is made on a wide scale, and many large indivisible units are started and only gradually brought to completion. For a number of reasons cited above, this inaugural build-up in the regulated industries was unusually large. Of course, actual output in this period was necessarily small, and the capital-product ratio rose.

But this introductory stage is, by nature, short-lived. It can last only so long as *new* plants are established at a faster pace than output rises in facilities that are brought to completion. The duration was less than a decade in the regulated industries for which relevant data are available. Also, it should be recalled that in the *aggregate* of the regulated industries this initial increase in the ratio for electric light and power, for telephones, and for electric railways was overshadowed by the sharp decline simultaneously in progress for the older industries—especially steam railroads and some of the older components included in the all other group. Accordingly, the capital-product ratio in the regulated industries as a whole moved downward throughout the 1880–1950 span. In manufacturing, this initial period of extensive expansion, characterized by the rise of a multitude of new firms and new industries, was accompanied and followed by the sweep of pervasive capital-demanding innovations which were the earmark of the industrial revolution. As a result the capital-product ratio remained on the rise until World War I.

The second stage of the pattern in the regulated industries is a natural outgrowth of the first and followed swiftly. Once many large installations are completed, output is free to expand with relatively

[5] Our use of *net*, rather than gross depreciated capital in the numerator of the capital-product ratio is warranted only by our judgment that it *more closely* approximates the volume of capital actually in use. Even if we had used gross capital, the general nature of the trends in capital-product ratios, already described, would have been undisturbed. In short, the imperfection of our measurements accounted for only a small part of the downtrend in the ratio of net capital to product.

little additional investment necessary. The capital-product ratio is therefore profoundly depressed.

In the third stage the drop in the capital-product ratio is perpetuated. Capital-saving inventions enhance the efficiency of plant and equipment. In some cases, existing facilities are put to more economical use. In addition, the growing relative importance of capital consumption, in the company of general technological advance, ensures that the stock of capital will be replaced at a progressively faster rate with units capable of greater productive service. Finally, the expansion of accrued depreciation serves to depress the *net* stock of capital, as ordinarily measured, in relation to that actually in use. For all of the foregoing reasons the capital-product ratio continues downward even after the influences at work in the second stage have completely lost their force. It is certain that these factors were significant not only in the regulated industries, but—in whole or in part—in many other major segments of the economy; for, at least since the 1920's, the downward trend of the capital-product ratio was nationwide.

From the general pattern described there are, to be sure, deviations. Even after the first stage of the pattern had ended, capital-*using* innovations occurred in the regulated industries and resulted, for a time, in rising capital-product ratios. This was the case in the early 1900's in electric light and power, and in the mid-1920's in telephones. But such deviations in the seventy-year experience of our industries have proved temporary. The dominating, pervading factor in this segment of the economy in the long run, once the initial period of gestation had been surmounted, was the steady flow of capital-*saving* devices and the persevering drop in the capital-product ratio.

In one of our components—at least in the brief period of its recorded history—the general pattern is barely perceptible at all. This is local bus lines—a component in which several distinctive forces were in operation during the twenty-five years of its activity covered by our records. Here, the gestation period lasted roughly as long as in other cases: from the early 1920's to the early 1930's. But this initial stage was followed by an extended period of stability, rather than decline in the capital-product ratio. Furthermore, in the years following World War II this stability was replaced by an abrupt advance, which placed the capital-product ratio at a level materially higher than the one prevailing twenty-five years earlier. This contrary behavior appears to have been attributable to three characteristics peculiar to local bus lines, coupled with the nature of the impact of the immediate postwar situation upon its business.

In the first place, there was a virtual absence of significant capital-saving innovations in the industry, owing to the technological conditions under which it operated. Instead of a variety of machines, layouts, central and subsidiary installations, and communication and transportation systems, the principal investment of the industry consisted of a single, relatively homogeneous unit—the bus. The limits to which its efficiency might have been expanded by increasing its speed or carrying capacity were obviously set not by technology, but by the municipal regulations in force in its service areas. Indeed there has probably been some *reduction* in the efficiency with which buses have been used in recent years, because of greater traffic and the slower pace at which they must operate.

Second, as street railways were gradually displaced, local bus lines were to an increasing extent required to maintain full schedules of service over given routes, with a consequent reduction in the average load per bus. Thus, in a sense, the gestation period of local bus transportation was extended by its continued, though piecemeal, expansion into new areas—a movement accelerated with the growth of suburbs in the post-World War II period. This tended to push the capital-product ratio up rather than down.

Third, the typical unit of capital investment is considerably smaller—that is, more "divisible"—for local bus transportation than for the regulated industries in general. New business arising from the growth and spread of the population in the post-World War II period was for the most part met by railroads, electric light and power, telephones, and other utilities by more intensive use of already constructed "central facilities" (road and terminals, generating plants, and central stations) coupled, of course, with *relatively* small supplementary investments such as in rolling stock and transmission lines. The capital-product ratio in these cases continued downward. But for the local bus transportation it meant simply the purchase of new buses, with virtually no offset in the more economical use of central facilities. And new lines established in new areas typically operated with smaller than average bus loads, at least initially. These considerations explain why the industry's capital-product ratio did not decline and suggest also why it tended to increase.[6] A substantial rise in the postwar years, however, was a necessary outgrowth of the special conditions then prevailing. For on the one hand, bus lines were induced to extend their services to

[6] For completeness, mention should also be made of capital-using innovations in buses, though these do not appear to have been quantitatively important. Reference is to the introduction of devices to improve the safety and comfort of passengers. Besides, in the case of a few lines, there had been conductors who were ultimately displaced by the introduction of automatic coin receptacles.

new suburban areas, and this required new investment along with the large-scale replacement of over-age or obsolete buses as postwar supplies became available. On the other hand, the total volume of fares dropped precipitously as wartime restrictions were lifted on the manufacture of private automobiles and on gasoline purchases. This factor accounts in the main for the rise in the capital-product ratio of local bus lines to about 1.7 in 1950, compared with about 0.7 in the war years and 0.9 in the late 1930's.

If our analysis of the situation for this component is true, then a decline in its capital-product ratio may be expected sometime in the period after that covered by the study. For as suburban areas grow less extensively and more intensively, the average load per bus should increase. An offsetting factor, however, may be the declining income elasticity of demand for bus service discussed in the previous chapter. Another offset may be the declining speed at which buses operate as auto traffic continues to increase.

Some Aspects of the Variation among Industries

One further difference among our components may be noted: the rather substantial variation in the *extent* of the declines in the capital-product ratio over the 1880–1950 span. Measured from the peaks to 1950, they vary from a decline of 93 per cent for electric light and power to one of 65 per cent for telephones. Furthermore, in one case—local bus lines—the ratio rose. It will be noticed, too, that the extent of variation was closely correlated with the initial standing of the capital-product ratio itself. The higher the ratio, the steeper the relative decline.

This is shown in Table 25, in which we have included the major divisions of mining and manufacturing industries. Changes in the capital-product ratio were measured in each case from the peak to the last date available—1950 for the regulated industries and 1948 for the others. The industries are ranked according to the size of their capital-product ratios at the initial date. The correlation between this rank and the degree of the ratio's subsequent decline is obviously nearly perfect.

This correlation has suggested the hypothesis that differences in the extent of decline in the capital-product ratio reflect variations in the *motivations* involved in the respective industries.[7] The more important the role played by capital in the productive process, the

[7] Cf. William Fellner, "Long-Term Tendencies in Private Capital Formation: The Rate of Growth and Capital Coefficients," in *Long-Range Economic Projection, Studies in Income and Wealth*, Vol. 16 (Princeton University Press for National Bureau of Economic Research, 1954), pp. 312–313.

TABLE 25

Relationship between Level and Magnitude of Decline in Capital-Product Ratios, Selected Industries

Industry	Capital-Product Ratios[a]		
	Peak Value	*1950*[b]	*Percentage Decline*[c]
Electric light and power	18.4	1.3	93
Steam railroads	15.9	2.7	84
All other regulated industries	12.6	0.9	92
Street and electric railways	6.9	2.3	67
Petroleum and natural gas	5.9	1.8	70
Telephones	5.2	1.9	65
Metal mining	2.7	1.0	63
Producers' supplies manufacture	1.7	0.9	48
Construction materials manufacture	1.4	0.8	43
Bituminous coal	1.3	0.9	31
"Other" mining	1.3	0.6	54
Capital equipment manufacture	1.3	0.7	46
Consumption goods manufacture	0.9	0.6	33
Anthracite	0.5	0.4	19

[a] All are based on values in 1929 dollars. However, the numerators in the ratios for regulated industries include fixed capital only. For other groups they include fixed, plus working capital.

[b] For groups other than regulated industries, 1948.

[c] Computed from unrounded data.

Source: Data for manufacturing industries, from Daniel Creamer, *Capital and Output Trends in Manufacturing Industries, 1880–1948* (National Bureau of Economic Research, Occasional Paper 41, 1954), Table 10, p. 58; data for mining industries, from Israel Borenstein, *Capital and Output Trends in Mining Industries, 1870–1948* (National Bureau, Occasional Paper 45, 1954), Table 13, p. 54.

greater the motivation for economizing its use. Plausible as it appears, this view is relieved of much of its force by the factors discussed below:

1. The innovations adopted by an industry are at times developed in its own laboratories. In such cases, research may be directed in one channel or another at the industry's will. But in many cases relevant research is conducted by supplying industries, or in laboratories with no initial industrial connection at all. The introduction of steel, the steam engine, and electricity, to cite perhaps the most important examples of the nineteenth and early twentieth centuries, were innovations whose effects extended into virtually every segment of the economy. Nor was the timing or the nature of their impact upon any given industry subject to its control. Electricity was fortuitously available from the industry's point of view; its use promised to increase profits. Whether it proved to be capital-saving or capital-using was incidental.

Thus, the steam engine was swiftly embraced by streetcar companies, generating a substantial flow of investment. The resulting smoke, smell, and soot, especially embarrassing in urban transportation, soon brought back the horsecar. Some decades later electric power was successfully introduced. But for the streetcar transportation industry, the timing and nature of these innovations were entirely adventitious. The relevant conclusion for our own problem should be obvious. Even supposing that high capital-product ratio industries have greater motivation for selecting capital-saving innovations, their ability to manifest this predilection in practice would be very narrowly limited.

2. Differences in the capital-product ratios often prove to be widely deceptive guides in judging differences in the relative importance of capital in operating costs. For variations in the former may reflect mainly discrepancies in the durability of the capital used. Thus two firms may each expend five thousand dollars per year for depreciation charges, five thousand for materials, and five thousand for labor costs. Assume that these are the total expenses and that profits are zero. Now in one firm the capital used may on the average last five years and in the other twenty years. Then in the first industry the ratio of fixed capital to product would be 1.7 and in the second 6.7. Yet the direct relative contribution of capital to the productive process—and its relative importance in operating costs—would be the same in each case. Data were presented earlier suggesting the wide variation in the average durability of capital in the several branches of the American economy.[8] There are also substantial differences in this regard among the regulated industries.[9] This does not deny, of course, that firms with high capital-product ratios will ordinarily have relatively high fixed charges for the use of money capital. Unless this were so, there would be no point to the motivation hypothesis at all.

It is even more relevant to point out, however, that differences in capital-product ratios offer virtually no guide to differences in the relative importance of labor costs among industries. Illustratively, we present the data of Table 26. This shows the relative importance of labor costs in selected periods for two segments of industry, one characterized by a very high capital-product ratio, the other by a relatively low capital-product ratio. For manufacturing, the proportion of labor is measured in relation to the value of net output—i.e. value added by manufacturing. For railroads, the importance of

[8] See pages 71–72.

[9] See tables relating to the derivation of capital consumption in Appendixes C through H.

TABLE 26

Capital-Product Ratios and Relative Importance of Labor Costs in Steam Railroads and Manufacturing, 1899, 1919, and 1939

	CAPITAL-PRODUCT RATIO[a]		RATIO OF SALARIES AND WAGES TO VALUE OF OUTPUT[b]	
Year	*Railroads*	*Manufacturing*	*Railroads*	*Manufacturing*
1899	6.94	0.80[c]	0.40	0.49
1919	3.52	1.02	0.55	0.52
1939	4.59	0.74[d]	0.47	0.47

[a] Ratio of values in 1929 dollars.

[b] Ratio of values in current dollars. For railroads, gross value of output; for manufacturing, value added.

[c] For 1900.

[d] For 1937.

Source: Capital-product ratios for manufacturing, from Daniel Creamer, *Capital and Output Trends in Manufacturing Industries, 1880–1948* (National Bureau of Economic Research, Occasional Paper 41, 1954), Table 8, p. 43; ratio of salaries and wages to value of output, from *Historical Statistics of the United States, 1789–1945* (Bureau of the Census, 1949), pp. 174 and 205–206.

labor costs is somewhat understated, since it is expressed in relation to the total (gross) value of output. Judged by the capital-product ratios, it might be supposed that the relative importance of labor in the railroads would be very much smaller. Yet, for the purposes at hand, the differences between the two industrial divisions in this regard are negligible. Surely, if labor-saving devices were welcomed in one, they would be welcomed with equal warmth in the other. It may also be noted that the proportion of labor costs to the value of output varied only moderately over time in the railroads, despite the sharp decline in the capital-product ratio for this segment during the same period. We must conclude that the motivation for reducing labor costs is likely to be as great in a high, as in a low capital-product ratio industry. If the reduction of labor costs could be accomplished *only* by adopting capital-using innovations, we may assume that they would both do so, with approximately equal vigor.

3. Industry is of course primarily concerned with the reduction of *total* costs. Whether the saving is made in the operating costs of labor or in the total cost of capital, provided they are of equal magnitude, the accounting conclusion in a statement of profit and loss will be much the same. It is a mistake, in any event, to assume that the gains accruing from capital-saving innovations are exclusively—or even primarily—in the capital account. This is demonstrated in Table 27.

In Table 27 we present data on labor productivity trends in two of the components—railroads and electric light and power—for

TABLE 27

Nine-Year Averages of Indexes of Capital-Product Ratios, Output per Man-Hour, and Capital-Labor Ratios for Steam Railroads and Electric Light and Power

(1939 = 100)

	STEAM RAILROADS			ELECTRIC LIGHT AND POWER		
Central Year of Nine-Year Average	*Capital-Product Ratio*	*Output per Man-Hour*	*Capital-Labor Ratio*	*Capital-Product Ratio*	*Output per Man-Hour*	*Capital-Labor Ratio*
1896	187.1	32.4	60.6	...	...	...
1900	145.2	35.2	51.1	...	...	...
1906	103.1	39.5	40.7	...	...	...
1910	96.1	43.2	41.5	...	...	...
1916	82.5	52.2	43.1	273.0[a]	43.1[a]	117.7[a]
1920	77.3	57.6	44.5	172.8[b]	46.0[b]	79.5[b]
1926	78.6	69.1	54.3	141.6	52.1	73.8
1930	97.1	75.9	73.7	149.5	57.9	86.6
1936	112.7	94.6	106.6	122.6	84.8	104.0
1940	67.7	115.8	78.4	84.4	124.5	105.1
1946	49.0	136.1	66.7	56.7	174.6	99.0

[a] For 1917 only.

[b] For 1922 only.

Source: Output per man-hour for 1916–50, from *Historical Statistics of the United States, 1789–1945* (Bureau of the Census, 1949), and Bureau of Labor Statistics; for years prior to 1916 for railroads, obtained by adjusting railroad employment data (from *Historical Statistics*) for changes in standard workweek, coupling with our own series on railroad output, and linking to index for later years.

Indexes of the capital-labor ratio are products of those for the capital-product ratio and output per man-hour.

which such figures were available. It will be noted that in both cases the indexes of output per man-hour rose sharply over the entire period of record. The declines in the capital-product ratios in these components during the same periods—reflecting in considerable measure capital-saving innovations—were steeper than in any other major divisions of the American economy.

The capital-labor ratios in Table 27 indicate that in railroads, taking the period as a whole, the gains in the productivity of labor were even greater than in that of capital. For the capital-labor ratio rose. In electric light and power there was a moderate decrease in this ratio, indicating a slightly greater relative advance in output per unit of capital (the reciprocal of the capital-product ratio) than in output per man-hour. It will be recalled that in both mining and manufacturing after World War I, capital-product ratios also declined under the impact of capital-saving innovations. In both of these divisions, in this period, the capital-labor ratio rose.[10]

[10] See Table 28.

From the above considerations, we may conclude that the simple tie between cause and effect supposed by the motivation hypothesis is much more tenuous than would at first appear. Its essence of truth lies in the fact that an industry characterized by high, fixed charges may be credited with a particularly intense desire to reduce them. But judged by their results, capital-saving as well as capital-using innovations have profoundly reduced the cost of labor—investing them both with a universal appeal for virtually all of industry, which was only enhanced by the advance in wages in progress over the entire period under review. Moreover, we have noted that the choice between one type of innovation and another is narrowly limited in an environment in which the fortuitous plays so significant a role.

Nevertheless, the observed correlation between the height of a capital-product ratio and the extent of its fall is an undeniable fact, which requires explanation. If the motivation hypothesis contributes but little to our understanding of this phenomenon, we must conclude that some other forces bear the principal responsibility. This role, we suggest, may be fulfilled by the three factors discussed below.

First, those components in which particularly high capital-product ratios were achieved are the very ones in which capital is characterized by a high degree of indivisibility. In such industries, as we have seen in the previous section, the way is smoothly paved for a subsequent and particularly sharp reduction in capital-product ratios as output expands in later years. This factor alone may account for a substantial portion of the observed correlation.

Second, the more diverse the physical stock of capital of an industry, the greater the chance that scientific advances will result in improving its efficiency. Large and expensive capital installations are likely to be characterized by a wider degree of variety in component units, materials, processes, and so forth, than smaller ones. Besides, complex facilities of this kind are probably more frequent in capital-extensive industries than in those in which man-power plays a relatively greater role. Hence it is in the former that there will be greater opportunity for improvements in capital efficiency. It should be emphasized that it is not a matter of motivation that is referred to here, but one of technological opportunity. We may reiterate that industry in general is interested in reducing *total* costs.

Third, there is no upper limit to the capital-product ratio, though there is a lower limit at least at zero, and as a practical matter somewhat above zero. Accordingly, at their peak, capital-product ratios may be very widely scattered. But as they decline they must converge toward, at least roughly, the same general minimum. There is thus some arithmetical compulsion in the finding that at the peak the variation among capital-product ratios is much greater than at the trough. And this finding is simply another way of stating that the highest capital-product ratios tend to fall by the largest relative amounts.

The Role of Wages and Interest

It follows from the conclusions of the previous sections that no simple or straightforward relationship may be expected between the secular trend of the capital-product ratio and the behavior of interest and wages. For we have seen that this ratio is affected by a variety of other factors. But even if we were to hold other factors constant—such as the stage of an industry's technological development, the degree of indivisibility of its capital units, and its rate of growth—the resulting picture would not be clear. The difficulty lies in the fact that capital-saving and capital-demanding innovations are not clear-cut alternatives. This is true in the sense that the availability of one or another type of innovation may be largely fortuitous from the industry's point of view, as described above. It is also true in terms of the *effects* of such innovations on the proportions in which the factors of production are combined and upon the pattern of operating costs.

Since the trend of the capital-product ratio was generally monotonically downward in the regulated industries, after an initial rise, we must turn to the other segments of the economy for examples of movements in both directions. In Table 28 we have assembled data bearing on this problem drawn from the studies, cited earlier in this chapter, of Creamer and Borenstein on manufacturing and mining, respectively. In both segments the period from 1880 to 1919 was characterized by a substantial rise in the capital-product ratio reflecting the many capital-using innovations introduced in this period. The result was, of course, a substantial economy in the use of labor, reflected both in the advancing output per man-hour and the rise in the capital-labor ratios shown here. A trend of this kind would, of course, have been encouraged by a rising level of wages relative to interest rates—a development which was in fact characteristic of the period. The establishment and expansion in these years of some of the regulated industries—such as electric light and power, telephones, and electric railways—were probably likewise facilitated by this trend, for these were all high capital-product ratio areas in relation to the rest of the economy.

TABLE 28

Capital-Product Ratio, Labor Productivity, and Capital-Labor Ratio in Manufacturing and Mining; Wages in Manufacturing; and Interest Rates, 1880–1948

(*all values in ratios in 1929 dollars*)

	MANUFACTURING INDEXES, 1929 = 100			MINING INDEXES, 1929 = 100				
Year	*Capital-Product Ratio*	*Output per Man-Hour*	*Ratio of Capital to Man-Hours*	*Capital-Product Ratio*	*Output per Worker*	*Ratio of Capital to Workers*	*Hourly Earnings in Manu-facturing*	*Long-Term Interest Rates*
1880	0.55	...	...	1.16[a]	26[a]	15[a]	...	4.46
1890	0.73	...	...	1.36[b]	29[b]	22[b]	$0.199	3.75
1900	0.79	53	48	...	...	...	0.216	3.30
1909	0.97	58	64	1.80	...	45	0.252	3.78
1919	1.02	66	76	2.30	62	69	0.529	4.78
1929	0.89	100	100	2.14	100	100	0.566	4.42
1948	0.65	135	99	1.33	180	111	1.350	2.79

[a] For 1879 only.
[b] For 1889 only.

Source: Basic data for manufacturing, from Daniel Creamer, *Capital and Output Trends in Manufacturing Industries, 1880–1948* (Occasional Paper 41, National Bureau of Economic Research, 1954). Basic data for mining, from Israel Borenstein, *Capital and Output Trends in Mining Industries, 1870–1948* (Occasional Paper 45, National Bureau, 1954). Hourly earnings in manufacturing for 1890–1919, from *Historical Statistics of the United States, 1789–1945* (Bureau of the Census, 1949), Series D124; for 1929 and 1948, from Bureau of Labor Statistics. Interest rates for 1900–1948 are average yields of twenty-year and fifty-year bonds extrapolated to 1880 by use of average of highs and lows for railroad bond yields; basic data, from *Historical Statistics* and *Statistical Abstract of the United States*, 1951, Bureau of the Census.

But now we turn to the subsequent years. Capital-saving innovations came to the fore in mining and manufacturing, and capital-product ratios declined. Would a rise in the level of wage rates relative to interest have *discouraged* this development, as it had encouraged the "opposite" trend in earlier years? It should be noted from the last two columns of Table 28 that in this second period taken as a whole wages rose, interest rates dropped, and the growing disparity between the two was even greater than that prevailing in the first. Yet the remaining data of the table suggest why capital-saving, no less than capital-using, innovations represented a favorable adjustment to this environment. For when capital-product ratios declined, output per man-hour continued to rise. In mining the rate of advance was even higher in the second period than in the first; in manufacturing the later increase in labor's productivity was somewhat smaller. In both segments the capital-labor ratio also rose in the second period, though at a slower pace than in the first. In short, capital-saving innovations resulted in even greater economies in the use of labor than in the use of capital.

In Table 29 we give some of the relevant data bearing upon the railroad segment—capital-product ratios, an index of wages, and long-term interest rates. If we consider the period from 1880 to 1910 we observe that the trend of interest was moderately downward and that of wages moderately upward, while the capital-product ratio dropped sharply. In the following forty years taken as a whole, the

TABLE 29

Capital-Product Ratios for Steam Railroads, Wages of Railroad Employees, and Interest Rates

Year	*Capital-Product Ratio*[a] (1)	*Index of Wages 1939 = 100*[b] (2)	*Long-Term Interest Rates*[c] (3)
1880	15.95	...	4.46
1890	9.84	29	3.75
1900	6.43	28	3.30
1910	4.35	35	3.84
1920	3.17	93	5.14
1930	4.23	89	4.40
1940	4.10	100	2.62
1950	2.66	132	2.71

[a] Ratio of values in 1929 dollars.
[b] Based on average hourly earnings in steam railroads, from Bureau of Labor Statistics.
[c] See note to Table 28.

prevailing trends in wages and interest were accelerated, while the decline in the capital-product ratio continued, though at a somewhat slower pace.

From these observations the following conclusions are suggested. Rising wage rates will of course encourage economies in the use of labor—but these may in fact accompany either a rising or a falling capital-product ratio. A progressive reduction in the cost of money capital would encourage investment in general, and would facilitate a rise in the capital-product ratio in particular, *if such an advance were generated by other forces*. But on the other hand a declining interest rate would not in any way inhibit a *reduction* in the capital-product ratio if it were induced by technological or other conditions. Both propositions are drawn directly from the experience of the 1880–1950 period. They suggest that the cost of money capital and of labor do not *determine* the capital-product ratio, nor in the period under review do they appear to have been the most important contributing influences. The determinants are the variety of factors described in the previous sections, taken together.

Secular Trends in Investment: Some Concluding Observations

The long-run trends in investment may be viewed as the proximate results of the secular patterns assumed by the marginal capital-product ratios and by changes in output. The present and the preceding chapters were designed to probe the forces which determined the long-run movements of these strategic components—output and the capital-product ratio—in the regulated industries. By this indirect route, we hoped to illumine the trend of investment itself.

Perhaps the most striking result of this branch of our analysis is the power of the factors which have dampened the capital-product ratios over the long run. Had these ratios remained unchanged, the secular pattern of net capital formation would have duplicated that of changes in output, and the trend in the physical stock of capital would have traced a path exactly like that of output. Though there is some resemblance in the trends, they are distinguished by large, significant, and systematic differences. Thus it is seen that the vigor of the advance in the stock of capital of the regulated industries is very much less than that of the rise in output; in some cases a pronounced retardation—or even a decline—occurred in the former, while the latter continued upward at a progressively expanding rate over the period of review. The difference lies in the trend of the capital-product ratio, which was definitely downward for all regulated industries in the aggregate, and for every component except local bus lines. It was this which dampened the flow of investment significantly in the total and in each of the components with the exception noted. In railroads, for example, the decline of the capital-product ratio accounts for the contraction in the stock of capital in the two decades following 1930, in the company of a continued *rise* in the secular trend of output. And differences in the pace of the decline in this ratio explain why the flow of net investment has remained more vigorous in telephones than in electric light and power. Of course, such "explanations" would remain in the category of tautologies if severed from the context in which they are made. Trends in the capital-product ratio explain nothing, except in terms of the underlying forces which they in turn reflect, as described earlier in this chapter.

It is in this sense, then, because of the downward trend in capital-product ratios, that the growth of the nation over the latter part of the 1870–1950 span required a progressively smaller flow of capital into the regulated industries. This was true despite the fact that output for all regulated industries in the aggregate, and for some of the components, had grown more rapidly *throughout* this period than did the national income or the population. The relevant data are shown in Table 30. Here, for each of the industrial divisions, the

TABLE 30

Value of Plant and Equipment of the Regulated Industries as Percentage of Net National Product, 1870–1950

(based on values in 1929 dollars)

Central Year of Nine-Year Average NNP	*All Regulated Industries*	*Steam Railroads*	*Electric Light and Power*	*Telephones*	*Street and Electric Railways*	*Local Bus Lines*	*All Other*
1870	122	105	...	...	1.60	...	16.3
1876	96	81	...	...	1.50	...	13.2
1880	80	79	...	0.12	1.64	...	11.0
1886	77	65	0.07	0.34	1.64	...	9.9
1890	77	64	0.57	0.39	2.65	...	9.6
1896	75	59	1.16	0.68	4.67	...	9.3
1900	66	60	1.99	1.42	6.85	...	8.4
1906	59	39	3.06	2.07	7.72	...	7.5
1910	67	42	5.06	2.37	8.35	[a]	8.9
1916	65	40	5.98	2.07	7.27	0.001	9.8
1920	58	35	5.52	1.76	5.96	0.004	9.6
1926	51	30	6.92	1.92	3.98	0.077	8.8
1930	63	34	10.30	3.56	3.55	0.159	11.6
1936	57	31	9.48	3.14	2.67	0.219	10.8
1940	38	24	7.56	2.62	1.43	0.289	8.3
1946	35	19	5.94	2.27	0.86	0.261	6.6
1950[b]	35	16	6.78	3.67	0.55	0.256	7.5

The numerator of the ratios is the value of plant and equipment taken at the beginning of the year (Appendix Tables B–1, C–1, D–1, E–1, F–1, G–1, and H–1); the denominator is the annual average of the net national product for the nine years centered in the year.

Source: Net national product in 1929 dollars, from revised annual estimates of Simon Kuznets, National Bureau of Economic Research (Variant I).

[a] Less than 0.001 per cent.

[b] For 1950 only.

value of plant and equipment at the beginning of a given year is expressed as a percentage of the nine-year annual average of the net national product centered in that year, with all values in 1929 dollars.

For all regulated industries in the aggregate, as the table shows, the stock of capital in the 1870 period was 122 per cent of the net national product. From this lofty level it declined almost without interruption to reach about 35 per cent in the post-World War II period. The drop means, of course, that *increases* in the net national product required progressively smaller additions to the physical capital stock of the regulated industries—i.e. smaller amounts of net capital formation. The same percentage also declined steadily for the railroads. For the other components, the trends were more complex. If the figures for 1930 and 1936 are ignored because of the sharp contraction in business activity, it will be observed that the value of plant and equipment as a percentage of the net national product was downward in the all other group after 1916, in local bus lines after 1940, and, of course, in street railways after 1910. In electric power, the ratio was steady between 1926 and 1950. Only in telephones did an increase persist throughout the period; in this component, it will be recalled, the decline in the capital-product ratio was relatively modest and had virtually ceased between the 1920's and 1950.

The same general picture develops when we compare investment directly, as in Table 31. Here, gross capital formation in the

TABLE 31

Gross Capital Formation of the Regulated Industries as Percentage of National Gross Capital Formation, 1876–1950

(based on nine-year averages; values in 1929 dollars)

Central Year of Nine-Year Average	*All Regulated Industries*	*Steam Railroads*	*Electric Light and Power*	*Telephones*	*Street and Electric Railways*	*Local Bus Lines*	*All Other*
1876	15.4	12.4	...	...	0.70	...	2.15
1880	16.3	13.5	...	...	0.60	...	1.88
1886	14.2	11.2	0.32	0.259	1.04	...	1.46
1890	15.9	11.2	0.62	0.31	1.93	...	1.84
1896	13.5	6.4	1.16	0.92	3.28	...	1.75
1900	12.6	4.3	1.79	1.36	3.46	...	1.62
1906	18.2	8.3	2.86	1.59	2.88	...	2.51
1910	19.9	9.8	3.36	1.46	2.01	...	3.31
1916	11.4	4.8	1.98	1.08	0.95	0.003	2.58
1920	11.3	4.1	2.50	1.28	0.77	0.040	2.53
1926	15.4	4.9	4.15	2.14	0.65	0.112	3.51
1930	15.8	4.5	4.10	2.54	0.63	0.166	3.92
1936	11.2	2.9	2.56	1.80	0.55	0.376	3.08
1940	7.1	2.1	1.51	1.16	0.21	0.226	1.92
1946	8.2	1.9	1.86	1.64	0.06	0.168	2.64
1950[a]	10.3	1.9	1.69	1.67	0.01	0.073	3.94

[a] For 1950 only.

Source: Gross capital formation for the United States from revised annual estimates of Simon Kuznets, National Bureau of Economic Research.

regulated industries is given as a percentage of gross capital formation in the nation as a whole. Here, too, the general trend in the last several decades was downward, reflecting primarily the sharper decline in the capital-product ratio in the regulated industries. In the aggregate the proportion dropped from a high of almost 20 per cent in the pre-World War I period to about half that in 1950. The trend was also materially downward, at least in the later years, in all of the components except those of the all other group.

The impact of the declining capital-product ratio is perhaps most distinctly revealed when it is recalled that aggregate output in the regulated industries rose more rapidly through most of the period of record than swiftly rising urban income, and even in later years moved forward at an approximately equal rate. In contrast, net capital formation barely kept abreast of the much slower advance of the total population. As Table 32 shows, the per-capita value of plant and equipment of the regulated industries reached a high of 368 dollars in 1930, and then drifted downward. To be sure, the

TABLE 32

Per-Capita Value of Plant and Equipment, Regulated Industries and Components, 1929 Dollars, 1870–1950

(*based on nine-year averages*)

Central Year of Nine-Year Average	*All Regulated Industries*	*Steam Railroads*	*Electric Light and Power*	*Telephones*	*Street and Electric Railways*	*Local Bus Lines*	*All Other*
1870	221	189	...	...	2.80	...	29.50
1876	239	202	...	...	3.80	...	33.10
1880	242	239	...	0.36	4.96	...	33.25
1886	254	214	0.22	1.12	5.41	...	32.80
1890	267	221	1.96	1.34	9.16	...	33.10
1896	281	221	4.38	2.57	17.60	...	35.20
1900	281	253	8.40	6.02	28.90	...	35.60
1906	286	187	14.85	10.03	37.50	...	36.20
1910	332	209	25.20	11.75	41.50	0.01	44.20
1916	340	209	31.20	10.80	37.90	0.06	51.20
1920	332	201	31.60	10.07	34.20	0.24	55.30
1926	333	192	44.60	12.40	25.70	0.33	57.10
1930	368	197	60.50	21.00	20.85	0.94	68.40
1936	329	178	54.80	18.15	15.40	1.25	62.40
1940	316	170	54.40	18.85	10.30	2.08	59.70
1946	294	158	50.30	19.18	7.27	2.21	56.25
1950[a]	321	150	62.00	33.50	4.97	2.33	68.40

[a] For 1950 only.
Source: Total continental population, from the Bureau of the Census.

per-capita value of plant and equipment rose throughout the period in electric light and power, telephones, local bus lines, and the all other group; but the increases in later years were modest. They were more than balanced in the total by the sharp reductions which set in for the railroads after 1900 and for street railways after 1910.

In closing this section, some remarks may be in order concerning the influence of the social environment in which the regulated industries operate. What effect did this have on the trends in output and investment? Obviously, a full-dress approach to this question—involving the changing scope, forms, and standards of public regulation—would carry us far beyond the purview of this study. Some broad observations may nonetheless be ventured.

The intervention of the public in those segments of the economy which have achieved utility or near-utility status appear to have had two general consequences of relevance to the present study: (1) the granting and protection of complete or limited monopoly positions, and (2) the maintenance of rates lower than those which would otherwise have prevailed. Both have probably had the effect of expanding output and capital formation. For the limits placed upon competition have greatly reduced the risk involved in investment in the regulated industries; and the risk element in some cases, in the absence of such protection, may have been prohibitive. The prospect of several telephone companies, for example, several electric light and power companies, or several local bus lines operating without limitation in the same areas, would seem likely to have retarded the establishment and growth of these industries. At the same time, the regulation of rates have seldom been permitted to depress profits below the levels required for the attraction of capital on a competitive basis with other industries.[11] There is some evidence, on the other hand, that if they had been permitted to go higher (toward the monopolistic levels they otherwise might in some cases have attained), the growth of consumption would have been significantly retarded.[12]

[11] Eli Winston Clemens, *Economics and Public Utilities* (1950), pp. 234–239, and G. Lloyd Wilson, *Transportation and Communications* (1954), pp. 140–144. Both, Appleton-Century-Crofts.

[12] Clemens, *op. cit.*, pp. 357–360. See also Wilson, *op. cit.*, pp. 25–27.

CHAPTER 7

Long Cycles

THROUGHOUT our description of the secular behavior of capital formation it was necessary to take frequent note of the giant, recurring swings which characterize these series. A meaningful definition of longer-term drift required some systematic method for penetrating—or seeing beyond—the short-term fluctuations. The use of nine-year moving averages removed in considerable measure the evidence of business cycles and "random" movements. In output this was generally sufficient, for in these series there is no pronounced evidence of long cycles.[1] Nor do clearly perceptible fluctuations of this nature appear in the annual increments in output. But in capital formation substantial swings, of considerable magnitude as well as duration, remained. For this reason special precautions were necessary in order to avoid a distorted picture of the secular trend. Either changes were measured from peak to peak or from trough to trough of the long cycles, or mathematical curves were fitted which generally pierced their midpoints, or—at a minimum—mental, informal account was taken of their behavior in comparing sequences of decade or nine-year averages. This requirement compels us to turn—at least briefly—to a description of the long cycles themselves, bearing in mind that such phenomena lie at the borderline of our central interest and that our data are but imperfectly suited to their analysis.

The Measurement of Long Cycles

Visually, the long cycles in the capital formation of all regulated industries are most clearly depicted in the center and lower panels of Chart 1. A first glance might suggest that little question could arise concerning their definition and measurement, given the magnitude of the towering waves under review. But this is true only in part. It makes considerable difference, for example, whether we focus attention upon the annual data or on the nine-year moving averages. The difference occurs primarily in the period from the 1870's through the 1890's. In the annual data, two substantial cycles appear with peaks in 1881 and 1893, and troughs in 1875, 1885, and 1896. It should be noted that the first of these is roughly coincident

[1] This is not to say that there is no evidence *at all* of long cycles in either output or changes in output. The point is that in these cases long cycles are not distinctly apparent in the raw data—either annual or nine-year moving averages. On the other hand, they are unmistakably present in the corresponding series for capital formation. However, if tested for *conformity* to long cycles, the output series would on this basis yield positive results.

with one of the more severe business cycles dated in the National Bureau of Economic Research chronology.[2] In the nine-year moving averages these two cycles are considerably smoothed, and it is possible to discern an underlying wave of greater duration than either, moving from a trough in 1876 to a peak at about 1891 and to a terminal trough in 1898. Aside from this, the difference in the timing of cycles in the annual data and in the nine-year moving averages are minor. Yet the exception is most significant. Whether to date two cycles or one during the years from the 1870's to the 1890's cannot be decided on purely empirical grounds.

The fundamental question on which a decision must turn concerns the very meaning of long cycles. Do they reflect the play of forces which extend *beyond* the range of ordinary business cycles, and comprise a distinctive causal nexus of their own? Were we able to identify such forces, we would possess a reliable guide for the statistical definition of these fluctuations. Or are long cycles *illusory*, in the sense that they reflect only the more or less chance juxtaposition of major and minor business cycles? Consistent with the latter thesis is the fact that each long cycle downturn is coincident with a major business depression. On the other hand, this is no more than would be expected if we were to assume that long cycles were an economic as well as a statistical reality. For a long cycle downturn would be *conducive* to major depressions.

These are questions which we may raise, but not answer, in the present brief survey. The final section of this chapter is designed to cast a modest light on some of the problems which arise in this connection. In the meantime we shall give principal attention to the hypothesis that long cycles are authentic reflections of forces extending *beyond* the duration of business cycles. Our decision is prompted primarily by the desire to make possible comparison with other studies conducted on a similar assumption. As in these other studies, we work with the nine-year moving averages, for these smooth out business cycle movements with reasonable effectiveness. But the underlying question, itself, we leave open. Measurements of long cycles based on nine-year moving averages are given for all regulated industries and, insofar as they occur, in each of the individual components in Tables 33 through 37. We also present measurements based on the annual data in Tables 38 through 43. But note that in the latter set a cogent question can be raised concerning *what* is being measured. For in the annual data business cycles, even the fairly small ones appear. We have felt that no

[2] Arthur F. Burns and Wesley C. Mitchell, *Measuring Business Cycles* (National Bureau of Economic Research, 1946), p. 78.

service would be performed, in the present connection, by dating all of these. Hence, we have concentrated simply on the *largest* waves which stand out rather clearly in the data. Such measurements provide some comparison with those based on the nine-year moving averages. But since the fluctuations marked off include at least one ordinary business cycle, they can be called *long* cycles only loosely.

The Pattern of Long Cycles

We direct attention first to Table 33, which summarizes the characteristics of long cycles as they appear in the nine-year moving averages of the gross capital formation, in constant dollars, of all regulated industries in the aggregate. Since the fluctuations appear much the same in net and gross investment, we have confined analysis to the latter.

The peaks and troughs presented in the first three columns are the successive high and low points as they appear in the nine-year moving averages. Though particular years are cited, they should be interpreted as designating the general neighborhood of a *period of years* in which long cycles change direction. This interpretation follows from our tentatively adopted concept of long cycles as recurrent patterns of economic events lasting longer than business cycles. It also results from the observation that if we had used seven-year or eleven-year moving averages (either of which would have smoothed the business cycles), our turning points would have been altered somewhat.

Columns 4 through 6 of the table present the duration of the expansions, contractions, and of the total cycles in the gross capital formation of the regulated industries. Measured in the nine-year moving averages, they vary from 17 to 22 years and average a little less than 20. Expansions are regularly longer than contractions, averaging 12 years as against 8. There is a suggestion, too, of a progressive decline over time in the length of the total cycles, but as the remaining columns of the table show, this was coupled with a sharp advance in amplitude.

The data appearing in columns 7 through 9 of Table 33 represent investment at the initial trough, peak, and terminal trough of each of the cycles. In the lower panel of the table these figures are given in millions of 1929 dollars. In the upper panel they are given in the form of relatives—the value at each turning point being expressed as a percentage of the average annual investment during the full course of the cycle in which it falls. The measures of amplitude in columns 10 and 11 are derived from the three previous columns by subtraction.

TABLE 33

All Regulated Industries: Dates, Duration, and Amplitude of Long Cycles in Gross Capital Formation, Based on Nine-Year Moving Averages

DATES OF LONG CYCLES			DURATION (YEARS)			LONG CYCLE VALUES AT:			AMPLITUDE OF:			AMPLITUDE (PER YEAR) OF:		
Trough (1)	*Peak* (2)	*Trough* (3)	*Rise* (4)	*Fall* (5)	*Total* (6)	*Initial Trough* (7)	*Peak* (8)	*Terminal Trough* (9)	*Rise* (10)	*Fall* (11)	*Rise and Fall* (12)	*Rise* (13)	*Fall* (14)	*Rise and Fall* (15)
						IN RELATIVES								
1876	1891	1898	15	7	22	61	122	116	61	6	67	4.1	0.9	3.0
1898	1910	1918	12	8	20	55	130	87	75	43	118	6.2	5.4	5.9
1918	1927	1935	9	8	17	72	134	62	62	72	134	6.9	9.0	7.9
1935	1946[a]		11	–	–	70	146	–	76	–	–	6.9	–	–
	Average		12	8	20	64	133	88	68	40	107	6.0	5.1	5.6
						IN MILLIONS OF 1929 DOLLARS								
1876	1891	1898	15	7	22	464	930	884	466	46	512	31.0	6.6	23.3
1898	1910	1918	12	8	20	884	2,113	1,415	1,229	698	1,927	102.4	87.2	96.4
1918	1927	1935	9	8	17	1,415	2,619	1,214	1,204	1,405	2,609	133.8	175.6	153.5
1935	1946[a]		11	–	–	1,214	2,542	–	1,328	–	–	120.7	–	–
	Average		12	8	20	994	2,051	1,171	1,057	716	1,683	97.0	89.8	91.1

[a] Terminal date of series rather than peak.

Source: Appendix Table K–2.

Thus the magnitude of the long cycles is evident here even more distinctly than in the chart. The extent of the movement in full, including rise and fall together, was equivalent on the average to more than 100 per cent of the average annual investment during a long cycle. As might be anticipated in a series in which the secular movement is upward, expansions exceed contractions with the former amounting on the average to nearly 70 per cent and the latter to 40 per cent. The *pace* of the movement was also greater during expansions, as shown in the columns giving amplitude per year. However, it is in keeping with the *declining* secular rate of increase in the capital formation of the regulated industries that contractions have grown progressively over time on both an absolute and relative basis. The amplitude of expansions, on the other hand, showed only a faint tendency to increase. Accordingly, the two movements were of almost equal magnitude in the most recent periods. Moreover, the amplitude of the whole cycle—rise and fall together—advanced sharply and steadily over the eighty-year period, from 67 per cent of the average annual investment in the 1876–98 cycle, to 118 per cent in 1898–1918, and to 134 per cent in the cycle which lasted from 1918 to 1935. These swings are measured from trough to trough. When taken from peak to peak the trend is about equally pronounced. Amplitudes advanced from 81 per cent in the first cycle lasting from 1891 through 1910, to 105 per cent in the second and to 148 per cent in the third. Of course, since our record covers only three and one-half cycles, conclusions concerning secular trends in their behavior must be tentative at most. In the evaluation of these secular changes, however, some further progress may be achieved through a comparative analysis of the individual components of the regulated industries.

A glance at Charts 4 through 9 will verify that swings of the kind described for the aggregate of the regulated industries do not appear, or are but indistinctly traced, in the capital formation of local bus lines or of street and electric railways. But they are clearly evident in the other components at least for a part, if not the whole, of the period of record. For these, descriptive analyses were prepared similar to the analysis compiled for the long cycles in the total. They are presented in Tables 34 through 43.

One important difference among these components lies in their reaction to the first of the cycles which appeared in the aggregate. It seems that this movement, beginning with the trough in 1876 and moving on to a peak in 1891 and to the terminal trough of 1898, is skipped, or is only partially reflected, in all of the components except railroads. It is primarily for this reason, of course, that this

TABLE 34

Steam Railroads: Dates, Duration, and Amplitude of Long Cycles in Gross Capital Formation, Based on Nine-Year Moving Averages

DATES OF LONG CYCLES			DURATION (YEARS)			LONG CYCLE VALUES AT:			AMPLITUDE OF:			AMPLITUDE (PER YEAR) OF:		
Trough (1)	*Peak* (2)	*Trough* (3)	*Rise* (4)	*Fall* (5)	*Total* (6)	*Initial Trough* (7)	*Peak* (8)	*Terminal Trough* (9)	*Rise* (10)	*Fall* (11)	*Rise and Fall* (12)	*Rise* (13)	*Fall* (14)	*Rise and Fall* (15)
						IN RELATIVES								
1876	1890	1899	14	9	23	73	127	60	54	67	121	3.9	7.4	5.3
1899	1910	1918	11	8	19	42	141	73	99	68	167	9.0	8.5	8.8
1918	1926	1935	8	9	17	88	134	50	46	84	130	5.8	9.3	7.6
1935	1946[a]	–	11	–	–	68	127	–	59	–	–	5.4	–	–
	Average		11	9	20	68	132	61	64	73	139	6.0	8.4	7.2
						IN MILLIONS OF 1929 DOLLARS								
1876	1890	1899	14	9	23	377	652	309	275	343	618	19.6	38.1	26.9
1899	1910	1918	11	8	19	309	1,038	539	729	499	1,228	66.3	62.4	64.6
1918	1926	1935	8	9	17	539	824	305	285	519	804	35.6	57.7	47.3
1935	1946[a]		11	–	–	305	572		267	–	–	24.3		
	Average		11	9	20	383	772	384	389	454	883	36.4	52.7	46.3

[a] Terminal date of series rather than peak.

Source: Appendix Table K–2.

TABLE 35

Electric Light and Power: Dates, Duration, and Amplitude of Long Cycles in Gross Capital Formation, Based on Nine-Year Moving Averages

DATES OF LONG CYCLES			DURATION (YEARS)			LONG CYCLE VALUES AT:			AMPLITUDE OF:			AMPLITUDE (PER YEAR) OF:		
Trough (1)	*Peak* (2)	*Trough* (3)	*Rise* (4)	*Fall* (5)	*Total* (6)	*Initial Trough* (7)	*Peak* (8)	*Terminal Trough* (9)	*Rise* (10)	*Fall* (11)	*Rise and Fall* (12)	*Rise* (13)	*Fall* (14)	*Rise and Fall* (15)
						IN RELATIVES								
	1910[a]	1917	–	7	–	–	110	76	–	34	–	–	4.9	–
1917	1927	1936	10	9	19	52	151	59	99	92	191	9.9	10.2	10.1
1936	1946[b]		10	–	–	72	149	–	77	–	–	7.7		
	Average		10	8	19	62	137	68	88	63	191	8.8	7.6	10.1
						IN MILLIONS OF 1929 DOLLARS								
	1910[a]	1917	–	7	–	–	356	247	–	109	–	–	15.6	–
1917	1927	1936	10	9	19	247	713	279	466	434	900	46.6	48.2	47.4
1936	1946[b]		10	–	–	279	575	–	296	–	–	29.6		
	Average		10	8	19	263	548	263	381	272	900	38.1	31.9	47.4

[a] Since the nine-year moving averages of gross capital expenditures show a steady rise through 1910, the long cycle analysis begins with this year.

[b] Terminal date of series rather than peak.

Source: Table K-2.

TABLE 36

Telephones: Dates, Duration, and Amplitude of Long Cycles in Gross Capital Formation, Based on Nine-Year Moving Averages

DATES OF LONG CYCLES			DURATION (YEARS)			LONG CYCLE VALUES AT:			AMPLITUDE OF:			AMPLITUDE (PER YEAR) OF:		
Trough (1)	*Peak* (2)	*Trough* (3)	*Rise* (4)	*Fall* (5)	*Total* (6)	*Initial Trough* (7)	*Peak* (8)	*Terminal Trough* (9)	*Rise* (10)	*Fall* (11)	*Rise and Fall* (12)	*Rise* (13)	*Fall* (14)	*Rise and Fall* (15)
IN RELATIVES														
	1908[a]	1917	–	9	–	–	108	99	–	9	–	–	1.0	–
1917	1927	1936	10	9	19	55	142	74	87	68	155	8.7	7.6	8.2
1936	1946[b]		10	–	–	60	155	–	95	–	–	9.5	–	–
	Average		10	9	19	58	135	86	91	38	155	9.1	4.3	8.2
IN MILLIONS OF 1929 DOLLARS														
	1908[a]	1917	–	9	–	–	161	147	–	14	–	–	1.6	–
1917	1927	1936	10	9	19	147	376	196	229	180	409	22.9	20.0	21.5
1936	1946[b]		10	–	–	196	510	–	314	–	–	31.4	–	–
	Average		10	9	19	172	349	172	272	97	409	27.2	10.8	21.5

[a] Since the nine-year moving averages of gross capital expenditures show a steady rise through 1908, the long cycle analysis begins with this year.

[b] Terminal date of series rather than peak.

Source: Appendix Table K-2.

TABLE 37

All Other Utilities: Dates, Duration, and Amplitude of Long Cycles in Gross Capital Formation, Based on Nine-Year Moving Averages

DATES OF LONG CYCLES			DURATION (YEARS)			LONG CYCLE VALUES AT:			AMPLITUDE OF:			AMPLITUDE (PER YEAR) OF:		
Trough (1)	*Peak* (2)	*Trough* (3)	*Rise* (4)	*Fall* (5)	*Total* (6)	*Initial Trough* (7)	*Peak* (8)	*Terminal Trough* (9)	*Rise* (10)	*Fall* (11)	*Rise and Fall* (12)	*Rise* (13)	*Fall* (14)	*Rise and Fall* (15)
						IN RELATIVES								
1898[a]	1913	1918	15	5	20	43	138	124	95	14	109	6.3	2.8	5.5
1918	1927	1935	9	8	17	72	129	70	57	59	116	6.3	7.4	6.8
1935	1946[b]		11	–	–	64	162	–	98	–	–	8.9	–	–
	Average		12	6	18	60	143	97	83	36	112	7.2	5.1	6.2
						IN MILLIONS OF 1929 DOLLARS								
1898[a]	1913	1918	15	5	20	116	371	333	255	38	293	17.0	7.6	14.7
1918	1927	1935	9	8	17	333	599	323	266	276	542	29.6	34.5	31.9
1935	1946[b]		11	–	–	323	816	–	493	–	–	44.8	–	–
	Average		12	6	18	257	595	328	338	157	418	30.5	21.0	23.3

[a] Since the nine-year moving averages of gross capital expenditures do not show any cyclical behavior prior to this year, the analysis begins with the cycle of 1898–1918.

[b] Terminal date of series rather than peak.

Source: Appendix Table K–2.

TABLE 38

All Regulated Industries: Dates, Duration, and Amplitude of Long Cycles in Gross Capital Formation, Based on Annual Data

DATES OF LONG CYCLES			DURATION (YEARS)			LONG CYCLE VALUES AT:			AMPLITUDE OF:			AMPLITUDE (PER YEAR) OF:		
Trough (1)	*Peak* (2)	*Trough* (3)	*Rise* (4)	*Fall* (5)	*Total* (6)	*Initial Trough* (7)	*Peak* (8)	*Terminal Trough* (9)	*Rise* (10)	*Fall* (11)	*Rise and Fall* (12)	*Rise* (13)	*Fall* (14)	*Rise and Fall* (15)
						IN RELATIVES								
1875	1881	1885	6	4	10	46	192	74	146	118	264	24.3	29.5	26.4
1885	1893	1896	8	3	11	51	174	69	123	105	228	15.4	35.0	20.7
1896	1910	1919	14	9	23	38	155	68	117	87	204	8.4	9.7	8.9
1919	1929	1933	10	4	14	49	141	29	92	112	204	9.2	28.0	14.6
1933	1948[a]		15	–	–	35	228	–	193	–	–	12.9	–	–
	Average		10.6	5.0	14.5	44	178	60	134	106	225	14.0	25.6	17.7
						IN MILLIONS OF 1929 DOLLARS								
1875	1881	1885	6	4	10	270	1,138	440	868	698	1,566	144.7	174.5	156.6
1885	1893	1896	8	3	11	440	1,498	592	1,058	906	1,964	132.3	302.0	178.5
1896	1910	1919	14	9	23	592	2,389	1,048	1,797	1,341	3,138	128.4	149.0	136.4
1919	1929	1933	10	4	14	1,048	2,999	618	1,951	2,381	4,332	195.1	595.3	309.4
1933	1948[a]		15	–	–	618	4,062		3,444	–	–	229.6		
	Average		10.6	5.0	14.5	594	2,417	675	1,824	1,332	2,750	166.0	305.2	195.2

[a] Tentative peak.

Source: Appendix Table B–1.

TABLE 39

Steam Railroads: Dates, Duration, and Amplitude of Long Cycles in Gross Capital Formation, Based on Annual Data

DATES OF LONG CYCLES			DURATION (YEARS)			LONG CYCLE VALUES AT:			AMPLITUDE OF:			AMPLITUDE (PER YEAR) OF:		
Trough (1)	*Peak* (2)	*Trough* (3)	*Rise* (4)	*Fall* (5)	*Total* (6)	*Initial Trough* (7)	*Peak* (8)	*Terminal Trough* (9)	*Rise* (10)	*Fall* (11)	*Rise and Fall* (12)	*Rise* (13)	*Fall* (14)	*Rise and Fall* (15)
						IN RELATIVES								
1875	1881	1885	6	4	10	43	199	70	156	129	285	26.0	32.2	28.5
1885	1893	1896	8	3	11	61	186	21	125	165	290	15.6	55.0	26.4
1896	1910	1919	14	9	23	18	182	52	164	130	294	11.7	14.4	12.8
1919	1923	1933	4	10	14	52	156	21	104	135	239	26.0	13.5	17.0
1933	1949[a]		16	–	–	30	173	–	143	–	–	8.9		
	Average		9.6	6.5	14.5	41	179	41	139	140	279	17.7	28.8	21.1
						IN MILLIONS OF 1929 DOLLARS								
1875	1881	1885	6	4	10	211	982	347	771	635	1,406	128.5	158.8	140.6
1885	1893	1896	8	3	11	347	1,064	122	717	942	1,659	89.6	314.0	150.8
1896	1910	1919	14	9	23	122	1,216	345	1,094	871	1,965	78.1	96.8	85.4
1919	1923	1933	4	10	14	345	1,035	140	690	895	1,585	172.5	89.5	113.2
1933	1949[a]		16	–	–	140	799	–	659	–	–	41.2		
	Average		9.6	6.5	14.5	233	1,020	238	787	836	1,623	102.0	164.7	122.4

[a] Tentative peak.

Source: Appendix Table C–1.

TABLE 40

Electric Light and Power: Dates, Duration, and Amplitude of Long Cycles in Gross Capital Formation, Based on Annual Data

DATES OF LONG CYCLES			DURATION (YEARS)			LONG CYCLE VALUES AT:			AMPLITUDE OF:			AMPLITUDE (PER YEAR) OF:		
Trough (1)	*Peak* (2)	*Trough* (3)	*Rise* (4)	*Fall* (5)	*Total* (6)	*Initial Trough* (7)	*Peak* (8)	*Terminal Trough* (9)	*Rise* (10)	*Fall* (11)	*Rise and Fall* (12)	*Rise* (13)	*Fall* (14)	*Rise and Fall* (15)
IN RELATIVES														
	1912[a]	1918	–	6	–	–	164	41	–	123	–	–	20.5	–
1918	1924	1934	6	10	16	25	161	28	136	133	269	22.7	13.3	16.8
1934	1949[b]		15	–	–	33	242	–	209	–	–	13.9	–	–
	Average		10	8	16	29	189	34	172	128	269	18.3	16.9	16.8
IN MILLIONS OF 1929 DOLLARS														
	1912[a]	1918	–	6	–	–	493.9	124.0	–	369.9	–	–	61.6	–
1918	1924	1934	6	10	16	124.0	812.7	143.0	688.7	669.7	1,358.4	114.8	67.0	84.9
1934	1949[b]		15	–	–	143.0	1,060.7	–	917.7	–	–	61.2	–	–
	Average		10	8	16	134	789.1	134	803.2	519.8	1,358.4	88.0	64.3	84.9

[a] Since this industry shows a steady growth in capital formation up to 1912, the long cycle analysis begins with this year, which represents the first peak.

[b] Tentative peak.

Source: Appendix Table D-1.

TABLE 41

Telephones: Dates, Duration, and Amplitude of Long Cycles in Gross Capital Formation, Based on Annual Data

DATES OF LONG CYCLES			DURATION (YEARS)			LONG CYCLE VALUES AT:			AMPLITUDE OF:			AMPLITUDE (PER YEAR) OF:		
Trough (1)	*Peak* (2)	*Trough* (3)	*Rise* (4)	*Fall* (5)	*Total* (6)	*Initial Trough* (7)	*Peak* (8)	*Terminal Trough* (9)	*Rise* (10)	*Fall* (11)	*Rise and Fall* (12)	*Rise* (13)	*Fall* (14)	*Rise and Fall* (15)
IN RELATIVES														
	1906[a]	1909	–	3	–	–	142	65	–	77	–	–	25.7	–
1909	1917	1919	8	2	10	74	127	87	53	40	93	6.6	20.0	9.3
1919	1929	1933	10	4	14	42	184	35	142	149	291	14.2	37.2	20.8
1933	1948[b]		15	–	–	31	300	–	269	–	–	17.9	–	–
	Average		11	3	12	49	188	62	155	89	192	12.9	27.6	15.0
IN MILLIONS OF 1929 DOLLARS														
	1906[a]	1909	–	3	–	–	237.8	107.9	–	129.9	–	–	43.3	–
1909	1917	1919	8	2	10	107.9	185.0	127.2	77.1	57.8	134.9	9.6	28.9	13.5
1919	1929	1933	10	4	14	127.2	556.8	106.1	429.6	450.7	880.3	43.0	112.7	62.9
1933	1948[b]		15	–	–	106.1	1,012.5	–	906.4	–	–	60.4	–	–
	Average		11	3	12	113.7	498.0	113.7	471.0	212.8	507.6	37.7	61.6	38.2

[a] Since this industry shows steady growth in capital formation up to 1906, the long cycle analysis begins with this year.

[b] Tentative peak.

Source: Appendix Table E–1.

TABLE 42

Street and Electric Railways: Dates, Duration, and Amplitude of Long Cycles in Gross Capital Formation, Based on Annual Data

DATES OF LONG CYCLES			DURATION (YEARS)			LONG CYCLE VALUES AT:			AMPLITUDE OF:			AMPLITUDE (PER YEAR) OF:		
Trough (1)	*Peak* (2)	*Trough* (3)	*Rise* (4)	*Fall* (5)	*Total* (6)	*Initial Trough* (7)	*Peak* (8)	*Terminal Trough* (9)	*Rise* (10)	*Fall* (11)	*Rise and Fall* (12)	*Rise* (13)	*Fall* (14)	*Rise and Fall* (15)
						IN RELATIVES								
	1907[a]	1919	–	12	–	–	205	40	–	165	–	–	13.8	–
1919	1923	1933	4	10	14	71	144	32	73	112	185	18.2	11.2	13.2
1933	1939	1950[b]	6	11	17	80	192	7	112	185	297	18.7	16.8	17.5
	Average		5	11	16	76	180	26	92	154	241	18.4	13.9	15.4
						IN MILLIONS OF 1929 DOLLARS								
	1907[a]	1919	–	12	–	–	355.6	69.3	–	286.3	–	–	23.9	–
1919	1923	1933	4	10	14	69.3	140.1	31.1	70.8	109.0	179.8	17.7	10.9	12.8
1933	1939	1950[b]	6	11	17	31.1	74.6	2.8	43.5	71.8	115.3	7.2	6.5	6.8
	Average		5	11	16	50.2	190.1	34.4	57.2	155.7	147.6	12.4	13.8	9.8

[a] Since this industry shows steady growth in capital formation up to 1907, the long cycle analysis begins with this year.

[b] Terminal date of series rather than trough.

Source: Appendix Table H-1.

TABLE 43

All Other Utilities: Dates, Duration, and Amplitude of Long Cycles in Gross Capital Formation, Based on Annual Data

DATES OF LONG CYCLES			DURATION (YEARS)			LONG CYCLE VALUES AT:			AMPLITUDE OF:			AMPLITUDE (PER YEAR) OF:		
Trough (1)	*Peak* (2)	*Trough* (3)	*Rise* (4)	*Fall* (5)	*Total* (6)	*Initial Trough* (7)	*Peak* (8)	*Terminal Trough* (9)	*Rise* (10)	*Fall* (11)	*Rise and Fall* (12)	*Rise* (13)	*Fall* (14)	*Rise and Fall* (15)
						IN RELATIVES								
1875	1881	1885	6	4	10	59	189	57	130	132	262	21.8	33.2	26.4
1885	1893	1896	8	3	11	39	189	80	150	109	259	18.6	36.0	23.4
1896	1912	1921	16	9	25	31	164	95	133	69	202	8.3	7.7	8.1
1921	1929	1933	8	4	12	48	145	34	97	111	208	12.1	27.8	17.3
1933	1950[a]		17	–	–	29	222	–	193	–	–	11.4	–	–
	Average		11	5	14	41	182	66	141	105	233	14.4	26.2	18.8
						IN MILLIONS OF 1929 DOLLARS								
1875	1881	1885	6	4	10	40	129	39	89	90	179	14.8	22.5	17.9
1885	1893	1896	8	3	11	39	190	81	151	109	260	18.9	36.3	23.6
1896	1912	1921	16	9	25	81	434	250	353	184	537	22.1	20.4	21.5
1921	1929	1933	8	4	12	250	756	177	506	579	1,085	63.3	144.8	90.4
1933	1950[a]		17	–	–	177	1,341	–	1,164	–	–	68.5	–	–
	Average		11	5	14	117	570	137	453	240	515	37.5	56.0	38.4

[a] Terminal date of series rather than peak.

Source: Appendix Table H-1.

initial swing is only dimly traced in the aggregate. Even in railroads it is the weakest of the long cycles, and its configuration—as noted above—is obscured by a succession of two larger-than-average business cycles. Its failure to appear in the telephone and electric light and power components is thus more understandable. These industries, a mere decade old or less, were in the flush of their early expansion when the peak of the initial long cycle in railroads was reached. The vacuum effect—described in Chapter 5—was at the height of its force. The flow of investment was further reinforced by the temporarily rising capital-product ratio characteristic of the gestation period. Hence, the weakest of long cycle downturns, that running from 1891 to 1898, left no perceptible imprint upon the pace of their expansion.

It will be noted in the tabular summaries (derived from nine-year moving averages) that turning point dates for the initial cycle are also omitted for the all other group. In the *annual* data two cycles appear before 1898, similar in timing to the subcycles in railroads, but very much weaker. In the nine-year moving averages they are completely ironed out. In the analysis of the all other group, however, a number of difficulties intrude. To be sure, within the component were two industries—gas utilities and pipelines—which were in a relatively early stage of vigorous expansion. Like telephones and electric light and power, their activity may not have reflected in any pronounced way the downturn of 1891–98. But most important is the fact that the method of estimation employed for the all other group in the earlier years resulted in smoothing the series artificially.[3] Hence, though adequate for the analysis of long-term trends, this series is insufficiently sensitive in this period to provide a reliable indication of the component's cyclical response. Although capital formation in the all other group actually rose during the 1891–98 contraction, it is of some interest that the pace of its advance was retarded during that time. From 1876 to 1891 the annual rate of gross capital formation advanced by 3.0 million 1929 dollars per year; during the 1891–98 period the annual rate of increase dropped to 2.3 million.

All of the other long cycles which are so pronounced in the aggregate of the regulated industries appear as well in each of the components barring, of course, local bus lines and street railways. The turning points occur at about the same time in every case, differing by a year at the most, except for the 1910 peak. Here there was somewhat greater variation, with the turn coming in 1910 in the railroads and in electric light and power, in 1908 in telephones,

[3] See Appendix H.

and in 1913 in the all other group. But even these discrepancies barely rate as significant, given the crudeness of most of our annual data prior to World War I, the use of nine-year moving averages, and the broad interpretation suggested above for the dating of long cycles in general.

There are, however, some significant differences in the amplitude of movement among the several components. It will be noted from the descriptive tables that expansions averaged 88 per cent in the capital formation of electric light and power and 91 per cent in telephones, but only 64 per cent in railroads. Contractions averaged 38 per cent in telephones, 63 per cent in electric light and power, and 73 per cent in railroads. If we recall the ratings given to these industries with respect to the model pattern of growth in Chapter 3, it will be noted that the amplitude of contractions varies directly, and the amplitude of expansion varies inversely, with the degree of maturity. This conclusion is in part confirmed by examination of the behavior of long cycles in the capital formation of railroads, telephones, and electric light and power considered individually. In each case contractions tend to deepen over time, as Tables 34, 35, and 36 show, while except for telephones, expansions tend to diminish.

Thus from both chronological and cross section study the following pattern emerges. In an industry's earlier days long cycles are barely evident in the progress of investment, if they appear at all. Later, the broad, vigorous expansion is interrupted by modest contractions. Gradually, the contractions deepen while expansions tend to grow weaker. It is through this process of cyclical behavior that the sharp upward slope of the secular growth trend slowly diminishes, and—in some cases—ultimately yields to descension. In this respect the secular role of long cycles is similar to that of business cycles,[4] though on a scale of magnified dimensions.

With the above in mind, we may return briefly to the two series in which long cycles were not distinctly apparent. Local bus lines were in the early stage of expansion at the time of the downturn beginning in 1927. That this contraction—the only one in the recorded history of this component—was omitted, is therefore fully in keeping with the general pattern described above. The street and electric railways component, on the other hand, is a special case.

It began as a virtually new industry in the 1880's. Like that of telephones and electric light and power, its early period of growth was not appreciably deterred by the long cycle contraction of 1891–98. As in the case of the other components, too, its capital formation

[4] Burns and Mitchell, *op. cit.*, pp. 412–416.

was finally enveloped in the sharp contraction of 1910–18, though in street railways the downturn started earlier (with the brisk business cycle dip of 1907). At that point, paths diverged. Under the impact of the vigorous competition of motor vehicles, extensive periods of sharply rising investment were out of the question for street railways. Capital formation moved in a precipitous, overshadowing decline, which was still in progress in 1950.

Even so, in the annual data of this series (see Chart 7) there is evidence of a response to long cycle fluctuations which is too faint to appear in the nine-year moving averages. The trough of 1919 was followed by an advance to 1923, then a drop to 1933, followed once again by expansion. All advances were weak and contractions powerful. The last expansion, beginning in 1933, was in fact cut off abortively six years later. Investment in street railways thus represents an illustration at the extreme of the general secular pattern of long cycle behavior. Expansions so swiftly lost their force, and contractions so rapidly gained power, that the evidence of long swings was all but submerged almost immediately after the industry's early period of growth under the impetus of the vacuum effect. By the end of the 1930's, long cycles in this series had apparently disappeared entirely.

It will be recalled that in the capital formation of regulated industries in the aggregate there was no apparent tendency for the amplitude of expansions to diminish over time, as we might expect in conformity with the general pattern. Instead, both contractions and expansions deepened progressively, though the increase in the latter was clearly more modest and less regular. Accordingly, the magnitude of long cycles as a whole was substantially augmented over time. This result is explained in some measure by the constant influx of new industries into the over-all composite. The expansion from 1898 to 1910 was reinforced by the sharply growing electric light and power, telephone, and electric railway components, none of which was significant in the previous expansion from 1876 to 1891. The expansion from 1918 through 1927 was bolstered by the development of an additional set of new industries including trucking, local bus lines, radio communication, and petroleum pipelines. Finally, television and air transportation helped to support the expansion which began in 1935 and continued to the very end of our period of study. Obviously, however, new industries alone are not sufficient to account for the unprecedented vigor of the latter advance. Investment in *all* components in this period mounted very sharply, and in some, such as telephones, pipelines, trucking and gas, the extent of the rise reached record levels. Indeed the magnitude of the fluctuations in the post-World War I period in general would remain something of a puzzle, even after allowing for the effects of the wars and the influence of maturation, unless our framework were broadened to permit a comparison with related movements in other segments of the economy.

Comparison with Other Economic Segments

In Table 44 are listed the dates of turning points of long cycles defined in nine-year moving averages of the gross national product,

TABLE 44

Long Cycle Turning Points in Selected Series

(*all value series in 1929 dollars*)

	Trough	*Peak*	*Trough*	*Peak*	*Trough*	*Peak*	*Trough*
Gross national product	1873	1883	1892	1905	1911	1926	1934
Gross construction	1873	1891	1897	1909	1917	1926	1935
Additions to population	1874	1884	1898	1910	1919	1924	1935
Number of dwelling units started		1889	1899	1909	1916	1925	1934
Expenditures on dwelling units		1891	1900	1909	1917	1925	1934
Capital formation of all regulated industries:							
Gross	1876	1891	1898	1910	1918	1927	1935
Net	1876	1890	1898	1909	1918	1926	1935

Source: Gross national product, gross construction, and additions to population, from Simon Kuznets, "Swings in the Rate of Secular Growth" (Work Memorandum No. 37, mimeographed, National Bureau of Economic Research, March 1952), Table 6. Dwelling units started and expenditures on dwelling units, from Leo Grebler, David M. Blank, and Louis Winnick, *Capital Formation in Residential Real Estate: Trends and Prospects* (Princeton University Press for National Bureau of Economic Research, 1956), Table 4.

As originally presented by Kuznets, nine-year moving averages in the additions to population were dated "by the last year rather than the midyear of the period on the ground that they are cumulative totals whose impact does not become effective until the addition is in fact made." In this table they are midyear, to conform with the dating of all the other series.

gross construction, annual additions to the population, and of two measures of residential building. For comparison the turning points for gross and net capital formation by the regulated industries are also given. The dates of the first three series in the table were taken from a study by Kuznets,[5] those on residential building from a

[5] Simon Kuznets, "Swings in the Rate of Secular Growth," (Work Memorandum No. 37, mimeographed, National Bureau of Economic Research, March 1952). His method for determining turning points for the gross national product and for gross construction differ from that employed for all the other series included in Table 44. Both the gross national product and gross construction are characterized by pronounced upward secular trends.

recent monograph by Grebler, Blank, and Winnick.[6] All of the value series employed were in 1929 dollars. The close relationship between the timing of long cycles in all of the series represented in the table, except the gross national product, is striking. Long swings occur almost simultaneously in gross construction, in additions to population, in residential building, and in the capital formation of the regulated industries. Only one important discrepancy is to be noted—that in the first peak, which occurs in 1884 in the population series and from five to seven years later in the others.

The agreement between swings in gross construction on the one side, and in residential building and regulated industry investment on the other, of course, is a near statistical necessity. For the first series is composed in large part of the second and a considerable portion of the third. Nevertheless, the series on residential building, on population increments, and on capital formation of the regulated industries are, from a statistical point of view, entirely independent. The regularity of agreement in the timing of long cycles in these cases suggests a significant causal nexus. Their behavior reflects either some common generator of their movements, or a direct interaction among the represented activities themselves.

Long cycles in the gross national product (and of course in all of its important components, except for construction[7]) are, for only part of the period, synchronous with those observed in the other segments of Table 44. And it should be noted that the cycles in the gross national product represent fluctuations in the *rate of growth* of this series,[8] rather than in its absolute values. Only the cyclical movements (consisting of two expansions and a contraction) in the post-World War I years are distinctly marked in the absolute figures. And it is only during this period that long swings are synchronous in the over-all level of business activity and in the regulated industries and residential building. This coincidence in the later years must have contributed in substantial measure to the power of the two postwar expansions, as well as to the unusual severity of the intervening contraction from the mid-1920's to the mid-1930's. For in these years the movements were mutually reinforcing.

Peaks and troughs were determined by plotting the nine-year moving averages on semilogarithmic scales and recording turns whenever the *slope* of the series "became significantly steeper or flatter." Thus turning points represent highs and lows in the *rate* of growth. In all of the other series of Table 44, peaks and troughs represent *absolute* highs and lows.

[6] Leo Grebler, David M. Blank, and Louis Winnick, *Capital Formation in Residential Real Estate: Trends and Prospects* (Princeton University Press for National Bureau of Economic Research, 1956), Table 4.

[7] See Kuznets, *op. cit.*, Table 6.

[8] See footnote 5, this chapter.

It is more difficult to interpret behavior in the years before World War I. Then the swings in the gross national product were quite different from those in all the other series of Table 44. It is possible that they were therefore mutually offsetting, and in this sense served as moderators. Nevertheless, the cycles which reached their peak about 1910 in the regulated industries and in residential building were very substantial. Throughout the pre-World War I period, furthermore, the long cycles in the gross national product appeared only in relative rates of growth, the absolute trend in the nine-year moving averages having been constantly upward. At the same time, of course, there were important shorter-term cycles in the Gross National Product, obscured by nine-year moving averages, which may have affected—and been affected by—the long swings in the other segments. Within the framework of the present study, it is not possible to explore these relationships. Some observations which bear upon the general problem, however, are given in the following section.

Some Theoretical Considerations

Though a full inquiry into the nature of long cycles would extend our analysis well beyond its intended purview, a few observations are ventured here concerning the relevance of some of our findings to the problem of causation. Hypotheses advanced in the past which are *directly* relevant to some or all of the regulated industries are limited to the theories of Einarsen and Isard[9] on reinvestment and transport-building cycles, respectively. We turn to these first, and later suggest other avenues of investigation which may—in the light of the facts adduced earlier in this chapter—prove fruitful.

The theory of reinvestment cycles observes that if a bulge in capital formation is at any time induced by a business boom or a war, or for whatever reason, replacement requirements at subsequent dates will tend to generate similar expansions. If all capital goods had the *same* life span, and if replacement decisions were based on purely *mechanical* considerations, subsequent cycles would duplicate the initial one exactly, and the duration from peak to peak would depend solely upon the durability of capital—except insofar as

[9] Johan Einarsen, *Reinvestment Cycles and Their Manifestation in the Norwegian Shipping Industry* (Oslo, University of Economics, 1938); "Reinvestment Cycles," *Review of Economic Statistics*, February 1938; and "Replacement in the Shipping Industry," *Review of Economic Statistics*, November 1946. See also J. S. Bain, "The Relations of the Economic Life of Equipment to Reinvestment Cycles," *Review of Economic Statistics*, November 1946.

Walter Isard, "A Neglected Cycle: The Transport-Building Cycle," *Review of Economic Statistics*, November 1942; "Transport Development and Building Cycles," *Quarterly Journal of Economics*, November 1942, and "The Transport-Building Cycle in Urban Development: Chicago," *Review of Economic Statistics*, November 1943.

booms, depressions, wars, and other "external" factors intruded. Although it is conceded that such ideal conditions are *never* satisfied, the existence of perceptible reinvestment cycles in practice must rest at least upon their rough approximation. In the regulated industries, in particular, we would expect (1) a considerable degree of concentration about some average life span among the different types of plant and equipment, and (2) some agreement between this average life span of capital and the observed duration of cycles. Neither of these conditions holds.

The fluctuations under review in the regulated industries lasted approximately twenty years and were about the same in all components. But the average life of capital varied widely among components, and in every case substantially exceeded the length of the cycle. The average life of capital in the railroads was fifty-eight years, in electric light and power thirty-seven, and in telephones twenty-eight.[10] Available information suggests also a considerable amount of variation within components. In railroads the life of equipment varied from twenty-five to forty years, while roadway items in general lasted two or three times as long.[11] In electric utilities the average life of equipment by type varied from twelve to seventy-five years, in telephones about the same, in gas utilities from eight to one hundred years. Utility structures varied in life from twenty to more than a hundred years.[12] There appears to be little ground for supposing that long swings in the capital formation of the regulated industries—at least in the United States—reflect in any considerable measure the periodic impulses associated with reinvestment cycles.

The facts at hand are similarly unfavorable to the transport-building cycle hypothesis formulated by Isard. These fluctuations are presumed to emanate from fundamental alterations in the mode of transportation, and because of their power and multifarious repercussions, are supposed to induce corresponding swings in housing and in the general level of business activity. A number of the preceding findings conflict with this hypothesis—at least as it may be employed to explain the fluctuations which have been called long cycles in this study. And it was so used by Isard.

In the first place, insofar as there are long swings in the general level of business activity, these appear to have run *counter* to long

[10] See Appendixes C, D, and E.

[11] K. T. Healy, "Regularization of Capital Investment in Railroads," in *Regularization of Business Investment* (Princeton University Press for National Bureau of Economic Research, Special Conference Series 4, 1954), pp. 162–195. See also Appendix A.

[12] Eli Winston Clemens, *Economics and Public Utilities* (Appleton-Century-Crofts, 1950), p. 198.

swings in the transportation and other regulated industries before World War I, and to have been synchronous with them later. The connection between the two, therefore, may not be the simple, straightforward cause-and-effect one supposed above. Second—and more important—it seems impossible to provide an explanation for each of the three and one-half swings during the 1870–1950 period in terms of specific transportation innovations. The only new development of major consequence along these lines in the years between 1870 and World War I was electric railways. But investment in this segment did not become significant until *after* the expansion period of our first cycle (from 1876 to 1891) had completely run its course. Indeed the rise in electric railway investment progressed most vigorously during the following contraction phase (from 1891 to 1898) and ended somewhere in the middle of the expansion phase of the second cycle (from 1898 to 1910).[13]

The only other major innovations of the same character in our period of study were the automobile and the airplane. But the start of the post-World War I long cycle expansion may be explained by a variety of factors—not the least of which was the huge accumulation of deferred investment requirements in all of the regulated industries during the war. The end of this expansion came along before any tentative termination date we might fix for the long-run growth of motor vehicle transportation, or even for the increments in its growth. Quantitative considerations alone preclude attributing the 1935–46 expansion to the development of air transportation. It would thus seem abundantly clear that the birth and growth of the different modes of transportation—important as they are—cannot be used to explain the appearance of the twenty-year cycles described in this chapter. Indeed if such innovations did generate cycles, it would appear that they must have been fluctuations of much greater duration than those now under consideration. Of course, it may be said that transportation *by nature* tends to expand in spurts, and that this in turn generates corresponding movements in other branches of economic activity, perhaps with substantial lags. So general a statement would not conflict with the facts. But it would leave still unexplained the heart of the problem: i.e. the particular factors which give rise to long swings in capital formation in transportation.

Both of the theories described above assumed that the swings in the capital formation of the regulated industries were *internally* generated—that is, due essentially to events within this segment of the economy itself. There remains the possibility that they reflect—

[13] The peak in the investment of street and electric railways occurred in 1903 in the nine-year moving averages, and in 1907 in the annual figures.

in whole or in part—events *outside* the segment. It would not conflict with the facts nor with considerations of plausibility, for example, to suppose that cycles in residential building induce those which have appeared in electric utilities, telephones, transportation, and the other regulated industries. There would remain the task, then, of explaining how residential building cycles arise. Of course, much attention has been given to this problem in the past—and much knowledge won,[14] though it cannot be said that a fully satisfactory explanation has yet been provided for the length of building cycles.[15]

It may be that the solution to this problem, and others, will be found in further investigations along lines recently charted by Kuznets. He suggests that the cycles in the capital formation of the regulated industries along with those in residential building may represent a joint reaction to the long swings in population increments. The latter in turn may mirror, with a lag, the long cycles in the aggregate (and per-capita) national income. As he puts it:

"One may argue that upswings in increase of product per capita, indicative of expansions in the rate of growth of economic welfare per head, induced greater inflow of people from abroad—if perhaps with a minor lag. The latter, as they cumulated, tended to prolong the upswing and downswing in the rate of growth of residential and related construction beyond the dates of the crests and troughs in the rate of growth of total and per capita national product. A contributory factor to the disparity in timing may have been the inability of the economy to generate capital resources needed in any combination of upswing in the rate of growth of flow of consumers and producers durables with that in the rate of growth of construction. When immigration ceased to be an important factor, and when limitations on the country's productive capacity ceased to be serious, swings in the rate of growth of construction, of other components of national product, and of national product itself, began to coincide. The implication of this shift for the accentuation of the amplitude of the swings in the rate of growth of national product, and for that matter, of the shorter fluctuations associated with business cycles is patent."[16]

Nevertheless, as may be expected, it is possible to raise questions

[14] Among the most illuminating investigations into underlying causal factors are those of Arthur F. Burns, "Long Cycles in Residential Construction," in *Economic Essays in Honor of Wesley Clair Mitchell* (Columbia University Press, 1935).

[15] Perhaps the most interesting econometric study of residential building cycles is J. B. D. Derksen's "Long Cycles in Residential Building: An Explanation" (*Econometrica*, April 1940). Derksen's effort to illuminate the duration of building cycles resulted in a model which yielded a cycle of twelve years. This, of course, conflicts with observed fluctuations of nearly twice that length.

[16] Kuznets, *op. cit.*, pp. 43–46.

concerning this (still developing) hypothesis to which answers are not at once apparent. In the years before World War I, swings in population increments largely ran counter to those in the rate of growth of the gross national product. How under these circumstances, we may inquire, were additions to population in this period translated into greater effective *monetary demand* for the services they were supposed to stimulate? And if demand itself moved in long cycles, we are justified in asking why the *output* of the regulated industries or output increments, did not reflect these swings more distinctly. Indeed, the need for further exploration is fully acknowledged by Kuznets, who writes:

"Yet, plausible as these relations seem, they require more exploration. Can we assume that variations in the *rate of increase* of product per worker, given the generally higher level of income in this country, necessarily affect the flow of immigrants? To what extent can we claim that such variations in the rate of growth of product per worker influenced people abroad, and what was the mechanism of this influence? Was it the assistance of foreign born already here that induced relations or friends to come, or was it some effective grapevine of letters and reports? Was there any connection between the rapidity of growth in this country and a similar course in countries of would-be immigrants, so that dislocation of industrialization widened the source of emigration in agreement with the timing of the fluctuations in the rate of growth here? Furthermore, can we assume that the newly arrived immigrants, with their relatively low purchasing power, had a truly major effect on residential construction? Were the swings in residential construction perhaps associated with those in the number of native born of native parentage—touched upon below? Alternatively, were the residential construction swings delayed beyond those in product per worker because, particularly in pre-World War I days, the economy did not have the capacity to accelerate the rates of growth of both consumer goods and some capital equipment *and* also of residential construction, so that construction swings had to wait until the limited capacity permitted an upswing? This argument might explain why the swings in residential construction lagged behind those in national product before World War I and coincided with them in post-World War I days.

"These questions should not be interpreted to mean that the association suggested . . . is necessarily illusory. They are rather intended to indicate both that the mechanism of these long swings is complex and that their further exploration promises to shed light on the past behavior of this country's economy—and perhaps also of other economies. The only hypothesis urged here is that immigration, arrivals and departures may have played a significant part in this mechanism."[17]

One additional avenue of investigation is suggested by the facts outlined in the two preceding sections. It concerns the possibility that the long swings in the investment of the regulated industries—and in that of residential building, too—are the result of the peculiar reaction of these industries, given their inherent characteristics, to ordinary business cycles. That both segments are *predisposed* to fluctuations of exceptional length (though not necessarily of twenty years) is well known. The details of financing and of capital budgeting are time-consuming and cumbersome.[18] Facilities are characterized by a high degree of indivisibility and exceptional durability. The planning horizon in the regulated industries is unusually distant.[19] The construction process itself is typically protracted, requiring in some cases as much as three years for completion.[20] And of course, once begun, such projects are not lightly abandoned in half-finished stages. Compounding these factors is an *institutional* tendency toward "lumpiness" in investment, even when the capital units are technically divisible. Thus freight cars are usually ordered and purchased in large quantities at a time, since frequent reconsideration of such decisions would be wasteful and troublesome. As explained by Hultgren: "If borrowing were necessary, underwriters and investors would not welcome a multiplicity of equipment trust issues, each secured by a small block of rolling stock. No one railroad typically buys cars in driblets; or at any rate small repetitive purchases can hardly account for any large part of total orders. On the contrary, orders for hundreds of thousands of freight cars, depending on the size of the road, are often placed at one time."[21]

All this lends to the regulated industries a high degree of inflexibility, a momentum which promotes continued movement in the same direction and discourages swift reversals. For reasons which are not entirely the same, residential building possesses a similar

[17] Simon Kuznets and Ernest Rubin, *Immigration and the Foreign Born* (National Bureau of Economic Research, Occasional Paper 46, 1954), pp. 33–34.

[18] See Edward W. Morehouse, "Regularization of Business Investment in the Electric Utility Industry," and K. T. Healy, "Regularization of Capital Investment in Railroads," in *Regularization of Business Investment* (Princeton University Press for National Bureau of Economic Research, 1954).

[19] See, for example, Michael Gort, "The Planning of Investment: A Study of Capital Budgeting in the Electric Power Industry," *Journal of Business*, April 1951.

[20] Morehouse, *op. cit.*, p. 220.

[21] Thor Hultgren, *American Transportation in Prosperity and Depression* (National Bureau of Economic Research, 1948), p. 167.

characteristic.[22] In these considerations there is the suggestion that an investment expansion, once under-way, will not be significantly deterred by a short and mild business cycle contraction. It is not without significance in this connection that *major* business depressions are roughly coincident with each of the long cycle downturns recorded in the capital formation of the regulated industries and of residential building. They were the contractions of 1873–79, 1893–94, 1907–08, and 1929–33—four of the six most severe depressions in United States history as ranked by the National Bureau of Economic Research.[23] A fifth—the decline of 1882–85—also powerfully depressed the capital flow, as Charts 1, and 4 through 9 show. The sixth—the downturn of 1920–21—is only faintly reflected; but this contraction occurred in the very early stage of a long cycle upswing and was itself short-lived and followed by brisk recovery.

Now a long cycle expansion period is one in which investment proceeds at a rate much faster than that warranted over the long run by fundamental growth factors. And the longer it proceeds, the more vulnerable it becomes to general business setbacks. It is possible that even before signs of a general depression appear, the pace of capital formation in one of the regulated industries or in residential building may be slackened, and this in itself may contribute to the onset of a general business decline. But however started, a business depression of major proportions is likely to depress the capital flow significantly in *all* the regulated industries and in residential building. With the one exception noted, it always has. And if the preceding expansion period has been protracted, the downturn may disclose a disparity of alarming proportions between existing capacity and the probable output requirements of the immediate future, which had been obscured by both the euphoria of the previous boom and the extensive period existing between the start of an investment project and its completion. Hence, given the high durability of capital in these segments of the economy, the contraction is likely to be an extended one, and to end only when long-term growth factors have once again brought demand abreast of the capacity to produce. As for long swings in population increments, they likewise may be explained in terms of major depressions. For it is these depressions, with their dramatic characteristics, which are widely reported and can be depended upon to retard for some time the influx of immigrants as well as the birth rate at home. And until the regulated industries and residential building were

[22] Burns, *op. cit.*, and Asher Achinstein, *Introduction to Business Cycles* (Crowell, 1950), Chapter 27.

[23] Burns and Mitchell, *op. cit.*, pp. 455–464.

once again revived, vigorous expansions in business activity would remain unlikely.

The exploration of such relationships, however, requires a framework different from that employed in the descriptive half of this chapter. Annual data would, at a minimum, be essential and, for some of the problems involved, monthly figures might well be found necessary. Such an investigation is precluded here by both the deficiencies of the materials at hand, and the major interest of the present study.

CHAPTER 8

The Evolution of Financial Structures

PARALLELING the physical growth of the regulated industries over the span from 1870 to 1950 was the ever-present need for money capital. The huge aggregations of equipment and structures for the railroads, electric power, telephones, and the other components entailed a draft upon the nation's savings which was at all times very substantial. In the nation's organized financial markets, the relative weight of those requirements was even greater. For the establishment and subsequent growth of the great business units characteristic of this segment of the economy typically necessitated accumulations of capital far greater than those at the immediate command of their organizers and managers. The acquisition of funds from other sources was a literal prerequisite for their development.

The particular manner in which such funds are acquired, however, necessarily changes over time, in response to the alterations in financial institutions, conventions, environmental factors, and the process of growth itself. It is to the broader pattern of such changes that we now proceed, with a view to discovering what, if any, persistent revisions have occurred in the means of financing the regulated industries over the eighty-year period studied. To focus attention upon the financial aspect of development, however, requires a different framework from that used in this volume so far. In previous analyses we have confined attention to the flow of real capital—to aggregates expressed in terms of constant dollars and considered representative, insofar as techniques of deflation permit, of physical quantities. Present purposes require centering upon the money flows themselves, unadjusted for price changes.

The Flow of Money Capital

A brief review of the general magnitude of these flows may provide a useful background for the financial analysis, for the trend of prices from 1870 to 1950 was sufficiently pronounced to make for significant differences between the flows of real and money capital. Broadly, the influence of prices was exercised in opposite directions in two periods. From the early 1870's through the late 1890's, the trend in the cost of plant and equipment was gently downward, as the solid line of Chart 23 shows. In this period, then, the sharp rise in real capital formation was slightly modified, or dampened, when translated into money terms. In the following years the opposite trend appeared and in much greater dimension. From the late 1890's to

CHART 23

Indexes of the Cost of Plant and Equipment of the Regulated Industries and the Wholesale Prices of All Commodities, 1870–1950

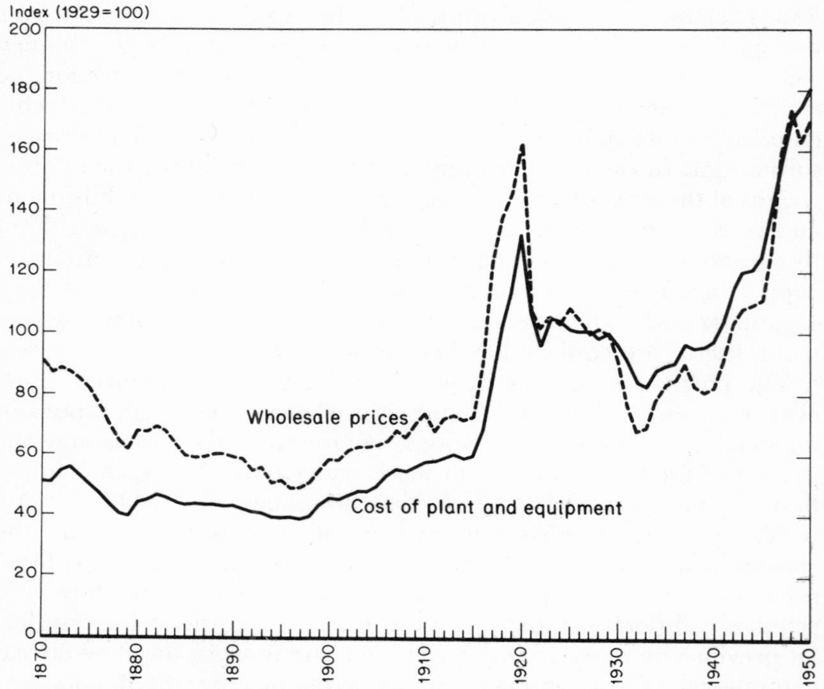

Source: Cost of utility plant and equipment, Appendix Table B-10; wholesale prices, Bureau of Labor Statistics.

the mid-1920's, the average price of capital goods increased two and one-half times. Between 1925 and 1950 there was a further rise of about 80 per cent. Over the period 1870–1950 as a whole, the chart shows, the advance in the cost of plant and equipment was considerably greater than that of the general level of wholesale prices. In the pre-1896 years, its decline was much more modest; its subsequent rise was more vigorous. In 1950 the cost of capital goods was fully three and one-half times as great as in 1870. Over the same period the general level of wholesale prices barely doubled. Hence the difference between the magnitude of the advance in the real, and in the money capital flows of the regulated industries reflected more than an alteration in the general price level; it mirrored, too, a revision in the *structure* of prices which rendered capital goods more costly in relation to others.

CHART 24

Gross Capital Formation, All Regulated Industries, 1874–1946

(nine-year moving averages)

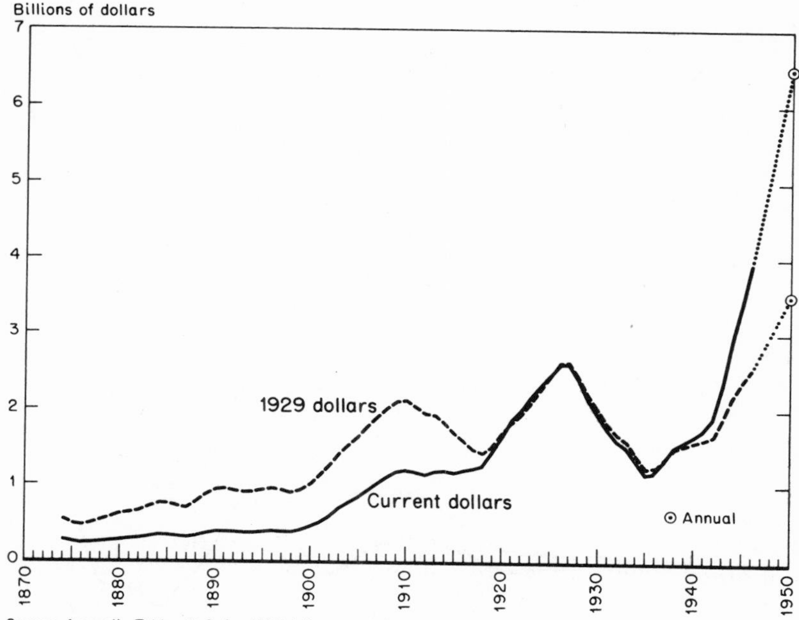

Source: Appendix Tables K-2, for 1929 dollars; K-6, for current dollars.

The effect is shown in Chart 24, which compares gross capital formation measured in current and in 1929 dollars. The general upward trend is very much more pronounced in the former. The gross flow of funds averaged between 200 and 300 million current dollars annually in the 1870's and 1880's. By the pre-World War I period, it exceeded one billion current dollars per annum, reached 2.6 billion in the 1920's and about 4.0 billion yearly in the 1940's. It will be recalled that this flow represents the expenditures of the regulated industries for plant and equipment; inventory accumulation, which is small in this segment of the economy, is omitted. Comparison may therefore be made with the gross expenditures of nonagricultural industry on plant and equipment as measured by the Department of Commerce. In 1950, when the gross flow of funds in the regulated industries amounted to 6.5 billion dollars, it represented 31 per cent of the national total. Since it is these expenditures which require long-term financing, the importance of the regulated industries in capital markets is patent.

CHART 25

Gross and Net Capital Formation, All Regulated Industries, Current Dollars, 1874–1946

(nine-year moving averages)

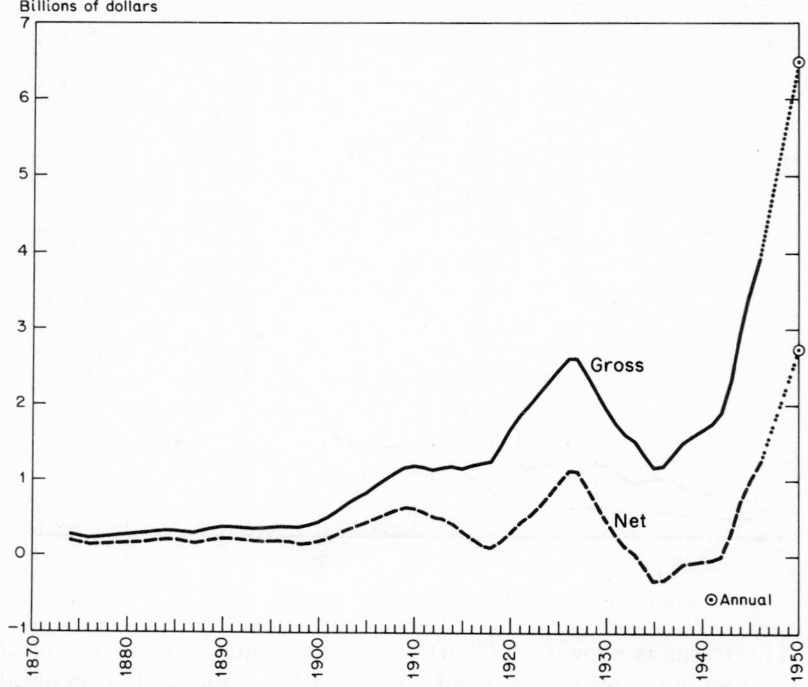

Source: Appendix Tables K-6, for gross capital formation; K-8, for net capital formation.

In Chart 25, the gross and the net flow of funds from the regulated industries are compared. The figures for these and related series are given in Table 45. Although in real terms, the pace of the advance in net capital formation in this segment of the economy was retarded after World War I, the secular trend of the net money flow continued upward throughout the period of record. But the rise is by no means as pronounced as in the gross flow. Indeed the difference between the two expands progressively and swiftly. This difference is of considerable importance, for it represents capital consumption measured in current prices—i.e. at *replacement* cost.

It was pointed out earlier that the normal process of growth ensures that capital consumption must ultimately equal and then exceed the magnitude of net capital formation.[1] This is true, whether

[1] See page 15.

TABLE 45

All Regulated Industries: Value of Plant and Equipment, Capital Formation, and Capital Consumption, Current Dollars, Nine-Year Moving Averages

(*in millions*)

Central Year of Nine-Year Average	*Value of Plant and Equipment*	*Gross Capital Formation*	*Net Capital Formation*	*Capital Consumption*
1876	5,218	224	134	90
1880	5,423	275	176	100
1886	6,503	314	183	131
1890	7,010	386	234	152
1896	7,861	390	186	204
1900	9,027	449	182	267
1906	12,695	927	505	423
1910	16,447	1,185	633	554
1916	25,474	1,193	210	988
1920	34,083	1,678	344	1,339
1926	39,614	2,614	1,125	1,496
1930	40,670	1,937	460	1,484
1936	38,790	1,178	−328	1,510
1940	41,984	1,663	−70	1,735
1946	57,512	3,942	1,264	2,678
1950[a]	78,453	6,488	2,736	3,752

[a] For 1950 only.
Source: Appendix Tables K-5, 6, 7, 8.

the flows are measured in real or in money (current dollars) terms. In the regulated industries a period of rough equality in these money flows came just before the turn of the century. After that capital consumption drew far ahead; even in 1950 when net capital formation reached a peak of 2.7 billion dollars, capital consumption was greater by about one billion.

The close connection between the real stock of capital and real net capital formation (the latter representing merely the change in the former) of course ceases to hold when these quantities are expressed in current dollars. For a price change will alter the money value of plant and equipment, either upward or downward, even in the absence of net capital expenditures. The trend of one cannot be derived from the other, as would be the case if the influence of prices were eliminated. In the light of the sharp general upward trend of prices, compounded as it was with the brisk flow of net capital expenditures, it is apparent that the growth of the money value of the plant and equipment of the regulated industries must have been enormous. The pace of the advance is depicted in Chart

CHART 26

Value of Plant and Equipment, All Regulated Industries, Current Dollars, 1874–1947

(nine-year moving averages)

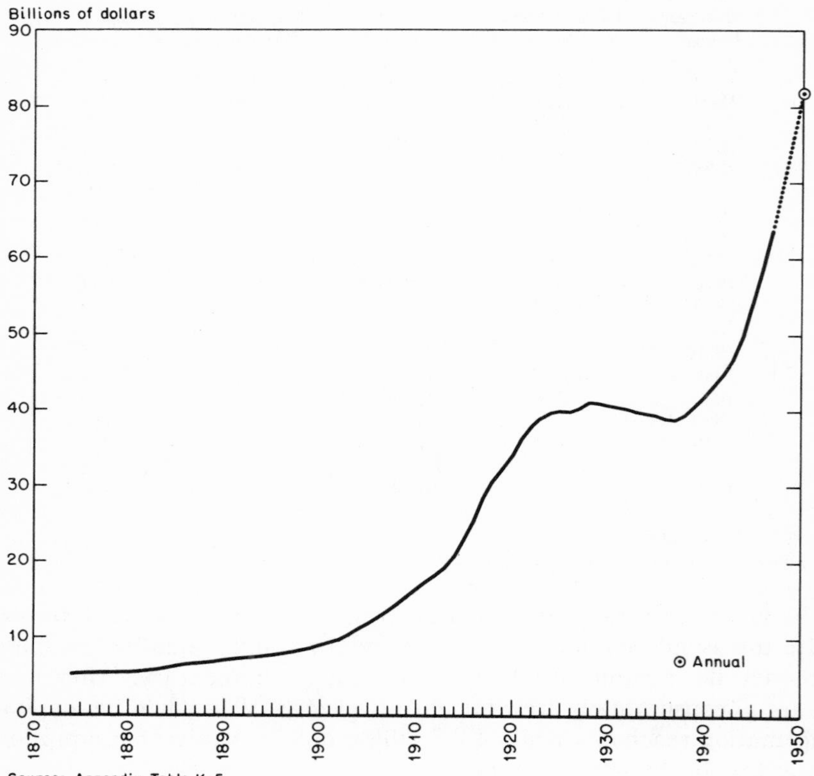

Source: Appendix Table K-5.

26. From somewhat more than five billion dollars in the 1870's, the money value of plant and equipment rose to about 10 billion just after the turn of the century, and then catapulted to 40 billion in the 1920's and—with the second postwar inflation—to nearly 80 billion at the beginning of 1950. The spectacular behavior of the money value of capital, however, should not be permitted to obscure the underlying trends of the physical quantities described in the previous chapters. For the *relationships* among these money flows, since the influence of prices is common to them all, are much the same as those which prevail among the real aggregates, despite the one important difference already pointed out. In this sense, even for

financial analysis, as we shall see in the following sections, these "real" trends are of paramount importance.

The Statistical Setting

A study of the financing of capital formation—in an industry or in the nation as a whole—requires a comprehensive view of the entire complex of the economic unit's financial transactions. For there is no way of tracing the route of a *particular dollar* obtained from some given source to any of the alternative uses to which it might be put; nor, since dollars are interchangeable, would there be any sensible purpose to such an undertaking. Hence, the sources and uses of capital funds must be analyzed in their entirety. For present purposes, since our principal interest is in secular development, we should require a *sequence* of such analyses, covering successive time intervals over as much of the 1870–1950 period as possible. We would in this way acquire a statistical portrait of the evolution of financial structures, and an opportunity to determine the dominant tendencies characteristic of it. Compilations framed with this end in view are presented for four of the principal components of the regulated industries—railroads, electric light and power, telephones, and street and electric railways; it was not possible to assemble appropriate materials for all regulated industries in the aggregate. The relevant data are given in Tables 46 through 49.

These tables provide information on all of the uses to which capital funds were put, and on all of the sources of these funds, during designated periods. Except for statistical errors, of course, the totals of sources and uses must balance. In the compilation at hand, however, only percentage distributions are given, although data on capital formation included at the bottom of the tables provide a guide to the *absolute* dimensions of the capital flow under review. This procedure was adopted for two reasons: (1) assuming that the time periods selected are reasonably representative, principal interest in our analysis actually centers in the proportions involved, rather than in the absolute magnitude of each of the items in the tables; (2) since the lengths of the intervals studied vary, and since the proportions of the industries covered also shift over time, comparison of the raw data underlying the tables would have been misleading. Nevertheless some of the characteristics of the basic data (given in Appendix J) may be noted before proceeding, in order to make the limitations of our tabulations clear.

In the earlier years the sources and uses of funds were approximated primarily by calculating the differences in corresponding balance sheet items from the beginning to the end of each of the

TABLE 46. Sources and Uses of Funds, Steam Railroads, 1880–1949: Percentage Distributions

	July 1, 1880 to June 30, 1890	*July 1, 1893 to June 30, 1907*	*July 1, 1907 to Dec. 31, 1916*	*July 1, 1914 to Dec. 31, 1920*	*Jan. 1, 1921 to Dec. 31, 1930*	*Jan. 1, 1931 to Dec. 31, 1940*	*Jan. 1, 1941 to Dec. 31, 1949*
Uses							
1. Gross capital expenditures[a]	85.9	74.0	108.8	78.6	120.3	121.6	80.4
(a) Road and equipment[a]	N	N	N	74.4	121.0	117.0	79.6
(b) Miscellaneous physical property[a]	9.9	N	4.6	4.2	−0.8	4.7	0.8
2. Current assets	4.1	17.0	2.6	8.1	−15.2	−3.7	18.8
(a) Inventories	0.6	2.7	2.3	14.8	−5.0	−4.0	4.5
(b) Receivables				5.8	−7.5	−2.6	1.9
(c) Cash and deposits	3.5	14.3	0.3	−0.8	2.3	4.2	10.1
(d) Other current assets				−11.7	−5.1	−1.3	2.3
3. Long-term securities, other than those in affiliated companies	N	N	N	−13.3	2.7	−12.2	1.5
4. Other assets	0	9.0	−16.1	26.6	−7.8	−5.8	−0.8
5. Total uses	100.0	100.0	100.0	100.0	100.0	100.0	100.0
Sources							
6. Retained profits	2.4	9.5	29.7	34.9	50.8	13.9	47.3
7. Depreciation charges			13.2	17.8	44.0	83.5	54.3
8. Current liabilities	7.3	11.9	2.3	21.5	−12.9	−20.3	9.2
(a) Tax liability	N	N	N	N	N	−0.2	4.1
(b) Other current liabilities	N	N	N	N	N	−20.1	5.1
9. Net new issues	90.3	73.7	63.2	3.3	25.8	14.3	−6.6
(a) Stocks	43.0	47.5	35.0	−3.0	14.8	11.9	−7.1
Common	N	N	N	−2.0	11.9	5.7	−5.8
Preferred	N	N	N	−1.0	2.9	6.2	−1.3
(b) Bonds	54.9	63.8	60.1	36.5	37.1	−22.6	−11.4
(c) (Less) investments in affiliated companies	−7.5	−37.6	−32.0	−30.2	−26.0	25.1	11.9
10. Other	0	4.8	−8.3	22.5	−7.8	8.6	−4.2
11. Total sources	100.0	100.0	100.0	100.0	100.0	100.0	100.0
Gross capital formation							
Millions of current dollars	2,687	2,978	5,280	3,021	8,088	2,874	7,020
Millions of 1929 dollars	6,069	6,382	8,945	3,365	7,961	3,246	5,067

Detail may not add to 100 because of rounding. N = Not shown separately. [a] Includes land.

TABLE 47

Sources and Uses of Funds, Electric Light and Power, 1881–1950: Percentage Distributions

	Jan. 1, 1881 to Dec. 31, 1912	*Jan. 1, 1913 to Dec. 31, 1922*	*Jan. 1, 1928 to Dec. 31, 1937*	*Jan. 1, 1938 to Dec. 31, 1950*
Uses				
1. Gross expenditure on plant and equipment[a]	89.1	78.2	87.4	94.5
2. Current assets	5.9	10.2	−0.2	8.7
(a) Inventories	N	N	N	3.2
(b) Receivables	N	N	N	1.2
(c) Cash and deposits	N	N	N	4.3
(d) Other current assets	N	N	N	[b]
3. Long-term securities, other than those in affiliated companies	3.3	3.1	16.4	−0.3
4. Other assets	1.7	8.5	−3.6	−2.9
5. Total uses	100.0	100.0	100.0	100.0
Sources				
6. Retained profits	4.9	5.3	7.3	12.8
7. Depreciation charges	2.7	10.2	16.3	37.5
8. Current liabilities	8.5	7.0	0.9	6.4
(a) Bills and accounts payable	2.7	6.8	N	2.1
(b) Tax liability } (c) Other short-term debt	5.8	0.1		
(b) Tax liability			N	4.1
(c) Other short-term debt			N	0.2
9. Net new issues	82.7	76.6	75.0	44.2
(a) Stocks	49.5	37.1	36.4	18.0
Common	42.0	24.4	N	N
Preferred	7.5	12.7	N	N
(b) Bonds	38.5	49.8	38.6	24.8
(c) (Less) investments in affiliated companies	−5.4	−10.3	N	1.4
10. Other	1.1	1.0	0.5	−1.0
11. Total sources	100.0	100.0	100.0	100.0
Gross capital formation				
Millions of current dollars	1,771	2,067	4,027	10,746
Millions of 1929 dollars	3,856	2,643	4,124	6,752

Detail may not add to 100 because of rounding.
N = Not shown separately.
[a] Includes land.
[b] Less than one-tenth of 1 per cent.

intervals studied. This was the method employed for railroads prior to 1914, for electric power prior to 1937, for telephones prior to 1913, and for street railways throughout the period for which data are presented. It can obviously provide only rough approximations of the magnitudes we seek, and its use affords another reason for confining our tabulations to percentage distributions. The most important source of distortion springing from the procedure followed in the earlier years is to be found in revisions in property valuations

TABLE 48

Sources and Uses of Funds, Telephones, 1877–1950: Percentage Distributions

	Jan. 1, 1891 to Dec. 31, 1902	*Jan. 1, 1903 to Dec. 31, 1912*	*Jan. 1, 1913 to Dec. 31, 1920*	*Jan. 1, 1921 to Dec. 31, 1930*	*Jan. 1, 1931 to Dec. 31, 1940*	*Jan. 1, 1941 to Dec. 31, 1950*
Uses						
1. Gross expenditure on plant and equipment[a]	84.6	86.5	93.7	87.2	113.8	92.7
2. Current assets	13.3	5.5	N	N	N	N
(a) Inventories	2.4	N	2.6	1.4	−3.0	0.8
(b) Receivables } (c) Cash and other current assets	10.9	N	3.1	2.1	−10.0	3.7
(c) Cash and other current assets		N				
(c) Cash and other current assets } 3. Long-term securities, other than those in affiliated companies			0.6	9.3	−1.9	2.2
3. Long-term securities, other than those in affiliated companies	2.0	6.4				
4. Other	0.1	1.7	0	0	1.7	0.6
5. Total uses	100.0	100.0	100.0	100.0	100.0	100.0
Sources						
6. Retained profits	−2.2	4.9	10.9	11.2	−7.4	2.1
7. Depreciation charges	8.5	14.7	47.4	31.9	107.2	38.4
8. Current liabilities	10.9	5.4	2.0	3.0	3.7	8.6
(a) Tax liability	N	N	3.8	2.3	2.5	3.1
(b) Other current liabilities	N	N	−1.8	0.7	1.2	5.5
9. Net new issues	82.6	74.8	39.6	53.9	−3.1	50.7
(a) Stocks	64.1		6.6	38.8	−7.1	8.5
(b) Bonds	18.5		36.2	19.2	4.8	45.5
(a) Stocks } (b) Bonds		80.1				
(c) (Less) investment in affiliated companies	N	−5.3	−3.1	−4.2	−0.8	−3.2
10. Other	0.2	0.2	0.1	0	−0.4	•0.2
11. Total uses	100.0	100.0	100.0	100.0	100.0	100.0
Gross capital formation						
Millions of current dollars	382	905	948	3,708	2,092	7,083
Millions of 1929 dollars	841	1,614	1,152	3,439	2,102	5,007

Details may not add to 100 because of rounding. N = Not shown separately. [a] Includes land.

TABLE 49

Sources and Uses of Funds, Street and Electric Railways: Percentage Distributions

	July 1, 1890 to June 30, 1902	*July 1, 1902 to Dec. 31, 1912*	*Jan. 1, 1913 to Dec. 31, 1922*
Uses			
1. Gross expenditure on road and equipment[a]	87.0	96.5	57.1
2. Current assets	2.0	4.7	8.9
(a) Inventories	0.4	N	N
(b) Receivables	0.7	N	N
(c) Cash and other current assets	0.9	N	N
3. Long-term securities, other than those in affiliated companies	5.0	−1.9	14.9
4. Other assets	6.0	0.7	19.0
5. Total uses	100.0	100.0	100.0
Sources			
6. Retained profits	1.4	2.2	−12.6
7. Depreciation charges		3.2	26.2
8. Current liabilities	4.8	12.8	13.4
(a) Bills and accounts payable	4.0	−0.6	6.2
(b) Interest, dividends, and taxes payable	0.7	1.6	19.6
(c) Other short-term debt		11.8	−12.4
9. Net new issues	88.2	84.0	66.9
(a) Stocks	49.6	44.2	−5.2
Common	N	N	−13.2
Preferred	N	N	8.0
(b) Bonds	38.6	54.1	81.1
(c) (Less) investments in affiliated companies	N	−14.3	−9.0
10. Other	5.7	−2.2	6.1
11. Total sources	100.0	100.0	100.0
Gross capital formation			
Millions of current dollars	1,134	1,410	1,087
Millions of 1929 dollars	2,663	2,643	1,292

Detail may not add to 100 because of rounding.
N = Not shown separately.
[a] Includes land.

—especially write-ups. They were particularly pronounced in the railroads before 1907 (when Interstate Commerce Commission regulations bearing on accounting procedures were strengthened) and in street railways before 1913. Their principal effect on our data is to inflate "expenditures on plant and equipment" on the uses side and "retained profits" and "net new issues" among the sources. Checks on the magnitude of distortion, given in Appendix J, suggest that in some of these earlier periods expenditures on plant and equipment may have been overstated for the railroads and electric power by as much as 24 and 15 per cent respectively. Such checks were not available for telephones or street railways, though general information indicates that the magnitude of write-ups may have been about the same for the latter and considerably smaller for the former.

In the later years (railroads after 1914, electric power after 1937, and telephones after 1913) the tabulations rest on a quite different foundation, and the apparent degree of accuracy is accordingly much higher. Distortions arising from changes in value were largely eliminated, for in the compilations in these years estimated series on capital expenditures, retained profits, depreciation charges, and net new issues were directly incorporated. The sources side and the uses side, each of which was in the main independently estimated, are in every case approximately in balance.[2] Nevertheless, taking the period of study as a whole, it is apparent that the data of Tables 46 through 49 are to be employed primarily for the detection of major trends and for the observation of the broader proportionate relations among the components. Fine differences must clearly be ignored. The presentation of percentage distributions, rather than the original data, was designed in part to encourage such interpretation.

The fairly long intervals for which sources and uses have been compiled also operate in this direction. Generally, the periods are in the neighborhood of a decade, and vary at the extremes from six to fifteen years, barring the initial interval for electric power, which covers the industry from its beginnings to the point at which comprehensive accounting data first became available. This telescoping of time, of course, obscures short-term movements. A brief period of heavy bond flotations followed by one of equally heavy redemptions may appear, in summary, as simply "no change" in one of our intervals. But insofar as that fault permits focusing upon the longer-term trends, it is in fact an advantage. So, from this point of view, is the netting-out of changes within the broad industry aggregates employed. For example, it is of interest that western railroad lines have in recent years grown in relation to the eastern lines. The composite changes over time, however, are also of interest, and it is upon these that emphasis is placed in this study.

The Sources and Uses of Capital Funds

Throughout this volume, the capital formation of the regulated industries is measured exclusively in terms of expenditures on fixed capital—plant, road, and equipment. Inventory accumulation is

[2] See Appendix J.

ignored as of little consequence. The basis for this judgment appears in the data in the upper panels of Tables 46–49. Generally, inventory accumulation accounted for less than 3 per cent of all uses of capital funds against at least 75 per cent for expenditures on plant and equipment. Only during the relatively brief period of war and postwar inflation in the railroad component—from 1914 to 1920—did inventory accumulation appreciably exceed this maximum level; and in the next two decades there was an offsetting liquidation. Only in street railways from 1913 to 1922, when contraction in physical terms was already under way, did expenditures on road and equipment fall appreciably below their minimum level. In all periods for which data are available, and in all components, inventory accumulation accounted for less than 2 per cent of all uses of funds, compared with more than 90 per cent for expenditures on plant and equipment.

Indeed, in the pattern of capital uses generally there appears to have been a considerable degree of stability over time among the several components. Cash and deposits were built up rather steadily by amounts varying in the main between 2 and 10 per cent of all dispositions. Investment in long-term securities was of about the same size, except for heavy liquidation by the railroads after 1914. Inventory accumulation was progressive but small. By far the most important use at all times was expenditures on plant and equipment. No such stability is to be found in the sources side of the tables. Here there is evidence of significant trends that apparently persisted throughout the time span covered, and radically altered the pattern of financing.

The first and most important of these is the pronounced and progressive shift over time toward internal financing. In the railroads this trend is in evidence in its most extreme form. In the 1880's, railroads secured 98 per cent of capital needs from outside. As in the case of all regulated industries, very little use then or at any other time—with one brief exception—was made of short-term credit. Ninety per cent of all capital requirements were met through the issue and sale of stocks and bonds. Gradually in the subsequent periods, the relationship between internal and external sources shifted. By the decade just preceding the entrance of the United States into World War I, internal sources had already mounted to the level of more than 40 per cent of all financial requirements. About two-thirds of this came from retained profits, the rest from depreciation charges. Net new issues of long-term securities provided nearly all remaining funds. Substantial use of short-term credit was made only during the inflationary surge of the immediately following years—during World War I and the brief adjacent postwar period

—when inventories were also accumulated in considerable volume. But even in these years, the proportion of total capital requirements financed internally increased, reaching more than 50 per cent.

The next three decades witnessed the climax of this trend. Between 1921 and 1940, 95 per cent of the industry's funds were generated internally, either through retained profits or depreciation charges. To be sure, stocks and bonds were issued in this period—amounting to 26 per cent of all sources in the 1920's and 14 per cent in the 1930's—but this financing was offset almost entirely by the liquidation of current liabilities. In the final decade of the 1940's, *all* capital needs were satisfied from internal sources. Long-term obligations, on balance, were actually reduced, although some short-term debt was incurred. And it should be borne in mind—as shown by the last two lines in Table 46—that this was a decade of very substantial investment. It may be rejoined that it was also a decade of financial as well as world-wide social and physical turbulence: during the first half railroads redeemed securities and in the second half floated new issues, while in the western sector of the country the expansion of roads offset the contraction in the eastern states. Nevertheless, our data for the 1941–49 period show the net results of these countervailing movements; taking the industry as a whole, and allowing as always in this study for short-term fluctuations, they complement neatly a secular trend clearly and steadily in evidence throughout the preceding years.

The same trend, but in modified form, appears in the other components. In electric light and power between 1881 and 1912, less than 8 per cent of capital funds were generated internally; 83 per cent was obtained through long-term securities. Between 1913 and 1922, 15 per cent of all capital requirements were obtained internally, between 1928 and 1937 more than 23 per cent, and between 1938 and 1950 more than 50 per cent. By the latter period net new issues accounted for only 44 per cent. Internal financing by street railways accounted for not much more than 1 per cent of all requirements between 1890 and 1902, and then rose to 5 per cent between 1902 and 1912 and to 14 per cent between 1913 and 1922. Unlike the first two components, however, the growth of retained profits did not contribute to this trend. As might be expected in an industry in which net growth ceased—and was followed by a decline—depreciation charges accounted for the entire expansion in internal sources.

In telephones the trend toward internal financing was more uneven than in any of the other components. Between 1891 and 1920 the contribution of internal sources mounted briskly, rising from 6 to nearly 60 per cent, with both retained profits and depreciation charges expanding. The succeeding decade, however, was one of unusually high investment and the rise in retained profits in this period was more than balanced by the *relative* decline in depreciation charges. Compared with the preceding war years, then, there was some reduction in the proportion of internal funds taken as a whole, though it remained greater than in all previous years. In the depressed 1930's, depreciation charges accounted for all capital requirements. In the decade of the 1940's, substantial expansion and some tendency toward a profit squeeze were coupled with the maintenance of the distinctive dividend policy of this component. Together, they contributed toward limiting the role of internal financing. The proportion of capital funds obtained through gross saving was somewhat below that of any of the intervals back to 1913, though still substantially above that of the intervals prior to 1913. Broadly, in this component, the trend toward internal financing was evident over the 1877–1950 span, though less distinct than in the other regulated industries.

The Anatomy of Internal Financing

In this section we explore the *reasons* underlying the secular advance in the rate of internal financing. We seek a *quantitative* explanation—that is, one which may be tested against, and weighed by, the data at our disposal. A first step toward this objective is to define the variables strategic for our problem.

Note, first, that we are dealing with a *ratio*—the proportion of all sources of capital represented by retained earnings and depreciation charges. In the appendix to this chapter we derive a formula which relates the various measurable factors influencing this ratio's secular trend. Within the framework adopted, the variables identified are exhaustive—i.e. they embrace, directly or indirectly, *all* the factors which affect the rate of internal financing. We summarize these below. Following the summary, we test their actual importance in the determination of the trends observed in the regulated industries. As might be expected in a financial analysis, all variables dealt with are measured in *current* dollars. Our formula is as follows:

$$r = \frac{\text{gross retained earnings}}{\text{total uses of funds}} = \frac{ab + k}{\alpha + \beta},$$

where r is the rate of internal financing, a is the net rate of savings, b is the profit rate, k is the depreciation rate, α is the net rate of capital flow, and β is the rate of capital consumption. Our numerator, therefore, breaks down the totality of gross retained earnings into its main components. Our denominator does the same for the total uses of funds. Since total uses are necessarily equal to the total sources of funds, our formula represents simply one way of expressing the rate of internal financing. The significance of the variables cited will become clearer in the further discussion of their definitions which follows.

DIRECTLY RELATED VARIABLES

Our formula isolates three variables, in the numerator, which vary *directly* with the rate of internal financing. The first of these is the net rate of savings (a), defined as the ratio of retained profits to total profits. Obviously, with *other things being equal*, an advance in the net savings rate would raise the rate of internal financing. The second factor is the profit rate (b), defined as the ratio of net profits to the value of total assets. If the profit rate advances while all other variables (including the net savings rate) remain unchanged, the rate of internal financing will also rise automatically. The final factor in this group is the depreciation rate (k), defined for our special purpose as the ratio of depreciation charges to the value of total assets. This, too, varies directly with the rate of internal financing, *ceteris paribus*.

INVERSELY RELATED VARIABLES

The formula isolates two variables in the denominator which vary *inversely* with the rate of internal financing. These are the net rate of capital flow (α) and the rate of capital consumption (β). The first is defined as the ratio of all capital uses, *net of capital consumption*, to the value of total assets. If numerator and denominator of this ratio were expressed in constant dollars, it would represent the rate of growth of an industry's assets (viewed as physical goods and command over physical goods). Measured in current dollars—as it is in our formulation—it roughly approximates this.[3] If the net rate of capital flow declines, other things being equal, the rate of internal financing must increase. Totally aside from the obvious algebra, this is understandable if we consider that the net flow of capital represents a *use* of funds. If total *uses* decline, while retained gross earnings remain unchanged, then the *rate* of internal financing automatically rises. The same consequence follows if the net rate of capital flow diminishes, while the other variables in our formulation remain unaltered.

The rate of capital consumption is defined as the ratio of capital consumption to the value of total assets. Since all our measurements are in current dollars, capital consumption covers the using up of

[3] See the appendix to this chapter.

capital (through wear, obsolescence, etc.) at replacement cost. The replacement of capital consumed, of course, also represents a *use* of funds. If the rate of capital consumption rose, while all the other variables remained unchanged, the rate of internal financing would decrease. Bear in mind that capital consumption is not the same as a depreciation charge. In the nineteenth century all industries experienced capital consumption, but in many of them—before the general spread of accounting practice—depreciation charges were zero.

We shall shortly investigate the behavior of the strategic ratios contained in this equation for the light they may cast upon the changing proportions of internal financing to the total sources of capital. But we pause first for a few additional remarks concerning the distinction our formula draws between capital consumption and depreciation charges.

In the earlier years of our study, especially, this distinction is crucial, though it is at all times important. For depreciation accounting was not widely adopted in industry at large nor in the regulated segment. Thus in the railroad component in 1880–90, though it is not shown separately in Table 46, zero is an excellent estimate of the volume of depreciation charges. The same estimate would not hold in other segments, but even here it is probable that there was some deficiency in usage. Insofar as there was, it was gradually eliminated by the pressure of regulating agencies, the courts, and finally the exigencies of the income tax. Depreciation accounting came more and more into use, and was applied to an ever wider range of the stock of capital. Other things being equal, this was a factor making for greater internal financing. But of course it cannot be contended that under such circumstances other things would actually have remained unchanged.

Thus, a reduction in the reported profit rate would result inevitably from the adoption of depreciation accounting in the early days of an industry in which capital was long-lived. Conceivably, gross saving could remain unchanged. On the other hand, however, there is some likelihood that a rise in depreciation charges would stimulate an advance in the rate of *net* retention. For there is an obvious motivation for maintaining dividends within some distance of the bounds of reported profits. Suppose, for example, that the retention rate had been zero before the adoption of depreciation accounting —and in some *firms* it probably was. Then the product ab in the above equation, as well as k, would have been zero. Our contention is that if the depreciation rate (k) had become positive under such circumstances it is unlikely that ab would have gone negative by a corresponding amount, i.e. dividend payments would not in general have been maintained for very long at the price of a reduction in the value of total assets. Because of financial convention, therefore, the adoption of depreciation accounting may have had the effect of increasing the magnitude of gross savings and of the proportion of all capital uses financed internally. Whatever its extent—and some light is cast on this below—the influence of this factor had probably petered out by the time of World War I, or somewhat earlier. For depreciation accounting had by then been generally adopted.

We shall now apply our formula to a quantitative analysis of the factors underlying the growth of internal financing. The essential data required are given in Table 50. For this tabulation we have computed estimates of α and β during the initial time interval covered in the sources and uses tables for each of the components, and for the corresponding final interval. The over-all time span covered is, then, thirty years for street railways, sixty years for telephones, and seventy years for the others. Thus, for the railroads,

TABLE 50

Net Rate of Capital Flow and Rate of Capital Consumption, Selected Components

(*per cent*)

	First Period[a]	*Nine-Year Average Centered in 1926*	*Final Period*[b]
Net rate of capital flow[c]			
Steam railroads	3.2	1.4	0.2
Electric light and power	14.2	8.6	3.2
Telephones	17.5	10.6	9.3
Street and electric railways	12.1	...	−1.5
Rate of capital consumption[d]			
Steam railroads	1.8	2.0	2.3
Electric light and power	7.3	4.5	4.5
Telephones	10.9	11.5	7.2
Street and electric railways	4.3	...	4.5

[a] July 1, 1880 to June 30, 1890 for railroads, January 1, 1881 to December 31, 1912 for electric power, January 1, 1891 to December 31, 1902 for telephones and July 1, 1890 to June 30, 1902 for street railways.

[b] January 1, 1941 to December 31, 1949 for railroads, January 1, 1938 to December 31, 1950 for electric power, January 1, 1941 to December 31, 1950 for telephones and January 1, 1913 to December 31, 1922 for street railways.

[c] Ratio of the average money capital flow, net of depreciation, to average value of assets in current dollars. Estimated by computing ratio of average net capital formation to average value of plant and equipment in current dollars.

[d] Ratio of average capital consumption to average value of assets in current dollars. Assets estimated by multiplying current dollar value of plant and equipment by 1.10.

the "first period" is July 1, 1880 through June 30, 1890, and the "final period" is January 1, 1941 through December 31, 1949. For convenience in appraising the long-term trends we have also provided figures for the nine years centered in 1926.

The upper panel of the table presents the estimates of the net rate of capital flow. These were computed by measuring the ratio of the average annual net capital formation during each of the periods to the annual average of the value of plant and equipment, with both numerator and denominator expressed in current dollars. Assuming that assets other than plant and equipment remained proportionately about the same in the long run, over the period of interest, this ratio would approximate the net rate of capital flow as defined above. Most important is the very substantial decline, reflecting the retardation in the rate of growth described in a previous chapter, in railroads, electric power, and street railways, and to a smaller extent, in telephones.

In the lower panel of the table are presented estimated rates of capital consumption. These were computed by measuring the ratio of the average annual capital consumption in current dollars in each period to the average annual value of plant and equipment, similarly figured, after inflating the latter by 10 per cent to allow for other assets. Since such data are most commonly reported in accounting statements in terms of original cost, it is worth emphasizing that our estimates of both capital consumption and the value of plant and equipment are in *current* dollars—as they must be to suit the requirements of the present analysis. Price corrections of a peculiarly difficult character were therefore a necessary element in their construction. It may be observed that over the period of analysis the rate of capital consumption rose in the railroads, remained about the same in street railways, and declined in electric power and in telephones. Even in the last two components, however, it is significant that the rate of capital consumption actually rose substantially *in relation to* the net rate of capital flow. For the drop in the latter was much greater than in the former. This means that in every case capital consumption represented an expanding proportion of all capital uses. Essentially, of course, this is a manifestation of the combined effects of the retarded rate of growth of output and the declining capital-product ratio, both of which are mirrored in the fall of the net rate of capital flow. As we shall see below, it is of much significance for financial analysis.

Some light on the factors underlying the long-run trend in the rate of internal financing may be obtained, initially, by appraising the situation which prevailed in the first period. The rates of internal financing at that time are given for each of the components of the regulated industries in the first column of Table 51. These figures, of course, were taken from Tables 46–49 on sources and uses of funds. Employing the formula developed above, they may be represented symbolically as follows:

$$r_1 = \frac{a_1 b_1 + k_1}{\alpha_1 + \beta_1},$$

where the subscript 1 indicates the first period.[4]

Now with these actual rates we may compare hypothetical ones, computed on the assumption that depreciation and net savings were just sufficient, in combination, to cover the capital consumption requirements of this period. The hypothetical rate may be expressed by the equation:

$$r_1' = \frac{a_1' b_1 + k_1'}{\alpha_1 + \beta_1} = \frac{\beta_1}{\alpha_1 + \beta_1}$$

where the primes indicate hypothetical values. It should be noted that r_1' is nothing more than the ratio of capital consumption to total capital uses in the first period.[5]

The values of r_1' for each of the components are given in the second column of Table 51. In the first column are given the *actual* rates of internal financing in the first period. The differences between the two sets of figures are striking. It is evident that the rates of internal financing in these early years provided only a small fraction of the funds required for the consumption of capital—in the

[4] Since we know the values of r_1, α_1, and β, it is possible to compute the numerators of these ratios. Thus in the case of the railroads, we may write:

$$0.024 = \frac{a_1 b_1 + k_1}{0.032 + 0.016}.$$

Hence $a_1 b_1 + k_1 = 0.0012$. This is a reasonable answer on the assumption that a, the net savings rate, was about 10 per cent, that b, the profit rate, was about 1 per cent and that k, the rate of depreciation, was zero. This seems to have been approximately the case, remembering the manner in which these terms have been defined for purposes of this analysis—in particular, that the profit rate is the ratio of reported net income to the value of *all* assets measured in current dollars. For relevant data on profits and savings of the railroads in this period, see *Historical Statistics of the United States, 1789–1945* (Bureau of the Census, 1949), pp. 201 and 205, and W. H. S. Stevens and E. S. Hobbs, "Analysis of Steam Railway Dividends, 1890–1941" (Interstate Commerce Commission, mimeographed, November 1943), p. 22.

[5] Thus, from the definitions of the variables, we may write:

$$\frac{B}{\alpha + \beta} = \frac{\frac{C}{A}}{\frac{N}{A} + \frac{C}{A}} = \frac{C}{N + C}$$

where C is capital consumption, N is the net capital flow, and A is the value of total assets.

TABLE 51

Comparison of Actual and Hypothetical Rates of Internal Financing

	r_1	r_1'	r_2'	r_2''	r_2
Steam railroads	0.024	0.33	0.42	0.92	1.02
Electric light and power	0.076	0.33	0.24	0.58	0.50
Telephones	0.063	0.38	0.30	0.46	0.41
Street and electric railways	0.014	0.26	0.27	1.50	0.14

Source: Dates of first and final periods, given in footnotes to Table 50. Actual rates of internal financing, from Tables 46 through 49. Values of α and β, from Table 50.

Definitions of the rates are as follows:

r_1 = actual rate of internal financing in the first period.

$r_1' = \frac{\beta_1}{\alpha_1 + \beta_1}$, where α = net rate of capital flow and β = rate of capital consumption and subscript 1 indicates first period values.

$r_2' = \frac{\beta_2}{\alpha_1 + \beta_2}$, where subscript 2 indicates final period values.

$$r_2'' = \frac{\beta_2}{\alpha_2 + \beta_2}$$

r_2 = actual rate of internal financing in final period.

case of the steam railroads and street railways, considerably less than one-tenth, and for the others less than one-fourth.

The discrepancies, of course, reflect the absence of depreciation accounting referred to above. They also illuminate the extent to which business properties were being overvalued in the earlier years, for new assets were capitalized with little or no offset for wear and tear, aging, or obsolescence. This was clearly a situation which could not under any likely circumstances persist indefinitely. Sooner or later the financial practices in vogue would have been certain to affect the yield accruing to investors in these industries. As yields declined with the continued write-up of assets, the availability of additional external capital would have diminished or have been dissipated entirely.[6] Totally aside from this, the more extensive use of depreciation accounting was subsequently encouraged or enforced by the regulations of public administrative agencies as well as by the nature of corporate interests under the income tax laws. Thus, in one sense, the substantial excess of capital consumption over the gross retention of funds in the first period was itself a factor which induced a sharp rise in internal financing in later years. Even if

[6] Of course partial and temporary correctives occurred in the latter decades of the nineteenth century during major business cycle crises and depressions, many of which had strong financial overtones. During such periods assets were written down, though the long-term trend remained upward. The views concerning business cycles expressed by Thorstein Veblen in *The Theory of Business Enterprise* (Scribner, 1935) are based largely on the observation of such phenomena.

there had been no change in the rate of growth, a rise in internal financing would have been necessary on the grounds outlined. This is shown by the figures in the third column of Table 51. Here, we have computed values of r in accord with the following equation:

$$r_2' = \frac{\beta_2}{\alpha_1 + \beta_2}$$

where the subscript 2 represents the final period. In particular, r_2' represents the rate of internal financing which *would* have existed in the final period if (1) the net rate of capital flow had remained as it was in the first period, and (2) internal financing had been just sufficient to meet the prevailing rate of capital consumption. For comparison, the actual rate of internal financing in the final period is shown in the last column of the table.

Thus, a substantial increase in internal financing over the seventy-year span of our study would have been necessary even if the rate of growth in the regulated industries had not been dampened. The need to cover replacement alone would have pushed the value of r up from 2 to 42 per cent in the railroads, from less than 8 to 24 per cent in electric power, from 6 to 30 per cent in telephones and from one to 27 per cent in street railways. Comparison with the last column of the table shows that in the first three components these hypothetical advances account for from one-third to two-thirds of the actual increase in internal financing over the period of study. In street railways the hypothetical rate of internal financing is even greater than the actual rate in the final period.

Employing the same general method, we may now evaluate the effect of the retarded net rate of capital flow. To do this, we compute a second hypothetical rate of internal financing for the final period, defined by the equation:

$$r_2'' = \frac{\beta_2}{\alpha_2 + \beta_2}$$

It is the rate which would provide internal funds just sufficient for capital consumption, *given the net rate of capital flow actually then in progress*. Thus, r_2'' differs from r_2' only in the net rate of capital flow assumed.

The difference in the figures in the third and fourth columns of Table 51, therefore, may be said to reflect the impact of this single factor in isolation. The retardation in the net rate of capital flow over the seventy years was sufficient alone to have raised the rate of internal financing from 42 to 92 per cent in railroads, from 24 to 58 per cent in electric power, from 30 to 46 per cent in telephones, and from 27 to 150 per cent in street railways. Moreover, comparison between the fourth and fifth columns of the table shows that this hypothetical rate was in every case, save street railways, very close to the actual rate of internal financing in the final period. This means, essentially, that the sharp rise in internal financing over the period of study may be accounted for primarily in terms of two factors: (1) the need for correcting the initial deficiencies in capital consumption allowances which existed in the first period, and (2) the expanding relative importance of capital consumption in all uses of capital, springing from the retarded rate of growth of total assets. For both of these factors—and these alone—are reflected in our computations of r''_2.

Given the rough nature of our data, we may judge that the figures in the fourth and fifth columns of Table 51 are in approximate equality for steam railroads, electric power, and telephones. Obviously, this is not so for street railways. The great excess of the required rate of internal financing (r''_2) over the actual rate in this case is of considerable significance. It is in fact a symptom of the disaster which, before the end of the final period of analysis, had already overtaken this component. (The final period for street railways—from the beginning of 1913 to the end of 1922—is much earlier than for other components.) Overexpansion and the general failure to adopt sound methods of finance had in the 1920's brought many lines to insolvency. Income, in the aggregate, was insufficient to meet capital replacement. As the competition of the automobile intensified, this industry contracted swiftly. The final period of our financial analysis was a time of transition, in which the contraction process in street railways was begun.

For the other components, the experiments above appear to provide a sufficient—though, of course, not necessary—explanation for the observed rise in internal financing. Nevertheless, we may inquire concerning the possible role of other influences. One interpretation of our analysis so far would suggest the conclusion that the rates of net savings (a) and depreciation (k) had been raised in keeping with the long-run advance in the relative importance of capital consumption, together with the need for correcting the initial deficiency in retention that was characteristic of the earlier years. Another possibility is that the rates of retention—a and k—remained the same, but that the profit rate (b) increased by an amount sufficient to accomplish the same end. Available data, however, do not support the latter thesis. There is some evidence that the profit rate (in the sense in which it has been defined in this section) remained about the same in the long run in the street railways which avoided insolvency, declined slightly in telephones and electric power,[7] and increased in the railroad component,[8] over the roughly seventy-year span. But cyclical fluctuations aside, none of these trends appears to have been pronounced. The substantial rise in internal financing in railroads, electric power, and telephones must have been accomplished, in the main, through boosts in the *rates* of retention.

Probing further, we may inquire concerning the influence of prices. The price level—as such—does not appear in our formula. No mention has been made of it as a factor tending to boost the rate of internal financing. And yet prices in general, and capital goods prices in particular, moved securely upward from the 1890's onward, cyclical movements aside. Depreciation charges must have fallen far short of capital consumption figured at reproduction cost through most of this period. For in all of our components the original cost of property was employed as the entire, or the principal base upon which such costs were levied. Was not the price level, then, an important factor stimulating the advance in internal financing—and one which we have thus far overlooked?

Our answer to this question must be negative. An advance in prices affects capital goods purchased for expansion as well as those purchased for replacement. Indeed it is unlikely that any element of capital costs would remain entirely unaffected. Hence, an inflation does not necessarily increase capital replacement requirements *relative to other uses*. To be sure, when prices rise, business concerns are compelled to boost their *accounting* rates of depreciation (levied on original costs) or the proportion of reported profits retained, or both, if replacement costs are to be met. But this would not increase the rate of internal financing; indeed, it would only keep it from falling. Reference to the definitions underlying our formula should clarify this:

$$r = \frac{ab + k}{\alpha + \beta} = \frac{\frac{RP}{PA} + \frac{D}{A}}{\frac{N}{A} + \frac{C}{A}}$$

where R = retained profits, P = total net profits, D = depreciation charges, N = net capital flow, C = capital consumption, and A = value of assets.

[7] Eli Winston Clemens, *Economics and Public Utilities* (Appleton-Century-Crofts, 1950), pp. 233–234.

[8] Stevens and Hobbs, *op. cit.*, p. 22.

A rise in prices would boost N, A, and C in the same proportion, so that the denominator of r would not be changed. If profits rose in proportion to prices, then so long as the net savings rate $\left(\frac{R}{P}\right)$ was maintained, the first term in the numerator (ab) would remain unchanged. If profits did not increase so rapidly, $\frac{R}{P}$ would need to be advanced in order to keep ab the same. Concerning the second term in the numerator, the results are fairly certain. Since D depends on the accounting rates of depreciation figured on a base of original costs, it would remain unchanged in inflation, or would rise only with a substantial lag. Hence, in order to maintain k unchanged, an advance in D would be necessary. In short, inflation requires a rise in *accounting* depreciation rates (affecting k through D) and perhaps a rise in the net rate of savings (a) simply to *maintain* the prevailing gross rate of internal financing (r). Since r advances substantially over the period of study, in the face of progressive inflation, it is apparent that k or a, or both, must have been boosted by very large amounts.

Finally, we may recall that our analysis of Tables 46 through 49 showed, in general, that *both a* and k were boosted over the period studied. Yet, one may ask why the net rate of savings (a) should share at all in an advance which is designed to provide internal funds primarily for capital replacement? Why should not k alone be expanded sufficiently for this purpose? One possible answer may be found in the numerous institutional obstacles to swift and extensive increases in accounting rates. In the face of these, especially in periods of broad price advance, the deficiency in the amount of internal funds generated was apparently more easily taken up, at least in part, by increases in a.

One of the characteristics of the regulated industries disclosed in the previous chapters casts a further light on the phenomena under review. We find that the rise in internal financing did little more—at most—than parallel the rise in the aggregate cost of replacing capital consumed, relative to all capital requirements. It would be wrong, nevertheless, to conclude that internal sources did not contribute to a net advance in productive power. For we have seen that a sharp and steady rise in the productivity of physical capital was an outstanding characteristic in this segment of the economy almost throughout the period of study. New plant and equipment was nearly always materially more efficient than the old facilities they replaced. Hence, retained earnings accomplished something more than the limited objective of keeping the physical capital stock intact. In some part they have also contributed to the expansion of productive capacity.

Long-Term Debt and Equity

Brief reference may be made to one other significant alteration in the pattern of financing of the regulated industries over the spans covered by our sources and uses tabulations. This is the shift from equity to debt financing evident in each of our components. Of course we refer to a shift in the *proportions* of these methods of raising capital. Financing through the issue of long-term obligations was substantial in the regulated industries from their very beginnings. Of our components, only in telephones in its earliest days was less than a third of all capital funds obtained through the incurrence of long-term debt. For in the segment of the economy in which our interest centers, the conditions are inherently propitious for such obligations. The shouldering of a substantial burden of fixed charges is indeed possible *only* in situations in which both borrowers and lenders may share a reasonable degree of confidence in their safety. The size and quasi-monopoly positions of the firm in the regulated segment provide the necessary qualifications. For they yield the promise of the magnitude and steadiness in the gross income flow which alone can render substantial long-term debt financing feasible.[9]

Such considerations suggest a persistent difference between the regulated industries and the remainder of the economy. Available data bear this out. At the end of 1946 in the regulated industries, in the aggregate, the total value of bonds and mortgages outstanding was 21.5 billion dollars and of stocks, 23.9 billion. For all nonfinancial corporations exclusive of utilities, the value of bonds and mortgages outstanding was 12.2 billion dollars and of stocks, 43.4 billion. Thus the ratio of fixed debt to stocks was 90 per cent in the regulated industries and less than 30 per cent in the others. Nor is this discrepancy to be accounted for only by differences in the size of firm. In nonfinancial corporations, exclusive of the regulated industries, with assets of 100 million dollars or more, the total of bonds and mortgages outstanding at the end of 1946 was 4.4 billion dollars against 14.3 billion in stocks.[10] The ratio of the former to the latter is little more than 30 per cent. One must conclude that distinctive circumstances in the regulated industries, aside from mere

[9] Cf. Simon Kuznets, "Factors in the Demand for Capital Funds" (Work Memorandum No. 43, National Bureau of Economic Research, mimeographed, May 1952), p. 21.

[10] *Statistics of Income for 1946, Part 2* (Bureau of Internal Revenue), Tables 4 and 6. Quoted in Kuznets, *op. cit.*, pp. 22–23.

size of firm, invite the use of long-term debt financing. The relatively stable character of their incomes, springing from positions of monopoly as well as—in some cases—the nature of their products, is surely one of these. The conditions of public regulation, as explained later, is another.

We return to the trend over time in the proportion of long-term debt financing, as evidenced in the data of Tables 46 through 49. In the railroads in the 1880's, 55 per cent of all sources of capital were obtained through bonds against 43 per cent through stocks. Of the net new issues (gross of investment in affiliated companies) in this period, then, bonds represented about 56 per cent. This proportion rose steadily for railroads as long as external financing remained a significant factor. In the 1914–20 period, bonds and mortgages accounted for all the long-term funds obtained and in the succeeding decade of the 1920's, for more than 70 per cent. The experience of the 1930's disclosed the dangers of so heavy a burden of fixed charges in a component which was more volatile than the average regulated industry and was subject—to boot—to the intense competition of related services. Between 1930 and 1950 fixed obligations in substantial volume were redeemed by the railroads. But by this time internal financing provided virtually all the funds required, in the aggregate, and there was no need for equity financing. Note, however, that internal financing itself materially enhanced the value of *existing* equity claims in the railroads. As pointed out earlier, neither in this nor in any of the other components did short-term debt assume much significance, except for very brief periods.

In the other regulated industries for which we have compiled data the swing to long-term debt financing was also pronounced. In electric light and power in the 1881–1912 period, bonds represented 43 per cent of total net new issues (gross of investment in affiliated companies). The advance in succeeding decades brought the proportion to 58 per cent in the final period of the 1940's. In this segment, external financing remained of considerable importance throughout our period of study, despite the rise in the magnitude of internal sources. In telephones the rise in the proportion of bonds, similarly figured, was from 22 per cent in the 1891–1902 period to 85 per cent in the 1940's. Even in the brief span of our record for street railways, the proportion rose from 44 to 100 per cent. Thus it is seen that in all components there was a marked shift from major reliance on stocks in the securing of external funds to major—or *complete*—reliance on fixed indebtedness.

Of course, the significance of this trend must be viewed in context. Its impact upon financial structures is substantially modified by the expansion of equity claims through internal financing. Nevertheless the trend remains important for financial markets in general as well as for the industries themselves and must be viewed, essentially, as a manifestation of a distinctive orientation in the regulated segment evident in their earliest records. The principal factor underlying the swing would appear to be the existence of regulation itself. For this was an influence which gathered force through the years as public controls were extended, reinforced, and generalized, and was superimposed on the other characteristics of these industries benign to the growth of long-term debt. Wherever public regulation establishes permitted returns on *total* investment, and wherever it includes interest payments in costs, it provides an inevitable bias in industry for debt financing. The rewards for "trading on the equity" in monopolistic industries, in which public regulation aims at a fair return on total investment, acquire in this way an extraordinary degree of security which cannot be approached in other sectors of the economy.

In addition, of course, other well-known characteristics contribute to the trend toward debt financing, but these are common to all corporate industry and are of much more recent origin. They are also less puissant as judged by the reaction of the corporate sector exclusive of the regulated industries. Perhaps the most significant of these are the rise in the corporate income tax and the growing importance in capital markets of institutional investors, restricted either by legal limitation or preference to the purchase of bonds, or both.

Appendix: The Derivation of the Equation for the Rate of Internal Financing

Holding prices constant, we may define all the uses (U) of capital as equal to capital consumption (C) plus the *net* growth in the value of assets (N), or

$$U = C + N \tag{1}$$

If each of these magnitudes is expressed in current values, rather than in constant dollars, the equation still holds, but then N must be defined as the net *flow of funds* during the period, since the *value* of assets would fluctuate also with prices. In either case, however, we may express N as a ratio to the value of assets (A), as in:

$$\frac{N}{A} = \alpha \tag{2}$$

Equation (2) is equivalent to the rate of growth of assets, if correction is made for price changes. If A and N are expressed in terms of current values, this is no longer true. Still, even in the latter case the long-run trend of α would roughly approximate the secular behavior of the net rate of growth, being materially distorted only if the price change is brisk and the finite intervals over which the growth rate is computed are substantial. For if values are measured in current dollars, both the numerator as well as the denominator are influenced by price fluctuations. Nevertheless, when measured in current dollars, we shall term α the net rate of capital flow, to distinguish it from the growth rate. And since for the consideration of financial relations this is most convenient, we shall deal throughout this appendix with actual money flows, uncorrected for price changes, and shall continue to measure total assets in terms of current dollars.

We shall measure C in terms of current dollars—i.e. at replacement cost. The rate of capital consumption may then be defined as:

(3) $$\frac{C}{A} = \beta$$

And since

$$N = \alpha A, \text{ and}$$
$$C = \beta A,$$

we substitute in 1 to obtain:

(4) $$U = \alpha A + \beta A$$

Now the sources (S) of money capital may be equated to retained profits (R) plus depreciation charges (D) plus all external sources of capital (E), as in:

(5) $$S = R + D + E$$

The net savings rate may therefore be expressed by:

(6) $$\frac{R}{P} = a$$

where P = net profits.

The profit rate may be expressed by:

(7) $$\frac{P}{A} = b$$

and the depreciation rate by

(8) $$\frac{D}{A} = k$$

It should be noted that D is not the same as C, defined above. The magnitude of D is the arbitrary result of the particular accounting convention used by industry. Conceivably, D could be zero, even though C—the actual capital consumption at replacement cost—were very large.

We may further write:

(9) $$R = aP,$$
(10) $$P = bA, \text{ and}$$
(11) $$D = kA$$

Substituting 10 in 9 we obtain:

(12) $$R = abA$$

Using these symbols we may express the rate of internal financing (r) by:

(13) $$r = \frac{R + D}{S},$$

the proportion of all sources of capital obtained from retained profits and depreciation. Substituting from 11 and 12 in the numerator of 13, we get:

(14) $$r = \frac{abA + kA}{S}$$

Since S and U must be equal we may substitute from 4 in the denominator of 14 to obtain:

$$r = \frac{abA + kA}{\alpha A + \beta A}$$

and canceling:

(15) $$r = \frac{ab + k}{\alpha + \beta}$$

Hence, we conclude that the rate of internal financing may be analyzed in terms of five ratios. It will vary *directly* with the net savings rate (a), with the profit rate (b), and with the depreciation rate (k). It will vary *inversely* with the net rate of capital flow (α) and the rate of capital consumption (β). All relationships hold with the usual *ceteris paribus* assumption. Nevertheless, the last phrase of these conclusions would come as a surprise unless it were recalled that we have distinguished between the rate of depreciation and that of capital consumption. *If* they were at all times equal we would be justified in writing:

$$r = \frac{ab + \beta}{\alpha + \beta} \tag{16}$$

In equation 16 the rate of internal financing varies *directly* with capital consumption, so long as ab is less than α, i.e. so long as the gross retention of funds does not already account for the *entire* volume, or more, of capital requirements.[11] But the postulate underlying this formulation is unrealistic. We have confined attention, therefore, to equation 15.

[11] The value of r could be greater than unity, as it was in the railroads in the 1940's, if the flow of funds from external sources were negative.

CHAPTER 9

Résumé and Prospect

IN this concluding chapter we assemble the principal findings developed earlier, and briefly appraise their significance for an understanding of the decades ahead. Our summary consists of five major parts.

In the first, we focus upon the major characteristics of the growth of the regulated industries. Here, we review the long-run behavior of capital formation. Then we embrace the trends of the two variables which, proximately, determine the secular path of investment—output and the capital-product ratio. Second, we follow with a summary of our exploration into the factors underlying these trends. Third, we recapitulate our findings on the form and nature of long cycles. Fourth, we review the secular patterns observed in the financing of the regulated industries, and summarize the explanation we developed for them. Finally, we essay a brief analysis of the outlook.

The Secular Pattern of Capital Formation

The productive facilities of the regulated industries, in the aggregate, experienced a substantial expansion over the period from 1870 to 1950. From about 270 million 1929 dollars per annum in the first decade of the period, net capital formation rose to more than one billion per year in the years just preceding World War I. In subsequent years the growth in facilities was extended, though the early vigor of the rise slackened somewhat. As a result, the accumulated stock of physical capital in the regulated industries rose from about 8 billion 1929 dollars in 1870 to nearly 30 billion around 1910 and to about 47 billion in 1950. Gross capital formation, supported by swiftly growing capital replacement requirements, advanced from less than one-half billion 1929 dollars per annum in the 1870's to more than five times this amount in the post-World War II period.

Great as the expansion was, it did not keep pace over the eighty-year span of study with that of the nation as a whole. The regulated industries accounted for about 15 per cent of the nation's gross capital formation in the 1870's, about 20 per cent in the years preceding World War I, and no more than 10 per cent in the period following World War II. The per capita value of plant and equipment in the regulated industries, measured in 1929 dollars, was 221 in 1870, 368 in 1930, and 321 in 1950. Here, and in the subsequent discussion of this section, references to capital in all cases pertain to quantities measured in constant dollars. Furthermore, in the regulated industries plant and equipment are taken as the *total* stock of reproducible capital, the small amount of inventories typically held being neglected. Capital formation, accordingly, refers to accumulations of plant and equipment.

The main components of the regulated industries segregated for special study include steam railroads, electric light and power, telephones, street and electric railways, and local bus lines. This quintuplet in the 1880's, insofar as its elements were in operation, accounted for about 90 per cent, and in the 1940's still took as much as 70 per cent, of the gross flow of investment of all regulated industries. The progress of capital formation in the five components over the period from 1870 to 1950 exhibited a number of significant characteristics in common. This feature of their behavior invited the use of a model pattern both as a descriptive device, and as a framework for comparative analysis. The model has the following properties. The secular path of net capital formation rises at an increasing rate, passes through an inflection point, and then continues its advance at a diminishing rate until its peak is attained. Subsequently it declines, after a time reaching zero and ultimately turning negative. The stock of capital follows a similar secular course, at least up to contact with the zero line. Its inflection point, however, is coincident with the peak in net capital formation. Its own peak is achieved when net capital formation becomes zero. We omit, for conciseness, the subsequent stages of the pattern, through which only street railways of all our components progressed in any significant degree.

Indeed, the degree of progression along the model secular pattern varied widely among our components. Judged by this standard, the most youthful was telephones. In this industry none of the key stages of the model pattern had by 1950 been completed, either in the growth of its stock of capital or of its net capital formation. Both rose at absolute rates which expanded progressively throughout the eighty-year span of study. Net capital formation in telephones averaged 240 million 1929 dollars per annum in the 1940's, more than twice the rate of the 1920's. The stock of capital increased fivefold between 1900 and 1930, and in the next twenty years doubled again.

The most mature of the components was street railways—an industry whose life span in nearly its entirety is covered by the period studied. In this component the application of electricity stimulated a spectacular advance in net capital formation, which, however, soon reached its peak in the middle of the first decade of the twentieth century. Net investment then turned downward swiftly, diminishing at an increasing rate until it reached zero around 1916. At that point the stock of capital was at its peak. Subsequent contraction brought it down to about 770 million 1929 dollars in 1950, compared to facilities with value of nearly four billion 35 years earlier.

Of the other components, steam railroads came closest to matching the maturity of the street railways—though it still remained a substantial distance away. In railroads the changeover from an increasing to a decreasing rate of growth in the stock of capital—the secular peak in net capital formation—occurred in the early 1880's; the crest in the stock of capital itself seems to have been reached in the early 1930's. But in the years between 1931 and 1950, the railroads did not progress very far along the following stage. In this period the constant dollar value of road and equipment declined from 24.1 to 22.6 billion, or by less than 10 per cent.

The remaining components—electric power, local bus lines, and the all other regulated industries group—were ranged between these extremes. They had all passed, though at widely different times, the first stage in the model pattern of development—that is, the point at which net capital formation changes over from an increasing to a decreasing rate of advance. But in electric power and the all other group the signs of maturity went no further. In both, the rate of growth in 1950 was still very brisk, and the upward trend in net capital formation showed no clear indication of a termination. Local bus lines, on the other hand, proceeded one stage further in the model: in the late 1930's it passed the point at which the secular path of net investment reached a peak. Of course the stock of capital continued to head upward in subsequent years, for investment in buses remained substantial; but the rise from a secular point of view proceeded by diminishing amounts.

In one respect there is agreement among *all* components in the secular trends in the stock of reproducible capital. In all cases, the *relative* rate of growth diminished, and from a very early date in the history of each. Taking changes over successive long cycles, the secular rate of advance in the regulated industries in the aggregate dropped from 3 per cent per annum to 1.6 per cent and finally to less than 0.1 per cent annually. In the railroads there was a drop from 2 per cent to less than 1 per cent and finally to a slightly negative annual change. Electric light and power dropped from an annual increase of nearly 20 per cent during the first cycle to about 5 per cent in the second and to less than 1 per cent in the third.

Over the entire time span, in telephones there was a reduction from a rate of nearly 12 per cent to one of less than 3 per cent, and in electric railways from an 8 per cent per annum rise to an average annual decline of nearly 6 per cent. Local bus lines, during its brief history dropped from an average increase of nearly 40 per cent to one of less than 8 per cent. Only in the all other group was the decline anything but constantly progressive. In this case the rate of growth remained unchanged at slightly more than 3 per cent during the first two cycles, and then dropped to 0.5 per cent in the final swing. Though inevitable, ultimately, in any industry, the early incidence of the tendency toward a retarded rate of growth was attributed in the body of this report to special characteristics surrounding the genesis of the regulated segment.

Barring a dramatic alteration in the average life of capital, the trend just described implies a necessary relationship over time between net capital formation and capital consumption. Unavoidably, the latter must match the former at a very early date, and then spring far ahead. Such was the case in the aggregate of the regulated industries and in each of the components. In the decade of the 1940's, when investment was extraordinarily high, capital consumption in the total of the regulated industries was three times as great as net capital formation; in the railroads it was twenty-five times, in local bus lines and the all other group three times, and in electric power two times as great as net capital formation. In telephones they were equal, but in tribute to the surge of investment in the last decade covered by our study, it was the first time since the 1890's that net capital formation had been so large in relation to capital consumption. Thus in all components in recent years (street railways remained in the process of contraction), large replacement requirements were the dominant element in the gross flow of capital. It is significant that an investment of nearly two billion 1929 dollars was required annually in the 1940's simply to keep the physical stock of capital of the regulated industries intact, and that more than one-fourth of the two billion was accounted for by railroads.

As suggested, the trend in the gross flow of capital presents a relatively buoyant picture. Even in the railroads, the sharp downward movement evident in net investment is almost obliterated in gross capital formation. In all other components except street railways, the trend of gross investment was distinctly upward. In the aggregate of the regulated industries, it leaped from less than 500 million 1929 dollars per annum in the 1870's to 2.6 billion in the 1920's and to more than 3.0 billion per annum in the years immediately following World War II. In the latter period it represented from 25 to 30 per cent of the national total of gross capital expenditures on plant and equipment by all nonagricultural industry.

Secular Trends in Production

The model pattern of growth employed in the analysis of capital formation may also be applied to production. In this framework, output is analogous to the stock of capital, and changes in output are analogous to net capital formation. The trends in these two categories, in general, differ widely but systematically. In particular, the regulated industries appear considerably less mature when judged by the behavior of production rather than by that of capital formation. In the aggregate, output of the regulated industries rose by progressively increasing amounts throughout the 1880–1950 span for which records are available. So did the increments in output. Trends of the same kind prevailed in telephones, electric power, and the all other group. The latter two components, as well as the aggregate of the regulated industries, had been in an appreciably later stage of development when appraised from the standpoint of capital formation. At least they had each reached the point at which net capital formation (analogous to output increments) had ceased to rise by increasing amounts.

Railroads and local bus lines ranked on a par when judged by the production maturity standard, each having completed the first two stages of the model pattern. In both cases the secular trend of production in the 1940's remained upward, but its rise progressed at a diminishing rate. In the railroads, it will be recalled, the stock of capital had reached its peak in the early 1930's. Local bus lines—alone among the components, except for telephones—reached the same stage of growth in output and in capital formation. Street railways had a slightly more youthful look in the production framework, though output in 1950 was heading secularly downward, and had been tending in this direction for at least twenty-five years.

Thus the relative rank of the industries with respect to maturity is nearly the same when judged by the behavior of production as by that of capital formation. But in the former framework, the various components appear to be in significantly earlier stages of development, reflecting systematic changes in their respective capital coefficients. The most striking feature in the behavior of their production in the aggregate, however, was the vigor of its rise. Measured in 1929 dollars, it rose from a little more than one billion in the 1880's to nearly twelve billion in the 1920's and to nearly twenty-six billion in the 1940's. Of course, over almost the entire 1880–1950 period the *relative* rate of increase in output diminished—

in the aggregate and in each of the components. But as might be expected from the trend patterns already defined, the reductions were not quite as great as the corresponding ones in capital formation, and the rates of increase prevailing were generally higher.

Capital Coefficients

It is thus apparent that capital formation failed by a considerable margin to reflect the full vigor of the growth of output. The coefficients relating these variables were patently subject to constant change. In the analysis of this relationship, two concepts were distinguished: the average and marginal capital-product ratios. The first may be defined as $\frac{C}{O}$, where C is the stock of reproducible capital and O is the volume of output, both measured in constant dollars. The marginal capital-product ratio may be defined as the ratio between the change in the stock of reproducible capital and the change in output, similarly measured—i.e. as $\frac{\Delta C}{\Delta O}$.

Over the seventy-year period for which records are available, the trends of average and marginal capital-product ratios in the regulated industries are marked by abrupt decline. The average ratio in the aggregate dropped from about 12 in the 1880's to 6.5 at the turn of the century, to 3.5 in the 1920's, and to 1.7 in 1950. In railroads the reduction was also continuous—and at a diminishing rate—throughout the period of study, after allowance for cyclical variations, dropping over the span from 16 in the 1880's to 3 in 1950. In the other components the reductions were more irregular, totally apart from those fluctuations common to them all, which stem from cyclical revisions in the level of business activity. In telephones and electric power, the first decade of operation was characterized by a rise in the ratio. So were the earlier years in street railways in which electrification was accomplished. Significant interruptions in the long-run decline occurred in addition in electric power in the first twelve years of the twentieth century, and in telephones in the late 1920's and 1930's. Nevertheless, the over-all reductions were extensive: from the 1890's to 1950, the ratio dropped from 15 to 2 in electric power, from 5 to somewhat less than 2 in telephones, from 6 to 2 in street railways, and from 10 to 1 in the all other group. Moreover, the trends in general exhibited the common characteristic of gradually losing momentum. In the aggregate, in railroads, and for most of the period in electric power, they were described with considerable accuracy by the downward branch of a Gompertz curve.

Only in local bus lines is there a material departure from the general pattern, though it must be borne in mind that the history of the industry is very brief. In this component the ratio rose from about 0.5 in the mid-1920's to 1.7 in 1950. Part of this advance was due to short-run factors relating to the war and its aftermath; but part was also due to distinctive characteristics of this component.

The trend of the *marginal* capital-product ratio was also downward in every industry group except local bus lines. Measuring changes from peak to peak in the first long cycle and from peak to peak in the last of the long swings in the 1880–1950 span, the ratio declined from 9 to 0.4 in the aggregate of all regulated industries, from 10 to —0.2 in railroads, from 17 to 0.6 in electric power, from 5 to 2 in telephones, from 6 to 4 in street railways, and from 11 to 0.4 in the all other group. The negative ratio during the last cycle in the railroads indicates that during the years 1927 through 1950 output increased while the stock of capital was being contracted. Thus, with a minor exception, advances in output over the period were accompanied by progressively smaller amounts of capital formation —in each of the regulated industries as well as in the aggregate. And the dimension of this change in the long-run relationship between demand for final product and investment was very substantial.

It may be noted that the average capital-product ratio in the regulated industries has in all periods greatly exceeded that prevailing in other segments of the economy, although in the light of the trends described above, the differences have diminished over time. In manufacturing in 1948 the capital-product ratio was 0.65, compared with 1.7 in the regulated industries. In mining the ratio was 1.3. Differences in the amount of capital *consumed* per dollar of output, however, are much smaller than the disparities would suggest. The average life of capital is appreciably longer in the regulated industries than in either of the other two segments.

Underlying Factors

As suggested above, the secular behavior of net capital formation may be illumined by an analysis of factors which appear to shape the long-run trends in output increments and in the marginal capital-product ratio. We proceed to a summary of these factors.

OUTPUT

In the early days of the regulated industries a rate of growth was established far greater than that of any possible long-run sustaining factors. This is recorded distinctly for each of our components. For example, in the 1890's, shortly after the beginnings of electric power, its output amounted to 31 cents per person in the United States,

0.07 per cent of the gross national product, and 0.2 per cent of our rough measure of urban income. A decade later per capita output had increased five times, its proportion of the gross national product had quadrupled, and its proportion of urban income had tripled. Similar spectacular advances were made in the same period by the budding telephone industry and by street railways, which as a virtually new industry was in the process of electrification.

Here is a manifestation of what we have termed the vacuum effect. It is characterized by the rush of resources into a segment of the economy in which profit opportunities appear extraordinarily high. Its power is always great, though it must depend, ultimately, on the size, flexibility, and mobility of available resources, and on the relative magnitude of the demands made upon them. It is fed by the overthrow of the competitive opposition of older industries. It is nurtured also by an income elasticity of demand which in a new industry, destined for success, is almost certain for a time to exceed the critical level of unity. It is ensured, temporarily at least, by the fact that the earliest productive units established will fall far short of the capacity the market may at the time successfully absorb. This is a virtual technological necessity in a nation as large and as sprawling as the United States, and is only reinforced by the fact that caution and experiment are typical business characteristics. Moreover, far-reaching technological improvements are almost certain in an industry's earlier years, and add even further to its powers of expansion. In the face of a potential market which is obviously growing swiftly and is far above the level that existing facilities can exploit, innovators extend capacity as rapidly as possible. Reports of their successes attract imitators from an ever-wider range. Capital is risked with steadily mounting confidence. All these factors in concert push output forward at a rate far in excess of the growth of the nation's aggregate purchasing power, urbanization, or any other factor which in the long run could sustain it. This was true, in the earlier years, of all the components of the regulated industries.

So great was the power of the vacuum effect in the regulated industries that some ultimate decline in the relative rate of growth was inevitable in later years. However, the performance of the components studied varied greatly. In some, a number of "invigorating" factors served to support the pace of output at a relatively high level throughout the period of study. In others, "retarding" influences gained the upper hand. Among the invigorating factors were:

1. The development of new uses for the product. In this category

was the gradual extension in the uses of electricity to stoves, refrigerators, dishwashers, and a variety of other household and industrial appliances.

2. Virtual immunity from competition. For technical as well as institutional reasons, telephone service was so situated.

3. Technological innovations and mass production. These encouraged consumption by permitting price reductions relative to the general price level.

4. Propitious social changes making for favorable shifts in consumer tastes. One change was the swift pace of urbanization in the United States, with favorable impact on nearly all of the regulated industries.

All of the invigorating factors were especially influential in the development of the electric power and telephone industries. Owing to their effects, the early swift rise of output in the two components was extended so that throughout the 1880–1950 span production rose at an ever-increasing absolute rate. But even in these vigorously growing components, retarding influences were manifest, though always overshadowed. Contrariwise, in our other components the invigorating influences were weak and the retarding factors stronger, so that the pace of production was perceptibly dampened and—as we have seen—these industries moved farther along the model pattern of growth on the road to maturity. The retarding influences were:

1. Ultimately, the older related industries were completely crushed, or thrust into a smaller facet of their function, which for some reason remained impregnable. Future advances, then, could not be fed by business stripped from competitors.

2. Once mass distribution had been attained, the income elasticity of demand tended to decline. This stemmed, in part, from the complete routing of older competition and the achievement of at least temporary market saturation. Future advances, at best, were thus limited only to those arising from national growth

3. Younger industries producing related goods or services ultimately arose to offer competition.

4. The very power of the vacuum effect tended to induce some later reduction in the rate of growth of output. The longer it lasted, the greater grew the danger of overextension.

Production of all industries in their earliest years expanded far more rapidly than the gross national product or even urban income. In electric light and power and in telephones this condition persisted throughout the 1880–1950 span. Nevertheless, even in these vigorously growing components, retarding influences were at least modestly in evidence. For electric utilities, there was the competition of public power. For telephones there was some indication of market saturation—i.e. a declining elasticity of demand, both with respect to price and income. Hence the differential in the rate of growth of the two industries, over their long-run sustaining factors, was gradually and quite significantly narrowed, although in both cases the rate continued slightly above that of urban income. For the special invigorating factors, so pronounced, had barely begun to peter out.

Railroads, street railways, and local bus lines lack the virtual immunity from competition characteristic of telephones. They also lack the technical resiliency which has enabled electric light and power to find a succession of new uses. Their older competitors—canals, horse-drawn vehicles, etc.—had long since been routed. The vacuum effect in these components subsided at an early date in the period of our study, and invigorating influences, tending to prolong swift growth, were weak. Thus, new competition proved swiftly crushing for street railways and slowly but firmly limited the growth of the railroads. For local bus lines, the chief retarding factor appears to have been a declining income elasticity of demand.

Accordingly, in 1950 production by street railways amounted to 0.2 per cent of the gross national product, less than one-sixth of the proportion prevailing just before World War I. For railroads the rate of increase in output dropped from one which far exceeded that of the gross national product before World War I to one which did little more than match the growth of population. In 1950 railroad output amounted to about fifty-six dollars per person, at 1929 prices, approximately the same as thirty years earlier. The rate of growth of production by local bus lines had also fallen significantly below that of the gross national product. Of course, during the period of the vacuum effect, growth in all three had been sufficiently great to exceed even that of the swiftly advancing *urban* income.

It may be noted that the growth of production in the all other group of regulated industries topped that of the gross national product and of urban income throughout the 1880–1950 span, reflecting the development of new industries. For all regulated industries in the aggregate, production rose from 7 per cent of the gross national product in 1890 to 12 per cent in 1910, to 14 per cent in 1930, and to 17 per cent in 1950, remembering that output is here measured as gross of the materials consumed. The pace of this advance was also greater than that of urban income up to the time of World War I; from that date onward the ratio of the output of all regulated industries to urban income was virtually steady.

CAPITAL-PRODUCT RATIOS

Underlying the trend of the capital-product ratio in the regulated industries was a definite sequence of events which was common to all components. The variations in capital-product ratio trends observed among the different segments are attributable to differences in the intensity and duration of the elements of this sequence. The general pattern may be described in terms of these stages.

Initially, there was a period of gestation in which preparatory investment was made on a wide scale, and many large indivisible units were started and only gradually brought to completion. This inaugural build-up was unusually large in the regulated industries, for a number of reasons including technological characteristics, the distant horizons envisaged by utility-builders, and the speculation which was rife at this stage in some of the components. Of course, actual output in this period was necessarily small, and the capital-product ratio rose.

But this introductory stage was, by nature, short-lived. It could last only so long as *new* plants were established at a faster pace than output rose in facilities that were brought to completion. The duration was less than a decade in the regulated industries for which relevant data are available. Furthermore, it should be recalled that in the *aggregate* of utilities this initial increase in the ratio for electric light and power, for telephones, and for electric railways was overshadowed by the sharp decline simultaneously in progress for the older industries—especially steam railroads and some of the older components included in the all other group. The capital-product ratio in the regulated industries as a whole accordingly moved downward throughout the 1880–1950 span. In manufacturing, the initial period of extensive expansion, characterized by the rise of a multitude of new firms and new industries, was accompanied and followed by the sweep of pervasive capital-demanding innovations which were the earmark of the industrial revolution. As a result the capital-product ratio remained on the rise until World War I or somewhat later.

The second stage of the pattern is a natural outgrowth of the first and followed swiftly in the regulated industries. Once many large installations were completed, output was free to expand with relatively little additional investment necessary. The capital-product ratio was therefore profoundly depressed.

In the third stage the drop in the capital-product ratio was perpetuated. Capital-saving inventions enhanced the efficiency of plant and equipment. These took the form, primarily, of piecemeal improvements in existing facilities. In some cases, the physical capital stock was also put to more economical use. In addition, the growing relative importance of capital consumption, in the company of general technological advance, ensured that the stock of capital would be replaced at a progressively faster rate with units capable of greater productive service. Finally, the expansion of accrued depreciation served to depress the *net* stock of capital, as ordinarily measured, in relation to that actually in use. For all of the foregoing reasons the capital-product ratio continued downward even after the influences at work in the second stage had completely lost their force. It is certain that these factors were significant not only in the regulated industries, but—in whole or in part—in many other major segments of the economy; for, at least since the 1920's, the downward trend of the capital-product ratio was nationwide.

From the general pattern described there are, to be sure, deviations. Even after the first stage of the pattern had ended, capital-*using* innovations occurred in the regulated industries and resulted, for a time, in rising capital-product ratios. This was the case in the early 1900's in electric light and power, and in the mid-1920's in telephones. But such deviations in the seventy-year experience of our industries have proved temporary. The dominating, pervading factor among utilities in the long run, once the initial period of gestation had been surmounted, was the steady flow of capital-*saving* devices and the persevering drop in the capital-product ratio. Among our components, the only one in which this general trend did not hold was local bus lines. Here, special characteristics of the industry, together with the particular events of the World War II period and its aftermath, served to maintain a rising capital-product ratio throughout the industry's relatively brief history.

In general, the *extent* of the decline in the capital-product ratio was closely correlated among industries throughout the nation, including the regulated segment, with the initial standing of the ratio. The highest ratios declined the most. This development appears to be due to three factors: (1) Those components in which particularly high capital-product ratios were achieved were the very ones in which capital is characterized by a high degree of indivisibility. In such industries, the way is smoothly paved for a subsequent and particularly sharp reduction in capital-product ratios as output expands in later years. (2) The more diverse the physical stock of capital of an industry, the greater the chance that scientific advances will result in improving its efficiency. Insofar as diversity is correlated with the relative size of capital installations, this increases the *opportunity* for improving capital efficiency in capital-extensive industries. (3) There is no upper limit to the capital-product ratio, though there is a lower limit at least at zero, and as a practical matter somewhat above zero. Accordingly, at their peak, capital-product ratios may be widely scattered. But as they decline, the presence of a lower limit tends to reduce their dispersion.

The influence of wage and interest rates upon the long-run trend of capital-product ratios in the regulated industries appears to have been secondary. Both rising and declining capital-product ratios were accompanied by advances in labor's productivity, with little, if any, significant difference in degree. Hence, the stimulus to economies in the use of labor provided by rising wage rates could—and did—find satisfactory outlets in *both* capital-saving and capital-using innovations. Progressive reductions in interest rates would (other things being equal) encourage investment in general, and would facilitate a rise in the capital-product ratio in particular *if such an advance were generated by other forces*. But on the other hand a decline in the cost of money capital would not in any way inhibit a *reduction* in the capital-product ratio if it were induced by technological or other conditions. Accordingly, neither the influence of wage rates nor of interest rates appeared to play a crucial role in determining the secular pattern of the capital-product ratio in the regulated industries.

CAPITAL FORMATION

The secular progress of capital formation is thus the result of the two streams of events already described: (1) those which determine the secular pattern of output and (2) those which determine the secular pattern of the capital-product ratio. In the early stage of development of the regulated industries, investment was generated in huge dimensions because of the combined operation of the vacuum effect upon output and the rise in the capital-product ratio characteristic of the gestation period. But after this period—and very soon after for most components—the situation altered materially. The effect of increases in demand for final product upon investment was significantly dampened by progressive reductions in the marginal capital-product ratio. Besides, numerous forces combined to retard the growth of output. In general, over the long run, there was a tendency for capital formation to follow the pattern of output, but it was in the main a less vigorous version because of the declining capital-product ratio. Though production in the aggregate of the regulated industries persistently outdistanced the gross national product throughout the period of record, investment, at least in the later years, barely maintained the much more leisurely pace of the growth of the population.

Long Cycles

The capital formation of the regulated industries is characterized by pronounced long cycles—a fact which at every point materially complicated the task of defining long-term trends. The cycles lasted on the average about twenty years. Their amplitude was considerable—averaging in expansions about 70 per cent, and in contractions about 40 per cent of the average annual investment during the cycles as a whole. A chronological as well as a cross section (by industry) analysis of these fluctuations yielded the following pattern. In the earlier days of a regulated industry long cycles were barely evident in the progress of investment, if they appeared at all. Later, the broad vigorous expansion was interrupted by modest contractions. Gradually, the contractions deepened while expansions tended to grow weaker. It was through this process of cyclical behavior that the sharp upward slope of the secular growth trend slowly diminished, and ultimately yielded to descension.

Chronologically, however, the tendency for expansions to weaken over time was offset in part by certain other economy-wide alterations in the environment, so that the magnitude of cycles taken as a whole increased progressively over the 1870–1950 span. In the post-World War I period, the swings in the regulated industries were paralleled by corresponding movements in the general level of business activity as measured by the gross national product. In these years, cycles in the two series were reinforcing. Prior to World War I long cycles in the gross national product appear primarily as swings in the secular *rate* of growth, and are not pronounced in the absolute figures. Furthermore, insofar as they do appear, their timing is not the same as in the regulated industries.

Though unmistakable in capital formation, long cycles are not pronounced in the output or in the annual output increments of the regulated industries. However, similar fluctuations—with almost precisely the same timing—are found in residential construction and in annual population increments.

Analysis of the duration of long cycles, together with the average life of capital and the variations about this average, suggests that they cannot be attributed to the periodic reinvestment impulses investigated by Johan Einarsen. The transport-building cycle hypothesis of Walter Isard was also rejected on the grounds that (1) it was impossible to tie each long cycle to a specific transportation innovation as the theory requires, and (2) a hypothesized relationship was lacking between the timing of cycles in the regulated industries and in the general level of business activity. It was suggested that further work along two lines in this area might prove fruitful. One would be to explore the connection between swings in population increments, the gross national product, and investment in the regulated industries and in housing, as proposed by Kuznets. The other would concern certain tendencies toward long swings inherent in the characteristics of the regulated industries and residential construction, and the nature of the impact of major business cycles upon investment in this setting. In line with the latter hypothesis, long swings in the investment of the regulated industries would be interpreted as a manifestation of the interaction between this segment and business activity in the economy as a whole, conditioned by institutional properties peculiar to the segment. Among these properties are the high durability and great indivisibility of the capital used, the tendency to "bunch" orders of even the more divisible capital units, the cumbersome nature of capital budgeting and financing practices, and the considerable length of the average capital construction period. All these factors inhibit swift reversals in the direction of investment.

Finance

The physical growth of the regulated industries over the span from 1870 to 1950 was coupled with an expanding need for money capital. The rise in the flow of money capital was further supported, however, by the secular upward drift in the price level over the eighty-year span, and by the advances in the *relative* prices of capital goods. In current prices, the gross capital expenditures of the regulated industries amounted to between 200 and 300 million dollars per year in the 1870's and 1880's; by 1950 they aggregated 6.4 billion dollars. The value in current dollars of their stock of plant and equipment approached 80 billion at the beginning of 1950, against about 5 billion in the 1870's. In the financing of the huge capital requirements implied by these figures, two outstanding changes occurred over the eighty years for which data were assembled. First, there was a gradual, steady, and pronounced shift from external to internal financing. Second, there was a shift in the *form* of external financing from stocks to bonds.

Over the period of record, which differed somewhat among the several components, the proportion of internal sources to total sources of funds rose from 2 to 100 per cent for the railroads, from 8 to 50 per cent for electric power, from 6 to 41 per cent for telephones, and from 1 to 14 per cent for street railways. These changes were analyzed in terms of the equation:

$$r = \frac{ab + k}{\alpha + \beta}$$

where r is the proportion of all sources of capital provided by retained profits and depreciation, a is the ratio of net savings to profits, b is the ratio of profits to total assets in current prices, k is the ratio of depreciation charges to total assets in current prices, α is the ratio of net capital flow to total assets in current prices, and β is the ratio of capital consumption at replacement cost to total assets in current prices.

Other things equal, the formula shows that the rate of internal financing (r) will vary *directly* with the net savings rate (a), with the profit rate (b) and with the depreciation rate (k). It will vary *inversely* with the net rate of capital flow (α) and the rate of capital consumption (β). Experimentally, it was possible to test the influence of some of these factors separately.

It was found that the rise in the rate of internal financing in the regulated industries was attributable in the main to two factors: (1) The need for correcting the initial deficiencies in capital consumption allowances which existed in the earlier years of our period of study. Depreciation charges in the latter decades of the nineteenth century were by a substantial margin inadequate to provide for the prevailing rate of capital consumption. (2) The expanding importance of capital consumption relative to *all* uses of capital over the period of study, springing from the retarded rate of growth of total assets. The latter trend mirrored, primarily, the retarded rate of growth of output together with the declining capital-product ratio.

Thus, alluding to our first factor, even if the regulated industries' rate of growth had been unchanged over the seventy years studied, a substantial increase in the rate of internal financing would have been necessary to cover replacement. This factor alone would have been sufficient to boost the gross retention rate from 2 to 42 per cent in railroads, from less than 8 to 24 per cent in electric power, from 6 to 30 per cent in telephones, and from one to 27 per cent in street railways. When the second factor—retarded rate of growth over the period—is taken into account, a possible explanation is provided for the *entirety* of the observed rise in the rate of internal financing. Thus, it was found that the influence of the decline in the net rate of capital flow was sufficient to induce a further boost in the gross retention rate of from 42 to 92 per cent in railroads, from 24 to 58 per cent in electric power, from 30 to 46 per cent in telephones, and from 27 to 150 per cent in street railways. In the first three components the aggregate "hypothetical" advance in the retention rate was roughly the same as had actually occurred over the period 1880–1950. In street railways the hypothetical advance was much greater than the actual one, indicating that in the later years in this component internally generated funds were insufficient to meet capital consumption requirements. This situation was symptomatic of both the financial difficulties which many street railways were then encountering and of the fact that this component was in the process of contraction.

The shift in the *form* of external financing, from stocks to bonds, was also pronounced and pervasive. The use of long-term debt is—and always has been—far greater in the regulated industries than in the other segments of the economy. It is encouraged by the form of public regulation as well as by certain other characteristics of these components. Its extension over time probably reflected in part the growth of public regulation in addition to the shift toward internal financing which boosted the value of existing equity claims. The trend was further promoted by certain economy-wide influences such as the adoption and subsequent rise in the corporation income tax. But the importance of special factors is attested by the much more pronounced trend evident in the regulated industries. The proportion of external funds secured through bonds in the railroads rose from 56 per cent in the 1880's to 70 per cent in the 1920's, after which external sources in general sank to negligible dimensions. In electric power the rise was from 43 per cent in the years before 1912 to 58 per cent in the 1940's. In telephones bonds accounted for 22 per cent of net new issues in the 1890's and for 85 per cent in the 1940's. In the brief span of the expansion of street railways, bonds advanced from 44 to 100 per cent of the external sources of long-term capital. Reflecting these trends, the relative importance of bonds in the capital structure by the 1940's was three times greater in the regulated industries than in all other nonfinancial corporations.

The Outlook

Despite the economic, political, and social turbulence of the eighty years from 1870 to 1950, the continuity of development in the regulated industries over this period is impressive. Our analysis disclosed the evolution of economic patterns of several kinds, embodying the intricate sequences of secular growth. The patterns themselves may be viewed as chains, in which the links from beginning to end are related events over successive units of time. In our segment of study, no breaks are revealed in these chains—no sudden discontinuities in which the events of one period of time are divorced from all perceptible relationship with those which have gone before, or those which come later. It is from this point of view that something may be said of the secular growth of the regulated industries in the years ahead. For knowledge of the factors which have shaped development in the 1870–1950 period must necessarily illumine long-run prospects.

We shall now focus briefly on the outlook through 1975. No specific forecast will be attempted. The problems involved in such an undertaking would extend well beyond the boundaries established for this study. The discussion will be confined to reflections, primarily qualitative, concerning the identity, power, and direction of the principal forces likely to shape the growth of the regulated industries over the twenty years ahead. A reasonably concise discussion necessitates the assumption that over the years through 1975 there will be no major wars.

One lesson from the past is that the *simplest* projections of the future are nearly certain to be seriously defective. To suggest, for example, that investment in the regulated industries will proceed in the future at the same percentage rate as that which prevailed in some period of the past would ignore the role of long cycles, the connection between demand for final product and capital formation, the susceptibility of the capital-product ratio to change, and the shifting role of other factors such as technology and competition in different stages of development. By the same token, some other popular and somewhat more sophisticated approaches are ruled out. Thus, to project output of the regulated industries at some constant ratio to the gross national product or to population would violate the pattern of the past in which such relationships have been subject to constant modification. And to derive investment from this projection by applying the currently prevailing capital-product ratio would ignore the virtual certainty that this ratio in the future will differ materially. In accord with the logic of our own historical analysis, an effort to illumine the future of investment must be directed, initially, to the factors underlying demand for final product.

Fundamental, of course, is the future growth of the nation as a whole. But even if some plausible assumptions are made concerning the growth of the population and its income, an analysis of the probable role of the regulated industries must grapple with a host of specific circumstances conditioning their relative behavior. The particular influences—summarized in the vacuum effect—which generated the spectacular advance in the years prior to World War I have obviously disappeared for all major components. Hence, a conflict of invigorating and retarding factors remains to be appraised. Virtually by definition, the latter are in ascension and the former in decline in established industries. Diminishing rates of growth in production are universal among our components. And in some, reductions are in progress relative to the nation's growth. But differences in degree of retardation are enormous.

Output in the street railway component has for some time tended downward absolutely, and no element of importance in past development can be employed for supporting a reversal of this trend. No grounds exist for supposing that the competition of the other means of transportation will abate. Nor is there any likelihood that the range of innovation possible within the framework of street railways can overcome the fundamental advantages of competitors. The general pattern of growth described earlier, however, suggests one alteration in the pace of the decline of this component. The absolute reductions in output from year to year should diminish. This would continue a tendency noticeable in the immediate past. It reflects simply the fact that the industry is reduced gradually to a smaller number of remaining strongholds in which street railways enjoy some particularly favorable adaptation, or in which bus lines and passenger cars face unusual obstacles which are but slowly surmounted. The industry's progress to ultimate extinction thus becomes more and more reluctant.

In much diminished degree, railroads also face progressive encroachment from competitors. But output in this component remained secularly upward throughout the period of study. Will this pace be maintained over the next twenty years? Here we encounter not only the fundamental advantages of competitors, but certain basic advantages retained by the component itself. The rate of expansion in the output of the railroads had been reduced to well below the pace of the gross national product to approximately—since World War I—the rate of growth of the population. The inherent advantages of trucks and air transportation herald further inroads. None of those factors which we have termed invigorating is likely in the case of the railroads to spur an accelerated extension of activity. On the other hand, some facets of remaining business—e.g. long hauls for bulky and heavy commodities—are more nearly impregnable than others. It would not conflict with past patterns of growth to suppose that the output of the railroads will continue upward over the next twenty years, nor to suppose that the pace of its advance will become subject to further retardation. Indeed, an extension in this segment of the trend toward retardation in the rate of growth poses the possibility of a decline before 1975 in railroad output per capita. This would not preclude future substantial increases in the absolute volume of railroad output, for they will depend in part upon the trend in population itself.

Continued growth, though at a materially slower pace, seems also in prospect for local bus lines. For the most important invigorating factor present in the early days of this industry had by 1950 been sharply reduced in importance. This was the presence of numerous cities in which streetcars had not yet been replaced by buses. By the 1950's, the opposition had been almost completely crushed. Also, on the retarding side, it appeared that with higher incomes American families were depending in greater degree upon the private passenger car for local transportation. The pace in the advance in local bus lines had begun to fall behind that of the gross national product. It still remained above that of the growth of population. Perhaps it will converge with the latter, or possibly dip somewhat lower in the score of years ahead, under the pressure of an income elasticity of demand materially less than unity. This is the prospect indicated, if we assume that the direction of the forces now influencing demand in this component are by nature irreversible. Perhaps the most important possibility of reversibility lies in the competitive relation between the bus and the private passenger automobile. If traffic conditions worsen, and the use of private cars is limited further, the bus will be the chief benefactor. (See note 10, page 92.)

This leaves the three most vigorously growing components—electric power, telephones, and the all other group. In all three cases the pace of growth was geared more closely to that of urbanization than to the somewhat slower rate of expansion of the gross national product. Nevertheless, the differential had narrowed progressively. In telephones the principal retarding influence was apparently gradual market saturation. Increases in national income lent a progressively weaker stimulus to output as an ever larger proportion had acquired access to, and used, communication facilities. Continuance of past trends for this component would suggest a reduction in the rate of growth over the period ahead to a level not much above that of the population.

Evidence of retardation was less pronounced in electric power. A rise more rapid than that of population appears assured for some time to come by the wide expansion in household uses gradually extending throughout the country. Industrial uses might also be somewhat further extended if it becomes technically possible to reduce costs through the application of atomic energy. Yet it would appear that the size of the electric power industry must depend more and more upon the growth of the nation itself. The special invigorating influences of its earlier days—such as the vacuum effect, the crushing of competition, radical innovations of the basic technological framework—have either passed entirely or have been materially diminished in degree. The expansion of public power, while limited, is a retarding factor which must not be overlooked. A growth rate much in excess of that of the gross national product, therefore, could persist only if some important *new* uses for electric power were developed. In the absence of these, in the decades ahead, the output of electric power should continue to converge toward that of the gross national product; in so doing, of course, it would continue a trend long in progress.

With respect to the prospects of the heterogeneous all other group, of course, less can be said of specific character. Experience would suggest, however, that if any new industry were developed in the immediate future to become part of this group, it would require considerably more than twenty years to assume substantial importance among the regulated industries in the aggregate—particularly since no such industry is now on the horizon. The declining rate of growth of the group as it stands has evidenced the passing of the vacuum effect in some of the leading elements such as trucking and air transportation. But the persistent vigor of these and some of the other industries included, such as gas utilities, has limited the decline in the group's rate of growth narrowly. Even in the course of the most recent years this component's expansion has outdistanced that of the economy as a whole by a considerable amount. A continuation of the modest decline in its rate of growth over the next twenty years would leave it still somewhat above the pace maintained by the gross national product over the last several decades.

Thus the general pattern of development, as shaped in the past, suggests for the next twenty years, taken as a whole, a brisk and continued expansion in output for the regulated industries in the aggregate. The limits of the rise, prospectively, are set by the pace of the growth of the nation. Barring some presently unforeseeable change, it is difficult to conceive, against the background of the past, of a future advance in the total output of the regulated industries much smaller than that of the population, or much greater than that of the gross national product. This at least is the promise implied by the patterns of the past, after allowance for the secular changes in progress or in view. Though brisk, a rise within these limits would imply a materially slower pace, relative to the nation's growth, than that which had prevailed secularly at any time previously. This slackening in the advance of the regulated industries mirrors the waning of invigorating factors and the rise of the forces of retardation which have been the faithful concomitants of maturity in the past.

In appraising the outlook for investment, however, the growth in demand for final product is no more important than the technical relationship likely to hold between product and capital. Will the decline in the capital-product ratio—in progress for so long in the regulated industries—continue in the years ahead? If so, will its reduction proceed at a rate which matches, or materially exceeds, or falls short of, that of the past? Such questions become susceptible to at least general answers in the present context only if it is understood that reference, as throughout this discussion, is to secular movements. For both the average and the marginal capital-product ratios fluctuate widely over short periods of time in response to cyclical and other short-range factors.

The decline in the capital-product ratio in progress in more recent years in all of the regulated industries segregated in this analysis, except local bus lines, has been attributable to capital-saving innovations. In a larger sense, it represents a concluding chapter in a technological pattern, a phase of scattered improvements within an over-all framework which, itself, has embodied the most advanced basic scientific achievements currently available. Only a technological *revolution*—a fundamental change in the framework itself—can seriously disturb this pattern, and launch a prolonged *advance* in the capital-product ratio. Such a revolution would be tantamount to the rise of a new industry in the place of the old. There is no evidence of so radical a change in the offing in the regulated industry segment.

Even substantial interruptions (aside, of course, from cyclical changes) to the reduction of the capital-product ratio have been uncommon. The incorporation of atomic energy in the generation of electricity could conceivably occasion in the electric power component a material deviation of this kind from the longer-term trend. But this would reflect a mere period of build-up—during which capital is created and not yet brought into use. Such periods are by nature short-lived, as we have seen. The use of atomic energy in this setting, since it would leave the basic structure of the electric power industry intact, does not promise to be capital-demanding from a long-run standpoint. This at least is the prospect suggested by plans now taking shape in the industry. In a situation in which technological applications are still so amorphous, however, well-grounded predictions over any extended period of the future are not possible. Nothing in the nature of atomic energy rules out the development of capital-demanding uses, and it may well be that some will materialize within the next twenty years in connection with one or more of the industries under review.

Nevertheless, in the light of prospects now in view, something may be said in support of a continued stream of capital-saving innovations in the years ahead, in extension of the trend under way for so long in the regulated industries. We might expect, of course, that the pace of the decline in the capital-product ratio in the future will be less pronounced than in the past. For we have observed the close correlation between the level of the ratio and the extent of its subsequent decline; we have noted the factors underlying this phenomenon; and we have witnessed the retardation of its descent in recent years. But the continuance of its decline, albeit at a diminished rate, is more likely than a rise in the same sense that technological revolutions are less frequent—and more dramatically foreshadowed—than a multiplicity of minor technical refinements. There are no distinct and present signs of imminent revolutions of this kind.

Not that the capital-saving innovations are necessarily undramatic. The widely heralded "automation" of industrial processes consists primarily of capital-saving devices. Thus, the construction of electronic railroad classification yards, which at present writing is mainly in the planning stage, promises immense economies in the use of freight cars. As has been true historically of most capital-saving devices, the innovation will likewise reduce manpower requirements. Generalized, this trend promises that the impact upon investment of future advances in the demand for final product are likely to be substantially modified by the changing technical relations between capital and output. The general patterns previously described illumine the probable dimensions of this effect. Net capital formation in the regulated industries in the aggregate had in recent years fallen appreciably below the pace of the advance of the total population; i.e. the per capita value of plant and equipment dropped materially. Owing to the retardation in the growth of output, as well as the diminishing capital-product ratio, this decline may proceed in the future. In absolute terms also, the advance in net capital formation had lost much of its earlier vigor; the secular *rate of increase* has clearly dropped since about 1910, and the trend in the volume of net investment itself appears to have been nearly horizontal since that date. The general conclusions reached above all point to an intensification of these signs of secular weakness—barring, of course, a radical upward shift in the pace of the long-term growth of the economy as a whole. Mention must be made, too, of a second fundamental qualification implicit in our analysis. Technological developments may of course arise at any time, and may be of sufficient import to alter significantly the capital-product ratio, the rate of obsolescence on existing capital, or the output prospects of the regulated industries. Such changes could operate toward lifting the pace of investment very substantially, and for an extended period of time. Nor is there any way of predicting technological innovations. Their most likely center, as suggested above, is in the application of atomic energy, and the possibility that particular uses not now on the horizon may materialize as practical realities.

From a financial standpoint—and with the qualifications cited—our analysis suggests that the regulated industries will play a more modest role in capital markets in the twenty years ahead. Of course, there are probably exceptions within the group, such as air transportation. But the general conclusion appears to hold for the group as a whole as well as for all the currently more important components. The impact of the retarded rate of growth, and the declining capital-product ratio, on this segment's demand for outside capital has been reflected in the past by the trends in progress in methods of financing. Reference, in particular, is to the gradual shift toward the internal financing of capital requirements notable for all the components for which relevant data were available. Only a powerful upward shift in the prospective growth rate of this segment, or a capital-demanding innovation of huge dimensions—neither of which is predictable on the basis of current knowledge—would be sufficient to arrest this trend in the future. Furthermore, persistence of the trend toward internal financing may be expected to stimulate in turn a continuance of the shift from stocks to bonds in net new issues. For while internal financing increased the value of equity claims, it would also make financially feasible the assumption of a greater volume of debt. But of course the choice between stocks and bonds is influenced by other factors, including the attitude of the providers of capital. Consequently, the nature of the future shifts in this respect among the regulated industries must remain indefinite.

Assuming that on the basis of the secular patterns defined in earlier chapters of this book, a particular set of figures had been established as the most probable trend values of net and gross capital formation over the years through 1975, at least one further adjustment would remain necessary for most of the practical uses to which such projections might be put. This would involve the provision of some notions concerning the timing of the investment. For the secular trend is an abstraction, being divorced from long cycles as well as from other shorter-term fluctuations. And the long cycles are sufficiently large and extensive to command attention even when strictly long-range problems are in view. Judging from average experience in the past, it would be necessary to allow for a long cycle contraction approximately 40 per cent below the average of the projected secular trend values, and for an expansion about 70 per cent above. We would expect the expansion to last 50 per cent longer than the contraction, with the cycle as a whole covering twenty years. We might further adjust the amplitude by allowing for a secular tendency for contractions to increase in intensity. But two considerations would remain, which in fact might transcend in importance the mechanical details already mentioned.

The first would concern the possibility of a discontinuity in historical experience. It is generally believed that recent advances in technical knowledge as well as political education have enabled society to modify business cycle fluctuations to a much greater degree than was possible in the past. If this is true, does it not also follow that *long* cycles in economic behavior will be materially modified? It would seem that gradual modification, though certainly not swift elimination, may indeed be expected. Long cycle contractions have been accompanied in the past by severe business depressions. If depressions of major magnitude are avoided, long cycle contractions will be less extended and less severe. For it has been characteristic of the latter that investment dropped to levels far below those justified by secular growth factors. The sharpness of this decline reflected the collapse of demand as well as of business expectations. If demand for final product were maintained, the decline in investment would be more modest. As a result, the succeeding long cycle expansion, in which investment typically outstrips secular growth factors, would also be more narrowly limited. In this way the severity of long swings would be gradually dampened, perhaps so effectively that their practical significance would diminish to negligible proportions.

It is even conceivable that the effect of long cycles on the aggregate income and output of the nation may be virtually eliminated with considerable promptness. Many believe that fiscal and monetary controls, at least in principle, could accomplish this. But it is not within the realm of the plausible that long swings in every segment of the economy would be suddenly stopped. For the past makes an imprint on the present and on the future which cannot be easily erased, even when the desire to do so is general and urgent. In particular, a prolonged expansion has been under way in the capital formation of the regulated industries as well as in that of residential building since the mid-1930's. It was extended well beyond its usual length by the effect of World War II and its aftermath. It was characterized, like all such expansions, by an investment flow which far exceeded the growth factors upon which it must depend in the longer run.[1] Thus, the physical stock of capital of all regulated

[1] For substantiation of this point in residential construction, see Leo Grebler, David M. Blank, and Louis Winnick, *Capital Formation in Residential Real Estate* (Princeton University Press for National Bureau of Economic Research, 1956), Chapter XVIII.

industries rose from 41.2 billion 1929 dollars at the beginning of 1946 to 48.4 billion at the end of 1950—an annual rate of increase of 3.3 per cent. This was approximately double the rate of growth of population during the same period. Roughly the same relationship has been extended into the mid-1950's. Yet the secular pattern of growth, taking into account demand factors as well as the trend of the capital-product ratio, suggests a long-run rate of increase in the plant and equipment of the regulated industries which may be *less* than that of population. It is of course possible that the maintenance of steadier incomes for the population in the future than in the past could promote a somewhat higher rate of secular growth for the regulated industries than would otherwise prevail. But barring an unforeseeable change in tastes or in technology, the difference would at most be slight, since expansions have always compensated more or less fully for the investment deficits incurred in contractions. The growth rate of the regulated industries temporarily achieved in the post-World War II period, as we have seen, is very substantially above the long-term trend, and hence may sooner or later slacken. This brings us to the second of the two problems that would remain on the timing of future investment: *when* will the next contraction in capital formation begin?

The lack of a fully tested and generally accepted theory of long cycles restricts an answer to this question primarily to empirical considerations. Long cycle expansions in the past have averaged twelve years in length. The current expansion had by 1955 been under way for some twenty years—four of which were war years characterized by investment restriction. Assuming some minimum comparability with the past, it would appear more likely that the bulk of the future contraction will fall in the ten or fifteen years ending in 1970 than in the ten or fifteen years ending in 1980. This likelihood is consistent with the prospects for residential buildings; the population pressures for housing are expected to be weaker in the first of these periods than they were in the immediate past or are likely to be in succeeding years.[2] The close relationship between long cycles in residential building and in the regulated industries previously described is thus consistent with the outlook for the incidence of these swings in the immediate future. On the other hand, it must be emphasized that our knowledge of the causal factors underlying long cycles is sketchy, at best. There are no unassailable theoretical reasons for assigning any particular time pattern for the long cycles of the future. Nor is our experience with the past documented over a sufficiently extended period to accord

[2] Grebler, Blank, and Winnick, *op. cit.*, Chapter XIX.

any considerable degree of reliability to a purely empirical forecast. Hence, our first approach to the question of timing, though perhaps the only one available, is not calculated to inspire confidence. Until more is known concerning the factors underlying such phenomena, our inability to predict their incidence, even in the broadest terms, must be conceded. Moreover, it is worth reiterating, the power of these cycles, as well as their impact upon the economy as a whole, may well be mitigated in the future by counteractions on the part of government and business which were unknown or but tentatively employed in the years prior to World War II. If so, the tendency for contractions to increase in intensity would be halted and reversed, to the distinct benefit of the nation's economic stability and the welfare of its citizens. Obviously, the accumulation of knowledge concerning these fluctuations must be ranked as one of the important factors necessary for bringing this goal closer to realization.

APPENDIXES

APPENDIX A

On the Derivation and Accuracy of Capital Formation Data

TABLES on the derivation of capital formation data for the combined regulated industries are presented in Appendix B, and for the individual industries, in Appendixes C through H. In general, the notes to these tables are designed to provide a sufficient guide to the procedures used. They include descriptions of the various steps taken in the process of estimation. They also include references, wherever possible, to internal checks on the accuracy of the estimates obtained. This appendix is intended to supplement the later ones in three ways: (1) Information is provided on the techniques of derivation of interest to the general reader, who in most cases would not wish to follow the tables in detail. (2) Several special tests of the accuracy of the data bearing on the more important components are presented. (3) A full discussion is provided for the derivation of the data for steam railroads. Quantitatively, the railroads are the most important component of all, and the problems involved were extraordinarily complex. Furthermore, a discussion of the nature of the decisions made and the techniques employed in that case should serve to illumine the rationale underlying the procedures followed in the others.

Tests of Accuracy

The analysis in the body of this report was confined to nine-year moving averages of the basic data. Such averages possess the advantage of smoothing the shorter-term movements and allowing a greater degree of concentration upon the longer-term movements in which our interest centers. Their use was also prompted by a regard for the margin of error characteristic of many of the estimates, especially those for years prior to World War I. For later years the materials available for constructing the various series on capital formation were relatively abundant. Accordingly, estimates for the years 1919 through 1950 are directly useful as annual data. For the earlier years, resources were meager. A variety of assumptions were required to build the statistical edifice of capital formation finally presented. The internal checks and the benchmarks available, we believed, were sufficient throughout, to ensure the essential verity of the longer-term trends of the series; but for certain years there was considerable chance of substantial errors. It is these errors in the annual data which the nine-year moving averages are intended to smooth—and for purposes of our analysis, to reduce materially. Some notion of the magnitude of the errors, and of the extent to which they are minimized by the nine-year moving averages, is provided by the tests described below. The most important tests are those relating to gross capital formation, since upon the accuracy of this series depends, in the main, that of all the others.

GROSS CAPITAL FORMATION

For the period after 1911 the Interstate Commerce Commission has compiled data on gross capital expenditures by the bulk of American railroads. Only relatively minor adjustments were necessary to approximate complete coverage. For the years prior to 1912 it was necessary to resort to the annual reports of state railroad commissions, which in some cases carried capital expenditures as well as other financial items for individual roads. Samples obtained for selected years were used to derive estimates of gross capital expenditures for all railroads. The samples ranged in size from 20 to nearly 70 per cent of the total and were designed, as far as possible, to provide representative geographical coverage. (Estimates of the accuracy of the samples are given in the more detailed discussion of railroad data in a succeeding section.) Primarily because of the high cost of transcribing, such samples were taken, on the average, for every third year. The greatest span between any two samples was four years. Estimates of gross capital expenditures for inter-sample years were interpolated, after adjustment for the price factor, by means of a series on miles of track operated.

Changes in miles of track operated provide an admittedly poor indicator of capital expenditures, primarily because they represent only one facet of investment and because of an indeterminate lag between expenditures and the completion of lines of track.[1] Consequently, for all years before 1910,[2] the year-to-year changes in gross capital expenditures—or in any other series derived from these—must be viewed as rough approximations. The problem before us now is to determine *how* rough these approximations are, and to what extent they are improved by the averaging process.

Unfortunately, there is no direct test of the accuracy of the method of interpolation employed for the gross capital expenditures series, or of the extent to which results are improved by use of the nine-year moving averages. Changes in miles of track operated were almost

[1] Also, a change in miles of track operated does not represent, strictly, a *gross* change in capital. In the present case, however, it may be taken as an approximation of this, since the relative importance of abandoned lines in the period before 1910 was negligible.

[2] The Interstate Commerce Commission figures begin in 1912, but samples from the state railroad commission reports were taken in 1910 and 1911.

CHART A-1

Comparison of Gross Capital Formation in Constant Dollars, Steam Railroads, 1912–1928, Reported and Interpolated

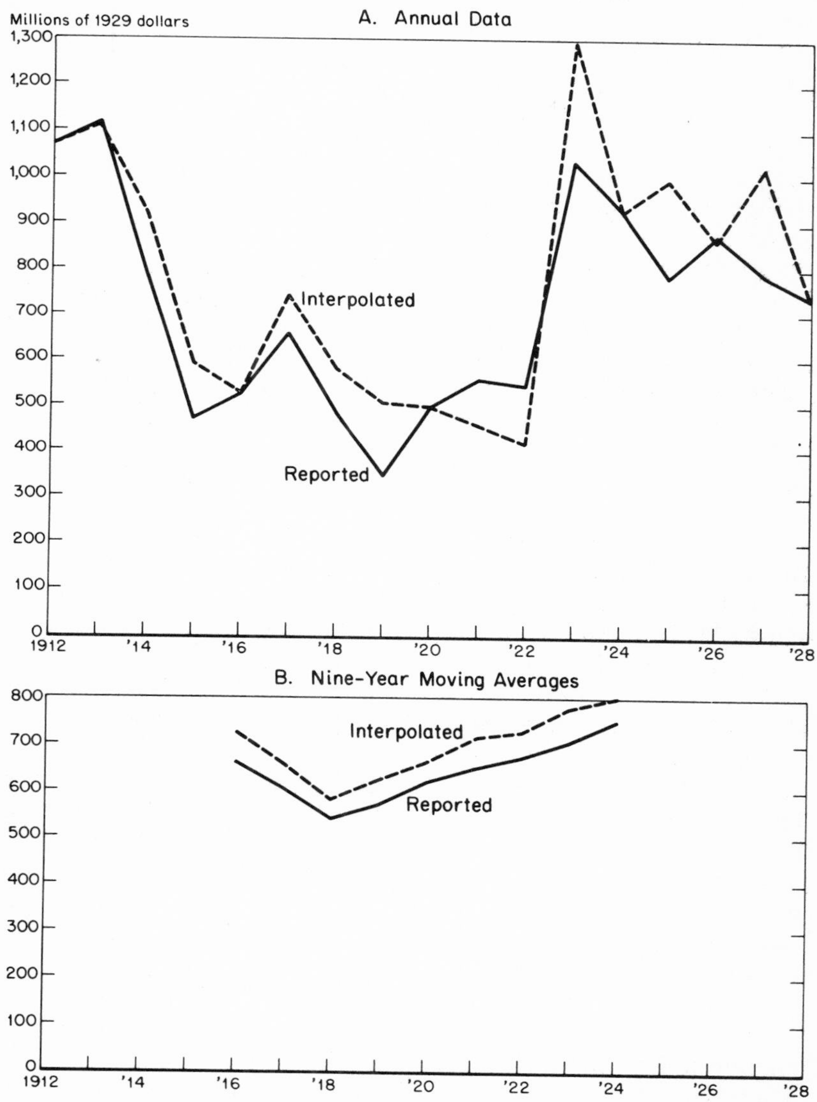

Source: Reported series, from Appendix Tables C-1 and K-2. Interpolation is based on data from *Statistics of Railways in the United States*, Interstate Commerce Commission, various years.

certainly a much more accurate indicator of capital expenditures in the earlier years, when construction of road and new lines was a substantially more important segment of total investment. And it is of course only for the earlier years that the method was employed. Nevertheless, it was deemed instructive—experimentally—to apply the same method of interpolation to the later years and compare results with the actually reported data.

The results of the experiment are shown in Chart A–1. As already indicated, in the actual use of the method for the period before 1912, sample data were available for every third year on the average, though not evenly spaced throughout. In the experiment it was assumed that every fourth year was known. As in the earlier period, changes in miles of track operated were used to interpolate for the intervening years. It was possible to work the experiment from 1912 only through 1928, since after that—unlike the earlier period—negative changes in track miles occur, and are of course inadmissible for interpolating gross capital expenditures.

In the first panel of Chart A–1, estimates derived from track mileage (between benchmark years) are compared on an annual basis with actually reported figures, after appropriate adjustment and deflation. The average absolute error for the entire period is 12 per cent, and the largest error for any year is 46 per cent (for 1919). In the computation of the average error, benchmark years were excluded so that the measure applies to the interpolated years alone. Of particular interest here, however, is the extent to which the errors are reduced by use of nine-year moving averages.

A comparison of the nine-year moving averages of the actual and interpolated series is shown in the second panel of Chart A–1. The average absolute error incurred is 8.6 per cent and the maximum error is 10 per cent (for 1921)—the former being less than three-fourths and the latter less than one-fourth of that found in the annual series. Perhaps equally important is the improvement obtained in the direction of movement. In the annual series the interpolated values move in the wrong direction seven out of sixteen times. In the nine-year moving averages, agreement in direction of movement is perfect.

It may be concluded, therefore, that the nine-year moving averages materially reduce the errors resulting from the interpolation method employed in estimating gross capital expenditures prior to 1910. There is a further presumption that the errors remaining in the nine-year moving averages are fairly small and that their direction of movement and turning points are reliable. In this connection, it should be borne in mind that the average error of 8.6 per cent found in the nine-year moving average of the interpolated series during 1914–26 is probably much greater than the actual error encountered when this method is used for the earlier period, for two reasons: (1) Track mileage was probably a much more accurate indicator of capital formation in the earlier period. (2) Samples were actually available, on the average, more frequently than every four years, the assumption employed in the illustration. On the other hand, of course, there are sampling errors in the benchmark estimates of gross capital expenditures in the years prior to 1912, not reflected in the experiment.

Checks of a somewhat similar order—and with somewhat similar results—are available for the electric light and power industry. For the years subsequent to 1919 data on gross capital expenditures were derived, after a number of adjustments, from annual series published by the Edison Electric Institute and the Federal Power Commission. For the earlier years in this case, too, the foundation for estimates was much more flimsy. The initial step in their derivation was the estimation of gross capital expenditures for intervals of five years, based on quinquennial reports of the Bureau of the Census and the Department of Labor. Estimates of gross capital expenditures during the five-year spans were derived in the main from changes over these periods in the total reported cost of plant and equipment after adjustment for property revaluations, retirements, and comparability of coverage. To test their accuracy, precisely the same methods were employed for estimating, from census materials, gross capital expenditures in the years 1923–27 and 1928–32. The results are compared below with totals of figures for the same years reported annually by the Edison Electric Institute:

	GROSS CAPITAL EXPENDITURES	
	Reported by Edison Electric Institute	*Estimated from Census Data*
1923–1927	$3,574,164,000	$3,549,898,000
1928–1932	2,821,263,000	3,063,137,000

In the first period the estimated total differs from the reported total by less than one per cent; in the second period the difference is 8.6 per cent.

The second step in deriving gross capital expenditures in the period before 1920 was to distribute the estimates for five-year totals among the individual years. A number of different but closely related methods were employed in the various subperiods prior to 1920, depending upon the materials available. The least promising was the one to which we were obliged to resort for the years between 1902 and 1912: that of deriving annual data by distributing the totals for 1902–07 and 1908–12 in accordance with the products of (1) estimated increase in generating capacity, and (2) a construction cost index. In turn, the annual increases in generating capacity were estimated by interpolating census data with a modified exponential trend.

The only *direct* check on this procedure related to a single year—1907. In that year the census asked plants in operation to report the cost of construction during the year and, in addition, conducted a survey of expenditures for plants under construction as of December 31, 1907. The total (appropriately adjusted to include construction of light and power departments of street railways and to exclude the cost of land) is 126 million dollars, a figure almost identical with that derived for 1907—125 millions—by the method of interpolation described above.

An additional—though indirect—test of the accuracy of the procedures described is obtained by employing the same methods of estimation to the years after 1920 (continuing the experiment begun above), for which reported data are available. This was done for the period 1921–32.[3] The comparison of reported and estimated gross capital expenditures is shown in Chart A–2. The average error for the annual data, depicted in the upper panel of the chart, is 16 per cent and at the extreme—in 1932—the estimated is more than double the reported figure. These errors, however, are sharply reduced when moving averages are employed, as shown in the lower panel of the chart. Since the shortness of the interval compared precluded a nine-year average, five-year moving averages were used. The average error in the five-year moving averages is 2.2 per cent, and the maximum error for any year is 13.6 per cent (for 1923). Thus, despite the crudeness of the method of interpolation employed, relatively accurate benchmark estimates limited the error in the five-year moving averages to tolerable dimensions. Furthermore, it should be noted that the direction of movement from year to year in the lower panel is correct in six out of seven cases; in the seventh case the year-to-year change is small.

A similar test is available for the telephone component. In this case, reported data on gross capital expenditures were available for the years subsequent to 1912. For the earlier years estimates were prepared from annual changes in the original cost value of plant

[3] It was not possible to continue the test beyond 1932 primarily because of the substantial write-downs in value of assets in immediately following years. Write-downs amounted to nearly one billion dollars in 1932–37.

CHART A–2

Comparison of Gross Capital Formation in Current Dollars, Electric Light and Power, 1921–1932, Reported and Estimated

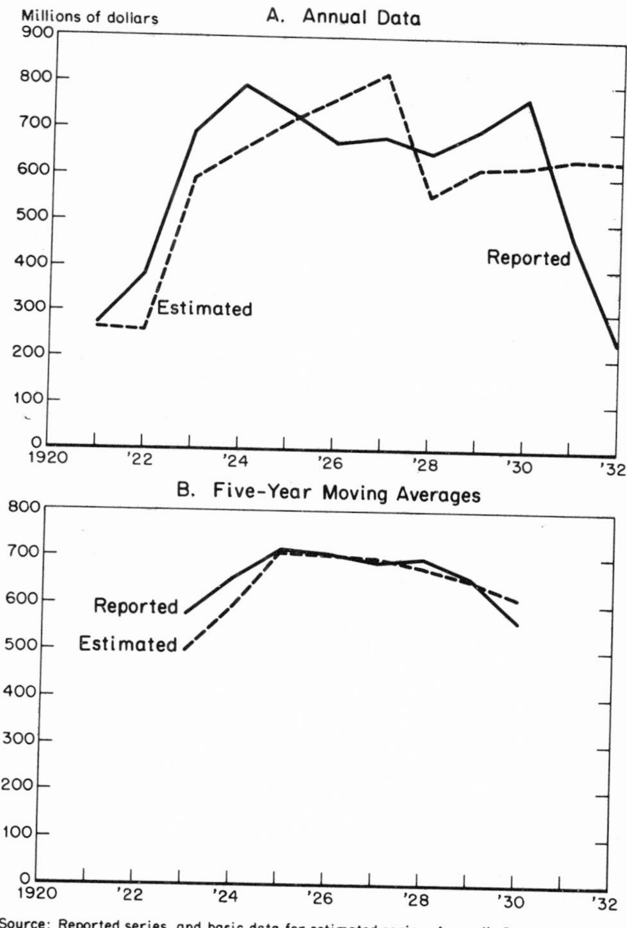

Source: Reported series, and basic data for estimated series, Appendix D.

and equipment, taken in conjunction with estimated annual retirements. Retirements each year were computed from depreciation figures and the average ratio, for the years 1913–17, between retirements and depreciation.

As a check on the reliability of the procedure, similar estimates of gross capital expenditures were computed for the years 1913–36 and compared with the reported figures for the same period.[4] In constructing the estimates the method employed was directly analogous to that used for the earlier period. The value of plant and equipment for the industry, available at five-year intervals, was completed for all years by interpolation with the value of plant and equipment of the Bell System. The average ratio during 1937–41 between retirements and depreciation was applied to depreciation in the years 1913–36 in order to estimate retirements. All computations were in terms of original cost dollars.

The results of this experiment are shown in Chart A–3. In the upper panel, the annual estimated figures differ from reported data on the average by 6.7 per cent; the maximum error for any year is 74 per cent (for 1933). Differences in the direction of year-to-year changes occur four out of twenty-three times. Here, too, very substantial improvement is achieved by the use of the nine-year moving averages shown in the lower panel. The average error is reduced to 4.9 per cent, the maximum error for any year, to 12 per cent (for 1917). The agreement in direction of year-to-year changes in the nine-year moving averages is perfect.

The above tests, conducted for the three most important components of the regulated industries, substantiate the assertions made at several points in this monograph. It is clear that the annual data in the years before World War I are subject to considerable error. At the same time it is apparent that the accuracy of the nine-year moving averages in these earlier years warrants a high degree of confidence. Both in level and in direction of year-to-year movement, errors appear to be well within the limits that may be considered tolerable for a study of long-term trends.

DEFLATION

Principal emphasis in the main text is placed upon the deflated series, for interest is most often centered upon the flow and stock of *real* capital. For no period in the eighty-year span covered by our data were indexes available which precisely fulfilled the variety of tasks for which they were required, such as deflating capital consumption or the stock of capital. A number of assumptions as well as

[4] The estimates were not extended beyond 1936 because: (1) Data for 1937–41 provided the basis in the experiment for the assumed ratio between retirements and depreciation. The estimates for these years would thus be forced into agreement with the reported figures. (2) The abnormally low retirements during World War II preclude the use of the method employed.

CHART A-3

Gross Capital Formation in Current Dollars, Telephones, 1913–1936, Reported and Estimated

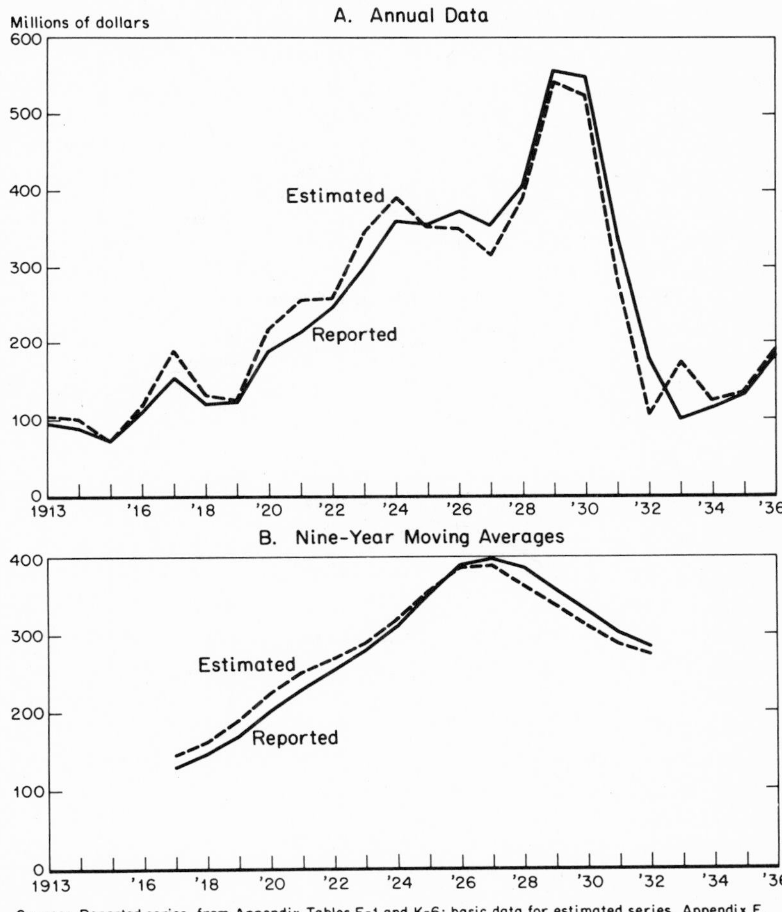

Source: Reported series, from Appendix Tables E-1 and K-6; basic data for estimated series, Appendix E.

adjustments of the original data were found necessary; they were subjected to independent checks wherever possible. For the earlier years, however, the sparsity of statistical resources constituted a special problem. For the later years construction cost indexes, more or less directly applicable to each of the components, were available. It was necessary to extend these indexes in the earlier years by combining data on wage rates, construction materials, and certain types of relevant equipment, where possible—in particular, for

CHART A-4

Comparison of Price Indexes, Experimental and Final Series, 1916–1934, Nine-Year Moving Averages

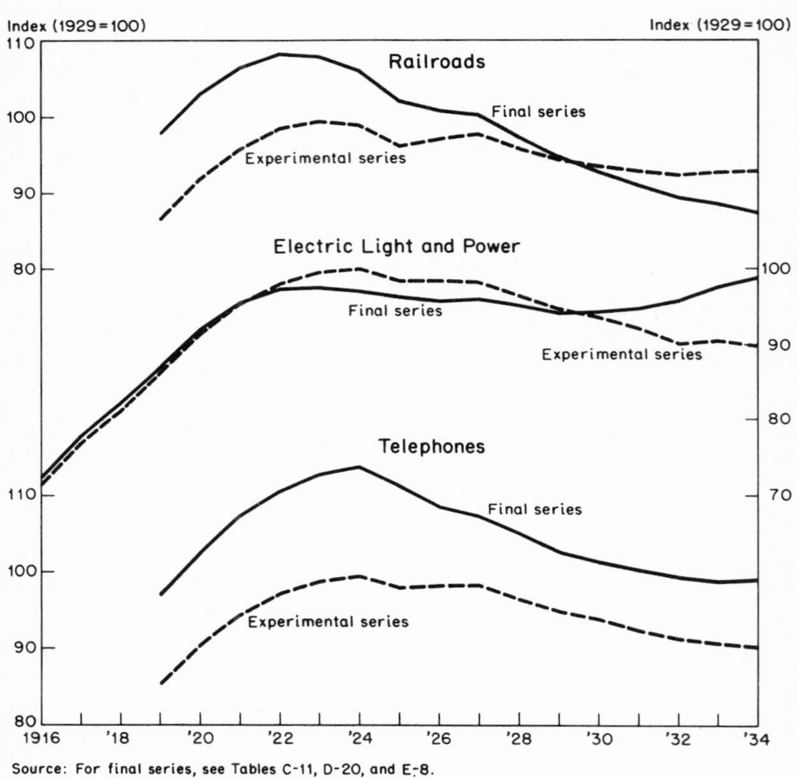

Source: For final series, see Tables C-11, D-20, and E-8.

railroads and telephones prior to 1915, and for electric power prior to 1912.

To test the accuracy of the methods used in the earlier years, we have applied them to the later years, thus extending these indexes forward experimentally so that they may be compared with the final series actually used. The experiment was carried forward as far as the continuity of the underlying data permitted—through 1938. The results of the test are given in Chart A–4. The nine-year moving averages of these series are shown for experimental and for final series for the railroad, electric power, and telephone components from 1916 or 1919 through 1934. The correspondence in all cases is fairly close, and the general trends quite similar. The maximum discrepancy between the two series in any year is 11.5 per cent in 1919 for the railroads, 10.5 per cent in 1934 for electric power, and 12.6 per cent in 1924 for telephones. The average discrepancy is 5.4 per cent for the railroads, 2.9 per cent for electric power, and 9.9 per cent for telephones. It is, of course, relevant to note that price fluctuations were very much more modest in the earlier years than in the period for which this test was conducted. Therefore the actual errors incurred may have been smaller than the results of the experiment would suggest.

NET CAPITAL EXPENDITURES AND CAPITAL CONSUMPTION

The qualifications of the accuracy of the series on gross capital expenditures noted above apply equally to net capital expenditures, except that in the latter case an additional problem arises—that involved in the estimation of capital consumption. The estimates made here of capital consumption (and in virtually all other places to the writer's knowledge) are to be viewed as rough approximations of the extent to which physical capital was used up, on the average, from year to year over the period. No attempt is made to measure the very short period (and usually small) changes which result from fluctuations in the intensity of capital utilization. The series do purport to measure the changes over time related to alterations in the stock and composition of capital. They are founded, ultimately, on estimates of the average length of life of property, and on estimates of the bases to which capital consumption rates are applied. A number of internal checks on the procedures used were available and are referred to in the tables of Appendixes C through H. Here, two *special* tests of the accuracy of our methods are presented for the telephone and railroad components.

In telephones, since our records cover the industry from its beginnings in the 1870's, the base for application of depreciation rates was built up by accumulating annual gross capital expenditures in constant dollars and subtracting retirements, also in constant dollars. An annual series of the gross physical fixed assets was thus developed, and to it rates of capital consumption (based on the average life of property) were applied. A check on this base is obtained by reference to an independently reported figure by the industry for the book value of plant and equipment. Our estimate for gross physical fixed assets in 1929 dollars at the end of 1950 was 8,708 millions. To obtain a comparable estimate from reported book value at the end of 1950 it is necessary to deflate the reported figure by a weighted average of our construction cost index for the previous twenty-eight years. The result of this deflation is a figure of 9,172 millions, about 5 per cent above the original estimate. Considering the opportunity for accumulation of errors over the seventy-year span, the difference may be adjudged small.

For the railroads it was necessary to use a much more complex method of estimation. In outline, it involved (1) deriving a series on the original cost value of road and equipment, (2) applying to this series appropriate depreciation rates to obtain capital consumption in original cost dollars, (3) deriving an index suitable for converting capital consumption from original cost to current dollars, and (4) applying another price index for converting capital consumption to constant dollars. As a check upon the various assumptions underlying the procedure, capital consumption is here computed by an independent method.

In this experimental method depreciation rates are applied to the gross capital expenditures in 1929 dollars each year from 1870 to 1950. On the basis of data obtained from Interstate Commerce Commission records, it is assumed that the average life of depreciable property was fifty years. Estimates of depreciation on property existing at the beginning of 1870 were obtained by using the figure on capital consumption previously derived for this year and reducing it progressively in subsequent years in accord with the estimates of retirements, until it falls to zero in 1925. The experimental series on capital consumption thus derived are compared with the final series employed in this study in Chart A–5.

The check series agrees closely in general drift and in level with the final series throughout. The discrepancies which occur for 1920 and subsequent years spring primarily from the marked swings which occur in the check series; these cycles, in turn, derive from the artificial assumption involved in applying depreciation rates to fifty-year spans of gross capital expenditures, which means adding one new year and dropping one old year with each successive calculation. However, the greatest of such discrepancies in any given year is less than 9 per cent; in the entire span 1920–50, the cumulative capital consumption calculated by the check method is within 3 per cent of the final estimates.

CHART A-5

Comparison of Capital Consumption, Steam Railroads, 1870–1950, Final and Experimental Series

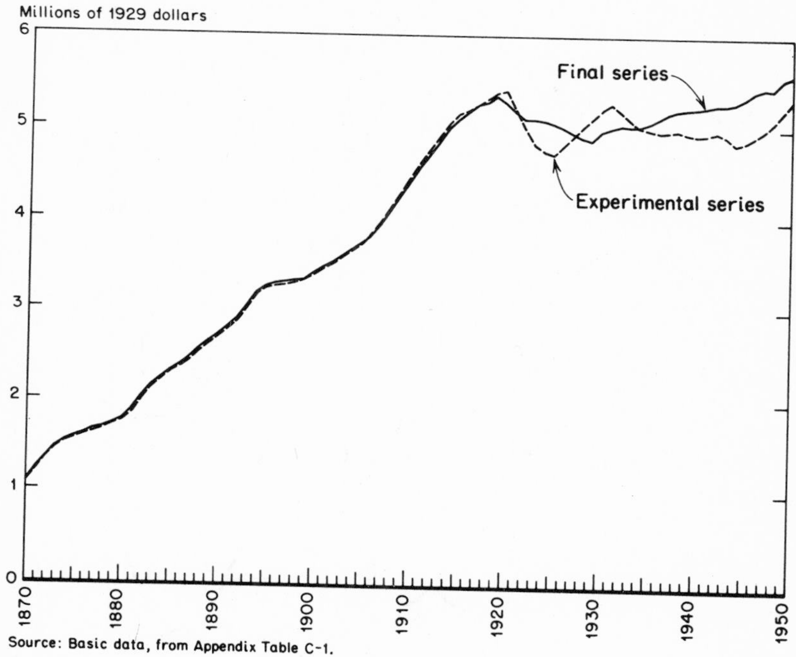

Source: Basic data, from Appendix Table C-1.

Reference may be made to one rough, though *direct*, test of the accuracy of the net capital formation series available for the railroad component. In this case it is possible to compare our series, based on various dollar-value estimates, with changes in the physical volume of several types of railroad investment goods. Perfect agreement cannot be expected for a number of reasons, entirely apart from the inevitability of statistical error. In the first place, data are not available on the physical volume of *all* types of investment goods. Second, changes in the stocks of these goods are gross differences; they include the effects of retirements as well as additions, but make no allowance for depreciation on existing stock. Third, no effort was made to combine the different types of investment goods into an over-all index, for the problems involved in weighting are considerable and would in themselves give rise to an indeterminate error of undoubtedly substantial size.

CHART A-6

Net Capital Formation in Constant Dollars, and Changes in Track and Equipment, Steam Railroads, Nine-Year Moving Averages, 1874–1946

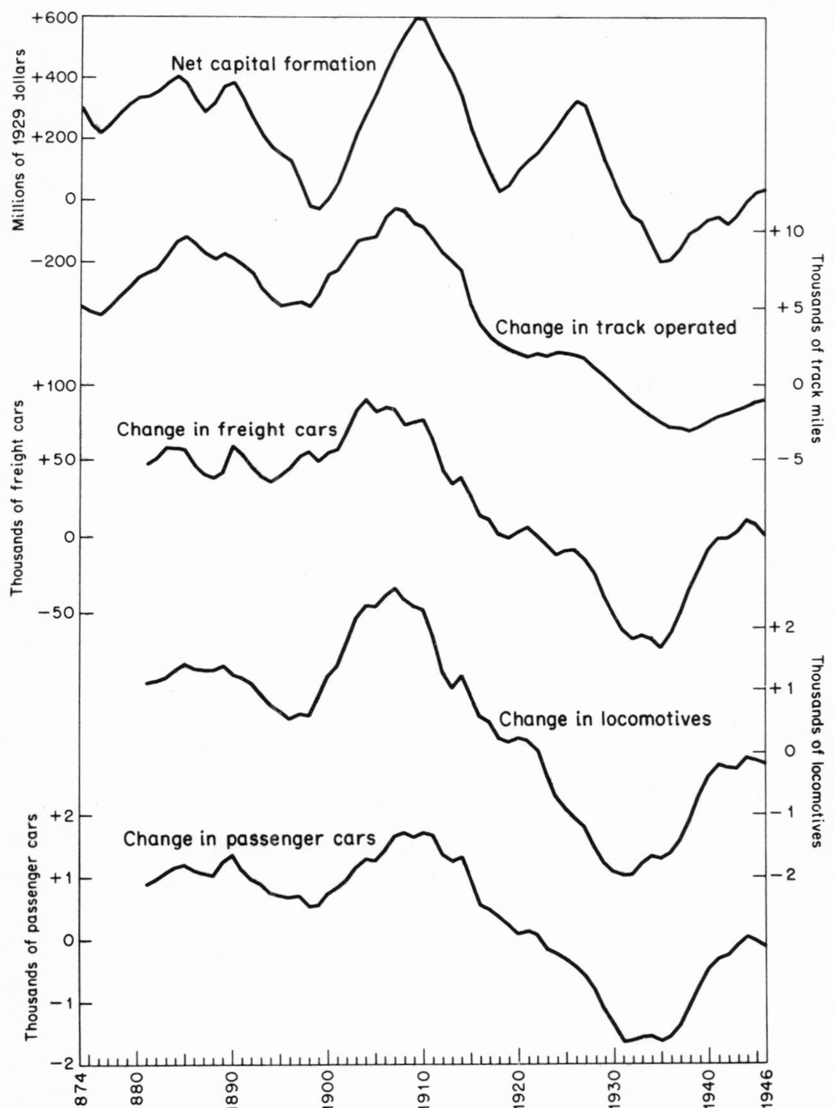

Source: Net capital expenditures, Appendix Table K-4; track and equipment changes based on reports of the Interstate Commerce Commission for 1890 and subsequent years, and on data from Poor's *Manual of Railroads* for earlier years. The ICC data, which refer to Classes I, II, and III railroads, were adjusted for each year to cover all roads.

For all these reasons, attention must be focused upon the broader characteristics of the series depicted in Chart A–6. If this is done, it will be seen that there is nearly perfect agreement between our own capital formation series and the data on physical volume considered together. In the one important exception, described below, the difference is attributable to the limitations of the physical volume series.

Initially, all series reach their all-time peaks in, or at the end of, the first decade of the twentieth century—in 1909 in our series on net capital formation, in 1907 in track and in locomotives, in 1904 in freight cars, and in 1910 in passenger cars. Prior to the 1898–1918 cycle, which culminated in this peak, the series in all cases fluctuate at a level about one-half to three-fourths of the way from the 1909 peak to the 1918 trough. The long cycle preceding the giant 1898–1918 swing also appears in all of the series, though it is less distinctly marked in freight cars. Turning to the later years, all series show a trough in the early thirties and a subsequent rise. In all cases investment after World War I appears substantially lower in general than in the earlier years.

The outstanding difference between our own and the physical volume series occurs in the 1920's. It is in this period, however, that retirements reached record levels far exceeding the rate of capital consumption, and for this reason, especially, changes in physical volume tend to understate the actual flow of investment. The tremendous volume of traffic in World War I, coupled with supply and labor shortages, precluded the maintenance of track, buildings, and rolling stock at accustomed standards and, at the same time, necessitated the general deferral of replacements. At the end of the war, extensive rebuilding and re-equipping were required. The flood of investment that occurred is not mirrored in the physical volume series because of the simultaneous retirement of obsolete equipment. It should be emphasized that in the twenties, railroad investment was directed toward improvements of many kinds rather than to extension of line. Thus signal systems were improved and in many cases installed for the first time in this period. Such improvements and other similar activities are not reflected in the physical volume series in Chart A–6. Average annual retirements in the twenties, compared with other decades are as follows:

	1929 Dollars[5] (millions)
1870–1879	5
1880–1889	10
1890–1899	10
1900–1909	14
1910–1919	171
1920–1929	1,204
1930–1939	222
1940–1946	360
1947–1949	620

A smaller but rather similar difference between our series on net capital formation and the physical volume series appears in the late 1940's. Again retirements rose sharply after World War II, exceeding the actual rate of capital consumption. This rise in retirements served to reduce the physical volume series, though there can be little doubt that the real rate of capital formation advanced after World War II as indicated in our series.

An Illustration: The Derivation of Data for the Railroads

The purpose of this section is to provide a detailed commentary upon the tables of Appendix C, which trace the derivation of capital formation data for the railroads. As noted, a very large proportion of the problems encountered and decisions made in constructing these series were common to all the components of the regulated industries. In this sense, the discussion will serve a more general purpose. The series described below are gross capital formation, capital consumption, net capital formation, and the value of road and equipment of the railroads, both in current and in constant dollars. Data are derived by years from 1870 through 1950. The annual figures are given in Table C–1. Nine-year moving averages are presented, along with those for all other components, in Appendix K.

In addition, a series on the book value of road and equipment was also derived, primarily because of its intermediate usefulness at several points in the estimation process. It will be discussed first.

BOOK VALUE OF ROAD AND EQUIPMENT

Content. This series represents the value of road and structures and equipment, gross of accrued depreciation, as carried on the books of the railroads. Under this heading is embraced all physical property of the railroads used directly or indirectly for transportation. Excluded is a small amount of physical property, such as hotels, not used for transportation.

[5] Tables C–11 and C–16.

Railroads have typically valued their property at cost and beginning with 1907 have been compelled to do so under Interstate Commerce Commission regulations.[6] However, since property is occasionally sold by one road to the other, valuations are not necessarily identical with the historical cost of production. Moreover, the period of consolidation in the 1880's and 1890's resulted in substantial upward revisions in the valuation of assets.

No deduction has been made in these figures for accrued depreciation. For present purposes, it was not necessary.

Derivation. From 1890 to 1950 data are available directly from ICC reports; they required adjustment only for undercoverage (based on the ratio between track mileage owned by reporting companies and by all companies) and, in the years prior to 1917, for shifting of dates from June 30 to December 31 for the sake of comparability with later years and with other series. The magnitude of the undercoverage blowup was small, ranging from 4 per cent in some of the earlier years to 1 per cent or less in the period after 1934. The original ICC figures along with the necessary adjustments are given in Table C–2.

For the period prior to 1890, the raw data available are those shown in columns 1–3 in Table C–3. The same figures, after correction for undercoverage, are given in columns 7–9. In 1890—the only year for which comparison is possible—the difference between the census and the ICC estimates is less than 3 per cent, after the undercoverage adjustment is made. On the other hand, Poor's estimate exceeds the ICC's by 9 per cent and that of the census by 12 per cent.

Though it was not possible to account for these differences, there are some reasons for believing that Poor's estimates are excessive rather than that the census and ICC figures err by nearly identical amounts. Poor's *Manual of Railroads* was compiled primarily for the presentation of individual company reports rather than national totals. Such aggregate figures as are presented could easily have been inflated by double-counting, especially if they were obtained by summing totals derived from state railroad commission reports, as seems likely. Many of the railroads reported to more than one state commission, and errors from this source alone could easily account for the differences in question.

Accordingly, the corrected census figures for 1880 and 1860 are accepted here after a small adjustment to the ICC level is made on the basis of the ratio between the two series in 1890. The figures for 1881–89 and 1876–79 are obtained by interpolation with reference

[6] Of course, the ICC permits occasional exceptions under special circumstances, but these are rare.

to the Poor's series. The figures for 1870–75 are obtained by straight-line interpolation between 1876 and the corrected census figures for 1860. These final estimates, as of January 1 in each year, are shown in column 11.

GROSS CAPITAL EXPENDITURES

Content. This series includes all expenditures (except those for land) charged to capital account by the railroads. Embraced here are all direct expenditures for equipment and road[7] and structures and also "general expenditures"—that is, expenses incurred incidental to actual purchase. The latter category, important only in the early days of the railroads, covers organization costs and such overhead items as taxes and legal expenses.

Derivation of Current Dollar Estimates. From 1912 to 1950 data on gross capital expenditures, including land, were obtained directly from the annual reports of the ICC for Class I and II roads, and required adjustment only for inclusion of other classes and for under-coverage by the same method as that described for physical assets. It was also necessary to shift the years prior to 1916 from a fiscal to a calendar year basis. The derivation of this series is shown in detail in the first nine columns of Table C–4.

For the period prior to 1912, the only source is the financial statements of individual companies contained in some of the annual reports of state railroad commissioners. Of course, not all states asked for information on gross capital expenditures. Furthermore, the behavior of individual states in this regard was erratic in that such information was obtained only in certain years.

Hence the method of selecting samples from the state reports was narrowly restricted by the nature of the source material. In some of the earlier years only three or four states obtained information on gross capital formation, and even in later years it was seldom included by more than ten states. Yet from the point of view of the accuracy of the results it is fortunate that most railroads pass through several states. For example, it was found in the sample for 1910 that roads accounting for 99 per cent of the assets of all roads reporting to the State of Wisconsin also reported to one or more of the three other states—Kansas, Indiana, and Minnesota. The significance of

[7] Since there has been some debate on the subject, it may be noted that ties and rails replaced in kind have been typically charged by the railroads to maintenance rather than to capital account. The excess cost of improvements is, of course, capitalized. In support of this practice is the observation that such replacements are made with a high degree of regularity and are postponable only in much narrower limits than the usual capital purchase.

this finding is twofold: (1) Railroading is not a local operation. The roads reporting to any one state will in fact operate in a wide variety of other states. (2) The roads reporting to any one state will represent a substantial proportion of all roads in the United States.

Samples from the state commissioner reports were chosen for the years 1873, 1877, 1880, 1882, 1887, 1891, 1892, 1896, 1900, 1904, 1907, 1910, and 1911. In general the objective was to choose an evenly spaced number of years. This objective was modified on occasion for several reasons: (1) For some years the available material was deemed insufficient, or not as adequate as in other years. (2) In order to clarify the material of one year (say 1892), it was at times necessary to explore the material of a previous year (1891), which in turn was utilized. (3) In one case—1910 and 1911—it was deemed important to explore more extensively the period concerned in order to date more accurately the occurrence of what appeared to be the all-time peak in gross capital expenditures.

The states selected for each of these years are listed in the footnote to Table C–5. For the years 1877, 1882, 1891, 1892, and 1900 they represent all those for which reports existed containing the desired information. In all cases an effort was made, insofar as the source material permitted, to represent the various geographical sections of the country. The sizes of the samples ranged from 20 per cent of the assets of all United States railroads to nearly 70 per cent, and they averaged 42 per cent for all sample years. The derivation of estimates of gross capital expenditures for all United States railroads in these sample years is illustrated in Table C–5.

In order to shed some light on the accuracy of the results, samples were taken in a "control" year—1914—and the results compared with the actually reported gross capital expenditures in that year—683 million dollars.[8]

The states included in the master sample for 1914 are shown in Table C–6 along with their respective book values of road and equipment and gross capital expenditures. The selection represents a grouping which was as similar in geographical representation as possible to the groupings actually employed in 1900, 1892, and other large sample years. In all, the sample roads in 1914 account for 59 per cent of the total fixed operating assets of all roads. An estimate of the gross capital expenditures for all roads, derived from this sample, comes to 660 million dollars, as shown in the first line of Table C–7. This is less than 4 per cent away from the actually reported figure for that year. The experiment suggests, therefore,

[8] This figure, which comes from Table C–4, includes an adjustment for undercoverage. It is for the fiscal year, and embraces expenditures for land.

that the sampling error in large sample years—specifically, 1877, 1882, 1891, 1892, 1896, 1900, and 1910—may be 4 per cent or less.

Estimates based on smaller samples were also derived from the 1914 material. While numerous combinations of states may have been tried, only five were selected here as roughly typical of the combinations which actually occurred in the small sample years. The states selected are given in the footnote to Table C–7, and the results of the experiment are given in the body of that table. The best estimate of gross capital expenditures in 1914, derived from Small Sample I, is 703 millions, just under 3 per cent more than the actual figure in that year. The poorest estimate, derived from Small Sample V, is 615 millions, about 10 per cent less than the true figure. These experiments suggest that sampling errors in the small sample years—specifically, 1873, 1880, 1887, 1904, 1907, and 1911—range from 3 to 10 per cent.

One other approach to appraising the probable error of these samples is possible. Since on the average each railroad operates in many states and few railroads operate in only one, there is a suggestion that the method of sample selection employed here provides results similar to those of random sampling. On this hypothesis[9]—namely, that the samples are random—a standard error was computed for 1907, which is one of the small sample years. The indicated standard error is 48 million dollars, or about 8 per cent of the estimated gross capital expenditures in that year. This falls within the range of errors for small samples suggested by study of the control year 1914, above.

For interpolating estimated gross capital expenditures in the intersample years, the three most relevant series would appear to be (1) changes in miles of track operated, (2) changes in miles of road owned or operated, and (3) changes in book value of road and equipment. Of these, the first has been considered here to be superior.

Miles of track operated is, of course, a more comprehensive indicator of capital formation than miles of road owned or operated, since it reflects the acquisition of additional track along already constructed lines and also of yard track, both of which are omitted

[9] This hypothesis would be true in particular if (1) there were independence between the ratio of the gross capital expenditures to the value of road and equipment of particular roads and their state classifications, and (2) if there were independence between this ratio and the appearance or the absence of gross capital expenditure data in state commission reports. The first of these conditions can be tested. One such test was applied to the data for the 1907 sample, with results consistent with the hypothesis. Variance within and between states differed by an amount much less than that which could be expected from chance five times out of a hundred.

from the latter series. Changes in book value of road and equipment is considered inferior because of the appearance of substantial write-ups in the valuation of assets, especially in the 1880's and 1890's. It is of interest that in the period 1912–28, for which a comparison is possible, changes in book value provided about the same results as those in track.[10] Yet it is most likely that book values were much *less* representative in the earlier period (when write-ups were so important[11]), and that track was *more* representative in the earlier period when expenditures for road represented a larger proportion of total expenditures.[12]

The derivation of the series employed on miles of track operated is shown in Table C–8. The interpolation of gross capital expenditures by means of this series is illustrated in Table C–9. It will be noted that in order to take account of price changes, use is made of an index of railroad construction costs. This index, which is widely used in our study, is described below.

Exclusion of Land. Before arriving at final estimates of gross capital expenditures in current dollars, however, it was necessary to exclude land, which is included in the recorded capital expenditures of the railroads. For the years 1917 through 1950 this was done on the basis of the ratio of land expenditures to total capital expenditures of Class I railroads, which may be derived from published ICC figures each year in the period. For 1880–1916, estimates of expenditures on land were obtained by interpolating between the ratio of expenditures on land to total gross capital expenditures of Class I roads in the years 1917–27 (which is 0.039) and the ratio of the value of land owned to the total value of road and equipment of all railroads in 1880 (which is 0.021) given by the census. For the years prior to 1880, the ratio 0.021 was used. These computations are shown in Table C–10.

Deflation. Estimates of gross capital expenditures in 1929 dollars were obtained for the years 1915 through 1950 by applying to the series on gross capital expenditures in current dollars the ICC railroad construction cost index after appropriate shift in base.

For the years prior to 1915 it was necessary to construct a special

[10] The average error was 13 per cent for annual estimates derived from track and 12 per cent for those derived from book values; the average error in five-year moving averages of these annual estimates was 7 per cent for track and 9 per cent for book value.

[11] Changes in the valuation of assets has been limited by ICC regulations since 1907.

[12] Rough estimates indicate that in the period prior to 1880, about 90 per cent of all capital expenditures were for road; between 1880 and 1917, about 70 per cent; and between 1917 and 1951, about 50 per cent or less. These figures are based primarily on differences in the value of road and equipment separately at the beginning of each of the years indicated above, as given by the census and the ICC.

index. Use was made of Shaw's index of the cost of construction materials; Shaw's index of the cost of locomotives and railroad cars; the indexes of lumber and building materials and of metals and implements, excluding pocket knives, from *Wholesale Prices, Wages and Transportation*; and indexes of wage rates in building trades. Weights were derived from an analysis of the composition of railroad expenditures in selected periods. The computation of this special index for the years 1840 through 1915 is illustrated in Table C–11, where the final index of the cost of road and equipment, from 1870 to 1950, is also shown.

CAPITAL CONSUMPTION

Original Cost Dollars. Capital consumption is defined here to mean capital which is "used up" either through depreciation or obsolescence.[13] The series presented in this study is based primarily on estimates of true composite depreciation rates, prepared especially for this purpose by the Bureau of Accounts, Cost Finding, and Valuation of the ICC. Use of depreciation charges as recorded by the railroads is precluded by the substantial revisions which have occurred over time in accounting practice, both voluntary and inspired by the ICC.[14]

The derivation of the capital consumption series is presented in Tables C–12 and C–13. The estimated depreciation rates obtained from the ICC are 1.54 per cent in 1917 and 1.72 per cent in 1949. The increase over this period is the composite result of two divergent tendencies. The life span of various types of railroad equipment as well as that of road and structures increased appreciably during these years. Yet at the same time, the relative importance of equipment in the aggregate of railroad property grew rapidly. The latter influence was predominant, and since the average life of equipment is less than that of road and structures, the net effect was a rise in the composite depreciation rate. Estimates of depreciation rates for the two types of property separately, along with their relative weights, as provided by the ICC, are as follows:

[13] Since replacement of ties and rails in kind are excluded from gross capital expenditures, they are also excluded from capital consumption.

[14] Before 1907 there appears to have been a virtual absence of depreciation accounting by the railroads: Beginning July 1, 1907, railroad operating expenses under the ICC's accounting rules required charges for depreciation on equipment at rates selected by the carriers and after January 1, 1935, at rates fixed by the Commission. Beginning on January 1, 1943, the Commission also required depreciation on road. Only small amounts of such depreciation had been voluntarily charged by the roads prior to that date. See W. H. S. Stevens and E. S. Hobbs, "Analysis of Steam Railroad Dividends" (mimeographed, Interstate Commerce Commission, 1943).

	Rate	Relative Weight
1917		
Road	0.86	0.74
Equipment	3.50	0.26
Composite	1.54	1.00
1949		
Road	0.82	0.65
Equipment	3.42	0.35
Composite	1.72	1.00

Estimates of composite depreciation rates for the years 1918–48 were derived by linear interpolation between 1.54 and 1.72.

Up to 1917 there are no data available on the average length of life of railroad property, except for scattered information in the files of the ICC. This information, scanty though it is, substantiates the conclusion drawn from a general knowledge of the development of the railroads—to wit, the durability of railroad capital was considerably enhanced. However, during the period 1890 to 1917—while the entire stock of railroad capital in constant dollars more than doubled—the book value of equipment rose from about 5 or 10 per cent of all railroad property to somewhat more than 25 per cent.[15] The opinion of the ICC's Bureau of Valuation, based on an examination of its own information, is that during the period these two factors were about evenly balanced and that, accordingly, the composite depreciation rate was not materially different from the 1917 figure. Hence, 1.54 per cent was used for each of the years 1870–1916, as shown in column 6 of Table C–12.

The depreciation rates prepared by the ICC are applicable to the original cost of railroad property, as estimated by that agency. Such estimates are available, as of January 1, for the years 1916–40 and 1947–50, and are shown in columns 1 and 2 of Table C–12. Since data for the latter span of years referred to Class I roads only, they were adjusted for inclusion of all roads as well as for undercoverage by ICC through use of the ratios given in column 4 of this table. The adjusted figures are presented in column 5. Data for the years 1916–1940 were adjusted for undercoverage by the same method used for series previously discussed, through use of the ratios given in column 4, Table C–2. Figures for the years 1941 through 1946 were linearly interpolated.

In securing estimates of original cost for the years before 1916, it was necessary to make some decision concerning the incidence of the write-ups in assets which is manifest in the 1916 figures. An

[15] The earlier figure is obtained from the annual report of the ICC. The latter figure is an unpublished ICC estimate.

initial guide to this decision is found in a comparison between the aggregate volume of gross capital expenditures during the entire period from 1870 through 1915, inclusive, and the difference between the book value of road and equipment at the beginning of 1870 and the original cost of road and equipment at the beginning of 1916. It was found that the former figure was greater than the latter by 239 million dollars.

This result suggests that the book value of road and equipment at the beginning of 1870 must have been closely in the neighborhood of the original cost, and that whatever net write-ups remained in 1916 had occurred in the intervening years. For the figure 239 millions is necessarily equal to retirements plus any write-ups existing at the beginning of 1870, and minus any write-ups which had occurred after 1870. It is highly unlikely that retirements alone were materially less than 239 millions, since this implies an almost negligibly small rate over the forty-six-year span considered.

Hence the book value of road and equipment has been accepted here as an approximation of the original cost, and—an equivalent assumption—239 million dollars was accepted as a minimum estimate of retirements over the forty-six-year period.[16] Through use of our annual series on gross capital expenditures, and through prorating the aggregate retirements of 239 million dollars, it was possible to interpolate estimates of original cost for the years 1870–1915, as shown in Table C–13. These estimates are in turn used in Table C–12 to derive a series on the volume of capital consumption in original cost dollars.

Current Dollars. Estimates of the original cost of railroad property by years from 1870 to 1949 have already been derived (see Table C–12). If a series were available on the reproduction cost new of railroad property in the same period, then it would be a simple matter to obtain price indexes appropriate for transforming capital consumption in these years from original cost to current dollars. The suggested procedure is indicated in the formula:

$$\text{(1)} \qquad \frac{Q_N P_N}{Q_N P_C}(q_N P_C) = q_N P_N$$

[16] The latter hypothesis is subject to some check. It was possible to obtain data on retirements from individual company statements included in the state railroad commission reports for Massachusetts in 1875, for Iowa, New York, and Michigan in 1896, and for New York in 1904. The average retirements rates were indeed very small—0.08 per cent in 1875, 0.16 per cent in 1896, and 0.16 per cent in 1904—though they yield larger, rather than smaller aggregate retirements over the 1870–1915 period than that assumed above. However, most state railroad commission reports included no information on retirements (even among those which contained gross capital expenditure information), and it is probable that in the states selected above the retirement rates were higher than the national average.

where $Q_N P_N$ is the reproduction cost new of railroad property in the year N, $Q_N P_C$ is the original cost of the property existing in that year, $q_N P_N$ is the capital consumption in the year N in current dollars.

The first step required by this procedure is derivation of a series on reproduction cost new. In this connection it should be noted that for selected years (as of January 1)—1937, 1940, 1945, 1946, 1947, and 1950—the ICC has published estimates of the reproduction cost new of railroad property. Appearances to the contrary notwithstanding, these figures are not in current dollars, as is required in the procedure above. For special purposes of administration, the Valuation Bureau based valuations upon the prices prevailing on the average in an arbitrarily selected period, including the current year as well as certain prior years. Besides, the period of price reference is not in all cases precisely defined, so that adjustment is not possible.

However the ICC has made available for this study unpublished estimates for these same years of the reproduction cost new of railroad property in 1910–14 dollars. The figures are given in column 1 of Table C–14. In succeeding columns of that table are shown the adjustments required to transform the series into current dollars. Table C–15 illustrates the derivation of capital consumption in current dollars in these selected years by the method described above.

Derivation of a series on reproduction cost new in current dollars for the remaining years is much more complex. The general method adopted here may best be described in terms of the formula:

$$(2) \qquad Q_N P_N = [Q_{N+1} P_{N+1} - G_{N+1} + R_{N+1}] \frac{P_N}{P_{N+1}},$$

where $Q_N P_N$ and $Q_{N+1} P_{N+1}$ are reproduction cost new at the end of the years N and $N + 1$ respectively, G_{N+1} is gross capital expenditures in $N + 1$, R_{N+1} is retirements in the year $N + 1$ valued new in the prices of that year, and P_N and P_{N+1} represent the cost of road and equipment in the years N and $N + 1$ respectively.

$Q_{N+1} P_{N+1}$ is known for several years—those given in Table C–15. All other data on the right side of the above equation are known for all years, with the exception of R. Once retirements in current dollars are known it will be possible to interpolate reproduction cost new between the years given in Table C–15 and to extrapolate for all the required years back of 1936.

The initial task, then, is to derive retirements. Although this can be done only crudely, a very wide margin of error is tolerable here since, as will be shown, these estimates will affect the final results only slightly. Their derivation is shown in Table C–16. Retirements in original cost dollars are obtained by adding to original cost of railroad property, at the beginning of any year, the gross capital expenditures during this year and subtracting this sum from the original cost at the beginning of the following year. The results are shown in the first column of Table C–16. In column 3 there is provided an index of the original cost of retirements which was obtained by assuming that the retirements in any year were originally purchased during a period ranging from twenty-eight to thirty-eight years previously. The final estimates of retirements in current dollars, given in column 5, were obtained by use of the formula:

$$R_{NN} = R_{Nc}(P_N/P_{29} \div P_c/P_{29}), \tag{3}$$

where R_{NN} is retirements in current dollars in the year N, R_{Nc} is retirements in the year N in original cost dollars, P_c/P_{29} is the index of the original cost of retirements, and P_N/P_{29} is the index of the cost of road and equipment in the year N.

Retirements are not estimated here for their own sake or even, ultimately, with the objective of deriving reproduction cost new. The *only* figure derived by their use, of ultimate interest here, is a cost index for transforming capital consumption from original cost dollars to current dollars. For this purpose a wide margin of error in these estimates is tolerable, as previously suggested. Indeed the effect of errors in the retirements estimate may be calculated from:

$$\frac{d\left\{\dfrac{Q_{N+1}P_{N+1} - G_{N+1} + R_{N+1}}{Q_N P_c}\right\}\dfrac{P_N}{P_{N+1}}}{dR_{N+1}} = \frac{\dfrac{P_N}{P_{N+1}}}{Q_N P_c}, \tag{4}$$

where the quantity of which the derivative is taken is the final index desired (derived from formulas 1 and 2), and R_{N+1} is retirements.

By use of this formula it is found that even if true retirements prior to 1916, when estimates rest on the weakest foundation, proved to be three times as great as those given in Table C–16, the error would have virtually no effect—much less than 1 per cent—upon the desired final cost of any year. Even if such an error had occurred in every year, its *cumulative* effect by 1915 would result in a change in the final index of less than 5 per cent. For the years after 1915, there is no reason to suspect the existence of a substantial error in one direction in every year, though large errors may have occurred in any given year. However, in the decade 1920–29, when estimated retirements are at their peak, a 50 per cent error in any year would be reflected in a deviation of about 2 per cent in the final index.

The estimates of reproduction cost new obtained by the use of formula 2 are given in Table C–17. It may be noted that this formula was used to interpolate between the estimates of reproduction cost new, provided by the ICC (as given after adjustment in Table C–15), and to extrapolate from the earliest ICC estimate (January 1, 1937) for the earlier years. Some indication of the accuracy of this method may be gained by experimentally extrapolating from the *latest* ICC estimate (January 1, 1950) and comparing the results with the ICC estimates for those years in which they are available. This was done with the following results (in millions of dollars):

Year (January 1)	*Reproduction Cost New as Estimated by:* ICC (adjusted)	Extrapolation from January 1, 1950
1947	45,043	45,173
1946	40,103	40,643
1945	38,282	38,647
1940	28,298	28,621
1937	27,070	26,612

The final cost index obtained by computing the ratio of reproduction cost new to original cost is given in column 1 of Table C–18. Capital consumption in current dollars, derived by applying this index to capital consumption in original cost dollars, is given in column 2.

Constant Dollars. Capital consumption in 1929 dollars was obtained simply by deflating the figures given in column 2 of Table C–18.

NET CAPITAL EXPENDITURES

Current and Constant Dollars. Net capital expenditures in current dollars was obtained by subtracting capital consumption from gross capital expenditures, both expressed in current dollars. Net capital expenditures in 1929 dollars may be computed either by a corresponding subtraction of the constant dollar series of gross capital expenditures and capital consumption or by deflating the current dollar series.

VALUE OF ROAD AND EQUIPMENT

Constant Dollars. Net capital formation in constant dollars by definition provides us with a measure of the change, by years, in the value of road and equipment in constant dollars—or the stock of capital. It is necessary now to secure a base figure for some year, to which these changes may be applied, in order to derive a series on the stock of capital itself. The derivation of this base is presented in Table C–19. It is founded on an unpublished estimate by the ICC of the reproduction cost, less depreciation of road and equipment of Class I roads in 1910–14 dollars. The final base derived represents reproduction cost, less depreciation for all roads in 1929 dollars. The result of applying the series on net capital formation to this base is the series on the value of road and equipment in 1929 dollars.

Current Dollars. This series was obtained from the one above simply by applying to it the index of the cost of road and equipment.

APPENDIX B

Notes and Tables on the Derivation of Capital Formation Data for All Regulated Industries

ESTIMATES of the value of plant and equipment, gross capital expenditures, capital consumption, and net capital formation for all regulated industries in the aggregate are presented in Table B–1. These estimates are based in the main on totals for the industries studied in detail here—steam railroads, electric light and power, telephones, street and electric railways, and local bus lines—with appropriate allowances for other industries in the group. Estimates for the others are based on less comprehensive and less refined materials than those employed for the five industries studied in detail. Hence the figures for the total may be somewhat less reliable than those for any of the individual components. However, the five industries account at all times for the bulk of the group's capital formation and, in earlier years, for nearly all of it.

Gross Capital Expenditures in Current Dollars, 1939–1950

Gross capital expenditures for all regulated industries in the aggregate for the years 1939–50 were derived as totals for four industry groups: railroads, transportation other than rail, communications, and public utilities. The data for each group are given in Table B–2. The series are based primarily on the data developed in this study (for steam railroads, electric light and power, telephones, street and electric railways, and local bus lines) and on the capital expenditures, as revised in August 1952, compiled jointly by the Department of Commerce and the Securities and Exchange Commission. Certain other sources were used and are given, along with other details of computation, in the footnotes to the table.

The estimates of total capital expenditures for the four groups of industries prepared by the Department of Commerce and the SEC, which are available only for 1939 and 1945–50, are shown in column 6 of Table B–2, for comparison with those compiled in this study. The two sets of figures are in close agreement for the year 1948, which is the benchmark for the Commerce-SEC data. Differences between them in other years are under 5 per cent, except for 1939. The Commerce-SEC figures include, while our data exclude for the most part, expenditures made by utilities for plant and equipment other than utility plant. It is also possible that the SEC reports reflect in some cases, gross additions to plant rather than gross capital expenditures; that is, they may not take account of changes in the value of construction work in progress. Moreover, the reports to SEC may sometimes have included the value of re-used equipment, even though the schedule calls for the exclusion of such equipment. Finally, since neither the series developed here nor the Commerce-SEC series is based on complete reports, both sets of data undoubtedly contain small errors occasioned by the inflation of sample figures.

1919–1938

Gross capital expenditures for 1919–38 were obtained from totals of (1) the industries covered in detail in this study; (2) estimates available for gas, pipelines, and telegraph in combination; (3) estimates prepared by us for motor transportation (except local bus lines) and services incidental to transportation; and (4) an allowance for all other industries. The data are shown in Table B–3. Data for gas, pipelines, and telegraph combined were obtained from Terborgh.[1] The derivation of the series for motor transportation and transportation services is shown in Tables B–4 and B–5. Since data covering capital formation in this field of activity have been compiled only for recent years, rough approximations for the years 1919–38 were made by the use of related economic series.

For the residual industries in the transportation and utilities group—water transportation, air transportation, pullman and express, water supply, irrigation, and radio broadcasting—estimates were added amounting to 3 per cent of total capital expenditures each year. This percentage was obtained from comparison of changes in book value for the above-mentioned groups and for all regulated industries for 1912–22 and 1922–48. The percentages for the two intervals were averaged with weights of 1 and 4, respectively, to yield an estimate appropriate for the years 1919–38.

The derivation of book values for 1912, 1922, and 1948 (and for specified earlier years back to 1880) is shown in Table B–6. Data for 1880–1922 are from Kuznets,[2] except as noted.[3] In addition to the industries listed by Kuznets we have included estimates for gas, motor transportation, air transportation, and radio broadcasting. The figures for 1948 are based on *Statistics of Income* (Bureau of Internal Revenue) after adjustment for complete coverage, and are shown in greater detail in Table B–7.

[1] George W. Terborgh, "Estimated Expenditures for New Durable Goods, 1919–1938," *Federal Reserve Bulletin*, September 1939.

[2] Simon Kuznets, *National Product since 1869* (National Bureau of Economic Research, 1946).

[3] See source to Table B–6.

1870–1918

Gross capital expenditures for the years 1870–1918 (Table B–9) were obtained from the totals for the five industries studied in detail together with estimates of the ratios of expenditures of these industries to expenditures of all regulated industries at certain benchmark dates. The ratios of changes in book value of the five industries to changes in book value of the entire group for the intervals 1870–80, 1880–90, 1890–1900, and 1900–12 were assumed to reflect the ratios of gross capital expenditures of the five industries to the total at the midpoints of the respective intervals. These ratios were interpolated linearly, and the 1875 ratio was extrapolated back to 1870. For 1907–18, the necessary ratios were derived by interpolation between the 1906 ratio and the average ratio, during the years 1919–22, of gross capital expenditures of the five industries to total transportation and public utilities. It is worth noting that the five industries accounted for more than 85 per cent of total gross capital expenditures at all benchmark dates except 1919, when the percentage had fallen to 75.

The complete series of gross capital expenditures in current dollars, for the entire period 1870–1950, is shown in Table B–1, column 3.

Gross Capital Expenditures in 1929 Prices

Gross capital expenditures in 1929 dollars (Table B–1, column 4) were derived by deflating the current dollar figures by an index of plant and equipment costs. This index, shown in Table B–10, is the implicit index obtained from totals of capital expenditures in current and 1929 dollars, for the five industries studied in detail. For convenience in further computations, Table B–10 also includes similar implicit price indexes for value of plant and equipment and capital consumption.

Capital Consumption, 1929 and Current Dollars

Capital consumption in 1929 dollars, derived in Table B–12, is based on totals for the industries studied in detail and on estimates for other transportation, communications, and utilities. Separate estimates were made for the relatively new industries (radio and television, air transportation, motor transportation, and transportation services) and for the "older" industries (gas, pipelines, telegraph, water transportation, irrigation, and water supply).

Data for the older industries were estimated for selected years of the period 1870–1922 (Table B–11) on the assumption that the relationship between capital consumption and book value was the same as that for the industries studied in detail. For the "newer" industries, a 1922 estimate was obtained from deflated book value and a depreciation rate. Data for the older and newer industries together for all years (1870–1922) were derived by linear interpolation between the estimates for 1870, 1880, 1890, 1900, 1912, and 1922.

An estimate for the older industries was obtained for 1948 (Table B–12) from BIR data on the assumption that the price index underlying depreciation charges is the same as for the five industries studied here; data for remaining years of the period 1922–50 were obtained by interpolation and extrapolation of the data for 1922 and 1948 by use of capital consumption in the five industries. Estimates of capital consumption for the newer industries were prepared for 1929–50 by the use of Department of Commerce and BIR data on depreciation, deflated to constant dollars; figures for 1923–28 were derived by linear interpolation.

Capital consumption in current dollars (Table B–1) was derived by inflating the constant dollar totals by an index of prices underlying capital consumption. This index is the implicit price index obtained (Table B–10) from totals of capital consumption in current and 1929 dollars for the five industries studied in detail.

Net Capital Expenditures, 1929 and Current Dollars

Net capital expenditures, shown in Table B–1 in both current and 1929 dollars, were obtained by subtracting capital consumption from gross capital expenditures.

Value of Plant and Equipment in 1929 and Current Dollars

The value of plant and equipment (Table B–1) in 1929 dollars was obtained from an estimate for January 1, 1870, and cumulation of net capital expenditures in succeeding years. The 1870 estimate is based on the total for the five industries studied in detail, inflated to represent all transportation, communications, and utilities by use of estimates of book values.

Value of plant and equipment in current dollars is derived from the constant dollar totals by inflation with the implicit price index for value of plant and equipment for the five industries.

APPENDIX B

TABLE B-1

Value of Plant and Equipment, Capital Formation, and Capital Consumption, All Regulated Industries, Annual Data, 1870–1951

(millions of dollars)

	Value of Plant and Equipment, January 1		Gross Capital Expenditures		Capital Consumption		Net Capital Expenditures	
Year	*Current Dollars* (1)	*1929 Dollars* (2)	*Current Dollars* (3)	*1929 Dollars* (4)	*Current Dollars* (5)	*1929 Dollars* (6)	*Current Dollars* (7)	*1929 Dollars* (8)
1870	4,437	8,053	452	888	67	131	385	757
1871	4,484	8,810	506	996	73	144	433	852
1872	4,899	9,662	457	837	87	159	370	678
1873	5,656	10,340	320	572	96	172	224	400
1874	5,993	10,740	186	353	96	181	90	172
1875	5,729	10,912	135	270	94	188	41	82
1876	5,486	10,994	133	284	91	192	42	92
1877	5,199	11,086	147	343	86	200	61	143
1878	4,828	11,229	143	357	81	202	62	155
1879	4,576	11,384	159	399	84	210	75	189
1880	4,594	11,573	339	765	95	217	244	548
1881	5,357	12,121	511	1,138	103	231	408	907
1882	5,850	13,028	470	1,009	115	248	355	761
1883	6,412	13,789	335	735	122	265	213	470
1884	6,502	14,259	241	546	121	276	120	270
1885	6,378	14,529	191	440	125	288	66	152
1886	6,342	14,681	253	580	129	297	124	283
1887	6,509	14,964	353	815	133	309	220	506
1888	6,683	15,470	328	761	140	324	188	437
1889	6,872	15,907	318	743	145	337	173	406
1890	6,982	16,313	338	788	152	354	186	434
1891	7,184	16,747	351	840	158	375	193	465
1892	7,212	17,212	566	1,384	162	396	404	988
1893	7,462	18,200	608	1,498	173	424	435	1,074
1894	7,845	19,274	361	916	180	455	181	461
1895	7,736	19,735	242	625	185	479	57	146
1896	7,754	19,881	229	592	195	500	34	92
1897	7,869	19,973	249	642	202	520	47	122
1898	7,757	20,095	312	776	218	543	94	233
1899	8,091	20,328	448	1,023	247	566	201	457
1900	9,021	20,785	496	1,088	273	597	223	491
1901	9,681	21,276	497	1,104	285	630	212	474
1902	9,788	21,750	548	1,186	309	665	239	521
1903	10,356	22,271	598	1,272	327	688	271	584
1904	10,925	22,855	661	1,395	344	726	317	669
1905	11,197	23,524	799	1,627	376	764	423	863
1906	12,072	24,387	1,027	1,952	422	806	605	1,146
1907	13,584	25,533	1,154	2,114	465	855	689	1,259
1908	14,789	26,792	1,078	2,034	483	901	595	1,133
1909	15,219	27,925	1,131	2,060	520	936	611	1,124

(continued on next page)

TABLE B–1 (continued)

Year	VALUE OF PLANT AND EQUIPMENT, JANUARY 1		GROSS CAPITAL EXPENDITURES		CAPITAL CONSUMPTION		NET CAPITAL EXPENDITURES	
	Current Dollars (1)	*1929 Dollars* (2)	*Current Dollars* (3)	*1929 Dollars* (4)	*Current Dollars* (5)	*1929 Dollars* (6)	*Current Dollars* (7)	*1929 Dollars* (8)
1910	16,326	29,049	1,352	2,389	557	975	795	1,414
1911	17,638	30,463	1,313	2,299	589	1,019	724	1,280
1912	18,411	31,743	1,337	2,305	621	1,059	716	1,246
1913	19,464	32,989	1,282	2,140	662	1,104	620	1,036
1914	20,517	34,025	1,008	1,732	669	1,143	339	589
1915	20,318	34,614	735	1,244	701	1,174	34	70
1916	20,706	34,684	912	1,333	817	1,195	95	138
1917	23,992	34,822	1,471	1,762	1,027	1,223	444	539
1918	29,951	35,361	1,171	1,164	1,245	1,249	−74	−85
1919	36,123	35,276	1,139	1,048	1,394	1,271	−255	−223
1920	39,785	35,053	1,726	1,368	1,756	1,361	−30	7
1921	46,384	35,060	1,439	1,335	1,482	1,370	−43	−35
1922	37,302	35,025	1,697	1,746	1,347	1,383	350	363
1923	33,937	35,388	2,740	2,642	1,480	1,403	1,260	1,239
1924	38,568	36,627	2,850	2,754	1,504	1,434	1,346	1,320
1925	39,503	37,947	2,578	2,535	1,494	1,462	1,084	1,073
1926	39,449	39,020	2,700	2,703	1,511	1,489	1,189	1,214
1927	40,516	40,234	2,650	2,655	1,529	1,512	1,121	1,143
1928	41,667	41,377	2,523	2,561	1,513	1,531	1,010	1,030
1929	41,728	42,407	2,999	2,999	1,549	1,549	1,450	1,450
1930	43,857	43,857	2,851	2,942	1,536	1,587	1,315	1,355
1931	43,584	45,212	1,670	1,782	1,503	1,623	167	159
1932	41,424	45,371	840	966	1,388	1,623	−548	−657
1933	37,560	44,714	533	618	1,367	1,610	−834	−992
1934	36,246	43,722	732	801	1,459	1,603	−727	−802
1935	37,898	42,920	857	922	1,472	1,597	−615	−675
1936	37,809	42,245	1,280	1,369	1,491	1,602	−211	−233
1937	38,021	42,012	1,842	1,859	1,586	1,612	256	247
1938	40,864	42,259	1,289	1,281	1,593	1,631	−304	−350
1939	39,855	41,909	1,331	1,328	1,606	1,637	−275	−309
1940	39,686	41,600	1,933	1,920	1,631	1,639	302	281
1941	40,475	41,555	2,297	2,135	1,762	1,661	535	474
1942	43,794	42,029	2,058	1,796	1,926	1,675	132	121
1943	48,430	42,150	1,312	1,101	2,005	1,682	−693	−581
1944	50,008	41,569	1,646	1,375	2,016	1,684	−370	−309
1945	49,842	41,260	1,976	1,609	2,095	1,698	−119	−89
1946	51,423	41,171	3,233	2,339	2,452	1,758	781	581
1947	58,495	41,752	5,362	3,385	2,944	1,863	2,418	1,522
1948	68,020	43,187	6,869	4,062	3,327	1,950	3,542	2,112
1949	77,416	45,299	6,537	3,697	3,589	2,046	2,948	1,651
1950	81,881	46,950	6,488	3,509	3,752	2,065	2,736	1,444
1951	87,254	48,394						

(Notes to Table B–1 on next page)

All data exclude investment in land and landrights. Columns 1 and 2 exclude accrued depreciation.

NOTES BY COLUMN

1 Col. 2 of this table times col. 7, Table B–10, for the year preceding each January 1.

2 For 1870: Total for steam railroads and street and electric railways (6,994 millions) inflated by 15.14 per cent to include other transportation, communications, and public utilities. The ratio of estimated 1870 book value for all utilities to the corresponding book value for railroads and street railways (see note to col. 2, Table B–9) provided the basis for inflating the plant and equipment figures. For later years the series was derived by cumulative addition of net capital expenditures (col. 8, this table). The value of street railway plant and equipment transferred from private to public ownership was deducted—326 millions for 1941, and 87 million for 1948 (see Appendix F).

3 Tables B–9 (1870–1918); B–3 (1919–38); and B–2, col. 1 (1939–50).

4 Col. 3 deflated by the index shown in Table B–10, col. 8.

5 Col. 6 inflated by the index shown in Table B–10, col. 9.

6 Table B–12.

7, 8 Col. 3 minus col. 5; col. 4 minus col. 6.

TABLE B–2

Gross Capital Expenditures, Excluding Land, Current Dollars: All Regulated Industries, 1939–1950

(*in millions*)

Year	*Total Transportation, Communications, and Public Utilities* (1)	*Railroads* (2)	*Transportation Other Than Rails* (3)	*Communications* (4)	*Public Utilities* (5)	*Commerce-SEC Totals* (for comparison with col. 1) (6)
1939	1,331	267	365	269	430	1,467
1940	1,933	462	543	334	594	
1941	2,297	566	499	483	749	
1942	2,058	684	403	398	573	
1943	1,312	483	313	183	333	
1944	1,646	581	479	205	381	
1945	1,976	569	574	300	533	1,948
1946	3,233	581	923	764	965	3,115
1947	5,362	873	1,298	1,308	1,883	5,125
1948	6,869	1,322	1,285	1,629	2,633	6,889
1949	6,537	1,357	887	1,234	3,059	6,684
1950	6,488	1,129	1,212	1,032	3,115	6,736

NOTES BY COLUMN

1 Total of columns 2 through 5.

2 Series prepared in this study (Table C–1).

3 Commerce-SEC data for 1939 and 1945–50 (*Survey of Current Business*, Department of Commerce, August 1952) interpolated for 1940–44 by use of the Commerce-SEC data published prior to August 1952.

4 The Commerce-SEC figures for communications appear to be higher than the levels indicated by other sources; they apparently include some expenditures for non-telephone plant and may possibly include expenditures for re-used equipment. The estimates for this group were therefore prepared as follows:

For 1939: Total for telephones (our series, Table E–1), telegraph (derived from Department of Commerce data for construction expenditures and an estimate for the ratio of construction to total plant and equipment expenditures) and radio (estimate derived from Federal Communications Commission data).
For 1945–50: An estimate for 1948 was prepared as the total for telephones, telegraph, and radio and television; the figure for radio and television was estimated from Bureau of Internal Revenue data. The ratio between our 1948 estimate (1,629 million) and the Commerce-SEC figure (1,742 million) was used to adjust the Commerce-SEC data for the years 1945–50.
For 1940–44: The data for 1939 and 1945 were interpolated by use of expenditures for telephones and telegraph combined; the data for telegraph were obtained from the Commerce figures for construction expenditures and an estimate of the ratio of construction to total plant and equipment expenditures.

5 Total for electric light and power (our series, Table D–1), gas (American Gas Association), and sewer and water (Commerce series on construction expenditures).

6 *Survey of Current Business*, August 1952.

TABLE B–3

Gross Capital Expenditures, Excluding Land, Current Dollars: All Regulated Industries, 1919–1938
(in millions)

	GROSS CAPITAL EXPENDITURES				
Year	*Industries Studied in Detail* (1)	*Gas, Pipelines, Telegraph* (2)	*Allowance for Motor Transportation* (3)	*Sum of Columns* 1–3 (4)	*Estimated Total* (5)
1919	751	155	200	1,106	1,139
1920	1,295	181	200	1,676	1,726
1921	1,170	137	90	1,397	1,439
1922	1,292	236	120	1,648	1,697
1923	2,265	245	150	2,660	2,740
1924	2,252	355	160	2,767	2,850
1925	2,003	300	200	2,503	2,578
1926	2,041	380	200	2,621	2,700
1927	1,966	427	180	2,573	2,650
1928	1,912	348	190	2,450	2,523
1929	2,243	369	300	2,912	2,999
1930	2,270	298	200	2,768	2,851
1931	1,248	243	130	1,621	1,670
1932	629	127	60	816	840
1933	380	57	80	517	533
1934	498	73	140	711	732
1935	586	86	160	832	857
1936	918	135	190	1,243	1,280
1937	1,386	162	240	1,788	1,842
1938	1,001	110	140	1,251	1,289

NOTES BY COLUMN

1 Includes steam railroads, electric light and power, telephones, street and electric railways, and local bus lines.

2 George W. Terborgh, "Estimated Expenditures for New Durable Goods, 1919–1938," *Federal Reserve Bulletin*, September 1939.

3 Table B–4, column 4, figures rounded. Includes services incidental to transportation.

5 Column 4 increased by 3 per cent to allow for all other transportation and utilities: pullman and express, water transportation, air transportation, water supply companies, irrigation, and radio broadcasting. This percentage was obtained from comparison of changes in book value for the above-mentioned groups and for all transportation and utilities for 1912–22 and 1922–48 (see Table B–6). The percentages for the two intervals were averaged with weights of 1 and 4, respectively.

TABLE B–4

Estimated Gross Capital Expenditures for Motor Transportation and Transportation Services, 1919–1938

(millions of dollars)

		ESTIMATED GROSS CAPITAL EXPENDITURES		
Year	VALUE OF BUSINESS MOTOR VEHICLES PRODUCED (1)	*Motor Transport* (2)	*Local Bus Lines* (3)	*Motor Transport except Local Bus Lines* (4)
1919	380	199	1	198
1920	380	199	–	199
1921	181	95	1	94
1922	246	129	11	118
1923	338	178	22	155
1924	343	179	18	161
1925	428	224	20	204
1926	425	222	22	200
1927	373	195	18	177
1928	410	214	24	190
1929	623	326	21	305
1930	418	218	17	201
1931	273	143	17	126
1932	138	72	13	59
1933	179	94	16	78
1934	320	167	24	143
1935	379	198	42	156
1936	463	242	53	189
1937	534	279	41	238
1938	334	175	30	145

NOTES BY COLUMN

1 For 1919–33, Simon Kuznets, *Commodity Flow and Capital Formation* (National Bureau of Economic Research, 1938); for 1934–38, Automobile Manufacturers Association. The value figures are at producers' current prices.

2 Col. 1 multiplied by 0.5227, the average ratio for available years 1939–49 of gross capital expenditures for all motor transportation and transportation services to the value of output of business motor vehicles at producers' prices (see Table B–5). The series includes estimated expenditures for services incidental to transportation.

3 Table G–1, col. 3.

4 Col. 2 minus col. 3. Includes services incidental to transportation.

TABLE B–5

Ratio of Gross Capital Expenditures for Motor Transportation to the Value of Business Motor Vehicle Factory Sales, 1939, 1945–1949

(millions of dollars)

	GROSS CAPITAL EXPENDITURES		VALUE OF SALES	
Year	*All Transportation Other than Rail* (1)	*Motor Vehicle Transportation* (2)	*Business Motor Vehicles* (3)	*Ratio of Column 2 to Column 3* (4)
1939	365	273	495	0.5515
1945	574	430	1,182	.3638
1946	923	691	1,043	.6625
1947	1,298	972	1,710	.5684
1948	1,285	962	1,858	.5178
1949	887	664	1,407	.4719
Average ratio				.5227

NOTES BY COLUMN

1 Table B–2. Includes air transportation, water transportation, oil pipelines, and street railways, as well as motor transportation.

2 For 1948, Commerce-SEC figure for motor transportation and local transit (1,005 millions) less our figure for street railways (43 millions). For other years, the 1948 ratio between expenditures for motor transportation and for all transportation other than rail was applied. The figures shown include expenditures for transportation services.

3 Automobile Manufacturers Association. Data refer to sales at producers' prices.

TABLE B–6

Book Values, Excluding Land: All Transportation, Communications, and Public Utilities, Selected Dates, 1880–1948

(in millions)

	June 30			*December 31*		
	1880	*1890*	*1900*	*1912*	*1922*	*1948*
1. Steam railroads	4,977	8,163	10,430	16,858	21,066	28,832
2. Street railways and other local transit	123	348	1,419	4,163	4,604	1,079
3. Telephones	18	69	386	1,047	2,139	9,703
4. Electric light and power	0	67	357	1,877	3,805	18,945
5. Telegraph	89	147	156	216	350	447
6. Pipelines	11	44	149	341	475	939
7. Gas	124	201	445	825	1,420	4,347
8. Motor transportation and transportation services	0	0	0	0	950	3,788
9. All other: pullman, water transportation, irrigation, waterworks, air transportation, radio and television	591	768	1,028	1,971	2,686	3,422
10. Total, all industries, lines 1–9	5,933	9,807	14,370	27,298	37,495	71,502
11. Total, lines 1–4	5,118	8,647	12,592	23,945	31,614	...
Changes in book value from preceding date						
12. Lines 1–9		3,874	4,563	12,928	10,197	34,007
13. Lines 1–4		3,529	3,945	11,353	7,669	...
14. Line 8		...	...	...	950	2,838
15. Line 9		...	...	...	715	736
Percentage ratios of changes in book value						
16. Line 13 to line 12		91.09	86.46	87.82	75.21	...
17. Line 14 to line 12		...	...	...	9.3	8.3
18. Line 15 to line 12		...	...	...	7.0	2.2

(Notes to Table B–6 on next page)

For 1880–1922, data are from Simon Kuznets, *National Product since 1869* (National Bureau of Economic Research, 1946), except as noted below:

Steam railroads: Book value figures in this study, deducting for land 2.10 per cent in 1880, 2.29 per cent in 1890, 2.52 per cent in 1902, 2.70 per cent in 1912, and 2.80 per cent in 1922. The deductions are based on the 1880 ratio of value of land to total book value and on the estimated percentages of capital expenditures devoted to land in later years.

Gas: Interpolated between the dates shown in Table B–8; it has been assumed that natural gas transmission and distribution were of negligible importance through 1922 and the figures refer to manufactured gas only. Kuznets did not include gas with public utilities.

Motor transportation: Average of two estimates. The first was derived by use of the average ratio during 1940, 1947, and 1948 between (1) capital assets of the motor transportation industry and (2) truck registrations inflated with prices of motor vehicles. This ratio was applied to the inflated truck registration figure for 1922. The second estimate made use of the ratio during 1940, 1947, and 1948 of (1) capital assets of motor transportation to (2) seven-year totals of the value of bus and truck production. This ratio was applied to the seven-year total of value of bus and truck production ending with the year 1922.

All other: The 1922 data for pullman and express (227 millions) are from ICC. Air transportation and radio are assumed zero through 1912. For 1922, rough estimates were made for air transportation (40 million) and radio (20 million).

For 1948, all figures are from *Statistics of Income* (Bureau of Internal Revenue), adjusted to include corporations not filing balance sheets and noncorporate assets (see Table B–7). The figure for electric light and power includes gas and other utility plant owned by electric utilities while data for earlier years refer to electric utility plant alone; this change in classification does not, however, affect our calculations. The 1948 figure for railroads includes pullman and railway express; since such companies are of minor importance, the change in classification has a negligible effect.

TABLE B-7

Capital Assets, Excluding Land: Transportation, Communications, and Public Utilities, 1948

(millions of dollars)

Railroads	26,247	
Lessors of railroad property	2,585	
Total, railroads		28,832
Local transit		1,079
Trucking		1,747[a]
Other motor vehicle transportation		1,311[a]
Pipelines		939
Water transportation		1,363
Air transportation		549
Transportation services		691
Other transportation		39
Telephone		9,703
Telegraph		447
Radio and television		212
Other communications		1
Electric light and power		18,945
Gas		4,347
Water supply		903
Other utilities		132
Public utility lessors		262
Total		71,502

Includes depreciation reserves. Based on BIR *Statistics of Income* data, adjusted to include corporations not filing balance sheets. The adjustment was made on the basis of the ratio of total compiled receipts for all corporations to total compiled receipts for corporations filing balance sheets, separately for returns with net income and with no net income within each industry.

[a] Adjusted BIR data—1,178 millions for trucking and 889 for other motor vehicle transportation—were raised 48.3 per cent for trucking and 47.6 per cent for other motor vehicle transportation to include noncorporate capital assets. These percentages are unpublished figures developed by SEC from BIR data.

TABLE B-8

Book Value of Plant and Equipment, Manufactured Gas

(millions of dollars)

Year	*Total Capital, Including Current Assets* (1)	*Plant and Equipment* (2)	*Plant and Equipment, All Years* (3)
1869	72		52
1889	259	189	189
1899	567	435	435
1904	725	535	535
1909	916		676
1914	1,252		924
1919	1,466		1,082

Columns 1 and 2 are from censuses of manufactures.

Column 3: for 1869, col. 1 times the 1889 ratio of col. 2 to col. 1; for 1909–19, col. 1 times the 1904 ratio of col. 2 to col. 1.

TABLE B-9

Gross Capital Expenditures, Excluding Land, Current Dollars, All Regulated Industries, 1870–1918

(millions of dollars)

Year	*Total for Industries Studied in Detail* (1)	*Ratio of Column 1 to Total for All* (2)	*Gross Capital Expenditures: All Transportation, Communications, and Utilities* (3)
1870	384		452
1871	430		506
1872	389		457
1873	272		320
1874	158		186
1875	115	0.8504	135
1876	114		133
1877	127		147
1878	124		143
1879	139		159
1880	298		339
1881	453		511
1882	419		470
1883	301		335
1884	218		241
1885	174	.9109	191
1886	229		253
1887	318		353
1888	294		328
1889	283		318
1890	300		338
1891	310		351
1892	497		566
1893	531		608
1894	314		361
1895	209	.8646	242
1896	198		229
1897	216		249
1898	271		312
1899	389		448
1900	432		496
1901	433		497
1902	478		548
1903	523		598
1904	578		661
1905	700		799
1906	902	.8782	1,027
1907	1,000		1,154
1908	921		1,078
1909	954		1,131

(concluded on next page)

TABLE B–9 (concluded)

Year	*Total for Industries Studied in Detail* (1)	*Ratio of Column 1 to Total for All* (2)	*Gross Capital Expenditures: All Transportation, Communications, and Utilities* (3)
1910	1,126		1,352
1911	1,079		1,313
1912	1,085		1,337
1913	1,027		1,282
1914	798		1,008
1915	575		735
1916	705		912
1917	1,123		1,471
1918	884		1,171
1919		.7458	

NOTES BY COLUMN

1 Includes steam railroads, electric light and power, telephones, street and electric railways, and local bus lines.

2 For 1885, 1895, and 1906, from ratio of changes in book value of industries studied to changes in book value for all industries for 1880–90, 1890–1900, and 1900–1912 respectively (see Table B–6); for 1919 (used for interpolation only), average of 1919–22 ratios of capital expenditures of industries studied to total expenditures of public utilities. The figure for 1875 was derived from the estimated ratio of changes in book value of industries studied to changes in book value for the total, 1870–80. The 1870 book values were estimated as follows (in millions):

Steam railroads	3,408	(our estimate with deduction of 2.10 per cent for land)
Street railways	67	(our estimate)
Telephones	0	
Electric light and power	0	
Gas	59	(interpolated between dates shown in Table B–8)
All other	467	
Total	4,001	

The all other category was estimated on the assumption that the relative change in book value during 1870–80 was the same as for steam railroads, street railways, and gas in combination.

3 Col. 1 divided by col. 2, with ratios shown in col. 2 interpolated linearly for years not shown; the 1875 ratio was extrapolated to 1870.

TABLE B–10. Derivation of Cost Indexes for Capital Stock, Capital Formation, and Capital Consumption, All Regulated Industries, 1870–1950

	TOTALS FOR INDUSTRIES STUDIED IN DETAIL[a] (*in millions*)						IMPLICIT COST INDEXES[b]		
	Value of Plant and Equipment, January 1		*Gross Capital Expenditures*		*Capital Consumption*				
Year	*Current Dollars* (1)	*1929 Dollars* (2)	*Current Dollars* (3)	*1929 Dollars* (4)	*Current Dollars* (5)	1929 *Dollars* (6)	*Value of Plant and Equipment*[c] (7)	*Gross Capital Expenditures* (8)	*Capital Consumption* (9)
1869	...	...	...	...	...	...	55.1	...	...
1870	3,852	6,994	384	754	58	114	50.9	50.9	50.9
1871	3,890	7,635	430	847	64	126	50.7	50.8	50.8
1872	4,240	8,355	389	712	76	139	54.7	54.6	54.7
1873	4,880	8,927	272	487	84	151	55.8	55.9	55.6
1874	5,166	9,264	158	300	84	159	52.5	52.7	52.8
1875	4,935	9,406	115	230	82	164	49.9	50.0	50.0
1876	4,723	9,473	114	243	79	167	46.9	46.9	47.3
1877	4,474	9,548	127	296	75	174	43.0	42.9	43.1
1878	4,154	9,670	124	309	70	175	40.2	40.1	40.0
1879	3,946	9,804	139	349	72	181	39.7	39.8	39.8
1880	3,954	9,971	298	672	82	187	44.2	44.3	43.9
1881	4,619	10,457	453	1,009	89	200	44.9	44.9	44.5
1882	5,055	11,269	419	900	100	216	46.5	46.6	46.3
1883	5,553	11,953	301	660	106	231	45.6	45.6	45.9
1884	5,641	12,383	218	494	106	241	43.9	44.1	44.0
1885	5,551	12,636	174	401	109	252	43.2	43.4	43.3
1886	5,527	12,785	229	525	113	260	43.5	43.6	43.5
1887	5,680	13,051	318	734	117	271	43.2	43.3	43.2
1888	5,842	13,514	294	682	123	284	43.2	43.1	43.3
1889	6,013	13,912	283	661	127	296	42.8	42.8	42.9
1890	6,115	14,278	300	699	134	312	42.9	42.9	42.9
1891	6,293	14,664	310	742	139	330	41.9	41.8	42.1
1892	6,316	15,076	497	1,215	142	348	41.0	40.9	40.8
1893	6,535	15,941	531	1,308	152	372	40.7	40.6	40.9
1894	6,868	16,878	314	796	158	400	39.2	39.4	39.5
1895	6,779	17,274	209	540	163	421	39.0	38.7	38.7

(continued on next page)

TABLE B-10 (continued)

TOTALS FOR INDUSTRIES STUDIED IN DETAIL[a] (*in millions*)

	Value of Plant and Equipment, January 1		*Gross Capital Expenditures*		*Capital Consumption*		IMPLICIT COST INDEXES[b]		
Year	*Current Dollars* (1)	*1929 Dollars* (2)	*Current Dollars* (3)	*1929 Dollars* (4)	*Current Dollars* (5)	1929 *Dollars* (6)	*Value of Plant and Equipment*[c] (7)	*Gross Capital Expenditures* (8)	*Capital Consumption* (9)
1896	6,775	17,393	198	511	171	439	39.4	38.7	39.0
1897	6,878	17,465	216	556	177	456	38.6	38.8	38.8
1898	6,778	17,565	271	674	191	475	39.8	40.2	40.2
1899	7,078	17,762	389	889	216	495	43.4	43.8	43.6
1900	7,872	18,157	432	947	239	523	45.5	45.6	45.7
1901	8,449	18,579	433	962	249	551	45.0	45.0	45.2
1902	8,543	18,989	478	1,034	270	582	46.5	46.2	46.4
1903	9,037	19,441	523	1,112	285	600	47.8	47.0	47.5
1904	9,537	19,953	578	1,220	300	633	47.6	47.4	47.4
1905	9,786	20,540	700	1,426	328	666	49.5	49.1	49.2
1906	10,544	21,300	902	1,716	369	704	53.2	52.6	52.4
1907	11,877	22,312	1,000	1,833	407	748	55.2	54.6	54.4
1908	12,912	23,396	921	1,737	423	789	54.5	53.0	53.6
1909	13,258	24,342	954	1,738	456	820	56.2	54.9	55.6
1910	14,196	25,260	1,126	1,990	488	854	57.9	56.6	57.1
1911	15,279	26,395	1,079	1,891	516	893	58.0	57.1	57.8
1912	15,888	27,395	1,085	1,871	544	929	59.0	58.0	58.6
1913	16,716	28,337	1,027	1,714	575	959	60.3	59.9	60.0
1914	17,542	29,093	798	1,372	576	984	58.7	58.2	58.5
1915	17,307	29,483	575	973	597	1,000	59.7	59.1	59.7
1916	17,576	29,458	705	1,031	689	1,007	68.9	68.4	68.4
1917	20,305	29,481	1,123	1,345	857	1,020	84.7	83.5	84.0
1918	25,240	29,806	884	879	1,029	1,032	102.4	100.6	99.7
1919	30,368	29,653	751	691	1,140	1,039	113.5	108.7	109.7
1920	33,275	29,306	1,295	1,026	1,438	1,115	132.3	126.2	129.0
1921	38,647	29,215	1,170	1,085	1,200	1,109	106.5	107.8	108.2
1922	31,084	29,193	1,292	1,329	1,079	1,108	95.9	97.2	97.4
1923	28,198	29,414	2,265	2,185	1,183	1,121	105.3	103.7	105.5
1924	32,108	30,478	2,252	2,175	1,198	1,142	104.1	103.5	104.9
1925	32,804	31,510	2,003	1,970	1,187	1,161	101.1	101.7	102.2

(concluded on next page)

TABLE B-10 (concluded)

Year	TOTALS FOR INDUSTRIES STUDIED IN DETAIL[a] (*in millions*)						IMPLICIT COST INDEXES[b]		
	Value of Plant and Equipment, January 1		*Gross Capital Expenditures*		*Capital Consumption*				
	Current Dollars (1)	*1929 Dollars* (2)	*Current Dollars* (3)	*1929 Dollars* (4)	*Current Dollars* (5)	*1929 Dollars* (6)	*Value of Plant and Equipment*[c] (7)	*Gross Capital Expenditures* (8)	*Capital Consumption* (9)
1926	32,680	32,319	2,041	2,044	1,196	1,178	100.7	99.9	101.5
1927	33,397	33,165	1,966	1,969	1,206	1,193	100.7	99.8	101.1
1928	34,167	33,942	1,912	1,941	1,189	1,203	98.4	98.5	98.8
1929	34,112	34,679	2,243	2,243	1,213	1,213	100.0	100.0	100.0
1930	35,708	35,708	2,270	2,342	1,197	1,237	96.4	96.9	96.8
1931	35,506	36,815	1,248	1,332	1,159	1,252	91.3	93.7	92.6
1932	33,679	36,893	629	723	1,075	1,257	84.0	87.0	85.5
1933	30,531	36,357	380	441	1,063	1,252	82.9	86.2	84.9
1934	29,483	35,546	498	545	1,127	1,238	88.3	91.4	91.0
1935	30,765	34,852	586	630	1,133	1,229	89.5	93.0	92.2
1936	30,658	34,253	918	982	1,139	1,224	90.5	93,5	93.1
1937	30,774	34,012	1,386	1,399	1,200	1,220	96.7	99.1	98.4
1938	33,057	34,193	1,001	995	1,184	1,212	95.1	100.6	97.7
1939	32,320	33,976	978	976	1,187	1,210	95.4	100.2	98.1
1940	32,186	33,740	1,358	1,349	1,197	1,203	97.4	100.7	99.5
1941	32,698	33,562	1,728	1,606	1,274	1,201	104.2	107.6	106.1
1942	35,400	33,968	1,583	1,381	1,393	1,211	114.9	114.6	115.0
1943	39,235	34,139	937	786	1,451	1,217	120.3	119.2	119.2
1944	40,547	33,707	1,035	865	1,456	1,216	120.8	119.7	119.7
1945	40,283	33,356	1,281	1,043	1,505	1,220	124.9	122.8	123.4
1946	41,432	33,179	2,084	1,508	1,719	1,232	140.1	138.2	139.5
1947	46,878	33,455	3,599	2,272	1,985	1,256	157.5	158.4	158.0
1948	54,140	34,384	4,856	2,871	2,195	1,287	170.9	169.1	170.6
1949	61,484	35,968	4,660	2,635	2,335	1,331	174.4	176.8	175.4
1950	65,021	37,268	4,009	2,168	2,444	1,345	180.3	184.9	181.7
1951	68,662	38,091							

[a] Includes steam railroads, electric light and power, telephones, street and electric railways, and local bus lines.

[b] Current dollar total, for each series, divided by 1929 dollar total.

[c] Refers to January 1 of succeeding year.

TABLE B–11

Capital Consumption, 1929 Dollars, All Transportation, Communications, and Public Utilities, Selected Dates, 1870–1922

(*in millions*)

	1870	*1880*	*1890*	*1900*	*1912*	*1922*
1. Book value, industries studied in detail	3,475	5,118	8,647	12,592	23,945	31,614
2. Book value, all other public utilities except those listed in line 6	526	815	1,160	1,778	3,353	4,871
3. Line 2 divided by line 1	0.1514	0.1592	0.1342	0.1412	0.1400	0.1541
4. Capital consumption, 1929 dollars, industries in line 1	114	187	312	523	929	1,108
5. Estimated capital consumption, industries in line 2	17	30	42	74	130	171
6. Book value: air transportation, radio and television, motor transportation and transportation services	0	0	0	0	0	1,010
7. Price index underlying book value (1929 = 100), industries in line 6						82.1
8. Book value in line 6 deflated to 1929 dollars						1,230
9. Capital consumption, 1929 dollars, industries in line 6						104
10. Capital consumption, 1929 dollars, all transportation, communications, and public utilities	131	217	354	597	1,069	1,383

Industries, studied in detail are steam railroads, electric light and power, telephones, street and electric railways, and local bus lines.

NOTES BY LINE

1, 2, 6 For 1870, see note on col. 2, Table B–9. Figures for 1880–1922 are from Table B–6; line 6 assumed zero through 1912.

4 See appendixes relating to the separate industries.

5 Line 3 multiplied by line 4.

7 Table B–10, average of col. 8 for the years 1911–22. An average twelve-year life is suggested by the depreciation rate.

9 Line 8 multiplied by 0.0847. This depreciation rate is based on the ratio of depreciation charges to book value for the included industries in 1948, as shown by BIR data.

10 Sum of lines 4, 5, and 9.

TABLE B-12

Capital Consumption, 1929 Dollars: All Regulated Industries, 1870–1950

(in millions)

Year	Total for Industries Studied in Detail (1)	OTHER TRANSPORTATION AND PUBLIC UTILITIES: Radio and Television, Air Transportation, Motor Transportation, and Services Incidental to Transportation (2)	All Other (3)	Total, Columns 2 and 3 (4)	All Transportation and Public Utilities (5)
1870	114			17	131
1871	126			18	144
1872	139			20	159
1873	151			21	172
1874	159			22	181
1875	164			24	188
1876	167			25	192
1877	174			26	200
1878	175			27	202
1879	181			29	210
1880	187			30	217
1881	200			31	231
1882	216			32	248
1883	231			34	265
1884	241			35	276
1885	252			36	288
1886	260			37	297
1887	271			38	309
1888	284			40	324
1889	296			41	337
1890	312			42	354
1891	330			45	375
1892	348			48	396
1893	372			52	424
1894	400			55	455
1895	421			58	479
1896	439			61	500
1897	456			64	520
1898	475			68	543
1899	495			71	566
1900	523			74	597
1901	551			79	630
1902	582			83	665
1903	600			88	688
1904	633			93	726
1905	666			98	764
1906	704			102	806
1907	748			107	855
1908	789			112	901
1909	820			116	936

(continued on next page)

TABLE B–12 (continued)

Year	Total for Industries Studied in Detail (1)	OTHER TRANSPORTATION AND PUBLIC UTILITIES: Radio and Television, Air Transportation, Motor Transportation, and Services Incidental to Transportation (2)	All Other (3)	Total, Columns 2 and 3 (4)	All Transportation and Public Utilities (5)
1910	854			121	975
1911	893			126	1,019
1912	929			130	1,059
1913	959			145	1,104
1914	984			159	1,143
1915	1,000			174	1,174
1916	1,007			188	1,195
1917	1,020			203	1,223
1918	1,032			217	1,249
1919	1,039			232	1,271
1920	1,115			246	1,361
1921	1,109			261	1,370
1922	1,108	104	171	275	1,383
1923	1,121	104	178	282	1,403
1924	1,142	105	187	292	1,434
1925	1,161	105	196	301	1,462
1926	1,178	106	205	311	1,489
1927	1,193	106	213	319	1,512
1928	1,203	107	221	328	1,531
1929	1,213	107	229	336	1,549
1930	1,237	111	239	350	1,587
1931	1,252	122	249	371	1,623
1932	1,257	110	256	366	1,623
1933	1,252	97	261	358	1,610
1934	1,238	101	264	365	1,603
1935	1,229	100	268	368	1,597
1936	1,224	105	273	378	1,602
1937	1,220	114	278	392	1,612
1938	1,212	137	282	419	1,631
1939	1,210	139	288	427	1,637
1940	1,203	144	292	436	1,639
1941	1,201	163	297	460	1,661
1942	1,211	158	306	464	1,675
1943	1,217	152	313	465	1,682
1944	1,216	149	319	468	1,684
1945	1,220	152	326	478	1,698
1946	1,232	191	335	526	1,758
1947	1,256	259	348	607	1,863
1948	1,287	300	363	663	1,950
1949	1,331	340	375	715	2,046
1950	1,345	341	379	720	2,065

(Notes to Table B–12 on next page)

NOTES BY COLUMN

1 Includes steam railroads, street and electric railways, and local bus lines; electric light and power, and telephones.

2 For 1922, from Table B–11; for 1929–50, derived by use of BIR and Department of Commerce data on depreciation, deflated to constant dollars. A twelve-year average life was assumed in preparing the deflator. For 1923–28, derived by linear interpolation.

3 For 1922, Table B–11; for 1948, obtained from the ratio of depreciation charges for these industries to the industries shown in col. 1 as reported by BIR, and capital consumption for the industries in col. 1. Data for remaining years of the period 1922–50, obtained by interpolation and extrapolation by use of col. 1.

4 For 1870, 1880, 1890, 1900, 1912, and 1922, from Table B–11; for other years of the period 1870–1922, obtained by linear interpolation; for 1923–50, col. 2 plus col. 3.

5 Col. 1 plus col. 4.

APPENDIX C

Tables on the Derivation of Capital Formation Data for Railroads

NOTE: A complete description of the derivation of the railroad data is given in Appendix A.

TABLE C-1

Value of Road and Equipment, Capital Formation, and Capital Consumption, Steam Railroads, Annual Data, 1870–1950

(millions of dollars)

	VALUE OF ROAD AND EQUIPMENT, JANUARY 1		GROSS CAPITAL EXPENDITURES		CAPITAL CONSUMPTION		NET CAPITAL EXPENDITURES	
Year	*Current Dollars* (1)	*1929 Dollars* (2)	*Current Dollars* (3)	*1929 Dollars* (4)	*Current Dollars* (5)	*1929 Dollars* (6)	*Current Dollars* (7)	*1929 Dollars* (8)
1870	3,787	6,886	380	747	56	110	324	637
1871	3,829	7,523	420	828	62	122	358	706
1872	4,172	8,229	379	694	73	134	306	560
1873	4,799	8,789	262	470	81	145	181	325
1874	5,076	9,114	148	282	80	153	68	130
1875	4,844	9,244	105	211	78	157	27	54
1876	4,630	9,298	104	222	75	160	29	62
1877	4,380	9,360	117	273	71	166	46	107
1878	4,061	9,467	114	284	67	167	47	117
1879	3,853	9,584	125	316	68	172	57	144
1880	3,852	9,728	282	639	78	177	204	463
1881	4,494	10,191	440	982	84	188	356	795
1882	4,922	10,986	398	858	94	203	304	655
1883	5,401	11,641	283	622	98	215	185	407
1884	5,482	12,048	199	453	98	223	101	230
1885	5,390	12,278	150	347	100	231	50	116
1886	5,354	12,394	206	474	103	237	103	237
1887	5,494	12,631	275	637	106	245	169	391
1888	5,626	13,022	251	581	110	255	141	326
1889	5,766	13,348	227	530	113	264	114	266
1890	5,827	13,614	231	538	116	270	115	268
1891	5,955	13,882	237	566	117	279	120	286
1892	5,936	14,168	407	993	118	288	289	705
1893	6,098	14,873	433	1,064	123	302	310	762
1894	6,363	15,635	190	485	125	319	65	166
1895	6,194	15,801	69	177	127	326	−58	−149
1896	6,104	15,652	48	122	130	329	−82	−208
1897	6,100	15,444	48	125	127	330	−79	−205
1898	5,867	15,239	82	207	132	332	−50	−126
1899	6,000	15,113	175	405	144	333	31	72
1900	6,560	15,185	205	452	155	341	50	110
1901	6,944	15,295	186	414	156	347	30	67
1902	6,898	15,362	200	430	164	353	36	77
1903	7,179	15,439	217	452	173	360	44	92
1904	7,455	15,531	250	524	175	367	75	157
1905	7,483	15,688	329	662	186	374	143	288
1906	7,940	15,976	474	883	205	382	269	501
1907	8,848	16,477	570	1,023	220	395	350	628
1908	9,527	17,105	575	1,042	227	411	348	630
1909	9,790	17,735	626	1,102	241	424	385	678

(continued on next page)

TABLE C–1 (continued)

Year	VALUE OF ROAD AND EQUIPMENT JANUARY 1		GROSS CAPITAL EXPENDITURES		CAPITAL CONSUMPTION		NET CAPITAL EXPENDITURES	
	Current Dollars (1)	*1929 Dollars* (2)	*Current Dollars* (3)	*1929 Dollars* (4)	*Current Dollars* (5)	*1929 Dollars* (6)	*Current Dollars* (7)	*1929 Dollars* (8)
1910	10,459	18,413	714	1,216	258	440	456	777
1911	11,265	19,190	653	1,114	268	457	385	657
1912	11,630	19,847	636	1,067	281	471	355	596
1913	12,184	20,443	682	1,116	296	484	386	632
1914	12,877	21,075	465	783	297	500	168	283
1915	12,687	21,358	281	467	307	510	−26	−43
1916	12,832	21,315	363	524	358	517	5	7
1917	14,776	21,322	562	657	449	525	113	132
1918	18,343	21,454	503	483	549	527	−46	−44
1919	22,309	21,410	401	345	622	535	−221	−190
1920	24,679	21,220	678	498	718	527	−40	−29
1921	28,841	21,191	591	554	552	517	39	37
1922	22,629	21,228	518	541	487	509	31	32
1923	20,367	21,260	1,103	1,035	543	509	560	525
1924	23,223	21,785	972	927	532	508	439	419
1925	23,270	22,204	791	782	510	504	281	278
1926	22,752	22,482	887	876	506	500	381	376
1927	23,132	22,858	804	790	503	494	301	296
1928	23,571	23,154	727	736	483	489	244	247
1929	23,120	23,401	860	860	487	487	373	373
1930	23,774	23,774	834	865	479	497	355	368
1931	23,273	24,142	349	389	450	501	−101	−112
1932	21,579	24,030	166	203	413	504	−247	−301
1933	19,434	23,729	112	140	403	503	−299	−363
1934	18,716	23,366	180	214	424	503	−244	−290
1935	19,453	23,076	171	200	433	507	−262	−307
1936	19,467	22,769	328	381	441	512	−113	−131
1937	19,491	22,638	565	613	477	518	88	95
1938	20,960	22,733	273	304	467	520	−194	−216
1939	20,220	22,517	267	297	469	522	−202	−225
1940	20,018	22,292	462	501	482	523	−20	−22
1941	20,533	22,270	566	569	522	525	44	44
1942	22,180	22,314	684	604	597	527	87	77
1943	25,369	22,391	483	401	635	527	−152	−126
1944	26,829	22,265	581	480	639	528	−58	−48
1945	26,905	22,217	569	452	672	534	−103	−82
1946	27,868	22,135	581	416	757	542	−176	−126
1947	30,769	22,009	873	564	844	545	29	19
1948	34,099	22,028	1,322	781	921	544	401	237
1949	37,695	22,265	1,357	799	942	555	415	244
1950	38,243	22,509	1,129	651	970	559	159	92
1951	39,213	22,601						

(Notes to Table C–1 on next page)

All data exclude investment in land and landrights. Columns 1 and 2 exclude accrued depreciation.

NOTES BY COLUMN

1 Col. 2 inflated by index of cost of road and equipment, col. 12, Table C–11.
2 Derived by applying net capital expenditures in 1929 dollars (col. 8) to reproduction cost less depreciation of road and equipment of all railroads in 1929 dollars on Jan. 1, 1937 (from Table C–19).
3 From Table C–10.
4 Col. 3 deflated by the index of cost of road and equipment, col. 12, Table C–11.
5 From Table C–16.
6 Col. 5 deflated by the index of cost of road and equipment, col. 12, Table C–11.
7 Col. 3 minus col. 5.
8 Col. 7 deflated by the index of cost of road and equipment, col. 12, Table C–11.

TABLE C-2

Derivation of Book Value of Road and Equipment of Steam Railroads, 1891–1951

(millions of dollars)

Year	Book Value of Road and Equipment Reported by ICC[a]		Adjustment Factor for Undercoverage (*based on track mileage*)[b]		Book Values Adjusted for Undercoverage		Final Estimate of Book Value of Road and Equipment
	June 30 (1)	*January 1* (2)	*June 30* (3)	*January 1* (4)	*June 30* (5)	*January 1* (6)	*January 1* (7)
1890	8,134		0.9736		8,354		
1891	8,445		.9774		8,640		8,497
1892	8,690		.9658		8,998		8,819
1893	8,938		.9653		9,259		9,128
1894	9,073		.9882		9,182		9,220
1895	9,203		.9918		9,280		9,231
1896	9,500		.9911		9,586		9,433
1897	9,709		.9918		9,790		9,688
1898	9,761		.9945		9,815		9,802
1899	9,962		.9946		10,016		9,916
1900	10,263		.9979		10,285		10,150
1901	10,405		.9941		10,467		10,376
1902	10,658		.9961		10,700		10,584
1903	10,974		.9962		11,015		10,858
1904	11,512		.9938		11,583		11,299
1905	11,951		.9950		12,011		11,797
1906	12,420		.9920		12,520		12,266
1907	13,030		.9900		13,162		12,841
1908	13,544		.9909		13,668		13,415
1909	13,949		.9913		14,071		13,870

(continued on next page)

TABLE C–2 (continued)

Year	BOOK VALUE OF ROAD AND EQUIPMENT REPORTED BY ICC[a]		ADJUSTMENT FACTOR FOR UNDERCOVERAGE (*based on track mileage*)[b]		BOOK VALUES ADJUSTED FOR UNDERCOVERAGE		FINAL ESTIMATE OF BOOK VALUE OF ROAD AND EQUIPMENT
	June 30 (1)	*January 1* (2)	*June 30* (3)	*January 1* (4)	*June 30* (5)	*January 1* (6)	*January 1* (7)
1910	14,922		0.9615		15,520		14,552
1911	15,990		.9588		16,677		16,099
1912	16,409		.9610		17,075		16,876
1913	17,008		.9648		17,629		17,326
1914	17,526		.9674		18,117		17,868
1915	17,884		.9672		18,490		18,316
1916	18,170		.9689		18,753		18,622
1917		18,320		0.9700		18,955	18,955
1918		19,083		.9762		19,543	19,543
1919		19,437		.9733		19,915	19,915
1920		19,802		.9760		20,277	20,277
1921		20,433		.9796		20,867	20,867
1922		20,925		.9787		21,405	21,405
1923		21,176		.9773		21,673	21,673
1924		21,981		.9772		22,404	22,404
1925		22,817		.9786		23,344	23,344
1926		23,481		.9814		23,929	23,929
1927		24,644		.9838		24,247	24,247
1928		25,221		.9860		24,640	24,640
1929		25,646		.9882		24,978	24,978
1930		26,283		.9893		26,528	26,528
1931		26,952		.9900		27,208	27,208
1932		27,007		.9898		27,367	27,367
1933		27,004		.9907		27,261	27,261
1934		26,853		.9904		27,125	27,125

(concluded on next page)

TABLE C–2 (concluded)

Year	BOOK VALUE OF ROAD AND EQUIPMENT REPORTED BY ICC[a]		ADJUSTMENT FACTOR FOR UNDERCOVERAGE (*based on track mileage*)[b]		BOOK VALUES ADJUSTED FOR UNDERCOVERAGE		FINAL ESTIMATE OF BOOK VALUE OF ROAD AND EQUIPMENT
	June 30 (1)	*January 1* (2)	*June 30* (3)	*January 1* (4)	*June 30* (5)	*January 1* (6)	*January 1* (7)
1935		26,627		0.9909		26,789	26,789
1936		26,447		.9917		26,622	26,622
1937		26,385		.9920		26,670	26,670
1938		26,598		.9929		26,753	26,753
1939		26,557		.9927		26,735	26,735
1940		26,503		.9937		26,662	26,662
1941		26,618		.9937		26,765	26,765
1942		26,651		.9938		26,801	26,801
1943		26,822		.9945		26,991	26,991
1944		27,137		.9947		27,298	27,298
1945		27,630		.9947		27,796	27,796
1946		27,993		.9941		28,199	28,199
1947		28,314		.9950		28,504	28,504
1948		28,733		.9951		28,785	28,785
1949		29,750		.9976		29,777	29,777
1950		30,639		.9977		30,710	30,710
1951		31,314		.9982		31,370	31,370

[a] *Statistics of Railways in the United States*, Interstate Commerce Commission, Annual Reports.

[b] Ratio of track-mileage owned by reporting companies to that owned by all companies, from source above.

TABLE C-3

Derivation of Book Value of Road and Equipment of Steam Railroads, 1860, and 1869–1890

(millions of dollars)

	BOOK VALUE OF ROAD AND EQUIPMENT, JUNE 30, REPORTED BY			ADJUSTMENT FACTOR FOR UNDERCOVERAGE (*based on track mileage*)[d]			BOOK VALUES ADJUSTED FOR UNDERCOVERAGE			FINAL ESTIMATES, JUNE 30	FINAL ESTIMATES, JANUARY 1
Year	*Census*[a] (1)	*Poor's*[b] (2)	*ICC*[c] (3)	*Census* (4)	*Poor's* (5)	*ICC* (6)	*Census* (7)	*Poor's* (8)	*ICC* (9)	(10)	(11)
1860	1,166			0.9735			1,198			1,229	
1869										3,276	
1870										3,481	3,378
1871										3,685	3,583
1872										3,890	3,788
1873										4,095	3,992
1874										4,299	4,197
1875										4,504	4,402
1876		4,087			0.9782			4,178		4,709	4,606
1877		4,180			.9800			4,266		4,774	4,742
1878		4,166			1.0000			4,166		4,700	4,737
1879		4,417			.9890			4,466		4,923	4,812
1880	4,839	4,654		.9766	.9938		4,955	4,683		5,084	5,004
1881		5,578			.9688			5,758		5,882	5,483
1882		6,035			.9307			6,484		6,422	6,152

(concluded on next page)

TABLE C-3 (concluded)

Year	Book Value of Road and Equipment, June 30, Reported by			Adjustment Factor for Undercoverage (*based on track mileage*)[d]			Book Values Adjusted for Undercoverage			Final Estimates, June 30	Final Estimates, January 1
	Census[a] (1)	*Poor's*[b] (2)	*ICC*[c] (3)	*Census* (4)	*Poor's* (5)	*ICC* (6)	*Census* (7)	*Poor's* (8)	*ICC* (9)	(10)	(11)
1883		6,685			0.9323			7,170		6,931	6,676
1884		6,925			.9535			7,262		6,999	6,965
1885		7,038			.9747			7,220		6,968	6,984
1886		7,255			.9905			7,325		7,045	7,006
1887		7,799			.9887			7,889		7,464	7,254
1888		8,344			.9761			8,549		7,954	7,709
1889		8,598			.9788			8,784		8,129	8,042
1890	8,121	8,789	8,134	0.9974	.9672	0.9736	8,142	9,087	8,354	8,354	8,242

[a] Census of Agencies of Transportation.
[b] *Poor's Manual of Railroads*, annual.
[c] *Statistics of Railways in the United States*, Annual Report.
[d] Ratio of track-mileage operated by reporting companies to that operated by all companies.

TABLE C–4

Derivation of Gross Capital Expenditures by Steam Railro

Year	GCE including land, Class I and II roads, reported by ICC[a]		Ratio of book value of road and equipment of Class I and II roads to that of all classes (ICC)[a]	
	Year ending June 30 (1)	*Year ending December 31* (2)	*Year ending June 30* (3)	*Year ending December 31* (4)
1912	551		0.9754	
1913	680		.9614	
1914	639		.9664	
1915	264[c]		.9644	
1916	281[c]	354[c]	.9655	0.9651
1917		572[c]		.9654
1918		488[c]		.9694
1919		382		.9681
1920		648		.9651
1921		565		.9661
1922		505		.9663
1923		1,076		.9671
1924		938		.9673
1925		803		.9638
1926		885		.9634
1927		814		.9641
1928		728		.9648
1929		875		.9651
1930		844		.9631
1931		353		.9629
1932		171		.9628
1933		114		.9616
1934		177		.9614
1935		194		.9613
1936		319		.9611
1937		549		.9614
1938		262		.9612
1939		255		.9612
1940		448		.9610
1941		552		.9610
1942		672		.9612
1943		475		.9615
1944		571		.9619
1945		582		.9615
1946		582		.9616
1947		863		.9618
1948		1,282		.9622
1949		1,319		.9618
1950		1,089		.9620

[a] *Statistics of Railways in the United States,* Annual Reports.
[b] Product of col. 3 or 4 of this table and col. 3 or 4 of Table C–2.

TABLE C-4

nt Dollars, 1912–1950 (*in millions*)

ADJUSTMENT FACTOR FOR UNDERCOVERAGE (BASED ON BOOK VALUE AND TRACK MILEAGE)[b]		GCE AFTER ADJUSTMENT FOR UNDERCOVERAGE		COL. 7 SHIFTED TO CALENDAR YEAR BASIS	FINAL ESTIMATE: COLS. 8 AND 9 AFTER EXCLUSION OF LAND EXPENDITURES
Year ending June 30	*Year ending December 31*	*Year ending June 30*	*Year ending December 31*		*Year ending December 31*
(5)	(6)	(7)	(8)	(9)	(10)
0.9374		588		660	633
.9276		733		708	679
.9349		683		483	465
.9328		283		292	280
.9355	0.9361	300	378		365
	.9424		607		562
	.9435		517		502
	.9449		404		401
	.9454		685		678
	.9455		598		592
	.9444		535		518
	.9451		1,139		1,099
	.9466		991		973
	.9459		849		791
	.9478		934		888
	.9506		856		804
	.9534		764		728
	.9548		916		859
	.9535		885		834
	.9531		370		350
	.9538		179		166
	.9524		120		113
	.9527		186		179
	.9533		204		171
	.9534		335		329
	.9546		575		565
	.9542		275		272
	.9551		267		267
	.9549		469		462
	.9550		578		566
	.9559		703		684
	.9564		479		484
	.9568		597		582
	.9558		609		569
	.9568		608		582
	.9571		902		870
	.9599		1,336		1,320
	.9596		1,375		1,357
	.9603		1,134		1,129

[c] Net of retirements. The failure to include data gross of retirements in those years may have reflected he negligible quantity of actual retirements during the war, similar to the situation during World Var II. In the immediate post-World War I year—1919—retirements amounted to 12 per cent of ross capital expenditures, but this undoubtedly reflected in part the deferred retirements of the war eriod.

TABLE C–5

Derivation of Gross Capital Expenditures of Steam Railroads from Samples in Selected Years

(millions of dollars)

Year Ending June 30	*Value of Road and Equipment*[a] *Sample Companies* (1)	*All Roads* (2)	*Ratio of Col. 1 to Col. 2* (3)	*Gross Capital Expenditures by Sample Companies* (4)	*Ratio of Col. 4 to Col. 1* (5)	*Gross Capital Expenditures of All Roads (col. 2 × col. 5)* (6)
1873	880	3,890	0.226	77	0.088	341
1877	2,331	4,709	.495	51	.022	104
1880	981	4,923	.199	31	.032	157
1882	3,416	5,882	.581	279	.082	482
1887	2,039	7,045	.290	80	.039	276
1891	5,141	8,354	.615	143	.028	234
1892	5,000	8,640	.579	145	.029	251
1896	4,180	9,586	.436	24	.006	58
1900	6,782	10,016	.171	171	.025	250
1904	3,700	11,583	.319	78	.021	243
1907	3,354	12,520	.268	153	.046	571
1910	8,225	15,520	.530	379	.046	714
1911	3,948	16,677	.237	183	.046	766

State reports from which samples were obtained are as follows: for 1873, Illinois, Ohio, and Pennsylvania; for 1877, California, Connecticut, Illinois, Massachusetts, Michigan, Minnesota, New York, Ohio, Pennsylvania, and Virginia; for 1880, Illinois, Iowa, and Pennsylvania; for 1882, California, Illinois, Iowa, Maine, Massachusetts, Michigan, New York, Ohio, Pennsylvania, Virginia, and Wisconsin; for 1887, Kansas, Pennsylvania, and Wisconsin; for 1891, California, Iowa, Kansas, Maine, Massachusetts, Michigan, New York, Ohio, Pennsylvania, Virginia, and Wisconsin; for 1892, California, Iowa, Kansas, Maine, Massachusetts, Michigan, New York, Pennsylvania, Virginia, and Wisconsin; for 1896, Iowa, Ohio, New York (large roads accounting for 78 per cent of total physical assets in the State), and Wisconsin; for 1900, California, Iowa, New York, Ohio, Pennsylvania, Virginia, and Wisconsin; for 1904, New York (large roads accounting for 82 per cent of total physical assets in the State) Ohio and Wisconsin; for 1907, Ohio and Wisconsin; for 1910, Indiana, Kansas, Minnesota, and New York; for 1911, Iowa, Minnesota, and Wisconsin.

[a] End of year for 1896, 1904, 1910, and 1911; beginning of year for other dates.

TABLE C-6

Book Value of Road and Equipment and Gross Capital Expenditures of Steam Railroads in Selected States, Year Ending June 30, 1914

(millions of dollars)

State	*Book Value of Road and Equipment, Beginning of Year*	*Gross Capital Expenditures*
Iowa	1,801.9	52.3
Kansas	1,475.1	27.5
Maine	171.6	5.2
Massachusetts	620.7	18.0
Michigan	1,621.5	75.4
New York	2,581.9	100.0
Texas	553.7	21.1
Virginia	1,575.6	69.2
Wisconsin	2,407.7	116.1
Total[a]	10,130.0	390.0

[a] Excludes duplications.

TABLE C-7

Estimation of Gross Capital Expenditures from Control Samples, Year Ending June 30, 1914

(millions of dollars)

Sample (1)	*Book Value of Road and Equipment, Beginning of Year*[a] (2)	*Gross Capital Expenditures*[a] (3)	*Ratio of Col. 3 to Col. 2* (4)	*Size of Sample*[b] (5)	*Estimated Gross Capital Expenditures of All Railroads*[c] (6)	*Percentage Error*[d] (7)
Large Sample	10,130.0	390.0	0.0385	0.591	660	−3.5
Small Samples						
I	4,929.4	202.2	.0410	.288	703	+2.8
II	6,398.4	243.5	.0381	.373	653	−4.5
III	5,531.8	207.3	.0375	.323	643	−6.0
IV	4,672.2	172.1	.0368	.273	631	−7.7
V	5,619.8	202.0	.0359	.328	615	−10.1

The large sample includes the nine states in Table C-6. The small samples include:

I. Iowa, Michigan, Wisconsin
II. Kansas, New York, Wisconsin
III. Iowa, Michigan, New York
IV. Kansas, Michigan, Virginia
V. Kansas, Michigan, New York

[a] Figures shown exclude duplications within each sample.

[b] Ratio of book value of road and equipment for roads in sample to that for all roads (17,139 million).

[c] Book value of road and equipment of all roads multiplied by col. 4.

[d] Reported gross capital expenditures of all roads, including land, is 693 million. See Table C-4, col. 7.

TABLE C–8

Derivation of Track Mileage, Steam Railroads, 1869–1911

Year Ending June 30	MILES OF ROAD (Single-Track) OPERATED	MILES OF ALL TRACK OPERATED		FINAL SERIES, MILES OF ALL TRACK[b]
	Poor's[a] (1)	*Poor's*[a] (2)	*ICC* (3)	(4)
1869	44,537			53,444
1870	49,883			59,859
1871	56,612			67,934
1872	63,236			75,882
1873	68,220			81,863
1874	71,327			85,591
1875	73,241			87,888
1876	75,452			90,541
1877	77,945	95,987		93,533
1878		100,479		97,910
1879		104,203		101,539
1880		110,202		107,385
1881		123,051		119,905
1882		135,667		132,199
1883		144,990		141,283
1884		152,758		148,853
1885		158,460		154,409
1886		164,229		160,030
1887		176,444		171,933
1888		188,156		183,346
1889		196,732		191,702
1890		205,120	199,876	199,876
1891			207,446	207,446
1892			211,051	211,051
1893			221,864	221,864
1894			229,796	229,796

(concluded on next page)

TABLE C-8 (concluded)

Year Ending June 30	MILES OF ROAD (Single-Track) OPERATED	MILES OF ALL TRACK OPERATED		FINAL SERIES, MILES OF ALL TRACK[c]
	Poor's[a] (1)	*Poor's*[a] (2)	*ICC* (3)	(4)
1895			233,276	233,276
1896			239,140	239,140
1897			242,013	242,013
1898			245,334	245,334
1899			250,143	250,143
1900			258,784	258,784
1901			265,352	265,352
1902			274,195	274,195
1903			283,822	283,822
1904			297,073	297,073
1905			306,797	306,797
1906			317,083	317,083
1907			327,975	327,975
1908			333,646[c]	338,214
1909			342,351[c]	347,038
1910			351,767[c]	356,583
1911			362,824[c]	367,791

[a] Averages of figures for December 31 of adjacent years.

[b] For 1911: col. 3 plus track-mileage of switching and terminal companies as reported by ICC (4,967 miles). For 1908–10, col. 3 times the ratio (1.01369) in 1911 of track-mileage including switching and terminal companies to track-mileage excluding such companies. For 1890–1907, col. 3; 1877–89, col. 2 linked to col. 4 by use of the 1890 ratio between the two series. For 1869–76, col. 1 linked to col. 4 by use of the 1877 ratio between the two series.

[c] Excludes switching and terminal companies.

TABLE C–9

Derivation of Gross Capital Expenditures, Including Land, by Steam Railroads, 1870–1912

(millions of dollars)

Year	Annual Increase in Track Mileage, Year Ending June 30[a] (1)	Index of Railroad Construction Costs, Year Ending June 30[b] (1929 = 100) (2)	Col. 1 × Col. 2 (3)	Gross Capital Expenditures for Selected Years, Year Ending June 30[c] (4)	Ratio of Col. 4 to Col. 3, and Interpolations (5)	Gross Capital Expenditures, Year Ending June 30 (col. 5 × col. 3) (6)	Gross Capital Expenditures, Year Ending December 31 (7)
1870	6,415	53.0	3,400		0.10327	351	388
1871	8,075	50.8	4,102		.10327	424	429
1872	7,948	52.7	4,189		.10327	433	387
1873	5,981	55.2	3,302	341	.10327	341	268
1874	3,728	54.1	2,017		.09681	195	151
1875	2,297	51.1	1,174		.09035	106	107
1876	2,653	48.3	1,281		.08390	107	106
1877	2,992	44.9	1,343	104	.07744	104	119
1878	4,377	41.6	1,821		.07300	133	116
1879	3,629	39.9	1,448		.06855	99.	128
1880	5,846	41.9	2,449	157	.06411	157	288
1881	12,520	44.5	5,571		.07505	418	450
1882	12,294	45.6	5,606	482	.08598	482	407
1883	9,084	46.0	4,179		.07947	332	290
1884	7,570	44.7	3,384		.07296	247	204
1885	5,556	43.6	2,422		.06645	161	154
1886	5,621	43.4	2,440		.05994	146	211
1887	11,903	43.4	5,166	276	.05343	276	282
1888	11,413	43.2	4,930		.05830	287	257
1889	8,356	43.0	3,593		.06317	227	233
1890	8,174	42.9	3,507		.06803	239	237
1891	7,570	42.4	3,210	234	.07290	234	243

(concluded on next page)

TABLE C–9 (concluded)

Year	Annual Increase in Track Mileage, Year Ending June 30[a] (1)	Index of Railroad Construction Costs, Year Ending June 30[b] (1929 = 100) (2)	Col. 1 × Col. 2 (3)	Gross Capital Expenditures for Selected Years, Year Ending June 30[c] (4)	Ratio of Col. 4 to Col. 3, and Interpolations (5)	Gross Capital Expenditures, Year Ending June 30 (col. 5 × col. 3) (6)	Gross Capital Expenditures, Year Ending December 31 (7)
1892	3,605	41.5	1,496	251	0.16778	251	418
1893	10,813	40.9	4,423		.13213	584	445
1894	7,932	40.0	3,173		.09647	306	195
1895	3,480	39.1	1,361		.06082	83	71
1896	5,864	39.3	2,305	58	.02516	58	49
1897	2,873	39.0	1,120		.03520	39	49
1898	3,321	39.1	1,299		.04524	59	85
1899	4,809	41.5	1,996		.05527	110	180
1900	8,641	44.3	3,828	250	.06531	250	212
1901	6,568	45.2	2,969		.05856	174	192
1902	8,843	45.7	4,041		.05180	209	207
1903	9,627	47.3	4,554		.04505	205	224
1904	13,251	47.9	6,347	243	.03829	243	258
1905	9,724	48.7	4,736		.05747	272	340
1906	10,286	51.7	5,318		.07666	408	490
1907	10,892	54.7	5,958	571	.09584	571	590
1908	10,239	55.5	5,683		.10703	608	596
1909	8,824	56.0	4,941		.11823	584	649
1910	9,545	57.8	5,517	714	.12942	714	740
1911	11,208	58.7	6,579	766	.11643	766	677
1912				588		588	

[a] Derived from Table C–8, col. 4 (increase from one year to the next).

[b] Averages of figures for adjacent calendar years, Table C–11, col. 12.

[c] Data for all years except 1912 are from Table C–5, col. 6; data for 1912 are from Table C–4, col. 7.

TABLE C–10
Derivation of Gross Capital Expenditures, Excluding Land, by Steam Railroads, 1870–1950
(millions of dollars)

Year	*Gross Capital Expenditures, Including Land* (1)	*Estimated Ratios of Gross Capital Expenditures on Land to Total Gross Capital Expenditures* (2)	*Gross Capital Expenditures Excluding Land: Col. 1 × (1 − Col. 2)* (3)
1870	388	0.0210	380
1871	429	.0210	420
1872	387	.0210	379
1873	268	.0210	262
1874	151	.0210	148
1875	107	.0210	105
1876	106	.0210	104
1877	119	.0210	117
1878	116	.0210	114
1879	128	.0210	125
1880	288	.0210	282
1881	450	.0215	440
1882	407	.0220	398
1883	290	.0225	283
1884	204	.0229	199
1885	154	.0234	150
1886	211	.0239	206
1887	282	.0244	275
1888	257	.0249	251
1889	233	.0254	227
1890	237	.0259	231
1891	243	.0263	237
1892	418	.0268	407
1893	445	.0273	433
1894	195	.0278	190
1895	71	.0283	69
1896	49	.0288	48
1897	49	.0293	48
1898	85	.0297	82
1899	180	.0302	175
1900	212	.0307	205
1901	192	.0312	186
1902	207	.0317	200
1903	224	.0322	217
1904	258	.0327	250
1905	340	.0332	329
1906	490	.0336	474
1907	590	.0341	570
1908	596	.0346	575
1909	649	.0351	626

(continued on next page)

TABLE C–10 (continued)

Year	*Gross Capital Expenditures, Including Land* (1)	*Estimated Ratios of Gross Capital Expenditures on Land to Total Gross Capital Expenditures*[a] (2)	*Gross Capital Expenditures Excluding Land: Col.* 1 × (1 – *Col.* 2) (3)
1910	740	0.0356	714
1911	677	.0361	653
1912	660	.0366	636
1913	708	.0370	682
1914	483	.0375	465
1915	292	.0380	281
1916	378	.0385	363
1917	607	.0736	562
1918	517	.0267	503
1919	404	.0082	401
1920	685	.0105	678
1921	598	.0110	591
1922	535	.0324	518
1923	1,139	.0312	1,103
1924	991	.0187	972
1925	849	.0682	791
1926	934	.0502	887
1927	856	.0610	804
1928	764	.0483	727
1929	916	.0615	860
1930	885	.0579	834
1931	370	.0568	349
1932	179	.0731	166
1933	120	.0629	112
1934	186	.0303	180
1935	204	.1608	171
1936	335	.0215	328
1937	575	.0173	565
1938	275	.0056	273
1939	267	.0000	267
1940	469	.0158	462
1941	578	.0200	566
1942	703	.0277	684
1943	497	.0272	483
1944	597	.0275	581
1945	609	.0656	569
1946	608	.0445	581
1947	902	.0321	873
1948	1,336	.0105	1,322
1949	1,375	.0131	1,357
1950	1,134	.0048	1,129

[a] The ratio of expenditures for land to total gross capital expenditures was estimated as follows: for years 1917–50, ratio of land expenditures to total gross capital expenditures of Class I roads (*Statistics of Railways in the U.S.*, ICC); for 1880, ratio of land owned to total value of road and equipment of all roads (Census of Transportation Agencies, 1880). This ratio was used for all years prior to 1880. Figures for years 1881–1916 were linearly interpolated using the average ratio of expenditures for land to total gross capital expenditures of Class I roads, during the 1917–27 period, as the 1917 ratio for interpolation.

TABLE C–11

Derivation of Index of Cost of Road and Equipment of Steam Railroads, 18

Year	INDEX OF COST OF Construction Materials (Shaw)[a] (1)	Metals and Implements[b] (2)	Lumber and Building Materials[b] (3)	Weighted Average of Cols. 2 and 3[c] (4)	Col. 1 ÷ Col. 4 and Inter- and Extrapolations (5)	Index of Cost of Constr. M. (col. 5 × col. 4) (6)
1840		158.3	88.7	102.6	0.8569	87.9
1841		158.6	90.2	103.9	.8569	89.0
1842		152.2	87.7	100.6	.8569	86.2
1843		147.0	85.0	97.4	.8569	83.5
1844		170.9	83.1	100.7	.8569	86.3
1845		142.0	86.1	97.3	.8569	83.4
1846		149.8	85.7	98.5	.8569	84.4
1847		154.6	87.3	100.8	.8569	86.4
1848		153.4	84.9	98.6	.8569	84.5
1849		160.1	78.7	95.0	.8569	81.4
1850		147.2	82.4	95.4	.8569	81.7
1851		131.0	78.4	88.9	.8569	76.2
1852		127.7	81.0	90.3	.8569	77.4
1853		149.3	83.2	96.4	.8569	82.6
1854		161.6	92.0	105.9	.8569	90.7
1855		149.3	83.4	96.6	.8569	82.8
1856		147.9	82.9	95.9	.8569	82.2
1857		145.0	84.7	96.8	.8569	82.9
1858		129.3	83.7	92.8	.8569	79.5
1859		129.0	79.6	89.5	.8569	76.7
1860		128.2	80.7	90.2	.8569	77.3
1861		127.0	87.8	95.6	.8569	81.9
1862		148.8	120.3	126.0	.8569	108.0
1863		181.0	142.8	150.4	.8569	128.9
1864		253.8	178.5	193.6	.8569	165.9
1865		280.3	146.9	173.6	.8569	148.8
1866		247.0	150.7	170.0	.8569	145.7
1867		229.3	144.2	161.2	.8569	138.1
1868		214.2	140.6	155.3	.8569	133.1
1869	126.4	202.4	133.8	147.5	.8569	126.4
1870		177.9	119.6	131.3	.8696	114.2
1871		169.2	122.1	131.5	.8823	116.0
1872		186.5	134.6	145.0	.8950	129.8
1873		190.5	138.6	149.0	.9077	135.2
1874		175.3	124.9	135.0	.9204	124.3
1875		167.9	115.9	126.3	.9331	117.9
1876		150.9	110.7	118.8	.9458	112.4
1877		134.0	101.5	108.0	.9585	103.5
1878		120.1	94.2	99.4	.9712	96.5
1879	95.8	115.6	92.8	97.4	.9836	95.8
1880		134.7	105.6	111.4	.9852	109.8
1881		123.8	105.9	109.5	.9869	108.1
1882		126.4	110.9	114.0	.9885	112.7
1883		120.0	108.3	110.6	.9902	109.5
1884		106.9	104.4	104.9	.9918	104.0
1885		102.1	102.1	102.1	.9934	101.4
1886		100.4	103.6	103.0	.9951	102.5
1887		100.6	102.0	101.7	.9967	101.4
1888		102.1	100.6	100.9	.9984	100.7
1889	100.0	100.0	100.0	100.0	1.0000	100.0

TABLE C–11

9 = 100 for all indexes except final series, col. 12)

Index of Wages in Building Trades[d] (7)	INDEX OF COST OF: Road (including construction)[e] (8)	Locomotives and Railroad Cars[a] (9)	Equipment[f] (10)	COMBINED INDEX OF: Cost of Road and Equipment, 1889 = 100[g] (11)	Cost of Road and Equipment, 1929 = 100[h] (12)	Year
50.0	72.7		158.3	81.3	34.8	1840
50.0	73.4		158.6	81.9	35.1	1841
50.7	72.0		152.2	80.0	34.2	1842
49.8	70.0		147.0	77.7	33.3	1843
50.0	71.8		170.9	81.7	35.0	1844
50.9	70.4		142.0	77.6	33.2	1845
52.2	71.5		149.8	79.3	33.9	1846
54.4	73.6		154.6	81.7	35.0	1847
54.1	72.3		153.4	80.4	34.4	1848
52.7	69.9		160.1	78.9	33.8	1849
50.7	69.3		147.2	77.1	33.0	1850
51.7	66.4		131.0	72.9	31.2	1851
52.1	67.3		127.7	73.3	31.4	1852
53.2	70.8		149.3	78.7	33.7	1853
54.9	76.4		161.6	84.9	36.3	1854
56.2	72.2		149.3	79.9	34.2	1855
56.7	72.0		147.9	79.6	34.1	1856
58.0	72.9		145.0	80.1	34.3	1857
56.3	70.2		129.3	76.1	32.6	1858
59.2	69.7		129.0	75.6	32.4	1859
58.8	69.9		128.2	75.7	32.4	1860
59.0	72.7		127.0	78.1	33.4	1861
62.5	89.8		148.8	95.7	41.0	1862
90.4	113.5		181.0	120.3	51.5	1863
84.5	133.3		253.8	145.4	62.2	1864
94.7	127.2		280.3	142.5	61.0	1865
99.9	127.4		247.0	130.4	60.0	1866
108.8	126.4		229.3	136.7	58.5	1867
109.0	123.5		214.2	132.6	56.8	1868
111.2	120.3		202.4	128.5	55.0	1869
109.1	112.2		177.9	118.8	50.9	1870
107.5	112.6		169.2	118.3	50.7	1871
107.8	121.0		186.5	127.6	54.6	1872
105.6	123.4		190.5	130.1	55.7	1873
104.7	116.5		175.3	122.4	52.4	1874
99.4	110.5		167.9	116.2	49.8	1875
93.3	104.8		150.9	109.4	46.8	1876
86.2	96.6		134.0	100.3	42.9	1877
82.6	90.6		120.1	93.8	40.2	1878
81.2	90.0		115.6	92.6	39.6	1879
84.0	99.5		134.7	103.0	44.1	1880
94.2	102.5		123.8	104.6	44.8	1881
97.0	106.4		126.4	108.4	46.4	1882
97.6	104.7		120.0	106.2	45.5	1883
99.1	102.0		106.9	102.5	43.9	1884
100.0	100.8		102.1	100.9	43.2	1885
100.2	101.6		100.4	101.5	43.5	1886
100.0	100.8		100.6	100.8	43.2	1887
100.6	100.7		102.1	100.8	43.2	1888
100.0	100.0	100.0	100.0	100.0	42.8	1889

(continued on next page)

TABLE C–11 (continued)

Derivation of Index of Cost of Road and Equipment of Steam Railroads, 1840–1950

(1889 = 100 for all indexes except final series, col. 12)

	INDEX OF						
Year	*Cost of Construction Materials* (Shaw)[a] (1)	*Wages in Building Trades*[d] (7)	*Cost of Road* (including construction)[e] (8)	*Cost of Locomotives and Railroad Cars* (Shaw)[a] (9)	*Cost of Equipment*[f] (10)	*Combined Index of Cost of Road and Equipment, 1889 = 100*[g] (11)	*Combined Index of Cost of Road and Equipment, 1929 = 100*[h] (12)
1890	99.2	101.5	100.1	100.0	100.0	100.1	42.9
1891	94.4	102.6	97.7	98.2	98.2	97.8	41.9
1892	89.3	104.7	95.5	97.0	97.0	95.7	41.0
1893	88.7	104.7	95.1	94.9	94.9	95.1	40.7
1894	84.2	102.2	91.4	93.0	93.0	91.6	39.2
1895	83.2	103.0	91.1	90.3	90.3	91.0	39.0
1896	84.5	104.7	92.6	89.7	89.7	92.3	39.5
1897	78.9	106.2	89.8	91.1	91.1	89.9	38.5
1898	82.2	107.6	92.4	95.5	95.5	92.7	39.7
1899	94.9	110.3	101.1	100.2	100.2	101.0	43.2
1900	100.9	115.1	106.6	101.6	101.6	106.1	45.4
1901	94.9	120.0	104.9	104.2	104.2	104.8	44.9
1902	97.1	126.9	109.0	105.4	105.4	108.6	46.5
1903	99.4	132.8	112.8	105.4	105.4	112.1	48.0
1904	96.1	135.8	112.0	106.8	106.8	111.5	47.7
1905	102.4	138.4	116.8	108.9	108.9	116.0	49.7
1906	113.6	146.8	126.9	111.6	111.6	125.4	53.7
1907	118.8	151.5	131.9	113.2	113.2	130.0	55.7
1908	109.8	161.2	130.4	114.9	114.9	128.9	55.2
1909	111.5	169.0	134.5	116.8	116.8	132.7	56.8
1910	114.8	175.7	139.2	118.7	118.7	137.2	58.7
1911	114.1	178.4	139.8	109.9	109.9	136.8	58.6
1912	115.2	182.5	142.1	114.1	114.1	139.3	59.6
1913	117.6	186.6	145.2	120.9	120.9	142.8	61.1
1914	109.5	190.7	142.0	110.0	110.0	138.8	59.4
1915	111.3	192.2	143.7	112.8	112.8	140.6	60.2

(concluded on next page)

TABLE C–11 (continuing col. 12)

Combined Index of Cost of Road and Equipment, 1929 = 100[h]

Year	(12)	*Year*	(12)	*Year*	(12)
		1930	96.4	1945	125.9
1916	69.3	1931	89.8	1946	139.8
1917	85.5	1932	81.9	1947	154.8
1918	104.2	1933	80.1	1948	169.3
1919	116.3	1934	84.3	1949	169.9
		1935	85.5		
1920	136.1	1936	86.1	1950	173.5
1921	106.6	1937	92.2		
1922	95.8	1938	89.8		
1923	106.6	1939	89.8		
1924	104.8				
1925	101.2	1940	92.2		
1926	101.2	1941	99.4		
1927	101.8	1942	113.3		
1928	98.8	1943	120.5		
1929	100.0	1944	121.1		

[a] From William H. Shaw, *Value of Commodity Output Since 1869,* National Bureau of Economic Research, 1947.

[b] *Wholesale Prices, Wages and Transportation,* Senate Report No. 1394, Part I. Column 2 is exclusive of pocket knives.

[c] Weights are 2 for metals and 8 for lumber and other building materials, reflecting their relative importance in the total volume of maintenance expenditures on road (including structures) by Class I roads in 1925, 1935, and 1945, as published in annual reports of the ICC.

[d] Derived from the following segments linked: 1907–1915—BLS union wage rates in building trades (*Historical Statistics of the United States*); 1890–1907—BLS index of average wages per hour in building trades (*ibid.*); 1840–90—wages per day in building trades (*Wholesale Prices, Wages, and Transportation,* Senate Report No. 1394, Part I).

[e] Weighted average of cols. 6 and 7 (1840–89) and cols. 1 and 7 (1890–1915). The weight used for wages is 40 per cent, reflecting the ratio of labor outlay to total outlay on maintenance of, and investment in, road (including structures) by Class I roads for the years 1925, 1935, and 1945, as published in the annual reports of the ICC.

[f] Cols. 2 and 9.

[g] Weighted average of cols. 8 and 10. Weights used were 9 and 1, respectively, and are based on the ratio of the cost of road (including structures) to total cost of road (including structures) and equipment for years 1880 and 1890–1908, as published in 1880 by the census and for the other years in the annual reports of the ICC.

[h] For 1915–50, ICC index of cost of road and equipment, base shifted; for 1840–1914, derived by linking col. 11 to ICC index of cost of road and equipment (1929 = 100) in 1915.

TABLE C–12

Derivation of Capital Consumption by Steam Railroads in Original Cost Dollars 1870–1950

(*in millions*)

Year	*Original Cost of Road and Equipment Excluding Land and Landrights, January 1, Adjusted*[a] (5)	*Depreciation Rates*[b] (per cent) (6)	*Capital Consumption Excluding Land and Landrights, Original Cost Dollars:* (col. 5 × col. 6) (7)
1870	3,378	1.5400	52
1871	3,757	1.5400	58
1872	4,175	1.5400	64
1873	4,553	1.5400	70
1874	4,813	1.5400	74
1875	4,959	1.5400	76
1876	5,063	1.5400	78
1877	5,165	1.5400	80
1878	5,280	1.5400	81
1879	5,392	1.5400	83
1880	5,515	1.5400	85
1881	5,795	1.5400	89
1882	6,231	1.5400	96
1883	6,626	1.5400	102
1884	6,906	1.5400	106
1885	7,102	1.5400	109
1886	7,249	1.5400	112
1887	7,452	1.5400	115
1888	7,723	1.5400	119
1889	7,970	1.5400	123
1890	8,193	1.5400	126
1891	8,420	1.5400	130
1892	8,653	1.5400	133
1893	9,055	1.5400	139
1894	9,482	1.5400	146
1895	9,668	1.5400	149
1896	9,733	1.5400	150
1897	9,778	1.5400	151
1898	9,822	1.5400	151
1899	9,901	1.5400	152
1900	10,071	1.5400	155
1901	10,271	1.5400	158
1902	10,452	1.5400	161
1903	10,647	1.5400	164
1904	10,859	1.5400	167
1905	11,103	1.5400	171
1906	11,425	1.5400	176
1907	11,890	1.5400	183
1908	12,450	1.5400	192
1909	13,014	1.5400	200
1910	13,629	1.5400	210

Note: Cols. 1 through 4 appear in the continuation of this table on the following two pages.

TABLE C–12 (continued)

Year	*Original Cost of Road and Equipment, Excluding Land and Landrights* (ICC), *January 1* *All Roads*[c] (1)	*Original Cost of Road and Equipment Excluding Land and Landrights, January 1, Adjusted* (5)	*Depreciation Rates*[d] (per cent) (6)	*Capital Consumption Excluding Land and Landrights, Original Cost Dollars:* (col. 5 × col. 6) (7)
1911		14,330	1.5400	221
1912		14,970	1.5400	231
1913		15,593	1.5400	240
1914		16,261	1.5400	250
1915		16,715	1.5400	257
1916	16,443	16,987	1.5400	262
1917	16,755	17,273	1.5400	266
1918	17,067	17,483	1.5456	270
1919	17,379	17,856	1.5512	277
1920	17,692	18,127	1.5569	282
1921	18,004	18,379	1.5625	287
1922	18,316	18,715	1.5681	293
1923	18,628	19,061	1.5738	300
1924	18,941	19,383	1.5794	306
1925	19,253	19,674	1.5850	312
1926	19,565	19,936	1.5906	317
1927	19,877	20,204	1.5962	322
1928	20,190	20,477	1.6019	328
1929	20,502	20,747	1.6075	334
1930	20,814	21,039	1.6131	339
1931	21,126	21,339	1.6188	345
1932	21,439	21,660	1.6244	352
1933	21,751	21,955	1.6300	358
1934	22,063	22,277	1.6356	364
1935	22,375	22,580	1.6412	371
1936	22,688	22,878	1.6469	377
1937	23,000	23,185	1.6525	383
1938	23,000	23,164	1.6581	384
1939	23,000	23,169	1.6638	385
1940	23,107	23,253	1.6694	388

Note: Primary data of original cost (cols. 1, 2) unavailable except for 1916–40 and 1947–51. Cols. 3 and 4 appear only for 1947–51 (next page).

[a] The January 1, 1870 figure for book value (from Table C–3, col. II) was assumed to represent original cost. Years 1871–1915 were obtained by interpolating between the data for 1870 and 1916 by reference to an annual series showing original cost January 1, 1870 plus cumulative gross capital expenditures from that date, as shown in Table C–13.

[b] For 1917–40, obtained by dividing column 1 of this table by col. 4 of Table C–2. Data in col. 3 of Table C–2 for years 1915 and 1916 were averaged to obtain the blow-up factor for 1916. For 1947–51, obtained by dividing col. 2 by col. 4. Years 1941–1946 linearly interpolated.

[c] W. H. S. Stevens, *Analysis of Steam Railway Dividends* (Interstate Commerce Commission), Table H.

[d] Unpublished data from the Bureau of Valuations, ICC, give figures for 1917 and 1949; those for intervening years were linearly interpolated, and the figures for earlier years were taken as identical with 1917.

TABLE C-12 (concluded)

Derivation of Capital Consumption by Steam Railroads in Original Cost Dollars

(*in millions*)

Year	*Original Cost of Road and Equipment, Excluding Land and Landrights,* (ICC), *January 1* *All roads* (1)	*Class* I *roads*[e] (2)	*Book Value of Road and Equipment of Class* I (ICC), *January 1* (3)	*Ratio of Book Value of Road and Equipment of Class* I *Roads* (ICC) *to That of All Roads*[f] (4)	*Original Cost of Road and Equipment Excluding Land and Landrights, January 1, Adjusted* (5)	*Depreciation Rates* (per cent) (6)	*Capital Consumption Excluding Land and Land rights, Original Cost Dollars:* (col. 5 × col. (7)
1941					23,570	1.6750	395
1942					23,886	1.6806	401
1943					24,203	1.6862	403
1944					24,519	1.6919	415
1945					24,836	1.6975	422
1946					25,153	1.7031	428
1947		24,035	26,898	0.9437	25,469	1.7088	435
1948		24,564	27,306	.9486	25,895	1.7144	444
1949		25,433	28,282	.9498	26,777	1.7200	461
1950		26,158	29,135	.9487	27,572	1.7200	474
1951		26,835	29,786	.9495	28,262		

[e] ICC, Bureau of Valuation, *Elements of Value of Property used in Common Carrier Service:* for 1947, E Parte No. 166, Exhibit No. 20; for 1948, Ex Parte No. 168, Exhibit No. 1; for 1949, 1950, and 195 unpublished.

[f] Col. 3 of this table divided by col. 7, Table C-2.

TABLE C-13

Derivation of Original Cost of Road and Equipment, and Retirements, 1870-1916

(*millions of dollars*)

Year	*Original Cost, January 1* (1)	*Original Cost, January 1, plus Gross Capital Expenditures since January 1, 1870* (2)	*Ratio of Col. 1 to Col. 2, and Interpolation* (3)	*Original Cost, January 1* (col. 2 × col. 3) (4)	*Retirements during the Year*[b] (5)
1870	3,378[a]	3,378	1.00000	3,378	
1871		3,758	.99970	3,757	1
1872		4,178	.99940	4,175	2
1873		4,557	.99910	4,553	1
1874		4,819	.99879	4,813	2
1875		4,967	.99849	4,959	2
1876		5,072	.99819	5,063	1
1877		5,176	.99789	5,165	2
1878		5,293	.99759	5,280	2
1879		5,407	.99729	5,392	2

(concluded on next page)

TABLE C-13 (concluded)

Year	Original Cost, January 1 (1)	Original Cost, January 1, plus Gross Capital Expenditures since January 1, 1870 (2)	Ratio of Col. 1 to Col. 2, and Interpolation (3)	Original Cost, January 1 (col. 2 × col. 3) (4)	Retirements during the Year[b] (5)
1880		5,532	0.99699	5,515	2
1881		5,814	.99668	5,795	2
1882		6,254	.99638	6,231	4
1883		6,652	.99608	6,626	3
1884		6,935	.99578	6,906	3
1885		7,134	.99548	7,102	3
1886		7,284	.99518	7,249	3
1887		7,490	.99487	7,452	3
1888		7,765	.99457	7,723	4
1889		8,016	.99427	7,970	4
1890		8,243	.99397	8,193	4
1891		8,474	.99367	8,420	4
1892		8,711	.99337	8,653	4
1893		9,118	.99307	9,055	5
1894		9,551	.99276	9,482	6
1895		9,741	.99246	9,668	4
1896		9,810	.99216	9,733	4
1897		9,858	.99186	9,778	3
1898		9,906	.99156	9,822	4
1899		9,988	.99126	9,901	3
1900		10,163	.99096	10,071	5
1901		10,368	.99065	10,271	5
1902		10,554	.99035	10,452	5
1903		10,754	.99005	10,647	5
1904		10,971	.98975	10,859	5
1905		11,221	.98945	11,103	6
1906		11,550	.98915	11,425	7
1907		12,024	.98884	11,890	9
1908		12,594	.98854	12,450	10
1909		13,169	.98824	13,014	11
1910		13,795	.98794	13,629	11
1911		14,509	.98764	14,330	13
1912		15,162	.98734	14,970	13
1913		15,798	.98704	15,593	13
1914		16,480	.98673	16,261	14
1915		16,945	.98643	16,715	11
1916	16,987	17,226	.98613	16,987	9

[a] Book value January 1, 1870.
[b] Derived from the year-to-year change in col. 4 and gross capital expenditures.

TABLE C–14

Derivation of Reproduction Cost New of Road and Equipment, Excluding Land and Landrights, of Steam Railroads in Selected ICC Reporting Years

(millions of dollars)

Year	RCN *for Class* I *Roads on December 31, Reported by* ICC, *in 1910–14 Dollars* (1)	*Book Value of Road and Equipment of Class* I *Roads on December 31* (ICC) (2)	*Ratio of Book Value for Class* I *Roads to That for All Roads*[a] (3)	RCN *for All Railroads on December 31, in 1910–14 Dollars*[b] (4)	*Index of Cost of Road and Equipment* (ICC), *1910–14 = 100* (5)	RCN *for All Railroads on December 31, in Current Dollars*[c] (6)
1936	17,726	24,974	0.9364	18,930	143.0	27,070
1939	17,890	25,116	.9420	18,992	149.0	28,298
1944	17,991	26,255	.9446	19,046	201.0	38,282
1945	18,090	26,587	.9428	19,188	209.0	40,103
1946	18,322	26,898	.9437	19,415	232.0	45,043
1949	18,996	29,135	.9487	20,023	282.0	56,465
1950	19,072	29,786	.9495	20,086	288.0	57,848

[a] Column 2 of this table divided by col. 7 of Table C–2.
[b] Col. 1 divided by col. 3.
[c] Col. 4 inflated by index in col. 5.

TABLE C–15

Derivation of Capital Consumption by Steam Railroads in Current Dollars, for Selected Years

(in millions)

Year	*Reproduction Cost New of Road and Equipment of All Railroads in Current Dollars, December 31* (1)	*Original Cost of Road and Equipment of All Railroads, December 31*[a] (2)	*Index of Cost of Road and Equipment on Original Cost Base*[b] (3)	*Capital Consumption in Original Cost Dollars*[c] (4)	*Capital Consumption in Current Dollars*[d] (5)
1936	27,070	23,185	1.1676	377	440
1939	28,298	23,253	1.2170	385	469
1944	38,282	24,836	1.5414	415	640
1945	40,103	25,153	1.5944	422	673
1946	45,043	25,469	1.7685	428	757
1949	56,465	27,572	2.0479	461	944
1950	57,848	28,262	2.0468	474	970

Investment in land and landrights is excluded.
[a] From Table C–12, col. 5.
[b] Col. 1 divided by col. 2.
[c] From Table C–12, col. 7.
[d] Col. 4 multiplied by col. 3.

TABLE C–16

Derivation of Retirements by Steam Railroads in Current Dollars, 1870–1949

(in millions)

Year	*Retirements During the Year in Original Cost Dollars*[a] (1)	*Average Annual Retirements during the Year in Original Cost Dollars*[b] (2)	*Index of Original Cost of Retirements, 1929 = 100*[c] (3)	*Ratio of Col. 12 in Table C–11 to Col. 3 of This Table* (4)	*Average Annual Retirements during the Year in Current Dollars (col. 2 × col. 4)* (5)
1870	1	2	34.8	1.4626	3
1871	2	2	35.0	1.4486	3
1872	1	2	34.7	1.5735	3
1873	2	2	34.4	1.6192	3
1874	2	2	34.5	1.5188	3
1875	1	2	34.3	1.4519	3
1876	2	2	34.2	1.3684	3
1877	2	2	34.3	1.2507	3
1878	2	2	34.2	1.1754	2
1879	2	2	33.8	1.1716	2
1880	2	3	33.5	1.3164	4
1881	4	3	33.4	1.3413	4
1882	3	3	33.7	1.3769	4
1883	3	3	33.6	1.3542	4
1884	3	3	33.7	1.3026	4
1885	3	3	33.8	1.2781	4
1886	3	3	33.5	1.2985	4
1887	4	3	33.4	1.2934	4
1888	4	3	33.2	1.3012	4
1889	4	3	33.3	1.2853	4

(continued on next page)

TABLE C-16 (continued)

Year	Retirements During the Year in Original Cost Dollars[a] (1)	Average Annual Retirements during the Year in Original Cost Dollars[b] (2)	Index of Original Cost of Retirements, 1929 = 100[c] (3)	Ratio of Col. 12 in Table C-11 to Col. 3 of This Table (4)	Average Annual Retirements during the Year in Current Dollars (col. 2 × col. 4) (5)
1890	4	4	34.2	1.2544	5
1891	4	4	36.0	1.1639	5
1892	5	4	38.6	1.0622	4
1893	6	4	40.8	.9975	4
1894	4	4	43.2	.9074	4
1895	4	4	45.4	.8590	3
1896	3	4	47.4	.8333	3
1897	4	4	49.5	.7778	3
1898	3	4	51.2	.7754	3
1899	5	4	52.8	.8182	3
1900	5	7	54.7	.8300	6
1901	5	7	56.1	.8004	6
1902	5	7	56.2	.8274	6
1903	5	7	55.0	.8727	6
1904	6	7	53.7	.8883	6
1905	7	7	52.2	.9521	7
1906	9	7	50.5	1.0634	7
1907	10	7	49.0	1.1367	8
1908	11	7	48.0	1.1500	8
1909	11	7	47.4	1.1983	8
1910	13	76	47.0	1.2489	95
1911	13	76	46.2	1.2684	96
1912	13	76	45.1	1.3215	100
1913	14	76	44.3	1.3792	105
1914	11	76	43.7	1.3593	103

(continued on next page)

TABLE C–16 (continued)

Year	Retirements During the Year in Original Cost Dollars[a] (1)	Average Annual Retirements during the Year in Original Cost Dollars[b] (2)	Index of Original Cost of Retirements, 1929 = 100[c] (3)	Ratio of Col. 12 in Table C–11 to Col. 3 of This Table (4)	Average Annual Retirements during the Year in Current Dollars (col. 2 × col. 4) (5)
1915	9	76	43.4	1.3871	105
1916	77	76	43.4	1.5968	121
1917	352	76	43.7	1.9565	149
1918	130	76	44.0	2.3682	180
1919	130	76	43.8	2.6553	202
1920	426	502	43.4	3.1359	1,574
1921	255	502	42.9	2.4848	1,247
1922	172	502	42.3	2.2648	1,137
1923	781	502	41.9	2.5442	1,277
1924	681	502	41.5	2.5253	1,268
1925	529	502	41.1	2.4623	1,236
1926	619	502	40.8	2.4804	1,245
1927	531	502	40.8	2.4951	1,253
1928	457	502	41.0	2.4098	1,210
1929	568	502	41.2	2.4272	1,218
1930	534	103	41.6	2.3173	239
1931	28	103	42.2	2.1280	219
1932	−129	103	42.9	1.9091	197
1933	−210	103	43.8	1.8288	188
1934	−123	103	45.2	1.8650	192
1935	−127	103	46.6	1.8348	188
1936	21	103	48.2	1.7863	184
1937	586	103	49.7	1.8551	191
1938	268	103	51.1	1.7573	181
1939	183	103	52.3	1.7170	177

(concluded on next page)

TABLE C-16 (concluded)

Year	*Retirements During the Year in Original Cost Dollars*[a] (1)	*Average Annual Retirements during the Year in Original Cost Dollars*[b] (2)	*Index of Original Cost of Retirements, 1929 = 100*[c] (3)	*Ratio of Col. 12 in Table C-11 to Col. 3 of This Table* (4)	*Average Annual Retirements during the Year in Current Dollars (col. 2 × col. 4)* (5)
1940	145	316	53.7	1.7169	543
1941	250	316	55.0	1.8072	571
1942	367	316	56.0	2.0232	639
1943	167	316	57.2	2.1066	666
1944	264	316	58.9	2.0560	650
1945	252	316	61.8	2.0372	644
1946	265	316	66.2	2.1118	667
1947	447	316	71.8	2.1560	681
1948	440	316	79.0	2.1430	677
1949	562	316	83.4	2.0372	644

[a] Obtained by use of the following formula: $R_N = O_N + G_N - O_{N+1}$, where R_N is retirements during the year in original cost dollars, O_N is the original cost of road and equipment at the beginning of the year, G_N is gross capital expenditures in current dollars during the year, and O_{N+1} is the original cost of road and equipment at the end of the year.

[b] Obtained from col. 1 by averaging the figures for each decade.

[c] Data for all years except 1870–77 inclusive were obtained by use of the following formula:

$$P_{ON} = \frac{P_{CN-38} + P_{CN-37} + \cdots + P_{CN-28}}{11},$$

where P_{ON} is the index of original cost of retirements made during year N, and P_{CN} is the index of cost of road and equipment in year N. The indexes of original cost of retirements for the years, 1870–77, were obtained by use of the following formulas:

$$P_{O77} = \frac{P_{CN-37} + P_{CN-36} + \cdots + P_{CN-29}}{9},$$

$$P_{O76} = \frac{P_{CN-36} + P_{CN-35} + \cdots + P_{CN-30}}{7},$$

$$P_{O75} = \frac{P_{CN-35} + P_{CN-36} + \cdots + P_{CN-30}}{6},$$

$$P_{O74} = \frac{P_{CN-34} + P_{CN-33} + \cdots + P_{CN-30}}{5},$$

$$P_{O73} = \frac{P_{CN-33} + P_{CN-32} + \cdots + P_{CN-30}}{4},$$

$$P_{O72} = \frac{P_{CN-32} + P_{CN-31} + P_{CN-30}}{3},$$

$$P_{O71} = \frac{P_{CN-31} + P_{CN-30}}{2},$$

$$P_{O70} = P_{CN-30}.$$

TABLE C–17

Derivation of Reproduction Cost New of Road and Equipment of Steam Railroads, Excluding Land and Landrights, in Current Dollars, 1870–1951

(in millions)

Year	*Reproduction Cost New, January 1*[a]	*Year*	*Reproduction Cost New, January 1*[a]
1870	3,972	1905	11,599
1871	4,053	1906	12,407
1872	4,454	1907	13,873
1873	5,173	1908	14,952
1874	5,536	1909	15,384
1875	5,353	1910	16,448
1876	5,189	1911	17,618
1877	4,977	1912	18,145
1878	4,676	1913	18,991
1879	4,494	1914	20,045
1880	4,550	1915	19,850
1881	5,345	1916	20,294
1882	5,866	1917	23,603
1883	6,470	1918	29,534
1884	6,623	1919	36,318
1885	6,585	1920	40,732
1886	6,626	1921	46,772
1887	6,874	1922	35,979
1888	7,098	1923	31,716
1889	7,345	1924	35,117
1890	7,500	1925	34,227
1891	7,743	1926	32,593
1892	7,794	1927	32,235
1893	8,029	1928	31,981
1894	8,399	1929	30,554
1895	8,275	1930	30,657
1896	8,299	1931	30,158
1897	8,451	1932	28,223
1898	8,282	1933	25,720
1899	8,619	1934	25,078
1900	9,551	1935	26,380
1901	10,237	1936	26,738
1902	10,305	1937	27,070
1903	10,866	1938	28,867
1904	11,427	1939	28,208

(concluded on next page)

TABLE C–17 (concluded)

Year	*Reproduction Cost New, January 1*[a]
1940	28,298
1941	29,304
1942	31,586
1943	36,049
1944	38,159
1945	38,282
1946	40,103
1947	45,043
1948	50,212
1949	55,557
1950	56,465
1951	57,848

[a] Interpolated between the years given in Table C–15, column 1, by use of the following formula:

$$Q_N P_N = [Q_{N+1} P_{N+1} - G_{N+1} + R_{N+1}] \frac{P_N}{P_{N+1}}$$

Where $Q_N P_N$ is reproduction cost new at the end of year N, G_{N+1} is gross capital expenditures in current dollars during year $N + 1$ (from Table C–10), P_N is cost of road and equipment in year N (from Table C–11, col. 12), and R_{N+1} is retirements valued new in the prices of that year. Extrapolated by use of this formula for years prior to January 1, 1937.

TABLE C–18

Derivation of Capital Consumption by Steam Railroads in Current Dollars, 1870–1950

(in millions)

Year	*Index of Cost of Road and Equipment on Original Cost Base*[a] (1)	*Capital Consumption, Current Dollars*[b] (2)
1870	1.079	56
1871	1.067	62
1872	1.136	73
1873	1.150	81
1874	1.079	80
1875	1.025	78
1876	.964	75
1877	.886	71
1878	.833	67
1879	.825	68
1880	.922	78
1881	.941	84
1882	.976	94
1883	.959	98
1884	.927	98
1885	.914	100
1886	.922	103
1887	.919	106
1888	.922	110
1889	.915	113
1890	.920	116
1891	.901	117
1892	.887	118
1893	.886	123
1894	.856	125
1895	.853	127
1896	.864	130
1897	.843	127
1898	.871	132
1899	.948	144
1900	.997	155
1901	.986	156
1902	1.021	164
1903	1.052	173
1904	1.045	175
1905	1.086	186
1906	1.167	205
1907	1.201	220
1908	1.182	227
1909	1.207	241

(continued on next page)

TABLE C–18 (continued)

Year	*Index of Cost of Road and Equipment on Original Cost Base*[a] (1)	*Capital Consumption, Current Dollars*[b] (2)
1910	1.229	258
1911	1.212	268
1912	1.218	281
1913	1.233	296
1914	1.188	297
1915	1.195	307
1916	1.366	358
1917	1.689	449
1918	2.034	549
1919	2.247	622
1920	2.545	718
1921	1.922	552
1922	1.664	487
1923	1.812	543
1924	1.740	532
1925	1.635	510
1926	1.595	506
1927	1.562	503
1928	1.473	483
1929	1.457	487
1930	1.413	479
1931	1.303	450
1932	1.171	413
1933	1.126	403
1934	1.168	424
1935	1.169	433
1936	1.168	441
1937	1.246	477
1938	1.217	467
1939	1.217	469
1940	1.243	482
1941	1.322	522
1942	1.489	597
1943	1.556	635
1944	1.541	639
1945	1.594	672
1946	1.769	757
1947	1.939	844
1948	2.075	921
1949	2.048	942
1950	2.047	970

[a] Column 2 of Table C–13 divided by col. 5 of Table C–12. Since reproduction cost new at the beginning of any year is in terms of prices of year just ended, the formula used here is as follows:

$P_N = R_{N+1}/O_{N+1}$, where P_N is index of cost of road and equipment in year N on original cost base, R_{N+1} and O_{N+1} are reproduction cost new and original cost, respectively, at beginning of year $N + 1$.

[b] Column 7 of Table C–12 multiplied by col. 1 of this table.

TABLE C–19

Derivation of Reproduction Cost Less Depreciation of Road and Equipment of Steam Railroads, January 1, 1937

(millions of dollars)

1. Reproduction cost less depreciation of Class I roads, 1910–14 dollars[a]	12,763
2. Book value of road and equipment of Class I roads, reported by ICC	24,974
3. Ratio of line 2 to January 1, 1937 figure in col. 7, Table C–2	0.9364
4. Reproduction cost less depreciation of all railroads 1910–14 dollars: line 1 divided by line 3	13,630
5. Index of cost of road and equipment, 1936; 1910–14 = 100[b]	143.0
6. Reproduction cost less depreciation, current dollars: line 4 inflated by line 5	19,491
7. Index of cost of road and equipment, 1936; 1929 = 100[c]	86.1
8. Reproduction cost less depreciation 1929 dollars: line 6 deflated by line 7	22,638

Investment in land and landrights is excluded.

[a] ICC unpublished estimate.

[b] ICC.

[c] From Table C–11, col. 12.

APPENDIX D

Notes and Tables on the Derivation of Capital Formation Data for Electric Light and Power

Gross Capital Expenditures, 1881–1920
(for privately owned plants)

For the years prior to 1921 no data bearing directly upon capital expenditures for electric light and power are available. Recourse must be made, therefore, to data on the value of plant and equipment, which were compiled for certain dates in the period. The problem of deriving a series on gross capital expenditures for this period is essentially one of adjusting changes in the values of plant and equipment for comparability, and for exclusion of land, elimination of write-ups, and inclusion of retirements.

EVALUATION OF DATA ON COST OF PLANT AND EQUIPMENT

The available data on cost of plant and equipment of the electric light and power industry through 1922 are given in Table D–2, column 1. The figure for December 31, 1898, is from the *Fourteenth Annual Report of the Commissioner of Labor* (1899), which includes the results of a special survey of the industry. All other data—for June 30, 1902, and the end of the years 1907, 1912, 1917, and 1922—are from the Census Bureau. Two questions of comparability arise primarily in connection with the census figures and are the result, in part, of changes in the schedule employed.

First, at least some of the establishments reporting to the census may have given the depreciated value of their plants in 1917 and 1922, when the schedule called for the *value* rather than the *cost* of plant and equipment, as in earlier years. Between 1912 and 1917, generating capacity increased 76 per cent, but the total value of plant and equipment rose only 40 per cent, despite the substantial increases in construction cost levels. The 1917 census report, commenting on the decline in per-capacity value, offered several explanations: (1) The installation of larger units led to economies in investment per kilowatt of generating capacity. (2) After generating plants had been properly constructed, the addition of generating units did not necessarily entail any appreciable increase in the investment in buildings or in much of the central station equipment. (3) Because of prevailing high prices, every effort was probably made to reduce capital outlays to a minimum. (4) The increasing number of very large stations eliminated duplication in buildings, equipment, and so forth. (5) Since the schedule called for the value of plant and equipment instead of the cost, many establishments may have reported the depreciated value of their plants.

The increase in the value of plant and equipment, per kilowatt of additional generating capacity, varied from $408 to $460 in the years prior to 1912, but declined to $228 for 1912–17, in the face of rising construction costs. While this decline is very substantial, it appears to have resulted largely from the nature of new construction during the period and from the first four factors indicated by the 1917 census report, rather than from noncomparability of the data for 1912 and 1917. The increase in the value of plant and equipment, in constant prices, per kilowatt of additional generating capacity, derived for 1912–17, is higher than for 1917–22 (there was no change in schedule between these two years), and is not far below the figures for 1922–27 and 1927–32. Moreover, the 1912–17 increase in value per kilowatt added is also in reasonable agreement with data on reported expenditures for plant and equipment (available from the Edison Electric Institute for 1921 and later years) per kilowatt of additional generating capacity. The increases in the reported value of plant and equipment per kilowatt of additional generating capacity, and the reported expenditures per kilowatt, in 1929 dollars, are[1]:

	Increase in Value per Kilowatt	*Expenditures per Kilowatt*
1912–1917	379	
1917–1922	260	
1922–1927	438	407
1927–1932	436	398

The second question concerns the precise content of the electric light and power industry as reported by the census. It seems fairly clear that other utilities were not included. Census agents were instructed to obtain separate estimates when book values embraced gas or other utilities in combination. This is further indicated by the above comparison of the change in value of plant and equipment per kilowatt of additional generating capacity between the years 1922 and 1927 and between 1927 and 1932. In 1922 and all prior years no separate estimates were published of the book value of utilities other than electric light and power owned by electric plants, while in subsequent years such specific figures were given. Still the increase in value of plant and equipment per kilowatt of additional generating capacity was in close agreement in the two periods 1922–27 and 1927–32, suggesting the relative purity of the 1922 estimate of the value of plant and equipment.

[1] Note that the tabulated figures are in constant dollars as opposed to the current dollar figures quoted earlier in the paragraph.

However, the census data for 1922 and previous years do not include the value of plant and equipment for some electric light and power plants operated in conjunction with electric railways but producing electric energy for sale. Where parent companies could not provide separate statistics, the entire property was included by the census in the electric railway report. In order to adjust for this omission, the figures given in Table D–2, column 1 were multiplied by the ratios of (a) revenue from electric service of all light and power plants, including power departments of street railways, to (b) revenue from electric service of the commercial light and power plants for which plant and equipment data are available. These ratios are shown in column 2 of Table D–2. The adjusted figures on value of plant and equipment are given in column 3. Since such data on revenues are not available for 1898, the 1902 ratio was applied to the plant and equipment figures for that year.

DEDUCTION FOR THE VALUE OF LAND

The census figures on plant and equipment include the value of land used in electric plant. Only fragmentary information is available on the proportion of expenditures for land to total capital expenditures or on the ratio of the value of land to total value of plant and equipment, though all of these are in fairly close agreement. The 1890 census of electric light and power plants in New York State shows the value of land and the total value of plant and equipment; land constitutes 9.4 per cent of the total. The Federal Trade Commission in its report, *National Wealth and Income*, uses a ratio of 10 per cent for 1922; its estimate is based on an analysis of the fixed capital accounts reported to the New York State Public Service Commission. Both of these estimates are somewhat higher than other available data for the United States as a whole. The *Fourteenth Annual Report of the Commissioner of Labor* presents detailed data on the distribution of plant and equipment costs for individual establishments. Land expense and total expense for plant and equipment were compiled in our study for forty-four large plants which accounted for approximately one-fourth of the total investment in the light and power industry in 1898. For these plants, land constituted 5.32 per cent of total investment. Chawner's estimate is 7.00 per cent for the years 1926–31.[2] It is based on data prepared by the engineering department of the Edison Electric Institute for the Federal Employment Stabilization Board.

[2] Lowell J. Chawner, *Construction Activity in the United States, 1915–37* (Department of Commerce, 1938).

Table D–3, column 1, shows changes in the value of plant and equipment, computed for selected periods through 1922 and derived from the figures given in Table D–2. Also given in Table D–3 are similar changes for the periods 1923–27 and 1928–32 derived from the census of electrical industries in those years. The latter figures are included for experimental purposes, developed later. It has been assumed that the value of plant and equipment at the end of 1880 was zero. Since the first commercial electric light plant was constructed in 1879, this is approximately correct.

In column 2 of Table D–3 are shown the relative deductions made for land. Our compiled figure of 5.32 per cent is used for the 1881–98 period. The Chawner estimate of 7.00 per cent is used for the 1928–32 period. The other ratios were obtained by linear interpolation. In column 3 the deductions for land expenditures are shown in absolute terms. The changes in value of plant and equipment, excluding land, are given in column 4.

CHANGES IN VALUE OF PLANT AND EQUIPMENT, FIVE-YEAR INTERVALS

In estimating retirements, which is the next major step in the derivation of gross capital expenditures, it was found necessary to distribute changes in value of plant and equipment by five-year intervals for the period before 1903. The procedures employed are described in this section.

Since no plant and equipment total prior to 1898 is available, we must first distribute the 1898 total by years. For this purpose the 1902 census is most useful since it shows, for all stations reporting, the year of beginning operations back to 1881. We may consider gross capital expenditures for prior years close to zero. As noted, the first plant is said to have been built in 1879; the 1890 census shows, for the year 1880, three plants with capital of $425,000, including current assets, and this figure apparently represents the total for the United States. Our final estimate of gross capital expenditures for the year 1881, when seven plants started operations, is only $206,000; expenditures in each of the two previous years, therefore, were probably less than $100,000.

The census series for number of stations beginning operations each year provides some indication of the extent of gross capital expenditures each year, but the average size of stations was increasing very rapidly during these early years of the industry's growth and it is necessary to make allowance for this factor. It was assumed that there was a regular geometric increase in average size per station throughout the period prior to 1902. The rate of increase was derived from data for cost per station, in constant prices, for New York State, estimated for the close of the year 1887 and the midpoint of 1896. Average cost per station is available for all stations in existence in New York in 1890 and 1902 and is shown in Table D–4; the averages include all plants—municipal as well as private—since no segregation of the data for 1890 are available. Table D–4 also shows all New York plants in operation in 1902 and 1890 classified by the year of installation. From these data, average cost per station was estimated for plants built in 1891–1902.[3] Average cost per station for plants built in 1881–90 is available from the 1890 census. The average for 1891–1902 was centered at the midpoint of 1896, since half the plants built in 1891–1902 were completed by that date; similarly, cost per station for plants built in 1881–90 was centered at the close of 1887. These average cost figures were deflated with a construction cost index, described below, to derive the average annual rate of growth in size per station—approximately 14 per cent. It is interesting to note that if size per station is measured by the growth in horsepower per station, similarly computed and centered, the rate of growth averages 17 per cent annually.

In column 1, Table D–5 shows the number of private stations existing in 1902, by year of beginning operations, as reported in the 1902 census; in column 2, the index for size of plant as derived above; in column 3, the construction cost index; and in column 4, the result of multiplying all of the first three columns together. Column 4 is the indicator of year-to-year changes in the value of plant and equipment. When applied to the total change in value of plant and equipment in the 1881–98 period (as given in column 4 of Table D–3), it yields the estimates of changes in value of plant and equipment, by years, given in column 5. Summing provides the five-year totals from 1881 through 1897, and a four-and-one-half-year total for 1898 to June 30, 1902, given in column 6.

CONSTRUCTION COST INDEX: 1880–1911 AND 1921–1923

The construction cost index used to convert the physical figures for 1881–1902 to money terms is shown in Table D–6. For convenience in later calculations, the index has been computed on the base

[3] Of the 228 privately owned stations reporting in 1902, 73 were constructed before 1890, and 155 after that date. Average cost per station was \$224,000 for all plants reporting in 1890 and \$441,000 for all plants reporting in 1902. If we let X represent cost per station for plants built in 1891–1902, we have

$$73 \times 224{,}000 + 155\,X = 228 \times 441{,}000$$
$$X = 543{,}000$$

1911 = 100 and has been shown for 1921–23. The index is based on (1) William H. Shaw's series for prices of electrical equipment, (2) Shaw's series for construction materials,[4] and (3) a series for wages in the building trades. Shaw's index for electrical equipment, available from 1889, is based for years prior to 1915 on his index for industrial equipment, derived from data on costs of various types of shop machinery purchased by the railroads, and has been extrapolated here to 1881 by linking the series in the Aldrich report for metals and implements, excluding pocket knives. Shaw's index for construction materials, available for 1879 and annually from 1889, is based on a composite of lumber and building materials prices and structural steel prices; it was extrapolated by him for years prior to 1890 by the use of selected series from the Aldrich report. The construction materials index has been interpolated here for 1880–89 by the use of a composite of the Aldrich report series for lumber and building materials (weight 4), and for metals and implements excluding pocket knives (weight 1); the basic series are shown in Table D–7. The third series used in the derivation of the construction cost index—wages in the building trades—is based for 1880–90 on the Aldrich report series for wages per day in the building trades,[5] for 1890–1907 on Bureau of Labor Statistics figures for average wages per hour in building trades (this series is a continuation of data in the Aldrich report), and for 1907–23 on BLS data for union wage rates in the building trades.

The three series described above were combined with weights derived from information shown by William W. Handy[6] on the composition of his index of electric light and power construction costs, available from 1911. The Handy publication shows the weights assigned the various major items entering into his construction cost index (e.g. buildings, mechanical equipment, electrical equipment) and the composition of these major items in terms of the relative weights of specific types of equipment, materials, labor, and so forth. Each of the detailed items shown there was classified in one of three categories—equipment, construction materials, and labor—and the sums of the weights thus derived were rounded. The weights used in the preparation of the index were equipment, 5; construction materials, 3; and labor, 2.

[4] Both series, from his *Value of Commodity Output since 1869* (National Bureau of Economic Research, 1947).

[5] *Wholesale Prices, Wages, and Transportation*, by Nelson W. Aldrich (Senate Report 1394, 52nd Cong., 2nd Sess., 1893).

[6] *The Yardstick of Public Utility Operations and Construction Costs* (Williams and Wilkins, 1929).

THE VALUE OF RETIREMENTS

The value of retirements during any period will depend on the value of plant and equipment installed during previous years, the average life of this plant and equipment, and the distribution of retirements around this average. It will be necessary to estimate gross capital expenditures for each five-year interval, then to estimate retirements of these expenditures in subsequent periods, to derive gross capital expenditures for the next interval, to estimate retirements of these expenditures, and so on for successive periods.

Our first step in this direction is to estimate the average life of the equipment installed during various periods. Average life of equipment for recent years may be estimated from data reported to the Federal Power Commission. Depreciation accounting is required by FPC's Uniform System of Accounts which became effective January 1, 1937, and an increasing number of companies are using a straight-line method of depreciation accounting. A satisfactory average for recent years may be obtained from the average depreciation rate reported by all companies using a straight-line method. For 1949, the average rate for such companies was 2.68,[7] a rate equivalent to an average life of 37.3 years. The depreciation rate charged in 1949 represents an average rate for all equipment in service, new and old. FPC data on generating capacity in service during 1946–48, by date of installation, indicate that the median age of the equipment in use was eighteen years for steam plant and twenty-three years for hydroelectric plant.[8] Hence, the average life implicit in the 1949 depreciation rate has been assumed here to refer to all equipment installed since 1928.

In earlier years, depreciation accounting was not generally practiced by the industry and there are no reliable accounting figures to serve as an indication of average life. For the early period we must rely on estimates of average useful life and of "proper" depreciation allowances made by various persons. An excellent compilation of such estimates is shown in the American Electric Railway Association Proceedings for 1912 (Report of the Committee on Life of Railway Physical Property to the American Electric Railway Accountants Association and the American Electric Railway Engineering Association). Estimates of the life of electric light and power plants were included in this compilation, devoted primarily to electric railway property. While the date of publication is 1912, the estimates compiled date back over a number of years,

[7] Federal Power Commission, *Electric Utility Depreciation Practices, 1949.*

[8] Federal Power Commission, *Electric Utility Cost Units*: Steam Electric Generating Stations (S–68), Hydroelectric Generating Stations (S–78).

some as far back as 1899. Ten estimates are presented for the life of electric plant; the sources cited include the Wisconsin Railroad Commission, engineering discussions, and estimates made in various rate cases. Of the ten available estimates, one is for an average life of fifty years and may be disregarded as being completely out of line with other data. The remaining nine estimates range from an average life of ten years to twenty-two years, and the average of these estimates is sixteen years. Corroboration of the reasonableness of these estimates is available from information shown in the 1907 Census of Street Railways (reprinted from the *Electric Railway Journal* of April 10, 1909). The average life of power plant equipment of the Chicago Union Traction Company is cited at sixteen years for all items; the average life of power plant equipment for the Milwaukee Electric Railway and Light Company is indicated as twenty years for most items, and ten or thirteen years for several types of equipment. In view of the nature of the available evidence, it is obvious that construction of a precise figure for any particular date is impossible. Nevertheless, the general order of magnitude appears fairly well established. Since estimates of average life typically lag behind experience, it was assumed that a 17-year average life might be ascribed to equipment installed prior to 1897. For the periods intervening between 1897 and 1928, average life was estimated by straight-line interpolation for each decade; a 22-year life was assumed for 1898–1907, a 27-year life for 1908–17, and a 32-year life for 1918–27.

Next, estimates of the distribution of retirements for equipment of different life expectancy are needed. Because little or no information is available on this question, we have prepared an approximate percentage distribution of retirements, by age of equipment, for equipment with an average life of thirty-seven years and have maintained this distribution, appropriately adjusted, for equipment with an average life of thirty-two years, twenty-seven years, twenty-two years, and seventeen years.

Reports of the Federal Power Commission for 1946, 1947, and 1948 show for steam plants, hydroelectric plants, and internal combustion plants, respectively, the generating capacity in service, by year of installation.[9] It was assumed, for the purpose of estimating the *distribution* of retirements, that all equipment may be treated as having the same average life. The FPC data, which represent nearly complete coverage of private electric utilities, were first adjusted to

[9] Federal Power Commission, *Electric Utility Cost Units*: Steam Electric Generating Stations (S–68), Hydroelectric Generating Stations (S–78), and Internal Combustion Engine Electric Generating Stations (S–85).

represent the entire industry, by the use of ratios of total generating capacity in each branch of the industry to generating capacity of the plants included in the FPC studies. Total generating capacity remaining in service in 1946–48 was classified by period of installation, the time periods corresponding to the periods for which census information is available: pre-1902, 1903–07, 1908–12, 1913–17, 1918–22, 1923–27, and 1928–32. The total capacity remaining in service, installed in each period, was compared with the net change in total generating capacity for the same periods as reported by the census (Table D–8). For instance, in 1902, the census reported a total generating capacity of 1,188,000 kilowatts (the figure actually used is the census figure adjusted to include power departments of electric railways); in 1946–48, 125,200 kilowatts of capacity which were installed prior to 1902 remained in service, or 10.5 per cent of the 1902 total. Similarly, total generating capacity increased by 1,578,500 kilowatts during 1903–07, and 461,300 kilowatts installed during this period remained in use in 1946–48, or 29.2 per cent of the total added during 1903–07.

Since data were not available for gross additions to generating capacity, the quantities of equipment remaining in service, by time of installation, had to be compared with the net changes in generating capacity for the same time intervals. As the gross additions were greater than the net, the ratios shown in Table D–8, column 6, should be reduced somewhat. The procedure followed was merely to round the ratios through the period 1908–12; for later years, the ratios were arbitrarily reduced slightly. From the cumulative distribution of percentages of equipment remaining in service for various periods after installation—for 45–50 years, 40–45 years, 35–40 years, and so on—we derive the percentage distribution of retirements shown in column 8.

The average age derived from this retirement schedule is 37.75 years, compared with 37.3 years derived from the depreciation rates of electric utilities in 1949. Thus, while the retirement distribution is based on generating facilities only and does not take account of transmission and distribution plant, it would seem to provide a satisfactory indicator of the distribution of retirements by age, and the average is in accord with the average for the entire industry.

Having obtained a percentage distribution of retirements of equipment with an average life of 37 years (37.75), we use the same relative distribution for equipment with an average life of thirty-two years, twenty-seven years, and twenty-two years, merely reducing the ages appropriate for each percentage by five years each time, as shown in Table D–9. The average life implicit in the retirement distributions used is 18 years for the period prior to 1897, 22.75 for 1898–1907, 27.75 for 1908–17, and 32.75 for 1918–27.

We can now proceed to estimate the actual value of retirements for the various time periods. We first estimate retirements for the entire period 1881–97. Using the figures for the increase in the value of plant and equipment by five-year intervals, obtained in Table D–5, and the retirement distribution shown in Table D–9, we may estimate the retirements, prior to 1897, of equipment installed during the years 1881–97. The computations, shown in Table D–10, part A, yield total retirements amounting to 0.0761 of the total increase in plant and equipment for the period before 1897. Since this ratio was not computed from an estimate of gross capital expenditures, but from the increase in the value of plant and equipment for 1881–97 (additions less retirements), an approximation of "gross increase in value of plant and equipment"[10] was obtained by dividing the series for the increase in the value of plant and equipment by the complement of 0.0761, or 0.9239. The same procedure was followed for the five-year intervals within 1881–97 as for the entire period.

The estimated gross increase in value of plant and equipment for each period to 1897 was entered in Table D–11, which shows the retirements of equipment installed, by five-year intervals, distributed by succeeding five-year intervals; for instance, of the equipment installed in 1881–82, 30 per cent was retired in 1898–1902, 20 per cent in 1903–07, and 10 per cent in 1908–12. The money value of these retirements (of equipment installed prior to 1897) was computed, thus making it possible to compute total retirements for the next interval, 1898–1902. The increase in the value of plant and equipment for 1898–1902, plus retirements during the same years, yields the gross increase in value of plant and equipment for this period (Table D–10). The gross figure, in turn, was entered in Table D–11, retirements of this equipment in later years computed, total retirements in 1903–07 and gross increase in plant and equipment for the same period derived, and so on for successive periods. The gross increase in value of plant and equipment for all periods is shown in Table D–10, part B.

The value of retirements derived by the procedure outlined above constitute the following percentages of capital assets at the beginning of the respective periods:

[10] This series is not called "gross capital expenditures" in Tables D–10 and D–11 (but rather, gross increase in value of plant and equipment) since an adjustment for write-ups is required, discussed below.

1898–1902	14
1903–1907	10
1908–1912	10
1913–1917	7
1918–1922	7
1923–1927	9
1928–1932	6

There are only scanty reported figures on the value of retirements to provide a basis for judging the reliability of our estimates, but such figures as are available indicate the estimates are reasonable. Reports to the Public Service Commission for the First District of New York State (New York City) for the years 1918–22 show total retirements for this period amounting to 6 per cent of fixed capital on hand at the end of 1917; our estimate for 1918–22 is 6.7 per cent. Unpublished data supplied by the Federal Power Commission for the value of retirements made by Class A and Class B utilities (which constitute over 98 per cent of all privately owned electric utilities) during the years 1938–42 indicate that retirements were approximately 8 per cent of the total value of electric plant existing at the end of 1937.

ADJUSTMENT FOR WRITE-UPS

The series derived in Table D–10, part B, would provide a satisfactory measure of gross capital expenditures, provided the book figures reported under value of plant and equipment represented actual original cost of construction and of equipment purchases. Actually in the power industry, as in other utilities, the book figures have been inflated above actual cost in many ways. Because of the crucial importance of rate regulation, and because of the importance of the valuation base in the determination of rates, there has always been a tendency to maintain the highest possible valuation. Write-ups above cost have resulted from many different types of financial operations. To mention but a few of those which figure prominently in the records of the Federal Trade Commission: mergers and consolidations of companies, the sale of property to a new company (which may or may not be controlled by the selling company) at a figure above cost, the capitalization of intangibles, the capitalization of potential earnings, the failure to write off the value of abandoned property at cost, or sometimes the failure officially to retire such property at all. The Federal Trade Commission, in its investigation of utilities, begun in 1928, published one hundred and one volumes on utility corporations which show numerous instances of such write-ups; in its summary report on electric utilities (*Utility Corporations, Vol. 72–A*), the FTC found total write-ups of 599 millions for ninety-one operating companies with total capital assets of 3,307 millions. Thus, write-ups constituted 18 per cent of the book value of capital assets for these companies.

Additional information on the amount of write-ups is available as a result of the activities of the Federal Power Commission. The commission's Uniform System of Accounts, which was made effective January 1, 1937, specifies that utility plant shall be carried on the books at the original cost at the time it was first devoted to public use. Where a company purchased property at a price in excess of original cost, the excess must be carried in an appropriate account, "Electric Plant Acquisition Adjustments," and must be amortized over a period of years. From the time of the adoption of the new system, the FPC was engaged in reclassifying plant accounts; this reclassification was virtually completed by 1950.

Two publications of the Federal Power Commission provide data on the amount of write-downs ordered by the FPC and by state public service commissions. The first (*Financial Records of the Electric Utility Industry, 1937–46*) indicates that from 1937 to 1946, downward revisions in plant accounts of 1,199 millions were ordered or approved by the FPC as the result of its reclassification and cost studies. Considerable additional amounts were ordered removed by state commissions. The FPC indicated that the total through 1946, including amounts ordered removed by state commissions, was approximately 1.5 billions. The second publication (*Report on the Reclassification and Original Cost of Electric Plant of Public Utilities and Licensees*, Serial No. A–38, 1950) indicates that total adjustments by the FPC made, and pending as of February 1950, were 1,603 millions, or 404 million above the 1946 total. If we add the 1946 total of 1.5 billion (which includes amounts written down by state commissions) and the additional amount written down by the FPC between 1946 and 1950 (404 millions), we obtain an estimated total of write-downs of 1,904 millions.[11] This figure compares with a total value of electric plant reported in the 1937 census of 11,936 millions.[12] Thus, write-ups constituted approximately 16 per cent of the book figures on the value of electric plant. This percentage corresponds very closely with the findings of the Federal Trade Commission.

No information is available as to the timing of the write-ups which

[11] The FPC ordered about 32 per cent of its total write-downs classified in the Electric Plant Acquisition Adjustments account, and required these amounts amortized over periods not in excess of fifteen years. The remainder was ordered removed from the property accounts immediately. For our purposes, we wish to consider the total write-downs, including the amounts classified as genuine acquisition adjustments.

[12] It is assumed that none of the write-downs was applicable to additions made after 1937, since the effectiveness of the FPC regulation would have prevented any write-ups.

were found; indeed such information could not be obtained without a detailed and comprehensive study of the financial history of all the major utilities. In its absence, we have uniformly reduced the figures for gross increase in value of plant and equipment by 16 per cent to derive the final estimates of gross capital expenditures by five-year intervals. These estimates are shown in Table D–12.

The Federal Trade Commission found that some companies wrote down the value of their capital assets during the depression of the thirties, but no estimate is available as to the amount of such write-downs. To the extent that write-downs occurred before 1937, our estimate of the proportion of write-ups for earlier years is too low and our estimates of gross capital expenditures are somewhat too high.

RELIABILITY OF THE ESTIMATES OF GROSS CAPITAL EXPENDITURES

Since our derivation of gross capital expenditures for the period prior to 1920 involved the preparation of many estimates, it is of interest to compare the results obtained by the procedure used with data on reported expenditures available for later years. Estimates of gross capital expenditures were prepared for 1923–27 and 1928–32, following the same procedure employed for earlier years, and compared with the figures reported by the Edison Electric Institute. This comparison is shown in Table D–12. For 1923–27, the estimated figure differs from the reported total by less than one per cent; for 1928–32, the estimated gross capital expenditures are 8.6 per cent higher than the reported figures. A reported figure on capital expenditures is available also for 1907, when the census asked plants in operation to report the cost of construction during the year and made a survey (somewhat incomplete) of expenditures for plants under construction as of December 31, 1907. The total of these items (appropriately adjusted to include construction by light and power departments of street railways and to exclude the cost of land) is 126 millions, a figure almost identical with that derived for 1907—125 millions—when our total for the period 1903–07 is distributed by years (Table D–15).

Several minor conceptual problems may be noted concerning the estimates of gross capital expenditures derived from the census data on the value of plant and equipment. There may be some lag in our gross capital expenditures series because the census canvasses were confined to plants in operation, and the plant and equipment figures as of the various dates would not include the value of construction work in progress for any plant not completed and operating at the date of the census survey. In addition, all companies in operation may not report the value of construction work in progress under value of plant and equipment; some may carry such work in a separate property account. For the early years, these factors may result in some errors in the timing of our series. To the extent that construction work in progress was not reported at the end of 1922, a certain amount of capital expenditures may be excluded from our series altogether. Finally, changes in the value of plant and equipment as reported by the census may reflect, to a small extent, transfers from private to municipal ownership, or vice versa. It is not believed that any significant error arises from this source; commercial plants accounted for 95–96 per cent of total plant and equipment during all census years 1902–32.

DISTRIBUTION OF GROSS CAPITAL EXPENDITURES BY YEARS

Total gross capital expenditures for 1881–97 and 1898–1902 (June) were distributed by years in accordance with the series derived in Table D–5, which represents the products of (1) number of stations beginning operations each year, (2) size of stations, and (3) a construction cost index. The annual series for this period is shown in Table D–13.

For the period (July) 1902–1912, it was assumed that there was a smooth growth in generating capacity of the industry, and gross capital expenditures were estimated from the increases in generating capacity, together with an index of construction costs. Estimates of generating capacity at the end of each year were made by interpolation of census data in accordance with a modified exponential trend, fitted by the method of average points for each of the periods 1902–07, 1912–17, and 1922–27. The derivation of the annual estimates of generating capacity is shown in Table D–14. The series for annual increases in generating capacity, multiplied by the index of construction costs previously obtained,[13] provided the basis for distributing total expenditures for 1902–07 and 1908–12 among the years within each period. The computations are shown in Table D–15. The final 1902 total is the sum of the six-month figure derived from the distribution for 1898–1902 (June) and the six-month figure derived from the distribution for (July) 1902–1907.

For 1913–20, the period dominated by World War I, the assumption of a smooth year-to-year increase in physical capacity of the industry would involve more serious error than for the earlier years. Information on increases in fixed capital was obtained from reports of the state public service commissions for California,

[13] The index for 1912 is based on the construction cost index compiled by W. W. Handy and described below, in the section on gross capital expenditures in 1929 dollars.

Massachusetts, and Ohio, and for the First District of New York State. Plant and equipment for this sample constituted about 30 per cent of total plant and equipment in the United States reported by the 1912 census. The total expenditures for 1913–17 were distributed among the five years in accordance with the annual increases in fixed capital shown by the sample. Since reported figures are available for the years 1921 and 1922, the reported gross capital expenditures for the two years were first subtracted from the total for 1918–22. The remainder, representing gross capital expenditures for 1918–20, was then distributed among the three years in accordance with the increases in fixed capital for these years shown by the sample data. The distribution of gross capital expenditures for 1913–20 is shown in Table D–16.

Gross Capital Expenditures, 1921–1937

The Edison Electric Institute reports "Construction Expenditures" for each year beginning with 1921. The figures are based on surveys made by the Institute and its predecessor, the National Electric Light Association, and are adjusted before publication to represent complete coverage of the industry. Coverage of the sample is high, published estimates of coverage being over 90 per cent for privately owned electric utilities. The EEI series includes expenditures for real estate and all equipment, including expenditures for replacements, additions, and betterments, as well as for new construction. An attempt was made by Edison Electric Institute to exclude expenditures for the purchase of existing properties, but it is possible that some such expenditures may be included for the years 1921–25.

The EEI data provide accurate estimates of capital expenditures as charged by electric utilities, but the figures may include, to a small extent, charges which have been written off the books by the Federal Power Commission and state public service commissions in recent years. The Federal Trade Commission, in its investigation of utility corporations, reported instances of write-ups of construction expenditures, as well as other types of write-ups.

The EEI data for 1926–37 are shown separately for private and municipal utilities; for prior years, however, only a combined total for the two segments of the industry is available. Estimates of total capital expenditures of privately owned plants were made for 1921–25 by multiplying the totals reported for private and municipal plants by the average ratio between expenditures of privately owned plants and all plants for the years 1926–28; privately owned plants accounted for 94 per cent of total expenditures during these years.

The EEI figures include the cost of land. Expenditures for land for

1926–31 were estimated at 7 per cent of total capital expenditures, as noted. An estimate for the year 1937 (and for later years as well) was obtained from unpublished data furnished by the Federal Power Commission on the value of land and the total value of additions of plant and equipment for the various types of production plant, transmission plant, distribution plant, and general plant. The deduction for land for 1921–26 was based on interpolation between the percentage used for 1881–98 and the percentage for 1926–31. The deduction for 1932–37 was derived by interpolation between the percentage for 1926–31 and the average percentage for 1937–42 shown by the FPC data for these years (2.29). These computations are given in Table D–17.

Gross Capital Expenditures, 1938–1950

For recent years, it is possible to obtain very accurate data on gross capital expenditures from reports made to the Federal Power Commission by Class A and Class B electric utilities. These utilities, generally the ones with gross revenues in excess of 250,000 dollars per year, constitute 98 per cent of all privately owned electric utilities in terms of assets and are required to report to the FPC. During the years 1941–43, the FPC obtained reports of actual capital expenditures of Class A and Class B utilities including expenditures for land. For other years of the period 1938–50, reports were obtained on the value of gross additions to electric plant each year; that is, the value of new plant was reported when the facilities were placed in service, regardless of when the actual expenditures were made. FPC also obtained reports on the value of construction work in progress at the end of each year. For the years 1938–40 and 1944–50, gross capital expenditures, including land, were derived by adding (algebraically) the value of gross additions placed in service and the net change in construction work in progress during the year. The Federal Power Commission supplied unpublished data on the total value of construction work in progress at the end of the years 1943–50; figures on construction work in progress at the end of the years 1937–40 were compiled from the reports for individual companies shown in the FPC annual publication, *Statistics of Electric Utilities in the United States*. The series for gross capital expenditures of Class A and Class B companies were adjusted to represent all privately owned utilities, on the assumption that these utilities represented 98 per cent of the total throughout the period under consideration.[14]

[14] Revenue from electric service reported by Class A and B companies for 1937 constituted 97.8 per cent of the electric service revenue reported by all privately owned plants in the 1937 census.

Deduction for expenditures for land was also made by the use of unpublished material supplied by the Federal Power Commission—data for the value of land and the total value of electric plant for additions placed in service during the years 1937–48 for virtually all Class A and B companies (a small amount of new plant was not classified in detail). The ratio between the value of land and total value of additions for the respective years was applied to the figures on gross capital expenditures to derive the value of land expenditures. Data on expenditures for land were not compiled by FPC for 1948–50; for these years, the average ratio of the value of land to total value of plant for 1945–47 was used. The derivation of the series for gross capital expenditures for 1938–50 is shown in Table D-18.

Gross Capital Expenditures, 1881–1950, in 1929 Dollars

The complete series for gross capital expenditures to 1950 was deflated with an index of construction costs on the base 1929 = 100. The construction cost index is based for the period 1911–50 on the index of electric plant construction costs developed by W. W. Handy and now compiled and published by Whitman, Requardt and Associates.[15] The Handy index is derived from series for building construction, various types of equipment, materials, labor, etc. It is intended to show typical steam plant experience and no purely hydroelectric companies were included in the surveys on which it is based, but no adjustment appears to be required on this account.[16] The Handy index is presented for five regions (the regional indexes differ from each other only because of the inclusion of separate wage figures for the various areas) and no series is shown for the United States as a whole. The five regional figures for each date were first combined into a U.S. average by the use of weights representing the approximate proportion of total generating capacity for each of the five regions, as reported by the census for 1902 and 1937. The Handy series includes annual figures through 1918 and data as of January 1 and July 1 for 1920 and for 1924 and later years; for 1919 and 1923, the index is available as of January 1 only; for 1921, for January 1 and September 1. No index was published for the year 1922. Where

[15] Semiannual bulletin, *Public Utility Construction Cost Indexes and Financial and Operating Ratios*.

[16] In Bulletin No. 53, which became available after this work was completed, indexes for steam and hydroelectric plant together are shown back to 1911 for each region, and the Atlantic Seaboard region is divided into North Atlantic and South Atlantic. An index based on the new figures would differ but slightly from the one used here. For 1950, the index derived from the more complete data now available is 1.6 per cent below the one used here.

possible, the construction cost index used here was prepared by averaging the reported figures for January (weight 1), July (weight 2), and January 1 of the following year (weight 1). For 1919, an average of figures as of January 1, 1919 and January 1, 1920 was used; for 1921, an average for January 1 and September 1; for 1923, an average for January 1, 1923 and January 1, 1924. The derivation of the construction cost index for 1911–50 (except 1922) is shown in Table D–19. The Handy index was interpolated for 1922 and extrapolated to 1881 by means of the construction cost index shown in Table D–6 and previously described, and the series was shifted to the base 1929 = 100, as shown in Table D–20.

The complete series for gross capital expenditures to 1950, in current prices, and in 1929 prices, is shown in Table D–1.

Capital Consumption in 1929 Dollars

Having obtained a complete series for gross capital expenditures of the electric light and power industry throughout the years, we next estimate annual capital consumption and net capital expenditures. As we have noted, in the electric light and power industry, depreciation accounting according to any uniform scheme has been practiced only in recent years and may be considered to date from 1937, when the Federal Power Commission's Uniform System of Accounts went into effect. Indeed, since a number of years elapsed before some companies adopted a systematic method of accounting for depreciation, it is only for the last few years that reported depreciation charges may be considered even to approximate "actual" capital consumption. Before 1937, companies generally used the retirement-reserve method of accounting for depreciation, or no standard method. Funds for the ultimate retirement of property were frequently set aside out of surplus in good years, while no charge for depreciation whatever may have been made when operations were less profitable.

We have estimated depreciation not from the reports of depreciation charges made by companies, but by the use of approximate estimates of average life of all plant and equipment. As was said above, seventeen years may be considered a fair approximation of average life during the early years of the industry's growth, and thirty-seven years may be considered a satisfactory approximation for recent years. The former figure was derived from various published estimates of the average life of electric plant; the latter is based on the average depreciation rate in the year 1949 for companies using a straight-line method of computing depreciation. In preparing our estimates of depreciation, an average seventeen-year life has been assumed for equipment *installed* in all years through 1900 and an average thirty-seven-year life for equipment *installed* in 1920 and later years. Average life for intervening years was derived by straight-line interpolation between these two figures.

Table D–21 shows the derivation of capital consumption in 1929 dollars for the years 1881–1936. Gross capital expenditures made in each year were divided by the estimated life of equipment to obtain the annual capital consumption of each year's plant and equipment additions; these figures are shown in column 3. In column 4, the annual figures are summed back through the appropriate number of years; total capital consumption for any year, as shown in this column, is the sum of the annual capital consumption for all the expenditures of prior years not yet fully depreciated. Finally, it was assumed that each year's expenditures may be centered at the midpoint of the year and that the expenditures of any year are depreciated at the end of the year by one-half the annual rate. The final estimates of capital consumption were therefore computed by taking two-year moving averages of the figures in column 4, centered in the second year. The results are shown in column 5 of Table D–21.

The estimates of depreciation, or capital consumption, for all years through 1936 were prepared from the series on deflated gross capital expenditures. Theoretically, it would be preferable to derive the depreciation estimates from a series for the deflated value of plant placed in service, since capital consumption does not begin until a plant is completed. However, the error involved is quite small; at most, depreciation may be charged slightly in advance of its actual occurrence. Since data on the value of plant placed in service are available for the years 1937–50 and since the value of construction work in progress is rather high for recent years, estimates of depreciation for these years were computed by the use of the deflated value of plant additions, rather than capital expenditures as the basic series. The data on the value of plant additions placed in service each year were first adjusted to include the value of plant additions made by small companies not reporting to the Federal Power Commission and to exclude the value of land. The value of gross additions was then deflated to 1929 dollars. The estimates of gross additions to plant and equipment, in 1929 dollars, are shown in Table D–22. Table D–23 shows the computation of the estimates of capital consumption for the years 1937–50 in 1929 dollars.

It is striking to note how large a proportion of expenditures represent replacement, even though there has been a rather steady increase in expenditures over the years. The figures are summarized below, in millions of 1929 dollars:

	Gross Capital Expenditures	*Net Capital Expenditures*	*Percentage of Net to Gross*
1880–1889	99.7	86.8	87
1890–1899	702.8	482.2	69
1900–1909	2391.5	1472.9	62
1910–1919	3042.9	1221.7	40
1920–1929	6076.1	3670.2	60
1930–1939	3415.5	160.6	5
1940–1949	5161.1	1727.5	33

Capital Consumption in Original Cost Dollars

Capital consumption in original cost dollars is shown in Table D–24. This series was computed in the same manner as the series in 1929 dollars, except that the base used to compute depreciation was gross capital expenditures in current prices for 1881–1936 and the value of plant additions in current prices for 1937–50.

It is of interest to compare the estimated series on capital consumption in original cost dollars with available reported figures on depreciation charges (Table D–25). Only in years since 1937 do the financial charges made for depreciation approximate our estimates of the actual capital consumption each year. The Federal Power Commission and state regulatory bodies have called attention repeatedly to the inadequacy of depreciation accounting prior to 1937. For example, the Federal Power Commission, reviewing its program of electric utility accounting reform, stated: "Moreover, depreciation accounting (prior to 1937) was a sorry state, inadequate reserves had been accrued and depreciation of retirement expense was determined generally in a haphazard fashion with little attempt to assign the cost of depreciation to operations on a systematic basis."[17]

Net Capital Expenditures

Net capital expenditures in 1929 dollars were derived by subtraction of the series for capital consumption from gross capital

[17] *Report on the Reclassification and Original Cost of Electric Plant of Public Utilities and Licensees, 1950.*

expenditures in 1929 dollars. Capital consumption and net capital expenditures in 1929 dollars are shown in Table D–1.

A series for net capital expenditures in current dollars, which also appears in Table D–1, was obtained simply by applying to the net capital expenditures in 1929 dollars the index of cost of plant and equipment shown in Table D–20. Capital consumption in current dollars, also shown in Table D–1, is the difference between gross and net capital expenditures in current dollars.

Value of Plant and Equipment

Since our series on gross and net capital expenditures extend back to the beginnings of the industry, we may derive a series on the value of physical assets in 1929 dollars, net after depreciation, simply by cumulating our figures on net capital expenditures in 1929 dollars each year. The results are presented in terms of 1929 prices in Table D–1. The value of plant and equipment in current prices, also given in this table, was obtained by applying to the constant dollar figures the index of the cost of plant and equipment shown in Table D–20.

The final figures, by years, for capital formation in electric light and power are given in Table D–1.

User-Owned and Publicly Owned Power Facilities

The development of commercial electric light and power utilities has been importantly influenced by the changing status of user-owned and publicly owned power facilities. In the early period of this industry's history, public power from a quantitative point of view was an insignificant factor, barely ever accounting for as much as 5 per cent of total facilities until the late 1920's. From the industry's inception in 1882 until the turn of the century, however, commercial electric utilities and user-owned electric power plants grew side by side. Initially, technological considerations made this feasible, since the interconnection of plants was not developed at once and the transmission of electricity over long distances[18] was difficult or impossible. Hotels, electric railways, and industrial establishments commonly built their own plants. As late as 1910 such user-owned facilities represented more than 40 per cent of the industry's capacity,[19] as shown in Table D–26.

[18] Before the introduction of alternating current, the maximum service area of a plant was one mile in diameter.

[19] User-owned plants represented an even larger percentage of *generating* capacity. Transmission and distribution facilities weigh much more heavily in the total physical assets of private utilities than of user-owned establishments.

From this date on, however, the growth of commercial utilities was greatly accelerated by the rapid extension of its market into these areas. As user-owned equipment became obsolescent through the swift pace of technological change, it was often abandoned in favor of the cheaper power supply provided by the expanding utilities. The period of major change-over in this respect appears to have ended by 1940, when the relative importance of user-owned facilities had declined to 13 per cent, although in very modest measure this trend is still in progress.

The beginning of the 1930's witnessed a new element in the industry's development. This was the expansion of public power, which more than doubled the size of its facilities in each of the succeeding decades, advancing from about 5 per cent of the industry's capacity in 1930 to 20 per cent in 1950. Taken in the aggregate, the rate of increase of electric light and power facilities of all types—private, public, and user-owned—reached a maximum in the decade of the twenties. Since 1930, however, total facilities have expanded by 32 per cent, private utilities by 27 per cent, and private utilities plus the still declining user-owned facilities by about 10 per cent. These discrepancies mirror the extension of public power.

The basic data on capital formation in user-owned and publicly owned electric light and power are shown in Tables D–26, D–27, and D–28, along with comparable series for the private utilities. Though annual data are presented for some of the series, it must be borne in mind that year-to-year changes are in no case reliable; they are useful only as indicators of longer-term trends, as will be evident from the description of their derivation, given below.

GROSS CAPITAL EXPENDITURES, PUBLICLY OWNED PLANTS EXCEPT FEDERAL

Estimates of gross capital expenditures for publicly owned plants except federal projects, were prepared for the period 1881–1922, as were the estimates for private establishments, by the use of data reported by the successive censuses on the value of plant and equipment. Municipal plants represented all the publicly owned facilities for this period (aside from some small federal projects), and these plants were canvassed by the Census Bureau in the same manner as private electric utilities. The increase in the value of plant and equipment reported for each of the periods 1881–1902 (June 30), 1902 (July 1)–1907, 1908–12, 1913–17, and 1918–22 was compared with the increases in the value of plant and equipment for the same periods for privately owned plants; the latter series was first adjusted to eliminate the effect of write-ups in the value of capital assets. The basic data are shown in columns 1–3 of Table D–29. It was assumed that the ratio of gross capital expenditures of municipal plants to gross capital expenditures of privately owned plants for each period was the same as the ratio of the respective increases in the value of plant and equipment (column 4) after this adjustment. Gross capital expenditures of publicly owned plants were therefore derived by multiplying gross capital expenditures of privately owned plants by the ratios of public to private increases in the value of plant and equipment. The results are shown in column 6 of Table D–29.

The series for gross capital expenditures thus derived for the periods 1881–1902 (June 30), 1902 (July 1)–1907, 1908–12, 1913–17, and 1918–22 were distributed among groups of years within each period, in accordance with the distribution for privately owned plants, to derive estimates for each half-decade. The computations are shown in Table D–30.

For the period 1923–50, estimates of gross capital expenditures of publicly owned plants, except federal, were derived by the use of data published by the Edison Electric Institute. The derivation of the estimates for this period is shown in Table D–31. For the years 1926–43, capital expenditures for the publicly owned sector of the industry are shown separately by EET; for 1923–25 and 1944–50, EEI presents only combined totals for gross capital expenditures of all utilities, privately owned and publicly owned (excluding federal projects). For 1923–25, expenditures for the publicly owned utilities were estimated by use of the average ratio, for the years 1926–28, of expenditures of publicly owned utilities to the total for private and public plants together. For 1944–50, estimates for the publicly owned segment were obtained by subtracting from the EEI series, which covers private and public electric plant, the series for gross capital expenditures for private utilities developed here. Deduction for the value of land included in gross capital expenditures as reported by EEI was made by the use of the same percentages used for privately owned utilities.

GROSS CAPITAL EXPENDITURES, FEDERAL PROJECTS

Estimates of gross capital expenditures of the federal government for light and power facilities have been prepared only for the period 1921–50, since data are not available to provide any basis of estimating expenditures in earlier years. However, expenditures in prior years were of minor importance and may be considered close to zero in analysis of investment trends in the industry.[20]

Expenditures of the federal government for power facilities were reported by the Federal Power Commission for the years 1940–43; these data are shown in column 6 of Table D–32. For other years, only approximate estimates of the level of expenditures can be prepared. Most federal projects serve jointly for the production of electric energy and for conservation and development—erosion control, flood control, irrigation, and the like—and no allocation of expenditures is regularly reported. For 1945–50, the *Electrical World* shows estimates of total federal expenditures, including expenditures of funds advanced by the Rural Electrification Administration. Since expenditures of REA funds by rural cooperatives are already included in our figures for gross capital expenditures of publicly owned plants, except federal, we deduct such expenditures from the *Electrical World* totals. It was assumed that REA funds advanced during any year represent capital expenditures of cooperatives during the succeeding years. The *Electrical World* figures for the years 1945–50, the deductions for expenditures of REA funds, and the estimates of expenditures for federal projects for 1945–49 are shown in columns 4 to 6 of Table D–32.

Estimates of expenditures of the federal government for power facilities for the intervals 1921–24, 1925–29, 1930–34, 1935–39, and for the year 1948 were obtained by use of FPC data on the net increase in generating capacity, taken in conjunction with the index of construction costs. Column 1 of Table D–32 shows the increases in generating capacity of federal plants, column 2 shows the index of construction costs, and column 3 shows the products of the two preceding series. The total gross capital expenditures for the years 1940–43 and 1945–50 (column 6) was compared with column 3 for the corresponding years. Gross capital expenditures were derived by multiplying column 3 by the ratio of total gross capital expenditures for 1940–43 and 1945–50 to the sums of the products of generating capacity and the construction cost index (column 3) for the same years.

[20] The 1937 census reported the total value of plant and equipment of federal and state establishments at 145 million dollars: Federal Power Commission data on generating capacity suggest that federal plants accounted for 97 per cent of the federal-state total, or for physical assets of approximately 141 million dollars. Generating capacity of federal plants was 833,000 kilowatts in 1937, and only 10,000 kilowatts in 1920, or 1.2 per cent of the 1937 total. If we assume that the increase between 1920 and 1937 in the value of federal light and power plant and equipment was proportional to the increase in generating capacity, then federally owned facilities would have been valued at only 1.7 millions at the close of 1920. Thus, it is apparent that federal expenditures in years prior to 1921 were of negligible importance.

Deduction for the value of land included in capital expenditures of the federal government was made by use of the same percentages of land expenditures to total gross capital expenditures as for privately owned utilities.[21] The computations are shown in columns 8 and 9 of Table D–32.

Since many of the federal projects are large undertakings and require several years to construct, there is a certain amount of lag in our estimates for 1939 and prior years, based as they are on the net increase in completed physical capacity. In addition, the data on generating capacity and construction costs can at best provide only a rough indication of capital expenditures, especially in view of the joint purpose of most federal projects and the difficult problems of cost allocation involved. It is therefore to be emphasized that the estimates of expenditures for the federally owned sector of the industry are crude approximations.

VALUE OF PLANT AND EQUIPMENT, PUBLICLY OWNED ELECTRIC UTILITIES, 1929 PRICES

The value of plant and equipment for publicly owned utilities, in 1929 prices, was obtained from the data on gross capital expenditures, in conjunction with estimates of capital consumption. The computations are shown in Table D–33. Gross capital expenditures, in current prices, were first deflated by the index of construction costs to obtain gross capital expenditures in 1929 prices. Estimates of capital consumption were prepared, in the same manner as for privately owned plants, by the use of data on gross capital expenditures and on average life of plant and equipment; the derivation of this series is shown in columns 3–7 of Table D–33. Net capital expenditures in 1929 prices (column 8) was obtained by subtracting capital consumption from gross capital expenditures. Finally, the value of plant and equipment, in 1929 prices, was obtained by cumulating net capital expenditures in each year.

VALUE OF PLANT AND EQUIPMENT, USER-OWNED FACILITIES, 1929 PRICES

The value of plant and equipment for user-owned electric light and power facilities was obtained primarily from data on user-owned generating capacity. The available data on user-owned generating

[21] Expenditures for land on federal projects are doubtless considerably higher, as a percentage of total capital expenditures, than on private establishments, since most are large hydroelectric projects which require a substantial outlay for land. In view of the approximate nature of the estimates of capital expenditures and the purpose for which they are presented, however, more precise figures on the percentage of expenditures for land were not compiled.

capacity—for the beginning of the years 1900, 1910, 1920, and annually for 1940–50—are shown in Table D–34, together with similar data for private and public electric utilities. The data for 1900–20 are from the Geological Survey; the data for 1940–50 are from the Federal Power Commission.

Since user-owned facilities do not, in general, involve long-distance transmission and require relatively small investment in distribution plant, estimates were made of the relationship between user-owned and utility-owned plants in investment per *unit* of generating capacity for available years—1900, 1910, and 1920 (Table D–35). It was assumed that electric railroads have investment in generating and distribution plant equivalent to that of the utility industry for the same capacity (but no transmission plant) and that other user-owned plant represents investment in generating capacity only (with no investment in transmission or distribution plant). Investment in (1) generating and distribution plant and in (2) generating plant, as percentages of total electric light and power investment, were obtained from 1950 data published by the FPC for Class A and Class B privately owned utilities (Table D–35, note to column 5). The former figure was weighted with the percentages of total user-owned capacity owned by electric railroads in 1900, 1910, and 1920 (column 3), the latter with the percentages of total user-owned capacity owned by other establishments (column 4) in the respective years. The results (column 5) show the value of plant and equipment per unit of generating capacity for user-owned establishments as ratios of the corresponding figures for electric utilities for 1900, 1910, and 1920.

Table D–36 shows the derivation of ratios of the value of plant and equipment for user-owned power facilities to the value of utility-owned plant and equipment. This series was obtained for 1900, 1910, 1920, and 1940–51 as the product of two sets of ratios: (1) the ratio of user-owned generating capacity to utility-owned capacity (column 1) and (2) the ratio between user-owned and utility-owned facilities in value of plant and equipment per unit of generating capacity (column 2). The 1920 figure for the latter series was extrapolated for 1940–51. The final series (column 3) was interpolated linearly for years intervening between 1900, 1910, 1920, and 1940; the 1900 ratio was used for all years prior to this date.

The series thus obtained was multiplied by the series for value of plant and equipment, in 1929 dollars, for electric utilities. The results—value of plant and equipment of user-owned electric light and power facilities in 1929 prices—are shown in Table D–26, column 5.

VALUE OF PLANT AND EQUIPMENT, PUBLICLY OWNED AND USER-OWNED, CURRENT PRICES

Value of plant and equipment, in current dollars, for publicly owned utilities and user-owned power facilities was obtained by multiplying the series in 1929 dollars (Table D–26) by the construction cost index. The results are shown in Table D–27.

Note: Table D–1 follows.

TABLE D-1

Value of Plant and Equipment, Capital Formation, and Capital Consumption, Electric Light and Power, Annual Data, 1881–1950

(*millions of dollars*)

	VALUE OF PLANT AND EQUIPMENT, JANUARY 1		GROSS CAPITAL EXPENDITURES		CAPITAL CONSUMPTION		NET CAPITAL EXPENDITURES	
Year	*Current Dollars* (1)	*1929 Dollars* (2)	*Current Dollars* (3)	*1929 Dollars* (4)	*Current Dollars* (5)	*1929 Dollars* (6)	*Current Dollars* (7)	*1929 Dollars* (8)
1881	a	a	0.2	0.5	a	a	0.2	0.5
1882	0.2	0.5	0.9	2.0	a	0.1	0.9	1.9
1883	1.1	2.4	1.0	2.3	0.1	0.2	0.9	2.1
1884	2.0	4.5	1.7	4.2	0.2	0.4	1.5	3.8
1885	3.4	8.3	2.2	5.6	0.3	0.7	1.9	4.9
1886	5.2	13.2	4.3	11.0	0.5	1.2	3.8	9.8
1887	9.0	23.0	7.2	18.4	0.8	2.1	6.4	16.3
1888	15.4	39.3	9.3	23.7	1.3	3.3	8.0	20.4
1889	23.4	59.7	12.4	32.0	1.9	4.9	10.5	27.1
1890	33.6	86.8	16.7	42.8	2.8	7.1	13.9	35.7
1891	47.8	122.5	14.2	38.8	3.5	9.5	10.7	29.3
1892	55.6	151.8	19.2	53.6	4.4	12.2	14.8	41.4
1893	69.2	193.2	18.5	51.7	5.5	15.3	13.0	36.4
1894	82.2	229.6	19.1	52.8	6.6	18.4	12.5	34.4
1895	95.6	264.0	22.6	69.1	7.2	22.0	15.4	47.1
1896	101.7	311.1	19.1	61.2	8.1	25.8	11.0	35.4
1897	108.1	346.5	32.9	92.2	10.8	30.3	22.1	61.9
1898	145.8	408.4	44.5	118.0	13.8	36.5	30.7	81.5
1899	184.7	489.9	50.4	122.6	17.9	43.5	32.5	79.1
1900	233.9	569.0	50.1	119.6	21.1	50.5	29.0	69.1
1901	267.4	638.1	68.2	165.9	24.0	58.4	44.2	107.5
1902	306.4	745.6	81.5	197.3	28.1	67.9	53.4	129.4
1903	361.4	875.0	82.5	202.7	31.6	77.7	50.9	125.0
1904	407.0	1,000.0	91.0	217.2	36.5	87.1	54.5	130.1
1905	473.5	1,130.1	100.2	234.1	41.2	96.3	59.0	137.8
1906	542.7	1,267.9	111.6	250.8	46.9	105.5	64.7	145.3
1907	628.9	1,413.2	125.0	269.4	53.0	114.3	72.0	155.1
1908	727.7	1,568.3	155.1	351.7	54.9	124.6	100.2	227.1
1909	791.8	1,795.4	180.7	382.8	64.4	136.3	116.3	246.5
1910	963.8	2,041.9	200.5	417.7	71.2	148.3	129.3	269.4
1911	1,109.4	2,311.3	229.5	454.5	81.3	161.1	148.2	293.4
1912	1,315.4	2,604.7	259.3	493.9	91.4	174.1	167.9	319.8
1913	1,535.4	2,924.5	148.6	288.5	94.6	183.6	54.0	104.9
1914	1,560.1	3,029.4	148.8	292.3	96.0	188.6	52.8	103.7
1915	1,594.7	3,133.1	124.4	234.3	101.3	190.8	23.1	43.5
1916	1,686.8	3,176.6	151.3	230.6	125.3	190.9	26.0	39.7
1917	2,109.9	3,216.3	284.3	358.5	152.7	192.5	131.6	166.0
1918	2,682.2	3,382.3	115.6	124.0	182.7	196.0	−67.1	−72.0
1919	3,085.2	3,310.3	145.9	148.6	191.8	195.3	−45.9	−46.7
1920	3,204.9	3,263.6	296.5	276.1	211.0	196.5	85.5	79.6
1921	3,590.6	3,343.2	271.0	271.0	198.7	198.7	72.3	72.3
1922	3,415.5	3,415.5	383.8	420.4	185.1	202.8	198.7	217.6
1923	3,317.0	3,633.1	693.4	725.3	203.8	213.2	489.6	512.1
1924	3,962.8	4,145.2	791.6	812.7	223.0	228.9	568.6	583.8

(continued on next page)

TABLE D–1 (continued)

Year	VALUE OF PLANT AND EQUIPMENT, JANUARY 1		GROSS CAPITAL EXPENDITURES		CAPITAL CONSUMPTION		NET CAPITAL EXPENDITURES	
	Current Dollars (1)	*1929 Dollars* (2)	*Current Dollars* (3)	*1929 Dollars* (4)	*Current Dollars* (5)	*1929 Dollars* (6)	*Current Dollars* (7)	*1929 Dollars* (8)
1925	4,606.0	4,729.0	736.6	757.0	238.4	245.0	498.2	512.0
1926	5,099.5	5,241.0	669.5	701.0	247.9	259.5	421.6	441.5
1927	5,426.8	5,682.5	683.1	729.8	256.0	273.5	427.1	456.3
1928	5,745.9	6,138.8	649.9	683.4	273.2	287.3	376.7	396.1
1929	6,214.7	6,534.9	699.4	699.4	300.5	300.5	398.9	398.9
1930	6,933.8	6,933.8	769.0	805.2	301.2	315.4	467.8	489.8
1931	7,089.5	7,423.6	469.4	503.1	305.6	327.5	163.8	175.6
1932	7,090.1	7,599.2	233.6	265.5	292.3	332.2	−58.7	−66.7
1933	6,628.6	7,532.5	128.7	143.6	296.3	330.7	−167.6	−187.1
1934	6,581.5	7,345.4	140.0	143.0	320.7	327.6	−180.7	−184.6
1935	7,010.4	7,160.8	187.1	187.9	323.4	324.7	−136.3	−136.8
1936	6,995.9	7,024.0	291.9	284.5	332.1	323.7	−40.2	−39.2
1937	7,166.4	6,984.8	454.1	406.5	361.4	323.5	92.7	83.0
1938	7,894.7	7,067.8	407.2	366.5	360.2	324.2	47.0	42.3
1939	7,899.3	7,110.1	346.9	309.7	364.5	325.4	−17.6	−15.7
1940	7,945.7	7,094.4	462.8	406.3	371.9	326.5	90.9	79.8
1941	8,171.4	7,174.2	590.9	497.4	390.1	328.4	200.8	169.0
1942	8,723.7	7,343.2	454.2	370.5	405.2	330.5	49.0	40.0
1943	9,051.8	7,383.2	254.7	206.1	413.9	334.9	−159.2	−128.8
1944	8,966.4	7,254.4	211.5	171.8	415.2	337.3	−203.7	−165.5
1945	8,726.4	7,088.9	361.6	287.0	427.0	338.9	−65.4	−51.9
1946	8,866.6	7,037.0	636.9	440.2	493.9	341.4	143.0	98.8
1947	10,325.5	7,135.8	1,234.8	735.4	585.4	348.6	649.4	386.8
1948	12,630.4	7,522.6	1,823.5	985.7	671.5	363.0	1,152.0	622.7
1949	15,068.8	8,145.3	2,075.7	1,060.7	751.6	384.1	1,324.1	676.6
1950	17,264.5	8,821.9	1,885.1	919.1	833.6	406.4	1,051.5	512.7
1951	19,145.3	9,334.6						

All data exclude investment in land. Columns 1 and 2 exclude accrued depreciation. Series cover privately owned electric utilities.

[a] Less than $100,000.

NOTES BY COLUMN

1 Col. 2 of this table times construction cost index, Table D–20, for the year preceding each January 1.

2 Derived from cumulative totals of net capital expenditures, col. 8, this table. It was assumed that the value of plant and equipment as of January 1, 1881 was zero.

3 Tables D–13, D–15, D–16, D–17, and D–18. The 1902 figure is the total of expenditures for January–June shown in Table D–13 and for July–December derived in Table D–15.

4 Col. 3, this table, deflated by the construction cost index, shown in Table D–20.

5 Col. 3 minus col. 7.

6 Tables D–21 and D–23.

7 Col. 8, this table, inflated by the construction cost index, shown in Table D–20.

8 Col. 4 minus col. 6.

TABLE D–2

Derivation of Book Value of Plant and Equipment, Electric Light and Power, Specified Dates, 1898–1922

(*thousands of dollars*)

	Value of Plant and Equipment, All Commercial Plants Included in Census Reports (1)	*Adjustment Ratios to Include Light and Power Departments of Street Railways* (2)	*Value of Plant and Equipment, All Commercial Plants* (3)
Dec. 31, 1898	265,182		286,688
June 30, 1902	482,720	1.0811	521,869
Dec. 31, 1907	1,054,034	1.1065	1,166,289
Dec. 31, 1912	2,098,613	1.1174	2,344,990
Dec. 31, 1917	2,933,017	1.1145	3,268,847
Dec. 31, 1922	4,229,356	1.0857	4,591,812

NOTES BY COLUMN

1 For 1898, *Fourteenth Annual Report of the Commissioner of Labor*, 1899; for 1902–22, successive reports of the Census of Electrical Industries.

2 For 1902–22: Based on the ratio of revenue from electric service of all commercial light and power plants, including light and power departments of street railways, to the corresponding revenue of commercial plants for which data on value of plant and equipment are shown in column 1. The data on revenue from electric service are from the Census of Electrical Industries.

3 Column 1 times column 2. The 1902 ratio was assumed for 1898.

TABLE D–3

Adjustment of Data for Value of Plant and Equipment to Exclude Value of Land, Electric Light and Power

(thousands of dollars)

Period	*Increase in Value of Plant and Equipment* (1)	*Deduction for Land* (per cent) (2)	*Deduction for Land,* (col. 1 × col. 2 ÷ 100) (3)	*Increase in Value of Plant and Equipment, Excluding Land,* (col. 1 minus col. 3) (4)
Jan. 1, 1881–Dec. 31, 1898	286,688	5.32	15,300	271,388
Jan. 1, 1899–June 30, 1902	235,181	5.56	13,100	222,081
July 1, 1902–Dec. 31, 1907	644,420	5.80	37,400	607,020
Jan. 1, 1908–Dec. 31, 1917	1,178,701	6.04	71,200	1,107,501
Jan. 1, 1913–Dec. 31, 1917	923,857	6.28	58,000	865,857
Jan. 1, 1918–Dec. 31, 1922	1,322,965	6.52	86,300	1,236,665
Jan. 1, 1923–Dec. 31, 1927	4,129,428	6.76	279,100	3,850,328
Jan. 1, 1928–Dec. 31, 1932	3,403,567	7.00	238,200	3,165,367

NOTES BY COLUMN

1 For 1881–1922, derived from Table D–2, col. 3. For 1923–32, derived from Table D–2, col. 3, for December 1922, and from Census of Electrical Industries for the close of 1927 and 1932. The census figures for 1927 and 1932 include all but an insignificant number of light and power departments of street railways. For 1927, utility plant of 902.6 millions was not reported by type. It was distributed between electric light and power and other utility plant in accordance with their relative values reported separately.

2 For 1881–98, compiled from data for forty-four plants shown in the *Fourteenth Annual Report of the Commissioner of Labor*, 1899. Plants Nos. 904–952 (except 915, 928, 933, 936, and 949) show total investment in plant and equipment of 62,938,000 dollars and investment in land of 3,348,000 dollars.

For 1928–32, Lowell J. Chawner, *Construction Activity in the United States, 1915–37* (Department of Commerce). Chawner's estimate is based on "the relationship of the cost of land to total capital expenditures over the six-year period, 1926–31, as indicated by figures prepared for the Federal Employment Stabilization Board by the engineering department of the Edison Electric Institute." Estimates of the percentage expenditure for land for other years, derived by linear interpolation between the percentages for 1881–98 and 1928–32.

TABLE D-4

Derivation of Rate of Increase in Size per Station, Electric Light and Power, 1881–1902

	NEW YORK STATE PLANTS	
	1902 (1)	*1890* (2)
1. Number of stations (including municipal)	256	139
2. Cost of plant and equipment (thousands of dollars)	112,999	31,184
3. Cost per station (thousands of dollars)	441	224

	NUMBER OF NEW YORK STATE PLANTS BY YEAR OF INSTALLATION	
	Privately owned plants in operation, 1902	*All plants in operation, 1890*
1902 (Jan. 1–June 30)	6	
1901	9	
1900	16	
1899	13	
1898	13	
1897	11	
1896	19	
1895	16	
1894	14	
1893	13	
1892	13	
1891	12	
1890	5	8 (Jan. 1–May 31)
1889	14	25
1888	17	31
1887	14	33
1886	12	14
1885	4	13
1884	4	3
1883	1	3
1882	...	2
1881	2	7

(Notes to Table D-4 on next page)

From Census of Electrical Industries, 1902, except that column 2 in the lower section of the table is from the 1890 Census, Vol. 6, Part 3.

Of the 228 private stations in existence in 1902, 73 were constructed prior to 1890 and 155 after that date. If we assume an average cost per station of \$224,000 for the 73 plants built prior to 1890 and an average of \$441,000 for the 228 plants in existence in 1902, we can derive the cost per station for the plants built during 1891–1902 as follows, where X represents the average cost of such plants:

$$155X + 73 \times \$224{,}000 = 228 \times \$441{,}000$$
$$X = \$543{,}000$$

This figure (\$543,000) may be centered approximately at the midpoint of 1896, since the lower section of col. 1 indicates that half the plants built 1891–1902 were completed by this date. Similarly, the average figure for 1881–90 (\$224,000) may be centered at the close of 1887; the lower section of col. 2 indicates that approximately half the plants built in 1881–90 were completed by this date. The figures for cost per station, in 1911 prices, are as follows:

	Cost per Station (thousands of dollars)	*Construction Cost Index* (1911 = 100)	*Cost per Station* (thousands of dollars, 1911 prices)
Dec. 31, 1887	224	77.4	289
June 30, 1896	543	61.8	879

Average cost per station, in constant prices, rose 204 per cent in the 8½-year period; this gain is equivalent to an increase at the rate of 14 per cent per year.

TABLE D–5. Distribution by Five-Year Intervals of Plant and Equipment Totals for 1898 and 1902, Electric Light and Power

Year	*Number of Private Stations in 1902, by Year of Beginning Operations* (1)	*Index of Size of Plant* (1881 = 100) (2)	*Index of Construction Costs* (1911 = 100) (3)	*Product of Columns* 1, 2, 3 (4)	*Change in Value of Plant and Equipment* (thousands of dollars) *By Years* (5)	*Five-Year Intervals* (6)
1881	7	100	87.5	613	227	
1882	27	114	90.1	2,773	1,027	1,254 (1881–82)
1883	25	130	86.8	2,821	1,045	
1884	43	148	80.5	5,123	1,898	
1885	49	169	78.0	6,459	2,392	
1886	86	192	77.7	12,830	4,752	
1887	127	219	77.4	21,527	7,974	18,061 (1883–87)
1888	142	250	77.7	27,584	10,217	
1889	168	285	76.7	36,724	13,603	
1890	198	325	77.2	49,678	18,401	
1891	157	370	72.5	42,115	15,600	
1892	190	422	71.0	56,928	21,087	78,908 (1888–92)
1893	161	481	70.9	54,906	20,338	
1894	144	548	71.7	56,580	20,958	
1895	166	624	64.8	67,122	24,863	
1896	129	711	61.8	56,682	20,996	
1897	170	811	70.8	97,612	36,156	123,311 (1893–97)
1898	195	924	74.7	134,594	49,855	
Totals 1881–98				732,671	271,388	
1899	178	1,053	81.4	152,571		
1900	152	1,201	83.0	151,518		
1901	185	1,368	81.5	206,260		
1902 (Jan. 1–June 30)	106	1,462	81.9	126,922		271,936 (1898–1902)
Totals 1899–1902				637,271	222,081	

NOTES BY COLUMN

1 Census of Electrical Industries, 1902.
2 Based on Table D–4; an annual increase of 14 per cent is assumed.
3 Table D–6, col. 4.

5 Total increase in value of plant and equipment for 1881–98 and 1899–1902, from Table D–3; total for 1881–98, distributed over the years in accordance with the series in col. 4, this table.

TABLE D-6

Derivation of Construction Cost Index, 1880–1911, and 1921–1923, Electric Light and Power

(1911 = 100)

Year	*Electrical Equipment* (1)	*Construction Materials* (2)	*Wages, Building Trades* (3)	*Construction Cost Index* (4)
1880	105.53	95.84	47.07	90.93
1881	97.00	94.80	52.81	87.50
1882	99.00	98.91	54.46	90.07
1883	93.98	96.21	54.76	86.81
1884	83.74	91.74	55.58	80.51
1885	79.93	89.40	56.05	78.00
1886	78.62	90.38	56.18	77.66
1887	78.82	89.20	56.11	77.39
1888	79.93	88.35	56.38	77.75
1889	78.32	87.63	56.11	76.67
1890	79.55	86.91	56.97	77.24
1891	72.39	82.68	57.50	72.50
1892	71.57	78.25	58.68	71.00
1893	71.68	77.73	58.73	70.91
1894	76.18	73.81	57.32	71.70
1895	62.78	72.89	57.79	64.82
1896	55.62	74.02	58.68	61.75
1897	76.28	69.18	59.50	70.79
1898	82.11	72.06	60.38	74.75
1899	88.04	83.20	61.85	81.35
1900	87.01	88.45	64.55	82.95
1901	86.09	83.20	67.25	81.46
1902	84.25	85.05	71.13	81.87
1903	79.14	87.11	74.48	80.60
1904	84.97	84.23	76.18	82.99
1905	84.76	89.69	77.65	84.82
1906	83.44	99.59	82.35	88.07
1907	87.32	104.12	84.93	91.88
1908	80.78	96.19	90.43	87.33
1909	90.29	97.73	94.78	93.42
1910	90.39	100.62	98.55	95.09
1911	100.00	100.00	100.00	100.00
1921	185.38	177.53	206.67	187.28
1922	172.80	175.98	193.91	177.98
1923	185.17	196.29	214.20	194.31

NOTES BY COLUMN

1 For 1889–1923, Shaw's index for electrical equipment, base shifted to 1911 (*Value of Commodity Output Since 1869*); index extrapolated to 1880 by means of Aldrich report index for metals and implements, excluding pocket knives (Part I of the report). The Shaw index is based, from 1915, on ICC indexes for accounts representing electrical equipment, and, for earlier years, on his index for industrial machinery.

(notes to Table D-6 continue on next page)

2 Based on Shaw's index for construction materials, available for 1879 and annually from 1889 interpolated with an index computed from the Aldrich group indexes for lumber and building materials and for metals and implements, excluding pocket knives, as shown in Table D-7.

3 Derived from the following three segments linked: 1907–23, BLS union wage rates in building trades; 1890–1907, BLS index of average wages per hour in building trades (this series is a continuation of data in the Aldrich report); 1880–90, Aldrich report, wages per day in building trades.

4 Derived from indexes in columns 1, 2, and 3 combined with weights of 5, 3, and 2, respectively.

TABLE D-7

Derivation of Index of Cost of Construction Materials, Electric Light and Power, 1879–1889

Year	*Construction Materials* (1911 = 100) (1)	*Metals and Implements, excl. Pocket Knives* (1860 = 100) (2)	*Lumber and Building Materials* (1860 = 100) (3)	*Average of Columns* 2 *and* 3 (1860 = 100) (4)	*Construction Materials* (1911 = 100) (5)
1879	83.92	90.2	115.1	110.12	83.92
1880		105.1	130.9	125.74	95.84
1881		96.6	131.3	124.36	94.80
1882		98.6	137.5	129.72	98.91
1883		93.6	134.3	126.16	96.21
1884		83.4	129.5	120.28	91.74
1885		79.6	126.6	117.20	89.40
1886		78.3	128.5	118.46	90.38
1887		78.5	126.5	116.90	89.20
1888		79.6	124.8	115.76	88.35
1889	87.63	78.0	124.0	114.80	87.63

NOTES BY COLUMN

1 Shaw index, base shifted.
2, 3 Aldrich report, Part I.
4 Average of columns 2 and 3 combined with weights of 1 and 4, respectively.
5 Column 1 interpolated with column 4.

NOTES TO TABLE D-8, BY COLUMN

1 Census of Electrical Industries.

2 For 1902–22, Table D-2, col. 2. No adjustment was required for 1927 and 1932.

4 Derived from col. 3.

5 Based on data reported by the Federal Power Commission (*Electric Utility Cost Units*: Steam Electric Generating Stations, Serial Pub. S-68; Hydroelectric Generating Stations, S-78; and Internal Combustion Engine Electric Generating Stations, S-85). The reported figures were multiplied by the ratios of total generating capacity of each type to generating capacity included in each of the FPC surveys.

7 Based on the ratios shown in column 6. Through 1912, the ratios in column 6 were merely rounded; for later years, these ratios were reduced to allow for the fact that gross additions to generating capacity were greater than the net additions on which information is available.

8 Derived from column 7.

TABLE D–8

Derivation of Distribution of Retirements, by Age of Equipment, Electric Light and Power

(*capacity data in thousands of kilowatts*)

Period	*Generating Capacity at End of Each Period, All Commercial Plants incl. in Census Reports* (1)	*Adjustment Ratios to Include Light and Power Departments of Street Railways* (2)	*Generating Capacity at End of Each Period, All Commercial Plants* (col. 1 × col. 2) (3)	*Net Change in Total Generating Capacity* (4)	*Generating Capacity Remaining 1946–48, by Date of Installation* (5)	*Column 5 ÷ Column 4* (6)
1881–1902	1,098.9	1.0811	1,188.0	1,188.0	125.2	0.105
1903–1907	2,500.2	1.1065	2,766.5	1,578.5	461.3	0.292
1908–1912	4,768.8	1.1174	5,328.7	2,562.2	1,524.9	0.595
1913–1917	8,411.9	1.1145	9,375.1	4,046.4	3,148.4	0.778
1918–1922	13,407.0	1.0857	14,556.0	5,180.9	4,599.4	0.888
1923–1927	24,383.3	1.0000	24,383.3	9,827.3	9,956.8	1.013
1928–1932	32,647.6	1.0000	32,647.6	8,264.3	8,849.2	1.071

DISTRIBUTION OF RETIREMENTS

Years after Installation	*Percentage of Equipment Remaining* (7)	*Years after Installation*	*Percentage of Equipment Retired* (8)
45–50	10	50	10
40–45	30	45	20
35–40	60	40	30
30–35	75	35	15
25–30	85	30	10
20–25	95	25	10
15–20	100	20	5

NOTES BY COLUMN ON FACING PAGE

TABLE D–9

Estimated Distribution of Retirements of Equipment, by Dates of Installation, Electric Light and Power

Years after Installation	PERCENTAGE RETIRED, OF EQUIPMENT INSTALLED DURING YEARS				
	1928–1947	*1918–1927*	*1908–1917*	*1898–1907*	*1881–1897*
5				5	15
10			5	10	10
15		5	10	10	15
20	5	10	10	15	30
25	10	10	15	30	20
30	10	15	30	20	10
35	15	30	20	10	
40	30	20	10		
45	20	10			
50	10				

Source: The percentage distribution of retirements for the period 1928–47 is from Table D–8, column 8. For earlier periods, the same percentage distribution was maintained, but the age of equipment retired was reduced five years for each period. For 1881–97, the percentages for the two earliest groups of retirements had to be combined.

TABLE D–10

Estimated Retirements and Gross Increase in Value of Plant and Equipment, Electric Light and Power

(thousands of dollars)

A. 1881–1897

Period	*Increase in Value of Plant and Equipment* (1)	*Percentage of Equipment Retired Prior to 1897* (2)	*Retirements of Values in Column 1 Prior to 1897* (3)	*Gross Increase in Value of Plant and Equipment* (4)
1881–1882	1,254	40	502	1,357
1883–1887	18,061	25	4,515	19,548
1888–1892	78,908	15	11,816	85,405
1893–1897	123,311	...		133,464
Total 1881–1897	221,534		16,853	239,775

B. 1881–1932, BY FIVE-YEAR INTERVALS

Period	*Increase in Value of Plant and Equipment* (1)	*Retirements of Equipment Installed in Prior Years* (2)	*Gross Increase in Value of Plant and Equipment* (3)
1881–1882			1,357
1883–1887			19,548
1888–1892			85,405
1893–1897			133,464
1898–1902 (June 30)	271,936	31,900	303,836
1902 (July 1)–1907	607,020	47,484	654,504
1908–1912	1,107,501	112,797	1,220,298
1913–1917	865,857	154,909	1,020,766
1918–1922	1,236,665	207,274	1,443,939
1923–1927	3,850,328	375,741	4,226,069
1928–1932	3,165,367	481,225	3,646,592

NOTES BY COLUMN

PART A

1 From Table D–5, col. 6.

2 From retirement distribution assumed for 1881–97 (see Table D–9).

3 Col. 1 times col. 2 divided by 100.

4 The ratio of retirements to the increase in the value of plant and equipment for the entire period 1881–97 is 0.0761. Since col. 1 is proportional to gross capital expenditures, col. 4 was derived by dividing all figures in col. 1 by 0.9239, the complement of this ratio.

PART B

1 For 1898–1902, Table D–5, col. 6; for 1902–32, Table D–3, col. 4.

2, 3 For 1881–97, from part A of this table. From 1898 on, col. 3 is the sum of cols. 1 and 2.

The estimated gross increase in value of plant and equipment for each period to 1897 was entered in Table D–11, and retirements of this equipment in later periods were computed by the use of the percentage distribution shown there. Thus, it was possible to compute total retirements for 1898–1902. The increase in the value of plant and equipment for 1898–1902 (col. 1), plus retirements during the same years (col. 2), yielded the gross increase in plant and equipment for 1898–1902 (col. 3). This figure, in turn, was entered in Table D–11, and retirements of this equipment in later years computed, total retirements in 1902–07 and gross increase in plant and equipment for the same period derived, and so on for successive periods.

TABLE D–11

Estimated Retirements, Electric Light and Power Facilities, 1898–1932

(dollar amounts in thousands)

Period	Gross Increase in Value of Plant and Equipment (1)	EQUIPMENT RETIRED 1898–1902 Per cent of col. 1	1898–1902 Amount (2)	1903–1907 Per cent of col. 1	1903–1907 Amount (3)	1908–1912 Per cent of col. 1	1908–1912 Amount (4)	1913–1917 Per cent of col. 1	1913–1917 Amount (5)	1918–1922 Per cent of col. 1	1918–1922 Amount (6)	1923–1927 Per cent of col. 1	1923–1927 Amount (7)	1928–1932 Per cent of col. 1	1928–1932 Amount (8)
1881–1882	1,357	30	407	20	271	10	136								
1883–1887	19,548	15	2,932	30	5,864	20	3,910	10	1,955						
1888–1892	85,405	10	8,541	15	12,811	30	25,622	20	17,081	10	8,541				
1893–1897	133,464	15	20,020	10	13,346	15	20,020	30	40,039	20	26,693	10	13,346		
1898–1902 (June 30)	303,836			5	15,192	10	30,384	10	30,384	15	45,575	30	91,151	20	60,767
1902 (July 1)–1907	654,504					5	32,725	10	65,450	10	65,450	15	98,176	30	196,351
1908–1912	1,220,298									5	61,015	10	122,030	10	122,030
1913–1917	1,020,766											5	51,038	10	102,077
Total Retirements			31,900		47,484		112,797		154,909		207,274		375,741		481,225

Column 1 is from Table D–10, part B, column 3; see footnote there to cols. 2 and 3.

Percentage distributions in columns 2–8 are from Table D–9. The value of retirements was derived by multiplying col. 1 by the appropriate percentage.

TABLE D–12

Gross Capital Expenditures, Current Dollars, Electric Light and Power, 1881–1922, Selected Intervals

(in thousands)

Period	*Gross Increase in Value of Plant and Equipment* (1)	*Gross Capital Expenditures* (2)	*Reported Gross Capital Expenditures* (3)
1881–1897	239,775	201,411	
1898–1902 (June 30)	303,836	255,222	
1902 (July 1)–1907	654,504	549,783	
1908–1912	1,220,298	1,025,050	
1913–1917	1,020,766	857,443	
1918–1922	1,443,939	1,212,909	
(For Comparison Only)			
1923–1927	4,226,069	3,549,898	3,574,164
1928–1932	3,646,592	3,063,137	2,821,263

NOTES BY COLUMN

1 From Table D–10, part B.

2 Column 1 multiplied by 0.84. Figures in column 1 were reduced 16 per cent to eliminate write-ups. See text discussion.

3 From Table D–17.

TABLE D–13

Gross Capital Expenditures, Current Dollars, Electric Light and Power, 1881–1902

(in thousands)

Year	*Series Proportional to Gross Capital Expenditures* (1)	*Gross Capital Expenditures* (2)
1881	613	206
1882	2,773	934
1883	2,821	950
1884	5,123	1,725
1885	6,459	2,175
1886	12,830	4,321
1887	21,527	7,249
1888	27,584	9,289
1889	36,724	12,367
1890	49,678	16,730
1891	42,115	14,183
1892	56,928	19,172
1893	54,906	18,490
1894	56,580	19,054
1895	67,122	22,605
1896	56,682	19,089
1897	97,612	32,872
Total 1881–1897	598,077	201,411
1898	134,594	44,504
1899	152,571	50,449
1900	151,518	50,100
1901	206,260	68,201
1902 (Jan. 1–June 30)	126,922	41,968
Total 1898–1902	771,865	255,222

Column 1 is from Table D–5, col. 4.

Column 2: Total gross capital expenditures shown in Table D–12 for 1881–97 and 1898–1902 distributed in accordance with series in column 1.

TABLE D–14

Derivation of Estimated Generating Capacity, Electric Light and Power, 1902–1912

(*thousands of kilowatts*)

	Generating Capacity, All Commercial Light and Power Plants (1)	*Estimated Generating Capacity, All Years* (2)
June 30, 1902	1,188	1,188
Dec. 31, 1902		1,307
Dec. 31, 1903		1,559
Dec. 31, 1904		1,829
Dec. 31, 1905		2,120
Dec. 31, 1906		2,432
Dec. 31, 1907	2,767	2,767
Dec. 31, 1908		3,196
Dec. 31, 1909		3,663
Dec. 31, 1910		4,172
Dec. 31, 1911		4,726
Dec. 31, 1912	5,329	5,329
Dec. 31, 1917	9,375	
Dec. 31, 1922	14,556	
Dec. 31, 1927	24,383	

Column 1 is from Table D–8, col. 3. Column 2 is derived from column 1, adjusted to a modified exponential trend by the addition of a constant derived by the method of average points for the years 1902–07, 1912–17, and 1922–27. Data for intercensal years were obtained by geometric interpolation between the adjusted data for available years.

TABLE D–15

Gross Capital Expenditures, Current Dollars, Electric Light and Power, 1902–1912

(thousands of dollars)

Year	*Estimated Increase in Generating Capacity from Preceding Year* (thousands of kws.) (1)	*Construction Cost Index* (1911 = 100) (2)	*Column 1 × Column 2* (3)	*Gross Capital Expenditures* (4)
1902 (June 30–Dec. 31)	119	81.9	9,746	39,568
1903	252	80.6	20,311	82,461
1904	270	83.0	22,410	90,982
1905	291	84.8	24,677	100,186
1906	312	88.1	27,487	111,594
1907	335	91.9	30,787	124,992
Total 1902–1907			135,418	549,783
1908	429	87.3	37,452	155,122
1909	467	93.4	43,618	180,661
1910	509	95.1	48,406	200,492
1911	554	100.0	55,400	229,460
1912	602	104.0	62,608	259,315
Total 1908–1912			247,484	1,025,050

NOTES BY COLUMN

1 Derived from Table D–14, col. 4.

2 Tables D–6 and D–19.

4 Total expenditures for 1902–07 and 1908–12, from Table D–12, distributed over the years within each period in accordance with the series in col. 3 of this table.

TABLE D–16
Gross Capital Expenditures, Current Dollars,
Electric Light and Power, 1913–1920
(*in thousands*)

Year	*Total Increase in Fixed Capital, Four States* (1)	*Gross Capital Expenditures, United States* (2)
1913	40,237	148,560
1914	40,305	148,812
1915	33,699	124,421
1916	40,990	151,341
1917	77,004	284,309
Total 1913–1917	232,235	857,443
1918	39,757	115,550
1919	50,205	145,917
1920	102,023	296,521
Total 1918–1920	191,985	557,988

Column 1 is based on data for additions to fixed capital in Massachusetts, California, Ohio, and the First District of New York (New York City), as reported to state public service commissions. For Massachusetts, figures are averages of changes in fixed capital for fiscal years ending June 30. The Ohio figures are: for 1913, average of changes for fiscal years ending June 30, 1913 and June 30, 1914; for 1914, one-half of net change June 30, 1913–June 30, 1914 plus one-third of net change June 30, 1914–December 1915; for 1915, two-thirds of net change June 30, 1914–December 31, 1915.

Column 2: Total expenditures for the stated period, distributed among years in accordance with column 1. The 1913–17 total is from Table D–12. The total for 1918–20 was obtained by deducting from the total for 1918–22 (Table D–12) the gross capital expenditures for 1921 and 1922 (Table D–17).

TABLE D–17

Gross Capital Expenditures, Current Dollars, Electric Light and Power, 1921–1937

(in thousands)

Year	*Gross Capital Expenditures, Privately Owned Plants* (1)	GCE, *Private and Municipal Plants* (2)	*Ratio, Column 1 to Column 2* (3)	GCE, *Including Land, Privately Owned Plants* (4)	*Expenditures for Land* (per cent) (5)	*Expenditures for Land (col. 4 × col. 5 ÷ 100)* (6)	*Gross Capital Expenditures Excluding Land (col. 4 minus col. 6)* (7)
1921		310,000		290,000	6.52	18,908	271,092
1922		439,000		410,600	6.52	26,771	383,829
1923		794,000		742,700	6.64	49,315	693,385
1924		908,000		849,000	6.76	57,392	791,608
1925		846,000		791,000	6.88	54,421	736,579
1926	719,900	766,400	0.9393	719,900	7.00	50,393	669,507
1927	734,500	779,400	0.9424	734,500	7.00	51,415	683,085
1928	698,800	755,900	0.9245	698,800	7.00	48,916	649,884
1929	752,000			752,000	7.00	52,640	699,360
1930	826,900			826,900	7.00	57,883	769,017
1931	504,700			504,700	7.00	35,329	469,371
1932	249,100			249,100	6.21	15,469	233,631
1933	136,100			136,100	5.43	7,390	128,710
1934	146,800			146,800	4.65	6,826	139,974
1935	194,600			194,600	3.86	7,512	187,088
1936	301,200			301,200	3.08	9,277	291,923
1937	465,200			465,200	2.38	11,072	454,128

NOTES BY COLUMN

1, 2 Edison Electric Institute Statistical Bulletins No. 11 and No. 17.

4 For 1926–37, col. 1; for 1921–25, col. 2 multiplied by 0.9354, the average ratio of col. 1 to col. 2 for 1926–28.

5 For 1921–22, from Table D–3; for 1926–31 from Lowell J. Chawner, *Construction Activity in the United States, 1915–37*; for 1937, from unpublished data furnished by the Federal Power Commission on the value of land and the value of all additions to plant and equipment; 1923–25, derived by linear interpolation between 1922 and 1926; 1932–36, derived by linear interpolation between the percentage for 1926–31 and an average for 1937–42 (2.29 per cent) derived from unpublished data supplied by the Federal Power Commission (see Table D–18).

TABLE D–18. Gross Capital Expenditures, Electric Light and Power, 1937–1950 (*thousands of dollars*)

Year	*Gross Additions to Electric Plant, Class A and B Utilities* (1)	*Construction Work in Progress, End of Year* (2)	*Change in Value of Const. Work in Progress from Preceding Year* (3)	*Gross Capital Expenditures Including Land, Class A and B Utilities* (4)	*Gross Capital Expenditures Including Land, All Companies* (5)	*Expenditures for Land* (per cent) (6)	*Expenditures for Land* (col. 5 × col. 6 ÷ 100) (7)	*Gross Capital Expenditures Excluding Land* (col. 5 minus col. 7) (8)
1937	303,000	264,401						
1938	397,300	273,642	+9,241	406,541	414,838	1.838	7,625	407,213
1939	369,200	253,785	−19,857	349,343	356,472	2.697	9,614	346,858
1940	405,100	312,820	+59,035	464,135	473,607	2.280	10,798	462,809
1941				591,919	603,999	2.169	13,101	590,898
1942				455,975	465,281	2.376	11,055	454,226
1943		295,247		254,258	259,447	1.815	4,709	254,738
1944	279,000	227,313	−67,934	211,066	215,373	1.780	3,834	211,539
1945	302,300	286,917	+59,604	361,904	369,290	2.089	7,714	361,576
1946	435,850	496,804	+209,887	645,737	658,915	3.340	22,008	636,907
1947	843,526	{ 886,449 836,403	+389,645	1,233,171	1,258,338	1.874	23,581	1,234,757
1948	1,560,878	1,106,603	+270,200	1,831,078	1,868,447	2.403	44,899	1,823,548
1949	1,925,472	1,265,413	+158,810	2,084,282	2,126,818	2.403	51,107	2,075,711
1950	1,904,001	1,254,315	−11,098	1,892,903	1,931,534	2.403	46,415	1,885,119

NOTES BY COLUMN

1 Unpublished data furnished by Federal Power Commission. This series represents the total value of electric plant placed in service each year by Class A and B utilities.

2 For 1937–40, compiled from reports for individual Class A and B companies shown in FPC's *Statistics of Electric Utilities in the United States* for the respective years.

For 1943–49, unpublished data furnished by FPC for Class A and B utilities. Two figures are shown for 1947, the first comparable with the data for earlier years, and the second comparable with figures for later years. The two figures differ because the first includes and the second excludes reported "construction work in progress" for two companies. All property of these companies was reported through 1947 under construction work in progress pending detailed classification of the project of which the property formed a part; the property was classified in the appropriate accounts in 1948.

For 1950, *Statistics of Electric Utilities in the United States.*

3 Based on year-to-year changes shown in col. 2.

4 For 1938–40 and 1944–50, col. 1 plus col. 3; for 1941–43, FPC, capital expenditures of Class A and B utilities.

5 Column 4 divided by 0.98, the ratio of assets of Class A and B utilities to all utilities, as estimated by FPC.

6 For 1938–47, based on unpublished data furnished by FPC on the value of land and total value of plant, for facilities placed in service during the respective years; for 1948–50, average percentage for 1945–47.

TABLE D–19

Derivation of Construction Cost Index, Electric Light and Power, 1911–1951

(1911 = 100)

	Atlantic Seaboard (1)	*North Central* (2)	*South Central* (3)	*Plateau* (4)	*Pacific* (5)	*United States Average for Specified Dates* (6)	*United States Average for Year* (7)
1911	100	100	100	100	100	100.0	100.0
1912	104	104	104	104	104	104.0	104.0
1913	102	102	102	102	102	102.0	102.0
1914	102	100	100	100	100	100.8	100.8
1915	106	105	107	103	103	105.2	105.2
1916	132	129	130	128	127	130.0	130.0
1917	160	154	157	155	156	157.0	157.0
1918	192	178	183	183	178	184.6	184.6
Jan. 1, 1919	202	184	188	187	182	191.7	194.6
Jan. 1, 1920	208	189	193	189	194	197.5	212.7
July 1, 1920	226	214	218	211	214	218.9	
Jan. 1, 1921	221	210	216	209	214	215.3	198.0
Sept. 1, 1921	183	176	183	178	185	180.6	
Jan. 1, 1923	189	179	182	179	178	183.2	189.4
Jan. 1, 1924	201	193	193	192	187	195.5	192.9
July 1, 1924	196	189	186	186	182	190.5	
Jan. 1, 1925	201	194	189	191	185	195.1	192.7
July 1, 1925	197	192	186	191	182	192.3	
Jan. 1, 1926	197	190	184	190	180	191.2	189.2
July 1, 1926	194	187	183	188	178	188.6	
Jan. 1, 1927	193	187	182	186	181	188.2	185.4
July 1, 1927	187	182	179	181	175	182.9	
Jan. 1, 1928	192	186	183	185	180	187.4	188.3
July 1, 1928	192	186	186	185	179	187.6	
Jan. 1, 1929	195	189	189	188	182	190.6	198.1
July 1, 1929	206	199	199	198	192	201.0	
Jan. 1, 1930	204	199	197	197	191	199.8	189.1
July 1, 1930	188	184	185	181	176	184.6	
Jan. 1, 1931	191	188	186	183	178	187.5	184.8
July 1, 1931	188	187	183	181	175	185.2	
Jan. 1, 1932	182	186	179	177	172	181.4	174.3
July 1, 1932	176	174	171	171	163	173.1	
Jan. 1, 1933	170	172	169	169	161	169.5	177.5
July 1, 1933	177	179	179	179	170	177.3	
Jan. 1, 1934	186	187	187	188	178	185.8	193.9
July 1, 1934	200	195	195	196	189	196.5	
Jan. 1, 1935	200	195	198	196	189	196.8	197.3
July 1, 1935	199	194	193	195	192	195.8	
Jan. 1, 1936	204	199	199	198	196	200.6	203.2
July 1, 1936	205	199	201	198	197	201.3	

(concluded on next page)

TABLE D–19 (concluded)

	Atlantic Seaboard (1)	*North Central* (2)	*South Central* (3)	*Plateau* (4)	*Pacific* (5)	*United States Average for Specified Dates* (6)	*United States Average for Year* (7)
Jan. 1, 1937	213	209	208	206	204	209.7	221.3
July 1, 1937	230	224	224	225	221	226.2	
Jan. 1, 1938	226	222	221	221	218	223.0	220.0
July 1, 1938	222	216	216	216	214	218.2	
Jan. 1, 1939	224	219	218	218	216	220.5	221.9
July 1, 1939	225	218	218	219	215	220.6	
Jan. 1, 1940	232	222	223	223	219	225.9	225.7
July 1, 1940	231	221	224	222	218	225.1	
Jan. 1, 1941	233	222	227	223	219	226.7	235.3
July 1, 1941	242	232	239	232	231	236.6	
Jan. 1, 1942	248	235	245	234	235	241.1	242.8
July 1, 1942	248	238	246	236	242	243.0	
Jan. 1, 1943	250	238	247	236	242	243.9	244.8
July 1, 1943	252	239	247	236	243	245.1	
Jan. 1, 1944	251	239	248	235	245	244.9	243.8
July 1, 1944	249	237	247	233	241	242.8	
Jan. 1, 1945	251	238	248	238	242	244.6	249.7
July 1, 1945	259	243	251	241	244	250.1	
Jan. 1, 1946	266	245	251	244	244	253.8	286.6
July 1, 1946	303	280	288	282	283	290.5	
Jan. 1, 1947	327	299	310	300	300	311.5	332.6
July 1, 1947	351	324	336	329	332	337.3	
Jan. 1, 1948	357	333	344	334	339	344.4	366.5
July 1, 1948	381	351	365	355	359	365.6	
Jan. 1, 1949	407	375	391	378	383	390.5	387.7
July 1, 1949	400	374	390	378	380	387.0	
Jan. 1, 1950	399	374	390	376	379	386.3	406.3
July 1, 1950	409	382	398	386	389	395.5	
Jan. 1, 1951	462	436	448	436	440	448.0	

NOTES BY COLUMN

1–5 Handy Index of Public Utility Construction Costs and Financial and Operating Ratios, semiannual bulletin, Whitman, Requardt and Associates. Figure for 1922 not available. The figure for January 1, 1951, col. 1, is that reported for the North Atlantic region, but 1950 data for the North Atlantic region are identical with those formerly shown for Atlantic Seaboard.

6 Average of cols. 1–5 combined with the following weights: Atlantic Seaboard, 4, North Central 3, South Central 1, Plateau 1, Pacific 1. The weights were derived from data on the distribution of generating capacity by region in 1902 and 1937, shown in the Census of Electrical Industries.

7 For 1912–18, col. 6; for 1919, average of figures for January 1, 1919 and January 1, 1920; for 1921, average of figures for January 1 and September 1; for 1923, average of figures for January 1, 1923 and January 1, 1924. Annual figures for all other years were obtained from averages of the indexes for January 1 (weight 1), July 1 (weight 2), and January 1 of the following year (weight 1).

TABLE D-20

Index of Construction Costs, Electric Light and Power, 1881–1950

(1929 = 100)

Year	Construction Costs	Year	Construction Costs
1881	44.2	1920	107.4
1882	45.5	1921	100.0
1883	43.8	1922	91.3
1884	40.6	1923	95.6
1885	39.4	1924	97.4
1886	39.2	1925	97.3
1887	39.1	1926	95.5
1888	39.2	1927	93.6
1889	38.7	1928	95.1
		1929	100.0
1890	39.0	1930	95.5
1891	36.6	1931	93.3
1892	35.8	1932	88.0
1893	35.8	1933	89.6
1894	36.2	1934	97.9
1895	32.7	1935	99.6
1896	31.2	1936	102.6
1897	35.7	1937	111.7
1898	37.7	1938	111.1
1899	41.1	1939	112.0
1900	41.9	1940	113.9
1901	41.1	1941	118.8
1902	41.3	1942	122.6
1903	40.7	1943	123.6
1904	41.9	1944	123.1
1905	42.8	1945	126.0
1906	44.5	1946	144.7
1907	46.4	1947	167.9
1908	44.1	1948	185.0
1909	47.2	1949	195.7
1910	48.0	1950	205.1
1911	50.5		
1912	52.5		
1913	51.5		
1914	50.9		
1915	53.1		
1916	65.6		
1917	79.3		
1918	93.2		
1919	98.2		

For 1911–50 (except 1922), from Table D-19, column 7; extrapolated to 1881 and interpolated for 1922 with index shown in Table D-6, column 4. Base shifted to 1929.

TABLE D–21

Capital Consumption, 1929 Dollars, Electric Light and Power, 1881–1936

(in millions)

Year	*Gross Capital Expenditures, Excluding Land* (1)	*Average Life of Plant and Equipment* (years) (2)	*Annual Capital Consumption of Expenditures in Column* 1 (col. 1 ÷ col. 2) (3)	*Sums of Column* 3 (4)	*Capital Consumption* (5)
1881	0.5	17	0.03	0.03	a
1882	2.0	17	0.12	0.15	0.1
1883	2.3	17	0.14	0.29	0.2
1884	4.2	17	0.25	0.54	0.4
1885	5.6	17	0.33	0.87	0.7
1886	11.0	17	0.65	1.52	1.2
1887	18.4	17	1.08	2.60	2.1
1888	23.7	17	1.39	3.99	3.3
1889	32.0	17	1.88	5.87	4.9
1890	42.8	17	2.52	8.39	7.1
1891	38.8	17	2.28	10.67	9.5
1892	53.6	17	3.15	13.82	12.2
1893	51.7	17	3.04	16.86	15.3
1894	52.8	17	3.11	19.97	18.4
1895	69.1	17	4.06	24.03	22.0
1896	61.2	17	3.60	27.63	25.8
1897	92.2	17	5.42	33.05	30.3
1898	118.0	17	6.94	39.96	36.5
1899	122.6	17	7.21	47.05	43.5
1900	119.6	17	7.04	53.95	50.5
1901	165.9	18	9.22	62.92	58.4
1902	197.3	19	10.38	72.97	67.9
1903	202.7	20	10.14	82.46	77.7
1904	217.2	21	10.34	91.72	87.1
1905	234.1	22	10.64	100.97	96.3
1906	250.8	23	10.90	109.99	105.5
1907	269.4	24	11.23	118.70	114.3
1908	351.7	25	14.07	130.49	124.6
1909	382.8	26	14.72	142.06	136.3
1910	417.7	27	15.47	154.49	148.3
1911	454.5	28	16.23	167.61	161.1
1912	493.9	29	17.03	180.58	174.1
1913	288.5	30	9.62	186.60	183.6
1914	292.3	31	9.43	190.61	188.6
1915	234.3	32	7.32	190.99	190.8
1916	230.6	33	6.99	190.77	190.9
1917	358.5	34	10.54	194.27	192.5
1918	124.0	35	3.54	197.81	196.0
1919	148.6	36	4.13	192.72	195.3

(concluded on next page)

TABLE D–21 (concluded)

Year	*Gross Capital Expenditures, Excluding Land* (1)	*Average Life of Plant and Equipment* (years) (2)	*Annual Capital Consumption of Expenditures in Column* 1 (col. 1 ÷ col. 2) (3)	*Sums of Column* 3 (4)	*Capital Consumption* (5)
1920	276.1	37	7.46	200.18	196.5
1921	271.0	37	7.32	197.12	198.7
1922	420.4	37	11.36	208.48	202.8
1923	725.3	37	19.60	217.94	213.2
1924	812.7	37	21.96	239.90	228.9
1925	757.0	37	20.46	250.02	245.0
1926	701.0	37	18.95	268.97	259.5
1927	729.8	37	19.72	278.05	273.5
1928	683.4	37	18.47	296.52	287.3
1929	699.4	37	18.90	304.52	300.5
1930	805.2	37	21.76	326.28	315.4
1931	503.1	37	13.60	328.65	327.5
1932	265.5	37	7.18	335.83	332.2
1933	143.6	37	3.88	325.64	330.7
1934	143.0	37	3.86	329.50	327.6
1935	187.9	37	5.08	319.86	324.7
1936	284.5	37	7.69	327.55	323.7

[a] Less than $100,000.

NOTES BY COLUMN

1 Table D–1, column 4.

2 An average life of seventeen years was assumed for plant and equipment installed in 1881–1900 and an average life of thirty-seven years for plant and equipment installed in 1920 and later years. Average life for other years was derived by linear interpolation between the figures for 1900 and 1920.

4 Cumulative totals of column 3 for appropriate number of years. The total for each year includes annual capital consumption of equipment installed in all prior years for which capital expenditures are not yet fully depreciated.

5 Two-year moving averages of figures in column 4 centered in the second year, on the assumption that expenditures made during any year are depreciated by one-half the annual rate during that year.

TABLE D–22

Value of Plant Additions Placed in Service, Electric Light and Power, 1937–1950

(thousands of dollars)

Year	*Gross Additions to Electric Plant, Class* A *and* B *Utilities* (1)	*Gross Additions to Electric Plant, All Companies* (2)	*Investment in Land* (per cent) (3)	*Investment in Land* (col. 2 × col. 3 ÷ 100) (4)	*Gross Additions to Electric Plant, Excluding Land* (col. 2 minus col. 4) (5)	*Construction Costs* (1929 = 100) (6)	*Gross Additions to Electric Plant, Excluding Land, 1929 Dollars* (col. 5 ÷ col. 6) (7)
1937	303,000	309,184	2.385	7,374	301,810	111.7	270,200
1938	397,300	405,408	1.838	7,451	397,957	111.1	358,200
1939	369,200	376,735	2.697	10,161	366,574	112.0	327,300
1940	405,100	413,367	2.280	9,425	403,942	113.9	354,600
1941	495,000	505,102	2.169	10,956	494,146	118.8	415,900
1942	459,000	468,367	2.376	11,128	457,239	122.6	373,000
1943	377,400	385,102	1.815	6,990	378,112	123.6	305,900
1944	279,000	284,694	1.780	5,068	279,626	123.1	227,200
1945	302,300	308,469	2.089	6,444	302,025	126.0	239,700
1946	435,850	444,745	3.340	14,854	429,891	144.7	297,100
1947	843,526	860,741	1.874	16,130	844,611	167.9	503,000
1948	1,560,878	1,592,733	2.403	38,273	1,554,460	185.0	840,200
1949	1,925,472	1,964,767	2.403	47,213	1,917,554	195.7	979,800
1950	1,904,001	1,942,858	2.403	46,687	1,896,171	205.1	924,500

NOTES BY COLUMN

1 Unpublished data supplied by the Federal Power Commission.
2 Column 1 divided by 0.98, the ratio of assets of Class A and B utilities to all utilities, as estimated by FPC.
3 Table D–17 and D–18.
6 Table D–20.

TABLE D–23

Capital Consumption, 1929 Dollars,
Electric Light and Power, 1937–1950

(millions of dollars)

Year	*Gross Additions Placed in Service, 1929 Dollars* (1)	*Average Life of Plant and Equipment* (years) (2)	*Annual Capital Consumption of Expenditures in Column 1* (col. 1 ÷ col. 2) (3)	*Sums of Column 3 and of Column 3, Table D–21* (4)	*Capital Consumption* (5)
1937	270.2	37	7.30	319.38	323.5
1938	358.2	37	9.68	329.06	324.2
1939	327.3	37	8.85	321.68	325.4
1940	354.6	37	9.58	331.26	326.5
1941	415.9	37	11.24	325.47	328.4
1942	373.0	37	10.08	335.55	330.5
1943	305.9	37	8.27	334.20	334.9
1944	227.2	37	6.14	340.34	337.3
1945	239.7	37	6.48	337.39	338.9
1946	297.1	37	8.03	345.42	341.4
1947	503.0	37	13.59	351.69	348.6
1948	840.2	37	22.71	374.40	363.0
1949	979.8	37	26.48	393.89	384.1
1950	924.5	37	24.99	418.88	406.4

NOTES BY COLUMN

1 Table D–22, col. 7.

2 See Table D–21, footnote to col. 2.

4 Cumulative totals of col. 3, this table, and of col. 3, Table D–21 for appropriate number of years. The total for each year includes annual capital consumption of equipment installed in all prior years for which capital expenditures are not yet fully depreciated.

5 Two-year moving averages of col. 4, centered in the second year.

TABLE D-24

Capital Consumption, Original Cost Prices, Electric Light and Power, 1881–1950

(millions of dollars)

Year	*Gross Capital Expenditures or Gross Additions Placed in Service* (1)	*Average Life of Plant and Equipment* (years) (2)	*Annual Capital Consumption of Expenditures in Column 1* (col. 1 ÷ col. 2) (3)	*Sums of Column 3* (4)	*Capital Consumption* (5)
1881	0.2	17	0.01	0.01	a
1882	.9	17	.05	.06	a
1883	1.0	17	.06	.12	0.1
1884	1.7	17	.10	.22	.2
1885	2.2	17	.13	.35	.3
1886	4.3	17	.25	.60	.5
1887	7.2	17	.42	1.02	.8
1888	9.3	17	.55	1.57	1.3
1889	12.4	17	.73′	2.30	1.9
1890	16.7	17	.98	3.28	2.8
1891	14.2	17	.84	4.12	3.7
1892	19.2	17	1.13	5.25	4.7
1893	18.5	17	1.09	6.34	5.8
1894	19.1	17	1.12	7.46	6.9
1895	22.6	17	1.33	8.79	8.1
1896	19.1	17	1.12	9.91	9.4
1897	32.9	17	1.94	11.85	10.9
1898	44.5	17	2.62	14.46	13.2
1899	50.4	17	2.96	17.37	15.9
1900	50.1	17	2.95	20.26	18.8
1901	68.2	18	3.79	23.95	22.1
1902	81.5	19	4.29	28.11	26.0
1903	82.5	20	4.13	31.99	30.1
1904	91.0	21	4.33	35.90	33.9
1905	100.2	22	4.55	39.90	37.9
1906	111.6	23	4.85	44.02	42.0
1907	125.0	24	5.21	48.25	46.1
1908	155.1	25	6.20	53.61	50.9
1909	180.7	26	6.95	59.43	56.5
1910	200.5	27	7.43	65.77	62.6
1911	229.5	28	8.20	72.85	69.3
1912	259.3	29	8.94	80.46	76.7
1913	148.6	30	4.95	84.29	82.4
1914	148.8	31	4.80	87.15	85.7
1915	124.4	32	3.89	88.42	87.8
1916	151.3	33	4.58	90.04	89.2
1917	284.3	34	8.36	95.45	92.7
1918	115.6	35	3.30	98.75	97.1
1919	145.9	36	4.05	99.01	98.9

(concluded on next page)

TABLE D–24 (concluded)

Year	*Gross Capital Expenditures or Gross Additions Placed in Service* (1)	*Average Life of Plant and Equipment* (years) (2)	*Annual Capital Consumption of Expenditures in Column* 1, (col. 1 ÷ col. 2) (3)	*Sums of Column* 3 (4)	*Capital Consumption* (5)
1920	296.5	37	8.01	107.02	103.0
1921	271.0	37	7.32	110.05	108.5
1922	383.8	37	10.37	120.42	115.2
1923	693.4	37	18.74	135.03	127.7
1924	791.6	37	21.39	156.42	145.7
1925	736.6	37	19.91	172.00	164.2
1926	669.5	37	18.09	190.09	181.0
1927	683.1	37	18.46	204.00	197.0
1928	649.9	37	17.56	221.56	212.8
1929	699.4	37	18.90	235.61	228.6
1930	769.0	37	20.78	256.39	246.0
1931	469.4	37	12.69	263.87	260.1
1932	233.6	37	6.31	270.18	267.0
1933	128.7	37	3.48	267.46	268.8
1934	140.0	37	3.78	271.24	269.4
1935	187.1	37	5.06	269.35	270.3
1936	291.9	37	7.89	277.24	273.3
1937	301.8	37	8.16	277.97	277.6
1938	398.0	37	10.76	288.73	283.4
1939	366.6	37	9.91	290.44	289.6
1940	403.9	37	10.92	301.36	295.9
1941	494.1	37	13.35	305.77	303.6
1942	457.2	37	12.36	318.13	312.0
1943	378.1	37	10.22	323.40	320.8
1944	279.6	37	7.56	330.96	327.2
1945	302.0	37	8.16	334.32	332.6
1946	429.9	37	11.62	345.94	340.1
1947	844.6	37	22.83	364.88	355.4
1948	1,554.5	37	42.01	406.89	385.9
1949	1,917.6	37	51.83	454.14	430.5
1950	1,896.2	37	51.25	505.39	479.8

[a] Less than $100,000.

NOTES BY COLUMN

1 For 1881–1936, gross capital expenditures, Table D–1, col. 3; for 1937–50, value of plant additions placed in service, Table D–22, col. 5.

2 Table D–21, col. 2.

4 Cumulative totals of col. 3 for appropriate number of years. The total for each year includes annual capital consumption of equipment installed in all prior years for which capital expenditures are not yet fully depreciated.

5 Two-year moving averages of figures in col. 4 centered in the second year, on the assumption that expenditures made during any year are depreciated by one-half the annual rate during that year.

TABLE D–25

Recorded Depreciation Charges and Computed Capital Consumption, Original Cost Prices, Electric Light and Power, 1912–1950

(millions of dollars)

Year	*Reported Depreciation Expenses* (1)	*Reported Depreciation Expenses Adjusted for Coverage* (2)	*Computed Capital Consumption* (3)	*Ratio, Reported to Computed Capital Consumption* (col. 2 ÷ col. 3) (4)
1912	18.0	20.1	76.7	0.262
1917	26.3	29.3	92.7	.316
1922	59.3	64.4	115.2	.559
1927	132.1	132.1	197.0	.671
1932	142.6	142.6	267.0	.534
1937	217.7	217.7	279.7	.778
1938	223.5	228.1	283.4	.805
1939	243.2	248.2	289.6	.857
1940	256.4	261.6	295.9	.884
1941	274.9	280.5	303.6	.924
1942	285.8	291.6	312.0	.935
1943	300.4	306.5	320.8	.955
1944	312.7	319.1	327.2	.975
1945	315.9	322.3	332.6	.969
1946	317.5	324.0	340.1	.953
1947	332.2	339.0	355.4	.954
1948	358.8	366.1	385.9	.949
1949	385.4	393.3	430.5	.914

NOTES BY COLUMN

1 For 1912–37, Census of Electrical Industries; for 1938–50, Federal Power Commission, *Statistics of Electric Utilities in the United States*. Figures cover Class A and B utilities.

2 For 1912–22: col. 1, this table, times col. 2 in Table D–2. For 1927–37, no adjustment required. For 1938–50, col. 1 divided by 0.98, the ratio of assets of Class A and B utilities to assets of all private electric utilities.

3 Table D–24.

Value of Electric Light and Power Plant and Equipment Owned by Electric Utilities and User-Owned, 1929 Dollars, 1882–1951

(*in millions*)

	VALUE OF PLANT AND EQUIPMENT, JANUARY 1					PER CENT OF TOTAL IN COLUMN 1			
		ELECTRIC UTILITIES				ELECTRIC UTILITIES			
Year	*Total, Cols.* 3, 4, 5 (1)	*Total* (2)	*Privately Owned* (3)	*Publicly Owned* (4)	USER-OWNED (5)	*Total* (6)	*Privately Owned* (7)	*Publicly Owned* (8)	USER-OWNED (9)
1882	1.1	0.6	0.5	0.1	0.5	54.5	45.5	9.1	45.5
1883	4.7	2.6	2.4	0.2	2.1	55.3	51.1	4.3	44.7
1884	8.7	4.8	4.5	0.3	3.9	55.2	51.7	3.4	44.8
1885	15.7	8.7	8.3	0.4	7.0	55.4	52.9	2.5	44.6
1886	26.2	14.5	13.2	1.3	11.7	55.3	50.4	5.0	44.7
1887	45.4	25.1	23.0	2.1	20.3	55.3	50.7	4.6	44.7
1888	76.1	42.1	39.3	2.8	34.0	55.3	51.6	3.7	44.7
1889	114.0	63.1	59.7	3.4	50.9	55.4	52.4	3.0	44.6
1890	163.9	90.7	86.8	3.9	73.2	55.3	53.0	2.4	44.7
1891	231.9	128.3	122.5	5.8	103.6	55.3	52.8	2.5	44.7
1892	288.1	159.4	151.8	7.6	128.7	55.3	52.7	2.6	44.7
1893	366.0	202.5	193.2	9.3	163.5	55.3	52.8	2.5	44.7
1894	434.7	240.5	229.6	10.9	194.2	55.3	52.8	2.5	44.7
1895	499.6	276.4	264.0	12.4	223.2	55.3	52.8	2.5	44.7
1896	591.2	327.1	311.1	16.0	264.1	55.3	52.6	2.7	44.7
1897	666.1	365.8	346.5	19.3	295.3	55.3	52.4	2.9	44.7
1898	778.4	430.7	408.4	22.3	347.7	55.3	52.5	2.9	44.7
1899	930.6	514.9	489.9	25.0	415.7	55.3	52.6	2.7	44.7
1900	1,077.9	596.4	569.0	27.4	481.5	55.3	52.8	2.5	44.7
1901	1,210.2	670.7	638.1	32.6	539.5	55.4	52.7	2.7	44.6
1902	1,410.5	783.0	745.6	37.4	627.5	55.5	52.9	2.7	44.5
1903	1,648.8	916.8	875.0	41.8	732.0	55.6	53.1	2.5	44.4
1904	1,877.8	1,045.9	1,000.0	45.9	831.9	55.7	53.3	2.4	44.3
1905	2,114.7	1,179.8	1,130.1	49.7	934.9	55.8	53.4	2.4	44.2
1906	2,369.0	1,324.0	1,267.9	56.1	1,045.0	55.9	53.5	2.4	44.1

(continued on next page)

TABLE D–26 (continued)

	VALUE OF PLANT AND EQUIPMENT, JANUARY 1					PER CENT OF TOTAL IN COLUMN 1			
		ELECTRIC UTILITIES				ELECTRIC UTILITIES			
Year	*Total, Cols. 3, 4, 5* (1)	*Total* (2)	*Privately Owned* (3)	*Publicly Owned* (4)	USER-OWNED (5)	*Total* (6)	*Privately Owned* (7)	*Publicly Owned* (8)	USER-OWNED (9)
1907	2,635.3	1,475.3	1,413.2	62.1	1,160.0	56.0	53.6	2.4	44.0
1908	2,917.5	1,636.0	1,568.3	67.7	1,281.5	56.1	53.8	2.3	43.9
1909	3,326.1	1,868.3	1,795.4	72.9	1,457.8	56.2	54.0	2.2	43.8
1910	3,767.3	2,119.7	2,041.9	77.8	1,647.6	56.3	54.2	2.1	43.7
1911	4,189.2	2,399.7	2,311.3	88.4	1,789.5	57.3	55.2	2.1	42.7
1912	4,633.6	2,703.2	2,604.7	98.5	1,930.4	58.3	56.2	2.1	41.7
1913	5,102.5	3,032.7	2,924.5	108.2	2,069.8	59.4	57.3	2.1	40.6
1914	5,195.4	3,147.0	3,029.4	117.6	2,048.4	60.6	58.3	2.3	39.4
1915	5,278.8	3,259.9	3,133.1	126.8	2,018.9	61.8	59.4	2.4	38.2
1916	5,257.0	3,311.3	3,176.6	134.7	1,945.7	63.0	60.4	2.6	37.0
1917	5,226.1	3,358.7	3,216.3	142.4	1,867.4	64.3	61.5	2.7	35.7
1918	5,384.6	3,532.3	3,382.3	150.0	1,852.3	65.6	62.8	2.8	34.4
1919	5,176.4	3,467.6	3,310.3	157.3	1,708.8	67.0	63.9	3.0	33.0
1920	5,009.0	3,428.0	3,263.6	164.4	1,581.0	68.4	65.2	3.3	31.6
1921	5,115.0	3,538.1	3,343.2	194.9	1,576.9	69.2	65.4	3.8	30.8
1922	5,206.3	3,640.0	3,415.5	224.5	1,566.3	69.9	65.6	4.3	30.1
1923	5,498.3	3,886.3	3,633.1	253.2	1,612.0	70.7	66.1	4.6	29.3
1924	6,194.0	4,426.2	4,145.2	281.0	1,767.8	71.5	66.9	4.5	28.5
1925	6,970.6	5,036.9	4,729.0	307.9	1,933.7	72.3	67.8	4.4	27.7
1926	7,652.2	5,592.1	5,241.0	351.1	2,060.1	73.1	68.5	4.6	26.9
1927	8,220.2	6,075.5	5,682.5	393.0	2,144.7	73.9	69.1	4.8	26.1
1928	8,790.7	6,572.5	6,138.8	433.7	2,218.2	74.8	69.8	4.9	25.2
1929	9,265.3	7,008.0	6,534.9	473.1	2,257.3	75.6	70.5	5.1	24.4

1930	9,727.8	7,445.1	6,933.8	511.3	2,282.7	76.5	71.2	5.3	23.5
1931	10,266.4	7,951.7	7,423.6	528.1	2,314.7	77.5	72.3	5.1	22.5
1932	10,388.4	8,143.3	7,599.2	544.1	2,245.1	78.4	73.2	5.2	21.6
1933	10,197.4	8,091.9	7,532.5	599.4	2,105.5	79.4	73.9	5.5	20.6
1934	9,857.9	7,919.3	7,345.4	573.9	1,938.6	80.3	74.5	5.8	19.7
1935	9,525.1	7,748.4	7,160.8	587.6	1,776.7	81.3	75.2	6.2	18.7
1936	9,367.3	7,717.3	7,024.0	693.3	1,650.0	82.4	75.0	7.4	17.6
1937	9,324.2	7,780.5	6,984.8	795.7	1,543.7	83.4	74.9	8.5	16.6
1938	9,419.1	7,962.7	7,067.8	894.9	1,456.4	84.5	75.0	9.5	15.5
1939	9,457.9	8,101.0	7,110.1	990.9	1,356.9	85.7	75.2	10.5	14.3
1940	9,421.2	8,178.1	7,094.4	1,083.7	1,243.1	86.8	75.3	11.5	13.2
1941	9,680.3	8,385.6	7,174.2	1,211.4	1,294.7	86.6	74.1	12.5	13.4
1942	10,070.7	8,736.6	7,343.2	1,393.4	1,334.1	86.8	72.9	13.8	13.2
1943	10,316.0	8,961.9	7,383.2	1,578.7	1,354.1	86.9	71.6	15.3	13.1
1944	10,263.0	8,950.0	7,254.4	1,695.6	1,313.0	87.2	70.7	16.5	12.8
1945	10,182.8	8,883.2	7,088.9	1,794.3	1,299.6	87.2	69.6	17.6	12.8
1946	10,143.5	8,880.7	7,037.0	1,843.7	1,262.8	87.6	69.4	18.2	12.4
1947	10,354.0	9,069.7	7,135.8	1,933.9	1,284.3	87.6	68.9	18.7	12.4
1948	10,936.0	9,618.3	7,522.6	2,095.7	1,317.7	88.0	68.8	19.2	12.0
1949	11,828.2	10,477.6	8,145.3	2,332.3	1,350.6	88.6	68.9	19.7	11.4
1950	12,866.7	11,495.3	8,821.9	2,673.4	1,371.4	89.3	68.6	20.8	10.7
1951	13,847.6	12,442.8	9,334.6	3,108.2	1,404.8	89.9	67.4	22.4	10.1

Detail may not add to totals because of rounding.

NOTES BY COLUMN

1 Column 2 plus col. 5.
2 Column 3 plus col. 4.
3 Table D–1.
4 Table D–33.
5 Column 2, this table, times col. 3, Table D–36; the 1900 figure for col. 3, Table D–36 has been extrapolated to 1882.

APPENDIX D

TABLE D-27

Value of Electric Light and Power Plant and Equipment Owned by Electric Utilities and User-Owned, Current Dollars, 1882–1951

(in millions)

January 1	Total, Cols. 3, 4, 5 (1)	ELECTRIC UTILITIES			USER-OWNED (5)
		Total (2)	Privately Owned (3)	Publicly Owned (4)	
1882	0.5	0.3	0.2	0.1	0.2
1883	2.1	1.2	1.1	0.1	1.0
1884	3.8	2.1	2.0	0.1	1.7
1885	6.4	3.5	3.4	0.2	2.8
1886	10.3	5.7	5.2	0.5	4.6
1887	17.8	9.8	9.0	0.8	8.0
1888	29.8	16.5	15.4	1.1	13.3
1889	44.7	24.7	23.4	1.3	20.0
1890	63.4	35.1	33.6	1.5	28.3
1891	90.4	50.0	47.8	2.3	40.4
1892	105.4	58.3	55.6	2.8	47.1
1893	131.0	72.5	69.2	3.3	58.5
1894	155.6	86.1	82.2	3.9	69.5
1895	180.9	100.1	95.6	4.5	80.8
1896	193.3	107.0	101.7	5.2	86.4
1897	206.3	114.1	108.1	6.0	92.1
1898	277.9	153.8	145.8	8.0	124.1
1899	350.8	194.1	184.7	9.4	156.7
1900	443.0	245.1	233.9	11.3	197.9
1901	507.1	281.0	267.4	13.7	226.1
1902	579.7	321.8	306.4	15.4	257.9
1903	681.0	378.6	361.4	17.3	302.3
1904	764.3	425.7	407.0	18.7	338.6
1905	886.1	494.3	473.5	20.8	391.7
1906	1,013.9	566.7	542.7	24.8	447.3
1907	1,172.7	656.5	628.9	27.6	516.2
1908	1,353.7	759.1	727.7	31.4	594.6
1909	1,466.8	823.9	791.8	32.1	642.9
1910	1,778.2	1,000.5	963.8	36.7	777.7
1911	2,010.8	1,151.9	1,109.4	42.4	859.0
1912	2,340.0	1,365.1	1,315.4	49.7	974.9
1913	2,678.8	1,592.2	1,535.4	56.8	1,086.6
1914	2,675.6	1,620.7	1,560.1	60.6	1,054.9
1915	2,686.9	1,659.3	1,594.7	64.5	1,027.6
1916	2,791.5	1,758.3	1,686.8	71.5	1,033.2
1917	3,428.3	2,203.3	2,109.9	93.4	1,225.0
1918	4,270.0	2,801.1	2,682.2	119.0	1,468.9
1919	4,824.4	3,231.8	3,085.2	146.6	1,592.6

(concluded on next page)

TABLE D–27 (concluded)

January 1	*Total, Cols. 3, 4, 5* (1)	ELECTRIC UTILITIES *Total* (2)	*Privately Owned* (3)	*Publicly Owned* (4)	USER-OWNED (5)
1920	4,918.8	3,366.3	3,204.9	161.4	1,552.5
1921	5,493.5	3,799.9	3,590.6	209.3	1,693.6
1922	5,206.3	3,640.0	3,415.5	224.5	1,566.3
1923	5,019.9	3,548.2	3,317.0	231.2	1,471.8
1924	5,921.5	4,231.4	3,962.8	268.6	1,690.0
1925	6,789.4	4,905.9	4,606.0	299.9	1,883.4
1926	7,445.6	5,441.1	5,099.5	341.6	2,004.5
1927	7,850.3	5,802.1	5,426.8	375.3	2,048.2
1928	8,228.1	6,151.9	5,745.9	405.9	2,076.2
1929	8,811.3	6,664.6	6,214.7	449.9	2,146.7
1930	9,727.8	7,445.1	6,933.8	511.3	2,282.7
1931	9,804.4	7,593.9	7,089.5	504.3	2,210.5
1932	9,692.4	7,597.7	7,090.1	507.6	2,094.7
1933	8,973.7	7,120.9	6,628.6	492.3	1,852.8
1934	8,832.7	7,095.7	6,581.5	514.2	1,737.0
1935	9,325.1	7,585.7	7,010.4	575.3	1,739.4
1936	9,329.8	7,686.4	6,995.9	690.5	1,643.4
1937	9,566.6	7,982.8	7,166.4	816.4	1,583.8
1938	10,521.1	8,894.3	7,894.7	999.6	1,626.8
1939	10,507.7	9,000.2	7,899.3	1,100.9	1,507.5
1940	10,551.7	9,159.5	7,945.7	1,213.7	1,392.3
1941	11,025.9	9,551.2	8,171.4	1,379.8	1,474.7
1942	11,964.0	10,379.1	8,723.7	1,655.4	1,584.9
1943	12,647.4	10,987.3	9,051.8	1,935.5	1,660.1
1944	12,685.1	11,062.2	8,966.4	2,095.8	1,622.9
1945	12,535.0	10,935.2	8,726.4	2,208.8	1,599.8
1946	12,780.8	11,189.7	8,866.6	2,323.1	1,591.1
1947	14,982.2	13,123.9	10,325.5	2,798.4	1,858.4
1948	18,361.5	16,149.1	12,630.4	3,518.7	2,212.4
1949	21,882.2	19,383.6	15,068.8	4,314.8	2,498.6
1950	25,180.1	22,496.3	17,264.5	5,231.8	2,683.8
1951	28,401.4	25,520.2	19,145.3	6,374.9	2,881.2

Detail may not add to totals, because of rounding.

Columns 1, 2, 4, and 5: Table D–26, columns 1, 2, 4, and 5 times construction cost index, Table D–20, for the year preceding each January 1.

Column 3 is from Table D–1, column 1.

TABLE D–28

Gross Capital Expenditures, Current Dollars, Electric Light and Power Privately Owned and Publicly Owned Utilities, 1880–1950, Five-Year Averages

(in millions)

	GROSS CAPITAL EXPENDITURES, EXCLUDING LAND					PER CENT OF TOTAL IN COLUMN 5			
Period	*Private Utilities* (1)	*Publicly Owned, Total* (col. 3 + col. 4) (2)	*Public, Except Federal* (3)	*Federal* (4)	*Total, Cols.* 1–4 (5)	*Private Utilities* (6)	*Publicly Owned, Total* (7)	*Public, Except Federal* (8)	*Federal* (9)
1880–1884	0.8	0.04	0.04		0.8	95.0	5.0	5.0	...
1885–1889	7.1	0.4	0.4		7.4	95.2	4.8	4.8	...
1890–1894	17.5	0.9	0.9		18.4	95.2	4.8	4.8	...
1895–1899	33.9	1.7	1.7		35.6	95.2	4.8	4.8	...
1900–1904	74.7	3.3	3.3		77.9	95.8	4.2	4.2	...
1905–1909	134.5	4.9	4.9		139.4	96.5	3.5	3.5	...
1910–1914	197.3	8.6	8.6		206.0	95.8	4.2	4.2	...
1915–1919	164.3	12.4	12.4		176.7	93.0	7.0	7.0	...
1920–1924	487.3	39.2	39.1	0.1	526.5	92.6	7.4	7.4	...
1925–1929	687.7	55.2	48.7	6.5	742.9	92.6	7.4	6.6	0.9
1930–1934	348.1	34.3	32.0	2.3	382.4	91.0	9.0	8.4	0.6
1935–1939	337.4	140.7	89.0	51.7	478.1	70.6	29.4	18.6	10.8
1940–1944	394.8	234.5	87.6	146.9	629.3	62.7	37.3	13.9	23.3
1945–1949	1,226.5	441.9	353.4	88.5	1,668.4	73.5	26.5	21.2	5.3

Detail may not add to totals because of rounding.

NOTES BY COLUMN

1 Table D–1.
3 Derived from Tables D–30 and D–31.
4 Table D–32. Estimates are not available through 1919 but average annual expenditures during these periods are believed to be very small, possibly less than 0.1 millions.

TABLE D–29

Gross Capital Expenditures, Current Dollars, Publicly Owned Plants except Federal, Electric Light and Power, Specified Intervals, 1881–1922

(in thousands)

Period	*Increase in Value of Plant and Equipment*			Ratio, Public to Private (col. 1 ÷ col. 3)	Gross Capital Expenditures, Excluding Land, Private Plants	Gross Capital Expenditures, Excluding Land, Publicly Owned Plants
	Publicly Owned Plants	Privately Owned Plants	Privately Owned, After Adjustment for Write-ups			
	(1)	(2)	(3)	(4)	(5)	(6)
1881–1902 (June 30)	22,020	521,869	438,370	0.05,023	456,632	22,937
1902 (July 1)–1907	20,859	644,420	541,313	.03,853	549,783	21,183
1908–1912	34,186	1,178,701	990,109	.03,453	1,025,050	35,395
1913–1917	50,310	923,857	776,040	.06,483	857,443	55,588
1918–1922	108,285	1,322,965	1,111,291	.09,744	1,212,909	118,186

NOTES BY COLUMN

1 Successive reports of the Census of Electrical Industries. Data cover municipal plants.

2 Table D–3.

3 Column 2 times 0.84, the ratio used to adjust the plant and equipment data for private plants to eliminate write-ups in the value of physical assets.

5 Table D–12, report on privately owned electric light and power.

6 Column 4 times column 5.

TABLE D-30

Gross Capital Expenditures, Current Dollars, Publicly Owned Plants except Federal, Electric Light and Power, Five-Year Intervals, 1881-1922

(in millions)

Period	*Gross Capital Expenditures, Privately Owned Plants* (1)	*Ratios to Total for Each Period* (2)	*Gross Capital Expenditures, Publicly Owned Plants* (3)	
1881–1884	3.8	0.0083	0.2	
1885–1889	35.4	.0775	1.8	
1890–1894	87.7	.1920	4.4	
1895–1899	169.5	.3711	8.5	
1900–1902 (June 30)	160.3	.3510	8.1	16.3 (1900–04)
1902 (July 1)–1904	213.0	.3874	8.2	
1905–1907	336.8	.6126	13.0	24.6 (1905–09)
1908–1909	335.8	.3276	11.6	
1910–1912	689.3	.6724	23.8	43.1 (1910–14)
1913–1914	297.4	.3469	19.3	
1915–1917	560.0	.6531	36.3	61.8 (1915–19)
1918–1919	261.5	.2156	25.5	
1920–1922	951.3	.7844	92.7	

NOTES BY COLUMN

1 Tables D-13, D-15, and D-20.

2 Ratios for groups of years in column 1 to totals for each available period: 1881–1902 (June 30), 1902 (July 1)–1907, 1908–12, 1913–17, and 1918–22.

3 Total gross capital expenditures, publicly owned plants, for available intervals, Table D-29, column 6, distributed by year in accordance with the ratios in column 2.

TABLE D-31

Gross Capital Expenditures, Current Dollars, Electric Light and Power, Publicly Owned Plants except Federal, 1923–1950

(*in millions*)

Year	*Gross Capital Expenditures, Including Land* (1)	*Investment in Land* (per cent) (2)	*Gross Capital Expenditures, Excluding Land* (3)
1923	51.3	6.64	47.9
1924	58.7	6.76	54.7
1925	54.7	6.88	50.9
1926	46.5	7.00	43.2
1927	44.9	7.00	41.8
1928	57.1	7.00	53.1
1929	58.7	7.00	54.6
1930	44.7	7.00	41.6
1931	37.2	7.00	34.6
1932	32.1	6.21	30.1
1933	27.9	5.43	26.4
1934	28.4	4.65	27.1
1935	42.5	3.86	40.9
1936	71.3	3.08	69.1
1937	88.5	2.38	86.4
1938	102.9	1.84	101.0
1939	151.6	2.70	147.5
1940	147.7	2.28	144.3
1941	106.0	2.17	103.7
1942	66.2	2.38	64.6
1943	51.6	1.82	50.7
1944	75.9	1.78	74.5
1945	74.5	2.09	72.9
1946	191.1	3.34	184.7
1947	339.2	1.87	332.9
1948	488.6	2.40	476.9
1949	716.7	2.40	699.5
1950	689.4	2.40	672.9

Column 1: Includes expenditures of rural cooperatives financed with Rural Electrification Administration funds. For 1926–43: Edison Electric Institute, Statistical Bulletin No. 11. For 1923–25: EEI figures for private and municipal plants combined (Statistical Bulletins 15 and 17) multiplied by 0.0646, the average ratio of expenditures of municipal utilities to the total for private and municipal plants during the years 1926–28. For 1944–50: EEI figures for expenditures of all utilities except federal (Statistical Bulletin No. 17) less gross capital expenditures, including land, of private utilities (Table D–18).

Column 2 is from Tables D–17 and D–18.

TABLE D–32

Gross Capital Expenditures, Current Dollars, Federal Plant, Electric Light and Power, 1921–1950

(in millions)

Period or Year	*Increase in Generating Capacity, Federal Plants* (000's kw) (1)	*Construction Costs* (1929 = 100) (2)	*Column 1 × Column 2* (3)	*Federal Gross Capital Expenditures, Including* REA (4)	*Expenditures of* REA *Funds* (5)	*Federal Gross Capital Expenditures, Excluding* REA (6)	*Federal Gross Capital Expenditures, Including Land* (7)	*Expenditures for Land* (per cent) (8)	*Federal Gross Capital Expenditures, Excluding Land* (9)
1921–24	4	96.1	384				0.7	6.61	0.7
1925–29	200	96.3	19,260				35.0	6.98	32.6
1930–34	74	92.9	6,875				12.5	6.06	11.7
1935–39	1,363	107.4	146,386				266.0	2.77	258.6
1940	294	113.9	33,487			50	50.0	2.28	48.9
1941	427	118.8	50,728			172	172.0	2.17	168.3
1942	846	122.6	103,720			233	233.0	2.38	227.5
1943	1,106	123.6	136,702			169	169.0	1.82	165.9
1944	564	123.1	69,428				126.1	1.78	123.9
1945	195	126.0	24,570	102	28	74	74.0	2.09	72.5
1946	...	144.7		105	57	48	48.0	3.34	46.4
1947	108	167.9	18,133	197	132	65	65.0	1.87	63.8
1948	498	185.0	92,130	340	225	115	115.0	2.40	112.2
1949	684	195.7	133,859	436	285	151	151.0	2.40	147.4
1950				771	327	444	444.0	2.40	433.3

NOTES BY COLUMN

1 Federal Power Commission, Production of Electric Energy and Capacity of Generating Plants.

2 Averages for appropriate years, from Table D–20.

4 Gross capital expenditures of the federal government for electric plant, including expenditures of funds advanced by Rural Electrification Administration; data from *Electrical World*, January 29, 1951.

5 Based on the year-to-year change in cumulative totals of REA funds advanced, shown in *Electrical World*, January 29, 1951. The increase in cumulative funds advanced during any year is assumed to represent capital expenditures for the following year.

6 For 1940–43, data compiled by FPC and shown in Edison Electric Institute, Statistical Bulletin No. 11; for 1945–50, col. 4 minus col. 5.

7 Column 6 for available years. For other years, col. 3 times 0.0018169, the ratio of total gross capital expenditures for 1940–43 and 1945–49 (col. 6) to the total of col. 3 for corresponding years.

8 Averages for appropriate years, Tables D–17 and D–18

TABLE D-33

Value of Plant and Equipment, Publicly Owned Electric Light and Power Plants, 1929 Dollars, 1881–1949

(in millions)

Year	*Gross Capital Expenditures, Publicly Owned Plants, Current Prices* (1)	*Construction Costs, Five-Year Averages for 1881–1939, Annual Data, 1940–1949* (1929 = 100) (2)	*Gross Capital Expenditures, 1929 Dollars* (col. 1 ÷ col. 2) (3)	*Average Life of Plant and Equipment* (years) (4)	*Annual Depreciation of Expenditures in Column 3* (col. 3 ÷ col. 4) (5)	*Appropriate Sums of* Column 5 (6)	*Capital* Consumption, *1929 Dollars* (7)	*Net Capital Expenditures, 1929 Dollars* (col. 3 minus col. 7) (8)	*Value of Plant and Equipment, December 31, 1929 Dollars* (9)
1881	0.05	43.5	0.1	17	...	...	...	0.1	0.1
1882	0.05	43.5	0.1	17	...	...	...	0.1	0.2
1883	0.05	43.5	0.1	17	...	...	...	0.1	0.3
1884	0.05	43.5	0.1	17	...	...	...	0.1	0.4
1885	0.4	39.1	1.0	17	0.1	0.1	0.1	0.9	1.3
1886	0.4	39.1	1.0	17	0.1	0.2	0.2	0.8	2.1
1887	0.4	39.1	1.0	17	0.1	0.3	0.3	0.7	2.8
1888	0.4	39.1	1.0	17	0.1	0.4	0.4	0.6	3.4
1889	0.4	39.1	1.0	17	0.1	0.5	0.5	0.5	3.9
1890	0.9	36.7	2.5	17	0.1	0.6	0.6	1.9	5.8
1891	0.9	36.7	2.5	17	0.1	0.7	0.7	1.8	7.6
1892	0.9	36.7	2.5	17	0.1	0.8	0.8	1.7	9.3
1893	0.9	36.7	2.5	17	0.1	0.9	0.9	1.6	10.9
1894	0.9	36.7	2.5	17	0.1	1.0	1.0	1.5	12.4
1895	1.7	35.7	4.8	17	0.3	1.3	1.2	3.6	16.0
1896	1.7	35.7	4.8	17	0.3	1.6	1.5	3.3	19.3
1897	1.7	35.7	4.8	17	0.3	1.9	1.8	3.0	22.3
1898	1.7	35.7	4.8	17	0.3	2.2	2.1	2.7	25.0
1899	1.7	35.7	4.8	17	0.3	2.5	2.4	2.4	27.4
1900	3.3	41.4	8.0	17	0.5	3.0	2.8	4.2	32.6
1901	3.3	41.4	8.0	18	0.4	3.4	3.2	4.8	37.4

(continued on next page)

TABLE D-33 (continued)

Year	Gross Capital Expenditures, Publicly Owned Plants, Current Prices (1)	Construction Costs, Five-Year Averages for 1881–1939, Annual Data, 1940–1949 (1929 = 100) (2)	Gross Capital Expenditures, 1929 Dollars (col. 1 ÷ col. 2) (3)	Average Life of Plant and Equipment (years) (4)	Annual Depreciation of Expenditures in Column 3 (col. 3 ÷ col. 4) (5)	Appropriate Sums of Column 5 (6)	Capital Consumption, 1929 Dollars (7)	Net Capital Expenditures, 1929 Dollars (col. 3 minus col. 7) (8)	Value of Plant and Equipment, December 31, 1929 Dollars (9)
1902	3.3	41.4	8.0	19	0.4	3.7	3.6	4.4	41.8
1903	3.3	41.4	8.0	20	0.4	4.0	3.9	4.1	45.9
1904	3.3	41.4	8.0	21	0.4	4.3	4.2	3.8	49.7
1905	4.9	45.0	10.9	22	0.5	4.7	4.5	6.4	56.1
1906	4.9	45.0	10.9	23	0.5	5.1	4.9	6.0	62.1
1907	4.9	45.0	10.9	24	0.5	5.5	5.3	5.6	67.7
1908	4.9	45.0	10.9	25	0.4	5.8	5.7	5.2	72.9
1909	4.9	45.0	10.9	26	0.4	6.1	6.0	4.9	77.8
1910	8.6	50.7	17.0	27	0.6	6.6	6.4	10.6	88.4
1911	8.6	50.7	17.0	28	0.6	7.1	6.9	10.1	98.5
1912	8.6	50.7	17.0	29	0.6	7.4	7.3	9.7	108.2
1913	8.6	50.7	17.0	30	0.6	7.7	7.6	9.4	117.6
1914	8.6	50.7	17.0	31	0.5	7.9	7.8	9.2	126.8
1915	12.4	77.9	15.9	32	0.5	8.1	8.0	7.9	134.7
1916	12.4	77.9	15.9	33	0.5	8.3	8.2	7.7	142.4
1917	12.4	77.9	15.9	34	0.5	8.3	8.3	7.6	150.0
1918	12.4	77.9	15.9	35	0.5	8.8	8.6	7.3	157.3
1919	12.4	77.9	15.9	36	0.4	8.8	8.8	7.1	164.4
1920	39.2	98.3	39.9	37	1.1	9.9	9.4	30.5	194.9
1921	39.2	98.3	39.9	37	1.1	10.6	10.3	29.6	224.5
1922	39.2	98.3	39.9	37	1.1	11.7	11.2	28.7	253.2
1923	39.2	98.3	39.9	37	1.1	12.4	12.1	27.8	281.0
1924	39.2	98.3	39.9	37	1.1	13.5	13.0	26.9	307.9
1925	55.2	96.3	57.3	37	1.5	14.6	14.1	43.2	351.1
1926	55.2	96.3	57.3	37	1.5	16.1	15.4	41.9	393.0
1927	55.2	96.3	57.3	37	1.5	17.1	16.6	40.7	433.7
1928	55.2	96.3	57.3	37	1.5	18.6	17.9	39.4	473.1
1929	55.2	96.3	57.3	37	1.5	19.6	19.1	38.2	511.3

(concluded on next page)

TABLE D–33 (concluded)

Year	Gross Capital Expenditures, Publicly Owned Plants; Current Prices (1)	Construction Costs, Five-Year Averages for 1881–1939, Annual Data, 1940–1949 (1929 = 100) (2)	Gross Capital Expenditures, 1929 Dollars (col. 1 ÷ col. 2) (3)	Average Life of Plant and Equipment (years) (4)	Annual Depreciation of Expenditures in Column 3 (col. 3 ÷ col. 4) (5)	Appropriate Sums of Column 5 (6)	Capital Consumption, 1929 Dollars (7)	Net Capital Expenditures, 1929 Dollars (col. 3 minus col. 7) (8)	Value of Plant and Equipment, December 31, 1929 Dollars (9)
1930	34.3	92.9	36.9	37	1.0	20.6	20.1	16.8	528.1
1931	34.3	92.9	36.9	37	1.0	21.1	20.9	16.0	544.1
1932	34.3	92.9	36.9	37	1.0	22.1	21.6	15.3	559.4
1933	34.3	92.9	36.9	37	1.0	22.7	22.4	14.5	573.9
1934	34.3	92.9	36.9	37	1.0	23.7	23.2	13.7	587.6
1935	140.7	107.4	131.0	37	3.5	26.8	25.3	105.7	693.3
1936	140.7	107.4	131.0	37	3.5	30.3	28.6	102.4	795.7
1937	140.7	107.4	131.0	37	3.5	33.2	31.8	99.2	894.9
1938	140.7	107.4	131.0	37	3.5	36.7	35.0	96.0	990.9
1939	140.7	107.4	131.0	37	3.5	39.6	38.2	92.8	1,083.7
1940	193.2	113.9	169.6	37	4.6	44.2	41.9	127.7	1,211.4
1941	272.0	118.8	229.0	37	6.2	49.8	47.0	182.0	1,393.4
1942	292.1	122.6	238.3	37	6.4	56.2	53.0	185.3	1,578.7
1943	216.6	123.6	175.2	37	4.7	60.3	58.3	116.9	1,695.6
1944	198.4	123.1	161.2	37	4.4	64.7	62.5	98.7	1,794.3
1945	145.4	126.0	115.4	37	3.1	67.3	66.0	49.4	1,843.7
1946	231.1	144.7	159.7	37	4.3	71.6	69.5	90.2	1,933.9
1947	396.7	167.9	236.3	37	6.4	77.5	74.5	161.8	2,095.7
1948	589.1	185.0	318.4	37	8.6	86.1	81.8	236.6	2,332.3
1949	846.9	195.7	432.8	37	11.7	97.3	91.7	341.1	2,673.4
1950	1,106.3	205.1	539.4	37	14.6	111.9	104.6	434.8	3,108.2

NOTES BY COLUMN

1 For 1881–1939: Table D–28. Average expenditures for each half-decade have been used for each year within the corresponding interval. For 1940–50, Tables D–31 and D–32.

2 Table D–20. The average for each half-decade to 1939 has been used for each year within the interval; annual data are shown for 1940–49.

4 Assumed same as for privately owned utilities, Table D–21 and D–23.

6 Sums of col. 5 for the plant and equipment additions of previous years still in service, as indicated by the average life data in col. 4.

7 Two-year moving averages of col. 6 centered in the second year.

9 Derived by successive addition of figures in col. 7.

TABLE D–34

Electric Light and Power Generating Capacity, Private and Public Utilities and User-Owned Facilities, 1900–1951

	CAPACITY					PER CENT OF TOTAL IN COLUMN 1			
		ELECTRIC UTILITIES				ELECTRIC UTILITIES			
January 1	*Total cols.* 3, 4, 5 (1)	*Total* (2)	*Privately Owned* (3)	*Publicly Owned* (4)	*User-Owned* (5)	*Total* (6)	*Privately Owned* (7)	*Publicly Owned* (8)	*User-Owned* (9)
	(horsepower, in thousands, of generators)								
1900	2,575	1,200	1,142	58	1,375	46.6	44.3	2.3	53.4
1910	11,878	5,225	4,974	251	6,653	44.0	41.9	2.1	56.0
1920	27,839	15,250	14,518	732	12,589	54.8	52.1	2.6	45.2
	(in thousands of kilowatts)								
1940	49,438	38,863	33,908	4,955	10,575	78.6	68.6	10.0	21.4
1941	50,962	39,927	34,399	5,528	11,035	78.3	67.5	10.8	21.7
1942	53,995	42,405	36,041	6,364	11,590	78.5	66.7	11.8	21.5
1943	57,237	45,053	37,442	7,611	12,184	78.7	65.4	13.3	21.3
1944	60,539	47,951	39,128	8,823	12,589	79.2	64.6	14.6	20.8
1945	62,066	49,189	39,733	9,456	12,877	79.3	64.0	15.2	20.7
1946	62,868	50,111	40,307	9,804	12,757	79.7	64.1	15.6	20.3
1947	63,066	50,317	40,335	9,982	12,749	79.8	64.0	15.8	20.2
1948	65,151	52,322	41,986	10,336	12,829	80.3	64.4	15.9	19.7
1949	69,615	56,560	45,381	11,179	13,055	81.2	65.2	16.1	18.8
1950	76,570	63,100	50,484	12,616	13,470	82.4	65.9	16.5	17.6
1951	82,850	68,919	55,175	13,743	13,931	83.2	66.6	16.6	16.8

For 1900–1920: Capacity, in terms of horsepower of generators—total, electric utility subtotal, and user-owned—from U.S. Geological Survey, Power Capacity and Production in the United States (Water-Supply Paper 579). Total electric utility capacity was distributed between private and public in the proportions 0.952 and 0.048 respectively; these figures were derived from the average proportions of gross capital expenditures of the two groups during 1880–1919.

For 1940–51: Capacity, in terms of kilowatts, from Federal Power Commission, Production of Electric Energy and Capacity of Generating Plants. "User-owned" includes generating capacity of electric railroads and manufacturing and mining plants.

TABLE D–35

Ratios of Value of Electric Light and Power Plant and Equipment per Unit of Capacity, User-Owned to Utility-Owned, 1900, 1910, and 1920

	ELECTRIC POWER CAPACITY (horsepower, in thousands, of generators)		CAPACITY, AS RATIO TO TOTAL USER-OWNED		
January 1	*Total, User-Owned* (1)	*Electric Railroads* (2)	*Electric Railroads* (col. 2 ÷ col. 1) (3)	*Other User-Owned* 1.0000 *minus* *Column* 3 (4)	*Value of Plant and Equipment per Unit of Capacity: User-Owned as Ratio to Utility-Owned* (5)
1900	1,375	935	0.6800	0.3200	0.7047
1910	6,653	3,091	0.4646	0.5354	0.6105
1920	12,589	4,360	0.3463	0.6537	0.5587

Columns 1 and 2: U.S. Geological Survey, Power Capacity and Production in the United States (Water-Supply Paper 579).

Column 5: col. 3 times 0.8447 plus col. 4 times 0.4072. The former figure represents the ratio of the value of generating and distribution plant to the total for generating, distribution, and transmission plant in 1950; the latter is the ratio of the value of generating plant to the total for generating, distribution, and transmission plant in 1950. It is assumed that electric railroads have investment in generating and distribution plant equivalent to that of the utility industry for an equivalent capacity (but no transmission plant) and that other user-owned utility plant represents generating capacity only. The 1950 ratios are based on data for Class A and B privately owned utilities shown by the Federal Power Commission in *Statistics of Electric Utilities in the United States*, 1950. The basic figures for 1950 are (in millions of dollars): generating plant 6,806.1; distribution plant 7,311.9; transmission plant 2,596.1.

TABLE D-36

Ratios of Value of User-Owned Electric Light and Power Plant and Equipment to Utility-Owned Plant and Equipment, 1900–1950

January 1	*Generating Capacity: Ratio, User-Owned to Utility-Owned* (1)	*Value of Plant and Equipment per Unit of Capacity: Ratio, User-Owned to Utility-Owned* (2)	*Value of Plant and Equipment: Ratio, User-Owned to Utility-Owned* (3)
1900	1.1458	0.7047	0.8074
1901			.8044
1902			.8014
1903			.7984
1904			.7954
1905			.7924
1906			.7893
1907			.7863
1908			.7833
1909			.7803
1910	1.2733	.6105	.7773
1911			.7457
1912			.7141
1913			.6825
1914			.6509
1915			.6193
1916			.5876
1917			.5560
1918			.5244
1919			.4928
1920	0.8255	.5587	.4612
1921			.4457
1922			.4303
1923			.4148
1924			.3994
1925			.3839
1926			.3684
1927			.3530
1928			.3375
1929			.3221

(concluded on next page)

TABLE D–36 (concluded)

January 1	*Generating Capacity: Ratio, User-Owned to Utility-Owned* (1)	*Value of Plant and Equipment per Unit of Capacity: Ratio, User-Owned to Utility-Owned* (2)	*Value of Plant and Equipment: Ratio, User-Owned to Utility-Owned* (3)
1930			0.3066
1931			.2911
1932			.2757
1933			.2602
1934			.2448
1935			.2293
1936			.2138
1937			.1984
1938			.1829
1939			.1675
1940	0.2721	0.5587	.1520
1941	.2764	.5587	.1544
1942	.2733	.5587	.1527
1943	.2704	.5587	.1511
1944	.2625	.5587	.1467
1945	.2618	.5587	.1463
1946	.2546	.5587	.1422
1947	.2534	.5587	.1416
1948	.2452	.5587	.1370
1949	.2308	.5587	.1289
1950	.2135	.5587	.1193
1951	.2021	.5587	.1129

NOTES BY COLUMN

1 Table D–34, col. 5 divided by col. 2.

2 For 1900–1920, Table D–35; the 1920 figure is used for 1940–51.

3 Col. 1 times col. 2 for available years; figures for other years were obtained by linear interpolation.

APPENDIX E

Notes and Tables on the Derivation of Capital Formation Data for Telephones

Gross Capital Expenditures in Current Dollars

THE series for gross capital expenditures represents actual cash outlays for plant and equipment chargeable to capital account, both for replacement and expansion. It excludes so-called "re-used equipment"—a mere intracorporate bookkeeping item which has appeared in several series published in the past for this industry.

1913–1950

The derivation of gross capital expenditures for the years 1913–50 is shown in Table E–2. Estimates of expenditures for the entire industry for the years 1939–50 were supplied by the American Telephone and Telegraph Company (column 6). For 1920–38, A.T. & T. supplied data on cash expenditures for the Bell system only (column 1) and on gross expenditures, including re-used equipment, for the Bell system and for the entire industry (columns 2 and 4). Cash expenditures for the industry were obtained from the data for gross expenditures, including re-used equipment (column 4), and the ratios of cash to gross expenditures for the Bell system in the same years (column 3). Since no data on actual cash expenditures were available for years prior to 1920, cash expenditures for the industry for the years 1914–19 were derived from data on gross expenditures, including re-used equipment, and the average ratio of cash to gross expenditures for the Bell system for the years 1920–21. Gross capital expenditures for 1913 are based on gross expenditures for the Bell system, including re-used equipment, and the average ratio, for 1914–17, of cash expenditures for the entire industry to gross expenditures for the Bell system. All the basic data are from A.T. & T.

1880–1912

Since no data for gross capital expenditures before 1913 were available, estimates for the earlier years were obtained from year-to-year changes in the value of plant and equipment, after adjustment, in conjunction with estimates of the value of property retired each year.

The derivation of the value of plant and equipment, in terms of original cost, is shown in Table E–3 for 1880, and in Table E–4 for the entire period 1880–1912.

Original cost at the end of 1880 was estimated from data shown in the census report for that year and from data shown in Exhibit 1360–A of the FCC Telephone Investigation;[1] the procedure is outlined in Table E–3. The census figures for value of plant and equipment in 1880 require adjustment both because they include write-ups for the American Bell Telephone Company and because no clear-cut distinction was apparently made between plant and equipment, and other assets. The value of plant and equipment for American Bell at the end of February 1881 was available from the FCC report; this figure was reduced to derive an estimate for the census date June 1, 1880 (line 4). Total assets of American Bell for this date (line 5) were obtained from the plant and equipment figure and the ratio of plant and equipment to all assets for the Bell system in 1885, as shown in FCC Exhibit 1360–A. Write-ups included in the census total for American Bell were estimated by subtracting the asset figure from FCC data (line 5) from the reported census total (line 2). A "corrected" census figure for total assets of all companies was then obtained by subtracting from the reported census total (line 1) the estimate of American Bell write-ups (line 6). A further adjustment, to include the assets of companies not reporting financial data to the census, was made by use of the ratio of miles of wire owned by reporting companies to miles of wire of all companies (line 8). Value of plant and equipment for all companies as of June 1, 1880 (line 9) was obtained from the corrected asset total, and the 1885 ratio of plant and equipment to total assets. Value of plant and equipment for the end of 1880 was derived by adding an estimate of capital growth between June 1, 1880 and the end of the year, as indicated in the table.

Table E–4 shows the derivation of the value of plant and equipment for all years 1880–1917. Figures for 1913–17 are included for convenience in later computations. Data for plant and equipment for the Bell system for 1885–1917, including land but excluding general equipment, are from FCC Exhibit 1360–A. Since the system comprised the entire telephone industry in 1885 and since an estimate for the entire industry for 1880 was derived in Table E–3, figures for the industry for 1881–84 were obtained by linear interpolation. The Bell system continued to account for the entire industry through the year 1893. The available figures for value of plant and equipment for these years thus required only a minor adjustment to exclude land and include general equipment. The allowances for these items was

[1] Report on the Investigation of the Telephone Industry in the United States (Federal Communications Commission, 1939), hereafter referred to by FCC exhibit number or as the FCC report.

determined from data for the Bell system for 1913–14, shown in FCC Exhibit 1364.

For 1894–1917, estimates were made of the value of plant and equipment for companies outside the Bell system. Data for the Bell system (column 1, Table E–4) for 1902, 1907, 1912, and 1917 were subtracted from census totals for the entire industry for these years (column 3). The resulting figures were interpolated linearly for intervening years. (Plant and equipment for non-Bell companies in 1893 was zero.) Value of plant and equipment for the entire telephone industry for 1894–1917, including land (column 5), represents simple sums of the figures for Bell and non-Bell companies. A final adjustment to exclude the value of land was made by the use of the percentage shown by the Bell system for 1913–14.

Estimates of retirements during the years 1880–1912 were based on depreciation rates and the relationship between depreciation and retirements. A depreciation rate of 10 per cent for the early part of the period considered was provided by A.T. & T.; this rate was used for the year 1880. The rate for the year 1950 is an average of the rates prescribed for ten companies by the FCC, adjusted to exclude land from the depreciation base. Rates for intervening years were obtained by linear interpolation between the rates for 1880 and for 1950, and are shown in Table E–5.

Relationships between retirement and depreciation were estimated by the use of data for 1913–17 and are shown in Table E–6. Depreciation for these years, in terms of original prices, was derived from the annual value of plant and equipment (Table E–4) and the depreciation rates shown in Table E–5. Retirements, also in original prices, were derived by subtracting from gross capital expenditures the annual change in the value of plant and equipment. The average ratio of retirements to depreciation for the five years 1913–17—approximately 0.40—provided the basis for estimating retirements in the years 1880–1912.

The derivation of gross capital expenditures for the period 1880–1912 is shown in Table E–7. Annual capital expenditures were obtained as sums of the annual changes in the value of plant and equipment (from Table E–4, column 6) and estimated retirements. The latter series (Table E–7, column 4) was derived from the value of plant and equipment and retirement rates obtained by multiplying the depreciation rates (shown in Table E–5) uniformly by 0.40. It was assumed that retirements were zero during the first three years of the industry's operation, 1878–80. Since companies outside the Bell system came into operation in 1894, and since such companies presumably made no retirements for the first few years, retirements for 1894–96 were determined from data on the value of plant and equipment for the Bell system only, taken in conjunction with the retirement rate. The value of plant and equipment at the end of 1879, needed in the computation of gross capital expenditures for 1880, was suggested by fragmentary data for securites authorized, shown in the FCC report.

Gross Capital Expenditures in 1929 Dollars

Gross capital expenditures in 1929 dollars were obtained by deflating the current dollar figures by an index of construction costs. The derivation of the construction cost index is shown in Table E–8 for 1915–50 and in Table E–9 for 1878–1915.

The construction cost index for 1915–50 is an average of indexes for the following four components: telephone apparatus, wages in the building trades, commercial buildings, and telephone poles in place. The series for telephone apparatus was developed by the Western Electric Company; the wage series is from the Bureau of Labor Statistics; the index for commercial buildings is that compiled by George A. Fuller Co. and published by the *Engineering News Record*; and the index for telephone poles was derived from Interstate Commerce Commission data. The index for telephone apparatus excludes the labor involved in the installation of apparatus and equipment and in developing equipment specifications.

The weights used in combining the four series were derived mainly from data shown in FCC Exhibit 1364 and from information furnished by A.T. & T. Slightly differing weights were used for the intervals 1915–24 and 1925–50. For the former period, the relative weights of equipment and plant (64 and 36 per cent) were obtained from balance sheet figures for 1913, 1915, 1917, and 1919 (FCC Exhibit 1364). Data shown in this exhibit also indicate that book value of plant is about equally divided between buildings and poles; each of these series was therefore assigned 18 per cent of the total weight. The labor component of installed equipment (22 per cent of total cost of installed equipment) was derived from data supplied by the BLS and A.T. & T. on the proportion of labor cost to total cost of installed equipment in 1950. The weight for the wage series was therefore set at 14 per cent (22 per cent of the 64 per cent for installed equipment). The remaining weight, 50 per cent of the total (78 per cent of 64 per cent for installed equipment) was assigned to the price index for telephone apparatus. For 1925–50, the weights were derived in an analogous manner. The relative weights for equipment and plant (70 per cent and 30 per cent) were based on balance sheet figures for 1929–35 shown in FCC Exhibit 1364; the weight for plant was divided equally between buildings and poles. The proportion of labor cost to total cost of installed equipment was assumed the same as in the earlier period.

For years prior to 1915, the construction cost index is based on three series: electrical equipment, construction materials, and wages in the building trades. The sources of these series are the same as those indicated in the notes to Table D–6, on electric light and power. The relative weights for equipment and plant (the latter is represented by construction materials) are based on balance sheet figures for 1913, 1915, 1917, and 1919, which indicate that equipment accounted for 64 per cent and plant 36 per cent of the total. Since 21 per cent of equipment cost represents labor (a slightly lower figure was used for the period than for later years), the weight for the equipment series, which excludes labor, was set at 51 per cent of the total (0.79 of 0.64). Unpublished data furnished by BLS covering the year 1947 suggest that 25 per cent of the cost of plant was labor cost. The weight for construction materials was thus derived as 75 per cent of 36 per cent. The remaining weight, 22 per cent, was assigned to the wage series; it reflects labor both for plant construction and for equipment installation.

Capital Consumption in 1880 Prices

1880–1917

Capital consumption was first computed in constant dollar totals, at 1880 prices. For this computation, it was necessary to derive a series on gross physical assets for 1879 and subsequent years, valued in 1880 prices. The derivation of the series for the years 1880–1917 is shown in Table E–10.

It was assumed, on the basis of information on the industry's development, that physical assets at the end of 1877 were zero. Physical assets at the close of 1879, in terms of 1880 prices, were derived from the totals of estimates of gross capital expenditures during 1878 and 1879, deflated to 1880 prices by use of the construction cost index described above. Physical assets at the close of 1880 were obtained by adding to the 1879 total the gross capital expenditures during 1880. It was assumed that no retirements were made during 1878–80, the first three years of operation. Physical assets for subsequent years were obtained by adding to the asset figure for the prior year gross capital expenditures for the current year, in 1880 dollars, and deducting retirements, also in 1880 dollars. Gross capital expenditures in 1880 dollars were obtained from the current dollar figures in Tables E–2 and E–7 and the construction cost index derived in Tables E–8 and E–9. Retirements in 1880 dollars were estimated from the retirement rates shown in Table E–7 and gross physical assets at the end of the preceding year, in 1880 dollars. Retirements for the years 1894–96 were based on physical assets for the Bell system alone, since other companies first came into operation in 1894 and presumably made no retirements for the first three years.

Capital consumption, in 1880 dollars, was obtained by multiplication of the series for gross physical assets and the appropriate depreciation rates, and is shown in column 6 of Table E–10.

1917–1950

Capital consumption was computed for each fifth year of the period 1917–37 (that is, for the census years 1917, 1922, 1927, 1932, and 1937) and annually for 1938–50. Capital consumption for intercensal years 1917–37 was derived by linear interpolation.

As with prior years, a series for gross physical assets in 1880 dollars provided the depreciation base, and the asset figures were derived by adding successively to the asset figures for prior years the net difference between gross capital expenditures and retirements, both in 1880 prices. The derivation of retirements is shown in Table E–11. Retirements were first computed in original cost prices (columns 1–6). The value of plant and equipment in terms of original cost was obtained for 1917 and every fifth year through 1937 from the census. Annual data on value of plant and equipment, at original cost, for 1938–49 are based on reports by Class A telephone carriers to the FCC, and were adjusted for complete coverage by use of the 1937 ratio between the value of plant and equipment for Class A companies and that for all companies reporting to the census; for 1950, FCC data for Class A and B companies were adjusted for coverage by use of the 1949 ratio between plant and equipment for such companies and the estimated total. Deduction for the value of land and right-of-way was made for 1917 by use of the ratio shown in FCC Exhibit 1364, and for 1942–50 by means of data shown in the FCC annual publication, *Statistics of the Communications Industry in the United States*; ratios of value of land to total value of plant and equipment for 1922–41 were derived by interpolation. The net changes in the value of plant and equipment excluding land, in terms of original cost, by five-year intervals through 1937 and annually thereafter, were compared with gross capital expenditures for the corresponding periods, also in terms of original prices. The difference between gross capital expenditures and the net increase in the value of plant and equipment, of course, represents retirement, in terms of original prices.

Retirements were converted from original cost prices to 1880 prices on the assumption that retired property had an average life varying from sixteen to twenty-eight years over the period considered; these figures were obtained from the depreciation rates. The index of prices underlying retirements was computed as an average of the construction cost index for eleven years appropriately centered at the year corresponding to the average date of installation. Retirements are shown in 1880 prices in column 10.

Gross physical assets in 1880 dollars, by five-year intervals for 1917–37 and annually for 1938–50 are derived in Table E–12. As previously noted, the figures were obtained by adding to the preceding asset total gross capital expenditures in 1880 prices and deducting retirements in 1880 prices. Finally, capital consumption in 1880 prices was obtained by multiplying the asset figures by the depreciation rates. Capital consumption for the intercensal years 1917–37 was derived by linear interpolation.

Capital Consumption, 1929 and Current Dollars

Capital consumption in 1929 dollars was obtained from the series in 1880 dollars by inflation of the figures with the construction cost index for the year 1929 on the base, 1880 = 100. Capital consumption in current dollars is derived by inflating the constant dollar totals with the construction cost index shown in Tables E–8 and E–9.

Net Capital Expenditures, 1929 and Current Dollars

Net capital expenditures, both in 1929 dollars and in current dollars, represents the difference between gross capital expenditures and capital consumption.

Value of Plant and Equipment, 1929 and Current Dollars

The value of plant and equipment, net of accrued depreciation in 1929 dollars, was computed by cumulative addition of net capital expenditures, in 1929 dollars. A base figure for January 1, 1880 was obtained from estimates of deflated gross capital expenditures for 1878 and 1879, with allowance for depreciation during 1879.

Value of plant and equipment in current dollars was derived by inflating the constant dollar totals with the construction cost index.

The final data on capital formation in telephones, by years from 1880 through 1950, are shown in Table E–1.

APPENDIX E

TABLE E–1

Value of Plant and Equipment, Capital Formation, and Capital Consumption, Telephones, Annual Data, 1880–1950

(millions of dollars)

Year	VALUE OF PLANT AND EQUIPMENT, JANUARY 1		GROSS CAPITAL EXPENDITURES		CAPITAL CONSUMPTION		NET CAPITAL EXPENDITURES	
	Current Dollars (1)	*1929 Dollars* (2)	*Current Dollars* (3)	*1929 Dollars* (4)	*Current Dollars* (5)	*1929 Dollars* (6)	*Current Dollars* (7)	*1929 Dollars* (8)
1880	3.8	8.5	5.5	10.8	0.5	0.9	5.0	9.9
1881	9.4	18.4	6.1	12.1	1.0	1.9	5.1	10.2
1882	14.3	28.6	6.3	12.2	1.5	3.0	4.8	9.2
1883	19.5	37.8	6.5	13.0	2.1	4.1	4.4	8.9
1884	23.4	46.7	6.6	14.1	2.4	5.1	4.2	9.0
1885	26.2	55.7	6.9	15.1	2.8	6.2	4.1	8.9
1886	29.7	64.6	1.2	2.7	3.4	7.4	−2.2	−4.7
1887	27.4	59.9	3.8	8.4	3.3	7.3	0.5	1.1
1888	27.8	61.0	5.0	10.9	3.5	7.7	1.5	3.2
1889	29.4	64.2	8.6	19.0	3.8	8.3	4.8	10.7
1890	33.9	74.9	8.6	18.9	4.4	9.7	4.2	9.2
1891	38.4	84.1	5.7	13.0	4.7	10.9	1.0	2.1
1892	37.4	86.2	7.6	17.7	5.0	11.6	2.6	6.1
1893	39.6	92.3	7.6	17.8	5.4	12.6	2.2	5.2
1894	41.8	97.5	22.8	53.0	5.9	13.6	16.9	39.4
1895	58.9	136.9	25.0	63.0	7.0	17.6	18.0	45.4
1896	72.4	182.3	28.9	75.4	8.5	22.3	20.4	53.1
1897	90.2	235.4	29.4	68.6	11.9	27.8	17.5	40.8
1898	118.5	276.2	34.5	76.7	14.6	32.4	19.9	44.3
1899	144.2	320.5	48.6	100.4	18.0	37.3	30.6	63.1
1900	185.6	383.6	57.4	115.9	21.7	43.8	35.7	72.1
1901	225.8	455.7	55.0	111.8	25.2	51.3	29.8	60.5
1902	254.0	516.2	63.4	126.9	29.0	58.0	34.4	68.9
1903	292.1	585.1	78.0	156.8	32.6	65.6	45.4	91.2
1904	336.6	676.3	77.2	150.9	38.4	75.0	38.8	75.9
1905	385.1	752.2	97.9	187.3	43.6	83.4	54.3	103.9
1906	447.6	856.1	129.6	237.8	51.3	94.2	78.3	143.6
1907	544.8	999.7	104.9	184.9	61.3	108.1	43.6	76.8
1908	610.6	1,076.5	59.9	108.3	64.9	117.4	−5.0	−9.1
1909	590.1	1,067.4	63.5	107.9	70.9	120.4	−7.4	−12.5
1910	621.1	1,054.9	88.5	146.9	74.3	123.3	14.2	23.6
1911	649.5	1,078.5	91.9	146.2	80.9	128.7	11.0	17.5
1912	688.8	1,096.0	113.1	182.5	82.9	133.8	30.2	48.7
1913	709.3	1,144.7	95.0	146.3	91.6	141.1	3.4	5.2
1914	746.7	1,149.9	89.3	138.4	93.8	145.4	−4.5	−7.0
1915	737.5	1,142.9	71.2	107.3	98.8	149.0	−27.6	−41.7
1916	730.3	1,101.2	108.7	158.2	103.2	150.2	5.5	8.0
1917	762.0	1,109.2	152.6	185.0	127.6	154.7	25.0	30.3
1918	940.0	1,139.5	118.9	133.3	143.2	160.6	−24.3	−27.3
1919	991.9	1,112.2	122.1	127.2	157.0	163.6	−34.9	−36.4

(continued on next page)

TABLE E–1 (continued)

Year	VALUE OF PLANT AND EQUIPMENT, JANUARY 1		GROSS CAPITAL EXPENDITURES		CAPITAL CONSUMPTION		NET CAPITAL EXPENDITURES	
	Current Dollars (1)	*1929 Dollars* (2)	*Current Dollars* (3)	*1929 Dollars* (4)	*Current Dollars* (5)	*1929 Dollars* (6)	*Current Dollars* (7)	*1929 Dollars* (8)
1920	1,032.7	1,075.8	188.3	155.3	202.1	166.7	−13.8	−11.4
1921	1,290.7	1,064.4	213.0	171.4	211.0	169.8	2.0	1.6
1922	1,324.9	1,066.0	245.5	219.2	193.7	172.9	51.8	46.3
1923	1,245.9	1,112.3	298.2	264.3	198.5	175.9	99.7	88.4
1924	1,355.0	1,200.7	359.8	314.1	209.2	182.6	150.6	131.5
1925	1,526.0	1,332.2	355.7	314.2	214.3	189.3	141.4	124.9
1926	1,649.4	1,457.1	371.6	334.3	217.7	195.9	153.9	138.4
1927	1,773.2	1,595.5	353.6	324.7	220.6	202.6	133.0	122.1
1928	1 870.5	1,717.6	404.8	390.5	217.0	209.3	187.8	181.2
1929	1,968.3	1,898.8	556.8	556.8	213.3	213.3	343.5	343.5
1930	2,242.3	2,242.3	548.9	550.5	216.7	217.3	332.2	333.2
1931	2,568.0	2,575.5	337.0	335.9	222.0	221.3	115.0	114.6
1932	2,698.7	2,690.1	177.5	191.2	209.3	225.4	−31.8	−34.2
1933	2,465.7	2,655.9	98.0	106.1	211.8	229.4	−113.8	−123.3
1934	2,338.6	2,532.6	112.7	111.4	228.4	225.8	−115.7	−114.4
1935	2,446.3	2,418.2	130.8	128.2	226.7	222.2	−95.9	−94.0
1936	2,371.3	2,324.2	180.8	178.9	221.0	218.7	−40.2	−39.8
1937	2,308.2	2,284.4	261.8	264.9	213.0	215.3	48.8	49.6
1938	2,309.3	2,334.0	236.7	232.5	215.4	211.5	21.3	21.0
1939	2,398.1	2,355.0	250.0	244.0	217.1	211.8	32.9	32.2
1940	2,446.4	2,387.2	310.0	311.0	210.9	211.6	99.1	99.4
1941	2,478.4	2,486.6	450.0	421.2	229.4	214.7	220.6	206.5
1942	2,877.0	2,693.1	370.0	340.1	242.7	223.1	127.3	117.0
1943	3,057.4	2,810.1	165.0	149.2	253.0	228.7	−88.0	−79.5
1944	3,020.6	2,730.6	185.0	164.5	255.6	227.2	−70.6	−62.7
1945	3,001.4	2,667.9	275.0	240.8	258.0	225.9	17.0	14.9
1946	3,063.8	2,682.8	730.0	551.7	301.6	227.9	428.4	323.8
1947	3,978.3	3,006.6	1,260.0	826.0	368.0	241.2	892.0	584.8
1948	5,478.7	3,591.4	1,551.0	1,012.5	402.9	263.0	1,148.1	749.5
1949	6,649.8	4,340.9	1,150.0	731.6	452.8	288.1	697.2	443.5
1950	7,519.6	4,784.4	945.0	570.4	495.9	299.3	449.1	271.1
1951	8,377.0	5,055.5						

All data exclude investment in land. Columns 1 and 2 exclude accrued depreciation.

NOTES BY COLUMN

1 Col. 2 inflated by the index of cost of plant and equipment for the year preceding each January 1 (Table E–8, col. 7, and Table E–9, col. 5).

2 For 1880, derived from estimates of gross capital expenditures in 1878 and 1879 (see note to col. 1, Table E–10) deflated to 1929 dollars, with allowance for depreciation during 1879. Other years derived by addition of net capital expenditures, col. 8, this table.

3 For 1913–50, Table E–2; for 1880–1912, Table E–7.

4 Col. 3 deflated by index of cost of plant and equipment (Tables E–8 and E–9).

5 Col. 6 inflated by above index.

6 Capital consumption as derived in 1880 dollars (Tables E–10 and E–12), adjusted to 1929 dollars by use of the index of plant and equipment costs for the year 1929 on an 1880 base (Table E–8).

7, 8 Col. 3 minus col. 5; col. 4 minus col. 6.

TABLE E–2

Gross Capital Expenditures, Current Dollars, Telephones, 1913–1950

(in millions)

	BELL SYSTEM			TELEPHONE INDUSTRY			
						A.T. & T.	
Year	*Cash, Excluding Re-Used Equipment* (1)	*Including Re-Used Equipment* (2)	*Ratio of Column 1 to Column 2* (3)	*Including Re-Used Equipment* (4)	*Cash, Excluding Re-Used Equipment* (5)	*Estimate of Cash Expenditures* (6)	*Gross Capital Expenditures* (7)
1913		94.0			95.0		95.0
1914		87.5		96.5	89.3		89.3
1915		71.3		77.0	71.2		71.2
1916		108.4		117.5	108.7		108.7
1917		149.7		165.0	152.6		152.6
1918		116.5		128.5	118.9		118.9
1919		122.2		132.0	122.1		122.1
1920	169	183.0	92.3	204	188.3		188.3
1921	193	208.5	92.6	230	213.0		213.0
1922	226	244.8	92.3	266	245.5		245.5
1923	286	306.8	93.2	320	298.2		298.2
1924	347	372.2	93.2	386	359.8		359.8
1925	341	370.9	91.9	387	355.7		355.7
1926	357	391.1	91.3	407	371.6		371.6
1927	340	383.6	88.6	399	353.6		353.6
1928	386	438.6	88.0	460	404.8		404.8
1929	541	602.2	89.8	620	556.8		556.8
1930	520	583.8	89.1	616	548.9		548.9
1931	319	388.1	82.2	410	337.0		337.0
1932	165	237.2	69.6	255	177.5		177.5
1933	94	160.1	58.7	167	98.0		98.0
1934	107	171.0	62.6	180	112.7		112.7

(concluded on next page)

TABLE E–2 (concluded)

	BELL SYSTEM			TELEPHONE INDUSTRY			
Year	*Cash, Excluding Re-Used Equipment* (1)	*Including Re-Used Equipment* (2)	*Ratio of Column 1 to Column 2* (3)	*Including Re-Used Equipment* (4)	*Cash, Excluding Re-Used Equipment* (5)	A.T. & T. *Estimate of Cash Expenditures* (6)	*Gross Capital Expenditures* (7)
1935	117	185.0	63.2	207	130.8		130.8
1936	165	239.3	69.0	262	180.8		180.8
1937	242	322.8	75.0	349	261.8		261.8
1938	220	296.3	74.2	319	236.7		236.7
1939						250	250.0
1940						310	310.0
1941						450	450.0
1942						370	370.0
1943						165	165.0
1944						185	185.0
1945						275	275.0
1946						730	730.0
1947						1,260	1,260.0
1948						1,551	1,551.0
1949						1,150	1,150.0
1950						945	945.0

NOTES BY COLUMN

1, 2, 4, 6 Obtained directly from A.T. & T., except that data for 1914–19 in column 4 are A.T. & T. data as given by Lowell J. Chawner in *Construction Activity in the United States, 1915–37* (Department of Commerce).

5 Col. 4 times col. 3 except as follows: For 1913, the average ratio, 1914–17, of col. 5 to col. 2, multiplied by the 1913 figure in col. 2. For 1914–19, col. 4 times the average 1920–21 ratio of cash expenditures to expenditures including re-used equipment in col. 3 (92.5 per cent).

7 For 1913–38, col. 5; for 1939–50, col. 6.

TABLE E–3

Derivation of Value of Plant and Equipment,
Telephones, December 31, 1880

(*millions of dollars*)

1. Total assets, telephone industry, June 1, 1880, reported in the 1880 census		15.7
2. Assets, American Bell Telephone Company reported in the 1880 census	9.5	
3. Value of plant and equipment, American Bell Telephone Company, February 28, 1881, from FCC Exhibit 1360–A	1.4	
4. Value of plant and equipment, American Bell Telephone Company, June 1, 1880, estimated	1.0	
5. Estimated value of all assets of American Bell Telephone Company, June 1, 1880 (line 4 divided by 0.64, the ratio of plant and equipment including land and excluding general equipment to total assets of the Bell system in 1885), FCC Exhibit 1360–A	1.6	
6. Estimated write-ups, American Bell Telephone Company assets, June 1, 1880 (line 2 minus line 5)	7.9	
7. Assets, telephone industry, June 1, 1880, for companies reporting to the census (line 1 minus line 6)	7.8	
8. Assets, telephone industry, June 1, 1880, all companies (line 7 divided by 0.78, the ratio of miles of wire for companies reporting financial data in the 1880 census to miles of wire for all companies)		10.0
9. Value of plant and equipment, telephone industry, June 1, 1880 (line 8 times 0.64)		6.4
10. Value of plant and equipment, telephone industry, end of 1880 (line 9 plus 3.2 millions, the estimated growth in the remainder of the year)		9.6

NOTES TO TABLE E–4,

BY COLUMN

1 For 1880, Table E–3, line 10. For 1885–1917, FCC Exhibit 1360–A, revised figure for 1895 supplied by A.T. & T. For 1881–84, linear interpolation between data for 1880 and 1885.

2 Col. 1 adjusted to exclude land and include general equipment (col. 1 times 0.98). General equipment accounted for 1.61 per cent and land for 3.58 per cent of the total value of plant and equipment for the Bell system in 1913–14 (FCC Exhibit 1364).

3 Includes land. The 1902 figure is that shown by the census for systems with incomes of 5,000 dollars or more since it exceeds the total dollars shown by census for all systems. The figures for 1907 and 1917 are as reported by the census. The 1912 total was derived from the census figure for systems with incomes of 5,000 or more (1,081.4 millions) and the average ratio, for 1907 and 1917, of value of plant and equipment for all companies to the figures for companies with incomes of 5,000 or more; the basic figures are (in millions of dollars):

	All Companies	*Companies with Incomes of 5,000 or More*
1907	820.4	794.1
1917	1,492.3	1,435.9

4 Necessarily includes general equipment for Bell system. For 1902, 1907, 1912, 1917: col. 3 minus col. 1. For 1903–16, derived by linear interpolation; for 1894–1901, derived by linear interpolation between 1902 and an estimate of 1.2 millions for Bell system general equipment in 1893 (1.6 per cent of col. 1).

5 Col. 1 plus col. 4.

6 For 1880–93, col. 2; for 1894–1917, col. 5 times 0.964, the ratio of plant and equipment, excluding land to the total including land for the Bell system, 1913–14 (FCC Exhibit 1364).

TABLE E–4

Derivation of Value of Plant and Equipment, Original Cost Dollars, Telephones, 1880–1917

(in millions)

End of Year	BELL SYSTEM: Including Land and Excluding General Equipment (1)	BELL SYSTEM: Excluding Land and Including General Equipment (2)	CENSUS TOTAL (3)	NON-BELL ENTERPRISES (4)	TELEPHONE INDUSTRY: Including Land (5)	TELEPHONE INDUSTRY: Excluding Land (6)
1880	9.6	9.4				9.4
1881	15.4	15.1				15.1
1882	21.2	20.8				20.8
1883	27.0	26.5				26.5
1884	32.8	32.1				32.1
1885	38.6	37.8				37.8
1886	38.3	37.6				37.6
1887	40.8	40.0				40.0
1888	44.4	43.5				43.5
1889	51.8	50.5				50.5
1890	58.5	57.3				57.3
1891	62.2	60.9				60.9
1892	67.6	66.3				66.3
1893	73.1	71.6				71.6
1894	77.7			17.6	95.3	91.9
1895	84.6			34.0	118.6	114.3
1896	95.2			50.4	145.6	140.4
1897	104.5			66.8	171.3	165.1
1898	118.1			83.2	201.3	194.1
1899	145.5			99.6	245.1	236.3
1900	180.7			116.0	296.7	286.0
1901	211.8			132.4	344.2	331.8
1902	250.0		399.0	149.0	399.0	384.6
1903	284.6			182.7	467.3	450.5
1904	316.5			216.4	532.9	513.7
1905	368.1			250.0	618.1	595.8
1906	450.0			283.7	733.7	707.3
1907	503.0		820.4	317.4	820.4	790.9
1908	528.7			329.5	858.2	827.3
1909	557.4			341.6	899.0	866.6
1910	611.0			353.7	964.7	930.0
1911	666.7			365.8	1,032.5	995.3
1912	742.3		1,120.6	378.3	1,120.6	1,080.5
1913	797.2			388.1	1,185.3	1,142.6
1914	847.2			397.9	1,245.1	1,200.3
1915	880.1			407.7	1,287.8	1,241.4
1916	946.3			417.5	1,363.8	1,314.7
1917	1,064.9		1,492.3	427.4	1,492.3	1,438.6

(notes to Table E–4 on previous page)

TABLE E-5
Depreciation Rates, Telephones, 1880–1950

(*per cent*)

Year	*Rate*	*Year*	*Rate*
1880	10.00	1915	6.80
1881	9.91	1916	6.71
1882	9.82	1917	6.62
1883	9.73	1918	6.53
1884	9.64	1919	6.43
1885	9.54		
1886	9.45	1920	6.34
1887	9.36	1921	6.25
1888	9.27	1922	6.16
1889	9.18	1923	6.07
		1924	5.98
1890	9.09	1925	5.89
1891	8.99	1926	5.79
1892	8.90	1927	5.70
1893	8.81	1928	5.61
1894	8.72	1929	5.52
1895	8.63		
1896	8.54	1930	5.43
1897	8.45	1931	5.34
1898	8.35	1932	5.25
1899	8.26	1933	5.15
		1934	5.06
1900	8.17	1935	4.97
1901	8.08	1936	4.88
1902	7.99	1937	4.79
1903	7.90	1938	4.70
1904	7.81	1939	4.61
1905	7.71		
1906	7.62	1940	4.51
1907	7.53	1941	4.42
1908	7.44	1942	4.33
1909	7.35	1943	4.24
		1944	4.15
1910	7.26	1945	4.06
1911	7.17	1946	3.97
1912	7.07	1947	3.87
1913	6.98	1948	3.78
1914	6.89	1949	3.69
		1950	3.60

For 1880, the rate is based on information provided by A.T. & T. whose records indicate that in 1884 the comptroller of the American Bell Telephone Company had suggested that a depreciation rate of 10 per cent was applicable to the original cost of plant and equipment.

For 1950: FCC has prescribed depreciation rates for various kinds of plant and equipment. These rates are based on engineering studies of wear, tear, obsolescence, inadequacy, and a knowledge of technical progress in the industry. The rates prescribed for ten companies averaged 3.5995 of plant and equipment, excluding land, during 1950.

Rates for the intervening years (1881–1949) were obtained by linear interpolation.

TABLE E–6

Derivation of Relationship between Retirements and Depreciation, Original Cost Dollars

(financial data in millions)

Year	*Value of Plant and Equipment December 31* (1)	*Change in Value of Plant and Equipment from Preceding Year* (2)	*Gross Capital Expenditures* (3)	*Retirements* (col. 3 minus col. 2) (4)	*Depreciation* (5)	*Ratio, Retirements to Depreciation* (col. 4 ÷ col. 5) (6)
1912	1,080.5					
1913	1,142.6	62.1	95.0	32.9	75.4	0.436
1914	1,200.3	57.7	89.3	31.6	78.7	0.402
1915	1,241.4	41.1	71.2	30.1	81.6	0.369
1916	1,314.7	73.3	108.7	35.4	83.3	0.425
1917	1,438.6	123.9	152.6	28.7	87.0	0.330
					Average	0.391

NOTES BY COLUMN

1 From Table E–4, column 6.
3 From Table E–2.
5 Column 1 for preceding year end times the depreciation rates shown in Table E–5.

APPENDIX E

TABLE E–7

Gross Capital Expenditures, Current Dollars, Telephones, 1880–1912

(in millions)

Year	*Book Value of Plant and Equipment* (end of year) (1)	*Change in Book Value of Plant and Equipment* (2)	*Retirement Rate* (per cent) (3)	*Retirements* (4)	*Gross Capital Expenditures* (5)
1880	9.4	5.5			5.50
1881	15.1	5.7	3.96	0.37	6.07
1882	20.8	5.7	3.93	0.59	6.29
1883	26.5	5.7	3.89	0.81	6.51
1884	32.1	5.6	3.85	1.02	6.62
1885	37.8	5.7	3.82	1.22	6.92
1886	37.6	−0.2	3.78	1.43	1.23
1887	40.0	2.4	3.74	1.41	3.81
1888	43.5	3.5	3.71	1.48	4.98
1889	50.5	7.0	3.67	1.60	8.60
1890	57.3	6.8	3.63	1.83	8.63
1891	60.9	3.6	3.59	2.06	5.66
1892	66.3	5.4	3.56	2.17	7.57
1893	71.6	5.3	3.52	2.33	7.63
1894	91.9	20.3	3.48	2.49	22.79
1895	114.3	22.4	3.45	2.62	25.02
1896	140.4	26.1	3.41	2.83	28.93
1897	165.1	24.7	3.37	4.74	29.44
1898	194.1	29.0	3.34	5.51	34.51
1899	236.3	42.2	3.30	6.40	48.60
1900	286.0	49.7	3.26	7.71	57.41
1901	331.8	45.8	3.23	9.23	55.03
1902	384.6	52.8	3.19	10.58	63.38
1903	450.5	65.9	3.15	12.12	78.02
1904	513.7	63.2	3.12	14.03	77.23
1905	595.8	82.1	3.08	15.81	97.91
1906	707.3	111.5	3.04	18.12	129.62
1907	790.9	83.6	3.00	21.25	104.85
1908	827.3	36.4	2.97	23.46	59.86
1909	866.6	39.3	2.93	24.24	63.54
1910	930.0	63.4	2.89	25.08	88.48
1911	995.3	65.3	2.86	26.57	91.87
1912	1,080.5	85.0	2.82	28.07	113.07
1913			2.78		
1914			2.75		
1915			2.71		
1916			2.67		
1917			2.64		

(Notes to Table E–7 on next page)

Figures shown have been rounded.

NOTES BY COLUMN

1 From Table E–4, col. 6.

2 First differences in data in col. 1. Value of plant and equipment at the end of 1879, 3.9 millions, is an approximation suggested by fragmentary data for capitalization of predecessor companies of A.T. & T. prior to 1880 (FCC report).

3 Forty per cent of the depreciation rate, Table E–5.

4 Col. 3 times the value of plant and equipment at preceding year end. It was assumed no retirements were made prior to 1881. In 1894–96 retirements relate to Bell system plant only. With the expiration of a basic Bell patent in 1893, competing enterprises entered the telephone industry. It is assumed that the new companies retired no plant during the first three years of their existence. The basic figures for the value of plant and equipment for the Bell system are (in millions of dollars): for 1893, 71.6; for 1894, 92.4; and for 1895, 115.3.

5 Col. 2 plus col. 4.

TABLE E–8

Derivation of Plant and Equipment Cost Indexes, 1915–1950, Telephones

(Columns 1–4, 1915 = 100)

Year	*Telephone Apparatus* (1)	*Commercial Buildings* (2)	*Telephone Poles in Place* (3)	*Wages in Building Trades* (4)	*Construction Cost Index* 1915 = 100 (5)	1880 = 100 (6)	1929 = 100 (7)
1915	100.0	100.0	100.0	100.0	100.00	130.06	66.32
1916	102.0	109.9	102.0	103.2	103.59	134.73	68.70
1917	132.3	121.1	117.0	109.7	124.37	161.76	82.49
1918	139.4	123.1	142.0	121.8	134.47	174.89	89.18
1919	143.4	129.2	168.0	139.5	144.73	188.24	95.99
1920	178.8	160.7	212.0	188.2	182.83	237.79	121.26
1921	189.9	144.5	220.0	191.7	187.40	243.73	124.29
1922	177.8	134.5	170.0	179.8	168.88	219.65	112.01
1923	166.7	150.7	177.0	198.7	170.15	221.30	112.85
1924	163.6	149.2	189.0	214.5	172.71	224.63	114.55
1925	158.6	148.4	185.0	222.9	170.68	221.99	113.20
1926	148.5	155.3	180.0	237.4	167.58	217.95	111.14
1927	140.4	151.4	183.0	245.4	164.19	213.55	108.90
1928	126.3	150.7	181.0	247.1	156.29	203.27	103.66
1929	116.2	154.6	174.0	250.5	150.78	196.10	100.00
1930	115.2	153.1	166.0	260.8	150.34	195.53	99.71
1931	125.3	138.4	149.0	261.6	151.26	196.73	100.32
1932	126.3	120.7	126.0	223.4	139.98	182.06	92.84
1933	127.3	119.2	125.0	217.2	139.23	181.08	92.34
1934	144.4	131.5	137.0	218.8	152.52	198.37	101.16
1935	146.5	128.3	139.0	221.2	153.85	200.08	102.03
1936	142.4	129.2	135.0	229.3	152.34	198.13	101.04
1937	126.7	143.8	141.0	245.2	149.18	194.02	98.94
1938	126.8	147.7	144.0	266.9	153.53	199.68	101.83
1939	129.1	149.9	138.0	268.8	154.51	200.96	102.48
1940	121.1	150.7	134.0	273.1	150.28	195.45	99.67
1941	130.5	158.3	154.0	283.1	161.08	209.50	106.83
1942	119.4	176.0	179.0	300.8	164.04	213.35	108.80
1943	119.4	183.1	188.0	303.0	166.79	216.93	110.62
1944	119.4	184.6	203.0	305.4	169.62	220.61	112.50
1945	119.4	185.3	213.0	311.8	172.19	223.95	114.20
1946	145.5	222.9	226.0	347.6	199.50	259.47	132.32
1947	168.2	272.1	247.0	397.6	230.02	299.16	152.55
1948	149.5	292.2	260.0	439.5	230.98	300.41	153.19
1949	152.0	293.7	271.0	457.8	236.98	308.22	157.17
1950	165.4	289.8	291.0	478.0	249.79	324.88	165.67

NOTES BY COLUMN

1 For 1915–36: Developed by Western Electric; includes all types of switchboards, substations, outside equipment, telephones, and miscellaneous. From *Telephone Investigation, Special Investigation Docket #1, Report on American Telephone and Telegraph Company, Profits and Price Trends* (Federal Communications Commission, June 14, 1937), Exhibit #2091, Appendix O, Sheets 1 and 2. Net change for 1937–50 was supplied by A.T. & T.

2 George A. Fuller Co. index composite of thirty-six major cost elements in warehouses, office, and loft buildings based on annual averages (of irregularly compiled indexes) published by the *Engineering News-Record* and shown in *Construction Volume and Costs, 1915–1950* (Department of Commerce, May 1951), Statistical Supplement to Construction and Building Materials.

(Notes continue on bottom of next page)

TABLE E–9

Derivation of Plant and Equipment Cost Index, 1878–1915, Telephones

(*1880 = 100, except Column 5*)

Year	*Electrical Equipment* (1)	*Construction Materials* (2)	*Wages in Building Trades* (3)	*Construction Cost Index* 1880 = 100 (4)	1929 = 100 (5)
1878	89.15	87.89	98.33	90.83	46.32
1879	85.82	87.25	96.66	88.60	45.18
1880	100.00	100.00	100.00	100.00	50.99
1881	91.92	98.91	112.19	98.27	50.11
1882	93.81	103.20	115.20	101.20	51.61
1883	89.06	100.39	116.34	98.12	50.04
1884	79.35	95.72	118.09	92.29	47.06
1885	75.74	93.28	119.08	90.02	45.91
1886	74.50	94.30	119.35	89.72	45.75
1887	74.69	93.07	119.21	89.45	45.61
1888	75.74	92.18	119.78	89.87	45.83
1889	74.22	91.43	119.21	88.77	45.27
1890	75.38	90.68	121.03	89.55	45.67
1891	68.60	86.27	122.16	85.16	43.43
1892	67.82	81.65	124.67	84.07	42.87
1893	67.92	81.10	124.77	83.99	42.83
1894	72.19	77.01	121.78	84.40	43.04
1895	59.49	76.05	122.77	77.88	39.71
1896	52.71	77.23	124.67	75.16	38.33
1897	72.28	72.18	126.41	84.16	42.92
1898	77.81	75.19	128.28	88.20	44.98
1899	83.43	86.81	131.40	94.90	48.39
1900	82.45	92.29	137.14	97.14	49.54
1901	81.58	86.81	142.87	96.48	49.20
1902	79.84	88.74	151.11	97.92	49.93
1903	74.99	90.89	158.23	97.59	49.77
1904	80.52	87.89	161.84	100.39	51.19
1905	80.32	93.58	164.97	102.52	52.28
1906	79.07	103.91	174.95	106.88	54.50
1907	82.74	108.64	180.43	111.22	56.72
1908	76.55	100.36	192.12	108.41	55.28
1909	85.56	101.97	201.36	115.47	58.88
1910	85.65	104.99	209.37	118.09	60.22
1911	94.76	104.34	212.45	123.24	62.85
1912	88.66	105.44	217.38	121.51	61.96
1913	96.89	107.53	222.29	127.34	64.94
1914	97.08	100.14	227.23	126.54	64.53
1915	102.31	101.78	229.07	130.06	66.32

Columns 1, 2, and 3 are from Table D–6, base shifted to 1880.

Column 4 is derived from indexes in columns 1, 2, and 3, weighted 51, 27, and 22, respectively.

3 Interstate Commerce Commissi on records. Simple average of cost indexes for eight regions for creosoted poles, given equal weight with simple average of untreated western cedar pole cost indexes for eight regions.

4 Bureau of Labor Statistics union wage rates in building trades.

5 Derived from indexes in columns 1, 2, 3, and 4 using weights of 50, 18, 18, and 14, respectively, for 1915–24, and of 55, 15, 15, and 15 for 1925–50.

APPENDIX E

TABLE E–10

Derivation of Capital Consumption, 1880–1917, 1880 Dollars
(*financial data in millions*)

Year	*Gross Physical Assets, End of Year, 1880 Dollars* (1)	*Retirements, 1880 Dollars* (2)	*Gross Capital Expenditures, 1880 Dollars* (3)	*Net Additions to Plant and Equipment, 1880 Dollars* (4)	*Depreciation Rate* (per cent) (5)	*Depreciation, 1880 Dollars* (6)
1879	4.39	–				
1880	9.89	–	5.50	5.50	10.00	0.44
1881	15.68	0.39	6.18	5.79	9.91	0.98
1882	21.28	0.62	6.22	5.60	9.82	1.54
1883	27.08	0.83	6.63	5.80	9.73	2.07
1884	33.21	1.04	7.17	6.13	9.63	2.61
1885	39.63	1.27	7.69	6.42	9.54	3.17
1886	39.50	1.50	1.37	−0.13	9.45	3.75
1887	42.28	1.48	4.26	2.78	9.36	3.70
1888	46.25	1.57	5.54	3.97	9.27	3.92
1889	54.24	1.70	9.69	7.99	9.18	4.24
1890	61.91	1.97	9.64	7.67	9.09	4.93
1891	66.33	2.23	6.65	4.42	8.99	5.57
1892	72.97	2.36	9.00	6.64	8.90	5.91
1893	79.48	2.57	9.08	6.51	8.81	6.43
1894	103.71	2.77	27.00	24.23	8.72	6.93
1895	132.89	2.95	32.13	29.18	8.63	8.95
1896	168.16	3.22	38.49	35.27	8.54	11.35
1897	197.47	5.67	34.98	29.31	8.45	14.20
1898	230.01	6.59	39.13	32.54	8.35	16.50
1899	273.63	7.59	51.21	43.62	8.26	19.01
1900	323.80	8.93	59.10	50.17	8.17	22.36
1901	370.40	10.44	57.04	46.60	8.08	26.16
1902	423.31	11.81	64.72	52.91	7.99	29.59
1903	489.89	13.37	79.95	66.58	7.90	33.43
1904	551.53	15.28	76.93	61.64	7.81	38.24
1905	630.03	17.00	95.50	78.50	7.71	42.55
1906	732.12	19.18	121.27	102.09	7.62	48.03
1907	804.37	22.02	94.27	72.25	7.53	55.14
1908	835.70	23.88	55.21	31.33	7.44	59.85
1909	866.22	24.51	55.03	30.52	7.35	61.41
1910	916.05	25.09	74.92	49.83	7.26	62.86
1911	964.40	26.19	74.54	48.35	7.17	65.64
1912	1,030.24	27.22	93.06	65.84	7.07	68.22
1913	1,076.15	28.69	74.60	45.91	6.98	71.94
1914	1,117.19	29.53	70.57	41.04	6.89	74.16
1915	1,141.69	30.25	54.75	24.50	6.80	75.97
1916	1,191.88	30.49	80.68	50.19	6.71	76.59
1917	1,254.82	31.40	94.34	62.94	6.62	78.87

(Notes to Table E–10 on next page)

Figures shown have been rounded; data were originally calculated with greater detail.

NOTES BY COLUMN

1 For 1879: Based on totals of estimates of capital expenditures for 1878 and 1879, deflated to 1880 dollars. It was assumed that no retirements were made during these years. The estimates of capital expenditures for 1878 and 1879 were suggested by fragmentary data available on capitalization of predecessor companies of the A.T. & T. prior to 1881 (FCC report). Capital expenditures in 1877 were under 100,000 dollars. The estimates, in original cost prices (millions of dollars), are

	Value of Plant and Equipment December 31	*Gross Capital Expenditures*
1878	0.4	0.4
1879	3.9	3.5

For other years, preceding year-end value plus col. 4.

2 Column 1 for preceding year times column 3 of Table E–7. It was assumed no retirements were made prior to 1881. For 1894–96, retirements were computed from data for the Bell system alone. Companies outside the Bell system first came into operation in 1894; it is assumed that such companies made no retirements during their first three years of operation. The procedure was the same as that followed for the industry as a whole. Gross physical assets for the industry as a whole at the end of 1893 are also gross physical assets for the Bell system. The basic figures for the Bell system alone are (in millions of dollars):

	Gross Capital Expenditures, Current Dollars	*Gross Capital Expenditures,* 1880 Dollars	*Retirements,* 1880 Dollars	*Gross Physical Assets, End of Year,* 1880 Dollars
1893				79.48
1894	7.4	8.77	2.77	85.48
1895	9.4	12.07	2.95	94.60
1896	13.2		3.22	

3 Current dollar figures in Tables E–2 and E–7 deflated by use of the construction cost index in Tables E–8 and E–9.

4 Column 3 minus column 2.

5 Table E–5.

6 Column 5 times column 1 for preceding year end.

TABLE E–11

Derivation of Retirements, 1880 Dollars, 1917–1950

(financial data in millions)

End of Year	Value of Plant and Equipment, Including Land: Class A Carriers (1)	Value of Plant and Equipment, Including Land: All Companies (2)	Percentage Devoted to Land & Right of Way (3)	Value of Plant & Equip., Excl. Land (4)	Net Change in Value of Plant & Equip. from Preceding Date Shown (5)	Gross Capital Expend., Total from Preceding Date Shown, Original Cost (6)	Retirements, Original Cost, Total from Preceding Date Shown (7)	Estimated Life of Retired Property (years) (8)	Index of Original Cost of Retirements (1880 = 100) (9)	Retirements, 1880 Dollars, Total from Preceding Date Shown (10)
1917		1,492.3	3.58	1,438.9						
1918										
1919										
1920						887.8	192.5	16	102.63	187.57
1921										
1922		2,205.2	3.22	2,134.2	695.3					
1923										
1924										
1925						1,738.8	425.6	17	112.06	379.80
1926										
1927		3,548.9	2.86	3,447.4	1,313.2					
1928										
1929										
1930						2,025.0	800.3	19	120.32	665.14
1931										
1932		4,791.9	2.50	4,672.1	1,224.7					
1933										
1934										
1935						784.1	561.5	20	149.47	375.66
1936										
1937	4,687.7	5,001.8	2.14	4,894.7	222.6					

(concluded on next page)

End of Year	Value of Plant and Equipment, Including Land: Class A Carriers (1)	All Companies (2)	Percentage Devoted to Land & Right of Way (3)	Value of Plant & Equip., Excl. Land (4)	Net Change in Value of Plant & Equip. from Preceding Date Shown (5)	Gross Capital Expend., Total from Preceding Date Shown, Original Cost (6)	Retirements, Original Cost, Total from Preceding Date Shown (7)	Estimated Life of Retired Property (years) (8)	Index of Original Cost of Retirements (1880 = 100) (9)	Retirements, 1880 Dollars, Total from Preceding Date Shown (10)
1938	4,796.8	5,118.2	2.06	5,012.8	118.1	236.7	118.6	21	169.69	69.89
1939	4,904.8	5,233.5	1.99	5,129.4	116.6	250.0	133.4	22	169.69	78.61
1940	5,071.3	5,411.1	1.91	5,307.7	178.3	310.0	131.7	22	178.73	73.69
1941	5,389.3	5,750.4	1.84	5,644.6	336.9	450.0	113.1	23	178.73	63.28
1942	5,648.2	6,026.7	1.76	5,920.6	276.0	370.0	94.0	23	187.48	50.14
1943	5,745.1	6,130.1	1.76	6,022.2	101.6	165.0	63.4	24	187.48	33.82
1944	5,852.8	6,245.0	1.76	6,135.1	112.9	185.0	72.1	24	196.25	36.74
1945	6,057.0	6,462.9	1.76	6,349.2	214.1	275.0	60.9	25	196.25	31.03
1946	6,682.0	7,129.7	1.76	7,004.2	655.0	730.0	75.0	26	196.25	38.22
1947	7,786.2	8,307.9	1.76	8,161.7	1,157.5	1,260.0	102.5	26	204.25	50.18
1948	9,106.0	9,716.2	1.76	9,545.2	1,383.5	1,551.0	167.5	27	204.25	82.00
1949	9,983.5	10,652.5	1.76	10,464.0	918.8	1,150.0	231.2	28	204.25	113.19
1950		11,418.9	1.76	11,217.9	753.9	945.0	191.1	28	211.41	90.39

Data in columns 5–7 and 10 for 1922–37 are totals for the five-year periods 1918–22, 1923–27, 1928–32, and 1933–37; figures for 1938–50 are for a one-year period.

NOTES BY COLUMN

1 From Statistics of the Communications Industry in the United States, Federal Communications Commission.

2 For 1917–37, Bureau of the Census; for 1938–49, figure for class A Carriers (col. 1) blown up by the ratio of total to class A (col. 2 divided by col. 1) in 1937; for 1950, FCC total for class A and B carriers (10704.1 millions) raised by use of the ratio of the 1949 figure for class A and B to the 1949 total (0.9374).

3 For 1917, based on data in FCC Exhibit 1364 for 1913–14 (Schedule A–6); for 1942–50, from same source as in col. 1. Ratios for 1922–41 were derived by linear interpolation.

4 Col. 2 times the difference 100 minus col. 3.

6 Table E–2.

7 Col. 6 minus col. 5.

8 Reciprocals of depreciation rates, Table E–5.

9 Derived from the construction cost index (Tables E–8 and E–9) by use of the formula

$$P_{ON} = \frac{P_{CN-L-5} + P_{CN-L-4} + \cdots + P_{CN-L} + \cdots + P_{CN-L+5}}{11}$$

where P_{ON} is the original cost of retirements made during year N, P_{CN} is the index of cost of construction in the year N, and L is the life in years of property retired in the year N (col. 8). Before 1938, the middle year of each five-year period is taken as the year N (1920 for 1918–22, 1925 for 1923–27, etc.).

10 Col. 7 divided by col. 9.

TABLE E-12

Derivation of Capital Consumption, 1917–1950, 1880 Prices

(*financial data in millions of dollars*)

Year	*Gross Capital Expenditures, 1880 Dollars* (1)	*Retirements, 1880 Dollars* (2)	*Gross Physical Assets, End of Year* (3)	*Depreciation Rate* (per cent) (4)	*Capital Consumption, 1880 Prices* (5)
1917			1,254.82		
1918				6.53	81.88
1919					83.45
1920	411.18 (1918–1922)	187.57 (1918–1922)			85.02
1921					86.58
1922			1,478.43		88.15
1923				6.07	89.72
1924					93.12
1925	803.36 (1923–1927)	379.80 (1923–1927)			96.52
1926					99.92
1927			1,901.99		103.32
1928				5.61	106.72
1929					108.77
1930	1,032.58 (1928–1932)	665.14 (1928–1932)			110.82
1931					112.87
1932			2,269.43		114.92
1933				5.15	116.97
1934					115.15
1935	402.48 (1933–1937)	375.66 (1933–1937)			113.32
1936					111.50
1937			2,296.25		109.77
1938	118.54	69.89	2,344.90	4.70	107.85
1939	124.40	78.61	2,390.69	4.61	107.99
1940	158.60	73.69	2,475.60	4.51	107.91
1941	214.78	63.28	2,627.10	4.42	109.48
1942	173.42	50.14	2,750.38	4.33	113.79
1943	76.06	33.82	2,792.62	4.24	116.61
1944	83.86	36.74	2,839.74	4.15	115.84
1945	122.79	31.03	2,931.50	4.06	115.20
1946	281.34	38.22	3,174.62	3.97	116.24
1947	421.22	50.18	3,545.66	3.87	122.98
1948	516.33	82.00	3,979.99	3.78	134.11
1949	373.06	113.19	4,239.86	3.69	146.90
1950	290.87	90.39	4,440.34	3.60	152.61

NOTES BY COLUMN

1 Derived from series in Table E–2, col. 7, deflated to 1880 by means of the construction cost index in Table E–8, col. 6.

2 From Table E–11, col. 10.

3 For 1917, Table E–10. For other years, derived by adding capital expenditures (col. 1) and deducting retirements (col. 2).

4 From Table E–5.

5 1918, 1923, 1928, 1933, and 1938–50 derived from col. 3 for preceding year end times col. 4; other years of period 1918–38 obtained by linear interpolation between available years.

APPENDIX F

Notes and Tables on the Derivation of Capital Formation Data for Street and Electric Railways

Scope of the Industry

FOLLOWING census practice, we have defined this industry to take in all privately owned railways within city limits, whatever the type of motive power, and all privately owned electric railways, whether located within or without city limits. Included are horse roads; cable roads; elevated steam railroads within cities; and electric railways, both surface, and subway and elevated. Investment in bus lines is excluded, as are the light and power departments of electric railways. Electrified divisions of steam roads are considered part of the industry only in those cases in which the road is solely electric and is conducted as a complete and separate operating unit.

Gross Capital Expenditures: Definition

Gross capital expenditures, as used in this report, represent all expenditures chargeable to capital account for additions, betterments, and replacements of road and equipment, with the exception of expenditures for land. Expenditures for original track are treated as capital expenditures, but replacement of track is considered a maintenance expense.

In the earlier years, there was a tendency among some companies to charge to current expense *all* expenditures for replacements.[1] As a result, gross capital expenditures in this period tend to be understated—a factor which has been taken into account in the derivation of estimates of capital consumption and net capital expenditures.

On the other hand, reports of gross capital expenditures for the early years tend to be overstated because many of the street railways were built under contract in speculative ventures, and the contractor was paid in stock of the operating company. The stock "payments" did not represent cash outlays and were, of course, considerably in excess of actual cash invested.

[1] See Report of Committee on a Standard System of Street Railway Accounting made to the Street Railway Accountants Association of America (1899) and American Street and Interurban Railway Accountants Association, Classification of Operating Expenses, Operating Revenues, and Expenditures for Road and Equipment for the Use of Electric Railways (1909).

Gross Capital Expenditures, 1922–1941

Data on capital expenditures for local transit facilities for 1922–41 were obtained from the reports of surveys made by the *Transit Journal* and its predecessor, the *Electric Railway Journal* (both, McGraw-Hill). Coverage of the surveys was variable, but the reported figures were adjusted by the two journals to represent estimated complete coverage of the industry. For the first year of the surveys, the reports received accounted for 20 per cent of the estimated total capital expenditures of the industry; by 1926, the reports covered approximately one-half the total electric railway mileage.

A number of adjustments of the reported figures were necessary, as shown in Table F–2. The data given for 1929–41 were corrected to exclude some expenditures for steam railroad electrification and some expenditures of public funds for rapid transit construction (columns 2 and 3); the approximate amounts involved were determined from the text discussions in the above-mentioned journals. The published figures were also adjusted to exclude expenditures for buses and other bus property (columns 4, 5, and 6). Figures available for expenditures for buses were raised to allow for other bus property, by the use of data compiled for bus companies in New York State in 1948. Finally, the series compiled by the *Transit Journal* and *Electric Railway Journal* include expenditures for Canada; these were eliminated by applying the ratio of average track-mileage for 1923–32 in the United States to the average for the United States and Canada together.

Gross Capital Expenditures, 1942–1950

Gross capital expenditures for 1942–49 are based on series compiled by the American Transit Association; the derivation of the data for these years is shown in Table F–3. The ATA figures include all expenditures for local transit made by electric railway, bus, and trolley bus lines, including expenditures by municipalities. Expenditures for buses are shown separately; total expenditures for bus property were obtained from the expenditures for buses and the ratio of investment in all bus property to investment in buses alone (columns 2 and 3). A special tabulation of expenditures for city-owned transit systems in cities with more than 100,000 population was provided by the ATA; the tabulation includes expenditures for both bus and rail systems. Since expenditures for all bus lines have already been deducted, we deduct only the estimated expenditures for city-owned rail systems.

Since data of the American Transit Association were available only through 1949 (and only partially in the latter year), a special estimate was required for 1950. It was prepared on the basis of the relationship during 1947–49 between capital expenditures, adjusted for price changes, and a series, available annually, on the number of surface railway cars and trolley coaches delivered.

Gross Capital Expenditures, 1870–1921

GROSS CAPITAL EXPENDITURES INCLUDING LAND, FOR SELECTED YEARS

Gross capital expenditures for the years ending June 30, 1902 and December 31, 1907 were derived primarily from data reported by the census for cost of construction and equipment during the year. The census figures were first adjusted to include expenditures of a small number of companies which did not report any financial data to the census. This adjustment, made on the basis of track-mileage, is shown in lines 1 to 6 of Table F–4.

A more important adjustment of the census data was necessary in order to include expenditures of companies with roads under construction at the close of the census year (Table F–4). The census canvasses were confined to properties in operation at some time during the census year, and no returns were obtained from roads under construction. Reports to the state railroad commissions of Massachusetts and New York provided some data with which to estimate such expenditures. The ratio of expenditures of roads under construction to those of roads in operation in the two states[2] was applied to the totals for expenditures of roads in operation in the United States to derive an estimate of expenditures in the United States for new roads.[3]

[2] For 1902, the comparison was based on the ratio between capital expenditures of roads not in operation and capital expenditures of roads in operation, as reported to the state railroad commissions. For 1907, gross capital expenditures of roads not in operation in the two states, as reported to the state commissions, were compared with gross capital expenditures of roads in operation as reported to the census. No complete tabulation of state reports was made in this study for the year 1907, but the 1902 data reported to the state commissions are in close accord with the figures reported by the census.

[3] It was necessary to take special account of two companies—the Interborough Rapid Transit Company of New York, for 1902, and the Hudson and Manhattan Company of New York and New Jersey for 1907. The Interborough was formed in 1902 and listed under physical assets 2½ million dollars, which represented the cost of the lease. This figure was not included in tabulating the ratio of expenditures of roads under construction to expenditures of roads in operation, since it is believed that its inclusion would tend to overstate expenditures for new roads. The sum was, however, added to the estimated gross capital expenditures of other roads under construction in deriving estimates of total gross capital expenditures of these roads (see Table F–4, line 6).

For 1907 (line 6d), it was necessary to make a separate estimate of expenditures of the

For the years 1870, 1881, 1890, 1896, and 1913, estimates of gross capital expenditures were derived from compilations of data on capital expenditures for individual companies reporting to state railroad commissions. The available samples accounted for the following percentages of total cost of road and equipment in the United States as a whole, as reported by the census:

1890	47.9
1896	37.3 (estimated—no census figure available)
1913	56.5

Gross capital expenditures for the United States were derived by applying the ratio of capital expenditures to the value of physical assets for the sample to the value of physical assets for the United States as a whole.[4]

The first step was to compile total physical assets for the United States as a whole. Physical assets for the United States were reported by the census for 1890 and a figure for the year ending June 30, 1913 may be readily derived from the census total for the year ending December 31, 1912. Estimates for the close of the calendar years 1870 and 1881 and for the year ending June 30, 1896 are shown in Table F–5; they were obtained by use of data shown in reports of the state railroad commissions.

Table F–6 shows the derivation of gross capital expenditures for

---

Hudson and Manhattan Company of New York and New Jersey, which opened the first part of its tunnel system in 1908. Since the total cost of the road was over 100 million dollars, a sizable volume of capital expenditures was doubtless made during the year 1907. Data for the value of road and equipment as of June 1906 are available for two of the three companies which were consolidated into the Hudson and Manhattan Company in December 1906, but for June 1907 and later years the only reported figure is the estimated cost of the road *when completed*, as measured by the par value of securities issued. Gross capital expenditures for the year ending December 31, 1907 were estimated as one-third the total change in physical assets between June 30, 1906 and June 30, 1909; the system was virtually completed by the latter date. It was necessary to estimate June 30, 1906 physical assets for one of the three constituent companies.

[4] Several alternative methods of inflating the sample figures were examined in detail and tested with census data for 1902 and 1907: (1) Gross capital expenditures per mile of new track for the sample were multiplied by new track-mileage for the United States. (2) Gross capital expenditures per mile of new track for the sample were adjusted to represent expenditures per mile for the United States (by use of the ratio of United States physical assets per mile to sample physical assets per mile) and then multiplied by total new track-mileage. (3) Gross capital expenditures for the sample were inflated by the ratio of the increase in physical assets of the United States since the last census year to the increase in physical assets of the sample states. In every instance, the results obtained by the use of these assumptions for 1902 and 1907, when reported data are available from the census, were less satisfactory than the results obtained by inflating the sample gross capital expenditures by the ratio of United States to sample physical assets.

the years ending December 31, 1870; December 31, 1881; June 30, 1890; June 30, 1896; and June 30, 1913. Gross capital expenditures during the year and the value of physical assets at the close of the reporting year were tabulated for all companies reporting the necessary information in each of the states included. Gross capital expenditures of new roads and of roads under construction were included wherever possible. Physical assets of roads not yet in operation were not included in the asset totals, since assets of such roads are not included in the totals reported by the census.

In order to obtain sufficiently large samples it was necessary in some instances to incorporate data on the change in physical assets during the year to represent gross capital expenditures. The procedure followed in these cases was to tabulate physical assets as of the beginning and end of the year for identical companies in states in which gross capital expenditures were not reported. Companies which underwent consolidation or which failed to report in one of the two years were excluded. Companies newly formed during the reporting year were included. Gross capital expenditures were taken as zero for companies for which assets declined, or showed no change, during the year. The percentage in each year of sample gross capital expenditures estimated by this method (i.e. by use of the change in physical assets) is as follows:

1870	81.5
1881	62.9
1890	0
1896	0
1913	38.3

The use of the change in the value of physical assets to represent gross capital expenditures is of course open to some question. However, a number of factors suggest that the errors involved in the present case are not serious. Errors resulting from the fact that the change in physical assets are equal to gross capital expenditures less retirements are reduced by the failure of many companies in this period to deduct retirements from their property accounts. Moreover, we have eliminated the major source of errors resulting from changes in the valuation of assets by excluding from our tabulations companies which consolidated during the year. The most extensive speculation and write-ups, in any event, occurred outside the period in which we have used the change in the value of physical assets—after 1881 and prior to 1913. Finally, although it is true that we have neglected to include the expenditures of roads which did not experience a gain in physical assets during the year, such roads accounted for but a small proportion of physical assets.[5] Furthermore, the gross capital expenditures of these roads were doubtless much lower (in comparison with their physical assets) than those of others.

Concerning the representativeness of the samples employed, only indirect tests are available. Estimates of United States gross capital expenditures were derived for the years 1902 and 1907 from census data for the three samples employed and were compared with the reported United States totals provided by the census. The percentage errors in the sample estimates are:

	1902	*1907*
Sample I (used for 1870, 1881, 1890)	+17.3	−12.7
Sample II (1896)	+28.0	−15.1
Sample III (1913)	+7.8	+0.4

Though these errors are large, it is interesting that they do not suggest a consistent bias since they are for the most part in different directions in the two years.

DEDUCTION FOR THE VALUE OF LAND

Estimates of the percentage of expenditures devoted to land for 1870, 1881, and 1890 were based in part on a compilation of data for cost of right-of-way and total cost for individual roads shown in the 1890 census report, with animal, electric, cable, and steam roads taken separately, and in part on the relationship between expenditures for right-of-way and total expenditures for *all* land derived from the reports of the railroad commissions of the First and Second Districts of New York State for 1910–13. The New York State reports for 1910–13 were also used for estimating the percentage expenditures for land in the United States as a whole for the year 1913. Estimates for 1896, 1902, and 1907 were derived by linear interpolation between the figures for 1890 and 1913. The percentage expenditures for land for each of the selected years 1870–1913 are shown in column 2 of Table F–7.

DEDUCTION OF CAPITAL EXPENDITURES OF LIGHT AND POWER DEPARTMENTS

The figures reported to the census for years prior to 1922 and, in most instances, those reported to the state railroad commissions

[5] Companies with declines in the value of assets accounted for the following percentages of sample assets:

1870	1.0
1881	5.6
1913	6.0

include the operations of light and power departments producing electric energy for sale. In the preparation of our data, we have treated the light and power departments owned by street railways as part of the electric light and power industry. We therefore deduct the estimated volume of capital expenditures for such establishments from our series on gross capital expenditures of the street railway industry.

The procedure was to recompute the gross increases in value of plant and equipment (net increases plus estimated retirements) for the electric light and power industry, excluding electric light and power departments of street railways, for the various census intervals (Table F–8, line 6). The gross increases in physical assets for the electric light and power departments of street railways (line 8) were compared with the gross increase in physical assets for the entire electric light and power industry (line 7). The ratios derived from this comparison (line 9) were applied to gross capital expenditures of the electric light and power industry for the appropriate years to obtain capital expenditures of light and power departments which must be deducted from the figures for street railways. This adjustment is shown in Table F–9.

GROSS CAPITAL EXPENDITURES, ALL YEARS, 1870–1922

For interpolating capital formation during inter-sample years, data on total length of line are available from the census for 1881–90 and data on track extensions are available from the *Electric Railway Journal* for 1907–22. For 1890–1907 the only series available is a series on total track-mileage shown by the *Electric Railway Journal*. The erratic changes in this series from year to year suggest that coverage is not uniform and preclude its use for the interpolation of capital expenditures.

Accordingly, capital expenditures for 1882–89 and 1908–21 were derived by interpolation between the figures for 1881 and 1890 and between 1907, 1913, and 1922 with a series representing the products of increases in track (net increase in line for 1881–90 and new track extended for 1907–22) and a construction cost index. The procedure is shown in Table F–10. The construction cost index, described below, is shown in Table F–11.

Gross capital expenditures for inter-sample years during 1890–1906 were obtained by simple linear interpolation between the data for the years ending June 30, 1890; June 30, 1896; June 30, 1902; and December 31, 1907. For the years 1871–80 a somewhat different procedure was followed. Both cable roads and elevated steam roads came into existence during the early 1870's; it seems probable that gross capital expenditures during the years between 1870 and 1881 were higher than during either terminal year, and examination of the change in physical assets between 1870 and 1881 suggests that this was the case. Gross capital expenditures in 1881 were first deducted from the increase in physical assets between the close of 1870 and the close of 1881; the remainder was then distributed equally over the ten years 1871–80 inclusive.

CONSTRUCTION COST INDEX

The index of construction costs used in conjunction with the track-mileage figures as an interpolating medium is shown in Table F–11. The index was computed back to 1850 (for convenience in later computations). It is based, for 1850–1915, on the series for (1) cost of road and structures, and (2) cost of equipment developed in the preparation of the construction cost index for steam railroads. These series were combined with weights of 8 and 2 respectively. The weights were obtained from data for total cost of equipment per mile of track and total cost of all facilities per mile of track for street and electric railways for 1886, 1891, 1896, 1901, 1906, and 1911, as reported by the Railroad Commission of Massachusetts. The final index was linked, in 1915, to the Interstate Commerce Commission construction cost index for steam railroads with the base shifted to 1929. The ICC index has been used as the construction cost index for 1915 and subsequent years.

GROSS CAPITAL EXPENDITURES IN 1929 PRICES

Gross capital expenditures in 1929 dollars were derived by deflating the series in current dollars with the construction cost index described above.

Capital Consumption in 1929 Dollars

The procedure followed in obtaining a series for capital consumption involved (1) computing estimates of "physical life" depreciation rates, (2) estimating physical life depreciation for each of the periods 1870–1902 and 1903–49, (3) estimating total capital consumption, including obsolescence, for each of the two periods, and (4) distributing depreciation through obsolescence over the individual years. The year 1902 was selected as the dividing point for the entire period because it may be considered to mark approximately the end of the horse railway. Census data available for this year facilitate the preparation of the necessary estimates.

RATES OF DEPRECIATION

Depreciation rates for all street and electric railways were prepared for 1870, 1881, 1890, 1902, 1912, and 1922 as averages of the rates for the various types of railways. These rates are based largely on estimated physical life of property and do not include obsolescence.

Their derivation is shown in Table F–12. The rate of depreciation for 1922 was obtained by the use of data shown by the Bureau of Internal Revenue in its Bulletin F (1942). This average, which apparently includes track property, was adjusted, with the track accounts assigned a rate of zero.[6]

For 1902, use was made of a compilation of estimates of the life of various elements of street railway property made by a large number of individuals, state commissions, publications, and others.[7] Average depreciation rates for 1902 and 1922 were based on selected items for which comparable data were available. The rate for 1902 was used for the prior years. A rate for 1912 was derived by linear interpolation.

No information is available on the life of horse roads and cable roads, and in the absence of any specific information, the depreciation rates for roads of this type were set at the same level as for electric railways.[8] The depreciation rate for elevated steam lines was set at the same level as for ordinary steam railroads for the same period. A rate for rapid transit lines (elevated and subway electric railways) was placed at 1.00 per cent on the basis of data available for the Hudson and Manhattan Company and the New York City rapid transit lines.

The rates for each type of road for selected years of the period 1870–1922 are shown in columns 8–10 of Table F–12. Depreciation rates for all classes of electric railway property for 1870, 1881, 1890, 1902, 1912, and 1922 (column 11) were derived by combining the rates for (1) animal, cable, and surface electric lines, (2) elevated steam lines, and (3) elevated and subway electric lines in accordance with the estimated physical assets or capitalization for each class of property at each of the dates. The rates for 1870–1902 were reduced by 25 per cent, and the rate for 1912 by 10 per cent to allow for the

[6] Track property is not generally depreciated but is replaced through charges to maintenance.

[7] American Electric Railway Association Procedings, 1912, Report of the Committee on Life of Physical Property.

[8] Some elements in horse railway property were doubtless shorter-lived than those in electric railway property: the cars, for instance, which were lighter. Track was also less durable. On the other hand, horse railways required a large investment in structures for stables, and the life of structures would be substantially greater than that of other classes of property.

fact that many roads charged all, or a large proportion of replacement expenditures to maintenance in this period; no adjustment was required for 1922. Replacement of track is treated as a maintenance expense in all years.

The depreciation rates for the years intervening 1870, 1881, 1890, 1902, 1912, and 1922 were interpolated to provide the series shown in column 3 of Table F–16. The same rate was used for 1922 and subsequent years for two reasons: (1) There was no pronounced change in the technological character of surface electric railway property after this period. (2) While subway and elevated lines became increasingly important in later years and the depreciation rate for this class of property presumably should have a greater weight, much of the increase in the physical assets of rapid transit lines was due to public investment.

GROSS PHYSICAL ASSETS IN 1929 DOLLARS

The next step in the preparation of estimates of capital consumption was the derivation of the property base, that is, the preparation of a series for total physical assets, in constant dollars. Estimates were prepared for the close of 1870 and 1881; for June 30, 1890; for June 30, 1902; quinquennially for the close of the years 1907–47; and for the close of 1949 and 1950.

For 1870, 1881, and 1890, it was assumed that the book values represented original cost. It was therefore necessary only to deduct the estimated value of land and to convert the book values, which are in terms of prices originally paid, to constant prices. Total physical assets in terms of book values are shown in Table F–13, column 1, for each type of road, and the deduction for the value of land is shown in columns 2–4. An index of prices underlying original cost was prepared by averaging the construction cost index for the thirty years preceding each date, using as weights gross capital expenditures in the corresponding year, in constant prices. The figures for original cost of physical assets, excluding land, when divided by the index of prices underlying original cost, yielded estimates of physical assets, in 1929 dollars, for the close of 1870 and 1881 and for June 30, 1890 (column 8).

Since the development of the electric railway had assumed considerable importance by 1902, and write-ups were by that time significantly reflected in the census data, the derivation of an estimate of physical assets in constant dollars for that year presented a special problem. Accordingly, by the use of our estimate of the value (in 1929 dollars) of physical assets in 1890, the percentages of property existing in 1890, which remained in use twelve years later, were estimated for the various types of roads; the details are shown in the note to column 5, Table F–13. To the estimated 1890 property remaining in service in 1902 (in 1929 prices) was added the total gross capital expenditures, in 1929 prices, over the period July 1, 1890–June 30, 1902, to derive total physical assets as of June 30, 1902 (column 8).

Estimates of physical assets for the close of 1907, 1912, and 1917—years of rather steady growth—were prepared by adding to the physical assets for each prior year considered here (1902 for 1907, 1907 for 1912, etc.), the total gross capital expenditures for the intervening years and deducting the estimated value of retirements during the same interval. The derivation of physical assets for these years is shown in Table F–14. Retirements for each period were estimated by the use of data for the value of physical assets in 1929 dollars (column 2) and the depreciation rate (column 3) fifteen years prior to the midpoint of each interval.[9]

After 1917, the development of bus transportation and transportation by auto resulted in a rapid decline in the importance of the electric railway. For this period, there would be serious error in the assumption that physical life of property alone contributed to the volume of retirements. Physical assets were therefore estimated from data on changes in the total mileage of track operated. The derivation of gross physical assets, in 1929 dollars, is shown in Table F–15; for 1922–32 in part A, and for 1937–50 in part B.

It will be noted that in this derivation separate account is taken of subway and elevated track and of surface track during the years 1922–32, with weights assigned in accord with respective per-mile capitalizations. In the 1937–50 period, however, the estimate of physical assets was derived from data for surface track alone, since almost all new investment in subway and elevated lines then was financed with public funds.

As a check on the use of track-mileage to represent gross physical assets, the same method of deriving physical assets for the independently estimated years 1907, 1912, and 1917 was employed, using 1902 as the base for the weighted track series. The figures obtained differ by less than 5 per cent from those derived by the use of retirements and gross capital expenditures.

A final adjustment of the estimates of gross physical assets (Table F–15, part B, column 4) was necessary to take account of transfers

[9] The depreciation rates computed for 1902 and prior years are equivalent to an average life of property of thirty-two to thirty-seven years. Since the value of retirements was computed for data on total physical assets in a prior year, the time span was set at fifteen years.

of electric railway assets from private to public ownership. A number of such transfers occurred in the years following 1917, but it is not possible to make specific allowance for all of them. Account was taken, however, of the two largest sales of street railway property to public authorities—that in New York City in 1940 and that in Chicago in 1947. The cost to New York City was deducted from the estimates of the value of physical assets for 1942 and later years, and the cost to Chicago was deducted for 1947 and 1949.[10]

The series for physical assets compiled in Tables F–13, F–14, and F–15 for selected dates in the period 1870–1949 was interpolated linearly to obtain a complete series for physical assets at the close of each year 1870–1949 (Table F–16, column 1). Average physical assets during each year were obtained from two-year moving averages of this series, centered in the second year (column 2). Estimates of annual depreciation, in 1929 dollars, are shown in column 4. They were prepared from the series on average physical assets during the year and a series for depreciation rates. The latter series is based on the estimates compiled for selected years of the period 1870–1922 in Table F–12, with estimates for intervening years derived by linear interpolation; the same rate was used for 1922 and all subsequent years.

RATES OF OBSOLESCENCE, 1870–1902 AND 1903–1949

One further series of estimates is needed to derive total capital consumption for street and electric railways: capital consumed through obsolescence. Such a series was prepared for each of the two periods 1870–1902 and 1903–49.

Physical assets, in 1929 dollars, less accrued depreciation, were first estimated for the close of 1870, 1902, and 1949. Gross physical assets for these dates are available from Table F–16. The procedure used in estimating total accrued depreciation at the end of the years 1902 and 1949 is shown in Table F–17. In deriving the estimate for 1902, gross capital expenditures in 1902 and prior years were listed back over a period of years so that the total listed equaled the gross physical assets as of the close of 1902. The 1902 depreciation rate (2.93 per cent) was applied to the gross capital expenditures of prior years, with consideration for the age of each year's plant additions

[10] The deductions made are in terms of the actual costs to the two municipalities and do not, strictly speaking, represent gross physical assets in 1929 dollars. But since so many different elements entered into the determination of the prices paid by the municipalities —elements which cannot be considered in detail here—no adjustment was made for the price level underlying the investment in the two transit systems. It is worth noting that a price index underlying original cost for all electric railway property, on the base 1929 = 100, is 90.7 for 1942 and 101.4 for 1947.

by 1902. Similarly, for 1949, accrued depreciation was computed with the use of the 1949 depreciation rate and data on gross capital expenditures of prior years. In this instance, the prior years included date back to 1927.[11]

No information is available to provide a basis for deriving total accrued depreciation for the close of 1870, and an estimate for this date was made on the assumption that the ratio between accrued depreciation and gross physical assets was the same as for 1902. Since total physical assets, in 1929 dollars, for 1870 were very small compared with the 1902 total (137.2 millions compared with 3,127.7 millions), even a large error in the estimate of accrued depreciation for 1870 would not seriously affect that calculation of total capital consumption for the period 1870–1902.

The derivation of total capital consumption and of the obsolescence rates for 1870–1902 and 1903–49 is shown in Table F–18. Total capital consumption for each period (line 5) was computed by adding to net physical assets (line 3) at the beginning of the period (January 1, 1871 and January 1, 1903) the gross capital expenditures during each period (1871–1902 inclusive and 1903–49 inclusive) and subtracting net physical assets at the end of the period (December 31, 1902 and December 31, 1949). From the figures for total capital consumption for each period (line 5) were subtracted the physical life depreciation derived in Table F–16. The remainders (line 7) yielded estimates of capital consumption through obsolescence for each of the two periods—1871 through 1902 and 1903 through 1949. It was assumed that these totals of depreciation through obsolescence were actually incurred, respectively, in the years 1890–1902, when the horsecar and cable car declined most precipitously, and in the years 1920–49, when the electric railway was displaced most rapidly by other means of transportation. An obsolescence *rate* for each period was obtained by dividing the total capital consumption through obsolescence by the average physical assets for each period (line 8) and then by the number of years in each interval. The

[11] The procedure is, of course, based on only a crude model of actual developments. Following our procedure, for example, the installation of property in use in 1902 dates back only to the year 1885, and all property installed during the years 1886–1902 is considered as remaining in use at the close of 1902. Actually, some property installed before 1885 remained in service in 1902 and some installed after 1885 was no longer in use in 1902. Similarly, we assume that property in service at the close of 1949 dates back only to 1927. The simplified model adopted tends to understate total accrued depreciation. To the extent that property was abandoned which was installed during the years considered here (1885–1902 for 1902 and 1927–49 for 1949), property which was installed in earlier years remained in service, with a higher percentage depreciation. The understatement of accrued depreciation is probably greater (percentagewise) for 1949 than for 1902, because of the greater importance of obsolescence in the later period.

obsolescence rates thus derived are 0.49 per cent for 1890–1902, and 1.42 per cent for 1920–49.

The derivation of *total* capital consumption for individual years of the period 1870–1950 is shown in Table F–19.

Net Capital Expenditures in 1929 Dollars

Net capital expenditures in 1929 dollars were obtained by subtracting capital consumption from gross capital expenditures, both in 1929 dollars.

Value of Plant and Equipment in 1929 Dollars

The value of plant and equipment, in 1929 dollars, net of accrued depreciation, was obtained by using as base the figure derived in Table F–18 for December 31, 1870 (January 1, 1871). The figure for January 1, 1870 was obtained by subtracting from this total net capital expenditures for the year 1870; the series for January 1, 1872 and subsequent years was obtained by successive addition to the January 1, 1871 base of net capital expenditures, in 1929 dollars.

Capital Consumption and Net Capital Expenditures in Current Dollars

Net capital expenditures in current dollars was derived by multiplying net capital expenditures in 1929 dollars by the construction cost index shown in Table F–11. Capital consumption in current dollars is the difference between gross capital expenditures and net capital expenditures, both in current dollars.

Value of Plant and Equipment in Current Dollars

The value of plant and equipment at the beginning of each year in current dollars, was obtained from the value of plant and equipment in 1929 dollars and the construction cost index for the year preceding each January 1.

The final figures on capital formation in street and electric railways are given in Table F–1, by years, from 1870 through 1950.

APPENDIX F

TABLE F-1

Value of Road and Equipment, Capital Formation, and Capital Consumption, Street and Electric Railways, Annual Data, 1870–1951

(millions of dollars)

	VALUE OF PLANT AND EQUIPMENT, JANUARY 1		GROSS CAPITAL EXPENDITURES		CAPITAL CONSUMPTION		NET CAPITAL EXPENDITURES	
Year	*Current Dollars* (1)	*1929 Dollars* (2)	*Current Dollars* (3)	*1929 Dollars* (4)	*Current Dollars* (5)	*1929 Dollars* (6)	*Current Dollars* (7)	*1929 Dollars* (8)
1870	64.7	108.2	4.0	7.3	2.2	4.0	1.8	3.3
1871	61.2	111.5	10.3	19.0	2.4	4.5	7.9	14.5
1872	68.3	126.0	10.3	17.5	3.0	5.1	7.3	12.4
1873	81.2	138.4	10.3	17.2	3.4	5.6	6.9	11.6
1874	89.9	150.0	10.3	18.3	3.5	6.2	6.8	12.1
1875	91.1	162.1	10.3	19.3	3.6	6.7	6.7	12.6
1876	93.3	174.7	10.3	20.6	3.6	7.2	6.7	13.4
1877	93.9	188.1	10.3	22.6	3.5	7.7	6.8	14.9
1878	92.6	203.0	10.3	24.3	3.4	8.1	6.9	16.2
1879	92.7	219.2	10.3	24.8	3.6	8.6	6.7	16.2
1880	97.9	235.4	10.3	22.1	4.2	9.1	6.1	13.0
1881	115.8	248.4	7.2	15.4	4.4	9.5	2.8	5.9
1882	119.0	254.3	13.6	28.2	5.0	10.4	8.6	17.8
1883	131.4	272.1	10.9	23.1	5.5	11.7	5.4	11.4
1884	133.8	283.5	10.5	23.3	5.8	12.9	4.7	10.4
1885	132.5	293.9	14.6	33.0	6.3	14.2	8.3	18.8
1886	138.5	312.7	17.8	40.1	6.8	15.4	11.0	24.7
1887	149.8	337.4	31.5	71.4	7.3	16.6	24.2	54.8
1888	173.0	392.2	29.2	66.1	7.9	17.8	21.3	48.3
1889	194.7	440.5	35.1	80.1	8.4	19.1	26.7	61.0
1890	219.7	501.5	43.4	99.1	11.0	25.1	32.4	74.0
1891	252.1	575.5	53.1	124.1	12.8	30.0	40.3	94.1
1892	286.6	669.6	62.8	149.9	15.2	36.2	47.6	113.7
1893	328.2	783.3	72.5	174.3	17.6	42.4	54.9	131.9
1894	380.7	915.2	82.2	205.0	19.5	48.7	62.7	156.3
1895	429.7	1,071.5	92.0	231.2	21.9	55.0	70.1	176.2
1896	496.6	1,247.7	102.1	253.3	24.8	61.5	77.3	191.8
1897	580.1	1,439.5	106.5	270.3	26.8	68.0	79.7	202.3
1898	646.9	1,641.8	110.8	272.2	30.4	74.6	80.4	197.6
1899	748.6	1,839.4	115.2	260.6	35.9	81.3	79.3	179.3
1900	892.3	2,018.7	119.6	258.9	40.6	88.0	79.0	170.9
1901	1,011.6	2,189.6	123.9	269.9	43.5	94.8	80.4	175.1
1902	1,085.4	2,364.7	132.8	280.2	48.7	102.7	84.1	177.5
1903	1,205.0	2,542.2	146.1	300.0	46.7	95.8	99.4	204.2
1904	1,337.5	2,746.4	159.5	328.2	50.8	104.5	108.7	223.7
1905	1,443.5	2,970.1	172.8	342.9	57.0	113.1	115.8	229.8
1906	1,612.7	3,199.9	186.2	343.5	65.9	121.6	120.3	221.9
1907	1,854.6	3,421.8	199.5	355.6	73.3	130.6	126.2	225.0
1908	2,045.9	3,646.8	130.6	234.5	76.0	136.5	54.6	98.0
1909	2,085.9	3,744.8	83.0	144.6	80.2	139.8	2.8	4.8

(continued on next page)

TABLE F–1 (continued)

Year	VALUE OF PLANT AND EQUIPMENT, JANUARY 1		GROSS CAPITAL EXPENDITURES		CAPITAL CONSUMPTION		NET CAPITAL EXPENDITURES	
	Current Dollars (1)	*1929 Dollars* (2)	*Current Dollars* (3)	*1929 Dollars* (4)	*Current Dollars* (5)	*1929 Dollars* (6)	*Current Dollars* (7)	*1929 Dollars* (8)
1910	2,152.3	3,749.6	123.6	209.1	84.6	143.1	39.0	66.0
1911	2,255.0	3,815.6	103.9	177.3	85.7	146.3	18.2	31.0
1912	2,254.1	3,846.6	76.7	128.3	89.4	149.5	−12.7	−21.2
1913	2,287.6	3,825.4	100.6	163.8	92.3	150.3	8.3	13.5
1914	2,357.1	3,838.9	94.6	159.3	88.9	149.7	5.7	9.6
1915	2,286.0	3,848.5	99.2	164.8	90.0	149.6	9.2	15.2
1916	2,325.9	3,863.7	81.6	117.7	103.2	148.8	−21.6	−31.1
1917	2,656.0	3,832.6	123.9	144.9	127.0	148.5	−3.1	−3.6
1918	3,273.8	3,829.0	143.5	137.7	153.7	147.5	−10.2	−9.8
1919	3,979.6	3,819.2	80.6	69.3	168.9	145.2	−88.3	−75.9
1920	4,353.5	3,743.3	131.5	96.6	306.7	225.3	−175.2	−128.7
1921	4,919.5	3,614.6	94.3	88.5	237.9	223.2	−143.6	−134.7
1922	3,709.6	3,479.9	132.8	138.6	212.4	221.7	−79.6	−83.1
1923	3,254.1	3,396.8	149.3	140.1	235.9	221.3	−86.6	−81.2
1924	3,534.4	3,315.6	109.8	104.8	229.9	219.4	−120.1	−114.6
1925	3,354.6	3,201.0	99.2	98.0	220.2	217.6	−121.0	−119.6
1926	3,118.4	3,081.4	90.2	89.1	218.3	215.7	−128.1	−126.6
1927	2,990.3	2,954.8	106.8	104.9	217.7	213.8	−110.9	−108.9
1928	2,897.1	2,845.9	106.4	107.7	206.8	209.3	−100.4	−101.6
1929	2,711.4	2,744.3	106.2	106.2	202.2	202.2	−96.0	−96.0
1930	2,648.3	2,648.3	100.7	104.5	188.0	195.1	−87.3	−90.6
1931	2,465.6	2,557.7	76.1	84.7	168.9	188.0	−92.8	−103.3
1932	2,204.1	2,454.4	38.3	46.8	148.0	180.8	−109.7	−134.0
1933	1,900.4	2,320.4	24.9	31.1	138.3	172.7	−113.4	−141.6
1934	1,745.2	2,178.8	41.1	48.8	137.7	163.4	−96.6	−114.6
1935	1,740.1	2,064.2	54.8	64.1	131.8	154.1	−77.0	−90.0
1936	1,687.9	1,974.2	64.4	74.8	124.7	144.8	−60.3	−70.0
1937	1,639.5	1,904.2	64.0	69.4	125.0	135.6	−61.0	−66.2
1938	1,694.6	1,838.0	54.4	60.6	114.7	127.7	−60.3	−67.1
1939	1,590.3	1,770.9	67.0	74.6	108.9	121.3	−41.9	−46.7
1940	1,548.3	1,724.2	62.1	67.4	100.2	108.7	−38.1	−41.3
1941	1,250.9	1,356.7	36.3	36.5	95.4	96.0	−59.1	−59.5
1942	1,289.4	1,297.2	8.2	7.2	101.6	89.6	−93.4	−82.4
1943	1,376.4	1,214.8	13.9	11.5	101.9	84.5	−88.0	−73.0
1944	1,375.9	1,141.8	15.5	12.8	97.7	80.7	−82.2	−67.9
1945	1,300.5	1,073.9	22.9	18.2	96.9	77.0	−74.0	−58.8
1946	1,278.0	1,015.1	39.2	28.0	102.4	73.2	−63.2	−45.2
1947	1,355.9	969.9	49.7	32.1	105.1	67.9	−55.4	−35.8
1948	1,311.0	846.9	42.8	25.3	101.4	59.9	−58.6	−34.6
1949	1,375.2	812.3	20.6	12.1	86.9	51.1	−66.3	−39.0
1950	1,313.8	773.3	4.9	2.8	47.2	27.2	−42.3	−24.4
1951	1,299.3	748.9						

(Notes to Table F–1 on next page)

All data exclude investment in land and landrights. Series for value of plant and equipment are net of accrued depreciation. Excludes publicly owned facilities.

NOTES BY COLUMN

1 Col. 2 inflated by index of cost of road and equipment (Table F–11) for the year preceding each January 1.

2 For 1871, Table F–18 (figure for December 31, 1870). For 1870, value of plant and equipment in 1871 minus net capital expenditures in 1870. Figures for other years were derived by successive addition of each year's net capital expenditures. For 1941, the cost of New York City lines transferred to public ownership in 1940 was deducted (326.2 millions); for 1948, the cost of Chicago lines transferred to public ownership in 1947 was deducted (87.2 millions).

3 Table F–9 (1870); Table F–10 (1881–89 and 1907–22); Table F–2 (1922–41); Table F–3 (1942–50). Data for 1871–80 were obtained by deducting gross capital expenditures in 1881 from the total increase in physical assets excluding land between 1870 and 1881 (Table F–13, col. 4) and distributing the remainder equally over the ten-year period; data for the calendar years 1890–1906 were obtained by linear interpolation between estimates for the years ending June 30, 1890, 1896, and 1902, and December 31, 1907 (shown in Table F–9).

4 Col. 3 deflated by the index of cost of road and equipment (Table F–11).

5 Col. 3 minus col. 7.

6 Table F–19.

7 Col. 8, inflated by the index of cost of road and equipment (Table F–11).

8 Col. 4 minus col. 6.

TABLE F–2

Gross Capital Expenditures, Street and Electric Railways, 1922–1941

(thousands of dollars)

Year	*Gross Capital Expenditures as Reported, United States and Canada* (1)	*Deductions for Expenditures of Steam Railroads and City Governments* (2)	*Gross Capital Expenditures Less Deductions* (col. 1 minus col. 2) (3)	*Expenditures for Buses* (4)	*Total Expenditures for Bus Property, United States and Canada* (5)	*Gross Capital Expenditures, Street Railways, United States and Canada* (col. 3 minus col. 5) (6)	*Gross Capital Expenditures, Street Railways, United States* (7)
1922	151,000	none	151,000	9,017	10,925	140,075	132,763
1923	180,000	none	180,000	18,509	22,426	157,574	149,349
1924	133,200	none	133,200	14,285	17,308	115,892	109,842
1925	123,630	none	123,630	15,680	18,998	104,632	99,170
1926	116,380	none	116,380	17,540	21,251	95,129	90,163
1927	130,052	none	130,052	14,368	17,408	112,644	106,764
1928	135,350	none	135,350	19,100	23,142	112,208	106,351
1929	135,470	2,420	133,050	17,300	20,961	112,089	106,238
1930	124,500	2,200	122,300	13,280	16,090	106,210	100,666
1931	132,230	37,984	94,246	11,540	13,982	80,264	76,074
1932	60,850	11,360	49,490	7,510	9,099	40,391	38,283
1933	46,190	6,907	39,283	10,720	12,988	26,295	24,922
1934	78,180	13,740	64,440	17,430	21,118	43,322	41,061
1935	116,730	24,923	91,807	28,040	33,973	57,834	54,815
1936	109,374	none	109,374	34,150	41,376	67,998	64,449
1937	100,510	...	100,510	27,250	33,016	67,494	63,971
1938	83,473	2,047	81,426	19,801	23,991	57,435	54,437
1939	107,384	...	107,384	30,300	36,711	70,673	66,984
1940	113,649	...	113,649	39,734	48,142	65,507	62,088
1941	105,287	...	105,287	55,250	66,941	38,346	36,344

NOTES BY COLUMN

1 From the *Transit Journal* and its predecessor, *Electric Railway Journal* (both, McGraw-Hill). Figures for 1934 and prior years include expenditures for locomotives; data for 1935 and subsequent years do not include such expenditures.

2 Data compiled by the *Transit Journal* and *Electric Railway Journal* for 1929–41 include some expenditures for steam railroad electrification and for subways built with city funds. Complete data on amount of such expenditures are not available, but the *Transit Journal* presented some of this information in text discussions.

The following adjustments were made:

For 1929 and 1930: Expenditures for locomotives deducted (*Transit Journal*, January 1936, p. 9).

For 1931: Deductions of 23,830,000, Pennsylvania Railroad, and 14,154,000, New York City (*Transit Journal*, January 1932, p. 9).

For 1932: Deductions of 8,320,000 and 1,540,000, Pennsylvania Railroad, and of 1,500,000, Reading Company.

For 1933: Expenditures for locomotives deducted, 2,780,000 (*Transit Journal*, January 1936). Two-thirds of expenditures for power, or 6,190,000, deducted. (*Transit Journal*, January 1934, states that power expenditures were "mainly" for trolley buses in New York City, and Pennsylvania Railroad.)

For 1934: Expenditures for locomotives deducted (*Transit Journal*, January 1936).

For 1935: Deductions of 20,000,000, New York City, and of one-third of expenditures for power, or 14,770,000. (*Transit Journal*, January 1934, indicates a "large portion" of power expenditures were for New York City and Pennsylvania Railroad.)

For 1936: No deductions needed (*Transit Journal*, January 1937).

For 1938: Deduction of the increase, between 1937 and 1938, in expenditures for ways and structures. (*Transit Journal*, January 1939, states that New York City and Philadelphia accounted for the increase in this item.)

For 1937 and 1939–41: No information available.

4 For 1925–41, from *Transit Journal* and *Electric Railway Journal*. The reported figures for 1922–24 show only combined totals for cars and buses, as follows (in thousands): 1922, 38,000; 1923, 78,000; 1924, 60,200. Deduction for the cost of cars was made by multiplying the above figures by 0.2373, the ratio in 1925 of expenditures for buses to expenditures for cars and buses.

5 Column 4 multiplied by 1.2116, the estimated ratio of expenditures for all bus property to expenditures for buses alone. This ratio was derived from data on total investment in bus property and investment in revenue vehicles for New York State companies at the end of 1948 (annual report of the New York State Public Service Commission).

7 Column 6 multiplied by 0.9478, the ratio of average track-mileage during the period 1923–32 in the United States to the average for United States and Canada together, obtained from data shown in the *Transit Journal*, January 1932.

TABLE F–3

Gross Capital Expenditures, Street and Electric Railways, 1942–1950

(thousands of dollars)

Year	*Gross Capital Expenditures, All Local Transit* (1)	*Expenditures for Buses* (2)	*Total Expenditures for Bus Property* (3)	*Expenditures for Electric Railways* (col. 1 minus col. 3) (4)	*Expenditures for City-Owned Transit Systems* (5)	*Expenditures for Privately Owned Transit Systems* (col. 1 minus col. 5) (6)	*Estimated Ratio, Expenditures for Railways to Total Transit Expenditures, Private Lines* (7)	*Expenditures for Privately Owned Electric Railways* (8)
1942	90,990	66,900	81,056	9,934	16,000	74,990	0.10918	8,187
1943	39,300	19,000	23,020	16,280	5,700	33,600	.41425	13,919
1944	65,592	39,162	47,449	18,143	9,500	56,092	.27660	15,515
1945	83,010	47,500	57,551	25,459	8,300	74,710	.30670	22,914
1946	143,700	84,500	102,380	41,320	7,500	136,200	.28754	39,163
1947	281,260	182,040	220,560	60,700	51,000	230,260	.21581	49,692
1948	241,500	107,300	130,005	111,495	83,000	158,500	.27002	42,798
1949	176,400	46,400	56,218	120,182	100,000	76,400	.27002	20,630
1950								4,900

NOTES BY COLUMN

1, 2 American Transit Association. Data include expenditures of municipalities. Figures for 1949 are estimates based on forecasts of prospective expenditures; the survey on which data for prior years are based was discontinued after 1948.

3 Col. 2 multiplied by 1.2116, estimated ratio of expenditures for all bus property to expenditures for buses alone. Based on New York State data for 1948 on investment in buses and in all bus property.

5 Special tabulation prepared by American Transit Association.

7 For 1942–47, col. 4 divided by col. 1. For 1948–49, average of the ratios for 1945–47.

8 For 1942–49, col. 6 times col. 7. For 1950, estimate based on (1) the product of the number of surface railway and trolley coaches delivered, and the construction cost index, and (2) the average ratio, for 1947–49, between capital expenditures and comparable data for equipment delivered, adjusted for construction costs. The basic figures are:

	Cars delivered, surface railway and trolley bus (1)	*Construction costs* (1929 = 100) (2)	*Col. 1* × *Col. 2* (3)	*Expenditures* (millions) (4)	*Ratio,* Col. 4 to Col. 3 (5)
1947	1,581	154.8	2,447	49.7	0.02031
1948	1,908	169.3	3,230	42.8	.01325
1949	953	169.9	1,619	20.6	.01272
1950	183	173.5	318		
			Average 1947–49		.01543

TABLE F–4

Gross Capital Expenditures Including Land, Street and Electric Railways, 1902 and 1907

(*thousands of dollars*)

	YEAR ENDING	
	June 30, 1902	*December 31, 1907*
1. Track-mileage, total	22,576.99	34,403.56
2. Track-mileage of companies reporting financial data	22,198.09	34,110.61
3. Ratio, line 1 to line 2	1.01707	1.00859
4. Gross capital expenditures, companies reporting financial data	126,682	184,918
5. Gross capital expenditures, all companies in operation (line 3 times line 4)	128,844	186,506
6. Gross capital expenditures, roads under construction		
(a) Ratio, gross capital expenditures of roads under construction to those of roads in operation, New York and Massachusetts	0.03989	0.03001
(b) First estimate, gross capital expenditures, roads under construction (line 5 times line 6a)	5,140	5,597
(c) Add gross capital expenditures, Interborough Rapid Transit, New York	2,500	–
(d) Add gross capital expenditures, Hudson and Manhattan, New York and New Jersey		29,618
(e) Total gross capital expenditures, roads under construction (sum of lines 6b, 6c, and 6d)	7,640	35,215
7. Total gross capital expenditures, including land (line 5 plus line 6e)	136,484	221,721

Lines 1, 2, and 4 from Census of Street and Electric Railways.

Line 6a: For 1902, based on data tabulated from reports of individual companies to the state railroad commissions. The 1902 expenditure figure for New York excludes expenditures of the Interborough Rapid Transit Company. For 1907, based on expenditures of roads under construction as reported to the state railroad commissions and expenditures of roads in operation as reported to the census. Excludes Hudson and Manhattan Company.

Line 6c, from report of the New York State Railroad Commission. Expenditures of this company were not included in computing the ratio of line 6a, since their inclusion would tend to overstate capital expenditures of roads not yet in operation.

Line 6d: Capital expenditures not reported. Expenditures were estimated as one-third of the change in physical assets between June 30, 1906 (for the three constituent companies which formed the Hudson and Manhattan Company in December 1906) and June 30, 1909 when the road was virtually completed.

For two of the constituent companies (Hudson and Manhattan Railroad Company and the New York and New Jersey Railroad Company) the cost of road and equipment on June 30, 1906 was reported by the New York Railroad Commission. For the third company (Hoboken and Manhattan Railroad Company), the cost of road and equipment as of December 1905 was reported by the New Jersey Railroad Commission. This figure was extended to June 30, 1906 on the basis of the relative change over this six-month period in the physical assets of the Hudson and Manhattan Railroad Company.

TABLE F–5

Book Values, Street and Electric Railways, Selected Years, 1870–1902

(*thousands of dollars*)

	YEAR ENDING				
	December 31, 1870	*December 31, 1881*	*June 30, 1890*	*June 30, 1896*	*June 30, 1902*
1. Connecticut	...	...	2,032	18,585	42,778
2. Massachusetts	5,306	9,829	24,128	58,292	108,581
3. New York	23,481	72,689	147,527	303,309	497,715
4. Pennsylvania	6,899	11,503	17,804	...	...
5. Sum of lines 2, 3, 4	35,686	94,021	189,459		
6. Sum of lines 1, 2, 3			173,687	380,186	649,074
7. United States total			389,357		2,167,634
Physical assets, sample states as ratio to United States					
8. Sample, sum of lines 2, 3, 4	0.48659	0.48659	0.48659		
9. Sample, sum of lines 1, 2, 3			0.44609	0.37277	0.29944
10. Book values, United States	73,339	193,224	389,357	1,019,894	2,167,634

NOTES BY LINE

1–4 Total physical assets of all roads reporting to state railroad commissions during the respective years, including roads which did not report gross capital expenditures, but excluding roads under construction. A single date has arbitrarily been assigned to the state data available for each year, although the reporting period actually varies from state to state. Data for Pennsylvania, 1881, refer to the year ending December 31, 1880. Reference is to the year ending September 30 in these cases: Massachusetts, 1870, 1881, 1890, and 1896; New York, 1870 and 1881; Connecticut, 1896.

No data are available from the Connecticut report for 1890; the figure shown above is from the census. For 1902, physical assets reported by the state commission is in close agreement with the census figure.

7 U.S. Census, Street and Electric Railways.

8 For 1890, line 5 divided by line 7. The 1890 ratio was extrapolated to 1881 and 1870.

9 For 1890 and 1902, line 6 divided by line 7. The average of the 1890 and 1902 ratios was used for 1896.

10 For 1890 and 1902, from line 7; for 1870 and 1881, line 5 divided by line 8; for 1896, line 6 divided by line 9.

TABLE F–6

Gross Capital Expenditures, Including Land and Including Power Departments, Street and Electric Railways; Selected Years, 1870–1913

(*thousands of dollars*)

	YEAR ENDING				
	December 31, 1870	*December 31, 1881*	*June 30, 1890*	*June 30, 1896*	*June 30, 1913*
1. Gross capital expenditures, sample	2,181	3,950	19,477	38,993	59,839
2. Physical assets, sample	35,403	95,688	186,401	380,031	2,611,354
3. Ratio, gross capital expenditures to physical assets, sample (line 1 divided by line 2)	0.06160	0.04128	0.10449	0.10260	0.02291
4. Physical assets, United States	73,339	193,224	389,357	1,019,894	4,624,602
5. Gross capital expenditures, United States, including land (line 3 times line 4)	4,518	7,976	40,684	104,641	105,950

The sample (lines 1 and 2) includes all companies in the following states for the respective years 1870, 1881, and 1890, Massachusetts, New York, Pennsylvania; 1896, Connecticut, Massachusetts New York; 1913, Connecticut, Massachusetts, Michigan, New York, Wisconsin (gross capital expenditures reported), and California, Illinois, Ohio, and Pennsylvania (gross capital expenditures estimated from changes in physical assets). Data on gross capital expenditures and physical assets were tabulated from statistics for individual companies shown in reports of the various state railroad commissions Gross capital expenditures of new roads and of roads under construction were included where possible physical assets of roads not in operation were not included in total physical assets, in order to conform with census practice. Gross capital expenditures for New York for 1870 and 1881 and for four state for 1913 (California, Illinois, Ohio, Pennsylvania) were estimated from the total increase in physical assets during the year for all identical companies with an increase in physical assets plus the expenditures of roads newly constructed during the year. Gross capital expenditures of new roads and road under construction were estimated in the following instances: For 1890, expenditures of roads not in operation in New York were derived from the increases in physical assets for identical companies showing an increase plus the physical assets for companies formed during the year; the same procedure was followed for the Second District of New York (the area outside New York City) for 1913. For Connecticut and Michigan, gross capital expenditures of roads not in operation for 1913 were derived from physical assets as of June 30, 1913 shown by new companies which reported for the first time in 1914.

For dates of state reports that vary from the dates assigned in the table, see first paragraph of note to Table F–5.

Total physical assets (line 4) through 1896 are from Table F–5. For 1913, the census figure (in thousands) reported as of December 31, 1912—4,596,563—was multiplied by 1.0061, the ratio, for the sample companies, of physical assets June 30, 1913 to estimated physical assets December 31, 1912. Physical assets for the sample as of December 31, 1912 were estimated from the figure for June 30, 1913 and 1/2 the change June 30, 1912–June 30, 1913.

TABLE F–7

Gross Capital Expenditures Excluding Land, but Including Power Departments, Street and Electric Railways; Selected Years, 1870–1913

Year Ending	*Cost of Right of Way As Per Cent of Gross Capital Expenditures* (1)	*Cost of Right of Way and Other Land As Per Cent of Gross Capital Expenditures* (2)	*Gross Capital Expenditures Including Land* (3)	*Expenditures for Land* (col. 2 × col. 3 ÷ 100) (4)	*Gross Capital Expenditures Excluding Land* (col. 3 minus col. 4) (5)
December 31, 1870	7.94	11.9	4,518	538	3,980
December 31, 1881	6.69	10.0	7,976	798	7,178
June 30, 1890	1.73	2.6	40,684	1,058	39,626
June 30, 1896		3.0	104,641	3,139	101,502
June 30, 1902		3.4	136,484	4,640	131,844
December 31, 1907		3.8	221,721	8,425	213,296
June 30, 1913		4.2	105,950	4,450	101,500

NOTES BY COLUMN

1 Based on averages of percentages for the various types of roads—animal 7.94, electric 0.29, cable 7.44, steam 0.09. These percentages were derived from data for individual roads tabulated from the 1890 census reports; the sample tabulated included all roads with physical assets of $500,000 or more and represented 76 per cent of the industry total.

The 1870 percentage is for roads operated by animal power. The 1881 figure is an average of the percentages for animal roads (weight 70), cable roads (weight 15), and steam roads (weight 15). The weight for steam roads is based on the gross capital expenditures of elevated steam roads in New York (the only steam roads of importance for this period) as a percentage of gross capital expenditures of all street and electric railways in the United States. The weight for cable roads was assumed equal to that for steam since the two groups were of approximately equal importance; the remaining weight was assigned to animal roads.

For 1890, the average is based on the percentages for electric roads (weight 6), steam roads (weight 2), cable roads (weight 1), and horse roads (weight 1). The weight for steam roads is based on the ratio of gross capital expenditures of New York elevated steam roads to the United States total for all roads; nominal weights were assigned to cable and horse roads; and the remaining weight was assigned to electric roads.

2 For 1870, 1881, and 1890, column 1 multiplied by 1.5, the ratio of expenditures for right of way and other land for New York State, 1910–13, to expenditures for right of way alone. This ratio was obtained from data shown in reports made to the New York State Public Service Commissions for the First and Second Districts for years ending June 30, 1910–13.

The 1913 figure is based on data for New York State for 1910–13; and 1896, 1902, and 1907 were derived by linear interpolation.

3 Table F–4 (1902 and 1907) and Table F–6 (other years).

TABLE F-8

Adjustment of Capital Expenditures to Exclude Power Departments: Ratio of Gross Capital Expenditures of Street Railway Light and Power Departments to Total Electric Light and Power Expenditures

(*financial data in thousands of dollars*)

	January 1, 1881– June 30, 1902	*July 1, 1902– December 31, 1907*	*January 1, 1908– December 31, 1912*
1. Net increase in value of plant and equipment, electric light and power industry, as reported to census	482,720	571,314	1,044,579
2. Net increase in value of plant and equipment, electric light and power industry, adjusted to include light and power departments of street railways	521,869	644,420	1,178,701
3. Line 2, excluding value of land	493,469	607,020	1,107,501
4. Line 1, excluding value of land	456,449	538,160	981,478
5. Retirements, electric light and power	46,380	43,922	103,078
6. Gross increase in physical assets, electric light and power industry, excluding power departments of street railways (sum of lines 4 and 5)	502,829	582,082	1,084,556
7. Gross increase in physical assets, electric light and power industry, including power departments of street railways	543,610	654,504	1,220,298
8. Gross increase in physical assets, power departments of street railways (line 7 minus line 6)	40,782	72,422	135,742
9. Ratio, gross capital expenditures of power departments of street railways to total gross capital expenditures, electric light and power industry (line 8 divided by line 7)	0.07502	0.11065	0.11124

NOTES BY LINE

1 Successive reports of the Census of Electrical Industries.

2, 3 Table D–3.

4 Line 1 times the ratios of line 3 to line 2.

5 Computed from the values in line 4 (which represent the increases in the value of physical assets for the electric light and power industry, excluding power departments of street railways) in the manner shown in Table D–11.

7 Table D–10, part B.

TABLE F–9

Adjustment of Gross Capital Expenditures, Street and Electric Railways, to Exclude Expenditures for Power Departments

(*thousands of dollars*)

		Gross Capital Expenditures, Street and Electric Railways (1)	*Gross Capital Expenditures, Electric Light and Power Industry* (2)	*Ratio, GCE of Power Departments of Street Railways to Total in Column 2* (3)	GCE *of Power Departments of Street Railways Included in Electric Light and Power Industry* (4)	*Gross Capital Expenditures Street and Electric Railways, Excluding Amounts for Electric Power Departments* (5)
1870	Calendar year	3,980	...	...	...	3,980
1881	Calendar year	7,178	206	0.07502	15	7,163
1890	Year ending June 30	39,626	14,549	.07502	1,091	38,535
1896	Year ending June 30	101,502	20,846	.07502	1,564	99,938
1902	Year ending June 30	131,844	76,068	.07502	5,707	126,137
1907	Calendar year	213,296	124,992	.11065	13,830	199,466
1913	Year ending June 30	101,500	203,938	.11124	22,686	78,814

NOTES BY COLUMN

1 Table F–7, col. 5.

2 Tables D–13, D–15, D–16. Figures for fiscal years 1890, 1896, and 1913 are averages of the figures for appropriate calendar years. For the fiscal year 1902, one-half the 1901 total was added to the total for the first six months of 1902.

3 Table F–8, line 9.

4 Column 2 multiplied by column 3.

5 Column 1 minus column 4.

TABLE F-10

Gross Capital Expenditures, Street and Electric Railways, 1881–1889, and 1907–1922

(thousands of dollars)

Calendar Year (except as noted)	*Increase in Length of Line or New Track Extended* (miles) (1)	*Index of Construction Costs, 1929 = 100* (2)	*Column 1 × Column 2* (3)	*Gross Capital Expenditures, Selected Years* (4)	*Ratio of Col. 4 to Col. 3, and Interpolations* (5)	*Gross Capital Expenditures* (6)
1881	99.93	46.8	4,676.7	7,163	1.5316	7,163
1882	192.11	48.3	9,278.9		1.4676	13,618
1883	163.94	47.2	7,738.0		1.4035	10,860
1884	174.17	45.1	7,855.1		1.3395	10,522
1885	257.98	44.3	11,428.5		1.2754	14,576
1886	330.29	44.4	14,664.9		1.2114	17,765
1887	621.64	44.1	27,414.3		1.1473	31,452
1888	609.27	44.2	26,929.7		1.0833	29,173
1889	785.62	43.8	34,410.2		1.0192	35,071
1890 (January 1–June 30)	498.36	43.8	21,828.2			
1890 (year ending June 30)			39,033.3	38,535	0.9872	
1907	1,672.0	56.1	93,799	199,466	2.1265	199,466
1908	1,174.5	55.7	65,420		1.9961	130,585
1909	774.7	57.4	44,468		1.8657	82,964
1910	1,204.8	59.1	71,204		1.7353	123,560
1911	1,105.0	58.6	64,753		1.6049	103,922
1912	869.4	59.8	51,990		1.4745	76,659
1913 (year ending June 30)			55,925	78,814	1.4093	
1913 (year ending December 31)	974.9	61.4	59,859		1.6802	100,575

(concluded on next page)

TABLE F-10 (concluded)

Calendar Year (except as noted)	Increase in Length of Line or New Track Extended (miles) (1)	Index of Construction Costs, 1929 = 100 (2)	Column 1 × Column 2 (3)	Gross Capital Expenditures, Selected Years (4)	Ratio of Col. 4 to Col. 3, and Interpolations (5)	Gross Capital Ependitures (6)
1914	716.5	59.4	42,560		2.2219	94,564
1915	596.0	60.2	35,879		2.7636	99,155
1916	356.3	69.3	24,692		3.3053	81,614
1917	376.7	85.5	32,208		3.8470	123,904
1918	313.8	104.2	32,698		4.3888	143,505
1919	140.6	116.3	16,352		4.9305	80,624
1920	176.6	136.1	24,035		5.4722	131,524
1921	147.1	106.6	15,681		6.0139	94,304
1922	211.4	95.8	20,252	132,763	6.5556	132,763

NOTES BY COLUMN

1 For 1881–90: net increase in length of line, derived from data on length of line each year shown in 1890 Census, Vol. 14, Part 1.

For 1907–22: track extensions, from the *Electric Railway Journal*. The 1907 figure is based on total track extensions for the United States and Canada; 1880 miles, times 0.8896, the average ratio for the years 1908–10 of track extended in the United States to track extended in the U.S. and Canada.

2 Table F-11.

3 Column 1 times column 2. Figure for year ending June 30, 1890 obtained by adding one-half the 1889 figure to the figure for January–June 1890; figure for year ending June 30, 1913 is an average of those for the calendar years 1912 and 1913.

4 Tables F-2 (1922) and F-9 (other years).

6 Column 4 for available calendar years; for others, column 3 times column 5.

TABLE F-11

Index of Construction Costs, Street and Electric Railways, 1850–1950

PART A: 1850 through 1915

Year	*Cost of Road and Structures, 1889 = 100* (1)	*Cost of Equipment, 1889 = 100* (2)	*Combined Index of Construction Costs, 1889 = 100* (3)	*Index of Construction Costs, 1929 = 100* (4)
1850	69.3	147.2	84.9	37.2
1851	66.4	131.0	79.3	34.7
1852	67.3	127.7	79.4	34.8
1853	70.8	149.3	86.5	37.9
1854	76.4	161.6	93.4	40.9
1855	72.2	149.3	87.6	38.4
1856	72.0	147.9	87.2	38.2
1857	72.9	145.0	87.3	38.2
1858	70.2	129.3	82.0	35.9
1859	69.7	129.0	81.6	35.7
1860	69.9	128.2	81.6	35.7
1861	72.7	127.0	83.6	36.6
1862	89.8	148.8	101.6	44.5
1863	113.5	181.0	127.0	55.6
1864	133.3	253.8	157.4	68.9
1865	127.2	280.3	157.8	69.1
1866	127.4	247.0	151.3	66.2
1867	126.4	229.3	147.0	64.4
1868	123.5	214.2	141.6	62.0
1869	120.3	202.4	136.7	59.8
1870	112.2	177.9	125.3	54.9
1871	112.6	169.2	123.9	54.2
1872	121.0	186.5	134.1	58.7
1873	123.4	190.5	136.8	59.9
1874	116.5	175.3	128.3	56.2
1875	110.5	167.9	122.0	53.4
1876	104.8	150.9	114.0	49.9
1877	96.6	134.0	104.1	45.6
1878	90.9	120.1	96.7	42.3
1879	90.0	115.6	95.1	41.6
1880	99.5	134.7	106.5	46.6
1881	102.5	123.8	106.8	46.8
1882	106.4	126.4	110.4	48.3
1883	104.7	120.0	107.8	47.2
1884	102.0	106.9	103.0	45.1
1885	100.8	102.1	101.1	44.3
1886	101.6	100.4	101.4	44.4
1887	100.8	100.6	100.8	44.1
1888	100.7	102.1	101.0	44.2
1889	100.0	100.0	100.0	43.8
1890	100.1	100.0	100.1	43.8
1891	97.7	98.2	97.8	42.8
1892	95.5	97.0	95.8	41.9
1893	95.1	94.9	95.1	41.6
1894	91.4	93.0	91.7	40.1
1895	91.1	90.3	90.9	39.8
1896	92.6	89.7	92.0	40.3
1897	89.8	91.1	90.1	39.4
1898	92.4	95.5	93.0	40.7
1899	101.1	100.2	100.9	44.2

(concluded on next page)

TABLE F-11 (concluded)

Year	*Cost of Road and Structures, 1889 = 100* (1)	*Cost of Equipment, 1889 = 100* (2)	*Combined Index of Construction Costs, 1889 = 100* (3)	*Index of Construction Costs, 1929 = 100* (4)
1900	106.6	101.6	105.6	46.2
1901	104.9	104.2	104.8	45.9
1902	109.0	105.4	108.3	47.4
1903	112.8	105.4	111.3	48.7
1904	112.0	106.8	111.0	48.6
1905	116.8	108.9	115.2	50.4
1906	126.9	111.6	123.8	54.2
1907	131.9	113.2	128.2	56.1
1908	130.4	114.9	127.3	55.7
1909	134.5	116.8	131.0	57.4
1910	139.2	118.7	135.1	59.1
1911	139.8	109.9	133.8	58.6
1912	142.1	114.1	136.5	59.8
1913	145.2	120.9	140.3	61.4
1914	142.0	110.0	135.6	59.4
1915	143.7	112.8	137.5	60.2

PART B: 1916–1950,
continuing column 4

Year	*Index of Construction Costs, 1929 = 100* (4)	*Year*	*Index* (4)	*Year*	*Index* (4)
1916	69.3	1930	96.4	1940	92.2
1917	85.5	1931	89.8	1941	99.4
1918	104.2	1932	81.9	1942	113.3
1919	116.3	1933	80.1	1943	120.5
		1934	84.3	1944	121.1
1920	136.1	1935	85.5	1945	125.9
1921	106.6	1936	86.1	1946	139.8
1922	95.8	1937	92.2	1947	154.8
1923	106.6	1938	89.8	1948	169.3
1924	104.8	1939	89.8	1949	169.9
1925	101.2				
1926	101.2			1950	173.5
1927	101.8				
1928	98.8				
1929	100.0				

NOTES BY COLUMN

1, 2 Table C-11, Steam Railroads.

3 Derived from column 1 and 2 combined with weights of 8 and 2 respectively. The weights were derived from data for total cost of equipment per mile of track and total cost of all facilities per mile of track for Massachusetts street and electric railways for 1886, 1891, 1896, 1901, 1906, and 1911.

4 For 1915–50: ICC construction cost index for steam railroads, base shifted. For 1850–1914: column 3 linked to the ICC construction cost index for steam railroads in 1915.

TABLE F–12

"Physical Life" Depreciation Rates, Street and Electric Railways

	WEIGHTS FOR COMBINING DEPRECIATION RATIOS						
	PHYSICAL ASSETS OR CAPITALIZATION (millions of dollars)				PER CENT OF TOTAL ASSETS OR CAPITALIZATION		
	Total (1)	*Animal, Cable, and Surface Electric* (2)	*Elevated Steam* (3)	*Elevated and Subway Electric* (4)	*Animal, Cable, and Surface Electric* (5)	*Elevated Steam* (6)	*Elevated and Subway Electric* (7)
1870 December 31	73	73			100.0	–	–
1881 December 31	193	159	34		82.4	17.6	–
1890 June 30	389	307	82		78.9	21.1	–
1902 June 30	2,140	1,968	172		92.0	8.0	
1912 December 31	4,243	3,827		416	90.2		9.8
1922 December 31	4,662	4,006		656	85.9		14.1

AVERAGE DEPRECIATION RATES

	Animal, Cable, and Surface Electric (8)	*Elevated Steam* (9)	*Elevated and Subway Electric* (10)	*All Roads* (11)	*All Roads, Adjusted for Accounting Practices* (12)
1870	4.14			4.14	3.11
1881	4.14	1.54		3.68	2.76
1890	4.14	1.54		3.59	2.69
1902	4.14	1.54	1.00	3.91	2.93
1912	3.39		1.00	3.16	2.84
1922	2.63		1.00	2.40	2.40

NOTES BY COLUMN

1–4 Physical assets for 1870, 1881, and 1890; capitalization for 1902, 1912, and 1922. Totals for 1870–90 are from Table F–5. Physical assets for elevated steam roads for 1881 are based on total physical assets for elevated roads in New York State as reported to the State Railroad Commission; physical assets for elevated steam roads in 1890 are from 1890 Census (U.S.), Vol. 14, Part 1. Capitalization (net of investments in other than railway property) for 1902 from Census, Street and Electric Railways. Capitalization for surface and for subway and elevated lines for 1912 and 1922 is from the census report of 1922. All track is allocated by census according to the principal type of track of the reporting company, the elevated and subway group including a minor amount of surface track and the surface group including some elevated and subway track.

8 For 1922: Based on data shown in the Bureau of Internal Revenue's Bulletin F, adjusted to exclude track; the depreciation rate for property other than track (3.55 per cent) was averaged with a zero rate for track, since track accounts are not depreciated but are renewed through charge to maintenance.

For 1870–1902: Based on the 1922 rate multiplied by the estimated ratio (1.573) of the depreciation rate in 1902 to the rate in 1922. The ratio was derived from data on depreciation rates for selected accounts (grading, paving, poles, structures, shop equipment, power equipment, track, and rolling stock) as reported in Bulletin F (assumed appropriate for 1922) and as averages of individual estimates shown in the American Electric Railway Association Proceedings, 1912, Report of the Committee on Life of Physical Property (assumed appropriate for 1870–1902). We have assumed the same rate for animal and cable lines as for electric.

For 1912, derived by linear interpolation.

9 Assumed the same as for steam railroads.

10 Depreciation rate for elevated and subway electric lines arbitrarily placed at 1.00 on the basis of fragmentary data available for New York City lines and for the Hudson and Manhattan Company.

11 Averages of columns 8–10 weighted with percentages of total assets or capitalization for each type of road shown in columns 5–7. For 1902, an average rate for elevated steam and elevated and subway electric lines (1.27) was used together with the total weight (8.0 per cent) for the two types of traction.

12 The depreciation rate for 1870–1902 was reduced 25 per cent and the rate for 1912 reduced 10 per cent to take account of the fact that many roads made replacements on a maintenance basis. Replacement of track is treated as maintenance throughout.

TABLE F–13

Gross Physical Assets in 1929 Dollars, Street and Electric Railways, 1870–1902

(*in millions*)

		Original Cost of Plant and Equipment Including Land (book values) (1)	*Percentage of Cost Devoted to Land* (2)	*Cost of Land* (col. 1 × col. 2 ÷ 100) (3)	*Original Cost of Plant and Equipment Excluding Land* (col. 1 minus col. 3) (4)	*Percentage of 1890 Property Remaining in 1902* (5)	*1890 Property Remaining in 1902* (col. 4 × col. 5) (6)	*Price Index Underlying Original Cost* (1929 = 100) (7)	*Total Physical Assets in 1929 Dollars* (8)
Dec. 31, 1870	Animal roads	73.3	11.9	8.7	64.6			47.1	137.2
Dec. 31, 1881	Animal roads	124.8	11.9	14.9	109.9				
	Cable roads	34.2	11.2	3.8	30.4				
	Steam roads	34.2	0.1	0.0	34.2				
	Total	193.2		18.7	174.5			49.2	354.7
June 30, 1890	Animal roads	195.1	11.9	23.2	171.9	10.0	17.2		
	Cable roads	76.3	11.2	8.5	67.8	50.0	33.9		
	Steam roads	82.1	0.1	0.1	82.0	80.0	65.6		
	Electric roads	35.8	0.4	0.1	35.7	90.0	32.1		
	Total	389.4			357.4		148.8	47.4	754.0
June 30, 1902	Total								2,973.3

NOTES BY COLUMN

1 Totals for 1870, 1881, and 1890 are from Table F–5. Total cost of steam roads for 1881 is based on total physical assets of elevated roads in New York State as reported to the state railroad commission; total cost of cable roads was assumed equal to that for steam roads; and cost of animal roads was derived as the residual. The 1890 figures for cost of various types of roads are from the 1890 Census, Vol. 14, part 1.

2 Percentages for cost of right of way (from footnote to column 1 of Table F–7) times 1.5, ratio of expenditures for right of way and other land to expenditures for land alone for New York State.

5 Percentages of property existing in 1890 which remained in service in 1902 were determined somewhat arbitrarily by use of available information on track-mileage of the various types of roads. The track-mileage of roads operated with animal power in 1902 was only 5 per cent of the 1890 total, but since some of the 1890 investment was usable for roads converted to electric power (e.g. the expenditures involved in grading, structures, and the like), it has been assumed that 10 per cent of the 1890 investment in animal roads remained in use in 1902. For cable roads, the 1902 track-mileage was 49 per cent of the 1890 total. Some cable railways were constructed after 1890; on the other hand, at least a portion of the investment in cable roads was salvaged when they were converted to electricity. It has been assumed that 50 per cent of the 1890 cable property remained in use in 1902. The mileage of roads operated by steam in 1902 was 24 per cent of the 1890 figure. Much of the plant and equipment of the elevated steam roads remained serviceable when they were converted to electric traction—the elevated structures themselves, a portion of the investment in track, and probably a large part of the rolling stock. It has therefore been assumed that 80 per cent of the 1890 property remained in use in 1902. Finally, for the electric roads in existence in 1890, a nominal deduction of 10 per cent was made for retirements between 1890 and 1902.

7 Derived from averages of the construction cost index (Table F–11) for the 30 years preceding each date, weighted with gross capital expenditures in 1929 dollars in each year. The index for 1870 was derived by averaging the construction cost index for years back to 1850, since commercial development of street railways dates from this period. The weights for years prior to 1870 were arbitrarily set at the 1870 level.

8 For 1870, 1881, and 1890, column 4 divided by column 7. For 1902, the amount of 1890 physical assets (754.0 millions) times 0.41634, the ratio of the amount for 1890 property still in use in 1902 (148.8 millions, col. 6) to original cost of 1890 plant and equipment (357.4 millions, col. 4), plus 2,659.4 millions, total gross capital expenditures in 1929 dollars, July 1890–June 1902 (from Table F–1).

TABLE F–14

Gross Physical Assets in 1929 Dollars, Street and Electric Railways, 1907, 1912, 1917

(*in millions*)

		DATA FOR RETIREMENT BASE							
Period	*Base for Retirements* (1)	*Physical Assets, 1929 Dollars* (2)	*Depreciation Rate* (3)	*Number of Years in Period* (4)	*Col. 3 × Col. 4* (5)	*Retirements* (col. 2 × col. 5) (6)	*Gross Capital Expenditures, 1929 Dollars* (7)	*Increase in Physical Assets* (col. 7 minus col. 6) (8)	*Total Physical Assets in 1929 Dollars, End of Period* (9)
July 31, 1902–Dec. 31, 1907	June 30, 1890	754.0	2.69	5.5	14.80	111.6	1,810.3	1,698.7	4,672.0
Jan. 1, 1908–Dec. 31, 1912	June 30, 1895	1,678.7	2.79	5.0	13.95	234.2	893.8	659.6	5,331.6
Jan. 1, 1913–Dec. 31, 1917	June 30, 1900	2,603.4	2.89	5.0	14.45	376.2	750.5	374.3	5,705.9

NOTES BY COLUMN

1 Retirements were estimated by use of data for depreciation rate and original cost 15 years prior to the midpoint of each period.

2 For 1890, from Table F–13. For 1895 and 1900, derived by linear interpolation between the estimates of original cost for 1890 and 1902, Table F–13.

3 For 1890, from Table F–12. For 1895 and 1900 derived by linear interpolation between the depreciation rates for 1890 and 1902 shown in Table F–12.

7 Table F–1.

9 For 1907, total physical assets in 1902 (2,973.3 millions, Table F–13), plus column 8 of this table. For 1912 and 1917, physical assets at the end of the preceding period, column 9, plus the increase in physical assets shown in column 8.

TABLE F–15

Gross Physical Assets in 1929 Dollars, Street and Electric Railways, Selected Years, 1917–1950

(millions of dollars)

PART A: 1917–1932

Year	*Surface Track* (miles) (1)	*Subway and Elevated Track* (miles) (2)	*"Equivalent" Surface Track* (3)	*Column 3 as Ratio to 1917* (4)	*Gross Physical Assets in 1929 Dollars* (5)
1917	44,119	716	51,279	1.00000	5,705.9
1922	43,005	927	52,275	1.01942	5,816.7
1927	39,682	1,040	50,082	.97666	5,572.7
1932	30,418	1,130	41,718	.81355	4,642.0

PART B: 1937–1950

Year	*Surface Track* (miles) (1)	*Column 1 as Ratio to 1932* (2)	*Estimated Gross Physical Assets* (3)	*Deductions for Assets Transferred to Public Ownership* (4)	*Gross Physical Assets in 1929 Dollars* (5)
1932	30,418	1.00000	4,642.0	...	4,642.0
1937	22,460	.73838	3,427.6	...	3,427.6
1942	16,950	.55724	2,586.7	326.2	2,260.5
1947	13,750	.45203	2,098.3	413.4	1,684.9
1949	10,704	.35190	1,633.5	413.4	1,220.1
1950	9,590	.31527	1,463.5	413.4	1,050.1

NOTES BY COLUMN

Part A

1, 2 Census, Electric Railways.

3 Column 1 plus ten times column 2. It was assumed that cost per mile of track for subway and elevated lines was ten times as great as for surface lines. This estimate was derived from census data for net capitalization per mile of track for the two groups of companies for 1907, 1912, 1917, and 1922.

5 Physical assets in 1917 (Table F–14) times column 4.

Part B

1 For 1932 and 1937: Census, Electric Railways. For 1942–50: American Transit Association, *Transit Fact Books*.

3 Physical assets in 1932 (part A, above) times column 2.

4 The transit system in New York City was transferred from private to public ownership in 1940 and that of Chicago in 1947. The cost to New York City (326.2 millions) has been deducted for 1942 and the total cost to New York City and Chicago (326.2 plus 87.2, millions) has been deducted for 1947, 1949, and 1950.

5 Column 3 minus column 4.

TABLE F-16

Capital Consumption by "Physical Life" Depreciation, Street and Electric Railways, 1870–1950

(millions of 1929 dollars)

Year	*Gross Physical Assets, End of Year* (1)	*Average Physical Assets during Year* (2)	*Physical Life Depreciation Rate* (per cent) (3)	*Physical Life Depreciation* (col. 2 × col. 3) (4)
1870	137.2	127.3	3.11	4.0
1871	157.0	147.1	3.08	4.5
1872	176.7	166.9	3.05	5.1
1873	196.5	186.6	3.01	5.6
1874	216.3	206.4	2.98	6.2
1875	236.1	226.2	2.95	6.7
1876	255.8	246.0	2.92	7.2
1877	275.6	265.7	2.89	7.7
1878	295.4	285.5	2.85	8.1
1879	315.1	305.3	2.82	8.6
1880	334.9	325.0	2.79	9.1
1881	354.7	344.8	2.76	9.5
1882	401.7	378.2	2.75	10.4
1883	448.9	425.3	2.74	11.7
1884	495.6	472.3	2.74	12.9
1885	542.6	519.1	2.73	14.2
1886	589.6	566.1	2.72	15.4
1887	636.6	613.1	2.71	16.6
1888	683.6	660.1	2.70	17.8
1889	730.5	707.1	2.70	19.1
1890	846.5	788.5	2.69	21.2
1891	1,031.4	939.0	2.71	25.4
1892	1,216.4	1,123.9	2.73	30.7
1893	1,401.3	1,308.9	2.75	36.0
1894	1,586.2	1,493.8	2.77	41.4
1895	1,771.2	1,678.7	2.79	46.8
1896	1,956.1	1,863.7	2.81	52.4
1897	2,141.1	2,048.6	2.83	58.0
1898	2,326.0	2,233.6	2.85	63.7
1899	2,510.9	2,418.5	2.87	69.4
1900	2,695.9	2,603.4	2.89	75.2
1901	2,880.8	2,788.4	2.91	81.1
1902	3,127.7	3,004.3	2.93	88.0
1903	3,436.6	3,282.2	2.92	95.8
1904	3,745.4	3,591.0	2.91	104.5
1905	4,054.3	3,899.9	2.90	113.1
1906	4,363.1	4,208.7	2.89	121.6
1907	4,672.0	4,517.6	2.89	130.6
1908	4,803.9	4,738.0	2.88	136.5
1909	4,935.8	4,869.9	2.87	139.8
1910	5,067.8	5,001.8	2.86	143.1
1911	5,199.7	5,133.8	2.85	146.3
1912	5,331.6	5,265.7	2.84	149.5
1913	5,406.5	5,369.1	2.80	150.3
1914	5,481.3	5,443.9	2.75	149.7
1915	5,556.2	5,518.8	2.71	149.6
1916	5,631.0	5,593.6	2.66	148.8
1917	5,705.9	5,668.5	2.62	148.5
1918	5,728.1	5,717.0	2.58	147.5
1919	5,750.2	5,739.2	2.53	145.2

TABLE F-16 (concluded)

Year	Gross Physical Assets, End of Year (1)	Average Physical Assets during Year (2)	Physical Life Depreciation Rate (per cent) (3)	Physical Life Depreciation (col. 2 × col. 3) (4)
1920	5,772.4	5,761.3	2.49	143.5
1921	5,794.5	5,783.5	2.44	141.1
1922	5,816.7	5,805.6	2.40	139.3
1923	5,767.9	5,792.3	2.40	139.0
1924	5,719.1	5,743.5	2.40	137.8
1925	5,670.3	5,694.7	2.40	136.7
1926	5,621.5	5,645.9	2.40	135.5
1927	5,572.7	5,597.1	2.40	134.3
1928	5,386.6	5,479.7	2.40	131.5
1929	5,200.4	5,293.5	2.40	127.0
1930	5,014.3	5,107.4	2.40	122.6
1931	4,828.1	4,921.2	2.40	118.1
1932	4,642.0	4,735.1	2.40	113.6
1933	4,399.1	4,520.6	2.40	108.5
1934	4,156.2	4,277.7	2.40	102.7
1935	3,913.4	4,034.8	2.40	96.8
1936	3,670.5	3,792.0	2.40	91.0
1937	3,427.6	3,549.1	2.40	85.2
1938	3,259.4	3,343.5	2.40	80.2
1939	3,091.2	3,175.3	2.40	76.2
1940	2,596.9	2,844.1	2.40	68.3
1941	2,428.7	2,512.8	2.40	60.3
1942	2,260.5	2,344.6	2.40	56.3
1943	2,162.8	2,211.7	2.40	53.1
1944	2,065.1	2,114.0	2.40	50.7
1945	1,967.5	2,016.3	2.40	48.4
1946	1,869.8	1,918.7	2.40	46.0
1947	1,684.9	1,777.4	2.40	42.7
1948	1,452.5	1,568.7	2.40	37.6
1949	1,220.1	1,336.3	2.40	32.1
1950	1,050.1	1,135.1	2.40	27.2

NOTES BY COLUMN

1 Based on physical assets at the close of 1870 and 1881, and at June 30, 1890 and 1902 (Table F-13), at the close of 1907, 1912, and 1917 (Table F-14), and at the close of 1922, 1927, 1932, 1937, 1942, 1947, 1949, and 1950 (Table F-15), with estimates for intervening dates derived by linear interpolation. In the preparation of estimates for the years 1938–41 inclusive, the value of New York City transit lines transferred from private to public ownership in 1940 (326.2 millions) was added to the 1942 value of physical assets prior to interpolation for the years 1938–41; the value of the New York City transit lines was then subtracted from the interpolated figures for 1940 and 1941. Similarly, the value of Chicago transit lines transferred from private to public ownership in 1947 was added to the 1947 value of physical assets prior to interpolation for the years 1943–46 inclusive.

2 Two-year averages of column 1 centered in the second year. The figure for 1870 was derived on the assumption that the increase for 1870–71 was the same as for 1871–72.

3 Based on estimates shown in Table F-12 for 1870, 1881, 1890, 1902, 1912, and 1922 with estimates for intervening years derived by linear interpolation. The same rate (2.40) was used for 1922 and all subsequent years.

TABLE F–17

Total Accrued Depreciation, Street and Electric Railways, 1902 and 1949

(millions of 1929 dollars)

Year	*Gross Capital Expenditures in 1929 Dollars, Assets in Use 1902* (1)	*Per Cent Accrued Depreciation, 1902* (2)	*Total Accrued Depreciation, 1902* (3)	*Year*	*Gross Capital Expenditures in 1929 Dollars, Assets in Use 1949* (4)	*Per Cent Accrued Depreciation, 1949* (5)	*Total Accrued Depreciation, 1949* (6)
1885	21.0	51.28		1927	95.7	54.00	
1886	40.1	48.35		1928	107.7	51.60	
1887	71.4	45.42		1929	106.2	49.20	
1888	66.1	42.49		1930	104.5	46.80	
1889	80.1	39.56		1931	84.7	44.40	
1890	99.1	36.63		1932	46.8	42.00	
1891	124.1	33.70		1933	31.1	39.60	
1892	149.9	30.77		1934	48.8	37.20	
1893	174.3	27.84		1935	64.1	34.80	
1894	205.0	24.91		1936	74.8	32.40	
1895	231.2	21.98		1937	69.4	30.00	
1896	253.3	19.05		1938	60.6	27.60	
1897	270.3	16.12		1939	74.6	25.20	
1898	272.2	13.19		1940	67.4	22.80	
1899	260.6	10.26		1941	36.5	20.40	
1900	258.9	7.33		1942	7.2	18.00	
1901	269.9	4.40		1943	11.5	15.60	
1902	280.2	1.47		1944	12.8	13.20	
				1945	18.2	10.80	
			586.5	1946	28.0	8.40	
				1947	32.1	6.00	
				1948	25.3	3.60	
				1949	12.1	1.20	
							433.9

NOTES BY COLUMN

1, 4 Table F–1. In estimating total depreciation accrued in 1902 and 1949, gross capital expenditures of prior years were entered back to the point where total gross capital expenditures equalled gross physical assets as of 1902 and 1949 (hence listing only part of the 1885 and 1927 expenditures).

2, 5 The 1902 depreciation rate (2.93 per cent) was used for all property in use in 1902 and the 1949 rate (2.40 per cent) for all property in use in 1949. It was assumed that capital expenditures of any year are depreciated by one-half the annual rate at the end of that year. Columns 2 and 5 were derived from the depreciation rates and the age of plant and equipment at the close of 1902 and 1949 respectively.

3 Sum of products, col. 1 times col. 2 divided by 100.

6 Sum of products, col. 4 times col. 5 divided by 100.

TABLE F–18

Derivation of Rate of Obsolescence, Street and Electric Railways, 1871–1902, and 1903–1949

(*financial data in millions of 1929 dollars*)

	Dec. 31, 1870	*Dec. 31, 1902*	*Dec. 31, 1949*	*Jan. 1, 1871– Dec. 31, 1902*	*Jan. 1, 1903– Dec. 31, 1949*
1. Gross physical assets	137.2	3,127.7	1,220.1		
2. Accrued depreciation	25.7	586.5	433.9		
3. Net physical assets (line 1 minus line 2)	111.5	2,541.2	786.2		
4. Total gross capital expenditures				3,435.4	5,506.5
5. Total capital consumption				1,005.7	6,848.1
6. Capital consumption: "physical life" depreciation				885.7	5,177.9
7. Capital consumption: obsolescence (line 5 minus line 6)				120.0	1,670.2
8. Average physical assets, 1890–1902 and 1920–49 inclusive				1,868.7	3,956.6
9. Total rate of obsolescence (per cent)				6.42	42.21
10. Annual rate of obsolescence (per cent)				0.49	1.42

NOTES BY LINE

1 Table F–16, column 1.

2 For 1902 and 1949: Table F–17. Accrued depreciation in 1870 was estimated by multiplying total physical assets by the ratio (0.18752) of accrued depreciation to total physical assets in 1902.

4 Table F–1.

5 For 1871–1902: net assets December 31, 1870 (line 3) plus capital expenditures 1871–1902 (line 4) minus net assets December 31, 1902 (line 3). For 1903–49: net assets December 31, 1902 plus capital expenditures 1903–49 minus net assets December 31, 1949 minus 413.4 millions, assets of New York and Chicago transit lines transferred from private to public ownership.

6 Table F–16, column 4.

8 Derived from column 2 of Table F–16.

9 Line 7 divided by line 8 times 100.

10 Line 7 divided by the number of years included in each period, thirteen for 1890–1902 and thirty for 1920–49.

TABLE F–19

Capital Consumption in 1929 Dollars, Street and Electric Railways, 1870–1950

(*in millions*)

Year	*Capital Consumption through Physical Life Depreciation* (1)	*Capital Consumption through Obsolescence* (2)	*Total Capital Consumption* (col. 1 plus col. 2) (3)
1870	4.0	...	4.0
1871	4.5	...	4.5
1872	5.1	...	5.1
1873	5.6	...	5.6
1874	6.2	...	6.2
1875	6.7	...	6.7
1876	7.2	...	7.2
1877	7.7	...	7.7
1878	8.1	...	8.1
1879	8.6	...	8.6
1880	9.1	...	9.1
1881	9.5	...	9.5
1882	10.4	...	10.4
1883	11.7	...	11.7
1884	12.9	...	12.9
1885	14.2	...	14.2
1886	15.4	...	15.4
1887	16.6	...	16.6
1888	17.8	...	17.8
1889	19.1	...	19.1
1890	21.2	3.9	25.1
1891	25.4	4.6	30.0
1892	30.7	5.5	36.2
1893	36.0	6.4	42.4
1894	41.4	7.3	48.7
1895	46.8	8.2	55.0
1896	52.4	9.1	61.5
1897	58.0	10.0	68.0
1898	63.7	10.9	74.6
1899	69.4	11.9	81.3
1900	75.2	12.8	88.0
1901	81.1	13.7	94.8
1902	88.0	14.7	102.7
1903	95.8	...	95.8
1904	104.5	...	104.5
1905	113.1	...	113.1
1906	121.6	...	121.6
1907	130.6	...	130.6
1908	136.5	...	136.5
1909	139.8	...	139.8

(continued on next page)

TABLE F–19 (continued)

Year	*Capital Consumption through Physical Life Depreciation* (1)	*Capital Consumption through Obsolescence* (2)	*Total Capital Consumption* (col. 1 plus col. 2) (3)
1910	143.1	...	143.1
1911	146.3	...	146.3
1912	149.5	...	149.5
1913	150.3	...	150.3
1914	149.7	...	149.7
1915	149.6	...	149.6
1916	148.8	...	148.8
1917	148.5	...	148.5
1918	147.5	...	147.5
1919	145.2	...	145.2
1920	143.5	81.8	225.3
1921	141.1	82.1	223.2
1922	139.3	82.4	221.7
1923	139.0	82.3	221.3
1924	137.8	81.6	219.4
1925	136.7	80.9	217.6
1926	135.5	80.2	215.7
1927	134.3	79.5	213.8
1928	131.5	77.8	209.3
1929	127.0	75.2	202.2
1930	122.6	72.5	195.1
1931	118.1	69.9	188.0
1932	113.6	67.2	180.8
1933	108.5	64.2	172.7
1934	102.7	60.7	163.4
1935	96.8	57.3	154.1
1936	91.0	53.8	144.8
1937	85.2	50.4	135.6
1938	80.2	47.5	127.7
1939	76.2	45.1	121.3
1940	68.3	40.4	108.7
1941	60.3	35.7	96.0
1942	56.3	33.3	89.6
1943	53.1	31.4	84.5
1944	50.7	30.0	80.7
1945	48.4	28.6	77.0
1946	46.0	27.2	73.2
1947	42.7	25.2	67.9
1948	37.6	22.3	59.9
1949	32.1	19.0	51.1
1950	27.2	16.1	43.3

Column 1 is from Table F–16. Column 2 is the second column of that table multiplied by the obsolescence rates derived in Table F–18: 0.49 for 1890–1902, and 1.42 for 1920–50.

APPENDIX G

Notes and Tables on the Derivation of Capital Formation Data for Local Bus Lines

THE figures presented include bus lines operated by street and electric railways, as well as independent local bus lines. Trolley bus operations are not included here, but with electric railways. Investment in municipally owned bus lines is not included.

Gross Capital Expenditures in Current Prices

1942–1950

Gross capital expenditures for 1942–49 are based on American Transit Association figures, adjusted to include bus property other than buses and to exclude public investment. The figures are shown in Table G–2; their derivation is given in Table F–3. Since data of the American Transit Association were available only through 1949 (and only partially in this last year), a special estimate was required for 1950. This estimate was derived by use of the relationship during 1947–49 between capital expenditures and the number of buses delivered, with adjustment for price changes.

1922–1941: STREET RAILWAY AFFILIATES

Unlike the American Transit Association series, data available for years prior to 1942 from the *Electric Railway Journal* and its successor, the *Transit Journal*, do not include expenditures of independent bus lines. The reported figures on expenditures of street railway affiliates for buses were adjusted to include espenditures for bus property other than vehicles, and to exclude expenditures of Canadian companies (Table G–3).

1909–1941: INDEPENDENT BUS LINES

Only scanty data are available for the derivation of estimates of capital formation by independent bus lines prior to 1942. Use was made of the 1937 census data for book value of plant and equipment of all independent bus lines in large cities. The growth of this investment over the years was estimated by the use of annual data for gross and net investment of New York City bus companies 1909–39 (Table G–5).

Table G–4 shows the derivation of the estimates of gross capital expenditures of independent bus lines for 1910–38. Estimates of expenditures of independent bus lines for 1939–41 were obtained by use of graphic correlation of such expenditures for 1929–38 with expenditures of street railway affiliates and with time. Data for independent bus lines and street railway affiliates together are shown in Table G–6.

Gross Capital Expenditures in 1929 Prices

Gross capital expenditures in constant prices were obtained by deflation of the current dollar figures with an index of cost of plant and equipment. This index is based on series for motor vehicles, commercial buildings, and garage equipment, as shown in Table G–7. The weight for motor vehicles is based on the ratio of the value of buses to all bus property as reported by companies in New York State in 1948; the remaining weight was divided equally between buildings and garage equipment.

Capital Consumption, Net Capital Expenditures, and Value of Plant and Equipment, 1929 Prices

Capital consumption in constant dollars was obtained on the assumption of a uniform average life of thirteen years over the period, derived from 1937 census data on depreciation expense. Gross capital expenditures in 1929 dollars for each year were divided by thirteen to find the annual capital consumption of *each year's* plant and equipment additions (Table G–8, column 1). A first approximation to the total capital consumption for any year (given in column 2) was obtained by summing the figures in column 1 for the thirteen preceding years. Since the expenditures of any year may be centered at the midpoint of the year, the figures shown in column 2 were corrected by the use of two-year averages centered in the second year (column 3).

Net capital expenditures were derived by subtracting the estimates of capital formation from gross capital expenditures. The value of plant and equipment net of accrued depreciation was obtained by cumulative addition of each year's net capital expenditures (Table G–1).

APPENDIX G

Capital Consumption, Net Capital Expenditures, and Value of Plant and Equipment, Current Prices

Current dollar estimates of net capital expenditures were obtained from the constant dollar figures inflated by the index of cost of plant and equipment described above. Capital consumption, in current prices, is the difference between gross and net capital expenditures, both in current prices. The value of plant and equipment in current prices is based on the series in constant prices inflated by the index of cost of plant and equipment for the year preceding each January 1.

The final figures on capital formation in local bus lines are presented by years, from 1910 through 1950, in Table G–1.

TABLE G-1

Value of Plant and Equipment, Capital Formation, and Capital Consumption, Local Bus Lines, Annual Data, 1910–1951

(millions of dollars)

	VALUE OF PLANT AND EQUIPMENT, JANUARY 1		GROSS CAPITAL EXPENDITURES		CAPITAL CONSUMPTION		NET CAPITAL EXPENDITURES	
Year	*Current Dollars* (1)	*1929 Dollars* (2)	*Current Dollars* (3)	*1929 Dollars* (4)	*Current Dollars* (5)	*1929 Dollars* (6)	*Current Dollars* (7)	*1929 Dollars* (8)
1910	a	a	0.1	0.1	a	a	0.1	0.1
1911	0.1	0.1	0.1	0.1	a	a	0.1	0.1
1912	0.3	0.2	0.1	0.1	a	a	0.1	0.1
1913	0.4	0.3	0.3	0.2	a	a	0.3	0.2
1914	0.7	0.5	0.2	0.2	0.1	0.1	0.1	0.1
1915	0.7	0.6	0.1	0.1	0.1	0.1	a	a
1916	0.6	0.6	0.2	0.2	0.1	0.1	0.1	0.1
1917	0.7	0.7	0.4	0.4	0.1	0.1	0.3	0.3
1918	1.1	1.0	1.5	1.3	0.2	0.2	1.3	1.1
1919	2.5	2.1	1.2	0.9	0.4	0.3	0.8	0.6
1920	3.7	2.7	0.2	0.1	0.5	0.3	−0.3	−0.2
1921	3.9	2.5	1.0	0.7	0.4	0.3	0.6	0.4
1922	4.0	2.9	11.3	10.1	0.9	0.8	10.4	9.3
1923	13.6	12.2	22.2	20.6	2.1	1.9	20.1	18.7
1924	33.2	30.9	17.7	16.5	3.5	3.3	14.2	13.2
1925	47.3	44.1	19.9	18.9	4.9	4.7	15.0	14.2
1926	61.4	58.3	22.1	21.9	6.3	6.2	15.8	15.7
1927	74.7	74.0	18.4	18.9	7.6	7.8	10.8	11.1
1928	82.6	85.1	23.6	24.1	9.2	9.4	14.4	14.7
1929	97.7	99.8	21.1	21.1	11.1	11.1	10.0	10.0
1930	109.8	109.8	16.9	17.9	11.9	12.6	5.0	5.3
1931	108.7	115.1	16.6	18.7	12.4	14.0	4.2	4.7
1932	106.6	119.8	13.3	15.6	13.0	15.2	0.3	0.4
1933	102.5	120.2	16.1	19.6	13.6	16.5	2.5	3.1
1934	101.2	123.3	24.1	27.7	15.9	18.3	8.2	9.4
1935	115.3	132.7	42.2	50.2	17.6	20.9	24.6	29.3
1936	136.2	162.0	53.0	63.2	20.2	24.1	32.8	39.1
1937	168.7	201.1	41.1	45.6	24.2	26.8	16.9	18.8
1938	198.1	219.9	30.0	31.6	27.0	28.4	3.0	3.2
1939	211.9	223.1	47.0	50.3	28.0	30.0	19.0	20.3
1940	227.6	243.4	61.4	63.7	31.6	32.8	29.8	30.9
1941	264.4	274.3	85.4	83.1	37.8	36.8	47.6	46.3
1942	329.6	320.6	66.8	59.6	45.5	40.6	21.3	19.0
1943	380.4	339.6	19.7	17.5	47.3	42.0	−27.6	−24.5
1944	354.8	315.1	40.6	35.8	48.4	42.7	−7.8	−6.9
1945	349.2	308.2	51.8	44.9	51.3	44.5	0.5	0.4
1946	355.8	308.6	97.0	72.0	64.1	47.6	32.9	24.4
1947	448.9	333.0	180.6	114.9	83.3	53.0	97.3	61.9
1948	620.8	394.9	115.7	67.4	97.9	57.0	17.8	10.4
1949	695.5	405.3	55.8	31.2	100.9	56.4	−45.1	−25.2
1950	680.0	380.1	45.3	25.3	97.4	54.4	−52.1	−29.1
1951	627.9	351.0						

(Notes to Table G-1 on next page)

All data exclude land and publicly owned facilities. Columns 1 and 2 exclude accrued depreciation.

[a] Less than $100,000.

NOTES BY COLUMN

1	Col. 2 inflated by index of cost of plant and equipment (Table G–7, col. 4), for the year preceding each January 1.
2	Derived by cumulating net capital expenditures, col. 8.
3, 6	Tables G–6 and G–8.
4	Col. 3 deflated by index of cost of plant and equipment (Table G–7, col. 4).
5, 8	Col. 3 minus col. 7; col. 4 minus col. 6.
7	Col. 8 inflated by above index.

TABLE G–2

Gross Capital Expenditures, Local Bus Lines, 1942–1950

(thousands of dollars)

	EXPENDITURES, PRIVATELY OWNED LINES		
Year	*All Local Transit* (1)	*Electric Railways* (2)	*Bus Lines* (3)
1942	74,990	8,187	66,803
1943	33,600	13,919	19,681
1944	56,092	15,515	40,577
1945	74,710	22,914	51,796
1946	136,200	39,163	97,037
1947	230,260	49,692	180,568
1948	158,500	42,798	115,702
1949	76,400	20,630	55,770
1950			45,300

Columns 1 and 2 are from Table F–3. Column 3: For 1942–49, col. 1 minus col. 2. For 1950, estimate based on (a) number of buses delivered multiplied by the construction cost index, and (b) the average ratio, for 1947–49, between capital expenditures and comparable data for equipment delivered, adjusted for construction costs. The basic figures are:

	Buses Delivered (number) (1)	*Index of Plant and Equipment Costs* (1929 = 100) (2)	*Column* 1 × *Column* 2 (3)	*Capital Expenditures* (millions) (4)	*Ratio, Column* 4 *to Column* 3 (5)
1947	12,029	157.2	18,910	180.6	0.009551
1948	7,009	171.6	12,027	115.7	0.009620
1949	3,358	178.9	6,007	55.8	0.009289
1950	2,668	178.9	4,773		
			Average 1947–49		0.009487

TABLE G-3

Gross Capital Expenditures, Local Bus Line Affiliates of Street and Electric Railways, 1922–1941

(*thousands of dollars*)

Year	*Total Expenditures, United States and Canada* (1)	*Expenditures, United States* (2)
1922	10,925	10,355
1923	22,426	21,255
1924	17,308	16,405
1925	18,998	18,006
1926	21,251	20,142
1927	17,408	16,499
1928	23,142	21,934
1929	20,961	19,867
1930	16,090	15,250
1931	13,982	13,252
1932	9,099	8,624
1933	12,988	12,310
1934	21,118	20,016
1935	33,973	32,200
1936	41,376	39,216
1937	33,016	31,293
1938	23,991	22,739
1939	36,711	34,795
1940	48,142	45,629
1941	66,941	63,447

Column 1 is from Table F-2, col. 5. Column 2 is column 1 times 0.9478, the ratio of street railway track-mileage for 1923–32 in the United States, to the total for United States and Canada (see footnote to Table F-2, column 7).

TABLE G–4

Gross Capital Expenditures, Independent Local Bus Lines, 1910–1939

(thousands of dollars)

Year Ending June 30	*Estimated Total Net Investment, Independent Bus Lines* (1)	*Annual Change in Column 1* (2)	*Estimated Gross Total Investment* (3)	*Depreciation* (original prices) (4)	*Gross Capital Expenditures* (col. 2 + col. 4) (5)	*Gross Capital Expenditures, Calendar Years* (6)
1909	461		622			
1910	321	−140	683	49	−91	59
1911	475	154	1,005	54	208	80
1912	347	−128	1,005	79	−49	90
1913	497	150	1,234	79	229	286
1914	742	245	1,449	97	342	244
1915	773	31	1,553	114	145	126
1916	757	−16	1,525	122	106	228
1917	986	229	1,818	120	349	434
1918	1,361	375	2,366	143	518	1,454
1919	3,565	2,204	4,441	186	2,390	1,191
1920	3,207	−358	4,455	349	−9	211
1921	3,288	81	4,716	350	431	1,031
1922	4,548	1,260	6,032	370	1,630	938
1923	4,319	−229	6,354	474	245	850
1924	5,274	955	7,568	499	1,454	1,347
1925	5,919	645	8,958	594	1,239	1,912
1926	7,800	1,881	11,575	703	2,584	2,032
1927	8,370	570	12,946	909	1,479	1,864
1928	9,602	1,232	14,925	1,016	2,248	1,704
1929	9,589	−13	16,144	1,172	1,159	1,160
1930	9,483	−106	16,645	1,267	1,161	1,607
1931	10,228	745	18,602	1,307	2,052	3,271
1932	13,258	3,030	23,446	1,460	4,490	4,659
1933	16,244	2,986	31,466	1,841	4,827	3,836
1934	16,619	375	33,969	2,470	2,845	4,085
1935	19,276	2,657	37,673	2,667	5,324	10,047
1936	31,088	11,812	51,652	2,957	14,769	13,777
1937	39,817	8,729	63,429	4,055	12,784	9,793
1938	41,639	1,822	69,038	4,979	6,801	7,274
1939	43,966	2,327	73,391	5,419	7,746	

(Notes to Table G–4 on next page)

NOTES BY COLUMN

1 Net total investment for bus lines in New York City (Table G–5, col. 2) times 1.73328, the ratio, as of December 31, 1937, between total investment of independent bus lines reported by the census (66,234 thousands) and gross investment of all bus companies in New York City (38,213), as estimated by averaging the figures for June 30, 1937 and June 30, 1938. The census figure includes municipal lines; offsetting this overstatement of assets is the census exclusion of bus lines in cities with population under 100,000 in 1930.

2 Derived from year-to-year changes shown in column 1.

3 Gross total investment for bus lines in New York City (Table G–5, col. 1) times 1.73328, the December 31, 1937 ratio between total investment of independent bus lines and investment of bus companies in New York City.

4 Column 3 times 7.85 per cent. The depreciation rate was derived from the 1937 census figures for depreciation expense and total investment of the following categories of bus operations (figures in thousands of dollars):

	Investment	*Depreciation Expense*
Subsidiaries of street railways	30,214	2,495
Successors of street railways, other corporate identity	46,959	3,974
All other	66,234	4,785
Total, above categories	143,407	11,254

6 Column 5 averaged for adjacent years.

TABLE G–5

Gross and Net Investment, Bus Companies, New York City, 1909–1939
(*thousands of dollars*)

June 30	*Gross Investment* (1)	*Net Investment* (2)
1909	359	266
1910	394	185
1911	580	274
1912	580	200
1913	712	287
1914	836	428
1915	896	446
1916	880	437
1917	1,049	569
1918	1,365	785
1919	2,562	2,057
1920	2,570	1,850
1921	2,721	1,897
1922	3,480	2,624
1923	3,666	2,492
1924	4,366	3,043
1925	5,168	3,415
1926	6,678	4,500
1927	7,469	4,829
1928	8,611	5,540
1929	9,314	5,532
1930	9,603	5,471
1931	10,732	5,901
1932	13,527	7,649
1933	18,154	9,372
1934	19,598	9,588
1935	21,735	11,121
1936	29,800	17,936
1937	36,595	22,972
1938	39,831	24,023
1939	42,342	25,366

Source: State of New York, Department of Public Service, Metropolitan Division, Transit Commission, Report for the Calendar Year 1939.

TABLE G-6

Gross Capital Expenditures, Current Dollars, Local Bus Lines, 1910–1950

(in millions)

Year	*Independent Bus Lines* (1)	*Affiliates of Street and Electric Railways* (2)	*Total* (3)
1910	0.1		0.1
1911	.1		.1
1912	.1		.1
1913	.3		.3
1914	.2		.2
1915	.1		.1
1916	.2		.2
1917	.4		.4
1918	1.5		1.5
1919	1.2		1.2
1920	.2		.2
1921	1.0		1.0
1922	.9	10.4	11.3
1923	.9	21.3	22.2
1924	1.3	16.4	17.7
1925	1.9	18.0	19.9
1926	2.0	20.1	22.1
1927	1.9	16.5	18.4
1928	1.7	21.9	23.6
1929	1.2	19.9	21.1
1930	1.6	15.3	16.9
1931	3.3	13.3	16.6
1932	4.7	8.6	13.3
1933	3.8	12.3	16.1
1934	4.1	20.0	24.1
1935	10.0	32.2	42.2
1936	13.8	39.2	53.0
1937	9.8	31.3	41.1
1938	7.3	22.7	30.0
1939	12.2	34.8	47.0
1940	15.8	45.6	61.4
1941	22.0	63.4	85.4
1942			66.8
1943			19.7
1944			40.6
1945			51.8
1946			97.0
1947			180.6
1948			115.7
1949			55.8
1950			45.3

Column 1: For 1910–38, Table G–4, col. 6. For 1939–41, expenditures were derived by means of graphic correlation of expenditures of independent bus lines for 1929–38 with expenditures of street railway affiliates, and with time.

Column 2: Table G–3.

Column 3: For 1910–41, col. 1 plus col. 2; for 1942–50, Table G–2.

TABLE G–7

Index of Cost of Plant and Equipment, Local Bus Lines, 1910–1950

(1929 = 100)

Year	*Motor Vehicles* (1)	*Commercial Buildings* (2)	*Garage Equipment* (3)	*Total Plant and Equipment* (4)
1910	130.4	48.0	66.7	117.3
1911	144.3	46.8	73.8	129.2
1912	135.0	45.5	69.0	121.0
1913	147.5	49.8	75.4	132.2
1914	125.0	50.8	75.4	113.9
1915	115.5	64.7	73.3	107.1
1916	107.6	71.1	81.7	102.0
1917	110.4	78.3	92.9	105.9
1918	121.0	79.6	126.8	117.8
1919	142.5	83.6	136.3	136.6
1920	160.7	103.9	169.0	156.3
1921	143.4	93.5	129.9	137.7
1922	116.6	87.0	92.7	111.8
1923	108.7	97.5	107.3	107.6
1924	107.5	96.5	116.6	107.3
1925	105.3	96.0	115.6	105.4
1026	100.0	100.5	109.3	100.9
1927	96.1	97.9	105.0	97.1
1928	97.1	97.5	105.8	97.9
1929	100.0	100.0	100.0	100.0
1930	94.0	99.0	93.1	94.4
1931	89.5	89.5	84.0	89.0
1932	87.1	78.1	75.6	85.3
1933	83.2	77.1	77.3	82.1
1934	87.6	85.1	82.1	86.9
1935	84.1	83.0	84.7	84.1
1936	83.3	83.6	89.2	83.9
1937	89.3	93.0	94.9	90.1
1938	95.4	95.5	91.1	95.0
1939	93.4	97.0	91.4	93.5
1940	96.7	97.5	92.8	96.4
1941	103.3	102.4	98.5	102.8
1942	112.5	113.8	105.9	112.0
1943	112.6	118.4	106.8	112.6
1944	113.2	119.4	108.5	113.3
1945	115.4	119.9	110.3	115.3
1946	133.7	144.2	135.4	134.8
1947	153.6	176.0	171.6	157.2
1948	168.0	189.0	187.0	171.6
1949	176.9	190.0	186.1	178.9
1950	176.0	187.5	196.4	178.9

(Notes to Table G–7 on next page)

APPENDIX G

NOTES BY COLUMN

1 BLS wholesale price index for motor vehicles for 1913–50, extrapolated to 1910 by use of Shaw's index for industrial machinery and equipment. (William H. Shaw, *Value of Commodity Output since 1869*, National Bureau of Economic Research, 1947.)

2 George A. Fuller Co. index of costs of commercial buildings, 1913–50 (published in *Engineering News-Record*), extrapolated to 1910 by use of the Engineering News-Record building cost index.

3 Marshall and Stevens Co. index of costs of garage equipment, 1913–50 (published in *Engineering News-Record*), extrapolated to 1910 by use of Shaw's index for industrial machinery and equipment.

4 Columns 1, 2, and 3 combined with weights of 82, 9, and 9 per cent respectively. The weight for motor vehicles is based on the ratio of the value of buses to the value of all bus property for companies in New York State in 1948 (data derived from Annual Report of the New York State Public Service Commission); the remaining weight was divided equally between structures and garage equipment.

TABLE G-8

Capital Consumption, Local Bus Lines, 1929 Dollars, 1910–1950

(in millions)

Year	*Annual Depreciation of Each Year's Capital Additions*[a] (1)	*Sums of Column 1*[b] (2)	*Capital Consumption*[c] (3)
1910	0.01	0.01	d
1911	.01	.02	d
1912	.01	.03	d
1913	.02	.05	d
1914	.02	.07	0.1
1915	.01	.08	.1
1916	.02	.10	.1
1917	.03	.13	.1
1918	.10	.23	.2
1919	.07	.30	.3
1920	.01	.31	.3
1921	.05	.36	.3
1922	.78	1.14	.8
1923	1.58	2.71	1.9
1924	1.27	3.97	3.3
1925	1.45	5.41	4.7
1926	1.68	7.07	6.2
1927	1.45	8.50	7.8
1928	1.85	10.34	9.4
1929	1.62	11.94	11.1
1930	1.38	13.29	12.6
1931	1.44	14.63	14.0
1932	1.20	15.76	15.2
1933	1.51	17.26	16.5
1934	2.13	19.34	18.3
1935	3.86	22.42	20.9
1936	4.86	25.70	24.1
1937	3.51	27.94	26.8
1938	2.43	28.92	28.4
1939	3.87	31.11	30.0
1940	4.90	34.56	32.8
1941	6.39	39.10	36.8
1942	4.58	42.06	40.6
1943	1.35	42.03	42.0
1944	2.75	43.34	42.7
1945	3.45	45.59	44.5
1946	5.54	49.62	47.6
1947	8.84	56.33	53.0
1948	5.18	57.65	57.0
1949	2.40	55.19	56.4
1950	1.95	53.63	54.4

[a] Gross capital expenditures in 1929 dollars (Table G-1, col. 4) divided by thirteen. An average life of thirteen years was derived from 1937 census data on depreciation expense. See footnote to Table G-4, col. 4.

[b] For 1910–22, cumulative totals of col. 1 for all preceding years; for 1923–50, cumulative totals of col. 1 for the thirteen preceding years.

[c] Two-year averages of col. 2 centered in the second year.

[d] Under $100,000.

APPENDIX H

Table on the Derivation of Capital Formation Data for All Other Regulated Industries

APPENDIX H

TABLE H-1

Value of Plant and Equipment, Capital Formation, and Capital Consumption, All Other Regulated Industries, Annual Data, 1870–1950

(in millions)

	VALUE OF PLANT AND EQUIPMENT, JANUARY 1		GROSS CAPITAL EXPENDITURES		CAPITAL CONSUMPTION		NET CAPITAL EXPENDITURES	
Year	*Current Dollars* (1)	*1929 Dollars* (2)	*Current Dollars* (3)	*1929 Dollars* (4)	*Current Dollars* (5)	*1929 Dollars* (6)	*Current Dollars* (7)	*1929 Dollars* (8)
1870	585	1,059	68	134	9	17	59	116
1871	594	1,175	76	149	9	18	67	132
1872	659	1,307	68	125	11	20	57	106
1873	776	1,413	48	85	12	21	36	63
1874	827	1,476	28	53	12	22	16	30
1875	794	1,506	20	40	12	24	8	15
1876	763	1,521	19	41	12	25	7	17
1877	725	1,538	20	47	11	26	9	21
1878	674	1,559	19	48	11	27	8	21
1879	630	1,580	20	50	12	29	8	22
1880	640	1,602	41	93	13	30	28	62
1881	738	1,664	58	129	14	31	44	95
1882	795	1,759	51	109	15	32	36	77
1883	859	1,836	34	75	16	34	18	40
1884	861	1,876	23	52	15	35	8	17
1885	827	1,893	17	39	16	36	1	3
1886	815	1,896	24	55	16	37	8	17
1887	829	1,913	35	81	16	38	19	43
1888	841	1,956	34	79	17	40	17	39
1889	859	1,995	35	82	18	41	17	40
1890	867	2,035	38	89	18	42	20	48
1891	891	2,083	41	98	19	45	22	53
1892	896	2,136	69	169	20	48	49	123
1893	927	2,259	77	190	21	52	56	137
1894	977	2,396	47	120	22	55	25	65
1895	957	2,461	33	85	22	58	11	27
1896	979	2,488	31	81	24	61	7	20
1897	991	2,508	33	86	25	64	8	32
1898	979	2,530	41	102	27	68	14	36
1899	1,013	2,566	59	134	31	71	28	62
1900	1,149	2,628	64	141	34	74	30	69
1901	1,232	2,697	64	142	36	79	28	64
1902	1,245	2,761	70	152	39	83	31	69
1903	1,319	2,830	75	160	42	88	33	72
1904	1,388	2,902	83	175	44	93	39	82
1905	1,411	2,984	99	201	48	98	51	103
1906	1,528	3,087	125	236	53	102	72	134
1907	1,707	3,221	154	281	58	107	96	175
1908	1,877	3,396	157	297	60	112	97	187
1909	1,961	3,583	177	322	64	116	113	206

(concluded on next page)

TABLE H–1 (concluded)

Year	VALUE OF PLANT AND EQUIPMENT, JANUARY 1		GROSS CAPITAL EXPENDITURES		CAPITAL CONSUMPTION		NET CAPITAL EXPENDITURES	
	Current Dollars (1)	*1929 Dollars* (2)	*Current Dollars* (3)	*1929 Dollars* (4)	*Current Dollars* (5)	*1929 Dollars* (6)	*Current Dollars* (7)	*1929 Dollars* (8)
1910	2,130	3,789	226	399	69	121	157	279
1911	2,359	4,068	234	408	73	126	161	280
1912	2,523	4,348	252	434	77	130	175	304
1913	2,748	4,652	255	426	87	145	168	280
1914	2,975	4,932	210	360	93	159	117	199
1915	3,011	5,131	160	271	104	174	56	95
1916	3,130	5,226	207	302	128	188	79	115
1917	3,687	5,341	348	417	170	203	178	214
1918	4,711	5,555	287	285	216	217	71	68
1919	5,755	5,623	388	357	254	232	134	124
1920	6,510	5,747	431	342	318	246	113	98
1921	7,737	5,845	269	250	282	261	−13	−13
1922	6,218	5,832	405	417	268	275	137	142
1923	5,739	5,974	475	457	297	282	178	175
1924	6,460	6,149	598	579	306	292	292	288
1925	6,699	6,437	575	565	307	301	268	264
1926	6,769	6,701	659	681	315	311	344	368
1927	7,119	7,069	684	686	323	319	361	366
1928	7,500	7,435	611	620	324	328	287	293
1929	7,616	7,728	756	756	336	336	421	421
1930	8,149	8,149	581	600	339	350	242	248
1931	8,078	8,397	422	450	344	371	78	81
1932	7,745	8,478	211	243	313	366	−102	−121
1933	7,029	8,357	153	177	304	358	−151	−181
1934	6,763	8,176	234	256	332	365	−98	−108
1935	7,113	8,068	271	292	339	368	−68	−76
1936	7,151	7,992	362	387	352	378	10	8
1937	7,247	8,000	456	460	386	392	70	66
1938	7,807	8,066	288	286	409	419	−121	−133
1939	7,535	7,933	353	352	419	427	−66	−73
1940	7,500	7,860	575	571	434	436	141	133
1941	7,777	7,993	569	529	488	460	81	68
1942	8,394	8,061	475	415	533	464	−58	−50
1943	9,195	8,011	375	315	554	465	−179	−149
1944	9,461	7,862	611	510	560	468	51	42
1945	9,559	7,904	695	566	590	478	105	88
1946	9,991	7,992	1,149	831	733	526	416	303
1947	11,617	8,295	1,763	1,113	959	607	804	508
1948	13,880	8,803	2,013	1,191	1,132	663	881	528
1949	15,932	9,331	1,877	1,062	1,254	715	623	351
1950	16,860	9,682	2,479	1,341	1,308	720	1,171	621
1951	18,592	10,303						

Derived by subtracting totals for steam railroads, electric light and power, telephones, street and electric railways, and local bus lines from the data for all regulated industries.

APPENDIX I

Notes and Tables on the Derivation of Output and Capital-Product Ratios for All Regulated Industries and Components

Derivation of Output Data for All Regulated Industries and Components

THE output figures presented here represent "gross" output; that is, they are based on the total physical outputs of the individual industries, expressed in terms of 1929 price levels, without deduction for the cost of fuel, materials, and services purchased from other industries or for depreciation. The estimates for all regulated industries in the aggregate were built up from subtotals for (1) transportation and (2) communications and other public utilities. The output index for transportation for 1890 and for the years 1920–40 is from Harold Barger, *The Transportation Industries, 1889–1946.*[1] This index was interpolated for the years 1891–1919 by reference to totals for steam railroads and street and electric railways combined (Table I–2). The index was completed for the years 1941–45 by use of an index of total transportation, except water, compiled from Barger's figures for individual industries, as shown in Table I–3, and extrapolated to 1950 by use of an index compiled by the Department of Commerce. Total transportation output was expressed in terms of 1929 dollars by multiplying the output index with estimated 1929 operating revenues (Table I–4).

Output for the communications and public utilities group was obtained by combining output series for electric light and power, gas, and telephones (all in terms of 1929 dollars) and adjusting the totals for these three industries to include other communications and public utilities. The latter adjustment was made in Table I–5 on the basis of the ratios of estimated output, in current dollars, of the three industries to output of all communications and public utilities, in current dollars.

The output figures for electric light and power and telephones are described in detail below. The output index for gas (Table I–6) for 1899–1942 is from Jacob M. Gould, *Output and Productivity in the Electric and Gas Utilities, 1899–1942,*[2] and was extended here to 1950 (Table I–7).

Estimates of the ratios of output in current dollars of electric light

[1] National Bureau of Economic Research, 1951.

[2] National Bureau of Economic Research, 1946.

and power, gas, and telephones to total communications and public utilities for 1929–50 are shown in Table I–8, and the derivation of the component series is shown in Tables I–9 through I–11. The adjustment required for the earlier years in order to raise the totals for the three industries to include other communications and public utilities was estimated, in the manner indicated in the footnote to column 5, Table I–5, by use of information on book value of plant and equipment for the three industries and for all communications and public utilities (Table I–12).

Individual Industries

STEAM RAILROADS

The sources of the output figures for railroads are described in my *Trends and Cycles in Capital Formation by United States Railroads, 1870–1950* (National Bureau of Economic Research, Occasional Paper 43, 1954).

ELECTRIC LIGHT AND POWER

Output of the electric light and power industry is shown in Table I–16 in index form and in terms of 1929 dollars. The index of output was obtained for 1902, 1907, and 1912–32 from Gould. The Gould index embraces publicly owned electric utilities as well as private companies; however, since the trend in current generated for private companies is virtually identical with the trend for all companies (private and public) through 1932, it has been used here through this date. Gould's index is based on sales of electric energy to ultimate consumers, with sales to various classes of consumers weighted separately in accordance with revenue per kilowatt-hour.

The index of output for the period prior to 1902 was obtained from a series for net current generated (total generated less losses). This series is based on data shown by the *Electrical World* for 1887, 1892, 1897, and 1902; estimates for intervening years were derived by geometric interpolation (Table I–17). Annual figures for the period 1902–12 were derived by interpolation of Gould's index with annual estimates of generating capacity which we compiled in the course of the preparation of estimates of gross capital expenditures.

The derivation of the output index for 1932–50 is shown in Tables I–18 and I–19. A weighted Edgeworth index was prepared for the years 1937, 1942, 1947, and 1950 from data on sales of electricity to three classes of ultimate consumers. The production index was interpolated between 1932 and 1937 by use of data for current generated by privately owned utilities and between 1937 and 1950 by means of figures for sales to ultimate consumers by Class A and Class B privately owned utilities.

TELEPHONES

Output of the telephone industry is shown in Table I–20, in index form and in terms of 1929 dollars.

The output index was derived for 1890 and quinquennially 1902–37 by use of census data for number of local and toll calls, combined with 1927 unit revenues as weights (Table I–21). Data for 1902–22 were adjusted for completeness of coverage, as shown in columns 4 and 5 of Table I–21. This index was interpolated for the remaining years in the period 1890–1937 by means of data for number of telephone conversations reported by the Bell system. It was extrapolated for 1938–50 by use of the Bureau of Labor Statistics output index for Class A carriers; the BLS measure is based on number of local and toll calls, combined with 1939 revenue per call as weights.

STREET AND ELECTRIC RAILWAYS

Output of street and electric railways for the years 1890–1950, is shown in Table I–22. The data refer to privately owned lines only.

The index for street and electric railways was derived by combining series for number of passengers (Table I–23) and freight car-miles (Table I–24) with 1939 unit-revenues as weights. The resulting index, available quinquennially for 1902–22 and annually for 1926–50 was interpolated for other years of the period 1907–37 and extrapolated for the year 1890 by use of an index of passenger traffic alone (Table I–25). The index was interpolated for the intervening years, 1891–1901 and 1903–06, by reference to output of other transportation and utility industries—railroads, electric light and power, and telephones (Table I–25). Trolley bus operations are included. It was necessary to make special estimates of passenger traffic for 1937–50, as shown in Table I–26.

LOCAL BUS LINES

Output of bus lines (Table I–27) is based on number of revenue passengers reported by the American Transit Association for 1922–37. As in the case of street railways, the special estimates of traffic shown in Table I–26 were needed for 1938–50.

ALL OTHER

Output for "all other" transportation, communications, and utilities was obtained by subtracting from the data for all utilities the totals for steam railroads, electric light and power, telephones, street and electric railways, and local bus lines.

TABLE I-1

Output and Capital-Product Ratios, All Regulated Industries, Annual Data, 1890–1950

Year	OUTPUT, 1929 DOLLARS (in millions)			CAPITAL-PRODUCT RATIOS, 1929 DOLLARS
	Transportation	*Communications and Public Utilities*	*Total*	
	(1)	(2)	(3)	(4)
1880			757	15.29
1881			838	14.46
1882			920	14.16
1883			977	14.11
1884			1,025	13.91
1885			1,107	13.12
1886			1,229	11.95
1887			1,351	11.08
1888			1,433	10.80
1889			1,563	10.18
1890	1,545	172	1,717	9.50
1891	1,674	183	1,857	9.02
1892	1,784	190	1,974	8.72
1893	1,756	194	1,950	9.33
1894	1,674	210	1,884	10.23
1895	1,784	222	2,006	9.84
1896	1,867	237	2,104	9.45
1897	2,014	258	2,272	8.79
1898	2,281	289	2,570	7.82
1899	2,547	334	2,881	7.06
1900	2,777	385	3,162	6.57
1901	2,980	478	3,458	6.15
1902	3,265	525	3,790	5.74
1903	3,458	580	4,038	5.52
1904	3,651	637	4,288	5.33
1905	4,055	719	4,774	4.93
1906	4,561	831	5,392	4.52
1907	4,672	914	5,586	4.57
1908	4,580	945	5,525	4.85
1909	4,938	1,007	5,945	4.70
1910	5,306	1,072	6,378	4.55
1911	5,435	1,133	6,568	4.64
1912	5,839	1,223	7,062	4.49
1913	6,097	1,282	7,379	4.47
1914	5,904	1,363	7,267	4.68
1915	6,281	1,374	7,655	4.52
1916	7,182	1,611	8,793	3.94
1917	7,909	1,796	9,705	3.59
1918	8,148	1,899	10,047	3.52
1919	7,835	1,996	9,831	3.59
1920	8,607	2,126	10,733	3.27
1921	6,768	2,045	8,813	3.98
1922	7,357	2,248	9,605	3.65
1923	8,525	2,580	11,105	3.19
1924	8,194	2,783	10,977	3.34

(concluded on next page)

TABLE I–1 (concluded)

Year	OUTPUT, 1929 DOLLARS (in millions)			CAPITAL-PRODUCT RATIOS, 1929 DOLLARS
	Transportation (1)	*Communications and Public Utilities* (2)	*Total* (3)	(4)
1925	8,525	3,048	11,573	3.28
1926	9,030	3,413	12,443	3.14
1927	8,865	3,702	12,567	3.20
1928	8,865	3,962	12,827	3.23
1929	9,196	4,325	13,521	3.14
1930	8,111	4,315	12,426	3.53
1931	6,851	4,219	11,070	4.08
1932	5,518	3,823	9,341	4.86
1933	5,849	3,770	9,619	4.65
1934	6,354	3,921	10,275	4.26
1935	6,603	4,176	10,779	3.98
1936	7,771	4,613	12,384	3.41
1937	8,442	4,902	13,344	3.15
1938	7,440	4,747	12,187	3.47
1939	8,359	5,145	13,504	3.10
1940	9,444	5,652	15,096	2.76
1941	11,532	6,360	17,892	2.32
1942	14,548	6,936	21,484	1.96
1943	17,132	8,010	25,142	1.68
1944	17,969	8,297	26,266	1.58
1945	17,721	8,432	26,153	1.58
1946	16,047	8,812	24,859	1.66
1947	16,856	9,893	26,749	1.56
1948	16,939	10,709	27,648	1.56
1949	15,394	10,993	26,387	1.72
1950	16,700	12,172	28,872	1.63

NOTES BY COLUMN

1 Index shown in Table I–2 times 1929 operating revenue derived in Table I–4.
2 Table I–5.
3 For 1890–1950: Column 1 plus column 2; data extrapolated to 1880 by use of figures for railroad output, Table I–13.
4 Ratio of value of plant and equipment in 1929 dollars (Table B–1) to total output, column 3, above.

TABLE I–2

Derivation of Output, Total Utilities: Transportation Output, 1890–1950

Year	*Index, Transportation, Barger* (1929 = 100) (1)	*Steam Railroads and Street and Electric Railways Combined* *Millions of 1929 Dollars* (2)	*Index* (1929 = 100) (3)	*Ratio of Column 1 to Column 3, and Interpolations* (4)	*Index, Transportation, All Years* (1929 = 100) (5)
1890	16.8	1,534	20.7	0.8116	16.8
1891		1,652	22.3	.8148	18.2
1892		1,756	23.7	.8181	19.4
1893		1,722	23.2	.8213	19.1
1894		1,638	22.1	.8246	18.2
1895		1,734	23.4	.8278	19.4
1896		1,809	24.4	.8310	20.3
1897		1,944	26.2	.8343	21.9
1898		2,197	29.6	.8375	24.8
1899		2,445	33.0	.8408	27.7
1900		2,655	35.8	.8440	30.2
1901		2,840	38.3	.8472	32.4
1902		3,091	41.7	.8505	35.5
1903		3,271	44.1	.8537	37.6
1904		3,431	46.3	.8570	39.7
1905		3,802	51.3	.8602	44.1
1906		4,251	57.4	.8634	49.6
1907		4,342	58.6	.8667	50.8
1908		4,237	57.2	.8699	49.8
1909		4,555	61.5	.8732	53.7
1910		4,878	65.8	.8764	57.7
1911		4,979	67.2	.8796	59.1
1912		5,332	71.9	.8829	63.5
1913		5,542	74.8	.8861	66.3
1914		5,355	72.2	.8894	64.2
1915		5,668	76.5	.8926	68.3
1916		6,466	87.2	.8958	78.1
1917		7,093	95.7	.8991	86.0
1918		7,275	98.2	.9023	88.6
1919		6,975	94.1	.9056	85.2
1920	93.6	7,633	103.0	.9087	93.6
1921	73.6				73.6
1922	80.0				80.0
1923	92.7				92.7
1924	89.1				89.1
1925	92.7				92.7
1926	98.2				98.2
1927	96.4				96.4
1928	96.4				96.4
1929	100.0	7,412			100.0

(concluded on next page)

TABLE I–2 (concluded)

Year	Index, Transportation, Barger (1929 = 100) (1)	Steam Railroads and Street and Electric Railways Combined: Millions of 1929 Dollars (2)	Steam Railroads and Street and Electric Railways Combined: Index (1929 = 100) (3)	Ratio of Column 1 to Column 3, and Interpolations (4)	Index, Transportation, All Years (1929 = 100) (5)
1930	88.2				88.2
1931	74.5				74.5
1932	60.0				60.0
1933	63.6				63.6
1934	69.1				69.1
1935	71.8				71.8
1936	84.5				84.5
1937	91.8				91.8
1938	80.9				80.9
1939	90.9				90.9
1940	102.7				102.7
1941					125.4
1942					158.2
1943					186.3
1944					195.4
1945					192.7
1946	174.5				174.5
1947					183.3
1948					184.2
1949					167.4
1950					181.6

NOTES BY COLUMN

1 Harold Barger, *The Transportation Industries, 1889–1946*; base shifted. The figure shown by Barger for 1889 is used here for 1890 since the data for the principal components, railroads and street railways, refer to the year ending June 30, 1890.

2 Table I–13, column 2, plus Table I–22, column 2.

5 Column 1 for available years. For 1891–1919, column 3 times column 4; for 1941–45, from Table I–3. For 1947–50, derived by linking to column 1 the index of transportation activity shown in the *Economic Report of the President, January 1951.*

TABLE I–3

Derivation of Output, All Regulated Industries: Transportation Output, 1941–1946

(1939 = 100)

Year	Index of Output, Total Transportation except Water (1939 = 100) (1)	CORPORATE SALES (in millions) Total Transportation (2)	Water (3)	Total except Water (4)	Coverage of Index in Column 1 (col. 4 ÷ col. 2) (5)	Index of Coverage (6)	Index of Output, Total Transportation except Water, Adjusted for Coverage (7)	Index of Output, Total Transportation (Barger) (8)	Index of Output, Total Transportation, All Years (9)
1939	100.0	7,364	664	6,700	0.9098	100.0	100.0	100	100
1940	112.4	7,769	832	6,937	.8929	98.1	114.5	113	113
1941	135.3	9,526	1,047	8,479	.8901	97.8	138.3		138
1942	177.3	11,527	729	10,798	.9368	103.0	172.1		174
1943	208.9	13,661	680	12,981	.9502	104.4	200.1		205
1944	217.3	14,307	726	13,581	.9493	104.3	208.3		215
1945	209.6	14,052	670	13,382	.9523	103.6	202.3		212
1946	192.1	13,786	523	13,263	.9621	105.7	181.7	192	192

NOTES BY COLUMN

1 Obtained by combining the individual indexes shown by Barger (*The Transportation Industries, 1889–1946*), for passenger and freight traffic of the various transportation industries except water, with 1939 revenues as weights.

2, 3 Department of Commerce, *National Income*, 1951 edition.

4 Column 2 minus column 3.

5 Ratio of sales of total transportation except water to all transportation.

6 Index of column 5.

7 Column 1 divided by column 6.

8 Harold Barger, *op. cit.*

9 Column 8 completed by interpolation with column 7.

TABLE I–4

Derivation of Output, All Regulated Industries: 1929 Operating Revenues, Transportation Industries

(*millions of dollars*)

1. Steam railroads	6,556
2. Pullman	84
3. Express companies	145
4. Street and electric railways	856
5. Local bus lines	165
6. Highway passenger transportation, not elsewhere classified	165
7. Highway freight and warehousing	195
8. Water transportation	476
9. Air transportation	34
10. Pipe lines	350
11. Services allied to transportation	170
Total	9,196

NOTES BY LINE

1, 4, 5 See output data for individual industries, Tables I–13, I–22, and I–27.

2, 3 Interstate Commerce Commission, *Statistics of Railways in the United States.*

6 Approximate estimate. Data shown in *Bus Facts* (National Association of Motor Bus Operators) for the late 1930's indicate that operating revenues for intercity bus lines were 70 to 80 per cent of those for city bus lines. Since line 6 also encompasses taxicabs we have assumed total revenues for this category the same as for local bus lines.

7 An estimate of revenues for intercity trucking (160 million) was obtained from Barger's estimate of ton-miles (4 billion) and his estimate of 1939 revenue per ton-mile (four cents). Since we wish to include local for-hire trucking and warehousing, this estimate was multiplied by 1.2176. The latter figure represents the ratio between (a) 1939 revenues for trucking and warehousing (1,080 million, based on the Commerce Department figure of 728 million for corporate sales, increased 48.3 per cent to include noncorporate business) and (b) Barger's 1939 revenue figure for intercity trucking (887 million).

The final figure obtained is far below the Commerce Department estimate of 1929 corporate sales for the trucking and warehousing industry. Since estimates of the level of activity in this industry for this period vary widely, we base our estimate of 1929 revenues mainly on Barger's figures so that it may be consistent with our output index.

8–11 Commerce Department estimates of corporate sales (*National Income,* 1951 edition).

APPENDIX I

TABLE I–5

Derivation of Output, All Regulated Industries: Output, Communications, and Public Utilities, 1890–1950
(*millions of 1929 dollars*)

Year	*Electric Light and Power* (1)	*Gas* (2)	*Telephones* (3)	*Total, Columns 1–3* (4)	*Coverage of Total Communications and Public Utilities* (5)	*Output, All Communications and Public Utilities* (6)
1890	7	58	15	80	0.464	172
1891	8	64	18	90	.493	183
1892	9	69	21	99	.522	190
1893	10	75	22	107	.551	194
1894	13	82	27	122	.580	210
1895	15	89	31	135	.609	222
1896	18	97	36	151	.637	237
1897	22	105	45	172	.666	258
1898	28	114	59	201	.695	289
1899	36	124	82	242	.724	334
1900	46	(151)	93	290	.753	385
1901	58	178	129	365	.764	478
1902	72	168	167	407	.775	525
1903	85	189	181	455	.785	580
1904	98	201	208	507	.796	637
1905	110	210	260	580	.807	719
1906	123	234	323	680	.818	831
1907	138	258	362	758	.829	914
1908	156	274	363	793	.839	945
1909	175	296	385	856	.850	1,007
1910	195	313	415	923	.861	1,072
1911	217	329	442	988	.872	1,133
1912	239	366	475	1,080	.883	1,223
1913	250	381	506	1,137	.887	1,282
1914	280	402	532	1,214	.891	1,363
1915	306	411	513	1,230	.895	1,374
1916	388	462	598	1,448	.899	1,611
1917	451	509	664	1,624	.904	1,796
1918	578	501	645	1,724	.908	1,899
1919	663	528	629	1,820	.912	1,996
1920	723	542	682	1,947	.916	2,126
1921	668	494	719	1,881	.920	2,045
1922	758	534	785	2,077	.924	2,248
1923	920	579	872	2,371	.919	2,580
1924	1,010	601	930	2,541	.913	2,783
1925	1,169	612	987	2,768	.908	3,048
1926	1,353	674	1,055	3,082	.903	3,413
1927	1,504	711	1,109	3,324	.898	3,702
1928	1,647	737	1,150	3,534	.892	3,962
1929	1,840	786	1,210	3,836	.887	4,325

(concluded on next page)

TABLE I–5 (concluded)

Year	Electric Light and Power (1)	Gas (2)	Telephones (3)	Total, Columns 1–3 (4)	Coverage of Total Communications and Public Utilities (5)	Output, All Communications and Public Utilities (6)
1930	1,905	797	1,190	3,892	0.902	4,315
1931	1,876	777	1,140	3,793	.899	4,219
1932	1,706	727	1,038	3,471	.908	3,823
1933	1,756	695	968	3,419	.907	3,770
1934	1,881	723	988	3,592	.916	3,921
1935	2,047	751	1,023	3,821	.915	4,176
1936	2,343	786	1,083	4,212	.913	4,613
1937	2,531	815	1,139	4,485	.915	4,902
1938	2,411	795	1,152	4,358	.918	4,747
1939	2,669	836	1,213	4,718	.917	5,145
1940	2,971	906	1,300	5,177	.916	5,652
1941	3,433	950	1,436	5,819	.915	6,360
1942	3,815	1,040	1,533	6,388	.921	6,936
1943	4,437	1,272	1,620	7,329	.915	8,010
1944	4,651	1,210	1,673	7,534	.908	8,297
1945	4,585	1,262	1,801	7,648	.907	8,432
1946	4,590	1,299	2,112	8,001	.908	8,812
1947	5,234	1,460	2,279	8,973	.907	9,893
1948	5,794	1,576	2,429	9,799	.915	10,709
1949	5,991	1,619	2,493	10,103	.919	10,993
1950	6,806	1,826	2,591	11,223	.922	12,172

NOTES BY COLUMN

1, 3 Data compiled in this study (Tables I–16 and I–20).

2 For 1899 and 1901–50, index shown in Table I–6 times 786 million, 1929 revenue as shown by J. M. Gould, *Output and Productivity in the Electric and Gas Utilities, 1899–1942*. For 1900, derived by linear interpolation: an estimate for 1889 (54 million) was obtained by extrapolating the 1899 figure with the change in book value of plant and equipment for manufactured gas (see Table B–8, capital formation for total); data for 1890–98 were derived by geometric interpolation between estimates for 1889 and 1899.

5 For 1929–50, Table I–8. For 1922: derived from the 1929 total for telephones, electric light and power, and gas (Table I–8) as a ratio of total communications and public utilities excluding radio (it was assumed radio was of negligible importance in 1922). For 1890, 1900, and 1912: extrapolated from 1922 by use of ratios of book value of industries included in the output index to total book value, communications and public utilities (see Table I–12); remaining years derived by linear interpolation.

TABLE I–6

Derivation of Output, Total Utilities:
Manufactured and Natural Gas Output Index, 1899–1950

Year	*Output Index* (1929 = 100)	*Year*	*Output Index* (1929 = 100)
1899	15.8	1925	77.8
		1926	85.8
1900	...	1927	90.4
1901	22.7	1928	93.8
1902	21.4	1929	100.0
1903	24.0		
1904	25.6	1930	101.4
1905	26.7	1931	98.9
1906	29.8	1932	92.5
1907	32.8	1933	88.4
1908	34.8	1934	92.0
1909	37.7	1935	95.5
		1936	100.0
1910	39.8	1937	103.7
1911	41.8	1938	101.1
1912	46.6	1939	106.3
1913	48.5		
1914	51.1	1940	115.3
1915	52.3	1941	120.9
1916	58.8	1942	132.3
1917	64.7	1943	161.8
1918	63.8	1944	153.9
1919	67.2	1945	160.6
		1946	165.3
1920	69.0	1947	185.8
1921	62.9	1948	200.5
1922	67.9	1949	206.0
1923	73.7		
1924	76.5	1950	232.3

For 1899–1942, J. M. Gould, *Output and Productivity in the Electric and Gas Utilities, 1899–1942.* For 1943–50, Table I–7.

TABLE I–7

Derivation of Output, All Regulated Industries: Manufactured and Natural Gas Output, 1943–1950

(1929 = 100)

	1940	*1942*	*1943*	*1944*	*1945*	*1946*	*1947*	*1948*	*1949*	*1950*
Output, Ratio to 1940										
1. Q Manufactured gas	1.00	1.130	1.188	1.223	1.362	1.421	1.554	1.514	1.444	1.442
2. Natural gas	1.00	1.226	1.665	1.496	1.495	1.522	1.744	2.007	2.155	2.560
3. V Value of manufactured gas	94.8	102.7	105.0	107.9	117.0	123.1	133.9	141.5	143.9	142.0
4. Value of natural gas	123.2	145.9	161.0	169.2	169.7	178.2	212.1	248.7	272.7	340.1
5. QV_0 Manufactured gas	94.8	107.1	112.6	115.9	129.1	134.7	147.3	143.5	136.9	136.7
6. Natural gas	123.2	151.0	205.1	184.3	184.2	187.5	214.9	247.3	265.5	315.4
7. V_1/Q Manufactured gas (line 3 divided by line 1)	94.8	90.9	88.4	88.2	85.9	86.6	86.2	93.5	99.7	98.5
8. Natural gas (line 4 divided by line 2)	123.2	119.0	96.7	113.1	113.5	117.1	121.6	123.9	126.5	132.9
9. $\Sigma(V_1 + QV_0)$ (sum of lines 3 through 6)	436.0	506.7	583.7	577.3	600.0	623.5	708.2	781.0	819.0	934.2
10. $\Sigma(V_0 + V_1/Q)$	436.0	427.9	403.1	419.3	417.4	421.7	425.8	435.4	444.2	449.4
11. Index, ratio to 1940 (line 9 divided by line 10)	1.000	1.184	1.448	1.377	1.437	1.479	1.663	179.4	184.4	207.9
12. Index, 1929 = 100		132.3	161.8	153.9	160.6	165.3	185.8	200.5	206.0	232.3

Extension of index prepared by J. M. Gould, *Output and Productivity in the Electric and Gas Utilities, 1899–1942*. Unweighted indexes for manufactured and for natural gas were combined in accordance with the Edgeworth formula based on 1940, in the manner shown by Gould in his Table A–18. The resulting index was linked to Gould's index in 1942. Q signifies the ratio of output in any year to 1940 output, V_0 the 1940 (base year) value of output and V_1 the given-year value of output.

NOTES BY LINE

1, 2 Based on sales to consumers, in millions of cubic feet, as reported by American Gas Association.

3, 4 Quarterly averages of revenue from sales to consumers, in millions of dollars, as reported by American Gas Association and shown in the *Survey of Current Business*.

10 Lines 3 plus 4 for 1940, plus lines 7 and 8 for the respective years.

12 Ratios of line 11 linked in 1942 to the index shown by Gould.

TABLE I–8

Derivation of Output, All Regulated Industries: Operating Revenues, Communications and Public Utilities, 1929–1950

(financial data in millions of dollars)

Year	*Telephones* (1)	*Telegraph* (2)	*Radio and Television* (3)	*Electric Light and Power* (4)	*Gas* (5)	*Local Utilities and Public Service, N.E.C.* (6)	*Total* (cols. 1 *through* 6) (7)	*Total* cols. 1, 4 *and* 5 (8)	*Ratio, Column* 8 *to Column* 7 (9)
1929	1,210	202	172	1,841	786	115	4,326	3,837	0.887
1930	1,239	183	125	1,914	800	120	4,381	3,953	.902
1931	1,201	155	130	1,890	770	148	4,294	3,861	.899
1932	1,062	120	96	1,723	726	140	3,867	3,511	.908
1933	977	120	92	1,676	680	131	3,676	3,333	907
1934	987	127	79	1,775	703	113	3,784	3,465	.916
1935	1,039	130	95	1,882	728	113	3,987	3,649	.915
1936	1,119	141	116	2,046	771	117	4,310	3,936	.913
1937	1,180	145	123	2,207	801	119	4,575	4,188	.915
1938	1,183	132	123	2,213	777	118	4,546	4,173	.918
1939	1,243	139	136	2,317	814	119	4,768	4,374	.917
1940	1,318	144	161	2,453	872	119	5,067	4,643	.916
1941	1,456	164	181	2,674	914	123	5,512	5,044	.915
1942	1,645	180	182	2,816	995	104	5,922	5,456	.921
1943	1,840	206	234	3,032	1,064	109	6,485	5,936	.915
1944	1,970	220	307	3,171	1,108	106	6,882	6,249	.908
1945	2,147	231	327	3,236	1,147	113	7,201	6,530	.907
1946	2,330	220	343	3,360	1,205	134	7,592	6,895	.908
1947	2,482	245	383	3,773	1,384	154	8,421	7,639	.907
1948	2,918	229	413	4,252	1,561	171	9,544	8,731	.915
1949	3,203	218	421	4,471	1,667	183	10,163	9,341	.919
1950	3,607	229	454	4,882	1,928	196	11,296	10,417	.922

NOTES BY COLUMN

1 Table I–9.
2 Federal Communications Commission, *Statistics of the Communications Industry in the United States*. Data cover large wire and ocean cable as well as radio telegraph carriers. No adjustment has been made for coverage since coverage is virtually complete

3, 6 Department of Commerce, National Income and Product of the U.S., 1929–1950. Data are "corporate sales."
4, 5 Table I–10, Table I–11.

TABLE I–9

Derivation of Output, All Regulated Industries: Telephones, Operating Revenues, 1929–1950

(millions of dollars)

Year	*Operating Revenues* *All Companies* (1)	*Class* A *Companies* (2)	*Ratios, Column* 1 *to Column* 2 *and Interpolations* (3)	*Operating Revenues, All Years* (4)
1929	1,210	1,135	1.066	1,210
1930		1,169	1.060	1,239
1931		1,139	1.054	1,201
1932	1,062	1,013	1.048	1,062
1933		935	1.045	977
1934		946	1.043	987
1935		999	1.040	1,039
1936		1,078	1.038	1,119
1937	1,180	1,140	1.035	1,180
1938		1,143		1,183
1939		1,201		1,243
1940		1,273		1,318
1941		1,407		1,456
1942		1,589		1,645
1943		1,778		1,840
1944		1,903		1,970
1945		2,074		2,147
1946		2,251		2,330
1947		2,398		2,482
1948		2,819		2,918
1949		3,095		3,203
1950		3,485		3,607

NOTES BY COLUMN

1 For 1929: Table I–20, footnote to column 2. For 1932 and 1937, Census of Electrical Industries.

2 Federal Communications Commission, *Statistics of the Communications Industry in the United States.*

4 Column 1 for available years; for other years, column 2 times column 3.

TABLE I–10

Derivation of Output, All Regulated Industries: Electric Light and Power, Operating Revenues, 1929–1950

(millions of dollars)

	Electric Utility Operating Revenues					
Year	*All Companies* (1)	*Electric Utilities Reported by* EEI (2)	*Ratio, Column 1 to Column 2 and Interpolations* (3)	*Operating Revenues, All Companies* (4)	*Electric Operating Revenues, Class* A *and* B *Companies* (5)	*Electric Operating Revenues, All Companies* (6)
1929	1,841	1,817	1.0132	1,841		
1930		1,894	1.0107	1,914		
1931		1,874	1.0083	1,890		
1932	1,723	1,713	1.0058	1,723		
1933		1,640	1.0220	1,676		
1934		1,710	1.0382	1,775		
1935		1,785	1.0543	1,882		
1936		1,911	1.0705	2,046		
1937	2,207	2,031	1.0867	2,207		
1938					2,169	2,213
1939					2,271	2,317
1940					2,404	2,453
1941					2,621	2,674
1942					2,760	2,816
1943					2,971	3,032
1944					3,108	3,171
1945					3,171	3,236
1946					3,293	3,360
1947					3,698	3,773
1948					4,167	4,252
1949					4,382	4,471
1950					4,784	4,882

Includes revenue from electric service to ultimate consumers and miscellaneous electric-service revenues.

NOTES BY COLUMN

1 For 1929: Table I–16, footnote to column 2. For 1932 and 1937, Census of Electrical Industries. Data cover revenue from sales of electric energy to ultimate consumers and miscellaneous electric-service revenues of private companies.

2 Edison Electric Institute, Statistical Bulletins.

4 Column 1 for available years; for other years, column 2 times column 3.

5 Federal Power Commission, *Statistics of Electric Utilities in the United States*.

6 Column 5 divided by 0.98, estimated coverage of Class A and B utilities.

TABLE I–11

Derivation of Output, All Regulated Industries:
Gas Sales, 1929–1950

(millions of dollars)

Year	*Manufactured Gas*	*Natural Gas*	*Total*
1929	444	342	786
1930	447	353	800
1931	435	335	770
1932	411	315	726
1933	378	302	680
1934	375	328	703
1935	372	356	728
1936	358	413	771
1937	360	441	801
1938	360	417	777
1939	365	449	814
1940	379	493	872
1941	388	526	914
1942	411	584	995
1943	420	644	1,064
1944	431	677	1,108
1945	468	679	1,147
1946	492	713	1,205
1947	536	848	1,384
1948	566	995	1,561
1949	576	1,091	1,667
1950	568	1,360	1,928

Source: American Gas Association. Data for each year for each component are for establishments producing manufactured gas or distributing natural gas in that year, except that manufactured gas data for 1929–31 are for plants manufacturing gas in 1931, and natural gas data for 1929–33 are for plants distributing natural gas in 1933.

TABLE I–12

Derivation of Output, All Regulated Industries:
Book Values of Plant and Equipment, Communications and Public Utilities

(in millions)

	1890	*1900*	*1912*	*1922*
1. Electric light and power	67	357	1,877	3,805
2. Gas	201	445	825	1,420
3. Telephones	69	386	1,047	2,139
4. Total (lines 1–3)	337	1,188	3,749	7,364
5. Water supply	237	255	275	343
6. Irrigation	63	102	343	523
7. Telegraph	147	156	216	350
8. Radio				20
9. Total (lines 1–3 and 5–8)	784	1,701	4,583	8,600
10. Ratio, line 4 to line 9	0.430	0.698	0.818	0.856

Source: All data are from Simon Kuznets, *National Product since 1869* (National Bureau of Economic Research, 1946), except figures for gas and radio which are from Table B–6 (lines 7 and 9, and note on "all other").

TABLE I–13

Output and Capital-Product Ratios, Steam Railroads, Annually, 1880–1950

Year	*Output Index* (1929 = 100) (1)	*Output, 1929 Dollars* (millions) (2)	*Capital-Product Ratios, 1929 Dollars* (3)
1880	9.3	610	15.95
1881	10.3	675	15.10
1882	11.3	741	14.83
1883	12.0	787	14.79
1884	12.6	826	14.59
1885	13.6	892	13.76
1886	15.1	990	12.52
1887	16.6	1,088	11.61
1888	17.6	1,154	11.28
1889	19.2	1,259	10.60
1890	21.1	1,383	9.84
1891	22.7	1,488	9.33
1892	24.1	1,580	8.97
1893	23.6	1,547	9.61
1894	22.4	1,469	10.64
1895	23.7	1,554	10.17
1896	24.7	1,619	9.67
1897	26.5	1,737	8.89
1898	29.9	1,960	7.78
1899	33.2	2,177	6.94
1900	36.0	2,360	6.43
1901	38.4	2,518	6.07
1902	41.7	2,734	5.62
1903	44.0	2,885	5.35
1904	46.0	3,016	5.15
1905	50.8	3,330	4.71
1906	56.6	3,711	4.31
1907	57.6	3,776	4.36
1908	55.9	3,665	4.67
1909	60.2	3,947	4.49
1910	64.5	4,229	4.35
1911	65.5	4,294	4.47
1912	70.3	4,609	4.31
1913	73.0	4,786	4.27
1914	70.1	4,596	4.59
1915	75.0	4,917	4.34
1916	86.3	5,658	3.77
1917	95.1	6,235	3.42
1918	98.0	6,425	3.34
1919	92.8	6,084	3.52

(concluded on next page)

TABLE I–13 (concluded)

Year	*Output Index* (1929 = 100) (1)	*Output, 1929 Dollars* (millions) (2)	*Capital-Product Ratios, 1929 Dollars* (3)
1920	102.2	6,700	3.17
1921	77.7	5,094	4.16
1922	82.9	5,435	3.91
1923	98.0	6,425	3.31
1924	92.4	6,058	3.60
1925	97.2	6,372	3.48
1926	102.4	6,713	3.35
1927	98.4	6,451	3.54
1928	98.1	6,431	3.60
1929	100.0	6,556	3.57
1930	85.7	5,618	4.23
1931	69.2	4,537	5.32
1932	52.4	3,435	7.00
1933	55.0	3,606	6.58
1934	59.7	3,914	5.97
1935	62.6	4,104	5.62
1936	75.5	4,950	4.60
1937	80.9	5,304	4.27
1938	65.9	4,320	5.26
1939	74.8	4,904	4.59
1940	83.0	5,441	4.10
1941	105.4	6,910	3.22
1942	147.3	9,657	2.31
1943	177.3	11,624	1.93
1944	182.5	11,965	1.86
1945	169.8	11,132	2.00
1946	142.0	9,310	2.38
1947	147.0	9,637	2.28
1948	141.9	9,303	2.37
1949	117.4	7,697	2.89
1950	128.9	8,451	2.66

NOTES BY COLUMN

1 For 1880–89, averages of data for adjacent fiscal years shown in Table I–14. For 1890–1915: from Harold Barger (*The Transportation Industries, 1889–1946*), with index base shifted to 1929 and data for fiscal years averaged. For 1916–46, Barger index, base shifted. For 1947–50, from Table I–15, base shifted.

2 Column 1 times railway operating revenues in 1929—6,556 millions. The 1929 revenue figure is based on data reported by the Interstate Commerce Commission for all railroads (6,486 millions) adjusted to include railroads not reporting to ICC by use of the ratio of track-mileage of reporting companies to track-mileage of all companies (0.9893).

3 Ratios of value of plant and equipment in 1929 dollars (Table C–1) to output, column 2 above.

TABLE I–14

Derivation of Output, Steam Railroads: Index of Output, 1880–1890

(mileage data in billions)

Year Ending June 30	*Passenger-Miles* (Poor's) (1)	*Freight Ton-Miles* (Poor's) (2)	*Passenger-Miles* (Census) (3)	*Freight Ton-Miles* (Census) (4)	*Passenger-Miles*[a] (5)	*Freight Ton-Miles*[a] (6)	*Index*[b] (1890 = 100) (7)	*Index*[c] (1929 = 100) (8)
1880			5.7	32.3	5.9	32.3	42.38	8.6
1881			6.5	38.1	6.6	37.7	48.90	9.9
1882	7.7	39.3	7.7	40.2	7.7	39.3	52.61	10.7
1883	8.5	44.1			8.5	44.1	58.76	11.9
1884	8.8	44.7			8.8	44.7	49.92	12.1
1885	9.1	49.2			9.1	49.2	64.79	13.1
1886	9.7	52.8			9.7	52.8	69.40	14.1
1887	10.6	61.6			10.6	61.6	79.53	16.1
1888	11.2	65.4			11.2	65.4	84.33	17.1
1889	12.0	68.7			12.0	68.7	89.05	18.1
1890	12.5	79.2	12.0	79.2	12.5	79.2	100.00	20.3

[a] For 1882–1890: Poor's data (columns 1 and 2). For 1880: census data (columns 3 and 4) adjusted to the level of Poor's series by use of the 1890 ratios between the two sets of figures (column 1 to column 3 and column 2 to column 4). For 1881, derived by interpolation of the data for 1880 and 1882 by use of census data for 1880–82 (columns 3 and 4).

[b] Derived from columns 5 and 6 weighted with unit-revenues for 1880 and 1890 in accordance with the Edgeworth formula. The 1880 unit-revenues (2.51 cents per passenger-mile and 1.29 per freight ton-mile) were obtained from the census; the 1890 unit-revenues (2.17 cents per passenger-mile and 0.93 cents per freight ton-mile) are from Poor's.

[c] Derived by linking column 7 in 1890 to the index shown by Barger (*The Transportation Industries, 1889–1946*), shifted to a 1929 base.

TABLE I–15

Derivation of Output, Steam Railroads: Index, 1939–1950

(1939 = 100)

Year	FREIGHT TON-MILES[a] (billions) (1)	PASSENGER-MILES[a] (billions) Commutation (2)	Coach (3)	Parlor and Sleeping Car (4)	Free Riders (5)	INDEXES (1939 = 100) Freight[b] (6)	Passenger[c] (7)	Total[d] (8)
1939	335	4.01	11.12	7.53	0.96	100.0	100.0	100.0
1947	658	6.01	27.67	12.26	1.26	196.4	197.8	196.6
1948	641	5.86	24.32	11.02	1.16	191.3	176.7	189.7
1949	529	5.48	20.27	9.35	1.20	157.9	149.9	157.0
1950	592	4.99	17.44	9.34	1.22	176.7	138.0	172.3

[a] Interstate Commerce Commission, *Statistics of Railways*. The classification follows that adopted by Barger (*The Transportation Industries, 1889–1946*). "Free riders" are estimated by subtracting parlor and sleeping car passenger-miles reported by the railroads from passenger-miles reported by the Pullman Company.

[b] Based on aggregate ton-mileage shown in column 1.

[c] Based on columns 2–5, combined with 1939 unit-revenues as weights. The 1939 unit-revenues (cents), from ICC, are:

Commutation	1.02
Coach	1.80
Parlor and sleeping car	2.98 (railroad unit revenue plus Pullman charge)
Free riders	0.65 (Pullman charge)

[d] Based on columns 6 and 7 combined with 1939 revenues from freight and passenger traffic as weights. The weights, from ICC data, are 3,293 millions for freight and 418 millions for passenger traffic. For comparison, the index for 1949 for passenger traffic and for total traffic was computed in accordance with the Edgeworth formula on a 1939 base. The resulting index for all traffic was identical with that shown in column 8.

TABLE I-16

Output and Capital-Product Ratios: Electric Light and Power, Annually, 1887–1950

Year	*Output Index* (1929 = 100) (1)	*Output, 1929 Dollars* (millions) (2)	*Capital-Product Ratios, 1929 Dollars* (3)
1887	0.28	5.2	4.42
1888	0.31	5.7	6.89
1889	0.35	6.4	9.33
1890	0.39	7.2	12.06
1891	0.43	7.9	15.51
1892	0.48	8.8	17.25
1893	0.57	10.5	18.40
1894	0.69	12.7	18.08
1895	0.82	15.1	17.48
1896	0.98	18.0	17.28
1897	1.17	21.5	16.12
1898	1.51	27.8	14.69
1899	1.98	36.4	13.46
1900	2.48	45.6	12.48
1901	3.18	58.5	10.91
1902	3.9	71.8	10.38
1903	4.6	84.7	10.33
1904	5.3	97.5	10.26
1905	6.0	110.4	10.24
1906	6.7	123.3	10.28
1907	7.5	138.0	10.24
1908	8.5	156.4	10.03
1909	9.5	174.8	10.27
1910	10.6	195.1	10.47
1911	11.8	217.2	10.64
1912	13.0	239.3	10.88
1913	13.6	250.3	11.68
1914	15.2	279.8	10.83
1915	16.6	305.5	10.26
1916	21.1	388.3	8.18
1917	24.5	450.9	7.13
1918	31.4	577.9	5.85
1919	36.0	662.6	5.00
1920	39.3	723.3	4.51
1921	36.3	668.1	5.00
1922	41.2	758.3	4.50
1923	50.0	920.3	3.95
1924	54.9	1,010.4	4.10
1925	63.5	1,168.7	4.05
1926	73.5	1,352.8	3.87
1927	81.7	1,503.7	3.78
1928	89.5	1,647.2	3.73
1929	100.0	1,840.5	3.55

(concluded on next page)

TABLE I–16 (concluded)

Year	*Output Index* (1929 = 100) (1)	*Output, 1929 Dollars* (millions) (2)	*Capital-Product Ratios, 1929 Dollars* (3)
1930	103.5	1,904.9	3.64
1931	101.9	1,875.5	3.96
1932	92.7	1,706.1	4.45
1933	95.4	1,755.8	4.29
1934	102.2	1,881.0	3.91
1935	111.2	2,046.6	3.50
1936	127.3	2,343.0	3.00
1937	137.5	2,530.7	2.76
1938	131.0	2,411.1	2.93
1939	145.0	2,668.7	2.66
1940	161.4	2,970.6	2.39
1941	186.5	3,432.5	2.09
1942	207.3	3,815.4	1.92
1943	241.1	4,437.4	1.66
1944	252.7	4,650.9	1.56
1945	249.1	4,584.7	1.55
1946	249.4	4,590.2	1.53
1947	284.4	5,234.4	1.36
1948	314.8	5,793.9	1.30
1949	325.5	5,990.8	1.36
1950	369.8	6,806.2	1.30

Column 1: For 1887–1912, Table I–17; for 1913–32, from J. M. Gould (*Output and Productivity in the Electric and Gas Utilities, 1899–1942*). For 1933–50, Table I–19.

Column 2: Column 1 times 1,840.5 (millions), 1929 revenue from sales to ultimate consumers plus miscellaneous electric-service revenues. This figure is based on 1929 revenues as reported by the Edison Electric Institute (Statistical Bulletin No. 13); the EEI figures were adjusted to the census level by the use of the average ratio (0.94942) between the two series in 1927 and 1932. The basic figures are (in millions of dollars):

	Census: Revenue from Sales to Ultimate Consumers and Miscellaneous Revenue	*Edison Electric Institute: Revenue*
1927	1,576.4	1,661.0
1929		1,938.5
1932	1,722.6	1,813.7

Column 3: Ratios of value of plant and equipment in 1929 dollars (Table D–1) to output, column 2 above.

TABLE I–17

Derivation of Output, Electric Light and Power: Index, 1887–1912

(1929 = 100)

Year	*Output Index* (1)	*Net Current Generated* (millions kw-h) (2)	*Output Index* (3)	*Estimated Generating Capacity* (millions kw) (4)	*Ratio, Column 3 to Column 4 and Interpolations* (5)	*Output Index* (6)
1887		131	0.28			0.28
1888		146	0.31			0.31
1889		163	0.35			0.35
1890		181	0.39			0.39
1891		202	0.43			0.43
1892		225	0.48			0.48
1893		269	0.57			0.57
1894		322	0.69			0.69
1895		385	0.82			0.82
1896		460	0.98			0.98
1897		550	1.17			1.17
1898		706	1.51			1.51
1899		905	1.93			1.93
1900		1,161	2.48			2.48
1901		1,489	3.18			3.18
1902 (yr. ending June 30)	3.6	1,687	3.6	1.19	3.025	
1902 (yr. ending Dec. 31)				1.31	2.996	3.9
1903				1.56	2.939	4.6
1904				1.83	2.881	5.3
1905				2.12	2.823	6.0
1906				2.43	2.766	6.7
1907	7.5		7.5	2.77	2.708	7.5
1908				3.20	2.654	8.5
1909				3.66	2.600	9.5

(concluded on next page)

TABLE I–17 (concluded)

Year	*Output Index* (1)	*Net Current Generated* (millions kw-h) (2)	*Outpui Index* (3)	*Estimated Generating Capacity* (millions kw) (4)	*Ratio, Column 3 to Column 4 and Interpolations* (5)	*Output Index* (6)
1910				4.17	2.547	10.6
1911				4.73	2.493	11.8
1912	13.0		13.0	5.33	2.439	13.0

NOTES BY COLUMN

1 J. M. Gould, *Output and Productivity in the Electric and Gas Utilities, 1899–1942.*

2 For 1887, 1892, 1897, and 1902: *Electrical World*, September 9, 1922. Total energy generated less losses. The *Electrical World* figure for 1902 has been assumed to refer to the census year, the year ending June 30. Data for other years were derived by geometric interpolation between available figures.

3 For 1902, 1907, and 1912: column 1; for 1887–1902, column 2 times the ratio of column 1 to column 2 for 1902.

4 Table D–14, derivation of gross capital expenditures.

6 For 1887–1901, 1907, and 1912: column 3. For other years, column 4 times column 5.

TABLE I–18

Derivation of Output, Electric Light and Power: Index, Selected Years, 1932–1950

	1932 (1)	*1937, Comparable with 1932* (2)	*1937, Comparable with Later Years* (3)	*1942* (4)	*1947* (5)	*1950* (6)
Residential sales						
Current sold (millions kw-h)	11,899	16,750	14,822	21,814	34,713	50,041
Revenue (millions of dollars)	626.9	716.5	645.7	813.7	1,090.8	1,476.5
Revenue per kw-h (cents)	5.269	4.278	4.356	3.730	3.142	2.951
Commercial and industrial sales						
Current sold (millions of kw-h)	47,835	72,674	65,202	101,129	127,899	158,829
Revenue (millions of dollars)	980.4	1,187.3	1,105.1	1,416.8	1,902.3	2,447.4
Revenue per kw-h (cents)	2.050	1.634	1.695	1.401	1.487	1.541
Other sales						
Current sold (millions kw-h)	2,414	3,905	11,988	16,747	22,235	26,011
Revenue (millions of dollars)	95.9	101.0	205.1	265.4	336.6	424.1
Revenue per kw-h (cents)	3.973	2.586	1.711	1.585	1.514	1.630
Index, 1932 = 100[a]	100	148.29				
Index, 1937 = 100[b]			100	150.79	206.84	268.97

[a] Prepared from sales and revenue data shown in columns 1 and 2 in accordance with the Edgeworth formula on a 1932 base.

[b] Prepared from sales and revenue data shown in columns 3–6 in accordance with the Edgeworth formula on a 1937 base.

Columns 1 and 2: Sales and revenue data, from Census of Electrical Industries. Data cover commercial establishments only. For 1932, residential corresponds to the census classifications "farm service" and "domestic." Commercial and industrial comprises the census classifications "commercial service" and "railroads." For 1937, residential includes the census classifications "residential or domestic" and "rural" and commercial and industrial includes the census categories "commercial and industrial" and "railroads and railways." Other includes the remainder of sales to ultimate consumers, with the exception of interdepartmental sales, which are not included here.

Columns 3–6: Sales and revenue data, from Federal Power Commission, *Statistics of Electric Utilities in the United States*. Data cover Class A and Class B utilities.

TABLE I–19

Derivation of Output, Electric Light and Power: Index, 1932–1950

(1929 = 100)

Year	*Production Index* (1929 = 100) (1)	*Current Generated* (millions of kw-h) (2)	*Sales to Ultimate Consumers* (millions of kw-h) (3)	*Ratio, and Interpolations, Column 1 to* *Col.* 2 (4)	*Ratio, and Interpolations, Column 1 to* *Col.* 3 (5)	*Production Index* (6)
1932	92.7	74,488		0.0012445		92.7
1933		76,668		.0012445		95.4
1934		82,079		.0012446		102.2
1935		89,330		.0012446		111.2
1936		102,293		.0012447		127.3
1937	137.5	110,464	92,012	.0012447	0.0014944	137.5
1938			87,811		.0014923	131.0
1939			97,314		.0014902	145.0
1940			108,420		.0014882	161.4
1941			125,527		.0014861	186.5
1942	207.3		139,690		.0014840	207.3
1943			161,285		.0014949	241.1
1944			167,812		.0015058	252.7
1945			164,250		.0015168	249.1
1946			163,247		.0015277	249.4
1947	284.4		184,847		.0015386	284.4
1948			203,018		.0015505	314.8
1949			208,297		.0015625	325.5
1950	369.8		234,881		.0015744	369.8

NOTES BY COLUMN

1 For 1932, J. M. Gould, *Output and Productivity in the Electric and Gas Utilities, 1899–1942*. For 1937, derived by multiplying the 1932 index by the index derived in Table I–18. For 1942–50, derived by multiplying the 1937 index by the index derived in Table I–18.

2 FPC, *Production of Electric Energy and Capacity of Generating Plants*. Data cover privately owned utilities.

3 FPC, *Statistics of Electric Utilities in the United States*. Data cover Class A and B utilities.

6 Column 1 for available years. For 1933–36, column 2 times column 4; for 1938–49, column 3 times column 5.

TABLE I–20

Output and Capital-Product Ratios, Telephones, Annually, 1890–1950

Year	*Output Index* (1929 = 100) (1)	*Output, 1929 Dollars* (millions) (2)	*Capital-Product Ratios, 1929 Dollars* (3)
1890	1.2	15	4.99
1891	1.5	18	4.67
1892	1.7	21	4.10
1893	1.8	22	4.20
1894	2.2	27	3.61
1895	2.6	31	4.42
1896	3.0	36	5.06
1897	3.7	45	5.23
1898	4.9	59	4.68
1899	6.8	82	3.91
1900	7.7	93	4.12
1901	10.7	129	3.53
1902	13.8	167	3.09
1903	15.0	181	3.23
1904	17.2	208	3.25
1905	21.5	260	2.89
1906	26.7	323	2.65
1907	29.9	362	2.76
1908	30.0	363	2.97
1909	31.8	385	2.77
1910	34.3	415	2.54
1911	36.5	442	2.44
1912	39.3	475	2.31
1913	41.8	506	2.26
1914	44.0	532	2.16
1915	42.4	513	2.23
1916	49.4	598	1.84
1917	54.9	664	1.67
1918	53.3	645	1.77
1919	52.0	629	1.77
1920	56.4	682	1.58
1921	59.4	719	1.48
1922	64.9	785	1.36
1923	72.1	872	1.28
1924	76.9	930	1.29
1925	81.6	987	1.35
1926	87.2	1,055	1.38
1927	91.7	1,109	1.44
1928	95.1	1,150	1.49
1929	100.0	1,210	1.57

(concluded on next page)

TABLE I–20 (concluded)

Year	*Output Index* (1929 = 100) (1)	*Output, 1929 Dollars* (millions) (2)	*Capital-Product Ratio, 1929 Dollars* (3)
1930	98.4	1,190	1.88
1931	94.5	1,140	2.26
1932	85.8	1,038	2.59
1933	80.0	968	2.74
1934	81.7	988	2.56
1935	84.6	1,023	2.36
1936	89.5	1,083	2.15
1937	94.2	1,139	2.01
1938	95.2	1,152	2.03
1939	100.3	1,213	1.94
1940	107.5	1,300	1.84
1941	118.7	1,436	1.73
1942	126.7	1,533	1.76
1943	133.9	1,620	1.73
1944	138.3	1,673	1.63
1945	148.9	1,801	1.48
1946	174.6	2,112	1.27
1947	188.4	2,279	1.32
1948	200.8	2,429	1.48
1949	206.1	2,493	1.74
1950	214.2	2,591	1.85

Column 1: For 1890–1937, Table I–21, column 8, base shifted. Index was extrapolated to 1950 by use of the BLS index for Class A carriers, which is based on local and toll calls combined with 1939 unit-revenues as weights (*Productivity Trends in Selected Industries: Indexes through 1950*).

Column 2: Column 1 times 1929 operating revenue—1,210 millions. The 1929 revenue figure is based on operating revenues of all companies reporting to ICC, adjusted to the level of census data for 1927 and 1932. The basic figures are (in millions of dollars):

	Census	ICC
1927	1,023.6	979.4
1929		1,172.9
1932	1,061.5	1,049.8

Column 3: Ratios of value of plant and equipment in 1929 dollars (Table E–1) to output, column 2, above.

TABLE I–21. Derivation of Output, Telephones: Index, 1890–1937 (*1927 = 100*)

Year	*Number of Calls* (millions) *Local* (1)	*Toll* (2)	*Sums of Number of Calls Times Weights* (3)	*Coverage of Data in Cols.* 1 *and* 2 (per cent) (4)	*Column* 3 *Adjusted for Coverage* (5)	*Output Index* (1927 = 100) (6)	*Index of Number of Calls, Bell System* (7)	*Output Index, All Years* (8)
1890	444	9	1,274	100	1,274	1.27	2.6	1.3
1891							3.0	1.6
1892							3.5	1.9
1893							3.5	2.0
1894							3.9	2.4
1895							4.3	2.8
1896							4.9	3.3
1897							5.7	4.0
1898							7.1	5.3
1899							9.6	7.4
1900							10.5	8.4
1901							14.0	11.7
1902	4,950	121	14,758	98	15,059	15.02	17.3	15.0
1903							18.4	16.3
1904							20.7	18.8
1905							25.2	23.4
1906							30.7	29.1
1907	10,161	240	30,067	92	32,682	32.60	33.7	32.6
1908							34.3	32.7
1909							37.0	34.7
1910							40.4	37.4
1911							43.7	39.8
1912	13,395	341	40,304	94	42,876	42.77	47.7	42.8
1913							49.3	45.6
1914							50.5	48.0
1915							47.1	46.2
1916							53.3	53.8
1917	19,366	443	56,915	95	59,910	59.76	57.7	59.8
1918							56.3	58.1
1919							55.2	56.7

(concluded on next page)

TABLE I–21 (concluded)

Year	*Number of Calls* (millions) *Local* (1)	*Toll* (2)	*Sums of Number of Calls Times Weights* (3)	*Coverage of Data in Cols.* 1 *and* 2 (per cent) (4)	*Column* 3 *Adjusted for Coverage* (5)	*Output Index* (1927 = 100) (6)	*Index of Number of Calls, Bell System* (7)	*Output Index, All Years* (8)
1920							60.1	61.5
1921							63.5	64.8
1922	21,235	666	67,293	95	70,834	70.66	69.5	70.7
1923							77.5	78.6
1924							83.0	83.8
1925							88.4	88.9
1926							94.8	95.1
1927	30,527	1,087	100,251	100	100,251	100.00	100.0	100.0
1928							107.0	103.7
1929							116.2	109.0
1930							118.3	107.3
1931							117.6	103.0
1932	29,077	971	93,744	100	93,744	93.51	110.6	93.5
1933							103.7	87.2
1934							106.5	89.1
1935							110.7	92.2
1936							117.7	97.6
1937	32,613	1,006	102,882	100	102,882	102.62	124.6	102.7

NOTES BY COLUMN

1, 2 Census of Electrical Industries. Data for 1890, 1927, 1932, and 1937 are for the entire industry. Data for 1902–17 are for systems with annual incomes of $5,000 or more; data for 1922 are for systems with annual incomes of $10,000 or more. For 1890, the reported census total (453 million) was distributed between local and toll calls in accordance with the 1902 proportions. For 1932, the reported total (30,048 million) was distributed between local and toll calls in accordance with averages of the 1927 and 1937 proportions.

3 Sum of Columns 1 and 2 weighted by 2.319 cents and 27.10 cents respectively, 1927 revenue per local call and per toll call as reported by the census.

4 Percentage ratio, miles of wire for companies covered in columns 1 and 2 to miles of wire for the whole industry.

5 Column 3 divided by column 4.

6 Based on column 5.

7 For 1890–1935: derived from data shown in the Federal Communications Commission Telephone Investigation, Exhibit 1360–A. For 1936–37: from data in the Quarterly Summary of Telephone Statistics, American Telephone and Telegraph Company.

8 Column 6 interpolated by use of column 7.

TABLE I–22

Output and Capital-Product Ratios, Street and Electric Railways, Annually, 1890–1950

Year	*Output Index* (1929 = 100) (1)	*Output, 1929 Dollars* (millions) (2)	*Capital-Product Ratio, 1929 Dollars* (3)
1890	17.6	150.6	3.33
1891	19.2	164.3	3.50
1892	20.6	176.4	3.80
1893	20.4	174.7	4.48
1894	19.7	168.5	5.43
1895	21.1	180.4	5.94
1896	22.3	190.4	6.55
1897	24.2	207.2	6.95
1898	27.7	237.2	6.92
1899	31.4	268.4	6.85
1900	34.5	294.8	6.85
1901	37.6	322.0	6.80
1902	41.7	357.0	6.62
1903	45.1	386.1	6.58
1904	48.5	415.2	6.61
1905	55.1	471.6	6.30
1906	63.1	540.0	5.93
1907	66.2	566.3	6.04
1908	66.8	571.5	6.38
1909	71.1	608.3	6.16
1910	75.9	649.3	5.77
1911	80.1	685.3	5.57
1912	84.5	722.9	5.32
1913	88.4	756.3	5.06
1914	88.7	758.8	5.06
1915	87.8	751.1	5.12
1916	94.4	807.6	4.78
1917	100.3	858.1	4.47
1918	99.3	849.5	4.51
1919	104.1	890.6	4.29
1920	109.1	933.4	4.01
1921	102.4	876.0	4.13
1922	108.7	929.9	3.74
1923	111.0	949.6	3.58
1924	108.7	929.9	3.57
1925	107.2	917.1	3.49
1926	107.2	917.1	3.36
1927	104.8	896.6	3.30
1928	101.2	865.8	3.29
1929	100.0	855.5	3.21

(concluded on next page)

TABLE I–22 (concluded)

Year	*Output Index* (1929 = 100) (1)	*Output, 1929 Dollars* (millions) (2)	*Capital-Product Ratio, 1929 Dollars* (3)
1930	91.2	780.2	3.39
1931	80.6	689.5	3.71
1932	67.7	579.2	4.24
1933	62.9	538.1	4.31
1934	65.3	558.6	3.90
1935	64.2	549.2	3.76
1936	66.3	567.2	3.48
1937	63.3	541.5	3.52
1938	58.7	502.2	3.66
1939	58.3	498.8	3.55
1940	57.7	493.6	3.49
1941	49.8	426.0	3.18
1942	60.5	517.6	2.51
1943	74.9	640.8	1.90
1944	78.0	667.3	1.71
1945	78.0	667.3	1.61
1946	76.3	652.7	1.56
1947	70.1	599.7	1.62
1948	54.6	467.1	1.81
1949	44.7	382.4	2.12
1950	39.6	338.8	2.28

Column 1: For 1890–1926, Table I–25, columns 7 and 3. For 1927–50, derived by combining series for number of passengers (Table I–23) and freight car-miles (Table I–24) with 1939 unit-revenues as weights (7 cents per passenger and 51 cents per freight car-mile), as shown by Barger in *The Transportation Industries, 1889–1946.*

Column 2: For 1890–1907, Table I–25, column 6. For 1908–37: column 1 of this table times 855.5 millions, estimated railway operating revenue in 1929. The estimate was obtained by adjusting the revenue data reported by the American Transit Association for electric railways and trolley buses (which include municipal lines) to the level reported for private lines by the Census of Electrical Industries for 1927 and 1932. The basic figures for operating revenue, in millions, are:

	Census	A.T.A.
1927	884.9	918.9
1929		887.4
1932	546.8	566.3

Column 3: Ratios of value of plant and equipment in 1929 dollars (Table F–1) to output, column 2 above.

TABLE I–23

Derivation of Output, Street and Electric Railways: Passenger Traffic, 1890–1950

(*in millions*)

	Revenue Passengers, Census				
Year	*Total* (1)	*Municipal Lines* (2)	*Private Lines* (col. 1 minus col. 2) (3)	*Revenue Passengers, American Transit Association* (4)	*Revenue Passengers, Private Lines, All Years* (5)
1890[a]	2,023		2,023		2,023
1902[a]	4,774		4,774		4,774
1907	7,441		7,441	7,440	7,441
1908				7,510	7,510
1909				8,000	8,000
1910				8,550	8,550
1911				9,030	9,030
1912	9,546		9,546	9,550	9,546
1913				9,980	9,970
1914				10,010	10,010
1915				9,900	9,880
1916				10,630	10,609
1917	11,305	39	11,266	11,300	11,266
1918				11,180	11,158
1919				11,720	11,697
1920				12,270	12,258
1921				11,520	11,508
1922	12,667	453	12,214	12,210	12,214
1923				12,480	12,430
1924				12,250	12,140
1925				12,090	11,933
1926				12,110	11,892
1927	12,175	588	11,587	11,850	11,587
1928				11,457	11,193
1929				11,303	11,032

(concluded on next page)

TABLE I–23 (concluded)

Year	Revenue Passengers, Census: Total (1)	Municipal Lines (2)	Private Lines (col. 1 minus col. 2) (3)	Revenue Passengers, American Transit Association (4)	Revenue Passengers, Private Lines, All Years (5)
1930				10,359	10,100
1931				9,189	8,950
1932	7,956	382	7,574	7,787	7,574
1933				7,290	7,049
1934				7,592	7,296
1935				7,485	7,141
1936				7,738	7,336
1937	7,737	728	7,009	7,438	7,009
1938					6,557
1939					6,484
1940					6,399
1941					5,448
1942					6,678
1943					8,326
1944					8,655
1945					8,683
1946					8,534
1947					7,815
1948					6,072
1949					4,945
1950					4,326

[a] Year ending June 30.

NOTES BY COLUMN

1, 2, 3 Successive reports of the Census of Electrical Industries. Data include pay-transfer passengers but not free-transfer passengers; includes trolley bus operators.

4 Shown in Barger, *The Transportation Industries, 1889–1946*. This series differs from the series in column 3 in that it includes municipal lines and, after 1917, does not include all pay-transfer passengers.

5 Column 3 for available years; for other years to 1937, column 3 interpolated by use of column 4. For 1938–50, data in Table I–26, column 6, linked in 1937 to column 3 above.

TABLE I-24

Derivation of Output, Street and Electric Railways: Freight Car-Miles, Electric Railways, 1902–1950

(*millions*)

Year	*Total* (1)	*Interurban* (2)	*Ratio, Column 1 to Column 2 and Interpolations* (3)	*Freight Car-Miles All Years* (4)
1902	9.13			9.13
1907	33.90			33.90
1912	35.75			35.75
1917	51.98			51.98
1922	56.23			56.23
1926		74.80		75.17
1927	79.21	78.80	1.005	79.21
1928		75.0	1.019	76.43
1929		76.8	1.032	79.26
1930		64.7	1.046	67.68
1931		53.5	1.059	56.66
1932	39.47	36.8	1.073	39.47
1933		32.3	1.067	34.46
1934		36.6	1.061	38.83
1935		40.2	1.056	42.45
1936		47.0	1.050	49.35
1937	47.29	45.3	1.044	47.29
1938		34.3		35.81
1939		37.0		38.63
1940		39.2		40.92
1941		44.2		46.14
1942		45.9		47.92
1943		49.3		51.47
1944		52.2		54.50
1945		49.3		51.47
1946		41.9		43.74
1947		43.2		45.10
1948		35.1		36.64
1949		32.7		34.14
1950		35.8		37.38

NOTES BY COLUMN

1 Census of Electrical Industries. The 1902 figure was derived from the reported total (24.33 millions) less the car-mileage of steam locomotives on the elevated lines of New York City (15.20 millions).

2 Interstate Commerce Commission, Electric Railways.

4 Column 1 for available years. For 1926, column 2 times the 1927 ratio of column 1 to column 2; for 1928–31 and 1933–36, column 2 times column 3; for 1938–50, column 2 times the 1937 ratio of column 1 to column 2.

TABLE I–25

Derivation of Output, Street and Electric Railways: 1890–1926

Year	*Index, Freight and Passenger Traffic 1929 = 100* (1)	*Index, Passenger Traffic 1929 = 100* (2)	*Index, Freight and Passenger Traffic 1929 = 100* (3)	*Output, Freight and Passenger* (millions of 1929 dollars) (4)	*Output: Railroads, Electric Light and Power, Telephones* (millions of 1929 dollars) (5)	*Output, Street and Electric Railways* (millions of 1929 dollars) (6)	*Output Index 1929 = 100* (7)
1890		18.3	17.6	150.6	140.5	150.6	17.6
1891					151.4	164.3	19.2
1892					161.0	176.4	20.6
1893					157.9	174.7	20.4
1894					150.9	168.5	19.7
1895					160.0	180.4	21.1
1896					167.3	190.4	22.3
1897					180.4	207.2	24.2
1898					204.7	237.2	27.7
1899					229.5	268.4	31.4
1900					249.9	294.8	34.5
1901					270.5	322.0	37.6
1902	41.7	43.3	41.7	357.0	297.3	357.0	41.7
1903					315.1	386.1	45.1
1904					332.2	415.2	48.5
1905					370.0	471.6	55.1
1906					415.7	540.0	63.1
1907	66.2	67.4	66.2	566.3	427.6	566.3	66.2
1908		68.1	66.8				
1909		72.5	71.1				

(concluded on next page)

TABLE I–25 (concluded)

Year	*Index, Freight and Passenger Traffic 1929 = 100* (1)	*Index, Passenger Traffic 1929 = 100* (2)	*Index, Freight and Passenger Traffic 1929 = 100* (3)	*Output, Freight and Passenger* (millions of 1929 dollars) (4)	*Output: Railroads, Electric Light and Power, Telephones* (millions of 1929 dollars) (5)	*Output, Street and Electric Railways* (millions of 1929 dollars) (6)	*Output Index 1929 = 100* (7)
1910		77.5	75.9				
1911		81.9	80.1				
1912	84.5	86.5	84.5				
1913		90.4	88.4				
1914		90.6	88.7				
1915		89.6	87.8				
1916		96.2	94.4				
1917	100.3	102.1	100.3				
1918		101.1	99.3				
1919		106.0	104.1				
1920		111.1	109.1				
1921		104.3	102.4				
1922	108.7	110.7	108.7				
1923		112.7	111.0				
1924		110.0	108.7				
1925		108.2	107.2				
1926	107.2	107.8	107.2				

NOTES BY COLUMN

1 Derived by combining series for number of passengers (Table I–23) and freight car-miles (Table I–24) with 1939 unit-revenues as weights (7 cents per passenger and 51 cents per freight car-mile), as shown by Barger (*The Transportation Industries, 1889–1946*).

2 Based on revenue-passenger data (Table I–23).

3 Column 1 interpolated by use of column 2.

4 Column 3 times 855.5 million, estimated railway operating revenue in 1929 (see footnote to column 2, Table I–22).

6 Column 4 interpolated by use of column 5.

7 Column 6 divided by 855.5 million, estimated railway operating revenue in 1929.

TABLE I–26

Derivation of Output, Street and Electric Railways: Revenue Passengers, Street and Electric Railways and Local Bus Lines, 1937–1950

(*millions of passengers*)

	Revenue Passengers, Electric Railway and Bus			*Revenue Passengers, Electric Railways, Total*	*Ratio, Electric Railway Passengers to Total Local Transit*	*Revenue Passengers, Private Lines*	
Year	*Total* (1)	*On Municipal Lines* (2)	*On Private Lines* (3)	(4)	(5)	*Electric Railway* (6)	*Bus* (col. 3 minus col. 6) (7)
1937	10,435.5		9,646	7,438.4	0.71280	6,876	2,770
1938	9,984.7	826.9	9,158	7,013.6	.70243	6,433	2,725
1939	10,252.3	880.1	9,372	6,958.0	.67868	6,361	3,011
1940	10,503.7	925.0	9,579	6,883.6	.65535	6,278	3,301
1941	11,301.5	2,787.3	8,514	7,095.4	.62783	5,345	3,169
1942	14,501.2	3,063.9	11,437	8,306.7	.57283	6,551	4,886
1943	17,918.0	3,774.8	14,143	10,348.0	.57752	8,168	5,975
1944	18,735.4	3,782.4	14,953	10,639.3	.56787	8,491	6,462
1945	18,981.9	3,781.3	15,201	10,637.2	.56039	8,518	6,683
1946	19,119.0	3,881.5	15,238	10,504.0	.54940	8,372	6,866
1947	18,287.0	3,774.6	14,512	9,662.0	.52835	7,667	6,845
1948	17,312.0	5,062.9	12,249	8,419.0	.48631	5,957	6,292
1949	15,251.0	4,608.0	10,643	6,951.0	.45577	4,851	5,792
1950	13,845.0	4,312.5	9,532	6,164.0	.44521	4,244	5,288

NOTES BY COLUMN

1, 4 American Transit Association, Transit Fact Books. Excludes pay-transfer passengers.

2 Unpublished data provided by American Transit Association for revenue passengers on publicly owned transit lines in cities over 100,000 population. The figures for each year include those companies which were publicly owned at the beginning of the year.

3 For 1938–50: A.T.A. Column 1 minus column 2, For 1937: Total of (a) figure for private and municipal electric railway traffic, excluding pay-transfer passengers (7,438 million) less the estimated portion of this traffic carried by municipal lines (9.4093 per cent, the ratio of municipal to total revenue passengers, including pay-transfer as derived from census data) and (b) bus passengers as reported by A.T.A. (2,997 million) less the census figure for traffic on municipally owned lines (89 million).

5 Column 4 divided by column 1.

6 Column 3 times column 5.

TABLE I–27

Output and Capital-Product Ratios, Local Bus Lines, Annually, 1922–1950

Year	*Output Index* (1929 = 100) (1)	*Output, 1929 Dollars* (millions) (2)	*Capital-Product Ratio, 1929 Dollars* (3)
1922	15.5	25.6	0.16
1923	25.4	41.9	.32
1924	38.0	62.7	.53
1925	57.1	94.3	.50
1926	77.2	127.5	.48
1927	88.1	145.5	.51
1928	94.4	155.9	.53
1929	100.0	165.1	.59
1930	94.3	155.7	.71
1931	87.7	144.8	.75
1932	80.9	133.6	.80
1933	78.9	130.3	.79
1934	90.4	149.3	.68
1935	99.8	164.8	.70
1936	120.6	199.1	.68
1937	130.2	215.0	.78
1938	128.1	211.5	.94
1939	141.6	233.8	.91
1940	155.2	256.2	.89
1941	149.0	246.0	1.07
1942	229.7	379.2	.87
1943	281.0	463.9	.82
1944	303.9	501.7	.71
1945	314.3	518.9	.67
1946	322.9	533.1	.67
1947	321.9	531.5	.84
1948	295.9	488.5	1.27
1949	272.4	449.7	1.55
1950	248.7	410.6	1.66

Column 1: Based on number of revenue passengers, data in Table I–26, column 7, linked to data in Table I–28.

Column 2: Column 1 times 165.1 millions, local bus line operating revenue in 1929 as reported by American Transit Association.

Column 3: Ratios of value of plant and equipment in 1929 dollars (Table G–1) to output, column 2, above.

TABLE I–28

Derivation of Output, Local Bus Lines:
Revenue Passengers, Local Bus Lines, 1922–1937

Year	*Revenue Passengers, Including Municipal* (millions)
1922	357
1923	585
1924	875
1925	1,313
1926	1,777
1927	2,028
1928	2,172
1929	2,301
1930	2,169
1931	2,018
1932	1,862
1933	1,816
1934	2,080
1935	2,297
1936	2,774
1937	2,997

Source: American Transit Association, Transit Fact Books. Figures for 1922–25 are based on total number of passengers (including free passengers) and the 1926 ratio (0.8845) of revenue passengers to total passengers. Data include passengers on municipal bus lines.

TABLE I–29

Output and Capital-Product Ratios, All Other Transportation and Utilities, Annually, 1890–1950

Year	*Output, 1929 Dollars* (millions) (1)	*Capital-Product Ratio, 1929 Dollars* (2)
1890	161	12.64
1891	179	11.64
1892	188	11.36
1893	196	11.53
1894	207	11.57
1895	226	10.89
1896	241	10.32
1897	261	9.61
1898	286	8.85
1899	318	8.07
1900	368	7.14
1901	431	6.26
1902	460	6.00
1903	501	5.65
1904	551	5.27
1905	602	4.96
1906	695	4.44
1907	744	4.33
1908	769	4.42
1909	830	4.32
1910	888	4.27
1911	926	4.39
1912	1,010	4.30
1913	1,073	4.34
1914	1,090	4.52
1915	1,156	4.44
1916	1,327	3.94
1917	1,481	3.61
1918	1,531	3.63
1919	1,544	3.64
1920	1,673	3.44
1921	1,432	4.08
1922	1,671	3.49
1923	1,896	3.15
1924	1,986	3.10
1925	2,034	3.16
1926	2,277	2.94
1927	2,460	2.87
1928	2,577	2.89
1929	2,894	2.67

(concluded on next page)

TABLE I–29 (concluded)

Year	*Output, 1929 Dollars* (millions) (1)	*Capital-Product Ratio, 1929 Dollars* (2)
1930	2,777	2.93
1931	2,682	3.13
1932	2,449	3.46
1933	2,621	3.19
1934	2,784	2.94
1935	2,891	2.79
1936	3,242	2.47
1937	3,613	2.21
1938	3,591	2.25
1939	3,985	1.99
1940	4,634	1.70
1941	5,442	1.47
1942	5,582	1.44
1943	6,356	1.26
1944	6,808	1.15
1945	7,449	1.06
1946	7,661	1.04
1947	8,468	.98
1948	9,166	.96
1949	9,374	1.00
1950	10,274	.94

Column 1: Derived by subtracting total output of steam railroads (Table I–13), electric light and power (Table I–16), telephones (Table I–20), street and electric railways (Table I–22), and local bus lines (Table I–27) from output of all transportation and utilities (Table I–1). For purposes of deriving output for the all other group, output of local bus lines, which is not available before 1922, was interpolated linearly between the 1922 figure and an assumed zero in 1909.

Column 2: Ratios of value of plant and equipment in 1929 dollars (Table H–1) to output, column 1 above.

TABLE I–30

Annual Changes in Output, All Regulated Industries and Components, 1880–1950

(millions of 1929 dollars)

Year	*Total*	*Steam Railroads*	*Electric Light and Power*	*Telephones*	*Street and Electric Railways*	*Local Bus Lines*	*All Other*
1880							
1881	81	65					
1882	82	66					
1883	57	46					
1884	48	39					
1885	82	66					
1886	122	98					
1887	122	98					
1888	82	66	1				
1889	130	105	0				
1890	154	124	1				
1891	140	105	1	3	13		18
1892	117	92	1	3	12		9
1893	−24	−33	1	1	−1		8
1894	−66	−78	3	5	−7		11
1895	122	85	2	4	12		19
1896	98	65	3	5	10		15
1897	168	118	4	9	17		20
1898	298	223	6	14	30		25
1899	311	217	8	23	31		32
1900	281	183	10	11	27		50
1901	296	158	12	36	27		63
1902	332	216	14	38	35		29
1903	248	151	13	14	29		41
1904	250	131	13	27	29		50
1905	486	314	12	52	57		51
1906	618	381	13	63	68		93
1907	194	65	15	39	26		49
1908	−61	−111	18	1	6		25
1909	420	282	19	22	36		61
1910	433	282	20	30	41		58
1911	190	65	22	27	36		38
1912	494	315	22	33	38		84
1913	317	177	11	31	33		63
1914	−112	−190	30	26	3		17
1915	388	321	26	−19	−8		66
1916	1,138	741	82	85	57		171
1917	912	577	63	66	50		154
1918	342	190	127	−19	−8		50
1919	216	−341	85	−16	41		13

(concluded on next page)

TABLE I–30 (concluded)

Year	*Total*	*Steam Railroads*	*Electric Light and Power*	*Telephones*	*Street and Electric Railways*	*Local Bus Lines*	*All Other*
1920	902	616	60	53	42		129
1921	–1,920	–1,606	–55	37	–57		–241
1922	792	341	90	66	54		239
1923	1,500	990	162	87	20	16	225
1924	–128	–367	90	58	–20	21	90
1925	596	314	159	57	–13	31	48
1926	870	341	184	68	0	34	243
1927	124	–262	151	54	–20	18	183
1928	260	–20	143	41	–31	10	117
1929	694	125	193	60	–10	9	317
1930	–1,095	–938	65	–20	–76	–9	–117
1931	–1,356	–1,081	–29	–50	–90	–11	–95
1932	–1,729	–1,102	–170	–102	–111	–11	–233
1933	278	171	50	–70	–41	–4	172
1934	656	308	125	20	21	19	163
1935	504	190	166	35	–10	16	107
1936	1,605	846	296	60	18	34	351
1937	960	354	188	56	–25	16	371
1938	–1,157	–984	–120	13	–40	–4	–24
1939	1,317	584	258	61	–3	23	375
1940	1,592	537	302	87	–5	22	669
1941	2,796	1,469	461	136	–68	–10	808
1942	3,592	2,747	383	97	92	133	142
1943	3,658	1,967	622	87	123	85	775
1944	1,124	341	214	53	26	38	453
1945	–113	–833	–66	128	0	17	640
1946	–1,294	–1,822	5	311	–14	14	214
1947	1,890	327	644	167	–53	–2	811
1948	899	–334	560	150	–133	–42	695
1949	–1,261	–1,606	197	64	–85	–39	207
1950	2,485	754	815	98	–43	–39	901

APPENDIX J

Sources and Uses of Funds

THE nature and limitations of the data on the sources and uses of funds were discussed in Chapter 8. This appendix presents, in Tables J–1 through J–7, the basic figures underlying the tabulations included in that chapter. Reference may also be made here to some estimates bearing upon the accuracy of these tables.

The figures for the earlier years are based primarily upon changes in balance sheet items. The most important source of error in this technique springs from write-ups, which are reflected in large part on the uses side in the physical property account, and on the sources side in securities outstanding and surplus. Such write-ups appear to have been of serious dimensions in railroads, electric power and street railways, but not in telephones. It was partly for this reason that the analysis in Chapter 8 was confined to the broader trends in *percentage distributions* of the financial items.

A change in the book value of plant and equipment (gross of depreciation) is equal to gross capital expenditures minus retirements, plus the influence of write-ups or write-downs. The estimates developed for gross capital expenditures and retirements elsewhere in this study make possible an approximation of the magnitude of these property revaluations for two of our components—railroads and electric power. The following tabulation expresses estimated write-ups (plus) or write-downs (minus), so derived, as a percentage of the change in book values of plant and equipment for the relevant periods:

Railroads	
1880–1890	+21
1893–1907	+24
1907–1916	+5
Electric light and power	
1881–1912	+15
1913–1922	+15
1928–1937	−2

The small negative figure for electric power during the 1928–37 period reflects the net result of two opposing tendencies. During the years 1928–32 apparent write-ups amounted to 872 million dollars; these were approximately balanced by write-downs during 1933–37 amounting to 933 millions.

In the later periods of the tables which follow, more refined methods were employed for estimating the sources and uses of funds, as described in the accompanying notes. Some impression of the accuracy of the compilations may be gained by the figures given in the lines labeled "discrepancy." These figures show the differences between the totals of the independently estimated sources and uses.

TABLE J–1

Sources and Uses of Funds: All Railroads, 1880–1916

(dollar amounts in millions)

	CHANGES IN BALANCE SHEET ITEMS FROM					
	July 1, 1880 to June 30, 1890		*July 1, 1893 to June 30, 1907*		*July 1, 1907 to December 31, 1916*	
	Amount	*Per Cent*	*Amount*	*Per Cent*	*Amount*	*Per Cent*
Uses						
1. Investment in road and equipment (book value)	3,510.3	85.9	4,092.8	74.0	5,287.9	108.8
2. Current assets	169.0	4.1	941.1	17.0	127.3	2.6
(a) Inventories	24.3	0.6	150.9	2.7	112.6	2.3
(b) Cash and other current assets	144.7	3.5	790.2	14.3	14.7	0.3
3. Long-term investments other than securities	405.3	9.9	[a]		223.0	4.6
4. Other assets	...		498.7	9.0	−780.4	−16.1
5. Total uses	4,084.6	100.0	5,532.3	100.0	4,858.0	100.0
Sources						
6. Surplus	97.5	2.4	526.6	9.5	1,442.7	29.7
7. Depreciation reserves	0	0	0	0	639.8	13.2
8. Current liabilities	299.4	7.3	660.7	11.9	111.4	2.3
9. Securities outstanding	3,687.7	90.3	4,079.7	73.7	3,069.2	63.2
(a) Capital stock	1,754.5	43.0	2,627.9	47.5	1,700.4	35.0
(b) Bonds	2,240.6	54.9	3,532.3	63.8	2,921.9	60.1
(c) (Less) securities held	307.4	−7.5	2,080.5	−37.6	1,553.1	−32.0
10. Other	...		265.4	4.8	−405.0	−8.3
11. Total sources	4,084.6	100.0	5,532.3	100.0	4,858.0	100.0

Detail may not add to totals because of rounding.

[a] Not shown separately.

Source of basic data: For 1880–90, *1890 Census of the United States*, Vol. xiv, Part 1, *Transportation by Land*; for subsequent periods, *Statistics of Railways in the United States*, Interstate Commerce Commission.

NOTES BY LINE

1 Changes in the book value of road and equipment are gross of depreciation. For the years prior to 1916, it is possible that some negligible amounts of depreciation had been deducted from book values; the original sources are not clear on this point.

3 Comprised of various categories of long-term investments including physical properties such as mines and timber tracts. Figures shown for the periods ending June 30, 1890 and December 31, 1916 are amounts outstanding on these dates, since neither the July 1, 1880 nor the July 1, 1907 figures were shown separately.

4 Not identified in detail before 1916. In that year, comprised working funds advanced to general and special agents, insurance, pension, and other funds; rents and insurance paid in advance; discount on capital stock and funded debt; property abandoned chargeable to operating expenses; and deferred assets and unadjusted debits.

6 In the earlier balance sheet statements this item was called "Profit and Loss."

7 Of the balance sheets that entered directly into this table, the statement for 1916 first included depreciation reserves. The earliest depreciation reserve figure is an ICC estimate of 170 million dollars for June 30, 1910. Accordingly, the entire depreciation reserve outstanding at the end of 1916 is assumed to have been accumulated during 1907–16 and the accumulation in the previous period is assumed to have been zero. While not strictly correct, it is a rough approximation. In 1907 the ICC first required the roads to provide for depreciation. It is known that such depreciation charged on a voluntary basis in previous years was very small.

9a, b For 1916, outstandings carried at par value; outstandings in prior years apparently at par value.

9c Securities held (mainly those of affiliated companies), carried in the balance sheets under assets, have been omitted from uses of funds and are here deducted from total securities outstanding, to eliminate intercompany duplications.

10 Not identified in detail prior to 1916. Included in that year: liability for provident funds, tax liability, premium on funded debt, insurance and casualty reserves, operating reserves, and other deferred liabilities and unadjusted credits.

TABLE J-2. Sources and Uses of Funds: Class I Railroads and Their Lessors, 1914–1949 (*dollar amounts in millions*)

	July 1, 1914 to December 31, 1920[a]		*January 1, 1921 to December 31, 1930*		*January 1, 1931 to December 31, 1940*		*January 1, 1941 to December 31, 1949*	
	Amount	*Per Cent*	*Amount*	*Per Cent*	*Amount*	*Per Cent*	*Amount*	*Per Cent*
Uses								
1. Total capital expenditures	2,582.5	78.6	7,879.0	120.3	2,917.2	121.6	6,908.1	80.4
(a) Road and equipment	2,444.0	74.4	7,929.0	121.0	2,805.0	117.0	6,836.0	79.6
(b) Miscellaneous physical property	138.5	4.2	−50.0	−0.8	112.2	4.7	72.1	0.8
2. Current assets	266.1	8.1	−996.4	−15.2	−88.2	−3.7	1,614.8	18.8
(a) Inventories	485.5	14.8	−324.9	−5.0	−94.9	−4.0	389.3	4.5
(b) Receivables	191.7	5.8	−492.1	−7.5	−62.6	−2.6	165.7	1.9
(c) Cash and deposits	−25.2	−0.8	152.4	2.3	100.9	4.2	863.0	10.1
(d) Other current assets	−385.9	−11.7	−331.8	−5.1	−31.6	−1.3	196.8	2.3
3. Long-term securities, other than those of affiliated companies	−438.2	−13.3	177.3	2.7	−292.6	−12.2	132.6	1.5
4. Other assets	875.0	26.6	−508.2	−7.8	−138.1	−5.8	−68.5	−0.8
5. Total uses	3,285.4	100.0	6,551.7	100.0	2,398.3	100.0	8,587.0	100.0
Sources								
6. Retained profits	1,289.7	34.9	2,513.0	50.8	336.7	13.9	3,801.9	47.3
7. Depreciation charges	657.3	17.8	2,178.0	44.0	2,017.7	83.5	4,367.0	54.3
8. Current liabilities	793.8	21.5	−635.6	−12.9	−490.5	−20.3	738.9	9.2
(a) Non-government	[b]		−4.0	−0.1	−159.4	−6.6	417.5	5.2
(b) Tax liability	[b]		[b]		−4.3	−0.2	331.1	4.1
(c) Other current liabilities	[b]		−631.6	−12.8	−326.8	−13.5	−9.7	−0.1
9. Net new issues	121.2	3.3	1,277.6	25.8	346.0	14.3	−531.6	−6.6
(a) Common	−75.5	−2.0	586.5	11.9	136.7	5.7	−467.0	−5.8
(b) Preferred	−37.0	−1.0	142.7	2.9	150.3	6.2	−107.9	−1.3
(c) Bonds	1,347.9	36.5	1,832.3	37.1	−547.4	−22.6	−913.5	−11.4
(d) (Less) investments in affiliated companies	1,114.2	−30.2	1,283.9	−26.0	−606.4	25.1	−956.8	11.9
10. Other	830.7	22.5	−387.9	−7.8	207.6	8.6	−340.3	−4.2
11. Total sources	3,692.7	100.0	4,945.1	100.0	2,417.5	100.0	8,035.9	100.0
12. Discrepancy	−407.3	...	1,606.6	...	−19.2	...	551.1	...

Detail may not add to totals because of rounding.

[a] The period July 1, 1914–December 31, 1920 covers Class I roads only; lessors are excluded.

[b] Not shown separately.

Source of basic data: *Statistics of Railways in the United States*, Interstate Commerce Commission, except as indicated.

NOTES BY LINE

1a For 1914–30, data derived from gross capital expenditure series including land, of Class I and II roads and their lessors reported by ICC, adjusted by the ratios 0.869 in 1914–20 and 0.987 in 1921–30 to eliminate expenditures of roads other than those covered in the table. These ratios reflect the proportion of expenditures of Class I and their lessors to Class I and II roads and their lessors in 1929 and 1930, and of Class I to Class I and II and their lessors in 1918. For 1931–49, gross capital expenditures for Class I and lessor roads were available separately.

1b Mines, timberlands, commercial power plants, hotels, and other non-railroad physical property, before subtracting reserves.

2a At cost less depreciation.

2b In 1914 and 1920 a portion of receivables may have been included with other current assets.

2c In 1914 a portion of deposits may have been included with other current assets. Beginning with 1941, includes an account called temporary cash investments which combined portions of various current accounts and holdings of U.S. Treasury certificates, marketable securities, time drafts receivable, demand and time loans, deposits, and other similar investments of a temporary character.

3 Cost less write-downs to reflect actual or anticipated impairment of value, exclusive of market fluctuations.

4 Includes unadjusted debits such as rents and insurance premiums paid in advance, and during the period 1931–49, deferred assets. The latter account and a corresponding "deferred liabilities" account included under "other" liabilities were grossly inflated in the 1920 balance sheet by the large number of claims and counterclaims developed by the railroads and the U.S. government as a result of federal operation of the railroads during the war. These claims, in general, did not represent cash flows, and their inclusion would have seriously distorted the sources and uses statement in adjoining periods. Therefore, for the periods 1914–20 and 1921–31 both deferred assets and deferred liabilities were eliminated, even though some actual cash transactions may thus have been inadvertently excluded from our statement. The changes in these eliminated accounts, and in total sources and uses including these accounts, are:

	July 1, 1914 to December 31, 1920	January 1, 1921 to December 31, 1930
Uses		
Deferred assets	−1,211.9	−1,659.6
Total uses	5,611.5	6,176.0
Sources		
Deferred liabilities	−1,882.5	−2,102.9
Total sources	6,597.0	3,737.6

6 Net income less cash dividends, plus (a) defaulted interest since 1929 (the difference between interest accruals, treated in income statements as an expense, and interest payments); (b) profit on road and equipment, except that after 1935 the profit on depreciable property was credited to depreciation reserves, and was not readily available for inclusion in retained income; (c) delayed income credits (available separately until 1942, thereafter included directly in net income).

7 Includes depreciation charges plus the value of retirements charge to operating expense. Source: Association of American Railroads, *Statistics of Railways of Class I, United States, Statistical Summary Numbers 3, 13, 27, and 35.* This compilation covers Class I roads and their lessors for this account and hence had to be reduced by 16.07 per cent for the period 1914–20 to eliminate lessors. The ratio represents book value of road and equipment of the lessors of Class I roads to the book value of road and equipment of Class I roads and their lessors on December 31, 1920.

8a Short-term loans, bills, and miscellaneous accounts payable.

8b Accrued tax liability includes payroll taxes in later years. Before the period 1931–40, taxes were included with "other" liabilities.

9a, b, c Common stock and preferred shares are at par values. Bonds represent cash raised, with the exception of bonds sold to other railroads which are valued at par. Except as noted, derived from Raymond W. Goldsmith's *A Study of Savings in the United States* (Princeton University Press, 1955 and 1956). Goldsmith's series on bonds include the railroad net bonds issued series of the National Bureau of Economic Research Corporate Bond Research Project plus equipment obligations and income bonds. His series on stocks represent the changes in stocks outstanding as reported by ICC adjusted for changes in intercorporate holdings, changes due to reorganization, changes due to stock dividends and to conversion of bonds, and for duplications. Net inter-railroad security sales were added back to the Goldsmith series. In the case of stocks, such data were directly available in Goldsmith's compilation. For bonds, the changes in inter-railroad holdings as reported by ICC were taken, except for the 1941–49 period when the effect of reorganization revaluations was seriously evident. The ratio of the change in inter-railroad holdings to net bonds issued during 1914–40 was employed to estimate net inter-railroad bond sales in this period.

To eliminate stocks and bonds issued by railroads other than those represented in our sources and uses statement, the series described above were reduced by 22.9 per cent in 1914–20, 8.5 per cent in 1921–30, 8.9 in 1931–40, and 7.7 in 1941–49. The ratios represent the proportion of the book value of road and equipment of railroads not included in our table to those covered by the original stock and bond series.

In addition, for completeness, changes in unpaid conditional sales contracts outstanding for Class I roads for 1938–49 were added to the debt data with an estimate for their lessors based on the value of road and equipment.

9d Investment in affiliated companies, reported in the ICC balance sheets under assets, have been excluded from uses of funds and are here deducted from net new issues to eliminate intercompany duplications.

10 Unadjusted credits and deferred liabilities.

12 Line 5 minus line 11.

TABLE J-3

Sources and Uses of Funds: Electric Light and Power Companies, 1881–1937

(dollar amounts in millions)

	CHANGES IN BALANCE SHEET ITEMS FROM					
	January 1, 1881 to December 31, 1912		*January 1, 1913 to December 31, 1922*		*January 1, 1928 to December 31, 1937*	
	Amount	*Per Cent*	*Amount*	*Per Cent*	*Amount*	*Per Cent*
Uses						
1. Investment in plant and equipment	2,098.6	89.1	2,130.8	78.2	3,461.9	87.4
(a) Electric light and power	2,098.6	89.1	2,130.8	78.2	3,215.0	81.2
(b) Electric railway, gas and other	[a]		[a]		246.8	6.2
2. Current assets	140.1	5.9	277.8	10.2	−9.7	−0.2
3. Long-term securities and investments	76.7	3.3	85.4	3.1	651.4	16.4
4. Other	40.8	1.7	231.9	8.5	−143.4	−3.6
5. Total uses	2,356.3	100.0	2,725.7	100.0	3,960.2	100.0
Sources						
6. Surplus	115.7	4.9	144.1	5.3	288.7	7.3
7. Depreciation reserves	64.4	2.7	277.4	10.2	646.2	16.3
8. Current liabilities	200.8	8.5	190.0	7.0	35.7	0.9
(a) Short-term debt	137.7	5.8	4.0	0.1	[a]	
(b) Bills and accounts payable, and other current liabilities	63.1	2.7	186.0	6.8	[a]	
9. Securities outstanding	1,948.5	82.7	2,086.9	76.6	2,969.5	75.0
(a) Common	989.8	42.0	664.5	24.4	1,441.8 (a and b combined)	36.4
(b) Preferred	176.9	7.5	345.2	12.7		
(c) Bonds	908.1	38.5	1,356.5	49.8	1,527.7	38.6
(d) (Less) Treasury securities	48.5	−2.1	105.8	−3.9	[a]	
(e) (Less) securities of other electric companies	77.8	−3.3	173.5	−6.4	[a]	
10. Other	26.8	1.1	27.5	1.0	20.1	0.5
11. Total sources	2,356.3	100.0	2,725.7	100.0	3,960.2	100.0

Detail may not add to totals due to rounding.

[a] Not shown separately.

January 1, 1881 is assumed to be the approximate beginning of the industry.
Source of basic data: Changes in balance sheet data derived from *Census of Electrical Industries: Central Electric Light and Power Stations.* Changes for the period 1881–1912 are the same as the value of balance sheet assets and liabilities on December 31, 1912, and in effect represent the net change in each account noted from the beginning of the industry until that date.

Data for 1881–1912 and 1913–22 cover electric light and power establishments, excluding insofar as possible the gas, electric railway, and other activities of composite companies. The extent to which other activities of composite companies are included in these periods is probably very small. Data for 1881–1912 and 1913–22 do not include street railway electric light and power departments which reported to the census in conjunction with the parent electric railway; such electric light and power departments are, however, included in our series on capital formation. For 1927–37, data do cover almost all electric power departments of street railways and they also include the electric railway, gas, and other activities of composite companies. As a result, the 1928–37 balance sheet changes shown refer to a broader industry composite than those for earlier periods.

Balance sheet data for 1881–1912 and 1913–22 have been adjusted to exclude intra-industry sales and purchases of securities, and lines 3 and 9 for these intervals are net of such intra-industry transactions (see footnote to lines 9d and e). Data for 1928–37 could not be corrected in similar fashion; line 3 for this period includes holdings of securities of other electric companies and line 9 represents the gross total of securities outstanding, without deduction for securities held by other electric companies.

NOTES BY COLUMN

1a, b 2 Some companies carried plant and equipment on their books at the entire cost of the properties, including write-ups, franchise values, and good will. Others showed depreciated values. For 1912, includes relatively small amounts of other physical property (see note to line 3). For 1927, utility plant of 902.6 millions, not identified by the census as to type, was distributed between electric plant and other utility plant in accordance with relative proportions of identifiable plant for the two groups.

3 Securities at cost, relatively small amounts of physical property that were neither electric or other utility plant, and sinking funds in 1937. Other physical property was included with plant and equipment in 1912. Sinking funds were included with other (line 4) in terminal years prior to 1937. Data for 1881–1912 and 1913–22 exclude Treasury securities and securities of other electric companies, while figures for 1928–37 include these items.

4 Identified as stock and bond discount, sinking and other special funds, and sundries in the 1912 census, and in 1937 as (a) deferred debits, unamortized debt discount and expense, extraordinary property losses, clearing accounts, and other deferred debits, (b) capital stock discount and expense, and (c) reacquired securities.

6 Shown in balance sheet statements as profit and loss, or deficit or surplus.

7 Comprised of depreciation and other reserves in 1881–1922, and of depreciation reserves only in 1928–37.

9a, b, c In 1937, common and preferred shares were carried at par value, the stated value of stock without par value if such stock has a stated value, or the value at which non-par stock was sold; bonds were carried at face value. Outstandings in prior years were apparently carried at similar values. For 1913–22 capital stock includes 33.2 million dollars of premium on capital stock and funded debt and 14.2 million of debenture shares shown separately on the latter date. Small amounts of cash invested in unincorporated properties are included with changes in common shares in each period.

9d, e For 1881–1912 and 1913–22, changes in Treasury securities and securities of other electric companies, shown in the balance sheets under assets, have been excluded from uses of funds and are here deducted from the securities outstanding component of sources of funds. Such an adjustment was not made for the 1928–37 period.

10 Identified as sundries in early census reports, and in 1937 as (a) deferred credits; unamortized premium on debt and other deferred credits, and (b) other reserves.

APPENDIX J

TABLE J–4

Sources and Uses of Funds: Class A and B Electric Light and Power Companies, 1938–1950

(dollar amounts in millions)

	January 1, 1938 to December 31, 1950	
	Amount	*Per Cent*
Uses		
1. Total capital expenditures	11,894.4	94.5
(a) Electric plant	10,782.3	85.6
(b) Gas and other plant	1,112.1	8.8
2. Current assets	1,099.0	8.7
(a) Inventories	405.0	3.2
(b) Receivables	147.6	1.2
(c) Cash and deposits	543.5	4.3
(d) Other	2.9	a
3. Investments, other than in associated companies	−43.0	−0.3
4. Other	−359.3	−2.9
5. Total uses	12,591.1	100.0
Sources		
6. Retained profits	1,652.5	12.8
7. Depreciation charges	4,857.4	37.5
8. Current liabilities	834.8	6.4
(a) Non-government	272.0	2.1
(b) Tax liability	532.0	4.1
(c) Other current and accrued liabilities	30.8	0.2
9. Net new issues	5,727.4	44.2
(a) Stocks	2,332.4	18.0
(b) Bonds	3,210.5	24.8
(c) (Less) investments in associated companies	−184.5	1.4
10. Other	−125.6	−1.0
11. Total sources	12,946.5	100.0
12. Discrepancy	−355.5	...

Detail may not add to totals due to rounding.

[a] Less than one-tenth of 1 per cent.

Source of basic data: Federal Power Commission, *Statistics of Electric Utilities in the United States*, except as noted. Covers Class A and Class B companies.

NOTES BY LINE

1a From Table XXI, Work Memorandum No. 35 (on file at the National Bureau of Economic Research).

1b Estimated as 23.32 per cent of total gross capital expenditures for gas plant and equipment, as reported by the American Gas Association for 1938–50 (4,769 millions). The estimate was derived as follows:

(1) Total capital expenditures for all gas plant and equipment for 1940–50, reported by American Gas Association, is 4,616.0 millions.

(2) Of this amount, companies deriving 50 per cent or more of operating income from natural gas are estimated to have spent 2,916.5 millions. This estimate was derived from the change in gas plant (less reserves) for such companies, January 1,

1940–December 31, 1950, plus depreciation and amortization charges 1940–50, as reported by FPC in *Statistics of Natural Gas Companies*.

(3) The balance for 1940–50 (1,699.5 millions) represents capital expenditures for gas of (a) the electric utilities, and of (b) gas companies, other than natural gas companies. It was assumed that the experience of the two groups was generally similar. Capital expenditures were therefore distributed between the two in accordance with book values of gas plant on December 31, 1948: (a) 2,062 millions for the electric utilities, and (b) 1,193 millions for the gas companies other than natural gas. The former is the balance sheet figure for "gas and other plant" for electric utilities as shown by FPC. The latter represents the difference between the value of capital assets for the gas industry, as reported by BIR, and the value of plant for natural gas companies as reported by FPC.

(4) Capital expenditures for 1940–50, allocated to electric utilities, amounted to 1,076.6 millions, or 23.32 per cent of total expenditures for gas plant for this period.

(5) It was assumed this percentage was applicable for capital expenditures of the entire period 1938–50.

2a Materials and supplies at cost.

2b Includes (i) notes and accounts receivable including debit balances subject to current settlement in open accounts with associated companies and drafts due in one year of issuance upon which associated companies are liable, (ii) balances due on subscriptions to capital stock, (iii) interest and dividends receivable, and (iv) other receivables. All accounts are after reserves in 1950.

2c Comprised of cash; special deposits for the payment of interest, dividends, and other purposes; petty cash funds; and temporary cash investments as demand and time loans, bankers' acceptances, Treasury certificates, and marketable securities.

2d Prepayments of insurance, rent, taxes, interest, and other items, and current accounts not noted previously.

3 Securities of nonassociated companies, relatively small amounts of other physical property that were neither electric nor other utility plant, and sinking and other funds. Securities were carried at cost less write-downs to reflect permanent impairment of value, exclusive of market fluctuations.

4 Deferred debits (unamortized debt discount and expense, clearing accounts, and other deferred debits), capital discount and expense, and reacquired securities.

6 Net income less cash dividends.

7 Includes depreciation and amortization charges of 4,595.1 millions plus 262.3 millions, estimated charges against income for the amortization of "plant acquisition adjustments," that is, plant purchased at prices in excess of original cost. During 1938–50, 187.3 millions of such excess plant values were written off; it was assumed that the write-downs were effected through charges to income. In addition, it is estimated that 75 millions was charged against income for reserves for similar plant values remaining on the books at the end of 1950. The latter estimate is based on Federal Power Commission records showing reserves of 44 millions carried against 186 millions of excess plant values by twenty-five large companies; total plant acquisition adjustments on the books December 31, 1950 were 320.7 millions.

8a Notes and accounts payable, and customers' deposits.

8b Taxes accrued. Includes interest on long- and short-term debt.

8c Dividends declared, matured interest on long-term debt, and current and accrued liabilities of an unspecified nature.

9a, b Par value of new issues of common and preferred shares, and bonds, less refunding, as shown in the *Electrical World* of February 29, 1951, and adjusted as noted below. These figures overstate the net amount of capital raised from the public through the sale of bonds and stocks since it was not possible to take account of the retirement of securities by methods other than refunding, such as sinking fund operations.

(1) *Electrical World* shows (in millions of dollars):

	Bonds		Shares
New issues	11,475.7		2,933.5
Refundings, bonds and shares combined		9,123.1	
Net new issues		5,286.5	

(Detail does not add to total because of rounding of annual data.)

(2) Refundings of 9,123.1 millions were allocated between bonds and shares, 91.4 per cent or 8,338.5 millions for bonds and 8.6 per cent or 784.6 millions for shares, based on the relative importance of public utility bond and preferred stock refunding issues floated during 1938–50 under authorization of the Securities and Exchange Commission. Source: *17th Annual Report*, SEC, 1951, Table 4. (Includes electric, gas, water, and communications companies. Before 1948, also includes street railway and bus companies.)

(3) New issues less refunding were therefore as follows (in millions of dollars):

	Bonds	Shares
New issues	11,475.7	2,933.5
Refunding	8,338.5	784.6
Net new issues	3,137.2	2,148.9

(4) Net new issues were reduced to 98 per cent, the proportion of assets of Class A and B electric companies to total assets of all privately owned electric utilities. The resulting figures, 3,074.7 millions for bonds and 2,106.1 millions for shares are 59.3 per cent and 40.7 per cent, respectively, of the total of net new issues. They compare closely with the proportionate net change in the outstanding book value during the period of the bonds and shares of seven electric light and power companies chosen at random. After eliminating the identifiable effects of security write-downs, the net increase of 614.5 millions in outstanding securities of the seven companies was accounted for 59.4 per cent by bonds and 40.6 per cent by stocks. Source: *Moody's Public Utilities* for various years: balance sheets and related data of the following companies excluding their subsidiaries: Ohio Edison, Pacific Power and Light, Consolidated Edison, Philadelphia Electric, Detroit Edison, Southern California Edison, and Cleveland Electric Illuminating.

(5) To net new share issues of 2,106.1 millions were added 226.3 millions of premiums and assessments on the capital stock of Class A and B companies.

(6) To net new bond issues of 3,074.7 millions have been added 135.8 millions of Class A and B company debt comprised of real estate mortgages, notes and unsecured certificates of indebtedness, other obligations maturing in more than one year from the date of issue, and advances from associated companies. To the extent that real estate mortgages are included in this source there is duplication of data obtained from the *Electrical World*.

Investments in associated companies, carried in the balance sheets under assets, have been excluded from uses of funds to eliminate intercompany duplication and are here deducted from the net new issues component of sources of funds.

10 Deferred credits (unauthorized premium on debt, customers' advances for construction, other deferred credits) and reserves, except those referred to elsewhere and property reserves.

12 Line 5 minus line 11.

TABLE J-5

Sources and Uses of Funds: Telephone Industry, 1891–1912

(dollar amounts in millions)

	CHANGES IN BALANCE SHEET ITEMS FROM			
	January 1, 1891 to December 31, 1902		*January 1, 1903 to December 31, 1912*	
	Amount	*Per Cent*	*Amount*	*Per Cent*
Uses				
1. Investment in plant and equipment (book value)	309.2	84.6	694.8	86.5
2. Current assets	48.6	13.3	44.0	5.5
(a) Inventories	8.7	2.4	[a]	
(b) Cash and other current assets	39.9	10.9	[a]	
3. Long-term securities, except those of other telephone companies	7.2	2.0	51.6	6.4
4. Other	0.3	0.1	13.4	1.7
5. Total uses	365.4	100.0	803.7	100.0
Sources				
6. Surplus	−7.9	−2.2	39.5	4.9
7. Depreciation reserves	31.0	8.5	117.8	14.7
8. Current liabilities	39.8	10.9	43.6	5.4
9. Securities outstanding		82.6	601.5	74.8
(a) Capital stock	234.2	64.1	643.9 (a and b combined)	80.1 (a and b combined)
(b) Bonds	67.5	18.5		
(c) (Less) securities of other telephone companies			20.7	−2.6
(d) (Less) Treasury securities			21.7	−2.7
10. Other	0.8	0.2	1.4	0.2
11. Total sources	365.4	100.0	803.7	100.0

Detail may not add to totals because of rounding.

[a] Not shown separately.

Data for 1891 are for the Bell system and are believed to be synonymous with the commercial telephone industry. Data for 1902 are for all commercial telephone enterprises, while those for 1912 relate to all commercial systems with annual incomes of $5,000 and over.

Source of basic data: For 1891, balance sheet data for December 31, 1890 as derived from *Annual Report, American Telephone and Telegraph Company, 1910*; for other years, derived from Census of Electrical Industries: Telephones.

NOTES BY LINE

1 Plant, equipment, and land primarily at cost, and capitalized franchise values and good will.

3 Shown in reports for 1902 and 1890 as securities of other companies; the small sums involved were assumed to represent stocks of non-telephone companies. For 1912 (and subsequent years) specifically refers to securities of non-telephone companies.

4 During 1903–12, includes sinking and other special funds.

6 Includes the premium on capital stock and the expense, discount, and premium on long-term debt. See also next note.

7 Depreciation and other reserves, except that the 1890 balance sheet included reserves with surplus.

9a, b Apparently at par values; includes installments received on stock subscriptions.

9c, d Securities of other telephone companies and Treasury securities, shown in the balance sheets under assets, have been excluded from uses of funds and are here deducted from securities outstanding, to eliminate intercompany duplications. For 1903–12, these items represent the totals reported at the terminal date for securities of other telephone companies and Treasury securities, since these data were not shown separately in the 1890 and 1902 balance sheets.

TABLE J-6

Sources and Uses of Funds: Bell Telephone System, 1913–1950

(dollar amounts in millions)

	January 1, 1913 to December 31, 1920		*January 1, 1921 to December 31, 1930*		*January 1, 1931 to December 31, 1940*		*January 1, 1941 to December 31, 1950*	
	Amount	*Per Cent*	*Amount*	*Per Cent*	*Amount*	*Per Cent*	*Amount*	*Per Cent*
Uses								
1. Capital expenditures for plant and equipment	862.4	93.7	3,537.0	87.2	1,950.0	113.8	6,650.0	92.7
2. Current assets								
(a) Inventories	23.8	2.6	55.3	1.4	−50.8	−3.0	57.8	0.8
(b) Receivables	28.7	3.1	84.8	2.1	−183.2	−10.7	265.5	3.7
(c) Cash and deposits	5.7	0.6	377.7	9.3	−32.1	−1.9	154.7	2.2
3. Other	[a]		[a]		29.9	1.7	42.1	0.6
4. Total uses	920.6	100.0	4,054.8	100.0	1,713.8	100.0	7,170.1	100.0
Sources								
5. Retained profits	104.9	10.9	450.9	11.2	−123.3	−7.4	153.2	2.1
6. Depreciation charges	458.0	47.4	1,287.8	31.9	1,786.8	107.2	2,758.0	38.4
7. Current liabilities								
(a) Non-government	−17.3	−1.8	28.0	0.7	20.1	1.2	396.7	5.5
(b) Tax liability	37.2	3.8	93.7	2.3	40.9	2.5	219.7	3.1
8. Net new issues	383.1	39.6	2,174.5	53.9	−52.3	−3.1	3,646.6	50.7
(a) Shares	63.8	6.6	1,567.2	38.8	−119.1	−7.1	611.5	8.5
(b) Bonds	349.7	36.2	775.9	19.2	79.9	4.8	3,268.4	45.5
(c) (Less) securities of subsidiaries	30.3	−3.1	168.6	−4.2	13.1	−0.8	233.3	−3.2
9. Other	0.6	0.1	...	...	−6.1	−0.4	11.7	0.2
10. Total sources	966.6	100.0	4,034.9	100.0	1,666.1	100.0	7,185.9	100.0
11. Discrepancy	−46.0	...	+19.9	...	+47.7	...	−15.8	...

Detail may not add to totals because of rounding.

[a] Not shown separately.

Note for 1931–40: Beginning with January 1, 1936, two companies (the Cincinnati and Suburban Bell Telephone Company and the Southern New England Bell Telephone Company) whose accounts had formerly been consolidated with other companies in the consolidated balance sheet of the Bell system were no longer consolidated. Data obtained from Bell system balance sheets during 1931–40 are based on statements including the two companies during 1931–35, and on statements excluding the two companies during 1935–40.

Source of basic data: *American Telephone and Telegraph Company, Annual Reports*, except as indicated below.

NOTES BY LINE

1 Data for 1913–19 are based on cash capital expenditures for the entire industry and the ratio (0.915) of Bell system capital expenditures including reused equipment to industry-wide capital expenditures including reused equipment during 1914–19 (Table E–2).

2a At cost. The balance sheet for 1930 includes a relatively small sum for general equipment, automobiles, and office furniture; changes in adjoining periods reflect this inclusion.

2b After reserves for uncollectible debts during 1941–50.

2c Beginning with the period 1921–30, includes temporary cash investments, comprised of securities acquired for the purpose of temporarily investing cash, such as time drafts receivable and time loans, bankers' acceptances, Treasury certificates, marketable securities, and other similar investments of a temporary character. In the period 1941–50, comprised of United States government obligations carried at market value.

3 Includes prepaid accounts, as rents and insurance, provident, insurance and other funds, and other deferred charges.

5 Net income less cash dividends. Beginning with 1932, includes proportional interest in deficit or profit of controlled companies not consolidated.

6 Includes depreciation charges plus the calculated value of plant retirements charged to operating expense. Depreciation charges include an estimate for the period August 1, 1918–July 31, 1919, when the properties of the Bell system were under federal control, based on the average relationship (5.307 per cent) between Bell depreciation charges during 1916–17 and the value of Bell plant and equipment at the close of 1915, 1916, 1917, applied to the value of Bell plant at the end of 1918.

The value of plant retirements charged to operating expense was estimated in accordance with the following assumptions:

The value of plant and equipment less depreciation and amortization reserves at the close of a period should be equal to its value at the beginning of the period plus capital expenditures for plant and equipment, less depreciation and amortization charges during the period. If the net plant value shown in the balance sheet at the end of a period is below the net value computed in the above manner, it is assumed that the difference is equal to plant that has been retired and charged to operations (or surplus). This book expense does not represent a cash payment, although it reduces stated profits; consequently it represents an internal source of funds. These retirements were calculated as follows (in millions of dollars):

1913–1920	50.2
1921–1930	64.0
1931–1940	112.5
1941–1950	412.2

7a Accounts and bills payable, including advance billing for service and customers deposits; dividends and other payables, except relatively small amounts of interest and rent; and certain other payables which are included in line 8b until 1941–50.

7b Unpaid taxes accrued, including through 1940 the relatively small non-government payables noted in line 8a.

8a Net cash sales of shares, derived as follows:

(1) The difference between the par value of shares outstanding of the Bell system held by the public (including installments received under employee purchase

plans) on terminal dates. Includes the common shares of the parent company (A.T. & T.) and the common and the relatively small amount of preferred shares of subsidiaries whose accounts are consolidated with those of the parent company in reports to shareholders.

(2) Less the par value of shares issued by the parent company to retire its bonds.

(3) Less the premium above par value paid by the subsidiary companies on retired preferred stock, except unspecified but small amounts included with premiums on bonds in 1937, 1938, and 1941.

(4) Plus the cash premiums above par value received by the parent company from the issuance of its own shares.

Included in this series of net new issues of shares for cash are two exchanges of securities not involving cash between the parent company (A.T. & T.) and other companies: (a) In 1918, A.T. & T. issued $6 million par value of shares for $7.5 million par value of common stock of the Bell Telephone Company of Pennsylvania, acquired from the New York Telephone Company and involving a premium of $1.5 million to A.T. & T. (b) In 1930, A.T. & T. issued $15 million par value of shares for 150,000 shares of no-par-value common stock of the Teletype Corporation which were valued at $200 per share by the board of directors of A.T. & T., and involved a premium of $15 million to A.T. & T.

The two exchanges of securities are included as sources (and as uses) of funds amounting to $7.5 million and to $30 million, respectively: The par value of A.T. & T. shares issued in exchange and the premiums received are included in the above steps 1 and 4, respectively. (However, step 4 does not include the estimated premium paid in bonds to A.T. & T. during 1913–20 [$7.0 million] and 1921–30 [$0.6 million] by bondholders converting their holdings to shares.)

Source: For 1913–35, *Investigation of the Telephone Industry in the United States*, FCC Exhibit 1360–B, Schedules 27A, 27B, 29B, and 38. For 1936–50, obtained directly from the American Telephone and Telegraph Co. or derived from *American Telephone and Telegraph Company, Annual Reports*.

8b Net cash sales of bonds derived as follows:

(1) The difference between the par value of bonds and notes of the Bell system held by the public on terminal dates.

(2) Plus the par value of bonds of the parent company (A.T. & T.) converted to shares.

(3) Plus premium above par value received by the parent company 1913–30, and the Bell system 1931–50, from the sales of its bonds, or less the discount for sales below par value.

(4) Less premiums above par value paid by the parent company 1913–30, and the Bell system 1931–50, on bonds called for redemption. In 1937, 1938, and 1941 included small but unspecified amounts of premium paid on retired preferred stock.

Source: Same as 8a.

8c Investments in subsidiaries not consolidated, shown in the balance sheets under assets, have been excluded from uses of funds and are here deducted from net new issues to eliminate intercompany duplications. Includes mainly securities of subsidiaries not consolidated at cost; also includes Bell system equity in subsidiaries not consolidated in excess of the investment in securities of these subsidiaries, investments in non-controlled telephone companies, and in sinking funds.

9 For 1913–20: Change in Bell system's liability to the employees benefit fund, comprised mainly of the employees pension fund (which was transferred to the Bankers' Trust Company as trustee in 1928). For 1921–30 and subsequent periods: Changes in the size of the pension fund reflected in the Bell system sources and uses of funds statement; includes primarily annual Bell contributions to the fund and the fund's acquisition and disposal of Bell securities.

For 1931–40: Refunds of revenues collected in prior years including interest thereon charged to surplus, and deferred credits.

For 1941–50: Same as for 1931–40, plus other charges and credits to surplus of a generally similar character.

TABLE J–7. Sources and Uses of Funds: Street and Electric Railway Companies (*dollar amounts in millions*)

	ALL STREET RAILWAY COMPANIES: CHANGES IN BALANCE SHEET ITEMS FROM					
	July 1, 1890 to June 30, 1902		*July 1, 1902 to December 31, 1912*		*January 1, 1913 to December 31, 1922*	
	Amount	*Per Cent*	*Amount*	*Per Cent*	*Amount*	*Per Cent*
Uses						
1. Cost of road and equipment, land, and other physical property	1,852.1	87.0	2,429.0	96.5	551.3	57.1
2. Cash and other current assets	43.5	2.0	117.9	4.7	85.6	8.9
(a) Cash	20.2	0.9	[a]		[a]	
(b) Bills and accounts receivable	14.9	0.7	[a]		[a]	
(c) Supplies	8.4	0.4	[a]		[a]	
3. Long-term investments, except securities of other electric railways	105.7	5.0	−47.4	−1.9	144.2	14.9
4. Other	127.6	6.0	17.3	0.7	183.7	19.0
5. Total uses	2,128.9	100.0	2,516.6	100.0	965.1	100.0
Sources						
6. Surplus	29.4	1.4	54.6	2.2	−122.0	−12.6
7. Depreciation and other reserves	[a]		80.8	3.2	252.4	26.2
(a) Depreciation reserves	[a]		[a]		[a]	
(b) Other reserves	[a]		[a]		[a]	
8. Current liabilities	101.2	4.8	322.4	12.8	129.8	13.4
(a) Short-term debt	[a]		296.2	11.8	−119.5	−12.4
(b) Bills and accounts payable	85.4	4.0	−15.0	−0.6	60.1	6.2
(c) Interest, dividends, and taxes payable	15.8	0.7	41.2	1.6	189.2	19.6
9. Securities outstanding	1,877.8	88.2	2,113.6	84.0	645.7	66.9
(a) Common }					−127.8	−13.2
(b) Preferred }	1,055.6	49.6	1,112.5	44.2	77.5	8.0
(c) Bonds	822.2	38.6	1,361.2	54.1	782.3	81.1
(d) (Less) Treasury securities	[a]		93.1	−3.7	76.8	−8.0
(e) (Less) securities of other electric railway companies	[a]		267.0	−10.6	9.5	−1.0
10. Other	120.6	5.7	−54.7	−2.2	59.0	6.1
11. Total sources	2,128.9	100.0	2,516.6	100.0	965.1	100.0

Detail may not add to totals due to rounding.

[a] Not shown separately.

Data include all street and electric railways and include electric light and power departments (and other operations) of street railway companies; such establishments are not included in our series on capital formation but are included with electric light and power companies. Data also include municipally owned roads. Such roads were of negligible importance through 1912; by 1932 they accounted for 2.5 per cent of assets of all companies engaged exclusively in electric railway operation.

Note for 1890–1902: Census data for 1890 were incomplete; no balance sheet data are available for non-reporting companies, who had assets of approximately 100 million dollars in 1890. Changes in both uses and sources of funds are thus overstated by about 100 millions for July 1, 1890–June 30, 1902.

Source of basic data: Changes in balance sheet data derived from the 1890 census report, *Transportation by Land*, and from *Census of Electrical Industries: Street and Electric Railways* for later years.

NOTES BY LINE

1 Includes, besides the specified properties, other utility property of composite companies such as electric light and power, gas, etc. (see above note on data included). Figures are book values and in many cases include value of franchises, capitalized earnings, good will, and the like.

3 Shown in reports for 1902 and prior years as "other permanent investments"; the sums involved were assumed to represent investments other than in electric railways. For 1912 and subsequent years, specifically excludes investments in other electric railways and in treasury securities.

4 Includes stock and bond discount; sinking and other special funds; interest, dividends, and rents receivable; and sundries.

6 Shown in balance sheets as profit and loss surplus and profit and loss deficit.

8a Identified in early census reports as "floating debt" and in later years as "loans and notes."

9a, b Includes small amounts of cash invested in unincorporated properties by municipalities and by individuals and partnerships; includes debenture stock for 1922.

9c For 1922 includes non-negotiable debt to affiliated companies, and real-estate mortgages.

9d, e Treasury securities and securities of other electric railways, carried in the balance sheets under assets, have been excluded from uses of funds in order to eliminate intercompany duplications and are here deducted from the securities outstanding component of sources of funds. For 1902–12, lines 9d and 9e represent the totals reported as of December 31, 1912; these items were not reported separately before 1912.

10 Sundries, and for 1922, premium on capital stock and funded debt.

APPENDIX K

Tables Presenting Nine-Year Moving Averages of the Data on Capital Formation, Output, and Capital-Product Ratios for All Regulated Industries and Components

APPENDIX K

TABLE K–1

Nine-Year Moving Averages of Value of Plant and Equipment, 1929 Dollars, All Regulated Industries and Components, 1874–1947

(*in millions*)

Nine-Year Moving Average Centered on January 1	*Total*	*Steam Rail-roads*	*Electric Light and Power*[a]	*Telephones*	*Street and Electric Railways*[a]	*Local Bus Lines*[a]	*All Other*
1874	10,203	8,657			151		1,395
1875	10,573	8,956			164		1,453
1876	10,880	9,201			177		1,500
1877	11,153	9,419			191		1,540
1878	11,452	9,664			204		1,578
1879	11,791	9,944			217		1,618
1880	12,163	10,256			231		1,659
1881	12,555	10,587			244		1,701
1882	12,955	10,924			258		1,741
1883	13,370	11,276			273		1,780
1884	13,824	11,658		42	292		1,822
1885	14,305	12,060	17	49	315		1,865
1886	14,771	12,440	26	55	343		1,907
1887	15,184	12,762	40	61	379		1,943
1888	15,563	13,043	57	66	423		1,976
1889	16,003	13,357	78	71	479		2,018
1890	16,530	13,730	102	76	548		2,074
1891	17,091	14,108	130	84	632		2,137
1892	17,638	14,444	162	98	733		2,201
1893	18,138	14,713	196	117	849		2,262
1894	18,603	14,923	235	141	983		2,322
1895	19,049	15,090	280	168	1,131		2,381
1896	19,498	15,234	329	201	1,292		2,441
1897	19,950	15,360	383	242	1,461		2,504
1898	20,344	15,414	445	289	1,636		2,559
1899	20,677	15,392	516	344	1,817		2,608
1900	21,024	15,362	598	403	2,003		2,657
1901	21,429	15,366	689	467	2,195		2,712
1902	21,919	15,425	792	536	2,390		2,776
1903	22,523	15,563	903	616	2,588		2,853
1904	23,241	15,784	1,023	700	2,789		2,945
1905	24,035	16,068	1,159	776	2,981		3,051
1906	24,898	16,414	1,315	843	3,154		3,173
1907	25,867	16,839	1,489	905	3,315		3,318
1908	26,919	17,329	1,681	962	3,460		3,486
1909	28,045	17,875	1,895	1,014	3,580		3,681

(concluded on next page)

TABLE K–1 (concluded)

Nine-Year Moving Average Centered on January 1	*Total*	*Steam Rail-roads*	*Electric Light and Power*[a]	*Telephones*	*Street and Electric Railways*[a]	*Local Bus Lines*[a]	*All Other*
1910	29,212	18,473	2,106	1,058	3,677		3,897
1911	30,348	19,071	2,314	1,090	3,749		4,124
1912	31,365	19,609	2,509	1,101	3,798		4,347
1913	32,257	20,078	2,693	1,105	3,818		4,563
1914	33,083	20,491	2,869	1,113	3,828	0.4	4,782
1915	33,775	20,824	3,010	1,119	3,835	0.7	4,986
1916	34,285	21,049	3,116	1,119	3,827	1	5,173
1917	34,654	21,199	3,198	1,116	3,802	1	5,339
1918	34,880	21,286	3,252	1,107	3,763	2	5,470
1919	35,031	21,306	3,319	1,103	3,714	3	5,586
1920	35,255	21,354	3,432	1,109	3,655	6	5,699
1921	35,618	21,453	3,604	1,135	3,581	11	5,834
1922	36,084	21,582	3,829	1,173	3,498	17	5,985
1923	36,626	21,738	4,085	1,224	3,401	26	6,153
1924	37,303	21,931	4,399	1,291	3,293	35	6,354
1925	38,121	22,174	4,763	1,383	3,182	46	6,574
1926	39,098	22,461	5,162	1,514	3,074	57	6,830
1927	40,230	22,784	5,607	1,681	2,972	70	7,115
1928	41,339	23,092	6,048	1,857	2,867	82	7,394
1929	42,238	23,308	6,424	2,018	2,756	92	7,639
1930	42,879	23,437	6,715	2,152	2,643	101	7,832
1931	43,313	23,503	6,928	2,258	2,530	109	7,984
1932	43,536	23,493	7,077	2,339	2,421	119	8,087
1933	43,609	23,436	7,171	2,402	2,316	132	8,149
1934	43,590	23,362	7,230	2,451	2,216	143	8,187
1935	43,374	23,222	7,250	2,463	2,118	157	8,163
1936	42,972	23,017	7,213	2,442	2,025	172	8,103
1937	42,548	22,821	7,166	2,420	1,904	189	8,049
1938	42,250	22,664	7,145	2,424	1,790	211	8,017
1939	42,075	22,556	7,149	2,455	1,683	235	7,998
1940	41,925	22,465	7,160	2,489	1,580	255	7,975
1941	41,816	22,404	7,167	2,528	1,480	272	7,966
1942	41,722	22,348	7,173	2,572	1,381	284	7,965
1943	41,666	22,268	7,180	2,647	1,285	296	7,990
1944	41,808	22,213	7,226	2,784	1,182	315	8,087
1945	42,219	22,210	7,343	3,001	1,081	333	8,250
1946	42,819	22,237	7,526	3,256	1,016	345	8,438
1947	43,526	22,269	7,747	3,519	955	348	8,687

Data exclude accrued depreciation and exclude land. For derivation, see the appendix relating to a given industry. Detail may not add to totals because of rounding and because of the inclusion in the total of small amounts for electric power prior to 1885, telephones prior to 1884, and for local bus lines prior to 1914, not shown in this table.

[a] Excluding publicly owned facilities.

TABLE K–2

Nine-Year Moving Averages of Gross Capital Expenditures, 1929 Dollars, All Regulated Industries and Components, 1874–1946

(in millions)

Nine-Year Moving Average Centered on	*Total*	*Steam Railroads*	*Electric Light and Power*[a]	*Telephones*	*Street and Electric Railways*[a]	*Local Bus Lines*[a]	*All Other*
1874	544	446			18		80
1875	490	398			20		71
1876	464	377			21		65
1877	498	409			21		65
1878	546	452			22		68
1879	589	490			22		70
1880	620	517			23		72
1881	637	530			24		71
1882	663	553			26		72
1883	714	592			31		76
1884	754	621		11	36		79
1885	752	609	11	12	42		78
1886	713	560	16	13	52		73
1887	694	528	20	13	62		72
1888	766	569	26	13	76		83
1889	872	637	31	14	93		98
1890	925	652	36	18	112		107
1891	930	619	43	25	133		110
1892	905	562	47	32	154		110
1893	892	511	55	38	176		111
1894	896	475	64	45	198		113
1895	922	460	73	54	216		118
1896	949	448	82	65	231		123
1897	918	383	95	76	244		120
1898	884	313	111	88	256		116
1899	923	309	128	99	266		120
1900	1,009	348	144	109	277		130
1901	1,124	408	163	122	287		144
1902	1,269	492	181	140	295		160
1903	1,418	583	198	153	304		180
1904	1,530	654	223	153	302		198
1905	1,638	726	252	153	289		218
1906	1,781	815	280	156	282		247
1907	1,904	891	309	159	271		275
1908	2,019	959	341	161	252		306
1909	2,102	1,025	349	161	233		334

(concluded on next page)

TABLE K–2 (concluded)

Nine-Year Moving Average Centered on	Total	Steam Railroads	Electric Light and Power[a]	Telephones	Street and Electric Railways[a]	Local Bus Lines[a]	All Other
1910	2,113	1,038	356	155	213		351
1911	2,035	992	354	141	193		355
1912	1,948	937	350	138	167		358
1913	1,918	894	350	147	157		371
1914	1,818	825	322	149	156	0.3	367
1915	1,670	728	292	147	140	0.4	362
1916	1,566	660	272	148	131	0.4	355
1917	1,459	603	247	147	127	0.5	334
1918	1,415	539	262	155	124	2	333
1919	1,515	567	310	169	122	4	344
1920	1,684	618	374	192	115	6	378
1921	1,818	647	433	209	113	8	408
1922	1,922	671	471	226	107	10	437
1923	2,087	705	538	247	103	12	482
1924	2,255	749	597	276	108	15	511
1925	2,437	789	644	321	109	17	557
1926	2,615	824	704	363	110	19	596
1927	2,619	807	713	376	104	20	599
1928	2,433	714	662	368	94	19	576
1929	2,196	627	588	345	86	20	531
1930	2,003	564	519	322	80	21	497
1931	1,805	489	462	299	78	24	453
1932	1,662	443	413	283	74	29	420
1933	1,584	429	382	269	70	31	402
1934	1,393	368	345	233	65	32	350
1935	1,214	305	290	199	62	36	323
1936	1,230	317	279	196	60	41	336
1937	1,360	358	305	222	59	48	368
1938	1,490	409	330	248	56	53	394
1939	1,524	430	337	252	52	52	401
1940	1,573	461	335	256	46	50	425
1941	1,600	469	336	263	40	48	445
1942	1,654	447	339	295	35	51	486
1943	1,888	476	380	361	32	60	578
1944	2,191	530	456	446	27	62	671
1945	2,389	563	528	493	20	58	726
1946	2,542	572	575	510	17	52	816

Data exclude land. For derivation, see the appendix relating to a given industry. Detail may not add to totals because of rounding and because of inclusion in the total of small amounts for electric power prior to 1885, telephones prior to 1884 and for local bus lines prior to 1914, not shown in this table.

[a] Excluding publicly owned facilities.

TABLE K-3

Nine-Year Moving Averages of Capital Consumption, 1929 Dollars, All Regulated Industries and Components, 1874–1946

(in millions)

Nine-Year Moving Average Centered on	*Total*	*Steam Railroads*	*Electric Light and Power*[a]	*Telephones*	*Street and Electric Railways*[a]	*Local Bus Lines*[a]	*All Other*
1874	174	146			6		22
1875	183	153			7		24
1876	191	159			7		25
1877	199	165			8		26
1878	208	171			8		27
1879	217	178			9		29
1880	227	186			10		30
1881	237	194			10		31
1882	248	201			11		32
1883	260	210			12		34
1884	273	219		5	13		35
1885	286	229	1	6	14		36
1886	300	238	2	7	16		37
1887	314	247	3	7	18		39
1888	328	255	5	8	21		40
1889	345	263	6	9	24		42
1890	363	273	8	10	28		44
1891	384	283	11	11	32		47
1892	405	292	13	13	37		49
1893	427	301	16	15	43		52
1894	450	308	20	18	49		55
1895	473	315	24	21	55		58
1896	498	322	28	24	62		61
1897	524	329	33	29	68		65
1898	551	334	39	34	75		68
1899	576	339	46	40	80		72
1900	604	344	53	46	86		76
1901	633	349	61	53	91		80
1902	665	354	69	60	97		84
1903	700	361	78	69	104		88
1904	737	370	87	77	110		93
1905	775	379	96	86	116		98
1906	813	390	106	94	121		102
1907	852	401	117	102	126		107
1908	893	413	128	109	132		112
1909	935	426	138	117	137		117

(concluded on next page)

TABLE K–3 (concluded)

Nine-Year Moving Average Centered on	*Total*	*Steam Railroads*	*Electric Light and Power*[a]	*Telephones*	*Street and Electric Railways*[a]	*Local Bus Lines*[a]	*All Other*
1910	978	440	148	124	141		124
1911	1,018	455	158	130	144		132
1912	1,056	468	166	134	146		141
1913	1,092	481	174	139	147		151
1914	1,127	492	181	143	148	0.1	163
1915	1,160	503	186	147	148	0.1	175
1916	1,198	511	190	152	157	0.1	188
1917	1,232	516	193	156	165	0.2	203
1918	1,263	519	195	159	173	0.3	217
1919	1,292	520	197	163	181	0.5	231
1920	1,321	519	202	166	189	0.8	244
1921	1,351	518	208	171	197	1	257
1922	1,380	515	215	175	204	2	269
1923	1,409	511	224	180	211	3	280
1924	1,438	506	234	185	219	4	291
1925	1,459	502	245	190	216	5	301
1926	1,483	500	258	195	213	6	310
1927	1,510	499	272	201	209	8	321
1928	1,534	498	286	206	205	9	330
1929	1,554	498	297	212	200	11	338
1930	1,570	498	306	216	193	12	345
1931	1,582	498	313	219	187	14	351
1932	1,592	500	319	220	179	16	358
1933	1,601	504	323	221	171	18	365
1934	1,610	507	325	221	163	20	374
1935	1,615	510	327	220	154	22	383
1936	1,617	512	326	219	146	24	390
1937	1,621	515	326	218	136	26	400
1938	1,629	517	326	217	127	29	412
1939	1,637	520	327	218	118	31	423
1940	1,647	522	328	218	110	34	434
1941	1,658	525	330	219	102	36	445
1942	1,674	528	332	220	95	38	460
1943	1,700	530	335	224	89	41	481
1944	1,734	533	339	229	82	44	507
1945	1,780	536	345	238	76	47	538
1946	1,825	540	354	247	70	49	567

For derivation, see the appendix relating to a given industry. Detail may not add to totals because of rounding and because of inclusion in the total of small amounts for electric power prior to 1885, telephones prior to 1884, and for local bus lines prior to 1914, not shown in this table.

[a] Excluding publicly owned facilities.

TABLE K-4

Nine-Year Moving Averages of Net Capital Expenditures, 1929 Dollars, All Regulated Industries and Components, 1874–1946

(in millions)

Nine-Year Moving Average Centered on	*Total*	*Steam Railroads*	*Electric Light and Power*[a]	*Telephones*	*Street and Electric Railways*[a]	*Local Bus Lines*[a]	*All Other*
1874	370	300			12		58
1875	307	245			14		47
1876	273	218			14		40
1877	299	244			13		38
1878	339	281			14		40
1879	372	312			13		41
1880	393	331			13		41
1881	399	337			14		40
1882	415	352			15		39
1883	454	382			19		42
1884	482	402		6	23		44
1885	466	380	10	6	28		41
1886	413	322	14	6	36		36
1887	380	281	17	5	44		33
1888	438	314	21	5	56		43
1889	527	373	25	5	69		56
1890	562	379	28	8	84		63
1891	546	336	32	14	101		64
1892	500	269	34	19	116		61
1893	465	210	39	24	133		59
1894	446	167	45	27	149		59
1895	449	145	50	33	160		61
1896	452	125	54	41	169		62
1897	394	54	61	47	176		56
1898	333	−22	72	54	181		48
1899	347	−30	82	60	186		49
1900	405	4	91	63	191		55
1901	490	59	102	69	196		64
1902	604	138	112	80	198		77
1903	718	221	120	84	201		92
1904	793	283	136	76	192		106
1905	864	346	156	67	173		121
1906	968	425	174	62	161		145
1907	1,053	490	192	57	145		169
1908	1,126	546	214	52	120		194
1909	1,167	599	211	44	97		216

(concluded on next page)

TABLE K–4 (concluded)

Nine-Year Moving Average Centered on	*Total*	*Steam Railroads*	*Electric Light and Power*[a]	*Telephones*	*Street and Electric Railways*[a]	*Local Bus Lines*[a]	*All Other*
1910	1,137	598	207	32	72		227
1911	1,017	538	196	11	49		223
1912	892	469	183	4	21		216
1913	826	413	176	8	9		219
1914	692	333	141	6	8	0.2	204
1915	510	226	106	[b]	−8	0.3	187
1916	368	149	82	−4	−26	0.3	166
1917	226	87	55	−9	−38	0.3	131
1918	151	21	67	−4	−49	1	116
1919	224	47	112	6	−59	3	113
1920	363	99	172	26	−74	5	135
1921	466	129	225	39	−83	6	151
1922	541	156	256	51	−97	8	168
1923	678	194	314	67	−108	9	201
1924	817	242	363	91	−111	11	220
1925	977	287	399	131	−107	12	256
1926	1,132	324	445	168	−102	12	285
1927	1,109	308	441	175	−105	12	278
1928	899	216	376	162	−111	10	245
1929	642	129	291	133	−114	9	193
1930	433	66	213	107	−113	8	152
1931	223	−10	149	81	−109	10	103
1932	71	−57	94	63	−105	13	63
1933	−16	−74	59	48	−101	13	38
1934	−216	−140	20	13	−97	13	−24
1935	−401	−206	−37	−21	−93	14	−60
1936	−388	−196	−47	−23	−86	17	−54
1937	−262	−157	−21	4	−77	22	−33
1938	−138	−108	4	31	−71	24	−18
1939	−114	−90	10	35	−66	20	−23
1940	−73	−61	7	38	−64	16	−10
1941	−57	−56	6	44	−63	12	−1
1942	−20	−80	8	75	−60	13	25
1943	188	−54	46	137	−57	19	97
1944	457	−3	117	217	−55	18	163
1945	609	27	183	255	−55	12	188
1946	717	32	221	262	−51	3	249

Data exclude land. For derivation, see the appendix relating to a given industry. Detail may not add to totals because of rounding and because of inclusion in the total of small amounts for electric power prior to 1885, telephones prior to 1884 and for local bus lines prior to 1914, not shown in this table.

[a] Excluding publicly owned facilities.

[b] Negative, less than $500,000.

TABLE K–5

Nine-Year Moving Averages of Value of Plant and Equipment, Current Dollars, All Regulated Industries and Components, 1874–1947

(in millions)

Nine-Year Moving Average Centered on January 1	*Total*	*Steam Railroads*	*Electric Light and Power*[a]	*Telephones*	*Street and Electric Railways*[a]	*Local Bus Lines*[a]	*All Other*
1874	5,190	4,398			82		711
1875	5,206	4,405			85		716
1876	5,218	4,407			89		721
1877	5,269	4,443			94		730
1878	5,290	4,457			98		732
1879	5,337	4,493			103		735
1880	5,423	4,564			108		743
1881	5,522	4,648			112		750
1882	5,649	4,757			117		760
1883	5,836	4,916			123		777
1884	6,070	5,113		20	132		801
1885	6,323	5,325	7	23	143		825
1886	6,503	5,474	10	26	155		839
1887	6,652	5,588	16	28	169		850
1888	6,740	5,648	22	30	187		854
1889	6,847	5,716	29	32	208		861
1890	7,010	5,824	38	34	236		878
1891	7,165	5,918	48	37	268		894
1892	7,303	5,985	58	42	307		910
1893	7,435	6,038	69	49	352		927
1894	7,533	6,049	82	59	402		940
1895	7,657	6,069	99	71	461		957
1896	7,861	6,136	120	88	532		985
1897	8,135	6,248	143	109	613		1,023
1898	8,394	6,337	170	132	697		1,058
1899	8,673	6,427	201	160	788		1,096
1900	9,027	6,567	235	191	889		1,144
1901	9,409	6,721	276	226	995		1,192
1902	9,876	6,925	325	265	1,109		1,252
1903	10,524	7,256	378	313	1,243		1,332
1904	11,268	7,648	439	365	1,388		1,428
1905	11,957	8,007	501	410	1,520		1,519
1906	12,695	8,398	578	454	1,647		1,618
1907	13,567	8,883	667	497	1,777		1,742
1908	14,462	9,377	773	542	1,893		1,876
1909	15,411	9,903	899	583	1,999		2,027

(concluded on next page)

TABLE K–5 (concluded)

Nine-Year Moving Average Centered on January 1	*Total*	*Steam Railroads*	*Electric Light and Power*[a]	*Telephones*	*Street and Electric Railways*[a]	*Local Bus Lines*[a]	*All Other*
1910	16,447	10,502	1,019	623	2,101		2,201
1911	17,363	11,030	1,136	655	2,175		2,366
1912	18,154	11,472	1,254	676	2,228		2,524
1913	19,177	12,056	1,407	693	2,296		2,725
1914	20,814	13,006	1,618	732	2,428	0.5	3,030
1915	23,013	14,323	1,853	773	2,631	0.8	3,433
1916	25,474	15,813	2,086	815	2,864	1	3,894
1917	28,582	17,725	2,339	882	3,160	2	4,474
1918	30,564	18,886	2,548	951	3,318	2	4,859
1919	32,055	19,718	2,743	1,006	3,418	3	5,166
1920	34,083	20,889	3,006	1,075	3,556	7	5,550
1921	36,172	22,049	3,330	1,163	3,671	12	5,946
1922	37,889	22,935	3,663	1,262	3,722	19	6,289
1923	39,063	23,467	3,968	1,354	3,690	27	6,556
1924	39,679	23,607	4,263	1,452	3,570	36	6,750
1925	39,895	23,434	4,598	1,556	3,388	46	6,873
1926	39,614	22,871	4,969	1,662	3,135	58	6,919
1927	40,312	22,942	5,377	1,800	2,997	70	7,125
1928	41,144	23,077	5,797	1,961	2,880	80	7,348
1929	41,032	22,656	6,093	2,085	2,699	88	7,412
1930	40,670	22,150	6,312	2,175	2,520	94	7,419
1931	40,498	21,784	6,525	2,264	2,367	100	7,459
1932	40,197	21,376	6,699	2,330	2,222	107	7,463
1933	39,792	20,923	6,857	2,379	2,082	116	7,435
1934	39,696	20,683	7,043	2,416	1,970	127	7,456
1935	39,251	20,288	7,151	2,434	1,852	139	7,388
1936	38,818	19,926	7,246	2,420	1,750	152	7,323
1937	38,713	19,810	7,366	2,396	1,644	170	7,327
1938	39,405	20,115	7,599	2,442	1,576	195	7,479
1939	40,759	20,855	7,873	2,521	1,535	226	7,749
1940	42,105	21,674	8,091	2,585	1,495	252	8,007
1941	43,442	22,501	8,283	2,655	1,452	276	8,275
1942	44,931	23,431	8,472	2,739	1,412	297	8,580
1943	46,890	24,521	8,742	2,925	1,374	325	9,003
1944	50,019	26,063	9,268	3,267	1,343	370	9,708
1945	54,211	28,027	10,059	3,734	1,324	422	10,645
1946	58,812	29,995	11,069	4,294	1,331	468	11,654
1947	63,641	31,888	12,227	4,905	1,332	501	12,787

Data exclude accrued depreciation and exclude land. For derivation, see the appendix relating to a given industry. Detail may not add to totals because of rounding and because of inclusion in the total of small amounts for electric power prior to 1885, telephones prior to 1884, and for local bus lines prior to 1914, not shown in this table.

[a] Excluding publicly owned facilities.

TABLE K–6

Nine-Year Moving Averages of Gross Capital Expenditures, Current Dollars, All Regulated Industries and Components, 1874–1946

(*in millions*)

Nine-Year Moving Average Centered on	*Total*	*Steam Railroads*	*Electric Light and Power*[a]	*Telephones*	*Street and Electric Railways*[a]	*Local Bus Lines*[a]	*All Other*
1874	275	225			10		41
1875	243	197			10		35
1876	224	182			10		31
1877	230	189			10		30
1878	247	204			10		31
1879	264	219			10		31
1880	275	229			10		32
1881	282	234			11		31
1882	294	244			12		32
1883	317	262			14		34
1884	336	276		5	16		35
1885	333	270	4	6	19		35
1886	314	247	6	6	23		32
1887	301	229	8	6	27		31
1888	327	243	10	6	33		35
1889	367	269	12	6	40		41
1890	386	273	13	8	48		44
1891	385	258	15	11	56		45
1892	371	233	17	13	64		45
1893	362	210	19	16	72		45
1894	362	194	23	19	81		46
1895	374	188	27	23	89		48
1896	390	184	31	29	96		50
1897	382	160	36	34	103		50
1898	376	134	43	41	109		49
1899	402	137	50	47	117		52
1900	449	157	58	52	124		58
1901	512	188	67	60	132		65
1902	598	235	76	71	141		76
1903	692	290	84	79	151		88
1904	762	334	96	80	152		99
1905	832	381	111	81	148		112
1906	927	439	125	85	148		130
1907	1,012	490	142	88	145		148
1908	1,093	536	161	92	137		167
1909	1,162	584	168	94	131		187

(concluded on next page)

TABLE K-6 (concluded)

Nine-Year Moving Average Centered on	*Total*	*Steam Railroads*	*Electric Light and Power*[a]	*Telephones*	*Street and Electric Railways*[a]	*Local Bus Lines*[a]	*All Other*
1910	1,185	599	173	93	122		199
1911	1,152	578	175	86	112		203
1912	1,125	555	178	87	99		209
1913	1,168	554	192	97	99		230
1914	1,172	540	185	103	105	0.3	242
1915	1,152	505	179	107	101	0.5	260
1916	1,198	508	186	118	104	0.5	282
1917	1,210	503	187	129	106	0.6	284
1918	1,257	485	214	146	109	2	301
1919	1,448	556	274	169	115	4	330
1920	1,682	632	348	201	116	6	379
1921	1,867	680	413	228	118	8	420
1922	2,005	716	456	253	115	11	454
1923	2,168	749	519	279	110	13	498
1924	2,322	786	575	310	113	15	523
1925	2,464	806	620	351	111	17	559
1926	2,620	833	675	388	111	19	594
1927	2,618	814	685	398	105	20	596
1928	2,407	710	634	385	93	19	566
1929	2,149	614	560	356	83	19	517
1930	1,945	547	494	329	77	19	479
1931	1,739	467	440	302	73	21	436
1932	1,587	414	397	283	68	25	400
1933	1,511	396	375	267	63	27	383
1934	1,322	331	342	232	58	28	331
1935	1,152	268	295	198	54	31	306
1936	1,181	280	295	195	52	36	323
1937	1,343	325	334	226	52	44	362
1938	1,513	388	371	256	50	50	398
1939	1,578	422	383	262	47	50	414
1940	1,666	468	386	268	43	49	452
1941	1,742	494	394	278	38	49	489
1942	1,897	496	414	330	35	56	566
1943	2,349	563	506	444	35	72	729
1944	2,964	680	670	588	32	80	914
1945	3,477	780	849	682	28	79	1,059
1946	3,942	842	993	737	24	75	1,271

Data exclude land. For derivation, see the appendix relating to a given industry. Detail may not add to totals because of rounding and because of inclusion in the total of small amounts for electric power prior to 1885, telephones prior to 1884, and for local bus lines prior to 1914, not shown in this table.

[a] Excluding publicly owned facilities.

TABLE K–7

Nine-Year Moving Averages of Capital Consumption, Current Dollars, All Regulated Industries and Components, 1874–1946

(in millions)

Nine-Year Moving Average Centered on	*Total*	*Steam Railroads*	*Electric Light and Power*[a]	*Telephones*	*Street and Electric Railways*[a]	*Local Bus Lines*[a]	*All Other*
1874	86	71			3		11
1875	88	73			3		11
1876	90	75			4		12
1877	92	76			4		12
1878	94	77			4		12
1879	97	79			4		13
1880	100	81			4		13
1881	104	84			5		14
1882	108	88			5		14
1883	114	92			5		15
1884	120	97		2	6		15
1885	126	101	1	3	6		16
1886	131	104	1	3	7		16
1887	136	107	1	3	8		17
1888	141	109	2	4	9		17
1889	146	112	2	4	10		18
1890	152	115	3	4	12		19
1891	159	117	4	5	14		19
1892	166	120	5	5	15		20
1893	172	122	6	6	18		21
1894	181	124	7	7	20		22
1895	191	127	9	9	23		23
1896	204	131	11	11	26		25
1897	218	135	13	13	29		27
1898	233	140	15	16	32		29
1899	249	145	18	19	35		31
1900	267	151	21	22	39		34
1901	287	157	25	26	42		36
1902	311	166	29	30	47		39
1903	339	175	33	36	51		43
1904	365	185	37	41	56		46
1905	392	194	42	46	60		49
1906	423	205	48	52	65		53
1907	454	217	53	58	69		57
1908	486	229	60	63	74		61
1909	522	242	67	69	78		65

(concluded on next page)

TABLE K-7 (concluded)

Nine-Year Moving Average Centered on	*Total*	*Steam Railroads*	*Electric Light and Power*[a]	*Telephones*	*Street and Electric Railways*[a]	*Local Bus Lines*[a]	*All Other*
1910	554	255	73	75	82		70
1911	585	266	79	80	84		76
1912	624	281	87	85	88		84
1913	685	306	98	92	93		96
1914	765	340	111	100	102	0.1	113
1915	858	381	124	109	111	0.1	134
1916	988	431	139	122	136	0.2	161
1917	1,084	461	150	136	152	0.2	184
1918	1,160	482	161	148	165	0.3	204
1919	1,250	509	172	159	182	0.5	226
1920	1,339	534	186	172	197	0.9	249
1921	1,414	551	199	184	210	1	269
1922	1,468	558	209	194	220	2	285
1923	1,500	553	217	203	228	3	297
1924	1,513	537	226	209	232	4	304
1925	1,490	511	236	211	220	5	306
1926	1,496	503	248	211	215	6	313
1927	1,513	499	261	214	210	8	321
1928	1,503	485	271	216	200	9	323
1929	1,488	470	279	216	190	10	323
1930	1,484	461	288	217	181	11	326
1931	1,480	453	297	218	171	12	328
1932	1,475	446	305	218	161	14	331
1933	1,483	445	315	218	152	16	338
1934	1,488	443	321	218	142	17	346
1935	1,496	442	328	218	133	19	355
1936	1,510	445	336	217	126	21	365
1937	1,552	458	347	219	120	24	385
1938	1,614	479	359	223	116	28	410
1939	1,675	503	369	225	112	31	435
1940	1,735	525	379	229	108	34	459
1941	1,802	551	390	233	105	38	486
1942	1,898	582	405	243	102	42	524
1943	2,049	624	430	260	101	49	586
1944	2,240	674	464	280	100	56	665
1945	2,457	725	506	307	99	64	756
1946	2,678	775	555	337	97	71	847

For derivation, see the appendix relating to a given industry. Detail may not add to totals because of rounding and because of inclusion in the total of small amounts for electric power prior to 1885, telephones prior to 1884, and for local bus lines prior to 1914, not shown in this table.

[a] Excluding publicly owned facilities.

TABLE K–8

Nine-Year Moving Averages of Net Capital Formation, Current Dollars, All Regulated Industries and Components, 1874–1946

(*in millions*)

Nine-Year Moving Average Centered on	*Total*	*Steam Railroads*	*Electric Light and Power*[a]	*Telephones*	*Street and Electric Railways*[a]	*Local Bus Lines*[a]	*All Other*
1874	190	154			7		30
1875	155	124			7		24
1876	134	107			7		20
1877	139	113			6		18
1878	153	126			7		18
1879	167	139			6		18
1880	176	148			6		18
1881	178	150			6		18
1882	185	156			7		18
1883	203	170			9		19
1884	215	179		3	10		20
1885	207	169	4	3	13		19
1886	183	142	5	3	16		16
1887	165	122	6	2	19		14
1888	186	134	8	2	24		18
1889	221	157	9	2	30		23
1890	234	158	10	3	36		26
1891	226	141	12	6	42		26
1892	206	113	12	8	48		25
1893	190	88	14	10	55		24
1894	181	70	16	11	61		24
1895	183	61	18	14	66		24
1896	186	53	20	18	70		25
1897	165	24	23	21	74		23
1898	143	−6	28	25	77		20
1899	153	−9	32	28	81		21
1900	182	6	36	30	85		24
1901	225	31	42	34	90		29
1902	287	70	47	41	94		36
1903	353	114	51	43	99		45
1904	397	149	59	39	96		53
1905	440	187	68	35	88		62
1906	505	234	78	33	83		77
1907	559	273	88	30	76		91
1908	608	307	101	29	64		107
1909	642	342	101	25	52		121

(concluded on next page)

TABLE K-8 (concluded)

Nine-Year Moving Average Centered on	Total	Steam Railroads	Electric Light and Power[a]	Telephones	Street and Electric Railways[a]	Local Bus Lines[a]	All Other
1910	633	345	101	18	40		128
1911	569	312	96	6	28		127
1912	503	274	91	2	11		125
1913	486	247	94	6	5		134
1914	410	200	74	4	4	0.3	129
1915	294	124	55	−2	−11	0.3	127
1916	210	77	48	−5	−32	0.3	121
1917	126	42	37	−8	−47	0.4	100
1918	96	3	53	−2	−56	1	97
1919	198	46	102	9	−67	4	104
1920	344	98	162	29	−81	5	130
1921	454	128	215	44	−92	7	151
1922	536	158	247	58	−106	9	169
1923	669	197	302	76	−117	10	202
1924	810	248	349	101	−118	11	219
1925	974	294	384	140	−110	12	253
1926	1,125	329	427	177	−103	13	281
1927	1,105	315	424	184	−105	12	275
1928	904	225	363	170	−107	10	243
1929	662	144	281	140	−107	9	194
1930	460	86	205	112	−104	8	154
1931	260	14	143	84	−98	9	108
1932	112	−32	92	65	−93	11	69
1933	28	−49	60	49	−88	12	45
1934	−167	−112	21	13	−84	11	−16
1935	−343	−174	−33	−20	−79	12	−50
1936	−328	−165	−41	−22	−73	15	−43
1937	−208	−133	−12	6	−67	20	−22
1938	−101	−91	12	33	−65	23	−12
1939	−97	−80	14	36	−64	19	−21
1940	−70	−58	7	39	−65	15	−8
1941	−60	−57	4	45	−66	11	3
1942	−1	−86	9	88	−67	13	41
1943	301	−61	76	184	−66	24	144
1944	725	6	206	308	−68	24	249
1945	1,019	54	343	375	−71	15	303
1946	1,264	67	438	400	−72	4	424

Data exclude land. For derivation, see the appendix relating to a given industry. Detail may not add to totals because of rounding and because of inclusion in the total of small amounts for electric power prior to 1885, telephones prior to 1884, and for local bus lines prior to 1914, not shown in this table.

[a] Excluding publicly owned facilities.

TABLE K–9

Nine-Year Moving Averages of Output, All Regulated Industries and Components, 1884–1946

(millions of 1929 dollars)

Nine-Year Moving Average Centered on	*Total*	*Steam Railroads*	*Electric Light and Power*[a]	*Telephones*	*Street and Electric Railways*[a]	*Local Bus Lines*[a]	*All Other*
1884	1,071	863					
1885	1,160	935					
1886	1,258	1,013					
1887	1,362	1,096					
1888	1,473	1,184					
1889	1,576	1,265					
1890	1,662	1,329					
1891	1,748	1,391	9				
1892	1,832	1,450	10				
1893	1,925	1,515	12				
1894	2,037	1,593	14	30	183		216
1895	2,166	1,681	18	38	196		234
1896	2,311	1,778	22	46	211		255
1897	2,476	1,882	27	58	227		282
1898	2,681	2,014	34	74	247		311
1899	2,920	2,172	42	91	271		344
1900	3,174	2,334	51	111	297		380
1901	3,470	2,524	62	136	329		420
1902	3,817	2,743	73	167	366		468
1903	4,152	2,945	85	201	402		519
1904	4,446	3,111	98	232	436		569
1905	4,755	3,287	113	264	471		620
1906	5,080	3,477	128	296	507		671
1907	5,388	3,650	144	327	544		723
1908	5,724	3,842	161	359	581		779
1909	6,068	4,039	178	392	619		837
1910	6,345	4,179	197	423	651		892
1911	6,596	4,313	217	444	674		943
1912	6,952	4,522	245	470	701		1,008
1913	7,417	4,808	278	503	733		1,087
1914	7,873	5,083	323	532	760		1,165
1915	8,256	5,289	375	556	787		1,238
1916	8,719	5,557	431	583	814		1,321
1917	8,914	5,611	479	610	831		1,367
1918	9,161	5,683	535	641	851		1,434
1919	9,587	5,886	606	679	872		1,523

(concluded on next page)

TABLE K–9 (concluded)

Nine-Year Moving Average Centered on	*Total*	*Steam Railroads*	*Electric Light and Power*[a]	*Telephones*	*Street and Electric Railways*[a]	*Local Bus Lines*[a]	*All Other*
1920	9,957	6,013	684	725	892		1,616
1921	10,265	6,092	771	768	904		1,694
1922	10,570	6,145	871	812	910		1,783
1923	10,850	6,148	974	863	916		1,886
1924	11,183	6,187	1,084	921	913		2,001
1925	11,492	6,171	1,208	980	904		2,136
1926	11,894	6,229	1,345	1,032	894	108	2,286
1927	12,057	6,129	1,469	1,071	867	122	2,398
1928	11,861	5,797	1,557	1,090	826	132	2,460
1929	11,710	5,524	1,640	1,094	782	139	2,530
1930	11,565	5,251	1,719	1,094	742	145	2,613
1931	11,381	4,961	1,796	1,091	702	150	2,682
1932	11,360	4,795	1,889	1,088	665	155	2,769
1933	11,418	4,669	1,987	1,087	629	162	2,884
1934	11,269	4,421	2,051	1,080	590	167	2,961
1935	11,389	4,342	2,136	1,083	558	176	3,095
1936	11,837	4,442	2,257	1,100	536	188	3,312
1937	12,787	4,828	2,449	1,145	519	201	3,645
1938	14,105	5,500	2,678	1,207	517	228	3,974
1939	15,757	6,357	2,962	1,278	526	263	4,371
1940	17,478	7,231	3,251	1,350	539	301	4,806
1941	19,008	7,917	3,500	1,430	551	336	5,273
1942	20,287	8,363	3,729	1,538	563	372	5,723
1943	21,905	8,953	4,043	1,663	574	407	6,265
1944	23,477	9,442	4,390	1,798	570	435	6,841
1945	24,731	9,693	4,725	1,931	558	457	7,367
1946	25,951	9,864	5,100	2,059	548	475	7,904

For derivation, see Appendix I. Detail may not add to totals because of rounding and because of inclusion in the total of small amounts for electric power prior to 1891, telephones, street and electric railways, and all other prior to 1894, and local bus lines prior to 1926.

[a] Excluding output of publicly owned facilities.

TABLE K–10

Capital-Product Ratios, All Regulated Industries and Components, Based on Nine-Year Moving Averages, 1884–1946

(1929 dollars)

Central Year	*Total*	*Steam Railroads*	*Electric Light and Power*[a]	*Telephones*	*Street and Electric Railways*[a]	*Local Bus Lines*[a]	*All Other*
1884	12.91	13.51					
1885	12.33	12.90					
1886	11.74	12.28					
1887	11.15	11.64					
1888	10.57	11.02					
1889	10.15	10.56					
1890	9.95	10.33					
1891	9.78	10.14	14.44				
1892	9.63	9.96	16.20				
1893	9.42	9.71	16.33				
1894	9.13	9.37	16.79	4.70	5.37		10.75
1895	8.79	8.98	15.56	4.42	5.77		10.18
1896	8.44	8.57	14.95	4.37	6.12		9.57
1897	8.06	8.16	14.19	4.17	6.44		8.88
1898	7.59	7.65	13.09	3.91	6.62		8.23
1899	7.08	7.09	12.29	3.78	6.70		7.58
1900	6.62	6.58	11.73	3.63	6.74		6.99
1901	6.18	6.09	11.11	3.43	6.67		6.46
1902	5.74	5.62	10.85	3.21	6.53		5.93
1903	5.42	5.28	10.62	3.06	6.44		5.50
1904	5.23	5.07	10.44	3.02	6.40		5.18
1905	5.05	4.89	10.26	2.94	6.33		4.92
1906	4.90	4.72	10.27	2.85	6.22		4.73
1907	4.80	4.61	10.34	2.77	6.09		4.59
1908	4.70	4.51	10.44	2.68	5.96		4.47
1909	4.62	4.43	10.65	2.59	5.78		4.40
1910	4.60	4.42	10.69	2.50	5.65		4.37
1911	4.60	4.42	10.66	2.45	5.56		4.37
1912	4.51	4.34	10.24	2.34	5.42		4.31
1913	4.35	4.18	9.69	2.20	5.21		4.20
1914	4.20	4.03	8.88	2.09	5.04		4.10
1915	4.09	3.94	8.03	2.01	4.87		4.03
1916	3.93	3.79	7.23	1.92	4.70		3.92
1917	3.89	3.78	6.68	1.83	4.58		3.91
1918	3.81	3.75	6.08	1.73	4.42		3.81
1919	3.65	3.62	5.48	1.62	4.26		3.67

(concluded on next page)

TABLE K–10 (concluded)

Central Year	Total	Steam Railroads	Electric Light and Power[a]	Telephones	Street and Electric Railways[a]	Local Bus Lines[a]	All Other
1920	3.54	3.55	5.02	1.53	4.10		3.53
1921	3.47	3.52	4.67	1.48	3.96		3.44
1922	3.41	3.51	4.40	1.44	3.84		3.36
1923	3.38	3.54	4.19	1.42	3.71		3.26
1924	3.34	3.54	4.06	1.40	3.61		3.18
1925	3.32	3.59	3.94	1.41	3.52		3.08
1926	3.29	3.61	3.84	1.47	3.44	0.53	2.99
1927	3.34	3.72	3.82	1.57	3.43	0.57	2.97
1928	3.49	3.98	3.88	1.70	3.47	0.62	3.01
1929	3.61	4.22	3.92	1.84	3.52	0.66	3.02
1930	3.71	4.46	3.91	1.97	3.56	0.70	3.00
1931	3.81	4.74	3.86	2.07	3.60	0.73	2.98
1932	3.83	4.90	3.75	2.15	3.64	0.77	2.92
1933	3.82	5.02	3.61	2.21	3.68	0.81	2.83
1934	3.87	5.28	3.53	2.27	3.76	0.87	2.76
1935	3.81	5.35	3.39	2.27	3.80	0.89	2.64
1936	3.63	5.18	3.20	2.22	3.78	0.91	2.45
1937	3.33	4.73	2.93	2.11	3.67	0.94	2.21
1938	3.00	4.12	2.67	2.01	3.46	0.93	2.02
1939	2.68	3.55	2.41	1.92	3.20	0.89	1.83
1940	2.41	3.11	2.20	1.84	2.93	0.85	1.66
1941	2.21	2.83	2.05	1.77	2.69	0.81	1.51
1942	2.07	2.67	1.92	1.67	2.45	0.76	1.39
1943	1.91	2.49	1.78	1.59	2.24	0.73	1.28
1944	1.79	2.35	1.65	1.55	2.07	0.72	1.18
1945	1.72	2.29	1.55	1.55	1.94	0.73	1.12
1946	1.66	2.25	1.48	1.58	1.98	0.73	1.07

Ratios of nine-year moving averages of value of plant and equipment, in 1929 dollars (Table K–1), to nine-year moving averages of output, in 1929 dollars (Table K–9).

[a] Excluding publicly owned facilities.

TABLE K–11

Annual Changes in Nine-Year Moving Averages of Output, All Regulated Industries and Components, 1885–1946

(millions of 1929 dollars)

Year	*Total*	*Steam Railroads*	*Electric Light and Power*[a]	*Telephones*	*Street and Electric Railways*[a]	*Local Bus Lines*[a]	*All Other*
1885	89	72					
1886	98	78					
1887	104	83					
1888	111	88					
1889	103	81					
1890	86	64					
1891	86	62					
1892	84	59	1				
1893	93	65	2				
1894	112	78	2				
1895	129	88	4	8	13		18
1896	145	97	4	8	15		21
1897	165	104	5	12	16		27
1898	205	132	7	16	20		29
1899	239	158	8	17	24		33
1900	254	162	9	20	26		36
1901	296	190	11	25	32		40
1902	347	219	11	31	37		48
1903	335	202	12	34	36		51
1904	294	166	13	31	34		50
1905	309	176	15	32	35		51
1906	325	190	15	32	36		51
1907	308	173	16	31	37		52
1908	336	192	17	32	37		56
1909	344	197	17	33	38		58
1910	277	140	19	31	32		55
1911	251	134	20	21	23		51
1912	356	209	28	26	27		65
1913	465	286	33	33	32		79
1914	456	275	45	29	27		78
1915	383	206	52	24	27		73
1916	463	268	56	27	27		83
1917	195	54	48	27	17		46
1918	247	72	56	31	20		67
1919	426	203	71	38	21		89

(concluded on next page)

TABLE K–11 (concluded)

Year	*Total*	*Steam Railroad*	*Electric Light and Power*[a]	*Telephones*	*Street and Electric Railways*[a]	*Local Bus Lines*[a]	*All Other*
1920	370	127	78	46	20		93
1921	308	79	87	43	12		78
1922	305	53	100	44	6		89
1923	280	3	103	51	6		103
1924	333	39	110	58	−3		115
1925	309	−16	124	59	−9		135
1926	402	58	137	52	−10		150
1927	163	−100	124	39	−27	14	112
1928	−196	−332	88	19	−41	10	62
1929	−151	−273	83	4	−44	7	70
1930	−145	−273	79	0	−40	6	83
1931	−184	−290	77	−3	−40	5	69
1932	−21	−166	93	−3	−37	5	89
1933	58	−126	98	−1	−36	7	115
1934	−149	−248	64	−7	−39	5	77
1935	120	−79	85	3	−32	9	134
1936	448	100	121	17	−22	12	217
1937	950	386	192	45	−17	13	333
1938	1,318	672	229	62	−2	27	329
1939	1,652	857	284	71	9	35	397
1940	1,721	874	289	72	13	38	435
1941	1,530	686	249	80	12	35	467
1942	1,279	446	229	108	12	36	450
1943	1,618	590	314	125	11	35	542
1944	1,572	489	347	135	−4	28	576
1945	1,254	251	335	133	−12	22	526
1946	1,220	171	375	128	−10	18	537

[a] Excluding output of publicly owned facilities.

INDEX